D1356559

Analyzing Genres in Political Communication

Discourse Approaches to Politics, Society and Culture (DAPSAC)

The editors invite contributions that investigate political, social and cultural processes from a linguistic/discourse-analytic point of view. The aim is to publish monographs and edited volumes which combine language-based approaches with disciplines concerned essentially with human interaction – disciplines such as political science, international relations, social psychology, social anthropology, sociology, economics, and gender studies.

For an overview of all books published in this series, please see
http://benjamins.com/catalog/dapsac

General Editors

Ruth Wodak, Greg Myers and Johann Unger
Lancaster University

Editorial address: Department of Linguistics and English Language,
Lancaster University,
Lancaster LA1 4YL, United Kingdom.
r.wodak@lancaster.ac.uk; g.myers@lancaster.ac.uk and j.unger@lancaster.ac.uk

Advisory Board

Volume 50

Analyzing Genres in Political Communication. Theory and practice
Edited by Piotr Cap and Urszula Okulska

Analyzing Genres
in Political Communication

Theory and practice

Edited by

Piotr Cap
University of Łódź

Urszula Okulska
University of Warsaw

John Benjamins Publishing Company

Amsterdam / Philadelphia

The paper used in this publication meets the minimum requirements of
the American National Standard for Information Sciences – Permanence
of Paper for Printed Library Materials, ANSI z39.48-1984.

Library of Congress Cataloging-in-Publication Data

Analyzing Genres in Political Communication : Theory and practice / Edited by Piotr Cap
and Urszula Okulska.
     p. cm. (Discourse Approaches to Politics, Society and Culture, ISSN 1569-9463 ; v. 50)
Includes bibliographical references and index.
1. Discourse analysis--Political aspects. 2. Public communication--Political
     aspects. 3. Journalism--Political aspects. 4. Mass media--Political aspects.
     5. Communication in politics. I. Cap, Piotr, editor of compilation. II. Okulska,
     Urszula, editor of compilation.
P302.77.A57   2013
320.01'41--dc23   2013020218
ISBN 978 90 272 0641 1 (Hb ; alk. paper)
ISBN 978 90 272 7148 8 (Eb)

John Benjamins Publishing Co. · P.O. Box 36224 · 1020 ME Amsterdam · The Netherlands
John Benjamins North America · P.O. Box 27519 · Philadelphia PA 19118-0519 · USA

Table of contents

Notes on contributors

Michael S. Boyd (michael.boyd@uniroma3.it) is an English language lecturer (*lettore*) in the Department of Foreign Languages and Cultures at the University of Roma Tre and an Adjunct Professor in the Faculty of Interpreting and Translation Studies at the LUSPIO University, Rome. He teaches courses in general English and applied discourse analysis. His research interests include CDA, political linguistics, new media, and (Critical) discourse analysis for translation and interpreting studies. He is the the author of articles on political discourse, ESP and new technologies. Recent publications include "(New) political genres for the masses? YouTube in the 2008 US presidential elections" in the volume *Genres on the Move. Hybridization and Discourse Change in Specialized Communication*, "Participation and recontextualization in the new media: Political discourse on YouTube" (forthcoming) and, with Claudia Monacelli, "Politics, (con)text and genre: Applying CDA and DHA to interpreter training".

Dr. **Peter Bull** (peb1@psych.york.ac.uk) is a Reader in Psychology at the University of York (United Kingdom), and a Fellow of the British Psychological Society. He holds first degrees in both Modern History (University of Oxford) and Psychology (University of Exeter), where he was also awarded his Ph.D. His principal research interest is the detailed microanalysis of interpersonal communication. He has over 90 academic publications concerned with this theme, principally in the form of refereed journal articles. He is the author of *The Microanalysis of Political Communication: Claptrap and Ambiguity* (2003), and *Communication under the Microscope: The Theory and Practice of Microanalysis* (2002).

Professor **Piotr Cap** (piotr.cap@gmail.com) is head of the Department of Pragmatics at the University of Łódź, Poland. His research interests are in cognitive pragmatics, (critical) discourse analysis, political linguistics, genre theory, business communication, and methodology of linguistic analysis. His monographic and edited publications include *Explorations in Political Discourse* (Lang, 2002), *Pragmatics Today* (Lang, 2005), *Legitimisation in Political Discourse* (Cambridge Scholars Press, 2006/2008), *New Approaches to Discourse and Business Communication* (Palgrave, 2009), *Perspectives in Politics and Discourse* (John Benjamins, 2010) and *Proximization: The Pragmatics of Symbolic Distance Crossing* (John

Benjamins, 2013). He is Founding Editor of the international journal *Lodz Papers in Pragmatics* (Mouton de Gruyter), Managing Editor of the *International Review of Pragmatics* (Brill) and member of advisory boards of several journals and book series in pragmatics and discourse analysis, including *Pragmatics: Quarterly Publication of the International Pragmatics Association*, and *Discourse Approaches to Politics, Society and Culture* (DAPSAC) (John Benjamins). He was a Fulbright Fellow at the University of California, Berkeley and Boston University, a Humboldt Fellow at the University of Munich, and has given talks in Europe, Asia, Australia and the Americas.

Anita Fetzer (anita.fetzer@phil.uni-augsburg.de) is a full professor of English linguistics at the University of Augsburg, Germany. She received her Ph.D. from Stuttgart University in 1993 and her habilitation in 2003, and is currently engaged in research projects on follow-ups in political discourse, and on the overt and non-overt realization of discourse relations. Her research interests focus on pragmatics, functional grammar, contrastive analysis, modality and evidentiality, and context. She has had a series of articles published on rejections, context, and political discourse. Her most recent publications are *Contexts and Context: Parts Meets Whole* (2011, with Etsuko Oishi), *Political Discourse in the Media* (2007, with Gerda Lauerbach), *Context and Appropriateness* (2007), and *Recontextualizing Context: Grammaticality Meets Appropriateness* (2004).

Bernhard Forchtner (b.forchtner@hu-berlin.de) is a Wilhelm-von-Humboldt Fellow at the Institute of Social Sciences, Humboldt University, Berlin. He obtained his doctoral degree from the Department of Sociology and the Department of Linguistics and English Language at Lancaster University, UK. His thesis explored the relation between public apologies, societal learning and self-righteousness. He has published in the field of memory studies, at the interface of sociological theory and critical discourse analysis, and on prejudice and discrimination. Recent publications include "Narrating a 'new Europe': From 'bitter past' to self-righteousness?' in *Discourse & Society*, "Critique and argumentation. On the relation between the discourse-historical approach and pragma-dialectics" in *Journal of Language and Politics* and "Embattled Vienna 1683/2010: right-wing populism, collective memory and the fictionalisation of politics" in *Visual Communication*.

Helmut Gruber (helmut.k.gruber@univie.ac.at) is an Associate Professor of Applied Linguistics at the University of Vienna. He studied Psychology, Applied Linguistics and Education at Vienna University. He has published in various fields of Applied Linguistics such as Critical Discourse Analysis, media studies, political discourse analysis, conflict communication, and Computer Mediated

Communication. He is co-editor of *Pragmatics*, the quarterly journal of the International Pragmatics Association (IPrA), and member of IPrA's consultation board.

Monika Kopytowska (monika.kopytowska@gmail.com) received her Ph.D. from the University of Łódź, Poland, where she is currently affiliated with the Department of Pragmatics. Her research interests revolve around media discourse and the pragma-rhetorical aspects of the mass-mediated representation of conflict, ethnicity, and religion. She has published internationally in linguistic journals and volumes and is now working on the dynamics of proximization in the news discourse. She is the co-editor of *Lodz Papers in Pragmatics*, the associate editor of *CADAAD Journal*, and the editorial board member of *The University of Nairobi Journal of Language and Linguistics*.

Michał Krzyżanowski (michal.krzyzanowski@oru.se) is Full Professor of Media and Communication Studies at Örebro University, Sweden, which he joined in 2013 after holding posts at the Universities of Aberdeen and Lancaster (UK), University of Vienna (Austria) and Adam Mickiewicz University, Poznań (Poland). He is specialized in Critical Discourse Analysis and has researched extensively on media and political communication in the context of Europe's social, political and institutional change. He also works on developing new, qualitative and integrative approaches in critical discourse studies (incl. discursive ethnography or discourse-conceptual analysis). Michał is Associate Editor of the *Journal of Language and Politics* and serves on editorial boards of such journals as, inter alia, *Critical Discourse Studies* or *Qualitative Sociology Review*. His recent book-length publications include: *Ethnography and Critical Discourse Analysis* (2011); *The Discursive Construction of European Identities* (2010); *European Public Sphere and the Media: Europe in Crisis* (with A. Triandafyllidou & R. Wodak, 2009); *The Politics of Exclusion: Debating Migration in Austria* (with R. Wodak, 2009); *Qualitative Discourse Analysis in the Social Sciences* (with R. Wodak, 2008; Polish translation 2011), *Discourse and Transformation in Central and Eastern Europe* (with A. Galasińska, 2008); *(Un)Doing Europe: Discourses and Practices of Negotiating the EU Constitution* (with F. Oberhuber, 2007).

Gerda Lauerbach (lauerbach@em.uni-frankfurt.de) has retired as Professor of English Linguistics and Applied Linguistics at Goethe University, Frankfurt/Main. Her teaching focused on semantics, pragmatics, conversation analysis and critical discourse analysis, her recent research on political discourse on television. She has published on discourse practice and ideology, on genre, preference and inference, on argument and rhetoric, and on the interaction of the visual and verbal modality in classroom and television discourse, also on political interviews, press conferences and talk show discourse.

Rowan R. Mackay (R.R.Mackay@sms.ed.ac.uk) has recently completed a Ph.D. in Linguistics at the University of Edinburgh, investigating multiple facets of multimodal legitimation with specific reference to American political spot advertisements. More general research interests fall under the unclear-cut categories of social semiotics, multimodality, and critical discourse studies.

Thorsten Malkmus (thorsten.malkmus@web.de) studied at universities in Frankfurt am Main, Paris and Southampton. He has received a Ph.D. in English Linguistics from the University of Frankfurt am Main, Germany. His doctoral dissertation provides an in-depth study of British and German election night speeches as part of the DFG-funded project "Television Discourse" (supervised by Gerda Lauerbach). He has taught English Linguistics at the University of Lüneburg, Germany. His main research interests include pragmatics, language and politics and (critical) discourse analysis.

Dr. **James Moir** (j.moir@abertay.ac.uk) is a senior lecturer in sociology at the University of Abertay Dundee, Scotland, UK with a research interest in the application of discourse analysis across a wide range of socio-psychological topics. This has involved the study of discourses of occupational identities; doctor-patient interactions and shared decision-making; the discursive construction of tourism as visual experience; Western discourse surrounding death and dying; higher education policy discourse, the media and political opinionation and, in this volume, fundamental differences in approaches to the study of political communication. Dr. Moir was recently a Senior Associate of the UK Higher Education Academy's Centre for Sociology, Anthropology and Politics (C-SAP).

Dr. **Katarzyna Molek-Kozakowska** (molekk@uni.opole.pl) is an Assistant Professor at the Institute of English Studies, Opole University, Poland. Trained as a linguist, she now specializes in discourse analysis and media studies. She has published articles on various aspects of mass-mediated political discourse, methodology of critical discourse analysis and critical media literacy, co-edited a two-volume book *Exploring Space: Spatial Notions in Cultural, Literary and Language Studies* (CSP, 2010), and authored a monograph *Discursive Exponents of the Ideology of Counterculture* (Opole University Press, 2011).

Dr. **Urszula Okulska** (u.okulska@uw.edu.pl) is Assistant Professor at the Institute of Applied Linguisitics, University of Warsaw. Her research interests include sociolinguistics (contemporary and historical), pragmatics, historical linguistics, text linguistics, discourse analysis and corpus linguistics. She has published the monograph *Gender and the Formation of Modern Standard English* (Lang, 2006), and co-edited volumes on global English from a European perspective (Lang, 2004), metalinguistic discourse (Lang, 2006), corpora in English-Polish contrastive linguistics (Universitas, 2006), discourse variation in communities, cultures and times (University of Warsaw, 2008), as well as on politics and discourse (John Benjamins, 2010) and age in language and culture (Mouton de Gruyter, 2011). The topics of her publications are additionally related to synchronic and diachronic aspects of language change, development of English specialized genres, professional/institutional communication, speech/discourse communities and the applicability of language corpora to sociolinguistic, discourse-pragmatic, and ethnolinguistic research.

Professor **Ruth Wodak** (r.wodak@lancaster.ac.uk) is Distinguished Professor of Discourse Studies at Lancaster University, UK, since 2004; she has remained affiliated to the University of Vienna as Full Professor of Applied Linguistics (since 1991). Besides various other prizes, she was awarded the Wittgenstein Prize for Elite Researchers in 1996 and an Honorary Doctorate from University of Örebro in Sweden in 2010. She is past-President of the *Societas Linguistica Europaea.* Her research interests focus on discourse studies; gender studies; language and/in politics; prejudice and discrimination; and on ethnographic methods of linguistic field work. She is member of the editorial board of a range of linguistic journals, co-editor of the journals *Discourse and Society, Critical Discourse Studies,* and *Language and Politics,* and co-editor of the book series *Discourse Approaches to Politics, Society and Culture* (DAPSAC). She has held visiting professorships in University of Uppsala, Stanford University, University of Minnesota, University of East Anglia, and Georgetown University; she is corresponding member of the Austrian Academy of Sciences and member of the *Academia Europaea.* In 2008, she was awarded the Kerstin Hesselgren Chair of the Swedish Parliament (at University Örebro). She has published 8 monographs, 26 co-authored monographs, over 50 edited volumes and c. 300 peer reviewed journal papers and book chapters. Recent book publications include *Qualitative Discourse Analysis in the Social Sciences* (with M. Krzyżanowski, 2008); *Migration, Identity and Belonging* (with G. Delanty, P. Jones, 2011), *The Discursive Construction of History. Remembering the Wehrmacht's War of Annihilation* (with H. Heer, W. Manoschek, A. Pollak, 2008), *The Politics of Exclusion. Debating Migration in Austria* (with M. Krzyżanowski, 2009), *The SAGE Handbook of Sociolinguistics* (with B. Johnstone and P. Kerswill, 2010) and *The Discourse of Politics in Action: 'Politics as Usual'* (revised edition 2011). See http://www.ling.lancs.ac.uk/profiles/Ruth-Wodak for more information on on-going research projects and recent publications.

Analyzing genres in political communication

An introduction

Piotr Cap and Urszula Okulska
University of Łódź, Poland / University of Warsaw, Poland

1. Aims and scope

The concept of genre in linguistics[1] has been addressed within several disciplines and empirical fields. The most notable contributions come, apparently, from Systemic Functional Linguistics (e.g. Halliday and Hasan 1989; Halliday and Martin 1993; Eggins and Martin 1997; Martin and Rose 2008), (new) rhetorical studies (e.g. Bazerman 1988; Freedman and Medway 1994), applied linguistics (e.g. Swales 1981, 1990; Bhatia 1993), discourse community studies (e.g. Barton 1994; Bex 1996), linguistic pragmatics (e.g. Levinson 1992), and Critical Discourse Analysis (e.g. Fairclough 1993, 1995; Chouliaraki and Fairclough 1999; Wodak and Meyer 2009). Arising from these disciplines is a rather intuitive notion of genre, a common sense (e.g. Gruber and Muntigl 2005) that discourse involves conventional use of stable utterance groups which follow recognizable patterns that suit the accomplishment of certain social goals.

Notwithstanding this consensus, the theoretical diffusion of work on genres has caused a great many questions to remain unanswered. To mention but a few – what components or stages do the utterance patterns comprise? What is their order and how does it change across different discourse domains? What are the conventional characteristics that typify a given genre and how much categorial fuzziness can be allowed in genre classifications? And finally, speaking of genre typologies, whose recognition counts the most in identifying a genre – the communicator's or the analyst's?

It seems that the existing, diversified body of research offers relatively little in the way of providing a comprehensive and organized set of answers to these and other questions. Such a conclusion must not be surprising given, as has been mentioned, the heterogeneous ancestry of genre analysis. Furthermore, the pace at which modern communication channels develop has the discursive styles and generic conventions undergo a continual change, modification, or hybridization. As a result, the methodological apparatus available to date is often unable to handle the new generic forms and needs updating.

The goal of the present collection is to provide such a comprehensive, in-depth, and, despite limitations, lasting update which will serve both theoretical and applied purposes. By giving a methodologically structured panorama of the major work directions in a specific field (political communication), the volume brings together the most important issues surrounding the contemporary genre theory in general. The choice of political communication as a thematic hub for discussion is not accidental. Political genres, while certainly fascinating in their own right, are also a natural setting for "macro" considerations. The generic composition of "political talk" (understood in the broad sense of the "political", see Section 3) invokes and reflects most (if not all) of the questions listed above. The liability to change, hybridization, and internalization of new discursive styles, the multilevel mediatized structure, etc., make political communication a genuinely representative microcosm of genre research.

This introductory chapter highlights and systematizes the most significant issues in exploring (political) genres, stressing the role a systematic account of the existing generic forms plays in defining a coherent and lasting research agenda for the investigation of new forms. It points to the benefits of genre analysis which draws upon a collective, organized input from different methodologies, and shows how to structure this input for the maximal explanatory power. Most importantly, it addresses the methodological repercussions of the twofold conceptual status of genre analysis, which relies on (i) general insights and theoretical preconceptions of the analyst, as well as on (ii) the continually updated information available from specific instants of the newly encountered discourse data (which oftentimes oppose the analyst's expert knowledge and his/her preconceptions).

Underlying the last point is an important aspiration and objective of the present chapter: to foreground – in line with the volume's structure – the characteristics, benefits, downsides, but also the apparent *synergy* of the theory- and data-driven approaches to analysis of (political) genres. The discussion addressing this objective suggests format and provides guidance for the reader's own meta-perspective assessment of the work on political genres exemplified by the consecutive articles in the volume. The selection of articles constitutes – cf. Section 3.1. below – a carefully structured set of (meta-)data revealing the potential, but also the possible limitations of the theoretical frameworks applied, in accounting for (political) genre forms at a number of levels: content- and reception-analytic, conceptual and classificatory.

2. General problems in genre analysis

Notwithstanding the diversity of approaches to genre analysis in the past few decades, several observations and research postulates can be described as common (Gruber and Muntigl 2005). This section gives a concise list of such observations, bringing up those of their elements that might need revision at the level of the particular research fields, e.g. political discourse. In so doing it paves the way for considerations (cf. Section 3) of how studies in the particular fields could possibly refine the conception of the communicative genre in general.

2.1 Genres as abstractions

Genres are often viewed as abstractions, i.e. as clusters of conventionalized and predictable ways of goal-oriented communicative acting arising from imperatives posed by constantly evolving socio-cultural situations. This view presupposes a dynamic relation between the functional and the linguistic side of genres; over time, functions are realized in an increasingly stable agglomeration of form (Giltrow and Stein 2009). Different discourse domains (from those involving highly predictable, transactional texts [Eggins 1994] to those involving less predictable, interactional texts [Coupland 2000]) are, at a given moment of time, at different stages of generic evolution and thus call for different analytic procedures and sensitivity. For instance, the fixed structure of appointment in a hairdresser's salon is easier to abstract and generalize upon linguistically, than the evolving, hybrid structure of political interviews (see Fetzer and Bull, this volume). The existence of such differences, often within the same social domain (e.g. political discourse where some forms of interaction are more conventionalized than others), leaves the analyst at the methodological crossroads. S/he can collect comparable linguistic data and attempt to find in them common, predictable, goal-oriented elements that are characterized by similar realizational patterns (Corbett 2006), or intuitively assume typical communicative functions hosted by the genre social context and then support the postulate through data search and systematization. Both approaches – which we refer to as data- and theory-driven, respectively – are on their own workable ways to structure individual analyses, yet for the generic picture of the entire discourse domain – such as political communication – one needs to put them in synergetic relationship. Conclusions regarding the "macro-genre" of the domain must rely on the data potential to elaborate on better established "component" genres, but also on the theory potential to propose data regularities among new, evolving or highly complex or hybrid genres. In such global considerations it seems quite pointless to emphasize which of the genres within the domain are "fixed enough" or ceasing to evolve or expiring, and which will continue to change, hybridize and migrate.

2.2   Genres and situational contexts

Genres activate certain situational contexts and are realized in these contexts. In other words, distinctive, familiar agglomerations of language data inform the participant (and, indirectly, the analyst) of being "in a genre" and make him/her assess and/or contribute to, the unfolding discourse in a specific way. Interestingly, in the case of complex and heterogeneous discourse domains (e.g. political communication), tracing the activation of a situational context and tracing its realization are two analytic endeavors of potentially different caliber. Contexts get normally activated through relatively stable and predictable language forms, and they may indeed be realized by similarly conventionalized forms, however they may also be realized by forms which diverge from the typical features of the genre. For instance, the US presidential inaugural (Cap 2002) will be immediately identified by its tone-setting introduction, the act of thanking the predecessor, the act of invoking continuity of beliefs and ideals, etc., all of which are relatively stable characteristics that make the addressee (and the analyst) approach the entire current manifestation of the genre (i.e. the whole speech) in the way most congruent with the recollection of the earlier manifestations. Still, there is no guarantee that the speaker will continue in the same manner his predecessors did; one should reckon with substantial alterations of content and style in the policy-setting segments as they can shape the distinctive identity – which is what the political speaker usually strives for. So, in methodological terms, analytic challenge and the division of analytic labor associated with context-activation and context-realization are frequently unequal and it is only the study of vast, generically complex discourse domains that can bring this discrepancy to light.

2.3   Genres as flexible macrostructures

Text linguistics (e.g. Dressler ed. 1978; de Beaugrande and Dressler 1981; Petöfi ed. 1988), early studies in text and discourse comprehension (e.g. van Dijk 1980; van Dijk and Kintsch 1983) and Systemic Functional Linguistics (esp. Hasan 1978; Halliday and Hasan 1989; Martin 1992; Martin and Rose 2008) have all contributed to the perception of genres as flexible macrostructures, monologic as well as dialogic patterns involving both obligatory and optional elements ("stages") occurring in a set order (see also Labov 1972; Ventola 1987; as well as Brown and

Yule 1983 [esp. Ch. 4] and McCarthy and Carter 1994 [esp. Ch. 1, 2]). For instance, news reports in the press characteristically consist of a headline, followed by a lead paragraph that summarizes the story, followed by a variable number of component paragraphs that spell out details. This specific characterization of a news report makes explicit the analytic problem pertinent to the general account of genres as flexible macrostructures. Since we do not know the number of paragraphs "acceptable" for a typical news report, we cannot judge whether/when the consecutive "optional" paragraphs (start to) detract from its conventional generic description. The accumulation of optional elements/stages in a macrostructure, which results from the macrostructure's openness to realize its global function with the aid of extra language forms, could thus lead to a theoretical (typological) problem. The more flexibly a macrostructure behaves in accommodating new topics and the sub-functions they carry, the lower becomes the level of generality (Werlich 1979; Longacre 1983) in describing the macrostructure as a genre; simultaneously, the more sub-genres arise that need their own, separate analytic treatment. Such implications of genres' flexibility were duly acknowledged in the 1990s in studies bridging the work on genres with the earlier work on prototype theory (see, for instance, Paltridge's [1995] interpretation of Rosch [1973]),[2] but, surprisingly enough, the later research seems to have abandoned the issue. Nowadays, attempts to account for specific functions of various genres and their change in the emerging, complex forms of social communication are highlighting it with new full force.

2.4   Genre relations in a social field

As may seem obvious at this point, genres are related to other genres in the social field in which they are relevant. There are fields – such as scientific communication (Bazerman 1988; Swales 1990; Valle 1997) or legal communication (Bhatia 1993) – where at least some of them exist side-by-side, contributing independently, in a modular manner, to the "hyper-genre" (Giltrow and Stein 2009) of the field.[3] For instance, "article" and "review" are two genres in the scientific written communication which rarely overlap in terms of (the sequence of) the language forms involved. The functions these forms perform can also be described as different; while articles are usually vehicles for conveying their authors' original ideas, the traditional function of reviews is to provide summaries (rather than thorough evaluations) of the ideas proposed by others.[4] However, in most cases, and especially within complex, hardly delimited, and dynamically constructed social fields, genres do not merely co-exist; they migrate through intertextual routes (e.g. Lemke 1985), colonizing the many different, particular situations that make up the field (see, e.g., Bazerman 2000). For example, a committee meeting in an organization often yields suggestions that get later incorporated in a written policy document (Ramallo, Lorenzo Suarez, Rodriguez-Yanez, and Cap 2009). The major corridor of change is thus *intertextuality* (Plett ed. 1991; see also Chouliaraki and Fairclough 1999; Wodak 2000; Fairclough 2006), and the driving force is the fluid and shifting character of genres occupying the complex and fast-evolving social fields. The analytic consequences are easy to observe: it may be straightforward to theorize, a priori, upon the content and the function of a political speech, just from its context and the general expert knowledge the analyst possesses, but what if the speech is received in the online multimodal embedding which involves music and image on a par with the speech text? (see Mackay on multimodal political ads, this volume). Do the standard methodological pre-conceptions still obtain or, more probably, a laborious data-driven investigation is necessary that will pile up the heterogeneous cues and turn them into a conclusion that both enriches the conception and applications of the principal genre (i.e. the political speech), and advances the idea of a new or related (sub-) genre (e.g. multimodal political advertising, involving the text of the speech as one of its constituents).

2.5   Genres and interpersonal roles

Genres assign interpersonal roles; using specific language forms by a genre participant tends to reflect and foster his or her distinctive identity and the role s/he has performed, performs, and may continue to perform, in social interactions with other participants. This is, however, no hard-and-fast rule; again (viz. 2.1), transactional discourses will invoke interpersonal roles far more predictably than interactional discourses do. A customer-retailer interaction involves, usually, language forms that are unlikely to redefine or modify the original, "opening" roles; for instance, one can hardly expect the customer to start persuading the retailer to buy one of his/her (retailer's) products for his/her (retailer's) own household use (though, hypothetically, it *could* happen). The topos of persuasion is normally reserved for the retailer and it constitutes (together with the relevant language forms) one of his/her professional identity elements. It is, in fact, an element that is *supposed* to get manifested anytime a professional encounter takes place. In contrast, many aspects of interpersonal roles in public discourse get only activated "on-demand", in situations which invite the communicators to (temporarily) suspend their prototypical roles and assume other roles which seem more relevant and more rhetorically effective at the given moment. For example, in TV studio debates, participants often defy the standard arrangement whereby they should respond, in a set order, to questions asked by the host. Instead of performing their prototypical roles throughout the debate, they react to what they consider the needs of the current situation and adopt, for example, a non-prototypical, more adversarial stance by asking questions directly to each other (see also Boyd on debates, this volume). Thus, they frequently employ language forms which transgress the conventional boundaries of the principal genre (i.e., here, the studio debate) and enter the territory of the "on-demand" genre, the interview in fact. The conclusion is that, especially in complex public discourses, genre interpersonal roles should be regarded as hierarchies of behavioral patterns, involving more and less typical and expected behaviors, manifested through different language arsenals.

3. Analyzing "political" genres

The way political genres are approached in this volume presupposes a relatively broad view of political communication, which we take to encompass all communicative acts whereby (representatives of) different social groups and institutions pursue their (particular) interests, needs, aspirations, and values (Fairclough 2006; Okulska and Cap 2010; Cap 2013). The pursuit of political goals always forces individuals or groups to assume both cooperative and competing positions in social interaction, thus upholding or contesting the existing power differential. On this view, "political communication" occurs within and between at least the following three domains: the state political system at national and trans-national level (e.g. government(s), parliament, political parties, elections, debates), the highly diversified sphere of governmental and non-governmental social institutions as well as the "grassroots" initiatives (businesses, NGOs, educational organizations, workplaces, etc. – but also extraparliamentary campaigns and social movements), and the media system. The role of the media is often to connect the former two, by constantly "depoliticizing" the settled practices of the stabilized political structures of the state and simultaneously "politicizing" the unstable, fluctuating, emergent tendencies and interests of the "lifeworld" or "civil society" (Muntigl 2002; Fairclough 1995, 2006).

Research in political genres is thus far best documented at the level of (mediatized) national politics; traditionally, such forms as political speeches (Cap 2002, 2008, 2010; Schäffner ed. 1997; Sauer 2002; Fairclough 2000; Muntigl 2002; Graham, Keenan, and Dowd 2004; Charteris-Black 2005; Dedaić 2006; Reisigl 2008; Bastow 2010; El-Hussari 2010), election posters (Richardson and Wodak 2009), policy papers (Muntigl et al. 2000; Krzyżanowski and Wodak 2010), (parliamentary) debates (Bayley 2004; Fetzer and Lauerbach eds. 2007; Wodak 2009; Ilie ed. 2010), press conferences (Ekström 2003, 2009; Ekström and Patrona eds. 2011; Jacobs 2011), and political interviews (Blum-Kulka 1983; Greatbatch 1988, 1998; Heritage and Greatbatch 1991; Okulska 2004, 2006a, 2006b; Fetzer and Lauerbach eds. 2007) have received most attention. This is rather unsurprising given the relatively stable language characteristics of these genres, but one could argue that such an apparent stability has been a constraining factor in the particular studies, rendering many of them self-contained. Thus, one goal of the present collection will be to show more extensively how genres of (trans-)national politics borrow from other genres in the public sphere (see esp. Wodak's chapter, on political vs. business meetings), and how they typically behave when migrating through various media channels (see esp. the chapters by Lauerbach, Molek-Kozakowska, Mackay).

Overall, research in genres in political communication – defined as broadly as above – poses important questions (and promises findings) for the theory of communicative genres in general. Here are the main reasons:

A. The heterogeneity of political genres essentializes the cornerstone issue in the genre theory, i.e. proposing typologies and hierarchies for which adequate methodological procedures could be designed and followed. Researching political genres is, without exaggeration, a continual struggle to maintain analytic consistency, in the face of all the possible evolutions a given genre is capable of. Let us take the process of mediatization as an obvious example. Is it possible for a genre to retain its distinctive features once it has felicitously migrated into the media domain? Or has the migration resulted in the new important distinctive features which can no longer be accounted for within the original theoretical framework of the genre? Recall the argument in 2.4: the analyst could theorize a priori, based on his/her expert knowledge, upon the form and function of a political speech *as such*, but do his/her pre-postulates and the research agenda still obtain if the speech is received in, say, an online multimodal embedding which has music and image accompany the speech text? It would seem logical to assume that the functionality of the particular language forms making up the text got affected/enhanced by the accompanying multimodal elements; thus, one way to proceed could be to identify the common function carriers at the textual and the extra-textual levels. That way, however, by altering the original methodological procedure to capture a new data instance, we virtually endorse a new generic being. Which is by no means a random possibility since in the area of political communication there are systematic connections between non-mediatized and (potentially) mediatized genres (policy documents vs. broadcast political speeches (live-announcing the policies); press releases vs. news conferences and media reports; etc.), and the more the material moves along such "chains" or "networks", the less is left of its "original" generic features, including the authorship features. One could say, in Bourdieu's words, that the "linguistic market" (Bourdieu 1992, 1993, 2005[5]), involving constant mediatization and recontextualization of content, continually updates the "value" of the original "linguistic capital" the political speaker possesses to maintain or change power relations through his/her discourse. Typically, content migration detracts from that capital: the more "distant" becomes the speaker from his/her original message, the less remains of his/her original goals and of the generic format the message follows (or rather, followed) to further these goals. The intensity of content migration in modern political communication is thus an adverse factor in considering anything like "authorship" a criterion to define (lasting/stable) generic features of that content.

B. Analysis of genres in political communication creates the need to revisit the central issues the genre theory has agreed upon, esp. with respect to properties taken as common to all or most of the communicative genres (viz. Sections 2.1–2.5). This is not to say that political genres undermine the rationale for the consensus as a whole; nonetheless, they exhibit cases which might need special treatment and extra caution on the part of the analyst. There are, as has been indicated in 2.1–2.5, at least five such case categories. First, abstracting the distinctive features of a political genre, both functional and linguistic, requires assessing the genre from a diachronic, evolutionary perspective, in order to judge its current liability (or a lack thereof) to a specific kind of inquiry which involves, in each situation, a uniquely appropriated ratio of theoretical pre-conception and data analysis. Second, political genres make explicit possible differences in the analytic challenge posed by the two usually disparate yet often fallaciously equated language formulas, of (i) context-activation and (ii) context-realization (thus prompting extra focus on the latter). Third, they cast the much-desired light on the theoretically unsound contradiction between the conventional stability of generic macrostructures, and their actual, situation-determined openness to accommodate optional language forms (as parts of optional stages in goal accomplishment). Fourth, political genres elucidate extremely well the many complex relations (and their research repercussions) that may hold within any set of genres occupying a social field, the kinds of connection that range between modular co-existence and hybridity. Fifth, analysis of genres in political communication refines the core conception of interpersonal roles in the genre theory; political genres do not assign stable or permanent interpersonal roles, they rather assign prototypical roles but at the same time allow frequent and often systematic shifts between the "center" and the "periphery" so to say, thus activating and sanctioning hierarchies of communicative acting.

C. Political communication, especially at the level of national politics, involves realization of macro-goals (winning an election race, soliciting legitimization of policies, etc.) through a continual build-up and implementation of constitutive practices such as, for instance, election campaign speeches, debates, advertising, all of which have their internal (micro-)structures. This brings us to the question whether there is possibly any "primary" or "prototypical" level or stage in the accomplishment of political goals at which genres are best identified, named, and classified. The ensuing question involves the status of a hypothetical "hyper-genre" of/in political communication in general: would such a broad concept, if ever defined, possess any explanatory power at all?

It seems that one should be skeptical with regard to both questions. The vast pragmatic research on discourse constructs conceptually similar to genres (see Levinson 1979, 1992, on activity types; Linell 1998, on communicative projects; Grundy 1995, on speech events; etc.) or on genres as such (Bauman 1992; Luckmann 1995; Thibault 2003; etc.) leaves little doubt: hierarchies of communicative acting are virtually infinite because intentionality and goal-enactment levels are infinite in the first place, and thus relatively stabilized "genres" can be potentially identified at more than one level of a given hierarchical structure – as long as the analyst sees some rationale to identify them. The election night broadcast (see Lauerbach, this volume; Malkmus, this volume) is a case in point, whose implications straddle the boundaries of political communication. Multiple parts of the broadcast scenario (speeches, interviews, analyses and comments, etc.) possess predictable generic characteristics at the level of their internal structure, but since most of them occur in the broadcast in a set order, according to conventionalized formulas and for a general purpose different from the specific roles they play as the program's isolated units, it is perhaps legitimate to call the whole scenario a (macro) genre, too. Thus, what endorses the recognition of a (political) genre is *not* the communication level or the genre's clusivity (i.e. whether it is potentially member of another genre); much rather, the stability of content-, form-, and goal-related aspects.

Looking for hyper-genres, functional macrostructures of/in political communication may be suffering from an inherent arbitrariness and lack of objectivity, but, paradoxically, it is often the awareness of these limitations at the macro-level that turns productive at the micro-level. Since the large discourse forms involving heterogeneous content are difficult to handle generically, the analyst gets a prompt to approach the component parts of the content in a bottom-up, data-driven fashion, in order to arrive at smaller-range but clearer-cut, results. Such an approach sheds light on the many different micro-functions of and ways in which constellations of different pieces of the same macro-content are *actually used*. As a result, the micro-functions of assigning social identities specific to different micro-contexts emerge as candidate criteria in genre typology, at least at the micro-level (Myers 2010[6]). For instance, one response to the heterogeneous nature of political interview, as well as to the sheer volume of content making up that (macro-[?])genre,[7] has been an attempt to narrow down the scope of analysis to the "adversarial political interview" (Bell and van Leeuwen 1994), so a clearer, more precise generic structure could be defined. Accordingly, the consecutive stages of "greeting/soliciting opinion/checking/challenging/entrapment/release" were successfully identified and described with the help of enough data to warrant sound conclusions. In that sense, while the "hyper-genre" as such does a limited amount of methodological work directly, it is still a concept that serves, indirectly, the discipline of the study, which research in political communication finely demonstrates.

3.1   This collection

Our goal in proposing this collection is (viz. Section 1) to make a contribution to the study of genres in political communication, and, by characterizing this complex enterprise from methodological, theoretical and empirical standpoints, offer insights that add to the analysis of communicative genres in general. Such a two-fold objective entails that we concentrate on the most distinctive traits of political genres which are at the same time the most useful in shedding light on the main tenets of the genre theory; this relationship has been captured, theoretically, in A–C above. The current question is which genres in political communication should be approached and within what structure, to address the three arguments empirically?

To answer the latter point first, we refrain from an attempt to devote each consecutive chapter to a "different" genre, thus precluding an impression that, by the end of the volume, the list has been exhausted. As was documented, neither the nature of political communication as a concept nor the nature of genres themselves, be they "political" or not, allow that. Instead of rigidly distinguishing between genres as such, we make an organized attempt to distinguish between *the ways political genres are usually worked on* – which involves the issues of what research knowledge is applied, what analytic aspirations are pursued, and what results are sought, in the different studies. Accordingly, the volume is divided into the **"theory-driven approaches" (Part I, six chapters)** and the **"data-driven approaches" (Part II, six chapters)**. The distinction between "theory-" and "data-driven" should be understood as an attempt to elucidate the difference between (but also the synergy of) the approaches which first propose, adopt or adapt methodological framework(s) and then proceed, top-down, to endorse it/them at the discourse analytic level of the specific genre instantiations; and those whose emphasis is on collecting and systematizing the bottom-level (novel) discourse data, to suggest "what else" or "what more" could be theorized about the genre from which the data were drawn.[8] Such a distinction and its repercussions can be elaborated on several planes which corroborate its validity. Most obviously, theory-driven approaches involve more expert knowledge (or sometimes, more "educated intuition" following from considerations of or even belonging to, the genre social context; viz. e.g. Ruth Wodak's expertise, see Note 1 in her chapter) on the part of the analyst than data-driven approaches do. At the same time, data-driven studies involve, more than theory-driven ones, dealing with data instances some of which contradict one another, making the analyst invest extra effort to establish, inductively, plausible regularities – or else, give up on his/her project altogether. These methodological characterizations are reflected in the type of content and form of genres that lend themselves to either approach. While the scope of data-driven analyses is pretty necessarily fragmentary and suited to provide some finely-focused additions to the theory via studying less established generic structures, theory-driven studies usually have their lens on the better established, conventionally recognized forms. Needless to say, since most (political) genres are in the process of continual change (conventionalization, hybridization, migration between thematic domains), the boundary between theory- and data-driven approaches remains fuzzy, thus calling for a possibly synergetic stance.

This brings us to the question which genres are represented in which of the volume parts. Notwithstanding the typological constraints, Part I deals (except for its last chapter) with genres that have been traditionally of interest to political discourse analysts (e.g. political speeches, political interviews, policy documents, etc.). As was discussed at the beginning of Section 3, these forms have indeed received a considerable attention (Fairclough 2006) – which can be considered a response to their relatively stabilized and thus readily "analyzable" structure, but also a factor further channeling and fixing their research agenda for the future. Nonetheless, the chapters in Part I suggest a number of interesting deviations from this agenda. In Part II, the issue of research consistency and de-fragmentation gets increasingly salient as the genres analyzed are often newly evolving forms (e.g. online advertisements, blogs) or the focus is on genre elements/components/features (e.g. conceptual metaphor and framing in debates, talk shows' role in campaigns, speeches in election night broadcasts, legitimation patterns in policy-setting speeches) some of which are considered (sub-)genres themselves (or the analyses make them deserve such a label). Altogether, one can see that – despite the reservations above – the list of genres in the collection is rather comprehensive; but more importantly, in certain cases (e.g. speeches) one genre is approached from two perspectives, theory- and data-driven, to capture its role as both an umbrella and a component category of description. The final general remark is that Part I chapters (except Chapter 6) are usually longer than Part II chapters since, in order to put forward any truly new claims (whether theoretical or empirical), Part I authors (Gruber, Lauerbach, Wodak) often need ample space to bring together multiple and long-worked-on theories relevant to a given ("old", "traditional") genre.

The opening chapter of **Part I**, by **Helmut Gruber**, is, in many ways, a comprehensive follow-up on the content of the present Introduction. It offers a largely theoretical overview of the relation between the different genre theories (e.g. Bazerman 1988 vs. Russell 1997 vs. Bhatia 1993, 2004 vs. Biber, Connor, and Upton 2007 vs. Martin and Rose 2008) and the knowledge obtained/available from the analysis of political genres, testing how far the theoretical concepts developed in several strands of genre theory (cf. Section 1 in this Introduction) could take us in the analysis of a type of political speech. In this vein, Gruber discusses a number of problems instances of political genres pose for the application of genre theories to political discourse, such as the discrepancy between the mode of production and the mode of delivery ("written to be spoken" texts), the heterogeneity of function aiming to suit a variety of audiences, etc. Gruber's conclusion is that a politically sensitive genre analysis must not only focus on generic features of political texts but also investigate registers and discourses which are realized in these texts. The discussion is catalyzed by insights from the study of the inaugural speeches of the Austrian chancellors in the last decade.

Next, there is **Anita Fetzer and Peter Bull**'s chapter on political interviews. It examines the genre of political interview accounting for its conceptualization in diverse, but, as Fetzer and Bull argue, not mutually exclusive research traditions. To capture the inherent complexity and dynamism of the genre, an approach based on methodological compositionality is adopted, subsuming ethnomethodological conversation analysis (Clayman 1988; Greatbatch 1998), critical discourse analysis (Fairclough 1995, 2001), pragmatics and sociopragmatics (Blum-Kulka 1983; Fetzer 2000; Wilson 1990), social psychology (Bull 2003), and media studies (Fetzer 2006; Fetzer and Lauerbach 2007). The approach recognizes sociopragmatics as the controlling theoretical category, offering an integrated frame of reference anchored to social, cognitive, and linguistic contexts. The authors' theoretical apparatus is put to work to advance the conception of political interviews as an essentially hybrid genre, accommodating the constraints and requirements of media communication and of professional discourse. The hybridity of the genre manifests itself in frequent departures from its prototypical (default) scenario i.e. involving the journalist as interviewer, who asks political questions, and the politician as interviewee, who answers political questions by giving political answers.

The third contribution in Part I, by **Michał Krzyżanowski**, deals with another "well established" genre, the policy document, which is innovatively scrutinized from two complementary perspectives marking two, apparently co-existing, generic and functional macrostructures: the policy-making and the policy communication. To corroborate empirically the rationale for adopting these two perspectives and for recognizing the corresponding macrostructures, the chapter works with European Union (EU) discourses on climate change (CC) as well as their transformation and change over time (2007–2011). Whereas the policy-making macrostructure encompasses regulations and projects of regulations governing actions on CC and introducing EU-wide measures, the (new) macrostructure of policy communication comprises sub-genres supporting "publicization" of CC policy and policy-relevant actions by explaining them to the public. The analysis of dynamic character of EU-CC discourses is framed theoretically by the elaboration of such notions as "discursive change" and "discursive shift" which are at the foundations of observing how discourses within/across different contexts change over time. As is argued in the chapter, a need exists to tackle a substantial discursive change which occurred in EU-CC policy recently and which to a large extent constitutes an adjustment of the EU-CC discourse to relevant Europe-specific as well as global politico-economic developments. As the chapter shows, the said transformation of the EU-CC policy discourse runs between two poles: from perceiving and constructing CC as a form of (more or less global) crisis and threat to showing its mainly economic aspects which, unless tackled, will be a major challenge to the future of (European) economy.

As the focus of the next two chapters becomes increasingly comparative (regarding genre manifestations across discourse domains as well as "sub-genres" within a genre, the latter issue initiated in Krzyżanowski's chapter) and thus spread among different though naturally related issues (both theoretical/definitional and empirical), further prospects open up for addressing, on a one-to-one basis, some specific features of (political) genres as defined in 3 A–C, or earlier.

The aim of **Gerda Lauerbach**'s chapter is to describe the genres and subgenres of television election night broadcasts, and the constraints on their order of sequential chaining. Election night broadcasts are shown to be instances of a macro-genre which consists of a complex, ordered assembly of interlocking genres (speeches, interviews, "breaking news" items, studio "waiting talks", etc.). As such, they can be taken to exhibit the characteristics of "outer" and "inner" generic structure (see e.g. Hasan 1985; Fairclough 1995; Levinson 1979; Luckmann 1986) in a particularly striking manner: their structure depends as much on the "outer" social and political context in which the event is situated as it does on an "internal" logic of communication and information economy. Altogether, Lauerbach's chapter is an important voice in the theoretical debate over such constructs and notions as hyper-generic structures (viz. C above), "chaining" (viz. A), or the fusion of socio-functional and form-related determinants of the genre's composition. The author contributes a top-down perspective on (the logic/rationality of) these concepts, herself providing a bottom-level verification based on, primarily, the British audiovisual and textual data.

The chapter by **Ruth Wodak** deals with the genre of meetings, seen as (the often underappreciated) sites of organizational power, strategic change, and hierarchy reification (Mumby 1988; Kwon et al. 2009; Wodak 2009). It recognizes the scarcity of and theorizes about the need for, systematic studies in the impact of specific rules and conventions underlying the realization of the (postulated) *prototype* genre of meetings *across* institutions, organizations, and social field, as well as in the influence of hierarchies, gender, politeness, contextual constraints, the meeting agenda, etc., on the choice of *specific discursive strategies* in spontaneous interaction. Accordingly, it compares various instances of brainstorming (away day) meetings with everyday routine meetings in political institutions (such as the European Parliament and the European Commission) and business organizations, with the aim of, first, describing similarities and differences – in respect to the prototype genre of meetings – across organizations and social fields; and of secondly investigating the impact of organizational knowledge of the prototype genre on presuppositions and context models of the participants related to the interaction and intended outcome of the meetings. Regarding the latter goal, the chapter prompts (however indirectly) considerations of the role of the communicator in identification of a genre, which eventually brings us to the dilemma voiced at the outset of this Introduction, i.e. "whose recognition counts the most in identifying a genre – the communicator's or the analyst's?"

The last chapter in Part I, written by **James Moir**, marks a transition between the two parts and is meant as venue for a methodological reflection. Its tackles a question the reader might have developed until that point of the volume; namely, given such a multitude and heterogeneity of (political) genres and the accompanying theoretical frameworks, is there a chance at all to find a controlling category of analysis *within* the existing genre theory, or should the search go beyond it? Moir opts for the latter in principle but warns against defining interdisciplinary categories and research tools *a priori*, on the basis of pre-formed analytic conceptions that may apply in one political communication context and genre but not another. To elucidate the dangers he scrutinizes (and eventually rejects) an approach based on reconciliation of political discourse studies and the social psychological research in persuasion (Bull 2007). Moir points to one central problem of this "integrated" approach: it involves long-established empirical preferences of each of the component theories. These empirical preferences (such as the socio-psychological focus on e.g. equivocation, applause-elicitation, and metaphorization) may be counterproductive in their collective over-determination of research in (new) bottom-level data the integrated approach is supposed to handle.

The six chapters in Part II are empirical/case studies; they work with amassment of bottom-level data sets, to provide – as has been said earlier – finely-focused additions to the theory of genres from which the data were drawn. Some of these additions can be considered subtle refinements of the conception of the well-established genres (e.g. speeches, debates), while some others should be viewed as points further sanctioning a given discourse structure as a "genre" – despite evolutionary dynamism, heterogeneity of form, etc. The latter concerns the newly evolving structures whose theoretical and typological scrutiny has a relatively short history (talk shows, online ads, blogs).

The first two chapters in **Part II**, by **Bernhard Forchtner** and **Thorsten Malkmus** respectively, re-address (viz. Gruber, Lauerbach) the genre of political speeches, enriching the theory of the genre by case analyses offering original data-driven insights in one of the most typical characteristics of the political speech, i.e. constructing the "us vs. them" opposition. In Forchtner's chapter, positive (self-)presentation of the "us" camp (and the ensuing negative presentation of the "them" camp) follows from a strategic application of the *rhetoric of the judge-penitence*, the "politics of apology" (Cunningham 1999; Nobles 2008). By confessing wrongdoing (in the past), the political speaker claims a moral high ground from which s/he is able to legitimize his/her own position (and future policies), as well as judge others through constructing them as morally inferior. Forchtner illustrates this strategy in the analysis of a 2003 speech by the then Danish PM Anders Fogh Rasmussen, in which the first public apology for Denmark's collaboration with the Nazi Germany helps establish credibility and moral ground for the country's engagement in the Iraq war. In Malkmus's chapter, the us vs. them dichotomy is examined in the context of speeches made as part of British and German election nights; and thus further, often setting-motivated, micro- and macro-builders of the opposition are identified such as pronominal uses, terms of address, evaluative expressions, stylistic routines, speech act sequences, etc. All those elements, abstracted from Tony Blair's winner speech at the British General Elections 1997 and Gerhard Schröder's winner speech at the German "Bundestagswahlen" 1998, are analyzed for patterns of ideological polarity with respect to van Dijk's (1995, 1998, 2009) socio-cognitive ideological square comprising the four corners: WE, THEY, GOOD, and BAD. Malkmus' study proves van Dijk's socio-cognitive approach is indeed well suited to handle the genre of political speeches involving ideological oppositions, at both macro and micro description levels. At the same time, it offers intercultural evidence for the us/them oppositions as stable features of the genre.

The third contribution in Part II, by **Michael Boyd**, is a study in the genre of debates. The chapter focuses on the final televised debate between the 2008 US presidential candidates Barack Obama and John McCain, and as such connects, on the genre content, form, and medium related planes, with several other texts in the collection. In terms of the content, it follows up on the issues of positive self-presentation and negative other-presentation undertaken by Forchtner and Malkmus. In terms of the genre form and medium, it offers a thoroughly data-based evidence of debates as a hybrid genre (Myers 2008; Halmari 2008) involving aspects of both political interviews (viz. Fetzer and Bull's text) and speeches (viz. Gruber). It is exactly the hybridity of the genre, claims Boyd, that allows participants of debates to force construals of different (competing) worldviews based on the same underlying concept(s) (the NATION AS FAMILY metaphor, in Boyd's text). Finally, in case study descriptive terms, Boyd's chapter shows in its analysis of the candidates' references to "Joe the Plumber" (an embodiment of a working-class everyman), how different strategies of de-contextualization, recontextualization, metaphorization and framing matter in *mediatized politics*.

The issue of mediatization is at the heart of the three final chapters in the volume, which explore the discourse of TV and electronic genres. The contribution by **Katarzyna Molek-Kozakowska** scrutinizes the nightly TV talk show (Scannell 1996; Hume 2000; Lorenzo-Dus 2009; among others) as a strategic persuasive genre in the American political campaigning. Working with a selection of shows (CBS's *Late Show with David Letterman*, CNN's *Larry King Live*, NBC's *Tonight Show with Jay Leno*) featuring the 2008 presidential candidates, Molek-Kozakowska explores, from the CDA perspective, the hybrid, "infotainment" conventions of the genre (Płudowski 2008), abstracting the properties that make it useful for the purposes of political persuasion and campaigning. It is demonstrated that the talk show's generic conventions are instrumental to such discursive strategies as the performance of sociability, the management of impression, the manufacture of authenticity, and the maneuvering between the institutional and personal domains of communication (see also Ilie 2001). Enactment of these strategies is sanctioned by the genre's macrostructure (cf. Lauerbach's theoretical account of hyper-genres in Part I) which involves a variety of (multimodal) subgenres: monologues/speeches, "simulated" conversations or interviews (viz. Fetzer and Bull, Part I), music performances, comedy routines, etc. It is shown in the chapter which of their (often multimodal) features are best utilized in talk shows and, vice-versa, how their implementations in the talk show structure inform, bottom-up, their original theories.

The problem of the adaptation of the well-established generic forms (e.g. [elements of] speeches) for the sake of the evolving mediatized forms continues in **Rowan Mackay**'s text, which adds insights from, now, a directly multimodal perspective. Studying Barack Obama's online advertisements from the 2008 election campaign, Mackay poses a novel and radical question that markedly complements the hybridity-focused discussions (based on relatively similar data) in chapters by Boyd and Molek-Kozakowska. The question goes: if a largely stabilized genre (here: political speech) is imported or implemented into a non-prototypical and rather new communicative setting (here: online advertising) to help perform a pragmatic function (here: legitimation), will it – as an established pattern – continue to dominate, or will the new setting/medium reduce its function to a necessarily supporting role? Mackay's own study only opens the debate, but her analysis offers enough data to accept changes in the hierarchy of legitimating tools: most notably, a shift away from the unquestioned primacy of text and talk genres (see also van Leeuwen 2005, 2007).

Monika Kopytowska's contribution on political blogs is the last in the "(new) media series"; mostly because blogging is such a recent, fluid and apparently uncontrollable phenomenon that questions arise (Giltrow and Stein 2009; Grafton 2009) about its current and future status as a "(political) genre" in the first place. To respond to this dilemma, Kopytowska adopts a rigorous, comparative corpus-based perspective on blogs written by prominent Polish and British politicians, as well as on the commentary posts, searching for systematic ways in which a common cognitive and axiological sphere of shared experience is created to replace the traditional uni-directional media-audiences relationship. The study, involving, among others, keyword and concordance analysis, endorses political blogs as a new generic form of social interaction and identity construction (Myers 2010) whereby strategic lexical, grammatical and functional means are deployed to enact a more equal and horizontal form of a dialectic relation (Miller and Shepherd 2009) between "political elites" and "ordinary citizens", the public/political and the private, the official and the informal, etc. Kopytowska demonstrates that what makes this dialectic relation possible is the mechanism of "proximization" (Cap 2006, 2008, 2013), allowing for the reduction of the temporal, spatial, axiological, cognitive and emotional distance between the blogger and his or her audience,[9] and thus for the mediation of experience and the creation of a virtual community around the "networked public sphere". Thus her approach aligns with and further corroborates (viz. the beginning of Section 3) the conception of political communication as a complex network of increasingly mediatized, inherently interactive/ collaborative practices of "the state" and "the lifeworld" or "civil society".

Summing up, the content of the particular chapters and the volume's structure as a whole have been profiled to enact two main goals: the "direct" goal to review/refine the conception of political communication through the analysis of its generic manifestations, and the "indirect" goal to enrich the genre theory with insights from the study of political genres. Approaching the chapters as sets of mutually interactive "meta-data" revealing possible avenues in genre research allows the reader to work out *an informed position* on what research tracks seem the most promising, what paths seem "dead-end streets", and what are the limits to which that knowledge could yield (new) typologies of (political) genres. Recognizing the status of (political) genre as a traditionally *classificatory* concept, we suggest that, given the current as well as the anticipated dynamism of (political) generic forms, prospective genre changes and the ensuing migrations between any typological "classes", "categories", etc., be best investigated on *methodological, rather than thematic,* planes. As demonstrated in the present collection, a methodological approach does *not* detract from the comprehensiveness of the thematic picture; quite conversely, it is often the need to exemplify an important theoretical point that determines inclusion of extra empirical data (viz. the role of Mackay's chapter which, on top of its "micro" input, invites the "macro" issues of genre migration, hierarchical ordering, generic dominance, etc.). Furthermore, any research agenda that is mindful of the questions of expert knowledge, analytic pre-conceptions, the synergetic, abductive relation between the theory-driven hypothesis, data verification and, conceivably, reformulation of the hypothesis, is naturally better suited to draw critically from the "common points" in genre theory (viz. 2.1–5). That is because each of these points represents a mix of deductive/inductive reasoning, the most striking example being perhaps the concept of genre as a "flexible macrostructure", a clear theoretical compromise. Finally, let us have the volume's message endorsed by an "applied" (rhetorical) question: what better way to teach (political) generic conventions (to a communicator, but notably, also to an analyst) than by elucidating the status of "expert knowledge", "analytic pre-conceptions", etc., etc., as factors allowing or disallowing to follow a convention, allowing or disallowing to alter it?

Notes

1. It is beyond the scope of this book to discuss work on genres in literary studies (which goes back to at least the 18th century when the term genre was borrowed from French), albeit one cannot deny the influence of that work on esp. early language studies. Establishing the literary-linguistic analytic link is usually attributed to Mikhail Bakhtin, whose many ideas and observations (concerning genres' heterogeneity, stability, predictability, etc.; cf. Bakhtin 1952–1953 [1986]) are still under constructive scrutiny by contemporary theorists (see Corbett 2006).

2. For further discussion of generic prototypes see, e.g., Wierzbicka (1983, 1989, 1990, 1999); McCarthy and Carter (1994); Witosz (2001); Vergaro (2002).

3. The concept of generic hierarchies and the rationality of distinguishing and naming super-ordinate and subordinate genres will be discussed in Section 3.

4. Recently, though, some scientific journals have proposed a hybrid form, *review article*, which demonstrates a fine balance between the summarizing, evaluative and novel content. Examples of such journals in the field of linguistics include *International Review of Pragmatics* and *Pragmatics and Society*.

5. See also Stråth and Wodak (2009) for an overview.

6. We take Myers' (2010) position as one prioritizing issues of use and function over content and form, in genre typology and description. While this position adds well to the explanatory power of the specific phenomena Myers (2010) is preoccupied with ("blogs and wikis"), we find problematic the status of function – at least as the sole or main criterion – in proposing typologies of broader generic forms, especially the "traditional" political genres (see the beginning of Section 3). Given the functional indeterminacy of content and form, at virtually any level of expression, from word to text, such an approach would cause genres to multiply beyond any typological framework. An alternative solution – though still intuitive and thus not meriting placement anywhere outside this note – would involve combining a possibly substantial number of both content/form- and function-oriented criteria. It seems that one candidate group reconciling the various strands of research in genres might be the four criteria of: content, setting, medium, and function (cf. Cap 2012). These could be used to determine prototypicality, status in the generic hierarchy, and the status of "genre" in the first place, based on *how many of the criteria are consistently matched in discourse throughout the socio-political field and the time-frame in which the genre has been operating*. For instance, Discourse of the War-on-Terror (Cap 2013) would claim a genre label through its default content (terrorist themes), typical function (legitimization), and a relative predictability of major communicative channels and venues. Inability to reach a "threshold number" of the criteria, or matching them partly, or differently at different stages of genre's development, would disqualify the genre as a genre, would brush aside a vast number of "ad hoc genres" arising in highly particularized contexts hindering their further development.

7. On the other hand, inclusion of political interview in the genre of, for instance, election night broadcast, makes more appropriate the "micro" prefix. It seems that, given the current state of research and the criteria it offers, any political genre could potentially belong into a "macro genre", while simultaneously encompassing a number of "micro genres".

8. Thus, our distinction appropriates findings from classic works on deductive (top-down) and inductive (bottom-up) modes of discourse/text comprehension and analysis (see e.g. Beaugrande 1991, 1997; Beaugrande and Dressler 1981; Kintsch 1988, 1989; van Dijk 1985; van Dijk and Kintsch 1983).

9. See also Myers (2010) for discussion of how markers of time and space can be used to construe social distance, through denoting in- and out-group memberships.

References

Bakhtin, Mikhail. 1952–1953 [1986]. *Speech Genres and Other Late Essays*, ed. by Caryl Emerson, and Michael Holquist. Austin, TX: University of Austin Press.

Barton, David. 1994. *Literacy: An Introduction to the Ecology of Written Language*. Oxford: Blackwell.

Bastow, Tony. 2010. "*Friends and Allies*: The Rhetoric of Binomial Phrases in a Corpus of U.S. Defense Speeches." In *Perspectives in Politics and Discourse*, ed. by Urszula Okulska, and Piotr Cap, 143–154. Amsterdam: Benjamins.

Bauman, Richard. 1992. "Contextualization, Tradition, and the Dialogue of Genres: Icelandic Legends of the *Kraftskald*." In *Rethinking Context: Language as an Interactive Phenomenon*, ed. by Alessandro Duranti, and Charles Goodwin, 125–146. Cambridge: Cambridge University Press.

Bazerman, Charles. 1988. *Shaping Written Knowledge. The Genre and Activity of the Experimental Article in Science*. Madison, WI: University of Wisconsin Press.

—. 2000. "Letters and the Social Grounding of Differentiated Genres." In *Letter Writing as a Social Practice*, ed. by David Barton, and Nigel Hall, 15–29. Amsterdam: Benjamins.

Beaugrande, Robert de. 1991. *Linguistic Theory: The Discourse of Fundamental Works*. London: Longman.

—. 1997. *New Foundations for Science of Text and Discourse*. Norwood, NJ: Ablex Publishing Corporation.

Beaugrande, Robert de, and Wolfgang Dressler. 1981. *Introduction to Text Linguistics*. London: Longman.

Bell, Philip, and Theo van Leeuwen. 1994. *Media Interview*. Kensington, NSW: University of New South Wales Press.

Bex, Tony. 1996. *Variety in Written English: Texts in Society, Society in Texts*. London: Routledge.

Bayley, Paul. (ed.). 2004. *Cross-Cultural Perspectives on Parliamentary Discourse*. Amsterdam: Benjamins.

Bhatia, Vijay. 1993. *Analysing Genre: Language Use in Professional Settings*. London: Longman.

—. 2004. *Worlds of Written Discourse*. London: Continuum.

Biber, Douglas, Ulla Connor, and Thomas Upton. 2007. *Discourse on the Move: Using Corpus Analysis to Describe Discourse Structure*. Amsterdam: Benjamins.

Blum-Kulka, Shoshana. 1983. "The Dynamics of Political Interviews." *Text* 3: 131–153.

Bourdieu, Pierre. 1992. *Language and Symbolic Power*. Cambridge: Polity Press.

—. 1993. *Outline of a Theory of Practice*. Cambridge: Polity Press.

—. 2005. "The Political Field, the Social Science Field, and the Journalistic Field." In *Bourdieu and the Journalistic Field*, ed. by Rodney Benson, and Erik Neveu, 29–47. Cambridge: Polity Press.

Bull, Peter. 2003. *The Microanalysis of Political Communication: Claptrap and Ambiguity*. London: Routledge.

—. 2007. "Political Language and Persuasive Communication." In *Language, Discourse and Social Psychology*, ed. by Ann Weatherall, Bernadette Watson, and Cindy Gallois, 15–33. Basingstoke: Palgrave.

Brown, Gillian, and George Yule. 1983. *Discourse Analysis*. Cambridge: Cambridge University Press.

Cap, Piotr. 2002. *Explorations in Political Discourse. Methodological and Critical Perspectives*. Frankfurt am Main: Peter Lang.

—. 2006. *Legitimization in Political Discourse: A Cross-disciplinary Perspective on the Modern US War Rhetoric*. Newcastle: Cambridge Scholars Press.

—. 2008. "Towards the Proximization Model of the Analysis of Legitimization in Political Discourse." *Journal of Pragmatics* 40: 17–41.

—. 2010. "Axiological Aspects of Proximization." *Journal of Pragmatics* 42: 392–407.

—. 2012. "On Genre Problems in (Political) Discourse." *Topics in Linguistics* 8: 11–16.

—. 2013. *Proximization: The Pragmatics of Symbolic Distance Crossing.* Amsterdam: Benjamins.

Charteris-Black, Jonathan. 2005. *Politicians and Rhetoric: The Persuasive Power of Metaphor.* Basingstoke: Palgrave.

Chouliaraki, Lilie, and Norman Fairclough. 1999. *Discourse in Late Modernity: Rethinking Critical Discourse Analysis.* Edinburgh: Edinburgh University Press.

Clayman, Steven. 1988. "Displaying Neutrality in Television News Interviews." *Social Problems* 35: 474–492.

Corbett, John. 2006. "Genre and Genre Analysis." In *Encyclopedia of Language & Linguistics 2nd Edition, vol. 5,* ed. by Keith Brown, 26–32. Oxford: Elsevier.

Coupland, Justine. (ed.). 2000. *Small Talk.* London: Longman.

Cunningham, Michael. 1999. "Saying Sorry: The Politics of Apology." *The Political Quarterly* 70: 285–293.

Dedaić, Mirjana. 2006. "Political Speeches and Persuasive Argumentation." In *Encyclopedia of Language & Linguistics 2nd Edition, vol. 9,* ed. by Keith Brown, 700–707. Oxford: Elsevier.

Dressler, Wolfgang. (ed.). 1978. *Current Trends in Textlinguistics.* Berlin: Walter de Gruyter.

Eggins, Suzanne. 1994. *An Introduction to Systemic Functional Linguistics.* London: Pinter.

Eggins, Suzanne, and James Martin. 1997. "Genres and Registers of Discourse." In *Discourse as Structure and Process,* ed. by Teun van Dijk, 230–257. London: Sage.

Ekström, Mats. 2003. "Epistemologies of TV-journalism. A Theoretical Framework." *Journalism: Theory, Practice and Criticism* 3: 259–282.

—. 2009. "Power and Affiliation in Presidential Press Conferences: A Study on Interruptions, Jokes and Laughter." *Journal of Language and Politics* 8: 386–415.

Ekström, Mats, and Marianna Patrona. (eds). 2011. *Talking Politics in Broadcast Media: Cross-cultural Perspectives on Political Interviewing, Journalism and Accountability.* Amsterdam: Benjamins.

El-Hussari, Ibrahim. 2010. "President Bush's Address to the Nation on U.S. Policy in Iraq: A Critical Discourse Analysis Approach." In *Perspectives in Politics and Discourse,* ed. by Urszula Okulska, and Piotr Cap, 99–117. Amsterdam: Benjamins.

Fairclough, Norman. 1993. *Discourse and Social Change.* Cambridge, MA: Polity Press.

—. 1995. *Media Discourse.* London: Edward Arnold.

—. 2000. *Analysing Discourse: Textual Analysis for Social Research.* London: Routledge.

—. 2001. *New Labour, New Language?* London: Routledge.

—. 2006. "Genres in Political Discourse." In *Encyclopedia of Language & Linguistics 2nd Edition, vol. 5,* ed. by Keith Brown, 32–38. Oxford: Elsevier.

Fetzer, Anita. 2000. "Negotiating Validity Claims in Political Interviews." *Text* 20: 1–46.

—. 2006. "'Minister, We Will See How the Public Judges You'. Media References in Political Interviews." *Journal of Pragmatics* 38: 180–195.

Fetzer, Anita, and Gerda Lauerbach. (eds). 2007. *Political Discourse in the Media: Cross-Cultural Perspectives.* Amsterdam: Benjamins.

Freedman, Aviva, and Peter Medway. (eds). 1994. *Genre and the New Rhetoric.* London: Taylor and Francis.

Giltrow, Janet, and Dieter Stein. (eds). 2009. *Genres in the Internet.* Amsterdam: Benjamins.

Grafton, Kathryn. 2009. "Situating the Public Social Actions of Blog Posts." In *Genres in the Internet*, ed. by Janet Giltrow, and Dieter Stein, 85–111. Amsterdam: Benjamins.

Graham, Phil, Thomas Keenan, and Anne Dowd. 2004. "A Call to Arms at the End of History: A Discourse-Historical Analysis of George W. Bush's Declaration of War on Terror." *Discourse and Society* 15: 199–222.

Greatbatch, David. 1988. "A Turn-Taking System for British News Interviews." *Language in Society* 17: 401–430.

—. 1998. "Conversation Analysis: Neutralism in British News Interviews." In *Approaches to Media Discourse*, ed. by Allan Bell and Peter Garrett, 163–185. Oxford: Blackwell.

Gruber, Helmut, and Peter Muntigl. (eds). 2005. *Approaches to Genre* (Special Issue of *Folia Linguistica* XXXIX/1-2). Berlin: Mouton de Gruyter.

Grundy, Peter. 1995. *Doing Pragmatics*. London: Edward Arnold.

Halliday, Michael A. K., and Ruqaiya Hasan. 1989. *Language, Context and Text: Aspects of Language in a Social-Semiotic Perspective*. Oxford: Oxford University Press.

Halliday, Michael A. K., and James Martin. 1993. *Writing Science: Literacy and Discursive Power*. London: Falmer Press.

Halmari, Helena. 2008. "On the Language of the Clinton-Dole Presidential Campaign Debates: General Tendencies and Successful Strategies." *Journal of Language and Politics* 7: 247–270.

Hasan, Ruqaiya. 1978. "Text in the Systemic-Functional Model." In *Current Trends in Textlinguistics*, ed. by Wolfgang Dressler, 228–246. Berlin and New York: Walter de Gruyter.

—. 1985. "The Structure of a Text." In *Language, Context, and Text: Aspects of Language in a Social-Semiotic Perspective*, ed. by Michael A. K. Halliday, and Ruqaia Hasan, 40–56. Victoria: Deakin University Press.

Heritage, John, and David Greatbatch. 1991. "On the Institutional Character of Institutional Talk: The Case of News Interviews." In *Talk and Social Structure*, ed. by Deirdre Boden, and Don Zimmerman, 93–137. Cambridge: Polity Press.

Hume, Ellen. 2000. "Talk Show Culture." Retrieved on 10 June 2009 from http://www.ellenhume.com/articles/talkshow1.htm

Ilie, Cornelia. 2001. "Semi-Institutional Discourse: The Case of Talk Shows." *Journal of Pragmatics* 33: 209–254.

—. (ed.). 2010. *European Parliaments under Scrutiny: Argumentative Strategies and Rhetorical Styles*. Amsterdam: Benjamins.

Jacobs, Geert. 2011. "Press Conferences on the Internet: Technology, Mediation and Access in the News." *Journal of Pragmatics* 43: 1900–1911.

Kintsch, Walter. 1988. "The Role of Knowledge in Discourse Comprehension: A Construction-Integration Model." *Psychological Review* 95: 163–182.

—. 1989. "The Representation of Knowledge and the Use of Knowledge in Discourse Comprehension." In *Language Processing in Social Context*, ed. by Rainer Dietrich, and Carl Graumann, 185–209. Amsterdam: North Holland.

Krzyżanowski, Michał, and Ruth Wodak. 2010. "Hegemonic Multilingualism in/of the EU Institutions: An Inside-Outside Perspective on the European Language Policies and Practices." In *Mehrsprachigkeit in europäischer Perspektive*, ed. by Heike Böhringer, Cornelia Hülmbauer, and Eva Vetter, 20–43. Frankfurt am Main: Peter Lang.

Kwon, Winston, Ian Clarke, and Ruth Wodak. 2009. "Organizational Decision-Making, Discourse, and Power: Integrating across Contexts and Scales." *Discourse & Communication* 3: 273–302.

Lemke, Jay L. 1985. "Ideology, Intertextuality, and the Notion of Register." In *Systemic Perspectives on Discourse. Volume 1*, ed. by James D. Benson, and William S. Greaves, 275–294. Norwood, NJ: Ablex Publishing Company.

Levinson, Stephen C. 1979. "Activity Types and Language." *Linguistics* 17: 365–399.

—. 1992. "Activity Types and Language." In *Talk at Work*, ed. by Paul Drew, and John Heritage, 66–100. Cambridge: Cambridge University Press.

Labov, William. 1972. *Language in the Inner City*. Oxford: Blackwell.

Linell, Per. 1998. *Approaching Dialogue*. Amsterdam: Benjamins.

Longacre, Robert. 1983. *The Grammar of Discourse*. New York, NY: Plenum Press.

Lorenzo-Dus, Nuria. 2009. *Television Discourse: Analyzing Language in the Media*. Basingstoke: Palgrave.

Luckmann, Thomas. 1986. "Grundformen der gesellschaftlichen Vermittlung des Wissens: Kommunikative Gattungen." *Kölner Zeitschrift für Soziologie und Sozialpsychologie Sonderheft 27 (Kultur und Gesellschaft)*: 191–211.

—. 1995. "Interaction Planning and Intersubjective Adjustment of Perspectives by Communicative Genres." In *Social Intelligence and Interaction: Expressions and Implications of the Social Bias in Human Intelligence*, ed. by Esther Goody, 175–188. Cambridge: Cambridge University Press.

Martin, James. 1992. *English Text. System and Structure*. Amsterdam: Benjamins.

Martin, James, and David Rose. 2008. *Genre Relations: Mapping Culture*. London: Equinox.

McCarthy, Michael, and Ronald Carter. 1994. *Language as Discourse: Perspectives for Language Teaching*. London and New York: Longman.

Miller, Carolyn, and Dawn Shepherd. 2009. "Questions for Genre Theory from the Blogosphere." In *Genres in the Internet*, ed. by Janet Giltrow, and Dieter Stein, 263–290. Amsterdam: Benjamins.

Mumby, Dennis. 1988. *Communication and Power in Organizations: Discourse, Ideology and Domination*. Norwood, NJ: Ablex Publishing Corporation.

Muntigl, Peter. 2002. "Politicization and Depoliticization: Employment Policy in the European Union." In *Politics as Text and Talk*, ed. by Paul Chilton, and Christina Schäffner, 45–79. Amsterdam: Benjamins.

Muntigl, Peter, Gilbert Weiss, and Ruth Wodak. (eds). 2000. *European Discourses on Unemployment: An Interdisciplinary Approach to Employment Policy-Making and Organizational Change*. Amsterdam: Benjamins.

Myers, Greg. 2008. "Analyzing Interaction in Broadcast Debates." In *Qualitative Discourse Analysis in the Social Sciences*, ed. by Ruth Wodak and Michał Krzyżanowski, 121–144. Basingstoke: Palgrave.

—. 2010. *The Discourse of Blogs and Wikis*. London: Continuum.

Nobles, Melissa. 2008. *The Politics of Official Apologies*. Cambridge: Cambridge University Press.

Okulska, Urszula. 2004. "Globalisation on the Polish Radio. The Case of Political Interviews." In *Speaking from the Margin. Global English from a European Perspective*, ed. by Anna Duszak, and Urszula Okulska, 239–259. Frankfurt am Main: Peter Lang.

—. 2006a. "English Borrowings in the Polish Media. Assimilation Processes and Gender." *Kwartalnik Neofilologiczny* 53: 208–231.

—. 2006b. "Pośredniość i bezpośredniość w dyskursie politycznym na przykładzie polskich i amerykańskich strategii uzyskiwania informacji w wywiadzie radiowym." [Directness and Indirectness in Political Discourse on the Example of Polish and American Requests for Information in the Radio Interview]. In *Korpusy w angielsko-polskim językoznawstwie kontrastywnym: Teoria i praktyka* [*Corpora in English-Polish Contrastive Linguistics: Theory and Practice*], ed. by Anna Duszak, Elżbieta Gajek, and Urszula Okulska, 183–209. Kraków: Universitas.

Okulska, Urszula, and Piotr Cap (eds). 2010. *Perspectives in Politics and Discourse*. Amsterdam: Benjamins.

Paltridge, Brian. 1995. "Working with Genre: A Pragmatic Perspective." *Journal of Pragmatics* 24: 393–406.

Petöfi, János. (ed.). 1988. *Text and Discourse Constitution. Empirical Aspects, Theoretical Approaches*. Berlin and New York: Walter de Gruyter.

Plett, Heinrich (ed.). 1991. *Intertextuality*. Berlin and New York: Walter de Gruyter.

Płudowski, Tomasz. 2008. *Komunikacja polityczna w amerykańskich kampaniach wyborczych* [*Political Communication in American Election Campaigns*]. Warszawa: Wydawnictwo Naukowe PWN.

Ramallo, Fernando, Anxo Lorenzo Suarez, Xoan Rodriguez-Yanez, and Piotr Cap. (eds). 2009. *New Approaches to Discourse and Business Communication*. Basingstoke: Palgrave.

Reisigl, Martin. 2008. "Analysing Political Rhetoric." In *Qualitative Discourse Analysis in the Social Sciences*, ed. by Ruth Wodak, and Michał Krzyżanowski, 96–120. Basingstoke: Palgrave.

Richardson, John, and Ruth Wodak. 2009. "Recontextualising Fascist Ideologies of the Past: Right-Wing Discourses on Employment and Nativism in Austria and the United Kingdom." *Critical Discourse Studies* 6: 251–267.

Rosch, Eleanor. 1973. "Natural Categories." *Cognitive Psychology* 4: 328–350.

Russell, David. 1997. "Rethinking Genre in School and Society: An Activity Theory Analysis." *Written Communication* 14: 504–554.

Sauer, Christoph. 2002. "Ceremonial Text and Talk. A Functional-Pragmatic Approach." In *Politics as Text and Talk*, ed. by Paul Chilton, and Christina Schäffner, 111–142. Amsterdam: Benjamins.

Scannell, Paddy. 1996. *Radio, Television and Modern Life*. Oxford: Blackwell.

Schäffner, Christina. (ed.). 1997. *Analysis of Political Speeches*. Clevedon: Multilingual Matters.

Stråth, Bo, and Ruth Wodak. 2009. "Europe-Discourse-Politics-Media-History: Constructing Crises." In *The European Public Sphere and the Media: Europe in Crisis*, ed. by Anna Triandafyllidou, Ruth Wodak, and Michał Krzyżanowski, 15–33. Basingstoke: Palgrave.

Swales, John. 1981. *Aspects of Article Introductions*. Birmingham: Aston University Press.

—. 1990. *Genre Analysis: English in Academic and Research Settings*. Cambridge: Cambridge University Press.

Thibault, Paul. 2003. "Contextualization and Social Meaning-Making Practices." In *Language and Interaction. Discussions with John J. Gumperz*, ed. by Susan Eerdmans, Carlo Prevignano, and Paul Thibault, 41–62. Amsterdam: Benjamins.

Triandafyllidou, Anna, Ruth Wodak, and Michał Krzyżanowski. (eds). 2009. *The European Public Sphere and the Media: Europe in Crisis*. Basingstoke: Palgrave.

Valle, Ellen. 1997. "A Scientific Community and Its Texts: A Historical Discourse Study." In *The Construction of Professional Discourse*, ed. by Britt-Louise Gunnarsson, Per Linell, and Brengt Nordberg, 76–98. New York, NY: Longman.

van Dijk, Teun. 1980. *Macrostructures: An Interdisciplinary Study of Global Structures in Discourse, Interaction, and Cognition*. Hillsdale, NJ: Erlbaum.

—. (ed.). 1985. *Discourse and Communication*. Berlin: Walter de Gruyter.

—. 1995. "Discourse Analysis as Ideology Analysis." In *Language and Peace*, ed. by Christina Schäffner, and Anita Wenden, 17–33. Aldershot: Dartmouth.

—. 1998. "Opinions and Ideologies in the Press." In *Approaches to Media Discourse*, ed. by Allan Bell, and Peter Garrett, 21–63. Oxford: Blackwell.

—. 2009. *Society and Discourse. How Social Contexts Influence Text and Talk*. Cambridge: Cambridge University Press.

van Dijk, Teun, and Walter Kintsch. 1983. *Strategies of Discourse Comprehension*. New York, NY: Academic Press.

van Leeuwen, Theo. 2005. *Introducing Social Semiotics*. London: Routledge.

—. 2007. "Legitimation in Discourse and Communication." *Discourse & Communication* 1: 91–112.

Vergaro, Carla. 2002. "'Dear Sirs, What Would You Do If You Were in Our Position?' Discourse Strategies in Italian and English Money Chasing Letters." *Journal of Pragmatics* 34: 1211–1233.

Ventola, Eija. 1987. *The Structure of Social Interaction: A Systematic Approach to the Semiotics of Service Encounters*. London: Frances Pinter.

Werlich, Egon. 1979. *Typologie der Texte. Entwurf eines textlinguistischen Modells zur Grundlegung einer Textgrammatik*. Heidelberg: Quelle&Meyer.

—. 1983. "Genry mowy" [Speech Genres]. In *Tekst i zdanie. Zbiór studiów* [*Text and Sentence. A Collection of Studies*], ed. by Teresa Dobrzyńska, and Elżbieta Janus, 125–137. Wrocław: PAN.

—. 1989. "Prototypes in Semantics and Pragmatics: Explicating Attitudinal Meanings in Terms of Prototypes." *Linguistics* 27: 731–769.

—. 1990. "'Prototypes Save': On the Uses and Abuses of the Notion of 'Prototype' in Linguistics and Related Fields." In *Meanings and Prototypes. Studies in Linguistic Categorization*, ed. by Savas Tsohatzidis, 347–367. London: Routledge.

—. 1999. *Język - umysł - kultura* [*Language - Mind - Culture*]. Warszawa: PWN.

Wilson, John. 1990. *Politically Speaking: The Pragmatic Analysis of Political Language*. Oxford: Blackwell.

Witosz, Bożena. 2001. "Gatunek - sporny (?) problem współczesnej refleksji tekstologicznej" [Genre - Controversial (?) Problem of Contemporary Textological Reflection]. *Teksty Drugie* 5: 67–85.

Wodak, Ruth. 2000. "From Conflict to Consensus? The Construction of a Policy Paper." In *European Discourses on Unemployment: An Interdisciplinary Approach to Employment Policy-Making and Organizational Change*, ed. by Peter Muntigl, Gilbert Weiss, and Ruth Wodak, 73–114. Amsterdam: Benjamins.

—. 2009. The Discourse of Politics in Action: Politics as Usual. Basingstoke: Palgrave.

Wodak, Ruth, and Michael Meyer. (eds). 2009. *Methods of Critical Discourse Analysis. 2nd Revised Edition*. London: Sage.

PART I

Theory-driven approaches

CHAPTER 1

Genres in political discourse

The case of the 'inaugural speech' of Austrian chancellors

Helmut Gruber

University of Vienna, Austria

The first part of this chapter provides an overview of the current state of genre theory in various fields of linguistics and discourse analysis. Based on this overview, a set of common features of genre definitions is presented that provides the theoretical basis for the empirical investigation. In the empirical part, the inaugural speeches of three Austrian chancellors (representing the two big Austrian political parties) during the last ten years are analyzed. After a short discussion of relevant contextual features (production process, audience design), lexical characteristics, generic and topical structures, and the co-articulation of topics are analyzed. Results show that, although delivered by politicians from two different political backgrounds, the speeches share many features in terms of lexis and generic structure. Differences become manifest at the topic structure and the co-articulation of topics. In conclusion, it is argued that a politically sensitive genre analysis must not only focus on generic features of political texts but also investigate registers and discourses which are realized in these texts.

1. Introduction

Since the 1980ies, linguists interested in "language in action" have been investigating the relationships between situational contexts, participants in typified speech events, and the recurring structural properties of the forms of talk they use, better known as "genres" of discourse. Much of this research has grown out of applied linguists' interests in the ways newcomers to certain contexts (academic, disciplinary, institutional, etc.) acquire an adequate "communicative competence" in their new environment and how they might be supported in doing so. Apart from investigating a variety of written and oral genres, several partly overlapping and partly distinct genre theories have been developed during these last decades. One of the aims of this chapter is to review the most relevant of them, to identify their conceptual and theoretical parallels and differences, and to suggest a conception of "genre" and related concepts which might be fruitfully used in the analysis of political language.

Investigations of political language have also been vastly conducted during the last decades (cf. journals like "Discourse & Society" or "Journal of Language and Politics"). Most of these studies were conducted under the auspices of Critical Discourse Analysis (CDA) and many of them have used the concept of genre as a theoretical notion without, however, developing a specific conception of "genre". CDA scholars (rather "uncritically") adopted the genre conception of Systemic Functional Linguistics or some other discourse linguistic school and applied it in their projects. One of the reasons for this might lie in CDA's "interdisciplinarity" (or "transdisciplinarity") which tends to combine a panoply of theoretical and methodological concepts in order to investigate socially relevant topics, uncover hidden ideological slants, and provide "prospective critique" (Reisigl and Wodak 2001, 33) of the phenomena under study.

The current chapter pursues a goal more modest than that of most CDA inspired research: it tests how far the theoretical concepts developed in several strands of genre theory can take us in the analysis of a type of political speech (i.e. the inaugural speech of the Austrian chancellor given after the formation of a new government [for analyses of other types of political speech see e.g. this volume's chapters by Forchtner and Malkmus]) which – although highly relevant for the Austrian political system – occurs only rarely and thus offers "members" (i.e. politicians) only very limited opportunities to become familiar with and ac-quire relevant genre knowledge. This effort may be misconstrued as the venture of a deliberately solitary ivory tower dwelling linguist who failed to notice the ad-vent of the age of interdisciplinarity (political theory, mass communication the-ory, and political sociology come to mind in this context) but it is my conviction that – prior to any engagement in inter-, trans-, or any other prefix + disciplinary project – any discipline has to make sure how far and in what respects it can in-vestigate a certain topic with its own concepts and methods. The current chapter presents a modest attempt in this vein.

The chapter is structured as follows: Section 2 presents a short overview of those genre theories which could be relevant for analyzing political language in general; in Section 3, I detail the political relevance of the chancellor's inaugural speech in the Austrian parliamentary system and give a short overview of previ-ous investigations of this genre. This is followed by a detailed analysis of the pro-duction process of inaugural speeches and the linguistic features of the speeches under investigation, their multiple audiences and their integration into several systems of genres of political and media discourse. In the last Section, 4, I try to integrate the discussion of the theoretical approaches in Section 2 with the empirical analysis in Section 3 and discuss which aspects of the speeches can be accounted for by the presented theories and which cannot. In closing, I suggest an enhancement of the existing genre theories through the integration of the concepts of "discourse" and "social field" into a genre theory which is relevant for the analysis of political communication.

2.   Genre theories

In this overview of current genre theories, I only discuss those aspects of the reviewed theories which are relevant for my investigation and refer readers to more comprehensive overviews in other recent publications (e.g. Biber, Connor, and Upton 2007; Lee 2001; Bhatia 2004).[1] The following section is diachronically organized, while the last subsection provides a short account of Fairclough's discourse theory (which shares some characteristics with Keller's approach to discourse analysis informed by the sociology of knowledge; Keller 2011).

2.1   Genre in the "New rhetoric" tradition

In North America, one major tradition of theorizing "genre" was initiated by scholars who refer to their approach as "new rhetoric" (Bazerman 1988; Berkenkotter and Huckin 1995; Freedman and Medway 1994). Originally combining insights from classical rhetoric, literary studies, and communication studies, these scholars stress the historical contingency and the cultural and historical situatedness of genres. Genres are viewed as purposeful, typified social actions which evolve as temporarily stable, yet flexible responses to recurring rhetorical situations (cf. Miller 1994). Genres are inextricably tied to social practices and the persons involved in these practices ("communities of practice"; Lave and Wenger 1991). In the "new rhetoric" view, a genre is not necessarily a linguistic entity, but rather "a social construct that regularizes communication, interaction and relations" (Bazerman 1988, 62). According to Russell (1997, 510) the notion of genre may also be applied to painting, clothing, architecture etc. Originally, "new rhetoric" informed investigations of genres focused mainly on mundane, everyday genre uses in "communities of practice" and on questions of how members of such communities gradually master the competent genre use (Berkenkotter and Huckin 1995). This ethnographic, micro-sociological approach (1) lacks a theoretically refined, systematic inventory for investigating the semiotic/linguistic properties of oral or written genres and (2) is unable to relate the micro-level of everyday practices to the meso- and macro-levels of wider institutional and/or cultural contexts of genre use (Englert, Mariage, and Dunsmore 2008). In order to tackle the second problem, Russell (1997) has integrated activity theory (Engeström 1987; Leontjew 1981) into the "new rhetoric" conception of genre. In this theory, the basic unit of analysis is the *activity system* which

> is any ongoing, object-directed, historically-conditioned, dialectically-structured, tool-mediated human interaction [...] These activity systems are mutually (re)constructed by participants using certain tools and not others (including discursive tools such as speech sounds and inscriptions). The activity system is the basic unit of analysis for both groups' and individuals' behavior, in that it analyzes the way concrete tools are used to mediate the motive (direction, trajectory) and the object (the 'problem space' or focus) of behavior and changes it.
>
> (Russell 1997, 508)

An activity system comprises three basic entities: the individual; the community it belongs to; and the activity the group is engaged in. These three basic entities are related by the factors which mediate between them: the social rules which govern the relation between individual and group; the 'tools' which mediate between the individuals and their activities; and the rules for the division of labor which mediate between a group and the activity it performs. "Individuals" in an activity system must not necessarily be "single persons": if an activity is performed by several groups[2] (who jointly constitute a "community"), the "individuals" in the activity systems are the single groups. Participants in an activity system learn to use typical tools (i.e. genres) to achieve certain means. In complex activity systems, "genre systems" (in Bazerman's 1994 sense) evolve which participants combine to organize interactions. The circulation of genres in systems (and the expectations which are related to these genres) (re)produces macro-social structures.

Russell's activity theoretic enhancement of new rhetoric's genre conception (partly) resolves the above mentioned problems of the theoretical gap between the micro- and macro- sociological levels. The conception of activity systems on several levels of complexity is a first step towards providing new rhetoric with a more sophisticated approach towards institutional and macro-societal communication. But as the discussion in Russell (1997) shows, complex activity systems (i.e. institutions), in which "simple" activity systems function as actors, might be categorically different from "simple activity systems" (e.g. a group of researchers who interact on a daily, informal basis will not develop their "interactivities" in a way which is similar to a complex university administration in which departments, administrative bodies, and other stakeholder groups interact). Thus, while providing an overarching notion for conceptualizing activities on various levels of social organization, the activity theoretical approach might conceal relevant differences between these levels. Furthermore, activity theory does not provide a theoretical account of how and why "genre systems" are combined for organizing interactions in complex activity systems.

2.2   Genre in Systemic Functional Linguistics

Within Systemic-Functional Linguistics (henceforth SFL; see, e.g., Halliday 1994), genres have been conceptualized in partly different ways (Cloran, Butt, and Williams 1996; Halliday 1994; Martin 1992). I will focus here on what has become to be known as Register & Genre Theory (RGT) (Eggins and Martin 1997; Martin and Rose 2008) as this approach is most often associated with SFL. Following SFL theory, RGT posits strong links between texts and contexts. According to Halliday's theorizing of language as "a social semiotic" (Halliday 1978), context is differentiated into "context of situation" and "context of culture". According to SFL, each text can only be understood (and analyzed) in relation to these two levels of context insofar as each situation is a manifestation of a specific culture and each situation is manifested through the unfolding text. The manifestation relation is bidirectional: each situation is manifested through an unfolding text, but at the same time the unfolding text manifests (construes) a certain type of situation. A second tenet of SFL is the metafunctional organization of language and context. According to SFL, language is organized along three metafunctions: the ideational (i.e. what an utterance is about), the interpersonal (i.e. the role relationships which are established by an utterance), and the textual (i.e. the semiotic mode in which an utterance is realized). Each text combines systematic choices from each of these metafunctions which contribute to its overall meaning.

In RGT, Martin has elaborated the SFL model into a comprehensive genre theory intended to model the relations between context and language. Following SFL, RGT views context as a semiotic system which comprises two levels: register and genre. Register (which corresponds to Halliday's "context of situation") varies in three dimensions – field, tenor, and mode which are realized in language as the ideational, interpersonal and textual metafunction, respectively. Each situational context is viewed as a specific combination of field, tenor, and mode choices. Register, however, needs to be realized by genre in order to become socially meaningful action (or, to use Martin's words: "register unconstrained by genre represents irrealis activity – what we may have stopped doing and/or might one day do"; Martin 1999, 32). Genre in RGT is "how things get done, when language is used to accomplish them" (Martin 1985, 250) or a "staged, goal-oriented social process" (Eggins and Martin 1997). Genres constrain register possibilities, organize them into socially meaningful, purpose-oriented activities and are used by interactants to accomplish social-semiotic actions; "register" is static whereas "genre" is dynamic (Lee 2001). So far, the RGT conception of registers and genres seems to be quite straightforward: register makes certain situation-specific topics, role-relationships and modes of expression (e.g. verbal vs. written) salient and genres combine certain choices on each dimension and realize them linguistically in order to reach a certain goal. But where is genre located in the RGT approach? – obviously it cannot be part of register as it organizes register variables, and hence RGT equates genre with "context of culture", i.e. culture is mapped as a system of genres (Martin 1999; Martin and Rose 2008). There is thus a sizable gap between situational context and cultural context with no theoretical notion (and level) mediating between.[3] Furthermore, a look at the concrete empirical work by RGT practitioners indicates that the conception of "genre" seems to acquire some "Janus-faced" (or circular) properties: on the one hand, at the theoretical level, genre is a highly abstract and general concept, because "culture" is viewed a system of genres. On the other hand, in practical research "genres" are identified and analyzed on very concrete levels of mundane interaction. Martin and Rose (2008), for instance, identify "story genres", "histories", "reports and explanations", and "procedures and procedural recounts" as genres which are relevant in secondary school education. This begs the question in which sense is a "protocol" (as a procedural genre) part of a "culture" (and part of which culture)? Of course, RGT theorists also see this problem and have (at least briefly) addressed it:

> [...] in a functional model of language and social context, there is more to say about genre as we move across strata and metafunctions. At the same time, the model assumed here does privilege genre as the ultimate level of abstraction, thereby giving genre responsibility for coordinating the recurrent configurations of meaning in a culture. In such terms, genre mediates the limits of our world – at the same time as offering systemic linguistics a holistic perspective on their meta-functionally and stratally diversified analyses.   (Martin and Rose 2008, 232)

In this quotation (and the whole section which precedes it), the authors acknowledge the problematic gap between the linguistic/semiotic properties of certain genres as they are investigated in empirical research and their abstract (social, semiotic) properties as organizing elements of (a) culture. Thus, much has to be done before RGT will develop a comprehensive theory of "context of culture" (i.e. genre). But there is also a second, inherent problem in the equation of genre with context of culture which RGT does not acknowledge: if genres are only identifiable and observable on the concrete level of their realizations in texts (i.e. language in context), how can their conceptualization at the abstract level of "context of culture" be accomplished without becoming circular?

All in all, SFL's and RGT's conception of genre provides a sophisticated methodology for the linguistic analysis of genres and their relation to context of situation (i.e. register), but it faces two problems when attempting to model contextual layers above the context of situation: (1) if there exists only one second layer of context (i.e. context of culture), it is extremely difficult to find theoretically sound bridging devices which mediate between the most global kind of context (culture) and the most limited one (situation) – this problem seems to have been acknowledged by RGT theorists and might be solved; (2) the problem of circularity of genre definitions is much more difficult to tackle from within RGT as it lies at the heart of the theory: if one were to abandon the idea that genres form the context of culture the whole theory would collapse. Still, RGT offers some advantages over the "new rhetoric" conception of genre: it provides a systematic methodology for investigating the linguistic properties of genres (as opposed to rather superficial linguistic ad-hoc analyses); and it assumes a theoretical level above the micro-social context (of situation) and posits a systematic relationship between situational context and higher levels of social organization. But, as has been shown above, this second advantage is also RGT's most problematic shortcoming.

2.3   The "Biber-Connor-Upton" approach to genre

Biber, Connor and Upton (2007) have recently presented a model of genre analysis which is based on previous approaches by Swales (e.g. Swales 1990) and Biber and his collaborators (e.g. Biber 1988). Swales' genre model (also known as "move-analysis") was originally developed in an EAP-teaching context but has received much attention outside the writing-pedagogy community as well. Swales posits a strong connection between "discourse communities" and "genres". *Discourse communities* in Swales' sense are characterized by a set of common public goals, some mechanisms of communication between their members, a certain, specific vocabulary, and – most importantly – their "ownership" of certain genres which are used for intra-community communication. The model thus presupposes that a "discourse community" has at least a certain degree of institutional organization. According to Swales, genres are classes of communicative events which share a common set of communicative goals and are structured into phases and moves. They are characterized by a systematic combination of choices regarding content, social positioning of users and communicative form. Thus, Swales – like RGT – stresses the connection between genres and contexts of use, but in his model "context" is not defined in terms of "situations" (of genre use) but rather in terms of social contexts of genre-using groups.

Biber's original model (e.g. Biber 1988) makes a strong distinction between the notions of "genre" and "text type". In Biber's view, "genres" are language users' everyday classifications of texts which do not necessarily reflect linguistic differences between groups of texts. Biber contrasts this everyday classification with a "scientific" empirical classification of texts ("typology") based on linguistic features. In order to arrive at a "text typology", a representative corpus of texts is annotated for several linguistic characteristics and then a multi-dimensional factor analysis is performed to identify the "underlying" linguistic factors which characterize different text types. Although there is some methodological and statistical doubt about factor analytic methods in the social sciences in general (as e.g. Lee [2001] has mentioned), Biber's text analyses have revealed a number of (very general) "text types" which are characterized by a configuration of typical "register values". Thus, in some respect, Biber's approach shares at least some basic conceptual similarities with the RGT model: both models assume that genres (or text types) are specific combinations of register choices (albeit the models vary significantly in their conception of "register") and both models apply a "bottom-up" methodology (i.e. they start with a close linguistic investigation of textual features and then proceed to higher levels of analysis). But while RGT (as all other genre models reviewed so far) posits a strong functional relationship between contexts and genres, Biber's text typology is merely interested in a "generalizable corpus-based description of discourse structures" (Biber, Connor, and Upton 2007, 12). In their 2007 book, the authors aim at combining Swales' move analysis with Biber's corpus based bottom-up approach. But instead of adopting Swales' "contextualism" (i.e. his basic assumption about the close connection between discourse communities and genres) they simply include his notions of "moves" and "phases" as genre structuring concepts above the clause level and show that both bottom-up analyses (i.e. lexically oriented investigations of "functional text units") and top-down analyses (i.e. corpus investigations of functional text-moves and phases) of texts tend to yield corresponding results.

Biber, Connor, and Upton's (2007) approach thus presents a methodology rather than a new theoretical perspective on genre: while Swales' original model relates genres to discourse communities and communicative purposes, the Biber, Connor, and Upton approach replaces this strand of theorizing with an elaborate set of computerized methods of automatic text analysis which yields text structures and discourse units without aiming at a functional explanation of the relationship between these structures and contextual features. Nonetheless, the model points at the necessary distinction between "register" as a (static) repository of linguistic choices and "genres" (text types) as structured and structuring linguistic realizations of register variables.

2.4   Bhatia's integration of the "socio-critical" perspective into a genre model

Bhatia's (2004) genre model is specifically designed for written genres in professional settings. It integrates insights from previous models developed in the North American rhetorical tradition, Systemic Functional Linguistics, the EAP-LSP-strand of genre research (i.e. Swales and his collaborators), in corpus linguistics (Biber and his collaborators), and in Fairclough's version of Critical Discourse Analysis. Bhatia proposes a four dimensional model of genre research procedures which comprises a textual, an ethnographic, a socio-cognitive, and a socio-critical perspective (Bhatia 2004, 160). As a guide to genre investigations, the model has undeniable value as it provides researchers with a flexible yet structured set of relevant aspects of genre dimensions and related analytic procedures. As a theoretical model, however, Bhatia's approach suffers from what could be called "additionalism", i.e. a tendency to adopt all relevant aspects of established genre theories while simultaneously neglecting the theoretical differences between them. Nonetheless, by integrating the "socio-critical" dimension into his research program, Bhatia hints at a relevant dimension of genre analysis neglected in most of the approaches reviewed so far. The socio-critical perspective links genre practices in a discourse community to aspects of power, ideology and change. The starting point for this "socio-critical perspective" in Bhatia's model is Fairclough's version of Critical Discourse Analysis (CDA).

Fairclough (1993) – while not contributing any new facets to the conceptualization of "genre"[4] – introduces a definition of "discourse" in his theory of CDA which, although widely used in CDA studies, has not been adopted in linguistic genre studies.[5] For Fairclough, discourse represents the "content dimension" of genres. He argues for using "discourse" for the subject matter a genre realizes because content enters genres always in "the mediated form of particular constructions" (Fairclough 1993, 128). Thus, "content" is never "neutral", but construed from a particular (social/ideological) position and this *content from a viewpoint* or *content with an attitude* is called "discourse". Discourses are not only associated with social group positions but partly independent of genres, i.e. they need a genre in order to be realized but they can be realized within different genres (Fairclough 1993, 125). This conception of discourse is compatible with newer sociological discourse theories in the tradition of the sociology of knowledge (Keller 2011). According to Keller, discourses are complexes of "utterance events" (*Äußerungsereignisse*) and practices which are related to each other by a structured process of meaning production and reconstruction by actors and analysts. Discourses do not only supply "meanings" but also "actor" and "subject positions", i.e. they construe social roles of interactants and of those they talk about. Thus, Fairclough's and Keller's conception of discourse[6] resemble each other insofar as (1) they posit a strong (dialectic) relation between "discourse" and the social group which uses it; (2) they conceptualize "discourse" as a meso- and/or macro-sociological phenomenon which organizes content positions ("types of knowledge"), social positions ("actor roles"), and "normative rules for utterance production" (Keller 2011, 208); the latter aspect is conceptualized in Fairclough's discourse theory as the relation between genres and discourses.

2.5   Preliminary conclusions

In the following, I summarize those aspects of the genre models which are relevant for this chapter and try to integrate them in a theoretical framework for my empirical analysis. All theories (except Biber's) conceive of genres as typified (and recognizable), structured,[7] goal-oriented social processes realized by means of a (or a combination of) semiotic system(s). The structured and goal-oriented nature of genres is reflected both in "external" genre classifications and in "internal" (linguistically analyzable) discursive characteristics. Genres are functionally related to situational and/or social-institutional contexts. The new rhetoric approach focuses on the relevance of the mundane, micro-social contexts of genre use in activity systems (or communities of practice). Although new rhetoric scholars concede that single genres may be combined into rather complex "systems of genres" (Bazerman 1994), the traditional version of their approach lacks a conceptual level of (meso- and/or macro-social) context to which "systems of genres" could theoretically be related. Only by enhancing this approach by integrating activity theory as a methodological and theoretical tool for grasping social structures at higher levels of social organization, genres in institutions could possibly be modeled. It is, however, doubtful whether the functioning of micro-social activity systems can be equated with the operating modes of meso- or macro-social activity systems (i.e. institutions).

RGT (and SFL) posits a macro-contextual level – context of culture – which is equated with "genre", i.e. RGT assumes that systems of genres constitute cultures and assumes no (analytic and theoretical) level between "context of culture" and "context of situation" (in which genres are realized). All approaches stress that genres draw on situational adequate linguistic resources, i.e. registers. Register is a static concept for theorizing situation-adequate linguistic resources whereas genre is a dynamic, goal-oriented conception of socio-semiotic activity (Lee 2001). This conception does not resolve the question of the relation between register/situation and genres. Both solutions proposed so far pose problems: it is not clear if the new rhetoric conception of genres as associated with micro-social activity systems (communities of practice) can fully account for genres or systems of genres which operate on more complex levels of social organization; and the RGT equation of "systems of genres" with "context of culture" does not provide any intermediate level of social organization between "context of culture" and "context of situation".

In my own theoretical framework, I propose to differentiate between two (often related) aspects of context on the theoretical level: the situational and the social context of genre realization. As shown above, most genre theories equate the situational constraints on "adequate language" for genre realization with "register". *Register* is a systematic choice of field, tenor, and mode variables (in the sense of RGT) which is associated with certain "contexts of situation". It provides a (static) semiotic mould for realizing a genre in a situation-adequate form (see Lee 2001). *Discourse*, on the other hand, is a form of practice-related meaning production tradition which is associated with a certain social group or field. Thus, discourse – in contrast to register – has a dynamic, directional character. *Genres* as typified (and recognizable), structured, goal oriented social processes are related to both discourses and registers. But while register contributes to the localized semiotic molding of a genre realization in a certain situational context, discourse contributes to its social (group specific) use: discourses specify who may use a certain genre as producer/recipient and which entities are talked about in a genre in which ways, i.e. the way social actors are represented (van Leeuwen 1996; Reisigl 2007). Discourses may also organize genres into "genre systems" and thus arrange the communicative practices in institutions/social fields. As members of social groups/fields (especially when these groups/fields have a certain degree of internal organization) are regularly engaged in certain communicative practices which are performed in certain kinds of situations, "register" (i.e. situational) and "discourse" (i.e. social) characteristics of genre realization may more or less coincide. If, however, genres are used in or adapted for situations in which they were not originally used or if different discourses/genres are mixed (see Fairclough 1993; Bhatia 2004), register characteristics and discourse features of a certain genre realization may become distinct and distinguishable.

So far, my discussion of "genre", "register", and "discourse" has been predominantly theoretical and based only on a review of the existing literature. The following empirical section shows how far the above conceptualization of the notions of "genre", "register", and "discourse" and their relationships can take us in the empirical analysis of a highly specialized political genre like the inaugural speech in the Austrian political system.

3.   The inaugural speech of Austrian chancellors

This study is based on the stenographic protocols of the Austrian parliament which are available online (http://www.parlament.gv.at/SERV/STAT/DOK/ index.shtml). These protocols are no verbatim transcripts of recordings from parliamentary sessions, but rather the result of a complex writing and editing process (Zima, Brone, and Feyarts [2010], who also report similar processes of producing parliamentary protocols in other European countries). Using these edited documents as a basis for an empirical investigation (rather than transcripts of recordings) is justified because (1) this investigation does not aim at scrutinizing the interactions between speakers and their audience and (2) because these protocols represent the official (historical) record of the Austrian parliamentary sessions.

The current section begins by providing a short account of the political relevance of the inaugural speech in the Austrian political system. I then give contextual information on the four inaugural speeches under investigation. Finally, I briefly discuss the (few) previous linguistic investigations of Austrian inaugural speeches. The major part of this section comprises the empirical analysis of the four speeches under investigation: their audience structure, their generic, lexical (registerial) and discursive characteristics.

3.1   The inaugural speech and its function in the Austrian parliamentary system

A visit to the website of the Austrian parliament (http://www.parlament.gv.at/ index.shtml) reveals "inaugural speeches" to be one of the few generic "tags" which are provided for searches. Thus, the term "inaugural speech" is used as an external genre label (cf. Section 2) and seems to signal a "members' category" relevant for differentiation between different types of parliamentary speeches. However, as Welan (1989) points out, the Austrian constitution makes no mention of this genre, nor of any obligation of the Austrian chancellor for delivering an inaugural speech. Welan, however, indicates an indirect obligation to do so: the constitution requires a new government to be introduced to the parliamentary assembly after being sworn in by the Austrian president. And, as Welan points out, the Austrian constitution explicitly stipulates that this "introduction" must comprise not only the names of the newly appointed members of government, but rather relevant fields of policy as well as the relevant political actions the new government intends to take. In this sense, inaugural speeches are typical "policy documents" (Reisigl 2007, 32; see also Krzyżanowski, this volume) as they deal with the political aims and intentions of the government and its plans for implementing this program. In the case of coalition governments, the inaugural speech focuses on areas of agreement between the parties involved and leaves out points of disagreement (Welan 1989). As this short characteristic shows, the inauguration speeches of Austrian chancellors differ in several relevant respects from inauguration speeches of e.g. American presidents which have been investigated under several angles so far (for a recent overview see Biria and Mohammadi 2012). The Austrian chancellors' inauguration speeches do not primarily aim at persuading an audience of a chancellor's political program and uniting the nation behind him but rather presents a repository of policy issues and the relevance the current government attributes to them.

The delivery of the inaugural speech marks the official endpoint of the successful formation of a government and represents the first parliamentary "highlight" for a new chancellor and thus its media coverage is high. In Austrian parliamentary elections, the constitution of the second chamber of Parliament (*Nationalrat*)[8] is determined under a system of proportional representation. After the election, the Austrian president (usually) entrusts the head of the strongest parliamentary party with the task of forming a new government. If no party reaches an absolute majority (which has been the case in Austria since the late 80s), a coalition government is usually formed.[9] The party negotiations which eventually lead to the formation of a coalition government may last for several weeks or months.[10] If the negotiations fail, the leader of the strongest party must receive another mandate for government formation from the Austrian president before he can start negotiations with another party (or he may officially withdraw from the negotiating process, in which case the president has to entrust another politician with the task of forming a government).[11] During the last ten years (the period under investigation here), the time which had elapsed between elections and the formation of a government (and the ensuing inaugural speech) was relatively long and coalition negotiations had lasted for months.

3.2   The inaugural speeches under investigation and their political context

Austria has seen four inaugural speeches since the year 2000 and all four speeches are associated with different patterns of personal and/or political change and continuation.[12] In 2000, Wolfgang Schüssel, then head of the conservative Christian Democratic Austrian People's Party (ÖVP) became chancellor of a coalition government which he had formed with Jörg Haider's right-wing populist Freedom Party (FPÖ). The formation of this government had been preceded by official coalition negotiations between the Social Democrats (SPÖ, which had gained the relative majority of votes in the elections in late 1999) and the ÖVP (which had only ranked third after SPÖ and FPÖ in the elections). These had been accompanied by unofficial negotiations between ÖVP and FPÖ. After the negotiations between SPÖ and ÖVP had officially failed, ÖVP and FPÖ swiftly formed a government with Schüssel as chancellor and FPÖ politician Riess-Passer as vice-chancellor. The formation of this government indicated a change (or even rupture) of two major political traditions in Austria: (1) since Jörg Haider had become leader of the freedom party in 1986 and had positioned it at the far-right of the Austrian political spectrum (comparable to the Front National in France and the Vlaams Belang in Belgium), an unwritten agreement between the other Austrian parliamentary parties had excluded the FPÖ from any forms of participation in the Austrian federal government; (2) since the early 70s, no ÖVP politician had held the office of Austrian chancellor, i.e. there had been an unbroken period of almost 30 years of SPÖ-led governments (and hence of SPÖ chancellors). Whereas the latter change would have probably caused some attention in the Austrian public and media, including the FPÖ in a coalition government not only caused fierce protests in Austria, but across Europe and elsewhere. As a consequence, the other EU countries imposed "bilateral sanctions" against the Austrian government which mainly consisted in diplomatic consequences but, which the ÖVP-FPÖ government cleverly used to denounce all domestic critics as "henchmen of the EU sanctioners".

Following a somewhat less than stellar performance of the FPÖ members of the new government and after severe tensions within the FPÖ related to its government policy, the FPÖ split into two parties in 2002: the (old, right wing extremist) FPÖ and the (newly founded, allegedly liberal-conservative) Alliance for the Future of Austria (BZÖ) which was founded by Jörg Haider and included all former FPÖ government members. As a consequence of the internal troubles of his coalition partner, chancellor Schüssel ended the coalition and called for elections. These were won by the ÖVP, but once again a coalition partner had to be found. Little wonder that after some negotiations, the ÖVP again formed a coalition government under Wolfgang Schüssel as chancellor with the recently founded BZÖ as a coalition partner in spring 2003.

After the legislation period had ended, the 2007 elections saw a return of the SPÖ as the relatively strongest party. As the SPÖ had often and openly pledged not to form a government with either the BZÖ or FPÖ, it had only one option for forming a coalition, namely negotiations with the ÖVP. Although the two parties had developed a substantial record of mutual political distrust and personal aversions over the last seven years, they eventually formed a coalition under Alfred Gusenbauer (SPÖ) as chancellor and Wilhelm Molterer (ÖVP) as vice-chancellor. Politically impeded by frequent tactical blockades imposed by his coalition

Table 1. Patterns of personal and political change in Austrian government formation since 2000

Domains of change / Persons	Personal	Political
Schüssel 2000 (February, 9th)	Change from Klima to Schüssel	Change from social-democratic dominated to conservative dominated government
Schüssel 2003 (March, 6th)	Continuation	Continuation
Gusenbauer 2007 (January, 16th)	Change from Schüssel to Gusenbauer	Change from conservative dominated to social democratic dominated government
Faymann 2008 (December, 3rd)	Change from Gusenbauer to Faymann	Continuation

partner, Gusenbauer managed to annoy not only most media representatives, but also many important officials of his own party by a combination of political clumsiness and rhetorical arrogance. As a consequence, he was replaced as head of the SPÖ by Werner Faymann in June 2008 and shortly afterwards ÖVP vice-chancellor Molterer decided to terminate the coalition with the SPÖ. The 2008 elections again brought a relative majority of votes for the SPÖ, which again – now under the leadership of Werner Faymann – formed a coalition government with the ÖVP (which had changed most of its leading personnel as a consequence of former vice-chancellor Molterer's unsuccessful attempt to surprise the SPÖ with parliamentary elections in a time of alleged party internal troubles) under party leader and vice-chancellor Josef Pröll.

This short description of the Austrian government history over the last ten years reveals two patterns of change and continuity: in 2000, the country saw a political as well as a personal change (from nearly 30 years of SPÖ-dominated governments to an ÖVP-led government and from former SPÖ chancellor Victor Klima to Wolfgang Schüssel); in 2003, political as well as personal continuity was maintained whereas 2007 again saw political and personal change. In 2008, we find political continuity with a personal change (from Gusenbauer to Faymann). Table 1 gives an overview of these two patterns (dates of inaugural speeches are in brackets in the first column after the respective chancellors' names).

Concerning the investigation of the inaugural speeches, these two intertwined patterns of change and continuity raise several research questions:

-   If a somehow conventionalized (temporally stabilized) genre of the "inaugural speech" exists in the Austrian political system, then its generic characteristics should be identifiable in all four speeches.
-   The second question which arises in this case is how (and to which extent) personal and political differences become manifest in these speeches.
-   If the "inaugural speech" is no conventionalized genre, the question arises which (political-ideological or personal-stylistic) influence most importantly the textual characteristics of the speeches.

3.3   Previous investigations of Austrian chancellors' inaugural speeches

Inaugural speeches of Austrian chancellors have not received much academic attention so far with the notable exception of an interdisciplinary project in which a corpus of all inaugural speeches between 1945 and 1987 was compiled and investigated from a legal, linguistic and mass-communication perspective (Gottschlich, Panagl, and Welan 1989). In his contribution to the volume, Panagl investigates the speeches as instances of "political language" from a lexical and a stylistic angle. He is interested in the political keywords with positive connotations (*Fahnenwörter*) and how changes in keywords co-occur with (or indicate) changes in the political environment. Furthermore, Panagl aims at identifying individual stylistic preferences of some Austrian chancellors (Panagl 1989). In a similar vein, Gottschlich (1989) conducts an advanced, computer aided content analysis of the inaugural speeches of Austrian social-democratic chancellors between 1970 and 1987 and identifies central topics and values/evaluations in the speeches. Like Panagl, he finds changing patterns in both areas and – generalizing to general policy trends – concludes pessimistically that Austrian present day politics lacks all visionary and programmatic elements without any progress in advanced organizational and/or problem solving capacities. Finally, Welan (1989) discusses the legal and constitutional premises of inaugural speeches as well as the concrete process of their intra-government planning, drafting and production. He also presents a "prototypical schema" for an inaugural speech which he bases on a political-rhetorical typology of statements in an "ideal" inaugural speech. His scheme resembles Pörksens' (2004) normative-rhetorical inventory of speech acts (or rhetorical moves) in a good political speech. Table 2 juxtaposes the two schemata and shows which categories correspond to each other; the grey shadings indicate which of the normative categories could be found in the speeches under investigation here (see 3.4).

Welan stresses that this ideal schema represents a "bureaucratic ideal" that is hardly ever met "in realis", whereas Pörksen claims that his schema represents

Table 2. Welan's and Pörksen's normative rhetorical schemata for inaugural (Welan) or political (Pörksen) speeches

Welan (1989)	Pörksen (2004)
Global analysis of current situation	Personal introduction of central theme
Presentation of central political fields, problem areas and their relations	Presentation of main thesis
Presentation of political priorities (and posteriorities)	
Justification of these priorities	Situation-based explanation of main thesis
	Comparative view on parallel and contrastive cases to integrate thesis in the course of political events
	Presentation of counter-positions and their refutation
	Conclusion
	Appeal to the audience
Setting time limits and deadlines for the political measures and programs	

the basis for a "political poetry" in which language serves as a tool for clarifying political questions and problems.

In an investigation which extends Gottschlich, Panagl and Welan's (1989) corpus until 1997, Ehtreiber (2003) investigates the "image of Austria" in Austrian chancellors' inaugural speeches. He identifies three central communicative functions of the speeches: (1) the "image-providing" function which is responsible for the first impression a new government makes on the general public; (2) the persuasive function through which the public is influenced to support the new government; (3) the informative function which informs the general public about the policy of the new government. Ehtreiber, however, does not relate these three functions to specific rhetorical moves or speech acts. He rather tries to apply Welan's (1989) categories for an "ideal inaugural speech" when he gives a (short) account of the generic characteristics of the speeches. The major part of his study consists of a diachronic investigation of keywords, semantic fields and metaphors in his corpus.

Hristozova-Weiss (2009) presents a case study of chancellor Gusenbauer's inaugural speech, the ensuing parliamentary debate and the representation of this whole parliamentary session in two print media. She is not interested in an investigation of genre characteristics of the texts, but rather in the intertextual practices which newspaper journalists employ either reporting or commenting on the speech and the following debate.

3.4   Genre aspects of the inaugural speeches

The above review of the existing literature has shown that only a few linguistic studies have been conducted on the inaugural speeches of Austrian chancellors and that these few studies have mainly focused on political keywords and individual styles of political orators. The two rhetorical "schemata" for inaugural speeches which have been proposed are normative rather than based on empirical analyses and as the overview in Table 2 shows, only few of the categories they propose could be found in the empirical data. This situation leaves a big research gap open which the following three sub-sections intend to close.

3.4.1   *The production of an inaugural speech*

The planning, drafting, and eventual production of an inaugural speech involves many persons and institutional resources. Firstly, the federal chancellery contacts the ministries and requests materials to be used for the speech. It may also provide guidelines regarding the major foci of political work the new government wants to pay special attention to (Welan 1989). Each ministry (i.e. each office of a minister) then compiles data, problem areas, interests, topics, political aims, and programmatic statements which might be of interest for the draft. As this process takes place under high time pressure (the compilation of materials cannot start before a government has been formed, in the present sample the inaugural speeches were delivered between 6 and 9 days after this event),[13] the quality of the inaugural speech depends to a large extent on the quality of the materials the ministries supply. Furthermore, the kinds of materials which are supplied may vary from simple statistical data to pre-formulated chunks of text. In any case, the speech's final formulation is prepared by the cabinet of the chancellor, sometimes also under cooperation of external experts. This short description of the production of an inaugural speech is based on Welan (1989) and not on any kind of empirical research.[14] It shows that the chancellor, although he is its "animator", acts only partly as "author" or "principal" of the speech (Goffman 1981). The authors and principals (including the chancellor) are the members of the chancellor's cabinet, external consultants, representatives of the coalition parties as well as the ministers' offices who supply the materials for the speech.

3.4.2   *The inaugural speech and its multiple audiences*

Inaugural speeches are major political events in the Austrian parliamentary system and as such are also major media events. Since 1970, the parliamentary sessions in which these speeches are delivered are broadcast live by the Austrian National broadcasting company ORF (personal e-mail from S. Steinlechner, ORF-archive). The broadcasting of the speeches adds an additional layer of complexity to the audience roles which they provide. In this section, I will give a short account of the layered audience role structure of the inaugural speeches. I will start by discussing for whom the speeches are intended to be relevant ("stakeholders") by their authors and then proceed to discuss the specific interactional setting of the speeches and the different audience roles it provides. In the last part of this section, I will show how the combination of different kinds of audience roles and stakeholder groups can contribute to explain the different systems of genres of which the inaugural speeches are part. Furthermore, the analysis of audience roles and stakeholder groups is an inquiry into the interpersonal aspects of the genre.

Stakeholder groups

I use the term "stakeholder groups" to refer to those groups of the general public who are identifiably affected by the announced policies in the speech and who can therefore be seen as its intended audience. The "official audience" of the speech is the parliamentary assembly as well as the members of the government (i.e. ministers). Coalition party MPs and government members will find their (at least general) political aims and values expressed in the speech whereas MPs from the opposition will not find many points of agreement. These different expectations become explicit in the applause phases during the speeches, during most of which only the MPs of the coalition parties applaud.[15] Nonetheless, all chancellors explicitly address all MPs in their speeches and at several points explicitly invite the MPs of the opposition parties for future cooperation (mostly in the closing section of their speeches, see below). Thus, the MPs and government members are not only the primary audience (cf. below) but also relevant stakeholders of the speeches, coalition party MPs being primary stakeholders whereas opposition party MPs could be termed "secondary" (or "adversary") stakeholders.

The second relevant group of stakeholders (which is non-present) is composed of the staff of ministers and leading officials in the ministries who supplied the source materials for the speeches (see Section 3.4.1) and who expect their issues to be mentioned. Of course, not all of the materials which were sent are used for the speeches, but selection and composition of the issues in the speeches are important political cues for the relative weight assigned to specific ministries and political issues.

A third group of non-present stakeholders comprises the many official representative organizations of various social groups ("chambers",[16] trade unions, NGOs, Churches) and the provincial governments. Although some MPs may be also members/officials of certain of these groups,[17] the respective organizations are relevant stakeholders in their own right. They are not directly involved in the planning and drafting of the inaugural speech, but they may nonetheless be affected by certain policies announced.

Another group of stakeholders are the media. To a small extent, media are stakeholders in the sense that they might be affected by certain media policy issues which are announced. But media policy (although it is mentioned in all four speeches) plays only a minor role in the speeches. To a larger extent, the media are stakeholders as it is part of their everyday business to report on domestic policy making the inaugural speech (and the following parliamentary debate) a major event for them. Both the chancellor and their advisors will be well aware of the close attention paid to their speeches by this stakeholder group.

The last and most amorphous group of stakeholders is the general Austrian public which can roughly be divided into supporters (voters), opponents (voters of opposition parties), and those generally uninterested in politics. Members of these three groups will have different expectations towards the speeches (positive, negative and none at all) and these potential expectations will be of relevance when the speeches are planned, drafted and delivered. But, independently of the individual affiliation of specific persons to one of these groups, everybody in Austria will be affected by the government's policy and hence by the policies announced by the chancellor.

Participant roles and their reflection in the speeches

In the case of the inaugural speeches, the *primary participants*[18] are the chancellor on the one hand and the national assembly on the other. The inaugural speech can be viewed as a complex "first turn" of a highly formalized exchange in which almost all primary participants will be involved in the ensuing debate. The members of government play a special role insofar as they may also participate in the parliamentary debate following the speech. However, they are not expected to comment upon the speech, but rather to explain or elaborate certain policy issues they plan to implement. Thus, the members of government could be characterized as *side participants* of the speech. The parliamentary stenographers, the journalists present and the visitors on the gallery (including the president of the republic) have the role of *bystanders* who are present, but do not have the right to interfere. There is a last audience group which can be characterized as 'indirect bystanders': the general public outside the plenary hall who can watch the speech (and part of the following debate) on TV. They have the same audience role as the visitors on the gallery, except that they watch the event via TV. In contrast to the physically present bystanders, their visual perspective is limited/guided by camera positions and the editorial work of the ORF. Thus, almost all relevant stakeholder groups (except of the MPs and the members of government) have the roles of direct or indirect bystanders.

This role distribution is reflected in the forms of audience reference in the speeches which comprise *greetings*, *direct addresses/appeals*, and *referential categorizations* (van Leeuwen 1996; Reisigl and Wodak 2001). At the beginning of their speech, each speaker explicitly *greets* the primary participants, i.e. the president of the National Assembly (who is also an MP and might participate in the following debate), the members of the National Assembly, the House itself (*Hohes Haus*), and – additionally – the Austrian president. The Austrian president as the highest representative of the republic is the only bystander who is explicitly greeted. The only exception from this pattern is the Schüssel I speech, which took place under very special political circumstances (cf. above). Accordingly, Schüssel I greeted not only the primary participants, but addressed all other stakeholder groups, foreign countries (*das Ausland*), and his critics explicitly at the beginning of the speech. *Direct addresses* of the MPs (or "the house", i.e. the primary audience) occur at move or phase boundaries in the speeches. Often, they are preceded by applause in response to the previous move or phase of the speech. MPs' instances of applause thus mark the end of moves and/or phases and speaker's direct addresses signal the beginning of a new move/phase. In the Schüssel II speech, some stakeholder groups (especially the "social partners", NGOs, and federal governments) are explicitly mentioned and invited for cooperation. Most stakeholder groups (the indirect bystanders) are not addressed but talked about, i.e. they are subject to *referential categorizations* (Reisigl and Wodak 2001). Table 3 gives a categorical overview of the explicitly mentioned stakeholder categorizations that are frequently construed as sensers/carriers of needs, feelings, wishes or attributes. The highest relative frequency value for each category is marked in bold.

All four speakers use general expressions like "the people" (*die Menschen*), "the Austrians", "the citizens", etc. most frequently to talk about the "indirect bystanders". The other categories show interesting individual differences between the four speeches that cannot be discussed in detail here. Schüssel I uses gender-related categories most often, whereas his second speech favors age- and family-related categorizations. In contrast, Gusenbauer uses education-related categorizations most often. Faymann uses mainly economy- and health-related categorizations and uses two categorization dimensions (integration/immigration and police) that do not occur in any other speech.

Table 3. Speakers/referring expressions (r.v. = raw value; r.p. = row percent; c.p. = column percent)

	Schüssel 2000			Schüssel 2003			Gusenbauer			Faymann			Total
	r.v.	r.p.	c.p.	r.v.	r.p.	c.p.	r.v.	r.p.	c.p.	r.v.	r.p.	c.p.	
Age	8	19.51	12.70	17	41.46	20.48	11	26.83	16.67	5	12.20	9.09	41
Economy	7	25.00	11.11	8	28.57	9.64	2	7.14	3.03	11	39.29	20.00	28
Education	1	6.67	1.59	3	20.00	3.61	8	53.33	12.12	3	20.00	5.45	15
Family	5	29.41	7.94	7	41.18	8.43	2	11.76	3.03	3	17.65	5.45	17
Gender	10	41.67	15.87	3	12.50	3.61	8	33.33	12.12	3	12.50	5.45	24
General expression	27	25.71	42.86	36	34.29	43.37	28	26.67	42.42	14	13.33	25.45	105
Health	5	16.13	7.94	9	29.03	10.84	6	19.35	9.09	11	35.48	20.00	31
Integration/Immigration	0	0.00	0.00	0	0.00	0.00	0	0.00	0.00	2	100.00	3.64	2
Police	0	0.00	0.00	0	0.00	0.00	1	25.00	1.52	3	75.00	5.45	4
Total	63 (100%)			83 (100%)			66 (100%)			55 (100%)			

The investigation of the forms of audience references has shown that different audience groups are addressed or referred to differently. While the primary audience is greeted and addressed at the beginning and during the speeches, only one bystander (the president of the republic) is greeted in all four speeches. The other bystanders (stakeholder groups) are only talked about and the categories used to talk about them make some characteristics salient and background others. The mentioning of some groups and the backgrounding (van Leeuwen 1996) of others may be interpreted as indications of interpersonal relevance attributed to certain groups by certain speakers.

The inaugural speech as part of a system of genres
Audience roles are also relevant for the speeches in terms of the system of genres (Bazerman 1994) in which the inaugural speech is embedded. The primary audience (i.e. the MPs) and the side participants (i.e. the ministers) are the only potential participants in the debate after the speech, whereas the journalists (i.e. one stakeholder group of the bystanders) react to the speech and the debate outside and after the speech event. All other stakeholder groups can only consume this media coverage of the parliamentary session.

Inaugural speeches are the main parts of a sequence of communicative actions as they are delivered during a parliamentary session. These parliamentary sessions may be segmented into three parts: the (short) pre-speech phase, the speech phase, and a lengthy post-speech debate. Each of these three parts is composed of specific genres.

The pre-speech phase of the inaugural speech session is rather short (5–15 minutes) and comprises mainly speech activities by the parliamentary president which structure the debate in the post-speech phase: (1) the president's reading of an official letter of the present chancellor in which he informs the house of parliament that he was commissioned to form a government by the Austrian president, and/or (2) the president's announcement of motions submitted by MPs before the session to be voted on at the end of the session. The third slot of the pre-speech phase consists of the president's announcement of the so-called "speaking time limitation" (*Redezeitbeschränkung*) in which the president announces how much speaking time each parliamentary party has been assigned.[19] The procedural nature of these activities is reflected by the fact that they are never talked about in the following phases.[20] Taken together, the single components of the pre-speech phase realize a genre which could be termed "procedural preliminaries". As the generic structure of the inaugural speeches is analyzed and discussed in the following section, I now turn to a discussion of the post-speech phase of the session. Each inaugural speech is followed by an official opening of the floor for the debate by the parliamentary president and the repeated mention of the speaking time limit (which is set to 20 minutes per speaker in this first part of the post-speech phase). The ensuing debate is pre-scheduled insofar as each party has handed in an ordered list of speakers who then deliver their "debate contributions", i.e. their reactions to the inaugural speech. The only flexibility in this order is introduced by the regulation that ministers may claim the right to speak at any time during the post-speech phase, but the range of topics they may talk about is limited to issues of their ministry. Additionally, each MP may claim the speaking right immediately after another's contribution in order to cope with factual errors.[21] In all debates, the chairmen of the parliamentary groups are the first speakers and opposition party speakers alternate with government party speakers. The order of speakers after the chairpersons is more or less determined by their prominence in their respective parties. Following this first sequence of 10–20 minute speeches (which is sometimes interrupted by an inserted "urgent question debate"), a second sequence of 5–10 minute debate contributions follows. This second part of the post-speech phase takes place after the live broadcast of the session[22] and comprises contributions from speakers which are less prominent. The last part of the post-speech phase follows at the end of the session and comprises debate contributions between 3–5 minutes by so-called "backbenchers".

MPs realize two (complementary) genres in this post-speech phase: coalition-party MPs praise the government program and the inaugural speech, whereas oppositional MPs criticize them (Gruber 2012). Two genres which occur in this phase are not directly related to the speeches, namely ministers' turns and factual corrections. Again, audience roles and genre use are clearly related: members of the primary audience (MPs) produce either praising or criticizing contributions and side participants (ministers) produce spontaneous statements. Whereas the genre of the pre-speech phase prepares the inaugural speech and the following debate, the genres of the post-speech phase respond to it. The three major phases of the session are thus integrated and reflect the centrality of the inaugural speech. The "urgent question" debates, in contrast, are clearly inserted into this system of genres as a reaction to the mass-communication possibilities the live broadcast of the session offers.

Apart from the direct-response genres, which are delivered orally during the parliamentary debate, a second class of reactive genres occurs in the media[23] during the days after the speech (cf. Hristozova-Weiss 2009) as a whole variety of reporting and commenting genres occurs in the electronic and print media. These genres report and comment on certain aspects of the speech and the following debate but also on reactions of representatives of relevant stakeholder groups (see Hristozova-Weiss 2009). A close analysis of these reactive genres is far outside the scope of this chapter. The only relevant aspect of this class of genres in this context is the clear relationship between audience roles and genre production: as noted above, journalists are in most cases immediate bystanders and they produce this second class of reactive genres which in turn also covers voices of other (indirect) bystander groups.

The inaugural speeches are thus part of two systems of genres: (1) they are the central part of the parliamentary session during which they are delivered and the producers and consumers of these genres are the members of the primary audience – this could be called the primary system of inaugural speech related genres; (2) this primary system of genres provides the basis for the secondary system of inaugural speech related genres (i.e. the media coverage of the speeches and the debates) which is produced by one group of bystanders (journalists), but consumed (or consumable) by all audience groups.[24]

3.4.3   *The generic structure of the inaugural speech: Register, discourse and genre*

The genre analysis of the four selected inaugural speeches was performed with regard to their structure and content: (1) move analysis deals with the generic structure(s) of the speeches; (2) corpus analysis of the main parts (see below) of the speeches investigates lexical differences and/or congruencies between them; (3) topical analysis of the main parts of the speeches helps to explain the obvious differences between the speeches which could not be accounted for by the first two analytical steps.

Phase and move analysis

In their correspondence to the classical rhetorical tri-partite scheme of intro-duction – main body of speech – closing sequence, the four speeches are sur-prisingly similar. The main bodies of the first three speeches (Schüssel I and II, Gusenbauer) are moreover divided into two subparts (with uneven length), so that the general generic pattern can be sketched in the following way ("/" = "or"; [...] = structural boundary; {...} = optional move; ^ = recursive move):

[Introduction] +
[main body of speech: {summary of government program/ sketching relevant
policy fields + formulation of policy aims beyond government term} +
topical policy issues] +
[closing phase]

The *introduction* contextualizes the formation of the respective government and government policies in the Austrian and European political and economic situa-tion. Accordingly, the introduction of the Schüssel I inaugural speech is extraor-dinary long and addresses mainly the negative reactions of the other EU members on the inclusion of the freedom party in the coalition. In this respect, the Schüssel

I introduction realizes a discourse of justification on the national level as it mainly addresses an audience outside Austria and uses argumentative topoi which present relevant aspects of the Austrian past and project it into the future (e.g. "Since WW II, Austria has always been a democratic country which is firmly rooted in the Western, humanitarian tradition and it will continue to be so"). In the other three introductions, the formation of the respective government coalition is justified from the perspective of the dominant coalition party (i.e. the chancellor's perspective). Additionally, the introductions serve to introduce the general discursive perspective under which the various policy issues in the main body of the speeches are presented. The introduction thus selects one discourse (in the discourse-sociological and/or Fairclough's sense) which frames the presentation in the main body of the speeches: in the two Schüssel inaugural speeches the dominating discourse is a ("the") political discourse (i.e. policy issues are framed as and presented as being motivated by certain – national or European – political consideration) whereas in the Gusenbauer and Faymann speeches the economic discourse dominates (i.e. policy issues are framed as and presented as being motivated by economic considerations).

The *main body* of the speeches represents the longest part of all four inaugural speeches and – in its minimal realization in the Faymann speech – comprises a series of topical moves which present all relevant issues of the government program. In the other speeches, the main body is introduced by a *summary of the government program* and/or a *short mentioning of the major political fields and policy principles* which are relevant for the following topical moves. In terms of the speeches' internal coherence (Mann and Thompson 1987), this first part represents a nucleus of policies and relevant policy fields which is then elaborated in a series of satellites in the following – much longer – part of the speech. In rhetorical terms, however, these nuclei comprise a series of catch phrases and political truisms which obviously serve to provide some political principles/aims which nobody in the (multi-layered) audience can disagree with. The largest part of the "main body" of the speeches consists of a *series of topical moves* which announce policy issues of the new government. These topical moves are either realized as a minimal topical move or as an enhanced topical move. A *minimal topical move* comprises only the announcement of a policy or a policy change and may be very short. An *enhanced topical move* elaborates this minimal structure by inserting two structural positions before the announcement of a policy or policy change. It has the following general structure:

[Catch phrase/ positive evaluation Austria/ general political comment/ description of situation/ problem formulation] +
{[appeal to fellow politicians/ appeal to relevant social groups]} +
^[announcing policy/ announcing policy change]

Both Schüssel and Gusenbauer show individual preferences for one specific option in the first structural slot of enhanced topical moves. Schüssel introduces topical moves by describing the (Austrian) situation in a certain policy field and then announces the government's policy (or policy change) on the respective topic. Schüssel II uses slogans/catch phrases to structure the series of topical moves in the main body of the speech. These slogans serve to organize longer stretches of topical moves into entities which could be called "chapters" in a written text. Gusenbauer introduces many topical moves with a general political comment followed by a topical policy announcement.[25] Faymann does not show any kind of preference for a certain kind of realization of enhanced topical moves, but rather uses all variants shown above. The second structural slot of the enhanced topical move (the appeal to fellow politicians/relevant social groups) is only realized when the policy announcement (which is the core element of a topical move) is supposed to be controversial. In these cases, the appeal is obviously aimed at pre-empting critique and/or objection.

The closing phase of the speeches is their shortest part by far. It comprises two kinds of speech activities: self-praise and appeals to others. Self-praise is a positive self evaluation of the government in the final part of the inaugural speech in which the new chancellor states that he and his government shall always and only pursue the best goals for the country, its inhabitants, and its future. This is followed by appeals for cooperation to the national assembly of the parliament in general and to the politicians of the opposition specifically. The closing phase is structured rather similarly in all four speeches.

Lexical analysis – register characteristics
Corpus analysis was performed for the main bodies of the speeches as they contain the relevant policy topics and fields. Thus, if topical differences exist, they should become manifest in lexical differences between these speech parts. A word list was computed for each of the four speeches (using the word count function of Atlas.ti and generating an Excel table for each speech), then sorted in descending frequency order of the words in each speech, and finally all function words were eliminated. As usual in corpus analyses, the absolute frequency of even the most frequent content words in the remaining lists is rather low in relation to the total number of words in each speech. For reasons of space, only those content words which occur in (almost) all speeches were incorporated in the further analysis and were conflated into the following content categories:

–   Future orientation: "future" (noun and adjective), auxiliary verb "will" (and its morphological forms)
–   Self reference: "I", "federal government", "we",[26] "our"

Table 4. Most frequent content word categories in the four speeches

	Schüssel I		Schüssel II		Gusenbauer		Faymann	
Total:	5263		6956		5578		4487	
self reference	112	2.13%	230	3.31%	131	2.35%	107	2.39%
future orientation	128	2.43%	141	2.03%	161	2.89%	76	1.69%
reference to Austria	23	0.44%	37	0.53%	21	0.38%	47	1.05%
reference to Europe	22	0.42%	27	0.39%	0	0.00%	34	0.76%
volition	21	0.40%	43	0.62%	29	0.52%	0	0.00%
obligation	55	1.05%	90	1.29%	53	0.95%	37	0.82%

- Austria: "Austria", "Austrian", "we", "our"
- Europe: "Europe", "European", "EU"[27]
- Modality: "want", "can", "must", "should"

Table 4 juxtaposes the categories of the most frequent content words in all four speeches. For the present analysis, the original lists were cut off at the absolute count of 10 occurrences/word in the longest speech (Schüssel II). The second column of each speech shows the relative frequency of the categories in the respective speech. Although the results come from four speeches given by three different politicians who represent two parties, the most frequent word categories are surprisingly similar.[28]

Thus, on the lexical level, the inaugural speeches realize – independently from political orientation and personal style – the same register, which can be characterized as "future-oriented and Austria- and (to a lesser degree) Europe-centered" on the ideational level, and as "government-centered and oriented towards what we (i.e. the government and Austrians) must/should and want to be done" on the interpersonal level. These characteristics show that the inaugural speeches are situated in the Austrian political field (Reisigl 2007) with its political register and that they are policy documents in which future issues of Austrian and European policy are addressed. But if these speeches are so similar (despite having been given by three politicians representing two parties), are there also differences between them?

Topical sequences in the four speeches
In order to provide a more detailed account of the topical aspects of the speeches, their main bodies, which comprise a series of minimal or enhanced topical moves, were investigated more closely. Table 5 gives an overview of the topics (i.e. political fields) mentioned in each of the four speeches (note that each topic may occur several times in the respective speech).

Table 5. Topics in the four speeches

Schüssel I	Schüssel II	Gusenbauer	Faymann
Administration	Administration		Administration (very short)
Agricultural		Agriculture	
	Constitution reform		
Culture	Culture	Culture	
Democracy policy			
National defense/security/ international policy		National defense	
Economy	Economy	Economy	Economy
			Economy/finances/family
Education	Education	Education	Education
Environment	Environment	Environment	Environment
EU	EU enlargement / EU	EU	EU / Austrian policy with regard to EU
Family	Family	Family	Family
Federal policy			
Finances	Finances	Finances	Finances
	Foreign policy	Foreign policy	
Gender	Gender	Gender	Gender
			General government policy
Health	Health / Health and social security	Health	Health
Human rights			
	Immigration	Immigration	Immigration
Labor market			Labor market
		Legal policy	Legal policy (very short)
	Media		
NS past			
	Policy towards past		
Security	Security	Security	Security
Social security administration	Social security	Social security	Social security
	Sports	Sports	
		Technology	
	Tourism		
	Transport		

This first overview again shows a considerable homogeneity of the speeches with some notable exceptions: Schüssel is the only chancellor to address issues of Austria's policy towards its (NS) past, democracy policy in general, and human rights policy. The mention of these topics might be due to the harsh criticism his coalition with an extreme right-wing party had received in- and outside Austria and which he wanted to calm by explicitly announcing policies in the relevant political fields. Several other policy issues are unique to the Schüssel speeches, namely "federal policy", "media policy", "tourism", and "transport". Thus, Schüssel's speeches could also be seen as documents of "overregulation" which announce policies (or policy changes) in a whole range of fields which remain unmentioned in other speeches. In general, however, Table 5 adds a new facet to the already familiar picture of the four speeches as being very similar.

Several differences between the speeches, however, become manifest, if the topical sequences in the speeches are scrutinized in more detail. Table 6 provides an overview of the topic sequences in each of the four speeches.

In Table 6, bold horizontal lines divide each speech's topical sequence list into three roughly equal parts. The criterion for division is the number of policy issues a certain topic comprises in relation to the total number of policy issues mentioned in the respective speech.[29] This overview reveals the first significant differences between the four speeches: the relative position of the topics differs in the four speeches. Both Schüssel speeches start with "EU-policy" and especially the second speech mentions a considerable amount of policy fields in relation to EU policy at the beginning of the main body (cells with grey background in Table 6). Issues of health policy, on the other hand, come very late in both of his speeches and social security issues are only mentioned at the end of first third and the beginning of the second third of his first speech and at the end of the last third in his second speech. In contrast, both Gusenbauer and Faymann begin their speeches with economic and financial policy issues in very prominent positions and also mention health policy in the first third of their speeches. Both background EU policy insofar as Gusenbauer mentions it at the end of the last third of his speech (and only with regard to a single policy issue) and Faymann mentions it at the end of the second third of his speech. Of course, the political and social contextualization of the speeches in their respective introductions (and thus the political, social and economic context made relevant by the four politicians) may influence which topic(s) come first in the main parts and which may be backgrounded. But this contextualization effect does not seem to account for all topical sequence differences: while Faymann took over office in 2008 at the onset of a severe economic and financial crisis (and thus his focus on economic and financial policy at the beginning of the main part of his speech is to be expected), Gusenbauer's inaugural speech in 2007 had not yet been overshadowed by economic crisis, but

Table 6. Order of topics and number of policy issues associated with groups of topics

Schüssel I	Schüssel II	Gusenbauer	Faymann
EU policy	EU policy	Economic policy	Economy
Army/security/ international policy	EU enlargement	Financial policy	General government policy
Financial policy	Policy towards past	Social security	Economic policy
Administration policy	Environmental policy	Health policy	Financial policy
Economic policy	Transport policy	(17 issues)	Family policy
Democracy policy	Immigration policy		Economy/finances/ family policy
NS past	Economic policy in border regions	Education policy	Financial policy
Federal policy	Crime policy	Gender policy	Health policy
Social security	Foreign policy	Family policy	Labor market
(12 issues)	Security policy	Cultural policy	Gender policy
	Foreigner policy	Technology	(10 issues)
Labor market	Security policy	Agriculture	
Social security administration	(25 issues)	Environmental policy	Economy
Family policy		(17 issues)	Social security
Gender policy	Constitution reform		Education
Human rights policy	Administration policy	Sports	EU policy/ Austrian policy with regard to EU
Security policy	Economy	Security	(11 issues)
Economic policy	Environment	Immigration	
(15 issues)	(22 issues)	Legal policy	Environmental policy
		Military policy	Administration policy (very short)
Agricultural policy	Tourism	EU policy	Security
Environmental policy	Sports	Foreign policy	Immigration policy
Education policy	Cultural policy	(18 issues)	Legal policy (very short)
Cultural policy	Media policy		(7 issues)
Health policy	Education		
(10 issues)	Health and social security		
	Financial policy		
	(14 issues)		

nonetheless economic and financial policy issues were the first two policy fields he mentions. Schüssel in 2000, on the other hand, paid very close attention to the national and international concerns against his coalition in the introduction of his first inaugural speech, but the policy issues which would be relevant to this come rather late in the speech's main body (at the end of the first third and in the middle of the second third). In 2003, Schüssel contextualizes his speech in terms of the outcome of the previous elections and his (allegedly) successful previous government, the only foreign policy aspect he mentions in the introduction is the war in Iraq. The pronounced focus on EU policy in the main body of his second speech is thus not foreshadowed in the introduction. Consequently, the position of a topic in the main body of the speeches depends only to a lesser degree on the actual political context made relevant in the introduction and reflects mainly the relative importance it is assigned by the respective speaker.

This sequential effect, however, cannot be attributed to generic aspects as the generic structures of the four speeches are very similar (see above). In order to determine how these sequential effects might be explained, we will focus on micro-sequential patterns in the speeches:

-   Family policy + gender policy: Schüssel I, Gusenbauer
-   security policy + immigration policy: Schüssel II, Gusenbauer, Faymann
-   agricultural policy + environmental policy: Schüssel I (and Schüssel II
    at the level of sequential moves within the "environment policy" topic),
    Gusenbauer
-   economic policy + financial policy: Gusenbauer, Faymann
-   health policy + social security policy: Schüssel II, Gusenbauer

This list shows that sequences of two topics (or sequential moves in some cases) co-occur in a non-random way: gender policy (i.e. policy towards women) is discussed in terms of family policy, immigration policy is related to "security", "agriculture" to "environment", "economy" to "finances" and "health" to "social security" in terms of sequential placement. These paired co-occurrences can be viewed as a linguistic realization of the "co-articulation"[30] of different discourses. Co-articulation is more than the simple sequential neighborhood of two adjacent topics in a speech. This can be shown by two short examples:

> Excerpt 1 (Gusenbauer 2007):[31]
> The rural area is of key importance for this government. This commitment demands substantial political steps. Between 2007 and 2013, Austria has EU-funds to the amount of 3,9 billion € at its disposal which are doubled through national co-financing.
> The "green pact" will be implemented as planned and rests on three pillars: a program for mountain farmers, a nation-wide environmental program and an investment program for strengthening the economic competitiveness of Austrian farmers.

In this excerpt, Gusenbauer starts a new topical move, which is indicated by applause from MPs of the coalition party to the previous sequence. The nominal group "rural area" (which is also in thematic position in the German original) introduces neither "agriculture", nor "environmental policy" in unambiguous terms; the same is true of the mention of the monetary funds and the term "green pact". Only the elaboration of the "three pillars" on which this green pact rests shows that agricultural and environmental policies are not only mentioned together, but that they are part and parcel of the same policy program.

The second example comes from Faymann's speech and shows how gender policy is explicitly related to family policy issues (as in the Gusenbauer and Schüssel speeches), but that both are co-articulated with equal treatment of men and women on the labor market and income inequalities.

> Excerpt 2 (Faymann 2008):
> Equal opportunities, equal treatment of women in the world of work, and the establishing of income justice are major aims of the Austrian government. In this context it will be relevant to develop childcare benefits further and to succeed in involving fathers in childcare. (*Applause of ÖVP MPs*)
> We intend to further enhance child care and eliminate existing deficits. This is especially true of day care of children below three years of age. The major point is to ensure child care quality, and to develop fundamental standards and pedagogical concepts.
> In the area of equal opportunity policy, the government is determined to develop in cooperation with the social partners a national action plan for equal treatment which is intended to enhance women's participation in the work force and which shall help to reduce differences in payment. (*Applause of SPÖ and ÖVP MPs*)

The beginning of Excerpt 2 represents the beginning of another new topical move. The topic sentence introduces two thematic elements, "equal treatment of women in the world of work" and "income justice". These two topical elements are elaborated in paragraphs 2 and 3, respectively. Although Faymann presents an issue of family policy in the second paragraph (enhancement of child care facilities), this issue is clearly articulated as a policy aimed at enhancing equal treatment of women and not as a family policy issue. Thus, both examples above show how linguistic resources (paragraph structure, thematic development, and coherence structure) are used for the co-articulation of different discourses (agriculture and environment discourse in the Gusenbauer speech; gender and family policy discourse with economic discourse in the Faymann speech). The Schüssel II speech is an example for the domination of an "EU-policy discourse" over almost all relevant topics, whereas Gusenbauer's speech illustrates the significant absence of EU-discourse.

This short analysis of topical sequences and micro-sequence pairs in inaugural speeches shows that a political-linguistic analysis which aims at a full explanation of agreements and differences between texts and talk in political communication cannot limit itself to genre and register features of the texts, but must consider discourse features as well. The analysis of the genres as well as of the systems of genre of which the inaugural speech is the central element has shown the speeches' functioning and embedding in the Austrian parliamentary system and their significance as media events. This generic aspect of the speeches, however, did not reveal any significant differences between the speeches. The same is true of the lexical analysis which, too, revealed that all four speeches realize the register of Austrian domestic policy, i.e. the genre reflects the linguistically relevant aspects (i.e. register aspects) of the situation in which it is used (see Section 2). Under a political-linguistic perspective, however, this result is not fully satisfying. As discussed in Section 3.2, the four speeches are embedded in an unfolding political situation which is characterized by two intertwined patterns of political/ideological and personal continuities and discontinuities. One can thus expect the inaugural speeches to exhibit differences as well as congruencies. The expected differences become visible at the level of topical sequences and discourses realized in the speeches. It could be shown that the relative relevance a speaker attributes to a certain topic corresponds to its sequential position (and the number of related issues) in the main part of the speech. The analysis of thematic structures, coherence relations and paragraph structures shows which discourse is realized, which discourses are co-articulated and which discourse is dominant in a speech. An analysis more detailed than possible here would have shown the linguistic/rhetorical means that are used by speakers for "co-articulating" discourses or for the "domination" of one discourse over another.

4. Discussion and conclusions

In this last part of the chapter, I want to integrate the results of the empirical analysis of the four inaugural speeches presented in Section 3 with the theoretical discussion of genre and discourse theories in Section 2. In doing so, I will argue that the inaugural speech meets all criteria for a "genre" which were established in Section 2 and that the genre "inaugural speech" is the central part of not one but two systems of genres. I will also argue that this result is not satisfactory for an analysis interested in the linguistic features indicating differences and parallels in the policies announced by the speakers. To account for this political-linguistic aspect of the speeches, the analytic approach has to be extended to integrate the concept of "discourse" into the analysis.

Section 2 concluded that the vast majority of the reviewed genre theories conceive of a genre as a typified, recognizable, structured, and goal oriented social process which is realized by means of one or more semiotic systems. This definition clearly leads us to classify the inaugural speech of the Austrian chancellors as a genre: the speeches have a rather *uniform internal structure* which consists of three phases (introduction – main part – concluding phase) which in turn comprise several distinct moves. The introduction contextualizes the speech within the national and international political situation. The main part of each speech comprises a set of minimal or enhanced topical moves in which several policies (or policy changes) are announced. The short concluding phase realizes appeals for cooperation to all MPs as well as to relevant stakeholder groups outside the immediate communication situation.

The overall *goal* of the genre is the introduction of the new government's policies and the planned implementation of these policies. This goal can be deduced from the Austrian constitution as well as from the form and content of the speeches. The *social process* which the genre fulfills is complex as was shown by the analysis of the stakeholder groups and audience roles as well as by the description of the speeches' production process. The realization of the genre involves a group of "authors" and "principals" (leading ministry officials, ministers, advisors, and the chancellor) but only one "animator" – the chancellor. The same complex picture emerges on the genre's audience side: the analysis of the speeches has shown that different stakeholder and audience groups are addressed and talked about in rather distinct ways. Greeting, appealing and nominating practices in the speeches thus clearly contribute to the differentiation of these recipient groups of the genre. The lexical analysis of the four speeches further shows that the genre draws on the register of Austrian domestic policy. This register contributes the most frequently used lexemes at the ideational and interpersonal planes of the speeches, regardless of the speakers' party-political affiliation and regardless of personal rhetorical styles. The investigation of the parliamentary sessions in which the inaugural speeches are embedded has shown that the genre is the central part of a system of genres. It is preceded by a rather fixed set of preparatory speech acts and it is followed by two different genres in the ensuing debate: praising and criticizing debate contributions by MPs of the government coalition and the opposition parties respectively.[32] Media coverage of the inaugural debate genre system constitutes a second system of genres focused on the inaugural speech, but that one could not be investigated in this chapter.

Apart from this general outcome of the study, the results also relate to certain theory-specific aspects discussed in Section 2. With regard to the "new rhetoric" genre approach's inclusion of activity theory, the results show that it seems difficult to trace the emergence and continuity of the "inaugural speech" genre back to the practices of an activity system. Several problems arise in this context:

1.   It is not clear which individuals constitute the activity system in which the inaugural speech serves as a relevant problem solving tool. Of course, the above mentioned "authors" and "principals" who are responsible for compiling the

materials for the speech and who are (partly) involved in its drafting are the first candidates – and a close ethnographic investigation would certainly reveal the relation between conflicting views and interests within this group and certain discursive features of the speeches.[33] But an activity system does not only comprise the "producing members" of a genre-using group but also its recipients. If we are to try to account for the recipient side of the genre, however, we would have to include the whole Austrian public in our activity system. But how would this benefit our understanding of the functioning of the genre? As the analysis has shown, different parts of the public (audience and stakeholder groups) are treated rather differently in the speeches and are also affected by the announced policies in very different ways. Thus, the concept of "activity system" is too narrow and undifferentiated to account for the complex production and consumption of the inaugural speech.

2. Activity theory attributes the emergence and temporal stability of a genre to the cooperation between an activity system's members and the necessity of arriving at a certain outcome which is beyond the capabilities of individual community members. Genres as emerging tools contribute to these joint outcomes, they are employed on the basis of existing genre knowledge, their usability is tested in several situations, and they are adapted if the outcomes of their use is inadequate. Applying this conception to the case of the inaugural speech shows its inadequacies: many "author"-members of the "production team" change in any instance of the realization of the genre, thus they do not have many occasions for practicing the genre. But how then, should they gradually learn to master it? – They might use their genre knowledge of political speeches in general because in certain respects inaugural speeches resemble any other political speech, but these similarities are insufficient to account for the discursive peculiarities of the inaugural speech. Thus, the activity theoretical approach to genre runs into (at least) two problems in explaining the emergence and discursive features of the genre and its use.

A possible solution to these problems can only be sketched here: as "new rhetoric" scholars mainly investigate the use and emergence of mundane genres, we could speculate that the activity theoretical view of the emergence of genres might only hold in contexts which Habermas has coined the "life-world" (Habermas 1988), whereas in "system-world" contexts (Habermas 1988), the explanation of genre emergence and use would have to take into account complex institutional structures, bureaucratic regulations and interaction patterns etc., and thus would need a more sophisticated analytical concept for complex social structures.

The RGT approach offers the notions of "context of situation" and "register" for explaining the immediate contextual aspects of genre use. As the analysis has shown, "register" is in fact important for explaining the ideational and interpersonal similarities of the four speeches. The register of Austrian domestic policy is the relevant linguistic context dimension in which the genre is used (i.e. the parliamentary session). But which status does the genre of the inaugural speech have in the Austrian political context? RGT posits only one theoretical level beyond the context of situation, and this is the context of culture, thus the inaugural speech should be part of Austrian culture. This, however, is not convincing at all as the genre is used very rarely and its use is limited to a very specific communicative situation with which most Austrians are probably not familiar. Thus, while it would make sense to claim that the genre of the inaugural speech is part of the Austrian political culture (or discourse), it would be implausible to claim that it is part of Austrian culture at large.

The above (Section 2) discussed major approaches to genre thus enable us to explain a considerable fraction of our results, but they also pose some theoretical problems in accounting for their apparent genre properties. One additional aspect has to be mentioned: so far, only those aspects of the four speeches were discussed which are congruent, i.e. their similarities. A political-linguistic analysis, however, must also strive to account for the political differences between the speeches. We would not expect speeches which are delivered by representatives of different political parties to conform in every respect, and a linguistic genre analysis intended to sufficiently characterize the genre of the inaugural speech should account for these differences.

In fact, the results showed significant differences between the four speeches in terms of topic sequences and in terms of discourses realized. The sequential placement of a topic is one relevant clue towards political differences, the second one is that certain topics were formulated within (or "articulated in") a discourse to which they do not originally belong (e.g. family policy in terms of economic discourse or environmental policy in terms of agricultural discourse) and in this way, emphasis can be put on different policies. The content-dimension above the level of lexis is thus crucial in accounting for the political differences between speakers and speeches. As Fairclough has already stated in 1993, content does not enter into texts in a neutral way but "contents [...] enter texts in the mediated form of particular constructions of them" (Fairclough 1993, 128). This is especially true of political texts, hence the concept of "discourse" was introduced in Section 2. In the realm of political communication, the concept of situational registers has thus to be complemented with the notion of "discourse", which refers to communicative social practices in social fields (in the sense of Bourdieu 2009). As social practices, discourses provide social positions for actors as well as perspectivized content matter and the semiotic resources for their realization. Discourses and genres do not exist in a 1:1 relation, i.e. a certain discourse may be realized by different genres and the same genre may be used for realizing different discourses (or an array of different discourses as the above results have shown, see also Fairclough 1993). The relationship between social fields (and of the corresponding "habitus"), discourses, genres and registers could only be sketched in this chapter and must be specified in further investigations of other genres in further social fields. It should, however, have become clear that existing genre theories need to be developed further in order to be able to account for genres outside the often limited social fields in which they were developed.

Notes

1. Investigations of genre which were conducted in the ethnography of communication framework (Gumperz and Hymes 1964) are not included in the following discussion as this approach never arrived at a theoretically reflected notion of "genre" (Günthner and Knoblauch 1995).

2. E.g. several research groups who co-operate in a research project.

3. There are, of course, (meta-)theoretical considerations which guide the SFL (and RGT) conception of only two levels of context, namely the recourse to Hjelmslev's differentiation between "connotative" and "denotative" semiotic systems (and the assumption that language is a denotative semiotic system whereas register and genre form a connotative semiotic) and SFL's adaption of Saussure's binary sign conception. A closer discussion of these theoretical aspects lies outside the scope of this chapter.

4. See, e.g., his definition of "genre" in Fairclough (1993, 125) which – although it is explicitly based on Bakhtin's genre concept – bears some resemblance to the RGT approach to genre.

5. See, e.g., the overview in Lee (2001) who explicitly links his conception of "genre" to Fairclough but does not even mention the concept of discourse in his article. Bhatia (2004) uses "discourse" in a very general sense of "language in action" which is comparable to Schiffrin's (1994) definition of discourse as "contextualized units of language" (Schiffrin 1994, 39).

6. Keller's complex sociological discourse theory, which integrates elements from Foucault's archeology of knowledge and the sociology of knowledge in the tradition of Berger and Luckmann, cannot be reviewed here in detail. For a detailed account see Keller (2011). Keller, however, does not seem to be aware of the rich linguistic literature on genre. In his opinion, genres have so far only been investigated at the level of "mundane interactions" which – according to him – show only "low degrees of organization" (Keller 2011, 227; transl. HG).

7. The structured (or staged) nature of genres is relevant insofar as it helps differentiate genres from simple speech acts: e.g. a question, although it might be realized by several kinds of syntactic structures, is a simple speech act and not a genre, because it has no internal functional stages (or moves), whereas question – answer sequences might form a genre (e.g. a news interview) because they developed specific functional stages of question – answer pairs.

8. I cannot provide an account of the Austrian parliamentary system as a whole here. For an overview see Zima, Brône, and Feyaerts (2010).

9. In principle, in this case also a minority government could be formed, but this is highly unusual in the Austrian political culture.

10. In the current investigation, the formation of government took between 65 days (2008) and 124 days (1999/2000).

11. In principle, the Austrian president may entrust any politician (and even non-politicians who – in his opinion – would be able to form a stable government) with the formation of a government, but in reality this has not been done so far.

12. This short historical account of Austrian government formations since 2000 follows mainly Löffler (2009).

13. Schüssel (2000): 8 days; Schüssel (2003): 6 days; Gusenbauer (2007): 7 days; Faymann (2008): 9 days between formation of government and inaugural speech.

14. But as inaugural speeches are typical policy documents, Wodak's (2000) account of the co-construction of an EU policy paper (see also Krzyżanowski, this volume) might also shed some light on the construction process of inaugural speeches. Although the construction of the policy paper in Wodak's investigation took four months and the inaugural speeches under investigation here had to be finished within less than 10 days, Wodak's conclusion that a policy paper comprises various voices and that "topics which were consensual get simpler and more precise whereas difficult, sensitive topics, which have to be negotiated at length, get vague and complex" (Wodak 2000, 112) will also apply to inaugural speeches.

15. Opposition party MPs may produce spontaneous interruptive comments (*Zwischenrufe*) during the speech which are not investigated here. For an account of this communicative practice in the Austrian parliament see Zima and Feyaerts (2010).

16. Austria has a unique system of compulsory membership in (occupational) organizations which represent relevant social groups and which are called "chambers". These chambers are not to be confused with trade unions (which exist independently from the chambers). Several of the (major) chambers which represent antagonistic social groups form the so-called "social partnership" which has a traditionally high influence on Austrian domestic policy although it has never had any official status in the political system.

17. Excepting representatives of Churches. Since the beginning of the 2nd Austrian Republic (1955), representatives of Churches may not be elected as MPs.

18. The participant role categories are described in detail in Zima and Feyaerts (2010) who base their work on Clark (1996) and Goffman (1981).

19. Speaking time is thus not limited on an individual basis, but for each party.

20. There is one relevant optional speech act: the "announcement of an urgent question". Urgent questions are specific parliamentary communicative actions in which a group of MPs may ask the government (or single ministers) questions which they deem 'urgent' and which the government (i.e. the chancellor) or minister has to answer publicly during a parliamentary session. The chancellor's or minister's reply is then in turn debated by the MPs.

21. In fact, there are three presidents of the parliament and they take turns during the sessions as they face a considerable work load during a parliamentary session. They ensure that a session is conducted in lawful ways and according to the parliamentary procedural rules.

22. This may severely impact the way the speakers deliver their speeches (cf. Zima et al. 2010) but an investigation of this aspect is outside the focus of the current paper.

23. The live broadcast of about 8 hours of the debate is a genre in itself insofar as it (1) influences relevant aspects of the debate (cf. above, and Zima, Brone, and Feyaerts 2010) and (2) provides viewers with a specific perspective on the debate which depends on camera positions and the switching between them (i.e. the broadcast director's work).

24. Of course, there is also a tertiary system of genres which is based upon this secondary one, namely the private conversations of the general audience and of relevant stakeholder groups on the media coverage of the speeches and of the debate. This tertiary system of genres cannot be investigated in a systematic way.

25. On an abstract level, these enhanced sequences resemble the main generic features of "policy documents" (Wodak 2000; see also Krzyżanowski, this volume), namely "presenting features of a given field" and "lines of action which should be taken in this field".

26. Of course "we" and "our" are potentially ambiguous as they may be used as an audience-excluding "we" which refers to the government only, but may also be used in an audience-including way which denotes government and audience, therefore both words are included in the "self reference" and the "Austria" categories.

27. In principle, "we" and "our", which are listed in the "self reference" and "Austria" category, could also refer to "Europe", but in fact they never do in the four speeches.

28. There is only one notable exception from this frequency pattern which concerns the Gusenbauer speech: it lacks the lexical complex "Europe" (at least in the list of the most frequent word categories, see also the next subsection).

29. e.g. Schüssel I contains 19 topics with a total of 37 policy issues mentioned, thus the list is divided into 3 parts, each of which contains roughly 12 policy issues; this ensures that topics which contain more policy issues are assigned higher weight than topics which contain only a few or one policy issue.

30. "Co-articulation" is a term from sociological discourse analysis (see Keller 2011; Fairclough 1993) which refers to the simultaneous realization of two or more discourses (where one discourse might be dominating) in one speech event.

31. For the sake of space, only the English translations (transl. HG) of the excerpts are presented, the German originals can be found at http://www.parlament.gv.at/SERV/STAT/DOK/index.shtml.

32. The occurrence of the inserted genre system of the "urgent question debate" which occurred in two of the four parliamentary sessions can be explained by the live-broadcast situation: opposition parties introduce urgent questions in the parliamentary debates in which the inaugural speech is delivered in order to receive media (and public) attention for their political agenda. The insertion of one genre system into another genre system is thus a consequence of the intensive media coverage the inaugural speech and its debate receive and points at the close interrelationship between politics and media in modern societies (see Okulska and Cap 2010, as well as Introduction to the present volume, esp. Section 3).

33. As did Wodak's investigation of an EU-policy paper and its gradual development within the EU bureaucracy (Wodak 2000).

References

Bazerman, Charles. 1988. *Shaping Written Knowledge. The Genre and Activity of the Experimental Article in Science.* Madison, WI: The University of Wisconsin Press.

—. 1994. "Systems of Genres and the Enactment of Social Intentions." In *Genre and the New Rhetoric*, ed. by Aviva Freedman, and Peter Medway, 79–105. London: Taylor & Francis.

Berkenkotter, Carol, and Thomas Huckin. 1995. *Genre Knowledge in Disciplinary Communication.* Hillsdale, NJ: Erlbaum.

Bhatia, Vijay K. 2004. *Worlds of Written Discourse. A Genre-Based View.* London: Continuum.

Biber, Douglas. 1988. *Variation across Speech and Writing.* Cambridge: Cambridge University Press.

Biber, Douglas, Ulla Connor, and Thomas Upton. 2007. *Discourse on the Move: Using Corpus Analysis to Describe Discourse Structure.* Amsterdam: John Benjamins.

Biria, Reza, and Azadeh Mohammadi. 2012. "The Socio-Pragmatic Functions of Inaugural Speech: A Critical Discourse Analysis Approach." *Journal of Pragmatics*, 44: 1290–1302.

Bourdieu, Pierre. 2009. *Entwurf einer Theorie der Praxis: Auf der ethnologischen Grundlage der kabylischen Gesellschaft.* Frankfurt am Main: Suhrkamp.

Clark, Herbert. 1996. *Using Language.* Cambridge: Cambridge University Press.

Cloran, Carmel, David Butt, and Geoffrey Williams (eds). 1996. *Ways of Saying, Ways of Meaning: Selected Papers of Ruqaya Hasan.* London: Cassell.

Eggins, Suzanne, and James R. Martin. 1997. "Genres and Registers of Discourse." In *Discourse as Structure and Process*, ed. by Teun van Dijk, 230–257. London: Sage.

Ehtreiber, Ewald. 2003. *"Alles für unser Österreich!" Das Bild Österreichs in den Regierungserklärungen der Zweiten Republik.* Frankfurt am Main: Peter Lang.

Engeström, Yrjo. 1987. *Learning by Expanding: An Activity Theoretical Approach to Developmental Research.* Helsinki: Orienta-Konsultit Oy.

Englert, Carol S., Troy Mariage, and Kailonnie Dunsmore. 2008. "Tenets of Sociocultural Theory in Writing Instruction Research." In *Handbook of Writing Research,* ed. by Charles MacArthur, Steve Graham, and Jill Fitzgerald, 208–222. New York: The Guilford Press.

Fairclough, Norman. 1993. *Discourse and Social Change.* Cambridge: Polity Press.

Freedman, Aviva, and Peter Medway. 1994. *Genre and the New Rhetoric.* London: Taylor & Francis.

Goffman, Erving. 1981. *Forms of Talk.* Philadelphia: University of Pennsylvania Press.

Gottschlich, Maximilian. 1989. "Regierungserklärungen als Modellfälle politischer Kommunikation." In *Was die Kanzler sagten: Regierungserklärungen der Zweiten Republik*, ed. by Maxmilian Gottschlich, Oswald Panagl, and Manfried Welan, 33–69. Wien: Böhlau.

Gottschlich, Maximilian, Oswald Panagl, and Manfried Welan. (eds). 1989. *Was die Kanzler sagten: Regierungserklärungen der Zweiten Republik.* Wien: Böhlau.

Gruber, Helmut. 2012. "Establishing Intertextual References in Austrian Parliamentary Debates. A Pilot Study." In *Proceedings of the ESF Strategic Workshop on Follow-ups Across Discourse Domains: A Cross-Cultural Exploration of their Forms and Functions,* ed. by Anita Fetzer, Elda Weizman, and Elisabeth Reber, 87–107. Würzburg: Universität Würzburg [online]. (URL: http://opus.bibliothek.uni-wuerzburg.de/volltexte/2012/7165/ URN:urn:nbn:de:bvb:20-opus-71656)

Gumperz, John, and Dell Hymes. (eds). 1964. *The Ethnography of Communication.* Menasha, WI: American Anthropological Association.

Günthner, Susanne, and Hubert Knoblauch. 1995. "Culturally Patterned Speaking Practices – The Analysis of Communicative Genres." *Pragmatics* 5: 1–32.

Habermas, Jürgen. 1988. *Theorie des kommunikativen Handelns*. Frankfurt am Main: Suhrkamp.

Halliday, Michael A.K. 1994. *An Introduction to Functional Grammar*. London: Edward Arnold.

—. 1978. *Language as Social Semiotic. The Social Interpretation of Language and Meaning*. London: Edward Arnold.

Hristozova-Weiss, Yordanka. 2009. *Die Parlamentsdebatte – Regeln und Improvisation*. Dissertation, Universität Wien.

Keller, Reiner. 2011. *Wissenssoziologische Diskursanalyse. Grundlegung eines Forschungsprogramms*. Wiesbaden: Verlag für Sozialwissenschaften.

Lave, Jean, and Etienne Wenger. 1991. *Situated Learning. Legitimate Peripheral Participation*. Cambridge: Cambridge University Press.

Lee, David. 2001. "Genres, Registers, Text Types, Domains, and Styles: Clarifying the Concepts and Navigating a Path through the BNC Jungle." *Language Learning & Technology* 5: 37–72.

van Leeuwen, Theo. 1996. "The Representation of Social Actors." In *Texts and Practices. Readings in Critical Discourse Analysis*, ed. by Carmen C. Coulthard, and Malcolm Coulthard, 32–70. London: Routledge.

Leontjew, Aleksei. 1981. *Problems for the Development of Mind*. Moscow: Progress.

Löffler, Manfred. 2009. *Regierungsbildung in Österreich aus koalitionstheoretischer Sicht*. Diplomarbeit, Universität Wien.

Mann, William, and Sandra Thompson. 1987. *Rhetorical Structure Theory: A Theory of Text Organization*. Marina del Rey: California Information Sciences Institute.

Martin, James R. 1992. *English Text. System and Structure*. Amsterdam: John Benjamins.

—. 1999. "Modeling Context: A Crooked Path of Progress in Contextual Linguistics." In *Text and Context in Functional Linguistics*, ed. by Mohsen Ghadessy, 25–63. Amsterdam: John Benjamins.

—. 1985. "Process and Text: Two Aspects of Semiosis." In *Systemic Perspectives on Discourse vol. 1: Selected Theoretical Papers from the 9th International Systemic Workshop*, ed. by James Benson, and William S. Greaves, 248–274. Norwood, NJ: Ablex.

Martin, James R., and David Rose. 2008. *Genre Relations. Mapping Culture*. London: Equinox.

Miller, Carolyn R. 1994. "Genre as Social Action." In *Genre and the New Rhetoric*, ed. by Aviva Freedman, and Peter Medway, 23–43. London: Taylor & Francis.

Okulska, Urszula, and Piotr Cap. (eds). 2010. *Perspectives in Politics and Discourse*. Amsterdam: John Benjamins.

Panagl, Oswald. 1989. "Die Regierungserklärungen der Zweiten Republik (1945–1987)." In *Was die Kanzler sagten: Regierungserklärungen der Zweiten Republik*, ed. by Maxmilian Gottschlich, Oswald Panagl, and Manfried Welan, 5–32. Wien: Böhlau.

Pörksen, Uwe. 2004. *Was ist eine gute Regierungserklärung? Grundriss einer politischen Poetik*. Göttingen: Wallstein Verlag.

Reisigl, Martin. 2007. *Nationale Rhetorik in Fest- und Gedenkreden. Eine diskursanalytische Studie zum "österreichischen Millennium" in den Jahren 1946 und 1996*. Tübingen: Stauffenburg.

Reisigl, Martin, and Ruth Wodak. 2001. *Discourse and Discrimination. The Rhetoric of Racism and Antisemitism*. London: Routledge.

Russell, David. 1997. "Rethinking Genre in School and Society: An Activity Theory Analysis." *Written Communication* 14: 504–554.

Schiffrin, Deborah. 1994. *Approaches to Discourse*. Oxford: Blackwell.

Swales, John. 1990. *Genre Analysis*. Cambridge: Cambridge University Press.

Welan, Manfried. 1989. "Regierungserklärungen in Recht und Politik." In *Was die Kanzler sagten: Regierungserklärungen der Zweiten Republik*, ed. by Maxmilian Gottschlich, Oswald Panagl, and Manfried Welan, 69–87. Wien: Böhlau.

Wodak, Ruth. 2000. "From Conflict to Consensus? The Co-Construction of a Policy Paper." In *European Union Discourses on Un/employment*, ed. by Peter Muntigl, Gilbert Weiss, and Ruth Wodak, 73–115. Amsterdam: John Benjamins.

Zima, Elisabeth, Geert Brône, and Kurt Feyaerts. 2010. "Patterns of Interaction in Austrian Parliamentary Debates." In *European Parliaments under Scrutiny: Discourse Strategies and Interaction Practices*, ed. by Cornelia Ilie, 135–164. Amsterdam: John Benjamins.

Zima, Elisabeth, and Kurt Feyaerts. 2010. "Participant Roles and Layered Intersubjectivity in Austrian Parliamentary Debates". Paper presented at the *Vierte Konferenz der Deutschen Gesellschaft für Kognitive Linguistik*, Bremen.

CHAPTER 2

Political interviews in context

Anita Fetzer and Peter Bull

University of Augsburg, Germany / University of York, UK

The genre of the broadcast political interview is examined from a compositional methodological approach, drawing on ethnomethodological conversation analysis, critical discourse analysis, sociopragmatics, social psychology and media studies. A distinction is proposed between the default and non-default political interview. In the prototypical (default) interview, there is the journalist as interviewer, who asks political questions, and the politician as interviewee, who answers political questions by giving political answers. In the non-default interview, this one-dimensional setting becomes blurred: in the employment of different semiotic codes and socio-cultural practices; in the inclusion of both public and private discourse identities; and in explicit accommodation to the audience's needs. To capture the inherent dynamics of the genre, it is proposed that political interviews be conceptualized as a hybrid genre, accommodating the constraints and requirements of both media communication and professional discourse.

1. Introduction

Political interviews are investigated in a number of analytic frameworks, which, from an interdisciplinary perspective, are not mutually exclusive but rather supplementary. While the conversation-analytic approach (Clayman and Heritage 2002) focuses primarily on the interactional organization and reconstruction of a communicative event thus highlighting the fact that a genre does not exist in isolation but is reconstructed in and through the process of communication, pragmatics (Jucker 1986; Wilson 1990) and critical discourse analysis (Fairclough 1998) investigate the specific functions of language with regard to language production and language comprehension. Pragmatics examines the dichotomy between what is said and what is meant by focusing on genre-specific strategies, such as evasiveness, indirectness or reformulation, and critical discourse analysis explicitly accounts for the interdependencies between discourse and social context, which are further differentiated in a socio-semiotic framework accommodating verbal and nonverbal means of communication (Bell 1977). Social psychological analyses have been focused on different aspects of such discourse, such as the frequency of interruptions (Beattie 1982; Bull and Mayer 1988), and on the analysis of question-response sequences, with particular regard to equivocation (e.g., Bull 2008; Bull, Elliott, Palmer and Walker 1996), based at least in part on a theory of equivocation proposed by Bavelas, Black, Chovil and Mullett (1990).

In the following section, the most important frameworks will be examined, focusing especially on particular interconnections and interrelationships.

1.1   Conversation analysis and political interviews

The research paradigm of ethnomethodological conversation analysis represents a micro-sociological perspective par excellence. It is based on the premise of the indexicality of social action focusing in particular on the domain of intersubjectivity. One of its major research questions is how separate individuals are able to know or act within a common world and how members negotiate or achieve a common context. This common context is synonymous with social context, which, like linguistic context, classifies into a local (or micro) social context and a global (or macro) social context (Schegloff 1987). Social contexts can be further distinguished with regard to a number of intermediate layers, such as meso social context regarding the delimiting frame of a particular speech event or genre, and more global institutional context (Drew and Heritage 1992). It is the intermediate layer anchored to the delimiting frame of genre which is of relevance to our examination of genres in general and political interview in particular.

The conversation-analytic investigation of political interviews has been based primarily on the analysis of turn taking, which has been assigned the status of an organizing principle, to which interactional and institutional roles are anchored. Political interviews are defined by the context-sensitive employment of the turn-taking system, viz. the participant-specific use of the adjacency pair question-answer: the interviewer employs the first part of the adjacency pair (or: the initiating format) and asks questions, and the interviewee employs the second part of the adjacency pair (or: the responsive format) and answers questions. The dynamics of the turn-taking mechanism allows for both a micro-perspective, examining the micro level of exchange, and a macro-perspective, examining the communicative exchange as a whole. Against this background, a political interview is not only interactionally organized on the micro level but also on the more remote level of genre with its constitutive opening, closing and topical-sequence sections. To interactionally organize the genre of a political interview, the interviewer and interviewee need to employ the participant-specific first, respectively second, part of the adjacency pair question-answer: the interactional role of interviewer is anchored to the employment of the initiating format and thus needs to ask a question or utter a greeting, while the interactional role of interviewee is anchored to the employment of the responsive format and thus needs to answer the question or respond to the greeting. Should an interviewer refrain from asking questions or should an interviewee refrain from answering questions,[1] the genre of a political interview cannot be interactionally organized.

The context-sensitive employment of the turn-taking mechanism in political interviews not only serves as the base for the definition of the interactional roles of interviewer and interviewee, but also for the genre-specific employment of backchannels, which are less frequent in political interviews than in ordinary talk (Heritage 1985). Furthermore, the genre-specific question-and-answer sequences serve as the foundation for the interactional organization of the genre's leitmotif of *neutralism*, as stated by Greatbatch (1988, 422). In the United Kingdom, the turn-taking system has remained quite stable since the rise of news and current affairs broadcasting in the 1950s. One important constraint making for this stability is the legal requirement of broadcast journalists since the inception of the BBC in the 1920s that they should maintain a formal neutrality.

From a genre-anchored perspective, the structured interplay of questions and answers assigns the interviewer's turns the status of questions, so even challenges, viz. questions questioning the appropriateness of answers, will count as questions, because their source is the interactional role of interviewer. The same kind of reasoning applies to the interactional role of interviewee. Turns produced by the interviewee count as answers, and their discursive content seems not of prime importance at that stage. That is why local deviations from the turn-taking mechanism tend to be resolved locally.

The turn-taking mechanism is undoubtedly a very important foundation for the definition of a political interview. But are question-answer sequences and interactional roles sufficient conditions for a thorough examination of political interviews?

1.2   Critical discourse analysis and political interviews

Critical discourse analysis has become a prominent research paradigm for a function-based analysis of language, language use, and discourse and communication. Language and language use, and discourse and discursive practices are seen as interactive concepts which are connected dialectically. While conversation analysis developed within the research paradigm of sociology opposing the then prevailing focus on macro-sociology and social structure by stressing the relevance of the micro domains of society and social context, critical discourse analysis is related closely to the theory and practice of critical theory, post-structuralism and post-modernity.

As regards methodology, critical discourse analysis has more recently adapted a variety of tools departing from purely linguistic and speech-act based examinations to the consideration of other semiotic resources, e.g. color, typography or images, to name but the most prominent ones. The extension of frame from mono-modal language to multimodal semiotic representation allows for an explicit account of the orchestration of multivoicedness and heteroglossia. To capture the diversity of society and culture, discourse analysis not only focuses on the investigation of discourse and discursive practice as delimited processes and products. Instead, these realizations are related explicitly to a wider frame of reference regarding possible forms and functions of intertextuality and interdiscursivity. In that frame of reference, political interviews are no longer seen as a structured interplay of questions and answers but rather as multi-voiced orchestrated encounters. To examine the use of language in such a frame of reference, a semantics- and discourse-based theory of grammar is needed.

Critical discourse analysis employs an integrated approach based on Systemic Functional Grammar (Halliday 1994), linguistic pragmatics and conversation analysis, and views meaning making and sense-making as contextual processes, as is stated explicitly by Jaworski and Coupland (1999, 41): "Construing language as discourse involves orienting to language as a form of social action, as a functioning form of social action embedded in the totality of social processes". Discourse is thus connected intrinsically with the construction of identity, social structure, reality and ideology. Against this background, it is crucial to distinguish between different layers and different types of meaning, viz. on the one hand between linguistic meaning, discursive meaning and social meaning, and on the other between meanings inferred, interpreted or decoded by the observer and those inferred, interpreted or decoded by the participants and their respective interactional, social and discursive roles, including their goals and intentions. As a necessary consequence of this distinction, meaning is neither a static construct situated in the text nor is it context-independent and given. Rather, meaning is dynamic and context-dependent: it is encoded and produced, and inferred, interpreted and decoded by the participants, as is mirrored by the discourse-analytic concepts of *acts of meaning making* and *acts of construction*. This does not only hold for the micro domain but also for ideology, which is seen as enacted in social practice (van Dijk 2009).

The dual status of discourse as process and product as well as its intrinsic dialectic connectedness with language use as discursive activity and with society, assign communicative genres the status of constructed, reconstructed and deconstructed frames of reference: "Discourse as part of social activity constitutes genres. Genres are diverse ways of acting, of producing social life, in the semiotic mode" (Fairclough 2003, 206). However, genres are neither stable nor normative. Rather, "genres are types. But they are types in a rather peculiar way. Genres do not specify the lexicogrammatical resources of word, phrase, clause, and so on. Instead, they specify the **typical** ways in which these are combined and deployed so as to enact the typical semiotic action formations of a given community" (Thibault 2003, 44). Against this background, discursive analyses of political interviews account for the identity of the participants as well as for subjectivity, they account for their use of style and styling, as well as intimacy, involvement and detachment, spelling out the inherent multimodal and multi-voiced discourses used within that particular genre.

Critical discourse based analyses (Bell and Garrett 1998; Fairclough 1995) of political interviews examine the specific functions of language regarding language production and language reception, such as medialization, conversationalization and ideology. Medialization looks at the impact of mass media on the production and reception of language, conversationalization considers the influence of mundane everyday talk on institutional discourse, and macro-oriented ideology is examined with respect to its manifestation in different types of discourse.

In critical discourse analysis, political interviews are not only examined from a top-down perspective as a genre which is embedded and dialectically connected with socio-cultural context and with other discourses but also as a multi-voiced encounter and media event, thus capturing the inherent complexity of the genre. But are these sufficient conditions to capture the subtle interactive processes inherent in the genre of a political interview?

1.3   Pragmatics and political interviews

Pragmatics is fundamentally concerned with communicative action and its felicity in context, investigating action with respect to the questions of what action is, what may count as action, what action is composed of, what conditions need to be satisfied for action to be felicitous, and how action is related to context. These research questions and the object of research require communicative action in particular to be conceived of as a relational concept, relating action and context, relating action and communicative action, relating communicative action and interlocutors, and relating interlocutors with the things they do with words in context.

The pragmatic-perspective paradigm does not represent a clearly delimited field of research but rather offers a general perspective towards the object to be examined. The perspective is thus shifted from an analysis of the language system and its constitutive parts to that of its rule-governed instantiation and embeddedness in context, considering its generalized and particularized conditions of use. That change in perspective has important consequences for methodology. To account for the parts-whole connectedness, a relational frame of reference is adopted, which accommodates the relation amongst the language system, language use and language users, and what they do with words in context, comprising linguistic context (or co-text), social context and cognitive context. Against this background, language is connected intrinsically with language use, and meaning is not seen as a product and given but rather as dynamic, multifaceted and negotiated in context. Language use is dependent on variability, and language users adapt to contextual constraints accommodating them not only in the formulation of utterances but also in their interpretation (e.g. Mey 2001). As in functional grammar and Systemic Functional Grammar (Givón 1993; Halliday 1994), the dynamic construct of meaning is a necessary condition for making linguistic choices.

In pragmatics, question-answer sequences are not restricted to the common-sense view of a question as a means of seeking information and the common-sense view of an answer as a means of providing information. Instead, questions and answers are employed strategically as they fulfill a number of communicative functions in discourse. In a political interview, for instance, a wh-question[2] can be employed to elicit unknown information by saying,

(1)   What figure?

(2)   Who comes first for you, the farmer or the consumer?

In (1), the interviewer requests the interviewee to provide specific information which may have been explicated in the preceding linguistic context or which may have been presupposed. In that setting, s/he requests the interviewee to spell out specific information in order to comment on it, elaborate on it and continue with a topical sequence of which the information is a constitutive part. The unknown information requested in (2) does not need to be spelled out as the addressee is requested to name one of the two alternatives, viz. the farmer or the consumer, which is to be assigned the status of new information in order to be commented on.

In that particular context questions can also be employed to request the addressee to carry out a specific communicative action, for example the ratification of an other-reformulation by agreeing or disagreeing with it, as is the case in (3):

(3)   Is this a commitment then?

Unlike the fairly clear-cut examples discussed above, in which the interviewee is requested to provide very specific information, the interviewer's employment of a question in the following example,

(4) Can you actually think of other alternatives?

does not generally have the communicative function of eliciting unknown information about the interviewee's ability to think of other alternatives. Instead, s/he is requested to provide one or more solutions to a specific problem. For these reasons, the employment of questions in a political-interview setting requires further specifications: not only does the employment of a question assign the interviewer the right to elicit unknown information, but it also puts constraints on the interviewee's answer which, in order to be appropriate, should consist of elaborate comments on some state of affair. Furthermore, by employing a question, the interviewer may not only initiate specific discourse topics and elaborate on them, but s/he may also close them. Thus, the linguistic structure of question can be used to perform a number of different speech acts in a political interview.

Pragmatic approaches to political interviews pay close attention to the meaning communicated beyond the literal level of what has been said (Jucker 1986; Lauerbach 2006). On the one hand, they analyze the dichotomy between *what is said* and *what is meant* firmly set in the research paradigm of speech act theory and its differentiation between direct and indirect speech acts (Austin 1976; Searle 1969), and adapt them to the contextual constraints and requirements of political discourse, for instance to the communicative strategy of hedging or to the construction of social reality (Searle 1995). On the other hand, they examine the strategic use of language, for example pronouns and metaphors (Bull and Fetzer 2006; Wilson 1990).

1.4   Social psychology and political interviews

The social-psychology paradigm (Bull 2003; see also Moir, this volume) is based on the detailed analysis of interpersonal communication, both verbal and non-verbal. Social psychological research on political interviews has been influenced by a number of theories, none of which were in the first instance devised for the analysis of political discourse (Bull and Feldman, in press). Specifically, these are: the social skills model of interaction (Argyle and Kendon 1967); equivocation theory (Bavelas, Black, Chovil and Mullett 1990; Bull 2008); and theories of face and facework (Brown and Levinson 1978, 1987; Goffman 1955).

According to the social skills model (Argyle and Kendon 1967), social behavior can be understood as a form of skill, involving processes comparable to those involved in motor skills, such as driving a car or playing a game of tennis. More recently, Argyle and Kendon's model has been significantly revised and updated by Hargie (e.g., Hargie and Marshall 1986; Hargie 1997, 2006a, 2006b). Although neither version of the model was intended to encompass political behavior, Bull (2011) has argued that it has significant implications for our understanding of what makes a successful politician. From this perspective, how politicians handle political interviews can be seen as a form of communicative skill. For example, Bull (2003) identified 35 different ways of equivocating in response to questions in political interviews. These can be seen as varying in their degree of communicative skill, ranging from the highly adroit to the completely inept (Bull 2010).

Equivocation, according to a theory proposed by Bavelas et al. (1990), characteristically occurs when people are posed questions to which all of the possible replies have potentially negative consequences, but where nevertheless a reply is still expected. Such questions create what is termed a *communicative conflict*, which is particularly prevalent in the context of political interviews. Although politicians are often castigated as slippery, evasive or downright deceitful, their evasive responses in interviews from this perspective may be regarded as more understandable reactions to situational factors, which create strong pressures towards equivocal communication.

In the context of political interviews, Bull et al. (1996; see also Bull 2008) have re-conceptualized equivocation theory in terms of *threats to face*. That is to say, politicians equivocate in order to avoid responses which will affect either positive or negative face (Brown and Levinson 1978, 1987), i.e. responses which may make them look bad or constrain their future freedom of action. Theories of face and facework have had a major influence on social psychological research on political interviews. For example, Bull (2008) proposed that whether or not a politician answers a question can be understood in terms of its *face-threatening structure*. Whereas equivocation typically occurs in response to questions which create communicative conflicts, in other circumstances answering the question may be the least face-threatening option. Thus, a major theoretical merit of this face analysis is parsimony: whether a politician equivocates or answers can arguably be understood within the same underlying theoretical conceptualization (Bull 2008).

1.5   Sociopragmatics and political interviews

A sociopragmatic perspective goes beyond the analysis of the rule-governed and strategic use of language. It also considers social and sociocultural aspects of communication in an explicit manner, assigning them the status of a constitutive part of communicative action, thus interfacing with the research paradigms of anthropological linguistics, interactional sociolinguistics, (critical) discourse analysis, and ethnomethodological conversation analysis. Sociopragmatics examines social parameters which affect the production and interpretation of utterances, placing language use in an external relation to language users. It is based on the premise that language use and social structure are connected dialectically, (re)constructing social and sociocultural context by confirming (or disconfirming) social values in interaction, for instance gender, power and social status. Consequently, the language user and her/his social roles and identities are at the heart of societal pragmatics, analyzing social and sociocultural context on the micro level of face-to-face interaction as well as on the macro level of institution.

The social perspective to pragmatics has shifted the focus of investigating context-dependent meaning from semantics-based methodologies to social context-based approaches and their premise of negotiated communicative meaning and sociocultural appropriateness, thus adding a further layer of meaning: social and sociocultural meaning. In this perspective, meaning is not given per se and carried as such into the utterance, metaphorically speaking. Language is assigned the status of a sociocultural construct which is used strategically by rational language users in context, considering possible perlocutionary effects their utterances may trigger as regards negative and positive politeness (Brown and Levinson 1987), for instance.

In a political interview, participants perform communicative acts in an intentional and strategic manner by intending their communicative act to count as a communicative act with a particular force. They perform different kinds of speech acts, such as requesting information, stating opinions or providing information. It is generally assumed that the interviewer requests the interviewee to provide specific information for the interviewer. But is that really the case? Does a political interview consist of an interviewer and interviewee exchanging speech acts? If a political interview is investigated with regard to language production and language comprehension, then it does consist of an interviewer, who produces speech acts, and an interviewee, who interprets speech acts. However, there is more to the interactional organization of a political interview than the constitutive parts of interviewer, interviewee and speech acts. Firstly, the ratified participants of a political interview do not only consist of the actual language producers of interviewer and interviewee, but also of the audience, in front of whom and for whom the political interview is performed. Secondly, an investigation of natural-language communication has to adopt micro (or bottom-up) and macro (or top-down) perspectives. This means that the individual speech acts should not be investigated in isolation but rather as constitutive parts of the whole interview.

In a sociopragmatic approach, genre is seen as an interactionally organized event, in and through which participants negotiate the communicative status of their contributions. Communicative meaning is not given per se, but rather seen as jointly constructed. Thus, the negotiation of intersubjective meaning is anchored to a micro level. The micro level is framed by macro frames, for instance by a communicative genre (Luckmann 1995), a communicative project (Linell 1998) or an activity type (Levinson 1979). The macro frame in turn is also framed by higher-order frames of references, such as institution or culture (Sarangi and Slembrouck 1996). The interdependence of a conversational contribution on both micro- and macro domains is a fundamental premise in natural-language communication. Since media communication is seen as a particular subset of natural-language communication, the former also feeds on these micro and macro domains. However, the interactive processes and products of a direct face-to-face interaction are also exploited in media communication, as conversational contributions are not solely produced for the direct (or first-frame) participants, but also, if not primarily, for the indirect (or second-frame) co-participants (Fetzer 2000). This has been shown by Clayman and Heritage (2002) for news interviews, where "adherence to news interview turn-taking procedures embodies a special 'footing' (Goffman 1981; Levinson 1988) in which the parties treat their talk as geared to the 'overhearing' news audience" (Clayman and Heritage 2002, 120).

In ordinary face-to-face communication, back channels, such as acknowledgements or the non-verbal cues of nodding and gaze, are assigned the function of signaling active listenership. Since those verbal and non-verbal cues are ambiguous in nature, they may be interpreted as signs of agreement or disagreement. This is also claimed by Clayman and Heritage (2002), to use their own words: "interviewers' withholdings of acknowledgments establish the news audience as an intended recipient of interviewee talk. However, these withholdings are important in an additional and significant way. Plainly, some acknowledgements verge on agreement with the interviewee's position or imply acceptance of its truth" (Clayman and Heritage 2002, 124). The inherent ambiguity of acknowledgements and other types of back channels is generally resolved in the process of negotiating intersubjective meaning in a direct face-to-face interaction by taking into consideration the communicative meaning of other contextual cues. In a political interview, however, meaning is negotiated in front of an audience who can closely monitor, if not scrutinize, the first-frame co-participants and their interaction in media communication. For this reason, the second-frame audience has access to information which the first-frame co-participants do not have as they can monitor only each other. They can neither monitor the second-frame audience and their comments, nor the set of the first-frame co-participants, of which they are a constitutive part. So, first-frame co-participants can repair possible misunderstandings with their direct communication partners without significant delay, should the communicative need arise, but they cannot repair possible misunderstandings with the second-frame audience in that manner.

In the framework of sociopragmatics, political interviews have been analyzed with respect to the interviewer and interviewee's clear-cut division of labor (Blum-Kulka 1983), which is deduced from the genre's constitutive speech acts, their felicity conditions, the participants' roles and their complementary rights and obligations. Here, the interactional role of interviewer is anchored to the speech act of question which assigns her/him the right to request the interviewee to provide answers to her/his questions. The interactional role of interviewee, by contrast, is anchored to the speech act of answer which assigns her/him the obligation to a dovetailed response containing the requested information. Furthermore, the interviewer has the right to ask follow-up questions if the interviewee does not answer a question to the interviewer's satisfaction. In a similar vein, political interviews are conceptualized as a negotiation of validity claims in mediatized contexts (Fetzer 2000), as a negotiation of roles and identities, and as a negotiation of individual intentions and collective purposes (Weizman 1998, 2006).

1.6   Compositional methodology and political interviews

Political interviews have been examined in a number of different frameworks, which have all been very important to capture the inherent complexity of the genre. Ethnomethodological conversation analysis is indispensable for the analysis of the genre, as it provides methodological tools for the analysis the genre's constitutive question-and-answer sequences based on the adjacency pair of question and answer, and possible refinements as regards preference organization. Furthermore, it gives us the tools to connect micro action with meso and macro action, looking at genre as a dynamic interactionally organized event. That particular outlook on political interviews has been adapted by the sociopragmatic perspective on political interviews.

Critical discourse analysis has offered a poststructuralist and postmodern perspective, pointing out that political discourse does not exist in isolation but rather is interconnected with other discourses which are embedded, imported or exported. Moreover, it has opened a window to look at discourse beyond language and language use, pointing out non-verbal communication as well as multimodality as indispensable tools for an appropriate analysis of discourse in society.

Social psychology has provided detailed research on political interview discourse, particularly with regard to the study of equivocation. It has been shown how several theories not developed in the first instance for the analysis of political discourse (notably, the social skills model, equivocation theory, and theories of face and facework) have been applied to the analysis of political interviews, thereby provided important insights into underlying social psychological processes.

Pragmatics has provided us with a perspective on language use as communicative action as well as with an important differentiation between what is said and what is meant, and between direct and indirect speech acts, and sociopragmatics has adapted important insights from ethnomethodological conversation analysis, critical discourse analysis, pragmatics and social psychology. It may, in fact, be described as a theoretical framework most visibly based on methodological compositionality, an approach to be followed in Sections 2–4 below.

The following section, *Political interviews: the default scenario*, analyses a political interview in its default (or prototypical) form. It shows that a default political interview generally constrains the co-participants to one-dimensional figures employing one-dimensional styles to discuss one-dimensional topics. The third section, *Political interviews: a multilayered genre*, extends the frame of investigation by examining the multilayeredness of the genre, illustrating the multi-voiced encounter with its multiple discursive identities, styles and topics. The fourth section, *Political interviews: a hybrid genre*, investigates the fuzziness of the genre, focusing on frame-breaks anchored to the private-public interface. A conclusion summarizes the results obtained.

2. Political interviews: The default scenario

In the age of mediatized mass democracies, political discourse in the media is an important means for ordinary people to encounter politics (Lauerbach and Fetzer 2007). This is particularly true of political debates (see, e.g., Boyd, this volume) and interviews, in which political information is transmitted in dialogue-anchored forms. Political interviews provide the opportunity, first, to translate politics, which has been frequently conceptualized as a macro structural phenomenon, into *text and talk* (Chilton and Schäffner 2002); second, to transfer macro-domain oriented politics to the micro domain; and third, to personify party-political programs, agendas and ideologies. Furthermore, the dialogic nature of the genre allows for the presentation of symbolic politics (Sarcinelli 1987) as a language game composed of questions and answers, in which the politician and journalist's argumentation and their underlying reasoning and negotiation of meaning are made explicit. This sort of contextualization facilitates and supports the comprehension of macro politics, making it more accessible to the general public.

Political parties tend to focus on the production of politics, which takes place behind the scenes, while politicians tend to focus on its presentation, which takes place in the public stage. On that stage, public agents co-construct, negotiate and contextualize politics, and it is the job of the politician to use all possible opportunities inherent in the contextual constraints and requirements of mass media to present her/his political agenda in a credible and responsible manner to a heterogeneous audience, whose members are potential voters.

The relationship between politics and the media is not an easy one (cf. Section 3 of this volume's Introduction; see also Okulska and Cap [2010], esp. Chapter 20). On the one hand, it is a happy symbiosis (Boorstin 1987), in which information on the part of the politician is exchanged for publicity on the part of the media. On the other hand, mass media is not only a neutral mediator of information but also a critical monitor of politics exercising control, while at the same time being under the commercial pressure in competition for audiences (Blumler and Gurevitch 1995; Negrine 1996). To account for these diverging needs, dialogic genres have become more and more popular for the producers of media communication, for the more and less active users of mass media, and for ordinary recipients.

Interviews in general and political interviews in particular are a prevalent discourse genre, which provides its agents with the opportunity to perform political actions in the public, mediatized arena. Politicians can go on air and make their party-political programs and agendas public. Journalists can go on air and demonstrate their professional skills by asking precise questions and critical follow-up questions. Within the discourse genre, the constitutive agents can perform a number of different, if not diverging roles: they can be politicians and journalists, members of parliament and members affiliated to particular media institutions, members or shadow members of government; they can be persuasive rhetoricians, eloquent media figures, caring family persons or simply good-looking and entertaining people. Against this background, political discourse is turning more and more into professional discourse.

Summarizing the results obtained from the examination of political interviews, a default political interview is defined by (1) clear-cut tasks and purposes, that is asking questions and giving answers, and eliciting information and providing the requested information, (2) clear-cut discourse roles, that is a journalist as interviewer and a politician as interviewee, and (3) a clear-cut use of language, that is non-emotional, neutral language. It is these factors which contribute to the presentation of political agents as one-dimensional figures.

3.   Political interviews: A multi-layered genre

To account for more recent changes in the discourse genre and media event of a political interview, a dynamic framework is introduced, which accommodates a top-down perspective accounting for the genre as a whole, and a bottom-up perspective accounting for the constitutive parts of the genre. Regarding the former, it considers relevant contextual constraints and requirements of sociocultural context anchored to discourse identity, discursive style, medialization and turn taking. Regarding the latter, it considers local-level language use as is reflected in turn-constructional units, communicative strategies and other semiotic practices. Moreover, it accommodates the connectedness between the genre's constitutive parts and the genre as a whole as well as the relevant transitions between the constitutive sections, feeding on the synergetic relation between conversation analysis and sociopragmatics. This does not only allow for the explicit accommodation between directly and indirectly communicated meaning, and conversationally implicated and inferred meaning, but also for the fundamental discursive premise of sequentiality and its local configuration as pre- and post-sequence, and its more global configuration as opening, topical and closing sections. But what consequences does such a dynamic outlook on communication entail? To find an appropriate answer to the question, the concept of communicative genre as defined by Luckmann (1995) and the concept of activity type as defined by Levinson (1979) are adapted to the contextual constraints and requirements of a political interview.

3.1   Political interview as communicative genre

In his sociology-anchored outlook on communication, Luckmann (1995) assigns communicative genre the status of a universal and locates it between micro-anchored communicative acts and macro-anchored institutional context, making explicit its intersubjective function as follows:

> Communicative genres operate on a level *between* the socially constructed and transmitted codes of 'natural' languages and the reciprocal adjustment of perspectives, which is a presupposition for human communicative interaction. They are a universal formative element of human communication. (…)
> Human communicative acts are *predefined* and thereby to a certain extent *predetermined* by an existing social code of communication. This holds for both the 'inner' core of that code, the phonological, morphological, semantic and syntactic structure of the language, as well as for its 'external' stratification in styles, registers, sociolects and dialects. In addition, communicative acts are predefined

and predetermined by explicit and implicit rules and regulations of the *use* of
language, e.g. by forms of communicative etiquette.   (Luckmann 1995, 177)

Adapting these constraints to a default interview, the clear-cut division of labor
between interviewer and interviewee can be upheld: the former seeks information and opinions by asking questions, and the latter provides information and
opinions by giving answers. However, the definition requires some refinement
with respect to discourse topic and media. First, interviewers and interviewees do
not generally seek and provide any type of information but information from the
public domains of life, in particular from the domains of politics and governmental affairs. There might also be the occasional request and provision of private-
domain based information, but this is generally accounted for by referring to the
political relevance of the issue in question. Second, the "inner" core and external
stratification constraints regulate the discursive style of a political interview and
restrict it to a non-emotional, neutral use of language. Third, due to its status as
mediated genre, the clear-cut division of labor needs to be extended to cover another constitutive participant: the audience (Fetzer 2006). For the communicative
genre-as-a-whole to be felicitous, the second-frame audience, that is the audience
watching the interview on TV (Fetzer 2000) or in some on-line forum, needs to
ratify the interviewer and interviewee's communicative acts. While the interviewer and interviewee's discursive styles need to be in accordance with the constraint
of neutralism, there is no such constraint for the second-frame audience. Should
there be active, face-to-face audience participation, as is the case with the more
recently introduced panel interview (Bull and Fetzer 2006), the first-frame audience also needs to act in accordance with the constraint of neutralism.

3.2   Political interview as activity type

Levinson's conception of activity type does not only accommodate sociology-
anchored premises but also a cognitive outlook on language use and communication. He defines activity type as "a fuzzy category whose focal members are
goal-defined, socially constituted, bounded events with *constraints* on participants, setting and so on, but above all on the allowable contributions" (Levinson
1979, 368).

The constraints have already been named in the analysis of Luckmann's concept of communicative genre. What is of relevance for this multi-layered examination is the definition of an activity type as a "fuzzy category". This does not only
explain the more recent changes in the dyadic political interview to the multi-
party configuration of a panel interview, in which members of the audience take

over the interviewer's role, but also the increase in the number of questions targeting the interviewee's private domains. Generally, this goes hand in hand with changes in the discursive style.

Closely connected with the cognitive concept of *fuzzy category* are *inferential schemata*, to use Levinson's (1979) own words:

> ... there is another important and related fact, in many ways the mirror image of the constraints on contributions, namely the fact that for each and every clearly demarcated activity there is a set of *inferential schemata*. These schemata are tied to (derived from, if one likes) the structural properties of the activity in question.
> (Levinson 1979, 370)

It is those inferential schemata, which provide a reasoning mechanism that enables us to interpret deviations from the default as a speaker-intended transmission of particularized communicative meaning (Fetzer 2000).

4.   Political interviews: A hybrid genre

More recent approaches to the analysis of political interviews have noted ongoing changes in the genre, such as changes in the participation framework reflected in active audience participation in panel interviews (Fetzer and Bull 2008), staged antagonism (Lauerbach and Fetzer 2007; Schegloff 1989), if not adversarialism (Lloyd 2004), increasing degrees of hybridization (Lauerbach 2004), conversationalization or medialization (Fetzer and Weizman 2006).

The multilayeredness of the genre is intrinsically connected with its degree of fuzziness and its degree of hybridity, which make its unbounded nature surface. That is to say, the political interview does not exist as such. Rather, it only comes into existence through the constitutive agents acting in accordance with the genre's constraints and requirements thereby turning an unpredictable communicative event into a predictable political interview. Against this background, a political interview can no longer be conceived of as a non-fuzzy, predictable event, as has been implicit in the earlier conceptions of a political interview as a relatively stable communicative encounter based on a clear-cut division of labor (Blum-Kulka 1983), or as an exchange of questions and answers anchored to the *leitmotif* of neutralism as is reflected in interactional and discursive roles, and style (Greatbatch 1988). By acting in dis-accordance with the constraints, for instance by interviewer and interviewees presenting themselves as multiply voiced, agents transcend boundaries and go beyond the constraints and requirements of non-fuzziness, linearity and predictability.

4.1   Critical incidents

Not acting in accordance with a discourse genre's constitutive constraints is also referred to as critical incident or frame break, the consequences of which are spelled out by Goffman as follows: "With frame breaks, then, there is typically a face-to-face phenomenon to look at – the context for negative experience" (Goffman 1986, 379), and "negative experience" is "negative in the sense that it takes its character from what it is not, and what it is not is an organized and organizationally affirmed response" (Goffman 1986, 379).

Critical incidents are reflected in disturbances caused by the constitutive agents' not acting in accordance with the constraints and requirements of the default genre. In a political interview, they can occur when unspoken constraints are made explicit, such as the rights of an interviewer[3] to introduce a discourse topic as in (5):

> (5)   IR   *no I have the right to say this is an interview and I'm sure you will recognise it because you understand the nature of political interviews Mr Heseltine as well as I do*

Critical incidents are also reflected in longer sequences of simultaneous talk, in which the agents fight for the floor, as in (6), and in making explicit the fact that the agenda of the interview has been agreed upon before the actual interview takes place as in (7):

> (6)   IE   well I understand the nature of the agreement
> IR   *[I have to I have to]*
> IE   *[that I entered into]* your programme
> IR   *[I do have I do have the right]*
> IE   *[that you seem to be breaking]*

> (7)   IE   *I've agreed to come on this programme not to discuss these issues, to discuss important factors about ideas, about the direction of policies, about where we should go in the nineteen nineties. That's what I agreed to do (…) Now can we just understand clearly the basis on which I came on this programme that we were going to talk about issues.* I will talk about issues because …

Critical incidents are further reflected in deviations from the interview's clear-cut division of labor anchored to the turn-takings system, that is interviewees employing the question format. Here, the clear-cut question-answer sequence is disturbed with local question-question sequences. Furthermore, there are deviations in the use of a non-emotional, neutral discursive style, as is the case with excerpt (8), in which the then Prime Minister John Major is referred to as "the boy who came from Brixton", and in which Tony Blair (IE) refers to his father as "dada":

(8) IR well John Major is presenting himself as *the boy who came from Brixton and … and* by contrast we all know erm your background and your appeal to middle England. Do you still consider yourself a socialist

IE I do in the sense of the values. I don't share the idea that socialism's about some fixed economic prescription. *And you know Jeremy my father came from a very poor background indeed.* He was brought up in in Govan, *his father erm his adopted father* was a rigger … but in fact *my dada* always used to see to me …

Other deviations from default discursive style are laughter, instances of affective language (e.g. waste time, hang on), non-neutral terms of address (e.g. terms of endearment), metapragmatic devices (e.g., you can correct me if I'm wrong, let me put this to you) and metadiscursive devices (e.g. this implies, what you are saying is). These devices signal a possible non-default scenario.

Frame breaks also occur with discourse-topic anchored references to the private-public interface, as is examined in the following.

4.2   Local non-defaults

The multilayeredness of a political interview surfaces in local non-default configurations, in which the participants act in dis-accordance with the genre's constraints and requirements, as is exemplified with the following two excerpts from an interview between the former British Prime Minister Tony Blair (IE) and the renowned journalist Jeremy Paxman (IR) (2003):

(9) IR_1 I want to explore a little further about *your personal feelings* about this war. Does the fact that George Bush and you are both *Christians* make it easier for you to view these conflicts in terms of good and evil?

IE_1 I don't think so no, I think that whether you're a Christian or not a Christian you can try and perceive what is good and what is is is evil.

IR_2 *you don't pray together* for example?

IE_2 *no we don't pray together Jeremy, no.*

IR_3 why do you *smile*?

IE_3 because erm erm erm erm *why do you ask me the question?*

IR_4 *because I'm trying to find out how you feel about it*

In (9) the interviewer refers to the private-public interface in an explicit manner thereby assigning it the status of a relevant discourse topic. He connects subjective-domain anchored feelings with the field of religion, which becomes particularly salient as the Prime Minister was criticized severely for his close ties with the American President George W. Bush. In its linguistic context, the private-public interface, politics and religion are connected in an explicit manner in the interviewer's turn IR_1. However, this local non-default is not restricted to one turn but elaborated on with respect to the act of praying in IR_2. The interviewee complies with the interviewer's request and answers the direct yes/no question of IR_2 with a straightforward negation in IE_2, addressing the interviewer with his first name "Jeremy". The interviewer aligns with that mode of communication and responds with a question targeting the interviewee's facial expression, his smile. This deviation from the default interview regarding topic and style results in a further deviation with the interviewee answering the interviewer's question by asking a question himself. What is relevant to our analysis is the linguistic realization of the non-default question. The interviewee starts his turn with a partial answer introduced by discourse marker "because" and then employs a number of hesitation devices before formulating the question. In IR_4, the interviewer aligns with the interviewee by formulating his turn with another token of the same discourse marker, but unlike the interviewee, provides the requested answer.

In (10), it is not the interviewer, or rather the audience member (AM), who refers to the private-public interface, but the interviewee himself. In his elaborate answer to the question why he is prepared to go to war without the support of the majority of people, he refers to his "honest belief", his "job as Prime Minister" and his "duty". These subjective-domain anchored references co-occur with the marker of common ground *you know* and with the explication of his personal reasoning process spelling out the pros and cons of going to war:

(10) AM But if that happened would you be prepared to go to war despite the fact that apparently the majority of people in this country would not be with you

      IE ... but erm erm *look* I understand that, *I mean*, I, it is not an easy task. Because I think the very first point that that Jeremy was making to me, is is the point that is most difficult for people, what is, *you know*, why now are we suddenly doing this and my answer to that is actually this does have a long history to it... *But it's my honest belief* that they do come together and *I think it's my job as Prime Minister even if frankly I might be more popular if I didn't say this to you, or said I'm well I'm having nothing to do with George Bush, I think it's my duty to tell it to you if I really believe it*, and *I do really believe it, I may be wrong in believing it, but I do believe it.*

While the interviewer's (AM) reference to the politician's private domain is explicitly accounted for when made an object of talk thereby assigning it discursive relevance, the politician uses private-domain references without accounting for their non-default status. Rather, he employs them strategically to reconstruct his discourse identity as a credible and responsible politician and Prime Minister, which has been challenged by the audience member's question.

Both Luckmann's concept of communicative genre and Levinson's notion of activity type are of importance for an analysis of political interviews in the media as they allow us to differentiate between default and non-default configurations. In non-default political interviews, the multilayered nature of the genre emerges in deviations from the discourse identities' clear-cut rights and obligations manifest in the genre's constitutive question-and-answer sequences, from the clear-cut public and political domains of reference and from the clear-cut neutral discursive style. Here, hybridity emerges locally and the clear-cut distinction between the private and the public becomes blurred. As a consequence of that, political interviews do not simply communicate "political reality" but rather *mediated political reality* (Fetzer and Johansson 2007).

4.3   Acts of confiding

In polyphony-anchored discourse analysis, political discourse comprises different types of talk, such as declaration, controversy and revelation (Charaudeau and Ghiglione 1997). While declaration and controversy are public modes of interaction, revelation, or confiding, as it is referred to in this contribution, is anchored to the private-public interface.

The act of confiding is examined in those contexts, where the politician is the confider of privileged information and where the interviewer and audience are the confidees. In ordinary discourse, the act of confiding has a decisive impact on the interpersonal relationship between the interactants by first, assigning the addressee the status of a privileged communication partner, and second, recontextualizing the relationship as a privileged one characterized by trust. The questions are then why politicians go on record with confidential information, and whether that disclosure would also have an impact on their interpersonal relationship with the audience.

In the following two excerpts, the interviewee provides confidential information[4] in her/his response to an interviewer question:

(11)   IR   Now the second point that I wanted to raise with you, that you made at the very beginning, was this one of the target date, that *you say 2000 is absolutely unrealistic. The EEC believes it's entirely realistic* and it's urging us to do it and is rather cross that we're not going for that date.

> IE *You see that is wrong Jonathan.* And *I* have to *tell you* that *I mean* I attended the councillors' and ministers' meeting erm in Luxembourg only two weeks ago, and *it is perfectly clear* <u>there are at least 3 maybe 4 erm countries within the EEC who are not in a position erm to stabilize by the year 2005</u>.

(12) IR Precisely which has therefore an impact on how the money can be spent and where it goes. *Now let me* take you a little bit to the future to the next spending round. *I don't expect you erm to tell me* how much you're going to go in there and ask your good friend Norman Lamont erm to have. I can imagine that you will be pressing for more money though

>   IE Well certainly we we've kept spending ahead of inflation every year since we've been in and <u>I have no intention of erm slowing down at the expense to the service at the present stage</u>.

In both excerpts, the interviewer's question is loaded with negatives, for instance *I don't expect you erm to tell me*, and semantic opposites, for example *absolutely unrealistic* and *entirely realistic*. The semantic opposition is not only reflected in language use but also in the sources, to which the non-compatible information is attributed. In (11), it is attributed to the conflicting parties "EEC" and the British minister, and in (12) to the minister of health and the minister of finance. Furthermore, there are explicit references to the appropriateness and truth of the utterances, namely "you see that is wrong Jonathan" with which the interviewee refutes the interviewer's claim that Britain is the only member who is "not going for that date".

In mediated political discourse, propositions are not generally refuted without providing the "true story", which is signaled by the metapragmatic markers *I have to tell you* and *I mean*. They introduce the "true information" that only the interviewee himself/herself has had access to the truth as it was her/him who attended the "councillors' and ministers' meeting" recently ("two weeks ago"), and for this reason is the only person in the studio who can give evidence that "there are at least 3 maybe 4 erm countries within the EEC who are not in a position erm to stabilize by the year 2005". By providing the confidential information, the politician re-constructs her/his credibility as a trustworthy politician which has been at stake in the interviewer's claim that Britain is failing European agreements (Fetzer 2002). Additionally, s/he presents her/himself as a responsible politician who goes on record with some selected information while at the same time keeping the utterance diplomatically unclear by not naming the other non-committing countries.

In (12) the interviewer employs the strategic move of stating explicitly that he does not "expect" the interviewee to "tell" her/him "how much" she/he is "going to go in there and ask" her/his "good friend Norman Lamont erm to have". The move is introduced by a reference to the appropriateness conditions, namely "now let me take you a little bit to the future to the next spending round". The interviewee cannot but comply with the requested information as the interviewer makes explicit, that she/he is fully aware of the fact that she/he requests confidential information that would only be discussed between good friends and colleagues, and therefore would be satisfied with a vague answer. The interviewee complies with the request and makes explicit her/his intention to "have no intention of erm slowing down at the expense to the service at the present stage". Analogously to the strategic move of making explicit private-domain anchored information, the interviewee employs the move to re-construct her/his credibility as a responsible minister of health: she/he makes explicit her/his intention which counts as a promise to accommodate her/his clients' needs while at the same time deconstructing the image of a non-cooperative, evasive politician.

Hybridity does not only manifest itself in the agents' multi-voiced performances presenting themselves as both political public figures and as private-domain anchored human beings, but also in the mediated genre's intertextual references. Within the genre of an interview, agents employ other genres, for instance small stories.

4.4   Small stories

Small stories are a constitutive part of a larger discourse. They occur as embedded sequences, and their interpersonal function is to express intimacy and solidarity (Coates 2003; Georgakopoulou 1997; Labov 1972). Regarding their communicative function, they convey contextualized arguments and advice. Like the act of confiding, they are anchored to the private-public interface, providing personal episodes of recent events, which need to be assigned public and political relevance in political discourse. Small stories are classified with respect to their reference to the past or future: the former recontextualize prior discourse, and the latter provide a context for what is to follow. So, do small stories also contribute to the reconstruction of credibility and responsibility in political interviews?

In the story under examination, the politician as the teller is also the protagonist, and analogously to the act of confiding, there is a tension between public-domain anchored speaking and private-domain anchored information. While the information given in the act of confiding is of immediate relevance to the politician's argumentation at a particular stage in an interview, the small story is of less immediate relevance to the argumentation, but rather fulfils a less straight forward function, as is the case with the following excerpt:

(13) IE *Let me just give you an example* I was down in Somerset the other day
      and *a woman who actually isn't a Liberal Democrat voter* came to me and
      said <u>they're sacking another teacher from my school what are you going</u>
      <u>to do about it? The answer from Labour is nothing. If you ask them what</u>
      <u>they're going to do about it</u> *say bye bye …*

In (13) the small story referred to as "an example" is told by Paddy Ashdown (IE)
who is also one of the protagonists. However, he is not the dominant and active
protagonist. In that scenario, this is a woman who is presented as "not a Liberal
Democrat voter". Rather, he portrays himself as a protagonist who listens to the
needs of others, who cares about them, who is open to advice, and, above all, is
not estranged from ordinary people. Thus, the small story is not of immediate
relevance to the politician's argumentation, but rather serves the interpersonal
function signifying solidarity. This is reflected in the use of the personal pronouns
I and *you* whose domain of reference is not clear-cut (Bull and Fetzer 2006).

Small stories provide political agents with the opportunity of presenting
themselves as private agents who are simple ordinary people. The stories are used
strategically to express alignment with the audience to reconstruct credibility and
responsibility.

5. Conclusions

This chapter has investigated the discourse genre of political interviews in the research paradigms of conversation analysis, critical discourse analysis, pragmatics,
social psychology, and sociopragmatics. While conversation analysis, critical discourse analysis, pragmatics and social psychology tend to analyze political interviews in a more constrained frame of reference, focusing on the research questions
of context-dependent turn-taking and interactional roles, on the representation
of social agents and ideology, on directness and indirectness, and on face-threats
and equivocation, sociopragmatics offers a more integrated frame of reference
anchored to social, cognitive, and linguistic contexts. It subsumes a number of
levels, such as the turn-taking mechanism, direct and indirectly realized communicative action, face-threatening acts, discursive roles and identity, etc.

Political interviews in the media have been examined as regards their interactional organization as a discourse genre and media event focusing on their
configuration as a default political interview with public media figures, public discourse topics, a non-emotional neutral discursive style and a clear-cut division of
labor anchored to the turn-taking system, the genre's constitutive speech acts, discourse identities and discursive style. There is a journalist as interviewer, who asks

political questions, and a politician as interviewee, who answers political questions by giving political answers.

The one-dimensional setting of default interview becomes blurred in a non-default interview, in which the mediated status of the genre becomes apparent in local deviations regarding discourse identity, topic and style. This is reflected in the employment of different semiotic codes and sociocultural practices, for instance naming and the use of informal and emotional language, in the discourse identities' attribution to both public and private domains of society, for instance portraying a politician as a member of government and as a family person, as well as in the explicit accommodation of the audience's needs. We find this in the more recent configuration of a political interview as a panel interview or in explicit references to the constitutive discourse identity of audience. In those contexts, the hybridity of the genre surfaces and the default one-dimensional setting is transformed into a multi-dimensional setting.

References to the private-public interface are not only found in the explicit accommodation of the audience. They are also used strategically: the interviewer generally employs references to the private domain to support her/his argumentation in her/his attempt to receive satisfactory, non-evasive answers, while the interviewee uses them to reconstruct her/his identity as a credible and responsible politician.

Acknowledgement

We are deeply grateful to our reviewers and to the editors for helpful comments on the first version of this chapter.

Notes

1. Political interviews may, of course, deviate from the participant-specific employment of the initiating and responsive formats. The deviations from a prototypical political interview are, however, only local phenomena and tend to be resolved in more or less controversial negotiation-of-meaning sequences (Fetzer 2000).

2. All examples are adopted from a corpus of 14 dyadic political interviews recorded between May and July 1990 from the BBC1-programme *On The Record*.

3. To facilitate readability, the transcription mode follows orthographic standards. IR denotes interviewer, IE denotes interviewee, and AM denotes a member of the audience. Utterances delimited by square brackets indicate simultaneous talk.

4. The private-domain anchored information made public is underlined, and linguistic indicators signaling that confidential information is elicited or forthcoming are presented in *italics*.

References

Argyle, Michael and Adam Kendon. 1967. "The Experimental Analysis of Social Performance." *Advances in Experimental Social Psychology* 3: 55–97.

Austin, John L. 1962. *How to do Things with Words*. Cambridge: Cambridge University Press.

Bavelas, Janet Beavin, Alex Black, Nicole Chovil, and Jennifer Mullett. 1990. *Equivocal Communication*. Newbury Park, CA: Sage.

Bell, Allan, and Peter Garrett. (eds). 1998. *Approaches to Media Discourse*. Oxford: Blackwell.

Blumler, Jay, and Michael Gurevitch. 1995. *The Crisis of Public Communication*. London: Routledge.

Blum-Kulka, Shoshana. 1983. "The Dynamics of Political Interviews." *Text* 3: 131–153.

Boorstin, Daniel. 1987. *Das Image – Der Amerikanische Traum*. Reinbek: Rowohlt.

Brown, Penelope, and Stephen C. Levinson. 1978. "Universals in Language Usage: Politeness Phenomena." In *Questions and Politeness*, ed. by Esther Goody, 56–110. Cambridge: Cambridge University Press.

—. 1987. *Politeness: Some Universals in Language Use*. Cambridge: Cambridge University Press.

Bull, Peter. 2003. *The Microanalysis of Political Communication: Claptrap and Ambiguity*. London: Routledge.

—. 2008. "'Slipperiness, Evasion and Ambiguity': Equivocation and Facework in Non-Committal Political Discourse." *Journal of Language and Social Psychology* 27: 324–332.

—. 2010. "Equivocation and Communicative Skill." In *The Interrelationship of Business and Communication*, ed. by Michael B. Hinner, 69–84. Frankfurt am Main: Peter Lang.

—. 2011. "What Makes a Successful Politician? The Social Skills of Politics." In *The Psychology of Politicians*, ed. by Ashley Weinberg, 61–75. Cambridge: Cambridge University Press.

Bull, Peter, Judy Elliott, Derrol Palmer, and Elizabeth Walker. 1996. "Why Politicians are Three-Faced: The Face Model of Political Interviews." *British Journal of Social Psychology* 35: 267–284.

Bull, Peter, and Anita Fetzer. 2006. "Who are *We* and Who are *You*? The Strategic Use of Forms of Address in Political Interviews." *Text & Talk* 26: 1–36.

Bull, Peter, and Ofer Feldman. forth. "Theory and Practice in Political Discourse Research." In *Grounding Social Sciences in Cognitive Sciences*, ed. by Ron Sun. Cambridge, MA: The MIT Press.

Charaudeau, Patrick, and Rodolphe Ghiglione. 1997. *La Parole Confisquée. Un Genre Télévisuel: Le Talk Show*. Paris: Dunod.

Chilton, Paul, and Christina Schäffner. 2002. "Introduction: Themes and Principles in the Analysis of Political Discourse." In *Politics as Text and Talk: Analytical Approaches to Political Discourse*, ed. by Paul Chilton, and Christina Schäffner, 1–41. Amsterdam: John Benjamins.

Clayman, Steven. 1992. "Footing in the Achievement of Neutrality: The Case of News Interview Discourse." In *Talk at Work*, ed. by Paul Drew, and John Heritage, 163–198. Cambridge: Cambridge University Press.

Clayman, Steven, and John Heritage. 2002. *The News Interview*. Cambridge: Cambridge University Press.

Coates, Jennifer. 2003. *Men Talk: Stories in the Making of Masculinity*. Oxford: Blackwell.

Ensink, Titus. 2006. "Pragmatic Aspects of Televised Texts. A Single Case Study of the Intervention of a Televised Documentary Program in Party Politics." *Journal of Pragmatics* 38: 230–249.

Fairclough, Norman. 1995. *Media Discourse*. London: Arnold.

Fetzer, Anita. 2000. "Negotiating Validity Claims in Political Interviews." *Text* 20: 1–46.

—. 2002. "'Put Bluntly, You Have Something of a Credibility Problem': Sincerity and Credibility in Political Interviews." In *Politics as Talk and Text: Analytic Approaches to Political Discourse*, ed. by Paul Chilton, and Christina Schäffner, 173–201. Amsterdam: John Benjamins.

—. 2006. "'Minister, We Will See How the Public Judges You'. Media References in Political Interviews." *Journal of Pragmatics* 38: 180–195.

Fetzer, Anita, and Elda Weizman. 2006. "Political Discourse as Mediated and Public Discourse." *Journal of Pragmatics* 38: 143–153.

Fetzer, Anita, and Marjut Johansson. 2007. "'I'll Tell You What the Truth Is': The Interactional Organization of Confiding in Political Interviews." *Journal of Language and Politics* 6: 147–177.

Fetzer, Anita, and Peter Bull. 2008. "'I Don't Mean You Personally, Forgive Me, I Mean Generally'. The Strategic Use of Pronouns in Political Interviews." *Journal of Language and Politics* 7.

Georgakopoulou, Alexandra. 1997. "Narrative." In *Handbook of Pragmatics*, ed. by Jef Verschueren, Jan-Ola Oestman, Jan Blommaert, and Chris Bulcaen. Amsterdam: John Benjamins.

Goffman, Erving. 1955. "On Face-Work: An Analysis of Ritual Elements in Social Interaction." *Psychiatry* 18: 213–231. Reprinted in Erving Goffman, 1967, *Interaction Ritual: Essays on Face to Face Behavior*, 5–45. Garden City, NY: Anchor.

—. 1986. *Frame Analysis*. New York, NY: Harper & Row.

Greatbatch, David. 1988. "A Turn-Taking System for British News Interviews." *Language in Society* 17: 401–430.

Hargie, Owen. 1997. "Interpersonal Communication: A Theoretical Framework." In *The Handbook of Communication Skills*, ed. by Owen Hargie, 29–63. London: Routledge (2nd edition).

—. 2006a. "Skill in Practice: An Operational Model of Communicative Performance." In *The Handbook of Communication Skills*, ed. by Owen Hargie, 37–70. London: Routledge (3rd edition).

—. 2006b. "Training in Communication Skills: Research, Theory and Practice." In *The Handbook of Communication Skills*, ed. by Owen Hargie, 553–565. London: Routledge (3rd edition).

Hargie, Owen and Peter Marshall. 1986. "Interpersonal Communication: A Theoretical Framework." In *The Handbook of Communication Skills*, ed. by Owen Hargie, 22–56. London: Croom Helm (1st edition).

Heritage, John. 1985. "Analysing News Interviews: Aspects of the Production of Talk for an Overhearing Audience." In *Handbook of Discourse Analysis Vol. III*, ed. by Teun van Dijk, 95–117. London: Academic Press.

Jucker, Andreas. 1986. *News Interviews. A Pragmalinguistic Analysis*. Amsterdam: John Benjamins.

Labov, William. 1972. *Language in the Inner City*. Philadelphia, PA: University of Philadelphia Press.

Lauerbach, Gerda. 2004. "Political Interviews as a Hybrid Genre." *Text* 24: 353–397.

—. 2006. "Discourse Representation in Political Interviews. The Construction of Identities and Relations through Voicing and Ventriloquizing." *Journal of Pragmatics* 38: 196–215.

Lauerbach, Gerda, and Anita Fetzer. 2007. "Introduction." In *Political Discourse in the Media*, ed. by Anita Fetzer, and Gerda Lauerbach, 3–30. Amsterdam: John Benjamins.

Levinson, Stephen C. 1979. "Activity Types and Language." *Linguistics* 17: 365–399.

Lloyd, John. 2004. *What the Media Are Doing to Our Politics*. London: Constable & Robinson.

Luckmann, Thomas. 1995. "Interaction Planning and Intersubjective Adjustment of Perspectives by Communicative Genres." In *Social Intelligence and Interaction*, ed. by Esther Goody, 175–188. Cambridge: Cambridge University Press.

Negrine, Ralph. 1996. *The Communication of Politics*. London: Sage.

Okulska, Urszula, and Piotr Cap. (eds). 2010. *Perspectives in Politics and Discourse*. Amsterdam: John Benjamins.

Sarcinelli, Ulrich. 1987. *Symbolische Politik*. Opladen: Wissenschaftlicher Verlag.

Schegloff, Emmanuel. 1989. "From Interview to Confrontation." *Research on Language and Social Action* 22: 215–240.

Searle, John. 1969. *Speech Acts*. Cambridge: Cambridge University Press.

—. 1995. *The Construction of Social Reality*. New York, NY: The Free Press.

Weizman, Elda. 1998. "Individual Intentions and Collective Purpose: The Case of News Interviews." In *Dialogue Analysis*, ed. by Svetla Cmejrkova et al. (eds), 269–280. Tübingen: Niemeyer.

Weizmann, Elda. 2006. "Roles and Identities in News Interviews: The Israeli Context." *Journal of Pragmatics* 38: 154–179.

Wilson, John. 1990. *Politically Speaking: The Pragmatic Analysis of Political Language*. Oxford: Blackwell.

CHAPTER 3

Policy, policy communication and discursive shifts

Analyzing EU policy discourses on climate change

Michał Krzyżanowski
Örebro University, Sweden

This chapter presents a closely related discursive and generic analysis of Europe-an Union policy on climate change. The analysis focuses on the years 2007–2011 when the EU climate change policy accelerated and underwent several signifi-cant shifts. At the discursive level, the analysis of the said shifts is framed by such concepts as "discursive change" and "discursive shifts" which help looking for both global/transnational frames and local, actor-specific appropriations/re-sponses to social, political and economic transformations. At the level of genre analysis, the chapter scrutinizes the EU climate-change policy dynamics by ex-amining discrepancies within/between the well-established field of "policy" and the relatively new field of "policy communication". As the analysis shows, while appropriating different facets of discursive change in local discursive shifts, the policy itself is dynamic and responsive to developments within both the EU and its more or less distant social, political and economic context. However, at the same time, the policy-communication remains relatively unchanged in its focus throughout the period of investigation thus showing that, whereas the EU policies such as those on climate change do change over time, such a change is often not communicated to the general public despite the actual presence of policy-communication genres which, at least hypothetically, should facilitate such process.

1. Introduction

The aim of this chapter is to present an in-depth analysis of transformation of Eu-ropean Union (EU) discourses on climate change (hereinafter: CC). The chapter presents examination of EU-CC narratives by pointing to their discursive em-bedding/framing and exploring their dynamics throughout the years 2007–2011 when the EU policy on CC clearly started to change its focus. As the chapter shows, the said transformation of the EU-CC policy discourse runs between two poles: from perceiving and constructing CC as a form of more or less global crisis and threat, to showing its mainly economic aspects which, unless tackled, will constitute a major challenge to the future of the (European) economy.

The analysis of the dynamic character of EU-CC discourses is framed theoretically by the elaboration of such notions as "*discursive change*" and "*discursive shift*" which help observing and interpreting how/why and in what way discourses within/across different contexts undergo transformation and change. As is argued in the chapter, a need exists to tackle a substantial discursive change which occurred in EU-CC policy recently (cf. below for details) and which to a large extent constitutes an adjustment of the EU-CC discourse to relevant Europe-specific as well as global politico-economic developments. In order to explore the said adjustment, the chapter relates "*discursive change*" (a term originally introduced by Fairclough 1992) which allows tracing the dynamics of discourse at the macro-level, to micro-level dynamics of discourse defined here as "*discursive shifts*" (cf. below). Whereas the macro designates in this case the larger (perhaps global) frames of contemporary public discourses (security, globalization, etc; cf. below; but also the general trend towards economization of many public discourses), the micro operates at the level of local dynamics of discursive responses to such global changes by different individual and collective actors (in our case, the EU, within its policy and related discourses – cf. Wodak [this volume]).

Coping with a diversity of genres located at different levels of generic hierarchies,[1] and used to both define/regulate and communicate EU policies on CC, the chapter highlights the evolving discrepancies which emerge – at both discursive and generic levels – between two emergent policy-relevant fields of action: on the one hand *the policy* itself and, on the other, *the policy communication*. While both of those fields provide delimitation of what might be seen as two co-existing "hyper-generic structures" (cf. Lauerbach [this volume]), the former encompasses such micro-generic forms – or (sub-)genres – as regulations and projects of regulations governing actions on CC and introducing EU-wide measures. On the other hand, the new field of policy communication comprises (sub-)genres which support "publicization" of CC policy and policy-relevant actions by explaining them to the public. As is argued, the development of the said discrepancy between policy and policy-communication genres also emphasizes a development of a discrepancy between, on the one hand, discursive construction and prescription of action (within policy discourse) and of interpretations of its importance and social, political and economic salience of those actions (within policy-communication discourse). Importantly, in the case of the analyzed CC policy, the said interpretations are provided, contrary to the expectations, not by external observing actors or recipients of policies (e.g. media or the public) but by the EU itself.

The chapter draws on the methodological apparatus of the Discourse-Historical Approach (DHA) in Critical Discourse Studies (for details and the scope of applications, cf. Krzyżanowski 2010; Reisigl and Wodak 2009; Wodak and Krzyżanowski 2008) which allows relating the macro- and mezzo-level of contextualization to micro-level analyses of texts which form discourses in focus of the investigation. Of particular importance here is also the application of the DHA to diachronic analysis of policy (and policy-communication) discourses by pointing to their transformation and change. That analysis follows an established set of studies which apply DHA methods to the analyses of policy discourses and their socio-political ontologies (cf. Krzyżanowski and Wodak 2010, 2011) as well as to the examination of political communication of the EU both within its institutions (cf. Krzyżanowski 2011; Wodak 2009) and in its recent externally-oriented Communication and Multilingualism Policies (cf. Krzyżanowski 2008, 2009a, 2012).

The chapter starts from a description of its theoretical framework which elaborates on the conception of discursive change and introduces the notion of discursive shifts which are, as indicated above, the key concepts of analyzing and interpreting localized, actor-specific responses to discursive change. The latter is also related to the current facets of socio-political transformation which are central to enacting discursive dynamics in both European and global context. On the other hand, different discursive shifts are observed on the example of "traditional" public discourses on CC such as those disseminated by the European media. In the following section, the chapter looks at the broadly-defined context of the study and elaborates on the general developments in European Union politics of recent decades along with the key discourses – of European democracy and European (knowledge-based) economy – which so far have been used to frame EU policy discourses across different fields. In that context, the development of EU climate change policy is described in detail along with the pivotal issue of "competition" between the EU and the USA in taking a leadership role in global politics of CC. The subsequent analytical part of the chapter starts from description of genres and sub-genres traditionally deployed in the European Union politics in general and in the EU-policy making in particular. It also includes a detailed description of the empirical material analyzed later on in the critical discourse analysis of EU-CC policy and policy-communication. That analysis examines sample policy and policy communication genres from 2007 and 2011 i.e. the so far turning moments of EU climate change policy.

2. Discursive change and discursive shifts

Since one of the central aims of this chapter is to scrutinize discursive dynamics in a selected politico-institutional context (of the EU), the theoretical framework of the article must allow relating socio-political dynamics – of the widely-understood context/s – to the transformation and change of discourses which are dialectically linked to the different facets of social (as well as political, economic and other) change. The core of the model proposed here differentiates between two central notions i.e. *"discursive change"* and *"discursive shifts"*. The former and the latter are seen as inherently interdependent with discursive change encompassing broader changes and dynamics of global nature and discursive shifts covering more or less localized responses to those changes constructed in dynamics of discursive practices of selected individual or collective actors.

Discursive change is conceptualized here in line with Fairclough (1992) who sees it as a form of social changes that

> do not just involve language, but are constituted to a significant extent by changes in language practices; and it is perhaps the one indication of the growing importance of language in social and cultural change that attempts to engineer the direction of change increasingly include attempts to change language practices.
>
> (Fairclough 1992, 6)

In his original set of discursive changes, Fairclough distinguished between such major forms of discursive change as "democratization", "commodification" or "technologization" of discourse. Of those three, surely the central one i.e. commodification needs closer attention here as it is also one of those facets of discursive change which can still – albeit in an altered form – clearly be observed nowadays. As Fairclough argues,

> commodification is a process whereby social domains and institutions, whose concern is not producing commodities in the narrower economic sense of goods for sale, come nevertheless to be organised and conceptualised in terms of commodity production, distribution and consumption.   (Fairclough 1992, 207)

Indeed, as Fairclough continues, key examples of commodification can be found within different social fields where, at least until recently, other values than those driving the field of economy were prevalent. Here, he points to the tendency whereby such previously un-economized sectors as, e.g., the field of public/higher education are "referred to as 'industries' concerned with producing, marketing and selling cultural or educational commodities to their 'clients' or 'consumers'" (1992, 207).

As is argued here, the commodification tendency has indeed been one of the central types of discursive dynamics of recent decades and underlies the development of perhaps even larger trend of the so-called *economization of discourse*. The latter is a way of approaching public and other discourse – and different real-world objects constructed therein – from the point of view of their overall "usability" for the local or global economy. Such is the case especially with regard to the discourses of the so-called Knowledge-Based Economy (or KBE; cf. Jessop 2008a, 2008b; Krzyżanowski and Wodak 2011; Wodak and Fairclough 2010) which has become a very prevalent frame of reference for many public discourses in Europe. To be sure, the EU policy and political discourses have not escaped that frame and have in fact been one of the key driving forces in providing various economization arguments.

The economization of discourse is, however, just one type of discursive change of relevance to the subsequent analysis of EU discourse on climate change, while other major forms of discursive change which are prevalent nowadays can also be traced in EU-CC narratives. Of the further changes, one can surely mention the *securitization of discourse* (in fact a form of an even larger process of *globalization of discourse*) which corresponds with rising global concerns about collective and individual safety and security, and which is a more or less general indication of how societies become increasingly insecure about the relation to their both immediate and distant environments (cf. also Beck 1992, for a relevant conception of *risk society*, or Nohrstedt 2011, for the idea of *threat society*). Indeed, the issue of climate change appears here as one of the central elements of global discursive changes which, heeding the overall securitization of discourses, increasingly conceptualizes climatic changes (especially those of the so-called anthropogenic i.e. human-induced nature) as one of the key threats to humanity now and especially in the future. As is also often the case, it is in this context that CC is often perceived as a form of "crisis" which, unlike in the past (cf. Koselleck 1959, 2006), is nowadays mainly constructed as an ongoing phenomenon that cannot be tackled unless a coordinated global response is in place.

Whereas discursive change encompasses macro-level frames of reference for the production and reception of discourses by specific (individual and collective) social actors, it surely requires a related category which would allow for the actual observing of the change in discourse at the micro-level (rather than in macro-terms). A category which suggests itself here is surely that of *discursive shifts*. The latter should mainly be seen in a relational way which looks at discourses historically or, more specifically, diachronically (cf. Krzyżanowski 2009b, 2010, 2012). It helps grasping systematically the actual multidimensional rather than unidirectional "shifts" in discourses over time.

In line with the Discourse-Historical Approach in CDA (cf. Reisigl and Wodak 2001, 2009; Wodak 2001), discourses are viewed here as "historical", i.e. as closely related to other discourse produced synchronically or diachronically, in the same or different contexts across different periods of time (Wodak 1996). Accordingly, discursive shifts are primarily based on the process of "recontextualization" (Wodak 2000; cf. also Bernstein 1990) of (elements of) different discourses, yet, rarely in a non-linear (1:1) way but in a process which allows for the simultaneous promulgation of different types of practices and entails the creation of new/hybrid discourses. Of course, as such, discursive shifts also necessarily rely on not only transformation but also certain amount of discursive continuity. On the one hand, the overt discursive continuity allows social actors to produce discourses which remain seemingly unchanged while in-fact already effectively recontextualizing elements of other discursive practices across spatial and temporal scales. On the other hand, covert discursive continuity (which can also be seen as overt discontinuity) acts in a way which shows discourse as profoundly changing while in fact retaining many of its former features. Indeed, as will be shown later on, while discursive shifts can surely be identified in some layers of EU-CC discourse, others are much more prone to display features of continuity rather than discontinuity (cf. below).

3.   European public discourses on climate change

Though this chapter tackles the rather underexplored field of EU-CC policy discourse, it must be mentioned that the Union's policy and related discourses on CC do not exist in a vacuum but in fact correspond to other public visions of CC widely disseminated in Europe's national public spheres. Within the latter, especially the media discourses have been widely scrutinized with the corresponding analyses focused predominantly on CC as a form of transnational crisis (cf. Berglez 2008; Berglez and Olausson 2010; cf. also Krzyżanowski 2009b). As the said media discourses constitute a vital frame of reference for the subsequent analyses, they are mentioned here mainly to illustrate the key tendencies while referring to key exemplary studies.

When approaching European media discourse on CC (cf. below for details), one surely needs to point to two sometimes contradictory conceptions which emerge from the media and related discourses. On the one hand, there exists a clear tendency to frame *CC as a general issue of interest and profound importance to the entire societies and all social groups*. Within that trend, CC is described mainly as a threat to the entire humanity which thus must be dealt with by entire societies or the global populace as a whole. On the other hand, the somewhat contradictory approach sees *CC as a problem which cannot be dealt by entire societies but mainly by selected social actors* who, due to their knowledge and expertise, are able to cope with different facets of CC. In this trend, such social actors as science (in general), politicians or institutions (e.g. the UN, the EU) are often referred to as those agents who are primarily responsible for leading the way in "combat" against CC.

While the aforementioned tendencies point to key discursive frames, they also must be considered from the point of view of "types" of the media in which they are put forward and where they are often combined (cf. below). On the one hand, in the quality media, one can observe a clear tendency towards the second of the aforementioned strands (necessity of social-wide response) though with a simultaneous emphasis on some actors' particular responsibility for tackling the problem. Here, one also needs to mention the fact that in the majority of countries, quality media provide views which draw on corresponding political agendas i.e. conservative and liberal views alike. On the other hand, in the tabloid media (especially the press), a tendency exists towards non-alignment to the national-political views on CC and instead towards presentation of CC as a threat and risk as well as a factor which – in a clearly populist tone obvious for the tabloids – is responsible for public fears and anxieties about their environment and general well-being now and in the future.

Of the studies which deal with qualitative media, one surely needs to point to the body of research proposed by Carvalho (2007; cf. also Carvalho 2005) who has provided a very extensive, diachronic analysis of the UK broadsheet newspaper discourses on CC. Dealing with the change of CC discourses in almost two decades between mid 1980s and early 2000s, Carvalho analyzed broadsheet discourses while covering the press in entirety of political views: from the left, through the center, to the right. As Carvalho suggests, the central frame of conceptualizing CC and CC-related response has taken place across the said spectrum along the lines of emphasizing the role of science in mainly informing (i.e. providing facts) about CC rather than tackling it. However, as Carvalho also shows, that tendency also undergoes a significant change over time and in line with different political views and ideologies (represented in different newspapers) where a shift occurs from viewing science as authoritative voice in explaining facts about CC to science's role and views being questioned in line with the former and the latter's frequent misalignment with political views and national policies. As Carvalho (2007) suggests:

> While the press acted jointly as spokespeople for the science establishment in the first few years (...) and enhanced its social authority and power, a radically different image started to emerge at the end of the 1980s, when climate change was politicized.
>
> (Carvalho 2007, 237)

While the politicization of CC has also been to some extent present in the tab-loid media, the latter have, quite contrary to the usual tendencies, displayed a somewhat different or perhaps even broader conceptualization of the problem. As evidenced by Boykoff (2008; cf. also Boykoff and Mansfield 2008, for alternative analysis; Boykoff and Boykoff 2007, for the analysis of US coverage), UK tabloid press generally displays some tendency towards "tabloidization" of the CC issue (through e.g. the frequent use of "doom" and "threat" arguments; especially in the headlines) while also pointing to a range of other issues and actors related to CC. Here, the aforementioned role of science is also thematized though mainly from the point of view of its sub-fields of ecology and meteorology which are re-ferred to as key sources of evidence that the often-questioned CC is in fact taking place. Further to the constructions of the role of science, a bulk of CC framing in tabloids refers to the field of politics thus pointing to the politicians' ability or, more frequently, inability, to respond to CC with relevant actions and policies (cf. politicization, above).

While the aforementioned research explores the national tendencies in tab-loid/quality reporting as well as interpretation of actions by national political and other actors, a different study by Olausson (2010; cf. also Olausson 2009) looks closely at how national media interpret wider actions on CC in either Eu-ropean or global dimensions. The author, who compares reporting on CC and related issues in a Swedish tabloid *Aftonbladet* and in a Swedish TV broadcast *Rapport,* distinguishes between three major frames of reporting which is clearly more "Europeanised than in case of the analyses presented above". As Olausson (2010, 143f.) argues, the three major frames are those of: (a) Construction of a discursive distinction of "Us" and "Them" between European Union and the USA as key global actors willing to tackle CC, (b) Legitimation of EU-CC policy and its actions in both European and global terms, and (c) Projection of traditionally national interpretation of actions onto the European level. Within the first frame, Olausson points to the overall tendency in presenting EU as predominantly posi-tive actor in both European and global actions on CC. Importantly, that "good" EU is juxtaposed with the (recently; cf. below) clearly negative position of the USA which is presented as the main perpetrator guilty of stalling a global deal on CC. Then, within the second frame, the acts of legitimizing EU policy rest on the premise in which no doubts are expressed anymore about the presence of CC as such (contrary to some trends in national reporting; cf. above). Here, it is also vital that the overall process of legitimizing the European policy is viewed from the rather non-objective point of view with a clear aim of "supporting European political power in relation to climate change" (2010, 147). Finally, the last frame points to the fact that, unlike in other instances of national reporting (cf. above), in the Swedish case one actually encounters an extension of typically national media reporting patterns onto the European level. This happens by means of e.g. using the traditionally national frame of self-glorification to present and interpret the salience of EU-CC policy.

4. The EU: Democratic and economic policy discourse in a multilevel system of governance

The European Union is a conglomerate of twenty-seven European states which span over more than 4 million square kilometers and count more than 500 million inhabitants. Unmatched in size by any other international organization, the EU is governed by a set of key institutions which include: The *Council of the EU* (EC)[2] which is the Union's ultimate decision-making and legislative body with some executive powers; the largest and one of the oldest institutions of the European integration – i.e. *the European Commission* (previously known as, inter alia, the "Commission of the European Communities" and thus often abbreviated as CEC)[3] – which is the EU public administration and the executive power of the Union which oversees the implementation of the EU policies in different fields; and *The European Parliament* (EP)[4] which is the only directly-elected EU institution which is (together with the EC) the Union's key legislative power which also possesses the ability to confirm or remove from office key EU officials (president of the EC, CEC president and commissioners, etc.).[5] Although the EP now also possesses policy-initiative abilities, the key driving force in EU-policy making is still the CEC, which also oversees the correct implementation (and tackles eventual infringements) of EU law across all of the Union's member states in over 15 policy fields.[6] That process is directed by the Commission's over 30 policy-departments (known as Directorates-General)[7] which also evolve according to the change in European social and economic conditions and with the Union's political priorities (cf. Kassim 2008). Whilst the CEC remains central in the EU policy-making and implementation, other bodies – namely the Council and the European Parliament – are involved in the legislative process (cf. Pollak and Slominski 2006, for details).

What is central from the policy point of view is that today's EU is a unique *multilevel system of governance* (cf. Hooghe and Marks 2003; Jessop 1995; Bache and Flinders 2004; Held 2006). Within the latter, EU politics and policy-making must be seen as inherently bound by the constant mediation between different (i.e. European, national and regional) levels of governance and between different level-specific institutions. That mediation must, however, be based on specific simultaneous bottom-up and top-down directions of policy making and implementation. Thus, contrary to many arguments on multilevel governance which relate it to processes of one-way top-down Europeanization i.e. the influence of EU policies on the domestic spaces of EU member states (cf., inter alia, Mény, Muller, and Quermonne 1996; or Green-Cowles, Caporaso, and Risse 2001), it is necessary to see the EU system as based on both- top-down and bottom-up logic which would allow for the policies to be not only produced or implemented at selected levels but to gain their legitimacy on all levels of the EU governance (cf. Krzyżanowski and Wodak 2011; also Krzyżanowski and Wodak 2010; Wodak and Fairclough 2010).

Since the Introduction of the 1993 Treaty of Maastricht (also known as the Treaty on the European Union, or TEU), we have seen the arrival of the European Union as a political organism moving beyond the strictly economic aims known from its earlier stages of development. Thus, ever since the TEU, we see a development of course of actions which lead to the "politicization of the EU" (Wiener 2004) as well as to making the Union the first supranational democracy of previously unparalleled proportions. However, with the accelerated development of the EU as both political organism and the multilevel system of governance and the subsequent "widening" and "deepening" of European integration (understood as, on the one hand inclusion of new members and, on the other, ever-closer cooperation within supranational level in Europe), questions about the so-called *democratic deficit of the EU* started to appear. Those questions – realized in diversity of EU-originating and related discourses – undertook the issue of ever-more complex relation between the supranational EU system and the broadly-perceived European citizenry which still remained closed within member nation-states and, except for the EP elections, had little direct impact on the form, shape and pace of the processes of European integration. Debates about the Union's democratic deficit (cf., inter alia, Majone 1994, 1998, 2005; Moravcsik 1998; Follesdal and Hix 2006; Pollak 2007; Eriksen 2009; Nicolaïdis 2010) aimed to show that, as such, the EU system is not socially representative and, acting through the intermediary of nation-state level, cannot become such either.

At the backdrop of arguments on its "democratic deficit", the EU started a course of policy actions which were supposed to make the EU system more comprehensive and more representative. Those actions resulted in the introduction of several new EU treaties (Amsterdam 1996; Nice 2000) of which the Draft Treaty Establishing a Constitution for Europe (produced by the so-called European Convention in 2002–2003; for details cf. Krzyżanowski 2010; Krzyżanowski and Oberhuber 2007) was a milestone introducing new aspects of EU multilevel democracy. That last treaty was never introduced and only its modified form was adopted (albeit not without obstacles) in 2007 under the name of Reform or

Lisbon Treaty. As it seems, however, despite undertaking several actions to improve its democratic image, the EU has still been unable to improve its public-wide support among European citizenry while Euroscepticism in Europe still remains on the rise (cf. Taggart and Szczerbiak 2008).

Yet, simultaneously to the developments of the "democratic discourse" in the EU described above, in early 1990s, the European Commission put rethinking of the European economy at the center of the EU policy. At that time, "a new collective sense of agency was needed at the highest level to drive an across-the-board agenda of systemic change and help create the conditions for a more competitive and cohesive Europe on the global stage" (Jones 2005, 247). Deriving its origins from the economically-driven policy actions of the 1990s, the highpoint of the economization of the EU policy is the European Union Lisbon Strategy implemented in the spring of 2000 (European Council 2000). The Lisbon Strategy is mainly legitimized by bi-dimensional challenges: global or external ones (associated with global competitiveness and the rise of the KBEs across the world) and local or internal ones (the reform of the European economic policy and its preparation of the then forthcoming Enlargement/s of the EU; cf. Dion 2005). In accordance with the strictly socio-economic rationale for the Strategy, the latter outlines its "new strategic goal" (European Council 2000, pt. 5) "to become the most competitive and dynamic knowledge-based economy in the world capable of sustainable economic growth with more and better jobs and greater social cohesion".

Following this criticism of its implementation progress (cf. Armstrong, Begg, and Zeitlin 2008; Zgajewski and Hajjar 2005; cf. also Kok Report 2004), the Lisbon Strategy was re-launched in early 2005 by means of strengthening its national implementation strategies. However, by 2010 it became clear that most of the goals of the Strategy were not achieved. The introduction in 2010 of the "new Lisbon" now called "Europe 2020" program (European Council 2010), allowed most of the ideas of Lisbon to remain in place in the new strategy whose implementation should take place in the coming years. However, despite the clear failure of Lisbon, its main result so far has been the fact of placing KBE-related discourse at the forefront of many policy debates in the European Union (both supranationally and nationally; cf. Fairclough and Wodak 2008). Accordingly, "the discourse of the 'KBE' has become a powerful economic imaginary in the last 20 years or so and, as such, has been influential in shaping policy paradigms, strategies, and policies in and across many different fields of social practice" (Jessop 2008b, 2) which include, as will be shown, the field of the Union's CC policy as well.

5. European Union's policy on climate change: An overview

Though developing mainly in the very turbulent period of the Union's transformation characterized by the clash between the aforementioned "democratic" and "economic" discourse of the EU in 1990s and especially 2000s, the EU-CC policy must be considered in a wider set of global developments as well as in the context of the ongoing competition between the EU and the USA. That competition, which saw the USA taking the undisputed role of a leader in global CC actions in the period between mid-1970s and late 1990s (cf. Vogler and Bretherton 2006), has since the debates about ratification of the 1997 Kyoto Protocol to the United Framework Convention on Climate Change (UNFCCC)[8] clearly shifted in favor of the EU. Throughout the first decade of the 2000s, the Union appeared as a global leader of CC policy by not only introducing its own EU-internal CC measures (cf. Oberthür and Roche-Kelly 2008, and below) but also by deciding (e.g. at the UNFCCC Conference of Partners – or COP – in Bonn and Marrakech in 2001 or at the EU Summit in Gothenburg in 2001; cf. Oberthür and Kelly 2008) to pursue the global ratification of Kyoto without the USA. As it seems, that trend very much prevailed until the 2010 Copenhagen UNFCCC-COP when the US-EU competition clearly receded thus making place for other forms of CC-related global struggle between developed and developing countries (cf. Bodansky 2010).

As such, the EU-CC policy starts in the year of 2000 when the First European Climate Change Programme (ECCP I) is introduced as a way of fulfilling the Union's Kyoto commitments which entered into force in 2005. The ECCP I[9] was mainly a large-scale consultative process undertaken with a wide range of stakeholders including, inter alia, EU institutions, EU member states as well as representatives of different industries and pro-CC activist groups. The ECCP I coincided with the development of policy on the EU's Emissions Trading Scheme (ETS) which was proposed in 2003 and entered into force in 2005 (i.e. along with Kyoto). The ETS was the first international trading scheme which set out initially national (EU Member State) and later on centralized EU-wide allocations for the limits of greenhouse gas emissions to its large-scale producers. In fact the ETS also constituted a milestone of the Second EU Climate Change Programme (ECCP II)[10] which was introduced in the year of 2005. Further to working out and later on improving the ETS, the ECCP II also encompassed actions in such areas as biofuels or taxation of vehicles. It also related the aims of CC policy to those of the (then still valid) Lisbon Agenda by means of coordinating measures to improve CC actions and the issues of economic growth and job creation.

It is in the process of implementation of ECCP II that one encounters the arrival of further major EU-CC policy milestones. First, in 2007, the European Council endorsed the so-called "20-20 by 2020" idea which meant that all EU member states would cut their greenhouse-gas emissions by 20% as well as increase to 20% the use of renewable energy by 2020 (in relation to 1990 levels). That idea was also at the forefront of the key CEC policy document of that period, i.e. the 2007 Green Paper on "Adapting to Climate Change" (see below for analysis). In the aftermath, in 2008, an EU Climate and Energy Package[11] was adopted which showed ways of implementing the previous measures and coordinating them strongly with other fields such as e.g. the EU Energy Policy. The Package also added yet another idea of including the issue of cutting energy use by 20% of projected 2020 levels (thus the project is now called "20-20-20"). As was decided upon accepting the Climate and Energy Package, the 20% goals (in all three fields) could be increased to 30% by 2030 in case a global Kyoto-related (or, by now, post-Kyoto) deal was reached.

While beyond 2010, the EU-CC policy stayed within the framework set out by ECCP I and II as well as by the EU Climate and Energy Package (cf. above), it also showed a further alignment of CC policy ideas to the renewed economic goals of the Union inscribed into Europe 2020 Strategy (cf. above) which was adopted by the Union almost simultaneously. It is in this context that the recent communications of the CEC – e.g. on "Energy 2020" (2010) or on "EU Roadmap 2050" (2011; cf. below for analysis) – are issued by pointing to further goals of the EU in climate and energy fields (now tied even more strongly than in the past).[12]

6.   Analysis

6.1   Classification of genres and selection of the empirical material

European Union policy making is characterized by immense diversity of interlocking textual and other genres. The former and the latter are situated at different levels of generic macrostructures.[13, 14] The central genres such as "policy document" encompass a number of micro-level generic variations (cf. below) used in the process of not only producing but also developing as well as, later on, implementing and communicating the EU policies.

The field of policy-making and implementation includes such notable subgenres as, inter alia, decisions, regulations, directives, resolutions, Presidency Conclusions, inter-institutional "communications", action plans, strategies and framework strategies, green papers, white papers, etc. – all of which carry different functions and are issued by different institutions or in an interinstitutional manner. Of the said genres, the key ones – also for the subsequent analyses – can be defined in a following way (in accordance with their policy-related functions, cf. European Communities 2006, 22):

- *Directive:* sets objectives that have to be achieved, but allows Member States to choose how to achieve them. Directives must normally be transposed into national legislation within two to three years after adoption.
- *Regulation:* creates binding legislation which automatically enters into force in all Member States on a given date, usually a few days after publication in the EU's Official Journal.
- *Decision:* can be addressed to Member States, companies or individuals and is fully binding on those to whom the decision is addressed. Some decisions take effect when they are notified to the addressee, others a few days after publication in the Official Journal.
- *Green Paper:* issued by the European Commission to stimulate debate and launch a process of consultation on specific topics.
- *White Paper:* issued by the European Commission to announce upcoming proposals for EU action in specific areas. At times a White Paper follows a Green Paper.

On the other hand, the emergent field of policy communication also highlighted and analyzed in this chapter includes various generic forms of texts used to explain the policy and provide its possible lines of interpretation to different stakeholders (of whom the general public remains, at least hypothetically, the key target). Among the sub-genres used within the generic macrostructure of EU policy communication, the key text-types are:

- *Leaflets and brochures* (usually with simplified summaries of policies)
- *Factsheets* (outlining "facts" in socio-political and economic reality as well as "policy-facts" i.e. regulations and other actions undertaken within respective fields in the EU)
- *Citizens' summaries* (outlining, in a simple manner, milestones of current and potential policy usually prior to its public consultations and other stakeholder debates)
- *Reports* (outlines of actions undertaken to date or reports from diverse actions such as consultations, working group series and so on).

The policy and policy-communication documents analyzed below are taken from two periods of EU-CC policy's recent development, namely 2007 and 2011, which are selected according to their relevance in terms of both EU-specific CC-policy developments and from the point of view of broader global developments. The year of 2007 is characterized in the EU context by the start of thinking about CC policies that would go beyond the Union's ECCPs (cf. above) as well as beyond the Kyoto provisions which expire in 2012. Accordingly, in 2007, the EU proposes the analyzed Green Paper in the process of debating the eventual EU Climate and

Energy Package (eventually adopted in 2008). At the same time, 2007 is also one of the final years of the US-American Republican administration of G. W. Bush which vehemently opposed ratification of Kyoto by the USA thus stalling further progress on the global CC deal. Globally, the year of 2007 also marks the start of post-Kyoto negotiations, particularly in the run-up to the 2010 major UNFCC-COP Conference in Copenhagen.

On the other hand, the year of 2011 marks the further stage of development of EU-CC policy when the latter was gradually moving towards elaboration of actions to be undertaken not only beyond Kyoto (2012) but especially until 2020. This, of course, happens in accordance with the EU general politico-economic provisions encapsulated in the "Europe 2020" strategy i.e. the cornerstone of EU economic policy after 2010 (cf. above). In extra-European terms, the year of 2011 also marks the highpoint of B. Obama's first Democratic administration in the USA. Whereas that administration has proven to be much more committed to a global CC deal than its Republican antecedents in the first decade of 2000s, its leading role was yet to be confirmed along with the details of global CC agreement that could potentially be supported by the US. Still in the global context, the year of 2011 also means the final stage of the validity period of the Kyoto protocol which would eventually expire in 2012 and fail to meet its targets.

In the following sections, the analysis of "policy" genres focuses on, on the one hand, the CEC Green Paper "*Adapting to climate change in Europe – options for EU action*" (European Commission 2007a), a 27-page-long document which, in line with the usual functions of green papers, was supposed to stimulate further policy-relevant debate and actions on EU-CC policy beyond 2010. The comparative analysis of EU-CC policy genres further includes examination of a CEC Communication entitled "*A Roadmap for moving to a competitive low carbon economy in 2050*" (European Commission 2011a). As is the case with all such communications, the analyzed 15-page text outlines a very likely policy action by describing its rationale and potential scope (NB: communications such as these often precede further publication of "white papers" and later on some more concrete policy measures in forms of regulations and directives). As is usually the case with the aforementioned genres, the analyzed policy documents use large number of specialized vocabulary and require specialist knowledge in the field of EU policy. By the same token, the documents also include numerous references to EU-relevant actions and measures (undertaken previously or to be undertaken in the future) thus limiting the scope of their readership to experts in the EU policy or at least to those members of the public who posses broad knowledge of the EU, its institutions, policies and its legislation. The documents are legal-like in their tone inasmuch they use e.g. very little modal structures thus presenting the Union's certainty in its course of CC-relevant policy actions.

On the other hand, the comparative analysis of "policy communication" genres encompasses documents from the same periods (2007 and 2011; cf. below for rationale) such as a brochure *"Combating Climate Change – The EU leads the way"* (European Commission 2007b) and a factsheet *"Climate Change"* (European Commission 2011b). Both of those documents clearly share their functions inasmuch they present policy "milestones" as well as potential (yet very positive) lines of their interpretation. The documents also share their text-internal generic features such as: layman language which, unlike in the policy, is devoid of specialized terminologies and abbreviations or large degree of multimodality, which, again unlike the policy, combines text with different suggestive images and simple diagrams emphasizing the presented "facts".

6.2   Steps and categories of analysis

The analysis conducted below follows the usual steps and categories of analysis developed within the Discourse-Historical Approach (DHA) in Critical Discourse Studies (cf. Reisigl and Wodak 2009; Wodak and Krzyżanowski 2008) which allows relating the macro- and mezzo-level of contextualization to micro-level analyses of texts which form discourses in focus of the investigation. The analysis encompasses two levels i.e. the so-called "entry-level analysis" which covers the thematic level of texts and the "in-depth analysis" which scrutinizes their further pragmatic and argumentative aspects (cf. Krzyżanowski 2010a, for details).

The general aim of the *entry-level* thematic analysis is to map out the contents of analyzed texts and thus to ascribe them to particular discourses to which the analyzed texts may belong. The key analytical categories of thematic analyses are *discourse topics* which "conceptually, summarize the text, and specify its most important information" (van Dijk 1991, 113). As in the majority of critical-analytic explorations of discourse, topics are also defined here by way of inductive analysis, i.e. by means of decoding the meaning of text passages – usually taking place via several thorough readings – and then ordering them into lists of key themes and sub-themes. The aim of the exercise is to decode the "limits" of discourses by defining their constituent topics (their contents and their hierarchies) embedded in the analyzed texts.

Undertaken after the investigation of key topics of discourse, *in-depth analysis* encompasses subsequent examination of the structures of discourse located "deeper" than its aforementioned contents. As such, the in-depth analysis is primarily argumentation-oriented and aims to reveal how different elements of discourse are endowed with pragmatic meaning and thus placed within different arguments according to the more-or-less strategic aims set up by the speakers/authors of texts.

Hence, the in-depth analysis encompasses not only the analysis and definition of larger "argumentation schemes" (van Eemeren and Grootendorst 1992), but also other supporting elements of discourse such as metaphors and other "means of linguistic realization" (Wodak et al. 1999).

Allowing for its argumentative character, the key category of in-depth analysis in the subsequent examination is that of *topos* (plural *topoi*) which originally derives from classic Aristotelian works on *Rhetoric* and *Topics*. Although they are considered differently in various argumentation-oriented studies (cf. Krzyżanowski 2010, for overview), topoi are viewed here as certain headings of arguments which, in a way, summarize the argument while also providing it with a necessary "skeleton" which is fleshed over by respective discourse contents. Therefore, the analysis aims to discover the links which are established in the course of analysis between the levels of mapping of those contents (i.e. topics) and establish the argumentation schemes (i.e. topoi) deployed, and related linguistic aspects. For this reason, this work shares a premise that:

> Topoi are not defined as abstract linking principles functioning at the deep structure level of argument, but as generic argumentative discourses, discursive forms, including both argument and conclusion. These forms are expanded, specified, 'filled in' according to the peculiarities of the case at hand.
>
> (Plantin 2006, 253–254, original emphasis)

Accordingly, this work analyses topoi and related elements of argumentation in terms of their discourse-pragmatic aspect – and subsequent identity-constructing role – rather than deductively looking for different universal "types" of arguments in the analyzed texts. In general, the aim of the analysis is to define the actual scope and qualitative features of different arguments constructing different positions by means of arguing in favor or against certain individual and collective ideas and views.

As part of the argumentation-oriented analysis, the subsequent examination also draws on categories from Theo van Leeuwen's (1996) theory on the *representation of social actors in discourse*. The latter helps looking for the various ways, in which certain social and political actors (e.g. the EU, USA etc.) are represented, portrayed and positioned in discourse, as well as endowed with social and political agency by means of different discursive moves (foregrounding/backgrounding, collectivization, etc). By the same token, other ways of constructing social groups and agency in discourses – e.g. by means of discursive strategies of reference/ nomination or predication (cf. Reisigl and Wodak 2001) – are also informing the subsequent in-depth analyses by looking at whether certain actors are named (or omitted) in the analyzed discourses as well as whether they are ascribed certain distinctive features vis-à-vis other individuals or collective, institutionalized or non-institutionalized actors referred to.

6.3   Analysis of the EU policy on climate change

The first of the analyzed EU policy genres, i.e. the 2007 CEC Green Paper, outlines diverse EU-internal actions on CC while emphasizing the necessity and modes of close collaboration between the EU and its Member States. The key topics of the document include: (a) Need for adapting to CC in Europe (cf. "Europe will not be spared" section, below), (b) Global aspects of CC, (c) European adaptation actions (including early action, action at the EU level as well as actions necessary at the level of Member States), (d) EU actions in such fields as, inter alia, energy, transport, health, water, marine and fisheries, (e) Adaptation in external actions as well as in climate research supported by the EU and in actions involving wider European society.

In general terms, the arguments expressed in the majority of the document are framed through different realizations of a *topos of crisis*. The latter generally points to the critical nature of the current CC situation as well as to the necessity of undertaking further actions in order to avoid imminent and future related dangers. A particularly illustrative part of the document dominated by the topos of crisis is its third section entitled "Europe will not be spared" in which a claim is put forward that

(1)   The effects of climate change in Europe and the Arctic are already significant and measurable. Climate change will heavily affect Europe's natural environment and nearly all sections of society and the economy. Because of the non-linearity of climatic impacts and the sensitivity of ecosystems, even small temperature changes can have very big effects.

(European Commission 2007a, 4)

As the example shows, the argument is augmented by means of exemplifying different types of dangers that stem from CC challenges. By the same token, those dangers are being ascribed to the diversity of social fields of which the rather unspecified "society" as well as "economy" are overtly nominalized. While the example also points to the natural aspects of CC, they are further developed later on in the document where it is argued that

(2)   There is overwhelming evidence that almost all natural, biological and physical processes (e.g. trees are blossoming earlier, glaciers are melting) are reacting to climatic changes in Europe and worldwide.

(European Commission 2007a, 5)

Here, some examples of natural changes are enumerated (trees, glaciers) by pointing to exemplary critical developments which are a prime evidence that CC is not a case of a purely scientific debate but, actually, a fact of life which additionally constitutes clear and present danger. While in the following parts of the document the topos of crisis is reframed by means of arguments encompassed by a *topos of economy* – which points to the economic aspects and implications of CC – the crisis-oriented presentation of climate situation still prevails. As is argued still on the same page of the document

> (3) Many economic sectors depend strongly on climatic conditions and will feel the consequences of climate change on their activities and businesses directly: agriculture, forestry, fisheries, beach and skiing tourism, and health. Reduced water availability, wind damages, higher temperatures, increased bushfires and greater disease pressure will lead to damage to forests. Increase in frequency and intensity of extreme events such as storms, severe precipitation events, sea floods and flash floods, droughts, forest fires, landslides cause damage to buildings, transport and industrial infrastructure and consequently impact indirectly on financial services and insurance sectors.
>
> (European Commission 2007a, 5)

Here, contrary to the previously rather vague presentation of natural implications of CC, a wide range of subfields of economy (agriculture, forestry, fisheries, etc.) is mentioned as directly affected by climatic changes. Importantly, the enumeration of natural aspects of CC returns though, unlike previously, it does not entail listing areas of the natural environment affected by CC as much as natural disasters (storms, severe precipitation events, sea floods, etc.) which are considered as detrimental to the aforementioned different sub-fields of the economy.

While the crisis-oriented framing of discourse on CC in EU policy is usually related to a general description of CC processes which underlie policy-relevant regulatory and other activities, an important part of the analyzed documents pertains to construction of the role of different institutional and other actors in tackling CC. While, for obvious reasons, the majority of such strategy focuses on EU as a central "global player" in tackling CC, it is vital that not the EU but those of whom it thinks in relation to CC are nominalized and foregrounded in discourse (albeit in a collective way). One such strategic move takes place by means of strategic focus on "developing countries", which the EU is willing to help via its not only European but also globally-relevant actions. As is argued in a section of the document devoted to "Integrating adaptation into EU external actions" (5.2: 21–24),

(4)   Climate change is a serious challenge to poverty reduction in developing countries and threatens to undo many development achievements. Poor communities in these countries depend highly on the direct use of local natural resources.   (European Commission 2007a, 22)

In a following passage, the same argument located within the *topos of global responsibility* is developed further when the role of developed countries is mentioned. While here, a historical dimension is added, it is also interesting that the EU as such is not mentioned but in fact the aggregation of "developed countries" is used to refer to those countries which are endowed with the major responsibility to act. What is vital, the USA is not nominated or foregrounded in this context in which it is usually mentioned as the main perpetrator in global CC (e.g. in the debates at the recent UNFCC-COP in Copenhagen in 2010; cf. Bodansky 2010). As is argued

(5)   Being responsible for most of the historic accumulation of anthropogenic greenhouse gas emissions in the atmosphere, developed countries will need to support adaptation actions in developing countries.
                                                        (European Commission 2007a, 5)

In fact, the non-mentioning of the US becomes salient in the document which later on describes those parts of the world which even have positive experiences of tackling CC that could be shared globally. In mentioning different areas Japan is nominalized as a country while the known opponents of the global CC (Kyoto) deal – such as US and Australia – are omitted while, paradoxically, their key regions (Southeast Australia, Southwest US) are deemed more important. Hence,

(6)   Impact analysis and good adaptation practices should be exchanged between industrialised regions facing similar problems, for example, in Japan, Southeast Australia, and Southwest US. Cooperation strategies with these countries should be further elaborated.   (European Commission 2007a, 23)

While the other analyzed policy document – i.e. the 2011 CEC Communication – has the overall pronounced aim of presenting a roadmap for EU-CC policy in near and distant future (until 2050), it pertains to a set of such topics as: (a) CC as one of the key challenges for the future EU policy in general, (b) Actions on transition to low-carbon economies across the EU (including the so-called sectoral actions within e.g. power-sector, industry, transport, etc), (c) Low-carbon future as an overall economic aim of the EU, and (d) The international dimensions of the current and future EU-CC policy. While, clearly, some of those topics (e.g. the idea of sector-related action convergence) resonate with the 2007 document analyzed above, other topics – especially those on e.g. international importance of EU actions (not on salience of international actions for the EU) – reflect a shift towards the agency of the EU as a global leader in CC-related actions.

The in-depth analysis of the 2011 document also points to some continuities as well as a set of important shifts in the framing of CC from the EU-policy perspective. First, from the outset of the document, we encounter a clear framing of the entire CC issue and its salience from a strictly economic point of view and by means of different realizations of the previously present (though not exactly dominant) *topos of economy*. The latter seems to now possess an overarching role in the EU-CC discourse which, as it appears, causes other arguments expressed previously (e.g. on CC as a global natural or human problem) to almost completely disappear. Importantly, the economic framing of CC is now overtly ascribed to the realization of the EU's economic policies (previously Lisbon, now "Europe 2020") with even the nominal structures (e.g. referring to "Europe 2020" slogan from EU economic policy and relating it to "20-20 by 2020" in the CC policy) supporting that shift. Even the overall rationale of the document points to the fact that

(7) This Communication sets out key elements that should shape the EU's climate action helping the EU become a competitive low carbon economy by 2050. The approach is based on the view that innovative solutions are required to mobilise investments in energy, transport, industry and information and communication technologies, and that more focus is needed on energy efficiency policies. (European Commission 2011a, 3)

Here, the mentioning of the "competitive low carbon economy" is central as it emphasizes the economic aspects in focus. The overall character of the language used in the passage (speaking about "economy", "investments", etc.) also emphasizes such a leading economy-oriented argumentation. The same type of vocabulary in fact prevails in the remainder of the document in which, again, economic statements like "low-carbon economy" are mentioned:

(8) The transition towards a competitive low carbon economy means that the EU should prepare for reductions in its domestic emissions by 80% by 2050 compared to 1990. The Commission has carried out an extensive modelling analysis with several possible scenarios showing how this could be done. (European Commission 2011a, 4)

In a different passage, issues of "investments", "prices" and "costs" become correspondingly central among the goals of the EU-CC policy:

(9)   A less ambitious pathway could lock in carbon intensive investments, resulting in higher carbon prices later on and significantly higher overall costs over
the entire period.   (European Commission 2011a, 5)

While, similarly to the 2007 document, the 2011 CEC Communication also the-
matizes the issue of the EU's global role in tackling CC, it does so in a clearly different manner. As is evident from the document – of which an entire section is
devoted to "The International Dimension" (pages 13–14) – while the EU is aware
of its global responsibility for CC-related actions, it also is mindful of the fact that
it cannot act alone. As it is argued

(10)   The EU with little more than 10% of global emissions will not be able to tackle
climate change on its own. Progress internationally is the only way to solve the
problem of climate change, and the EU must continue to engage its partners.
                                                      (European Commission 2011a, 13)

Hence, a clear reference is made to the fact that also the engagement of other important global players (here we have another implicature which suggests the role
in fact not taken by the US; cf. above) is important further to the EU-originating
actions. Importantly, while the overall argument of the passage is slightly negative
in tone (note the strategic "non-reference" to the US), the language as such is still
very politically-correct by referring to other important actors as "partners".

Importantly, when those partners are finally nominalized, it is by now logical
(in line with the deployed discursive strategies of not naming the US) that the
American role in the process is not thematized. Accordingly, it is suggested that

(11)   A number of Europe's key partners from around the world, such as China,
Brazil and Korea, are addressing these issues, first through stimulus pro-
grammes, and now more and more through concrete action plans to promote
the 'low carbon economy'. Standstill would mean losing ground in major
manufacturing sectors for Europe.   (European Commission 2011a, 13)

As it becomes clear, the EU now sees China, Brazil, Korea and other emergent
economies as its key partners (partially in line with the post-Copenhagen 2010
discourse; cf. above) as well as, in some cases, as certain role models which already implement the solutions soon needed in the European context. Though
here, we encounter yet another metonymical reference to the aforementioned
countries as "partners", it is vital that the eventually economically-framed argument (e.g. the reference to "manufacturing sectors" as well as, again, to the "low-
carbon economy") implicitly points to the competition between the EU and its
partners. As is argued at the end of the passage, the global cooperation is not as

much about tackling CC globally as much as it is about sharing CC-related solutions which could be fruitful to the European economic development and should thus be introduced and implemented in the EU context.

6.4   Analysis of EU policy communication on climate change

The two analyzed EU-CC policy communication texts carry the aim of presenting the milestones of EU policy to the public as well as of legitimizing that policy by means of presenting facts on CC which make that policy indispensable. While the 2007 "*Combating Climate Change*" brochure presents CC as such by moving onto description of different EU actions (altogether framed as an "integrated response"; European Commission 2007b, 5), the 2011 factsheet on "*Climate Change*" follows a largely similar pattern by outlining key aspects of CC which is "happening now" (European Commission 2011b, 2) as well as emphasizes the EU actions, albeit also in the more global context of e.g. the Kyoto commitments.

The in-depth analysis of the two selected policy-communication genres also points to the fact that the deployed discourse remains largely unchanged over time and, unlike the clearly dynamic policy genres (cf. above), it remains within the same type of overall framing of both CC and of the EU role in CC-related response.

The 2007 policy-communication brochure starts from introducing the general framing of CC and related policy in terms of crisis and threat (*topos of crisis*) by pointing to the important changes seen as dangers which are directly related to CC. As is argued

(12)   Climate change is one of the greatest threats facing the planet. If the Earth's temperature rises by more than 2 °C above pre-industrial levels, climate change is likely to become irreversible and the long-term consequences could be immense.   (European Commission 2007b, 3)

Hence, the argument represented in the passage not only encompasses nominalizing/predicating CC as "one of the greatest dangers facing the planet" but also points to the fact that it is the process of the more general industrialization that is to blame for the development of CC (NB: this, by the way, is contrary to the pro-industry economizing arguments expressed in the policy, cf. above). While some economic aspects of CC are also mentioned in the following passage (second sentence), the overall argument still remains within the crisis-oriented argumentation which is in this particular case reduced to such basic human needs as that of "fresh water":

(13)   In many parts of the world there would not be enough fresh water to go round. Extreme weather events causing physical and economic damage would become more frequent. Economies could go into decline from the cost of dealing with a different climate.   (European Commission 2007b, 3)

In a tone which is somewhat resembling the policy discourse, the policy-communication framing also points to the (leading) role of the EU in tackling CC locally and globally. Here, one first encounters the general pre-legitimation which describes an overall necessity for an "integrated energy and CC policy":

(14)   An integrated energy and climate change policy signals the launch of a new industrial revolution to transform the way we produce and use energy, and the types of energy we use.   (European Commission 2007b, 5)

while, in the further part of the document, the EU's role as a global leader in such a "response" is argued for:

(15)   The EU is not starting from scratch in tackling climate change. The EU has been progressively strengthening its measures to increase energy efficiency, limit emissions from factories and cars, and encourage energy savings for a number of years.   (European Commission 2007b, 10)

Importantly, as is argued, the EU has for a long time been thinking about CC and has already put in place many measures which may support CC's reduction. Importantly, the leading role of the EU constructed here does not entail the competitive discourse (between the EU and the US or other "partners", cf. above) and instead focuses on CC-related policies (e.g. on "energy") undertaken within the EU as such. Thus, one encounters here a construction of the EU as a leader not by taking the leading actions as much as by becoming an example to others on how to tackle CC.

However, the discourse directed against the US (and other Kyoto defectors such as Australia) eventually comes to the fore when an argument is put forward that

(16)   Even though the United States and Australia have not ratified the protocol and are therefore not formally contributing to the objective, the EU has gone ahead with concrete measures to achieve its emission targets, which take each member state's level of economic and industrial development into account.
(European Commission 2007b, 10)

Hence, yet again, the construction of EU's leading role is portrayed by means of showing its unique commitment to integrated actions in different (policy) fields as well as arguing that EU is committed to tackling CC – or in fact "going ahead" in that process – by taking actions not pursued elsewhere. Importantly, unlike in the policy genres, the US is mentioned here nominally thus providing the public (i.e. the key target group of policy-communication) with the example of who is different than the EU and who is not undertaking appropriate measures to tackle CC in global terms.

The other, 2011 policy-communication text largely follows the same logic as the aforementioned 2007 policy-communication document and provides a conglomerate of arguments which are rooted in, on the one hand, *topos of crisis*, and, on the other hand, in the topos of EU-leadership which is realized by means of overtly positive construction of the role of the EU and its anti-CC actions. While here, some of the 2011 policy arguments related to the economization of EU-CC discourse sift through, it is vital that the overall framing still remains within the same elliptic construction which runs from the argument on CC as crisis to that on the role of the EU.

The opening arguments on CC as crisis refer to the usual issues mentioned in relation to the change in global climate as well as provide their legitimation by means of recalling to different authorities such as experts, panels and so on:

(17)   There is unequivocal evidence that the Earth's climate is warming. By 2005, the average global temperature was 0.76 °C above the level in pre-industrial times, according to the UN Intergovernmental Panel on Climate Change (IPCC), which brings together hundreds of the world's leading experts. The average temperature is rising by around 0.2 °C every 10 years.

(European Commission 2011b, 2)

In this context of CC "facts" and "experts" (note the use of meteorological facts otherwise widely used in different instances of media discourse, cf. above), a mentioning of greenhouse gases (GHGs) is also made by referring to them as one of the key reasons for CC:

(18)   The vast majority of the world's leading climate experts attribute this warming mainly to a build-up of greenhouse gases (GHGs) emitted by human activities, in particular the burning of fossil fuels – coal, oil and gas – and the destruction of forests. Greenhouse gases are so called because they trap the sun's heat in the atmosphere in the same way as the glass of a greenhouse.

(European Commission 2011b, 2)

While such mentioning is a usual element of the majority of CC-related discourse, the very strong emphasis on GHGs in the opening of the document seems to be to some extent strategic since, later on, the European Union's unique role in tackling CC is exemplified by means of its policy to tackle GHGs. As is argued later on in the document,

(19) The world's first and biggest international GHG emissions trading system, the EU ETS has made climate change a boardroom issue for companies by putting a price on their carbon emissions.   (European Commission 2011b, 3)

The presentation of the EU's unique role is then also framed by means of a set of general statements. As is argued in the 2011 policy-communication document:

(20) Long in the forefront of international efforts to tackle climate change, the European Union is committed to becoming a highly energy-efficient, low-carbon economy. It has set itself some of the world's most ambitious climate and energy targets for 2020 and is the first region to have passed binding legislation to ensure they are achieved.   (European Commission 2011b, 3)

Here, in overall terms, we see yet another realization of the EU-leadership topos which is augmented by temporal statements which claim that EU is "long in the forefront" on tackling CC. Importantly, that "tackling" takes place, yet again, not as much by means of undertaking globally-responsible actions as much as it is by "setting itself" the pronounced "ambitious targets" including making them legally binding. Hence, one yet again encounters the construction of the EU role by means of self-reference to the Union's own CC actions as exemplary and central for the rest of the world.

7.   Conclusions: Discursive shifts in EU discourses on climate change

As has been shown, the European Union discourse on climate change is characterized by a large degree of *discursive change* which helps framing not only the EU-specific perceptions of CC (in terms of crisis/threat, as evidenced by the leading *topoi*) but also the Union's actions against both European and global facets of climatic change. In this context, the EU discourse should be perceived as, in fact, a part of many global public discourses (cf. above for overview of often similar media discourses) in which responses to the unprecedented worldwide changes such as CC are constructed. Those constructions, as is usually the case, are undertaken by means of framing CC in terms of combination of globally-related arguments with descriptions of different types of local (in the current case EU-specific) activities and responses.

However, as the in-depth look provided by the above analysis suggests, the key element of the EU's discursive response to CC lays in a set of micro-level *discursive shifts* which occurred in the analyzed period. The main of such shifts pertains to the promulgation of general discourses about CC – e.g. by perceiving it by means of different "facts" and as a certain type of "crisis" – with the recent political discourses of the EU in which a clear (renewed) emphasis has been made on the economic aspects of European integration and EU policy-making (cf. recent increase in arguments framed by the *topos of economy*).

Hence, as it seems, the EU-CC discourse recently undergoes a significant *economization*. It is in line with that shift that, in fact, the EU-CC discourse evolves over the analyzed period by moving from the more crisis-oriented arguments on CC (and the necessity of a corresponding policy) to looking at CC as a predominantly economic challenge and a major obstacle to building a globally-competitive European Knowledge-Based Economy. (In fact, a similar shift towards economization has also been recently observed in other EU policy fields such as, e.g., EU Language and Multilingualism Policy; cf. Krzyżanowski and Wodak 2011). It is also in accordance with the aforementioned shift that a significant change occurs in the EU discourse which, as it appears, points to the fact that the EU is gradually less committed to tackling CC for reasons related to its impact on the future of European (and other) societies and of the humanity as a whole and instead turns towards looking at CC as an obstacle to the Union's recent and current politico-economic projects (i.e. the "late" Lisbon Strategy or the current "Europe 2020" program).

The said, central shift in the EU-CC policy discourse must be considered especially salient from the point of view of the two analyzed sub-fields of policy making i.e. the policy itself as well as the policy-communication. In the former, the key shift occurs between crisis-like framing of discourse still in the year of 2007, to the increasing economization of the EU-CC discourse in 2011. As this shift may imply, the CC discourse becomes adjusted in its course to the present-day general policy frames of the EU (i.e. focus on the economy, especially of the European KBE) which, in turn, may be considered – albeit only partially – as the Union's responses to the changing socio-political and economic situation (ongoing Financial Crisis, etc.). By the same token, while the arguments on the EU leadership in global response to CC remain an almost steady element of the analyzed policies, it is vital that the qualitative features of that construction do change over time. Hence, while in 2007 the EU-CC discourse still revolves around creating an image of the Union as a strong actor (especially vis-à-vis the USA), in the year of 2011 we already see a construction of somewhat weaker role of EU as a leader – or perhaps of a coordinator – of a response which must be undertaken by many "partners" around the globe. This peculiar discursive "weakening" of the Union's role seems to correspond to the general change in the EU-CC policy in which it gradually becomes clear that a more narrow focus on EU-internal measures might be necessary in the absence of a global agreement and solid worldwide legal measures on tackling the climate change.

On the other hand, the rather novel policy-communication discourse analyzed above seems to be much less prone to changes over the period in which the majority of policy-communication texts focus on a similar set of issues (this is further supported by no dynamics of the scrutinized texts which both in 2007 and in 2011 are indeed both discursively and generically similar). Hence, at both of the analyzed moments of time, policy-communication revolves around, on the one hand, facts about CC (thus proving that CC in fact exists and must be tackled) and, on the other hand, around the construction and legitimation of the EU's role as a long-term global leader in fight against the CC (cf. the steady use of *topos of global responsibility*). While, as indicated above, some elements of the changing policy and related discourse do penetrate into the policy-communication (as by 2011 there is some presence of arguments related to economy by 2011), it must still be emphasized that, unlike in the policy, policy communication rests on discursive (and generic) continuity rather than discontinuity.

Accordingly, a final remark yields itself with regard to the generic and discursive dynamics in the sub-fields of CC-related policy making. Whereas, as indicated in the analysis, the policy itself is more dynamic and clearly responds to developments within both the EU and its more or less distant social, political and economic context, it seems that the policy-communication strategically remains unchanged in its focus. Hence, whereas the policies do change over time, such a change is apparently often not communicated to the general public (and other recipients of policy-communication). Instead of being informed about the Union's changing (and increasingly economic) motivations with regard to CC, those affected by the EU-CC are actually still being presented with the usual mixture of CC-related facts and of the corresponding EU identity-making discourse. The former and the latter are communicated in lieu of actual information and communication on the de-facto scope (and pivotal change) of the relevant policies which, perhaps, would not now meet public expectations and thus would not resonate well among the European populace.

Acknowledgement

This chapter is based on the guest lecture which I delivered at the Universities of Bergen and Örebro in 2011. I am grateful to colleagues from Bergen and Örebro for their valuable comments. I am particularly indebted to Peter Berglez for his valuable ideas and literature suggestions when preparing the lecture and the early version of this chapter.

Notes

1.   See the discussion of generic structures, hyper/macro/proto-genres, and generic chains, in Section 3 of this volume's Introduction. See also chapters by Lauerbach and by Wodak (this volume).

2.   Cf.: http://www.consilium.europa.eu

3.   Cf.: http://ec.europa.eu

4.   Cf.: http://www.europarl.europa.eu

5.   Further key EU institutions include: *The Court of Justice of the EU* (http://curia. europa.eu), *The European Court of Auditors*, as well as, since 2009, *The European Central Bank* (http://www. ecb.int).

6.   For details, cf. http://ec.europa.eu/policies/index_en.htm

7.   For details, cf. http://ec.europa.eu/about/ds_en.htm

8.   The 1997 Kyoto Protocol to United Framework Convention on Climate Change (cf. http:// unfccc.int) was until its expiry in 2012 the main document spelling out percentage-based commitments of the world's industrialized economies on cutting greenhouse-gas emissions. It was considered the main international legal document outlining the global response of climate change in the first years of 2000s. Its full implementation was progressively stalled by the United States which, under the presidency of G. W. Bush in 2000–2008 opposed its ratification (cf. Helm 2008, for further details). In view of Kyoto's eventual expiry in 2012, the UNFCCC-COP conferences in recent years have been working (without success) on reaching a new global deal beyond 2012.

9.   For further details and all relevant documents, cf. http://ec.europa.eu/clima/policies/eccp/first_en.htm

10.   Cf. http://ec.europa.eu/clima/policies/eccp/second_en.htm

11.   Cf. http://ec.europa.eu/clima/policies/package/index_en.htm

12.   Cf. Oberthür and Roche-Kelly (2008) for a detailed description of key documents forming the EU-CC policy.

13.   See – viz. Note 1 – the discussion of generic structures, hyper/macro/proto-genres, and generic chains, in Section 3 of this volume's Introduction. See also chapters by Lauerbach and by Wodak (this volume).

14.   Note that the notion of "generic macrostructure" used here (cf. Introduction to the volume, for details) is not to be mistaken with that of "semantic macrostructures" used widely within e.g. the so-called Socio-Cognitive Approach in Critical Discourse Analysis (cf. e.g. van Dijk 1984).

References

Armstrong, Kenneth, Iain Begg, and Jonathan Zeitlin. 2008a. "Is There a Convincing Rationale for the Lisbon Strategy?" *Journal of Common Market Studies* 46: 427–435.

Azmanova, Albena. 2009. "1989 and the European Social Model. Transition without Emancipation?" *Philosophy and Social Criticism* 35: 1019–1037.

Bache, Ian, and Matthew Flinders. (eds). 2004. *Multi-Level Governance*. Oxford: Oxford University Press.

Beck, Ulrich. 1992. *Risk Society: Towards a New Modernity*. London: Sage.

Berglez, Peter. 2008. "What is Global Journalism?" *Journalism Studies* 9: 845–858.

Berglez, Peter, and Ulrika Olausson. 2010. The 'Climate Threat' as Ideology: Interrelations between Citizen and Media Discourses. Paper presented at the conference *Communicating Climate Change II – Global Goes Regional*, 11–12 October 2010, Hamburg, Germany.

Bernstein, Basil. 1990. *The Structuring of Pedagogic Discourse*. London: Routledge.

Bodansky, Daniel. 2010. "The Copenhagen Climate Change Conference: A Postmortem." *The American Journal of International Law* 104: 230–240.

Boykoff, Maxwell T. 2008. "The Cultural Politics of Climate Change Discourse in UK Tabloids." *Political Geography* 27: 549–569.

Boykoff, Maxwell T., and Jules Boykoff. 2007. "Climate Change and Journalistic Norms: A Case-Study of US Mass-Media Coverage." *Geoforum* 38: 1190–1204.

Boykoff, Maxwell T., and Maria Mansfield. 2008. "'Ye Olde Hot Aire'*: Reporting on Human Contributions to Climate Change in the UK Tabloid Press." *Environmental Research Letters* 3/2008.

Carvalho, Anabela. 2005. "Representing the Politics of the Greenhouse Effect: Discursive Strategies in the British Media." *Critical Discourse Studies* 2: 1–29.

—. 2007. "Ideological Cultures and Media Discourses on Scientific Knowledge: Re-Reading News on Climate Change." *Public Understanding of Science* 16: 223–243.

Dion, David-Pascal. 2005. "The Lisbon Process: A European Odyssey." *European Journal of Education* 40: 295–313.

Eriksen, Erik-Oddvar. 2009. *The Unfinished Democratisation of Europe*. Oxford: Oxford University Press.

European Commission. 2006. *The European Climate Change Programme: EU Action against Climate Change*. Brussels: European Communities.

—. 2007a. *Adapting to Climate Change in Europe – Options for EU Action*. (Green Paper from the Commission to the Council, the European Parliament, The European Social Committee, and the Committee of the Regions; COM(2007) 354 final). Brussels: The European Commission.

—. 2007b. *Combating Climate Change – the EU Leads the Way*. Brussels: The European Commission.

—. 2011a. *A Roadmap for Moving to a Competitive Low Carbon Economy in 2050*. (Communication from the Commission to the Council, the European Parliament, The European Social Committee, and the Committee of the Regions; COM(2011) 112/4). Brussels: The European Commission.

—. 2011b. *Climate Change*. Brussels: The European Commission.

European Council. 2000. *Presidency Conclusions – Lisbon European Council 23– 24 March 2000*. Brussels: Council of the European Union.

—. 2010. *Presidency Conclusions –European Council 25–26 March 2010*. Brussels: Council of the European Union.

Fairclough, Norman. 1992. *Discourse and Social Change*. Cambridge: Polity Press.

Fairclough, Norman, and Ruth Wodak. 2008. "The Bologna Process and the Knowledge-Based Economy: A Critical Discourse Analysis Approach." In *Education and the Knowledge-*

Based Economy in Europe, ed. by Bob Jessop, Norman Fairclough, and Ruth Wodak, 109–127. Rotterdam: Sense Publishers.

Follesdal, Andreas, and Simon Hix. 2006. "Why There is a Democratic Deficit in the EU: A Response to Majone and Moravcsik." *Journal of Common Market Studies* 44: 533–562.

Green-Cowles, Maria, James Caporaso, and Thomas Risse. (eds). 2001. *Transforming Europe: Europeanisation and Domestic Change*. Ithaca, NY: Cornell University Press.

Held, David. 2006. *Models of Democracy*. 3rd edition. Cambridge: Polity Press.

Hooghe, Liesbet, and Gary Marks. 2003. *Unraveling the Central State, But How? Types of Multi-Level Governance*. Vienna: Institute for Advanced Studies.

Howarth, David. 2007. "Internal Policies: Reinforcing the New Lisbon Message of Competitiveness and Innovation." *Journal of Common Market Studies* 45: 89–106.

Jessop, Bob. 1995. "The Regulation Approach, Governance and Post-Fordism: Alternative Perspectives on Economic and Political Change?" *Economy and Society* 24: 307–333.

—. 2008a. "The Cultural Political Economy of the Knowledge-Based Economy and its Implications for Higher Education." In *Education and the Knowledge-Based Economy in Europe*, ed. by Bob Jessop, Norman Fairclough, and Ruth Wodak, 13–40. Rotterdam: Sense Publishers.

—. 2008b. "Introduction." In *Education and the Knowledge-Based Economy in Europe*, ed. by Bob Jessop, Norman Fairclough, and Ruth Wodak, 1–12. Rotterdam: Sense Publishers.

Jessop, Bob, Norman Fairclough, and Ruth Wodak. (eds). 2008. *Education and the Knowledge-Based Economy in Europe*. Rotterdam: Sense Publishers.

Jones, Hywel Ceri. 2005. "Lifelong Learning in the European Union: Whither the Lisbon Strategy?" *European Journal of Education* 40: 247–260.

Judt, Tony. 2010. *Ill Fares the Land*. London: Penguin.

Kassim, Hussein. 2008. "'Mission Impossible', but Mission Accomplished: The Kinnock Reforms and the European Commission." *Journal of European Public Policy* 15: 648–668.

Kok Report. 2004. *Facing the Challenge: The Lisbon Strategy for Growth and Employment. Report from the High Level Group chaired by Wim Kok*. Luxembourg: Office for Official Publications of the European Communities.

Koselleck, Reinhart. 1959. *Kritik und Krise. Eine Studie zur Pathogenese der Burgerlichen Welt*. Freiburg: Alber.

—. 2006. "Crisis." *Journal of the History of Ideas* 67: 357–400.

Krzyżanowski, Michał. 2008. Multilingualism and the Democratic Image of the EU: Perspectives from the European Public Sphere. Paper presented at the Workshop 'Bottom-Up Europe', Salzburg Centre for European Studies, University of Salzburg, 9 May 2008.

—. 2009a. "Discourses about Enlarged and Multilingual Europe: Perspectives from German and Polish National Public Spheres." In *Language, Discourse and Identity in Central Europe*, ed. by Patrick Stevenson and Jenny Carl, 23–47. Basingstoke: Palgrave.

—. 2009b. "Europe in Crisis: Discourses on Crisis-Events in the European Press 1956–2006." *Journalism Studies* 10: 18–35.

—. 2010. *The Discursive Construction of European Identities: A Multilevel Approach to Discourse and Identity in the Transforming European Union*. Frankfurt am Main: Peter Lang.

—. 2011a. "Political Communication, Institutional Cultures, and Linearities of Organisational Practice: A Discourse-Ethnographic Approach to Institutional Change in the European Union." *Critical Discourse Studies* 8: 281–296.

—. 2012. "(Mis)communicating Europe? On Deficiencies and Challenges in Political and Institutional Communication in the European Union." In *Intercultural Communication, Past and Present*, ed. by Barbara Kryk-Kastovsky, 185–215. Amsterdam: Benjamins.

Krzyżanowski, Michał, and Florian Oberhuber. 2007. *(Un)Doing Europe: Discourses and Practices of Negotiating the EU Constitution*. Brussels: P.I.E.-Peter Lang.

Krzyżanowski, Michał, and Ruth Wodak. 2010. "Hegemonic Multilingualism in/of the EU Institutions: An Inside-Outside Perspective on the European Language Policies and Practices. In *Mehrsprachigkeit aus der Perspektive zweier EU-Projekte: DYLAN Meets LINEE*, ed. by Heike Böhringer, Cornelia Hülmbauer, and Eva Vetter, 115–135. Frankfurt am Main: Peter Lang.

Krzyżanowski, Michał, and Ruth Wodak. 2011. "Political Strategies and Language Policies: The 'Rise and Fall' of the EU Lisbon Strategy and its Implications for the Union's Multilingualism Policy." *Language Policy* 10: 115–136.

Majone, Giandomenico. 1994. "The Rise of the Regulatory State in Europe." *West European Politics* 17: 78–102.

—. 1998. "Europe's 'Democratic Deficit': The Question of Standards." *European Law Journal* 4: 5–28.

—. 2005. *Dilemmas of European Integration. The Ambiguities and Pitfalls of Integration by Stealth*. Oxford: Oxford University Press.

Mény, Yves, Pierre Muller, and Jean-Louis Quermonne. (eds). 1996. *Adjusting to Europe: The Impact of the European Union on National Institutions and Policies*. London: Routledge.

Moravcsik, Andrew. 1998. *The Choice for Europe: Social Purpose and State-Power from Messina to Maastricht*. Ithaca, NY: Cornell University Press.

Nicolaïdis, Calypso. 2010. "The JCMS Annual Review Lecture – Sustainable Integration: Towards EU 2.0?" *Journal of Common Market Studies* 48: 21–54.

Nohrstedt, Stig-Arne (ed.). 2011. *Communicating Risks – Towards the Threat-Society?* Göteborg: Nordicom.

Oberthür, Sebastian, and Claire Roche-Kelly. 2008. "EU Leadership in International Climate Policy: Achievements and Challenges." *The International Spectator* 43: 35–50.

Olausson, Ulrika. 2009. "Global Warming – Global Responsibility? Media Frames of Collective Action and Scientific Certainty." *Public Understanding of Science* 18: 421–436.

—. 2010. "Towards a European Identity? The News Media and the Case of Climate Change." *European Journal of Communication* 25: 138–152.

Plantin, Christian. 2006. "On Casting Doubt: The Dialectical Aspect of Normative Rules in Argumentation." In *Considering Pragma-Dialectics*, ed. by Peter Houtlosser, and Agnès van Rees, 245–257. Mahwah, NJ: Lawrence Erlbaum Associates.

Pollak, Johannes. 2007. *Repräsentation ohne Demokratie. Kollidierende Modi der Repräsentation in der Europäischen Union*. Wien/New York: Springer.

Pollak, Johannes, and Peter Slominski. 2006. *Das Politische System der EU*. Vienna: Facultas WUV-UTB.

Reisigl, Martin, and Ruth Wodak. 2001. *Discourse and Discrimination. Rhetorics of Racism and Anti-Semitism*. London: Routledge.

—. 2009. "The Discourse-Historical Approach (DHA)." In *Methods of Critical Discourse Analysis* (2nd edition), ed. by Ruth Wodak, and Michael Meyer, 87–122. London: Sage.

Taggart, Paul, and Alex Szczerbiak. (eds). 2008. *Opposing Europe? The Comparative Party Politics of Euroscepticism*. Vols. 1 and 2. Oxford: Oxford University Press.

van Dijk, Teun A. 1984. *Prejudice in Discourse*. Amsterdam: Benjamins.

van Dijk, Teun A. 1991. "The Interdisciplinary Study of News as Discourse." In *Handbook of Qualitative Methods in Mass Communication Research*, ed. by Klaus Bruhn-Jensen, and Nicholas Jankowski, 108–120. London: Routledge.

Vogler, John, and Charlotte Bretherton. 2006. "The European Union as a Protagonist to the United States on Climate Change." *International Studies Perspectives* 7: 1–22.

Wiener, Antje. 2004. "Die Verfassung Europas. Konturen eines europäischen Konstitutionalismus." *Integration* 27: 176–185.

Wodak, Ruth. 1996. *Disorders of Discourse*. London: Longman.

—. 2000. "Recontextualization and the Transformation of Meanings: A Critical Discourse Analysis of Decision Making in EU-Meetings about Employment Policies." In *Discourse and Social Life*, ed. by Srikant Sarangi, and Malcolm Coulthard, 185–206. Harlow: Pearson Education.

—. 2001. "The Discourse-Historical Approach." In *Methods of Critical Discourse Analysis*, ed. by Ruth Wodak and Michael Meyer, 63–94. London: Sage.

—. 2009. *The Discourse of Politics in Action: Politics as Usual*. Basingstoke: Palgrave.

Wodak, Ruth, and Norman Fairclough. 2010. "Recontextualizing European Higher Education Policies: The Cases of Austria and Romania." *Critical Discourse Studies* 7: 19–40.

Wodak, Ruth, and Michał Krzyżanowski. (eds). 2008. *Qualitative Discourse Analysis in the Social Sciences*. Basingstoke: Palgrave.

Wodak, Ruth, Rudolf de Cillia, Martin Reisigl, and Karin Liebhart. 1999. *The Discursive Construction of National Identity*. Edinburgh: Edinburgh University Press.

Zgajewski, Tania, and Kalila Hajjar. 2005. *The Lisbon Strategy: Which Failure? Whose Failure? And Why?* (Egmont Papers No. 6). Brussels: Royal Institute for International Relations.

CHAPTER 4

The television election night broadcast

A macro genre of political discourse*

Gerda Lauerbach

University of Frankfurt am Main, Germany

Election night broadcasts are instances of a macro-genre which consists of a complex, ordered assembly of interlocking genres. The emergent character of the news, the liveness of the broadcast and its multi-focal character make for a number of typical genres and genre sequences. The chapter provides an overview of the area of research and a framework of analysis, drawing on DA, CA, systemic functional linguistics, pragmatics, semiotics and sociology. The genres studied are reports and comments (soft and hard news, audio-visual presentation of statistics) and Declaration sequences, comprising a running-up sequence (reports, interviews), and the Declaration of results at constituency level. The data are from the BBC election night on the 1997 UK parliamentary elections. The focus is on the discourse of journalists, not of politicians, and on the interplay of the verbal and visual channels.

1. Introduction

Television broadcasts on the results of national elections have managed to hold on to their status as national media events, in Europe and elsewhere, even in times of the new media. In spite of multi-channel fragmentation, they are still able to draw sizeable audiences, a fact which causes fierce competition between the major national channels. Media corporations send their best presenters into the arena, their most skilful interviewers, their most competent political experts and most creative statistics wizards. The transmissions are planned as meticulously as is possible for an event that is carried live, will go on for hours, if not all night, and is happening simultaneously in a multitude of different places. They provide excellent data of the ways in which experienced political journalists, all kinds of experts and high-ranking politicians interact on a topic of great national import and in doing so construct a wide range of genres and generic configurations of political discourse. The eventual results of such collaborative discursive constructions are particular instances of a macro-genre which consists of a complex, ordered assembly of interlocking genres. All this is achieved under conditions of liveness and the emergent character of the news as the election results are coming into the studio – first from the national polling organizations, later from official sources.

Television election nights have become rituals of transition in the political life of a nation. Structurally, such broadcasts occupy the third position in the discursive chain of Election Campaign – Election – Broadcast of the Election Results. After the election campaign and the casting of the votes on election day, television stages the third discursive event of the elections, that of making the results known all over the nation. Election night broadcasts thereby provide closure to a fundamental act of political participation. Their function goes however beyond the mere publication of the results. Television also provides the social space in which the elections results can be publicly discussed, evaluated against the context of the election campaigns, used to speculate on the next government, its members and policies, and on the role of the opposition, the shadow cabinet and so on. Politicians, experts, invited representatives of the powerful social institutions and even ordinary people can, under the direction of the journalists, engage in a battle of interpretation over what the results of the election mean (cf. Stiehler 2000). Television thus presents a stage on which (and stage directions according to which) the participants involved can transform the numerical election results into social and political facts. Also, by opening its forum to many different points of view, television presents a multitude of perspectives on the election from which viewers can construct their own. The viewers for their part, and only on this night, are not just the passive overhearing audience of the normal news bulletin. Those who have voted are in fact the newsmakers of the day – how they have voted is after all what the program is about (Lauerbach 2007, 316f.). Some channels take this into account, for example by inviting a studio audience and providing the rare opportunity for participation, or by interviewing "the man in the street".

Election night broadcasts realize a macro-genre of political discourse. They are composed on the one hand of the constituent genres and sub-genres that are typical of such broadcasts, and on the other hand of genres which they share with related macro-genres (e.g. with television news bulletins, current affairs magazines, etc.). Their discourse is political discourse, dedicated to making the results of a national election publically known and to discussing what these results mean to the nation at large and to its citizens. In this respect it is akin to news discourse. More generally, it is also mediated discourse, which fact subjects it to the constraints and potentialities of television. The great potential of television, which sets it apart from e.g. radio and the print media, is of course its audiovisuality.

Election night discourse also originates from a central studio, while the news it reports is being made in a multitude of places outside of the studio. Also, it is live discourse, which imposes its own specific determinants (cf. Marriott 2000). It is discourse that is broadcast over a period of many hours and as such develops its own dynamics and information economy. Above all, however, the discourse of election night is journalistic discourse. For although political actors are the newsmakers of mediated political discourse, so that the discourse is always about them, they do not necessarily have to be present. This is different for the journalists and the audience – both are constitutive of media discourse within any discursive domain. Thus journalistic discourse *about* politics is the overarching category which embeds the discourse of and with politicians. Moreover, it is journalistic discourse which keeps the gate through which the discourse of politicians enters the stage of the media. All of these characteristics have consequences for the types of genres, sub-genres and genre-chains to be found in this macro-genre.

The aim of this chapter is to describe some of the genres, sub-genres and generic configurations of one such national election night broadcast (see also Malkmus [this volume] for a detailed analysis of *political speeches* in election night broadcasts). The data selected from my corpus of broadcasts on the US (2000), Germany (1998) and the UK (1997) elections is the BBC 1 transmission during the night following the UK 1997 general elections. I focus on the British data, rather than on the North American or German ones, for the following reasons: Due to the British and US election systems (first past the post or winner takes all), the British and American election night broadcasts are much longer and more comprehensive than the German one, thereby promising richer descriptions of the characteristics of the macro-genre under study. This is because, due to Germany's mixed system of personalized proportionate representation, the results become known much faster, in a matter of hours, so that the corresponding television broadcasts are rather more sparse variants of the genre. Also, in contrast to the US election night broadcast, the UK one has a proper ending with a clear winner and loser, which the equally long and comprehensive US 2000 presidential election night does not. It may be remembered that it took five weeks, several recounts of the votes of the state of Florida and the decisions of various courts, state and federal, until at last the US Supreme Court decided that G. W. Bush had won the 2000 election over Al Gore.

Before proceeding to closer scrutiny of the data in Sections 3 to 5 of this chapter, however, a few remarks on the category of genre and on my model of analysis are in order.

2.   Genre

The term *genre* refers here to non-literary genres as they are studied in disciplines like sociology, linguistic pragmatics or discourse analysis. Such communicative genres are theorized as located at the transition points between society/the social order/the social situation or context on the one side, and language/language use /discourse or text on the other (Luckmann 1986; Fairclough 1995, 2003; Hasan 1985a–c). Levinson (1979) speaks of "activity types", which have developed as conventionalized patterns of linguistic and other semiotic types of communication in order to deal with recurring social "problems". These "problems" belong to a genre's external (social, institutional) sphere of motivation, while its characteristic internal (discursive, textual) structure is constructed through the discursive practices of working through those problems (Fairclough 1995, 2003; Luckmann 1986; Kress 1993). The external-internal relation is constitutive of genres and highlights their function as points of articulation between context and text (Hasan 1985a–c), between social practice and discourse practice (Fairclough 1995, 2003). Genres can vary across cultures, times, social classes and sub-cultures (Luckmann 1986; Günthner and Luckmann 2001) and social change can manifest itself in the change and hybridization of genres (Luckmann 1986; Fairclough 1995, 2003), as can language change (Bakhtin 1986). Genres can be mixed within one text, where they can occur in hierarchical order and in generic chains (Fairclough 1995, 2003), as they do in election night broadcasts.

Genres are crucial for understanding what is happening on the social plane and what is being meant discursively. They provide standardized frames of interpretation and genre-specific schemata for inferring implicit meaning (Levinson 1979). At the same time, they supply the schemata for discursive action and interaction. Genres have their own "style", e.g. the generic norm for talk is considered to be everyday conversation (Crystal and Davy 1969). The generic norms of everyday conversation are modified in the transition to other genres, for example with respect to linguistic characteristics like prosody in radio talk (Crystal and Davy 1969), or to constraints on conversational contributions in news interviews (Heritage and Greatbatch 1991). "Universal" pragmatic principles like speech act conditions, the inferential model of Gricean conversational logic and norms of politeness must likewise be adjusted for institutional genres like classroom teaching and courtroom discourse (Levinson 1979), and no doubt for many other genres as well, not least those of political discourse. The same goes for preference organization in political interviews (Lauerbach 2004; see also Fetzer and Bull, this volume).

For Systemic Functional Linguistics, with its tradition of studying language in context, genre as conventionally patterned language use is a case of variation in

context. Various forms of contextual variation are distinguished: dialect as variation according to regional or diachronic context, code as variation according to
social contexts of socialization (class, education), and register as variation according to context of situation. Genre is related to register as a form of situational variation. Register as situationally specific language use is defined through its three
variables of field (what is going on in a situation: the subject matter and the social
activity engaged in), tenor (who is taking part, including the role relationships
between the participants), and mode (what part the language and other semiotic
resources play). Typical instances of register are the occupational varieties: the
language (or the discourse, cf. Fairclough 1995) of politics, of law, journalism,
pedagogy, caretaking, etc.

The category of genre is determined by a particular selection from, or a specific contextual configuration of the register variables of field, tenor and mode
(Hasan 1985a–c). Relating this to approaches like Luckmann's (1986, 1988), a
contextual configuration can be considered on a par with the "external" structure
of a genre. In parallel to the three dimensions of register, Hasan's model of genre is
likewise characterized by three functional components: a generic semantic potential associated with the social activity engaged in (related to field), a generic structure potential (related to tenor) and a generic textural potential (related to mode).
Together, Hasan's three potentials constitute the resources of semiotic meaning
for constructing the "internal" structure of a genre.

I shall follow Hasan's (1985a–c) model for analyzing genre, but combine it
with Goffman's (1981) differentiation of the speaker role into the three participant roles of his "production format": animator, author and principal. Put simply,
the animator is the one uttering the words, the author the one who has selected
the contents to be expressed and the way in which they are formulated, and the
principal the one whose position is being expressed and who is committed to
and responsible for it in the legalistic sense (1981, 145). Whenever we use the
term "speaker", we imply that all three roles converge, or at least that they do
so in everyday talk. Goffman had indeed mainly institutional communication in
mind when first writing about this (as in radio talk or courts of law), but the differentiation is also helpful and necessary for modes of everyday talk like quoting,
storytelling, joking or mocking. For the analysis of television text with its added
visual component, it is essential. Two further concepts of Goffman's with which
he accounts for the dynamics of changes in participant roles, are "footing" and
"footing change". Footing refers to the special alignments between participants'
identities and relations which exist in a particular state of talk. These can change
with a change of the type of addressee, of the type of discourse or genre, of the
topic and so on. Most commonly, a change in type of addressee is involved, and
most commonly, a change in code follows (Goffman 1981, 126–127). Like the

roles of the production format, footing and footing changes refer to general qualities and processes of talk. For complex institutional genres like those of television
talk, how they are realized is an important part of a genre's profile.

According to Hasan, any analysis of genre must address itself to the three
interrelated domains of field, tenor and mode; respectively, to a genre's semantic,
structural and textural potential. The analysis of field focuses on the purpose of
the social activity, the topics dealt with, as well as participants' goals (which may
converge with or diverge from the overall purpose), and their agendas regarding
those topics and goals. However, not all types of social activity are goal-oriented
or strategic (Fairclough 2003). The talk over the garden fence, for instance, a classic example of phatic communication, has proved notoriously difficult for analysis
in terms of purpose, goals, strategy and structure. Fairclough proposes an orientation along the lines of Habermas' (1984) distinction between communicative
and strategic communication, which associates the first with the life-world and
the second with institutional interaction. Life-world discourse is assumed to be
less structured and to be governed by what Habermas terms communicative rationality, while strategic interaction is more strictly structured, even ritualized at
times, and is subject to instrumental rationality. The question that these two types
of discourse-orientation raise for analysis is, however, if they do indeed occur
in strict distribution in natural, everyday, communicative interaction on the one
hand and in institutional, strategic interaction on the other. There are a number
of indications that they do not. The work of conversation analysis has shown for
instance that genres of everyday conversation are governed by a number of rules
and principles (e.g. rules for turn-taking, principles like conditional relevance
or preference organization) which can be and are applied quite strategically in
everyday conversation and thereby produce predictable structures like pre-sequences (cf. Levinson 1983). There are, in this type of discourse, also a number
of techniques for circumventing or violating the principles which are structurally relevant. Institutional, strategic discourse on the other hand, which tends to
be ritualized to different degrees and predictably structured, is becoming more
and more subject to processes of conversationalization and personalization, as
Fairclough has repeatedly shown. Political discourse in the media is no exception
to this process, and election night broadcasts are a good example of this.

The analysis in terms of tenor looks at genre-specific participant roles and
role-specific activities (which is where Goffman's production format will prove
useful), and to the sequential structure in which these are typically worked
through. This includes the question as to which of these activities are obligatory,
i.e. constitutive of the genre, and which ones are optional (cf. the concept of "flexible macrostructure" discussed in Section 2.3 of this volume's Introduction). In
the political interview for instance (see Fetzer and Bull, this volume), the roles of

interviewer and interviewee are constitutively associated with the activity of asking questions and responding, respectively. This constraint produces a certain basic sequential structure, which can however become more elaborate if a number of optional activities are realized (Lauerbach 2000). Another issue is the study of the typical identities and inter-subjective relations of a genre's participants and of how they can change (footings and footing changes). Taking again the mass media interview as an example, the question arises how participants attend to these. Do they construct the interview's topics collaboratively, co-constructing the same topical agenda, or are they pursuing diverging or even conflicting agendas, which for the political news or current affairs interview might well be the expected orientation? What are the strategies used to do the latter and yet remain within the limits of the genre?

Finally, the analysis based on mode has to reconstruct, on the one hand, a genre's typical relations of lexical, syntactic and pragmatic cohesion, as well as those of semantic and topical coherence, not only on the level of what is explicitly expressed but also on the level of what is presupposed and implicated (cf. Levinson 1979 and above). What comes under scrutiny here on the other hand is how language and other semiotic modalities (speech, writing, print, gesture, kinesics, image, music, sound, etc.) are used in a genre. This is of course relevant for all types of mediated discourse in newspapers, magazines, television, film, advertising and so on. The visual component plays an important role in constructing the meanings of television, and political discourse is no exception to this.[1] For some genres of mediated political discourse, the power of images and the effects of audio-visuality can hardly be overestimated (cf. Mackay's chapter on multimodal ads, this volume).

3.   The BBC Election Night 1997: Data and method

The text on which the analyses in this chapter are based is the BBC 1 transmission of the results of the 1997 UK parliamentary elections, beginning at 9.55 pm on May 1st, 1997 and ending at around 6 am on May 2nd.[2] This clearly delimited macro-text of eight hours duration can be taken as the instantiation of a macro-genre which consists of a complex, ordered assembly of interlocking genres. This macro-genre exhibits the characteristics of "external" and "internal" generic structure (as described in Section 2) in a particularly striking manner. Its structure depends as much on the external social and political context in which the event is situated as it does on internal logics of communication and of information economy. The external structure of the broadcast is due first of all to the election system used. It makes a difference if a country has a system of proportional representation where results become relatively quickly known, as in Germany, or if it has a personalized majority rule system as in the UK. In the UK general election of 1997, the votes in 624 constituencies in England, Scotland and Wales had to be counted separately, each constituency sending their own Member of Parliament to Westminster. In fact, the last result came in shortly before 6 am the following morning and the broadcast ended shortly after that. The beginning of the broadcast five minutes before the polling stations closed at 10 pm on election day was likewise determined by the external context. Thus the specific configuration of the external context in terms of the election system in use, the organization of the processes of voting and of counting the ballots, as well as the attendant political and organizational personnel distributed over a large number of locations determine programming and duration of the broadcast, the number of media participants involved, the number of results presented and of live two-way interactions done between studio and constituencies or other locations ("live two-ways"), of how many political interviews are conducted and political speeches held.

Following Hasan (1985a–c) as discussed in Section 2, the internal structure of the broadcast depends on the generic semantic, structural and textural potentials provided by the contextual configuration described. Thus the UK general election of 1997 provides the "field" or "generic semantic potential" of the text. This will comprise that the election was won in a landslide victory by the Labour Party under Tony Blair and after 18 years of conservative rule (first under Margaret Thatcher, then John Major), that the third major party in the UK, the Liberals, played a minor role, how the parties have conducted their election campaigns, what their main policy statements were, what the future cabinet will look like, and so on.

The "tenor" or "generic structural potential" is determined by the multiple participants involved in constructing this macro-text according to their participant roles and goals. There are five constitutive participant groups: the election officials who announce the results; the British electorate whose votes have provided them; the politicians, political managers and functionaries who campaigned for them; the media corporation BBC with its many journalists, political and statistical experts which presents the broadcast; and last but not least the mass audience which watches it. The BBC had correspondents and camera teams in the constituencies of the three main party leaders, in those of the cabinet members of the Conservative Party and of the possible Labour shadow cabinet candidates, as well as in a great number of other seats, either "marginals", where the outcome was uncertain, or in seats which were particularly interesting for other reasons.

As to "mode", or textural potential, extensive planning, expenditure and preparation were required to ensure that this night-long spectacle, with its great number of participants, its modal character of liveness and of emerging news, and not least with the complexities of its sophisticated electronic studio (cf. Schieß 2007) and a large number of camera teams on location, would come across to the audience as an ordered, comprehensible and entertaining whole. Thus, the massive human, technological and economical resources of the BBC provided a large part of the "generic textural potential" of the night. It was up to the presenter David Dimbleby and his backstage crew to draw on this potential in the most efficient manner possible (cf. Lauerbach 2007).

Still following Hasan, the "internal" generic structure of the election night broadcast is constructed by participants' selections from the semantic (field), structural (tenor) and textural (mode) potentials provided by the particular contextual figuration of the genre. The participants are constrained in this by the rights and obligations of their social and interactional roles with respect to the kinds of genres and generic sequences they can generate. They are however also constrained by a much more general logic of cohesion and coherence inherent to the semiotic systems used. In this respect, election night broadcasts are like news bulletins (cf. Montgomery 2007, 38–41). They differ from those however in a number of ways: they are not only live but also largely unscripted, the news they report emerges throughout the night, and the background knowledge shared by the participants increases throughout the night. As a consequence of the latter, processes of news development and reporting that normally evolve over the space of several days or weeks (like quoting from previous news and news sources and from the reactions thereto) are observable within the course of one night (cf. Lauerbach 2006). The information economy mentioned above will of course also be affected by this dynamic, and it is an interesting question to study just how this works.

Like any other genre, macro-genres exhibit what in conversation analysis is called global and local structure, generated by global and local management systems. Turn-taking for instance is a local, turn-by-turn management system (Sacks, Schegloff and Jefferson 1974), while openings, closings and topic changes are organized by global management systems (Schegloff 1972; Schegloff and Sacks 1973; cf. also Levinson 1983 for an overview). In our case, the BBC started its broadcast at 9.55 pm. The first five minutes were used by the presenter David Dimbleby to introduce the program and to predict, on the basis of the opinion polls, "a very, very exciting political night". He stressed the presence of BBC journalists at places all over the country, introduced the studio interviewer and the statistics presenter, both of whom delivered a taste of things to come. The presenter then introduced the studio with its large, multi-functional monitor wall, its computer section and experts and the central presenter's table with the BBC's political editor and a political expert from Essex University. In a live two-way to a helicopter flying over the Midlands, Dimbleby talked to the BBC's "roving reporter" who characterized himself as the man for "the sort of a low-brow, down-at-heel counterpoint to your intellectual analysis in the studio". In two further live two-ways Dimbleby asked correspondents for reports from Blair's and Major's constituencies. Then, at 10 pm exactly, he announced the result of the exit poll: "There it is, ten o'clock and we say Tony Blair is to be Prime Minister and a landslide is likely". This announcement marks the end of the well-planned opening section and jumps into the middle section of the broadcast with a splash.[3] The middle section itself, of almost exactly 8 hours' duration, ends with a final summary of the results and with images from Labour's celebration at the Royal Festival Hall in London. The closing section is brief. The presenter announces "the end of a most dramatic night in British politics which has seen the virtual wipe-out of the Tory party in Britain".

With eight hours' video-recording available, it was clear that not all of this material could be transcribed. The project's design rested on the decision that the basic unit of analysis should be based on a heuristic notion of genre and that a start should be made with interviews. Under the guidance of the author, graduate students and a number of research assistants[4] viewed the tapes in teams of two or three with the aim of producing a "macro-transcript". The "macro" was supposed to represent the presenter's interventions and the sequence of genres throughout the broadcast. How to recognize then where a genre starts and ends? This was fairly easy: whenever the presenter makes a transition to something else, which usually involved a change of topic, of participants and/or setting and/or modality and/or direct/indirect audience address. This hands-on method worked in most cases. What sometimes proved to be more difficult was to recognize what it was that was being done in generic terms. For example, the category interview branched into sub-genres of political, expert and vox pop interview, that of speeches into victory/acceptance and concession speech and other sub-types. There were various sub-types of reports, analysis, comment and of presenting election results. Some genres were clearly demarcated and defined, others more fuzzy, some reflected a coherent order, others did not. If no label could be found, a description of what was happening was supplied. On the basis of this macro-transcript, detailed transcriptions of types of genres (interviews, reports, live two-way reports and interviews, speeches, etc.) were done. In all cases, the visual and the verbal channel were transcribed in parallel according to the transcription conventions shown in Appendix 1. The macro-transcript however proved to be invaluable for providing an overview of the genres of the text and it also supplied ample evidence of different types of generic chaining.

As mentioned above, there are genres that election nights share with other news genres (reports, analysis, comment, interviews), and others which are specific to election nights (live two-way reports from constituencies, reports of results, declarations, computer-supported interpretation of results, acceptance and concession speeches, and others). Other types of genres are specific to the liveness of the program (like studio talk while waiting for breaking news, self-reflexive reports and comments), yet others are owed to the fact that election nights are macro-texts of long duration (like re-caps and summaries). The genres selected for closer analysis in this section are those considered most typical for the macro-genre of election night broadcast as realized by the BBC on election night 1997. They are typical in that they are not shared with other macro-genres like news bulletins and current affairs magazines; in that they capture the qualities of liveness and those of the long duration of the broadcast, during which an increasing store of shared knowledge is built between the participants, e.g. the journalists, the experts, the politicians and the audience. They are also typical in that they reflect the quality of the spatial diversity of the broadcast through the frequent interactions between studio and outside locations. Also, they are genres that have so far not been studied within the framework of the election night project.[5]

In what follows, the focus will be on election night reports in various sub-generic variants and in particular generic configurations or genre chains: reports from outside locations like constituencies, reports on exit poll results, reports on "real" results, reports of live transmissions of the official declaration of results at constituency level. Nor have we yet looked at the ways in which the results are interpreted and commented on by presenter and experts. Another genre studied is the kind of live studio talk that is done in so-called "running-up sequences", while e.g. the declaration of a particular result is awaited, and then the official declaration of a particular constituency's result. This new focus shifts the attention from the discourse of politicians in interviews or speeches to that of election officials and journalists, from political to journalistic discourse. Also, reports and interpretation of election results rely heavily on audiovisual support, so that audio-visual analysis will be an important and necessary feature of the analyses presented below. The same holds for the feature of liveness of the broadcast, which gives rise to specific manifestations both on the level of genre sequencing and of generic profile. Also, the data exhibits various types of genre chains, syntagmatic chains, as well as simple paradigmatic ones. The genres studied are presented in a loosely chronological order rather than a systematic one, in the hope that this may create a feeling for the way this macro-text evolves.

4. Reports

Reports are a journalistic news genre and as such subject to news standards which have evolved in the print news. They have to answer to the "five w's and one h": what happened where and when, who was involved, how did it happen, and why –

and in this order, so that texts can be cut easily from the end by the editor (cf. Bell 1991). Whatever journalists report has to be recent, newsworthy and relevant to their addressees, and it has to be attributed or attributable to reliable sources. Also, news reports are not normally about what is going to happen. Quite a few of the reports in election nights are, however, an exception to these requirements.

4.1   Early down-the-line reports: "Soft" news

Down-the-line reports or live two-ways in the data are reports by outside correspondents and reporters. The journalists, accompanied by a camera team, are as a rule located in key constituencies or counts and are called on by the presenter in the studio to set the scene and mood early in the night while still waiting for the news to develop, in this case for the exit poll results. There are two brief such reports from the constituencies of Tony Blair and John Major at the beginning of the program, cf. excerpt 1:[6]

Excerpt 1. Setting the scene

00:04:04 shot1	LS of David Dimbleby in the studio, seated at desk, camera zooms on Dimbleby	DAVID DIMBLEBY <DD>: We'll be back with him later on. And two battle hardened correspondents back at the frontline tonight, John Simpson in Sedgefield with
00:04:10 shot 2	LS of David Dimbleby, at table front left; behind him large video wall displaying election logo, changing to split screen with live shots of John Simpson in (heading TOS:) Sedgefield (l) and Kate Adie in (heading TOS:) Huntingdon (r); then Simpson takes up entire video wall; Dimbleby looking at table monitor in front of him, then turning towards video wall	Tony Blair, and Kate Adie with John Major at Huntingdon. John! JOHN SIMPSON <JS>: Well this is Newton Aycliffe Sport
00:04:17 shot 3	MS of John Simpson, BG sports centre with flags saying "Sedgefield"	Centre, which is at the heart of Tony Blair's constituency and uh indeed behind me (.) there is a definite air of excitement. People are expecting (.) the/ the vote for (.) possibly the next Prime Minister is about to be counted any moment, and there could be a turnout of eighty-two percent.

00:04:33 shot 4	DD in front of video wall, JS and KA split screen; then KA alone; DD looking at video wall	DD: And Kate Adie. KATE ADIE <KA>: Well here in Huntingdonshire
00:04:37 shot 5	MS of Kate Adie against bank of flowers framing stage: heading "*B B C* Huntingdon"	the Conservatives are at least=er **happily** confident of re-electing John Major, it is (.) [studio sound intruding: *Big Ben starts striking ten o'clock*] one of the safer seats in the country. But on the wider s:/ scene, we're gonna have to wait about (.) five hours until we hear from the Prime Minister himself.

The requirements for news discourse to refer to reliable sources are obviously relaxed for this type of "soft news"-report. When John Simpson, in shots 2 and 3, testifies to "a definite air of excitement" behind him at Tony Blair's count, the audience may look to the visual channel for confirmation of this statement. All they will see, however, is long empty tables awaiting the ballots to be counted "any moment", and a few people standing about in the space of an otherwise empty gym. So they just have to believe the journalist's judgment. And when he predicts a possible high turnout of 82% in Tony Blair's constituency, presumably someone has told him. Yet he presents this as his own discourse, assuming the footing not only of animator and author, but also of the principal of this information (Goffman 1981). The source discourse of the information thus remains implicit or "unsignalled" (Fairclough 1988), which leads to vagueness with respect to principalship. The same applies to Kate Adie in shot 5 when she refers to the conservatives in John Major's constituency being "happily confident" of re-electing him. There are no visual cues at all to this as she is filmed standing in front of a bank of flowers framing a stage, and no mention is made verbally as to how the speaker came by this evaluation. However, when she reminds the audience that Major's seat "is one of the safer seats in the country", common knowledge also plays a role. In this excerpt, the journalists seem to be their own sources by virtue of their profession and of being eyewitnesses at the places they are reporting on. What also plays a role, no doubt, is that what is being reported is of no great political import. It emphasizes tenor rather than field, "soft news" with a focus on interpersonal expectations and attitudes rather than "hard news" about "real" politics. While what is being reported is being expected to be true, the requirement for producing the evidence does not have to be observed.

This is also the case in many early down-the line reports from constituencies with "interesting" campaign histories. An example is a cluster of four starting at 40 minutes into the night, touching on the doubtful reputation of a Conservative candidate being challenged by a journalist Labour candidate (Tatton), on a self-disclosed homosexual Labour candidate fighting a staunchly anti-gay Conservative candidate (Exeter), on two millionaires fighting it out in Putney, and on quoting the Tory candidate of a strong Tory seat with "The Tories could put a donkey up here and it would still win" (Reigate). These highly personalized reports do not provide any new information. They re-present old news of the campaign and re-activate shared knowledge. By grouping these reports together in a battery of human interest items, their gossipy entertainment character is emphasized. Although the journalists are located at the constituencies they describe, as exhibited on the visual channel by name and location captions at the bottom of the screen, the information they convey does not really depend on their presence at these places. This is the BBC blatantly doing entertainment and titillation, with the implicit promise of providing the sequels to these stories later in the night.

Are such reports still political discourse? Well, politicians are human, and gossip and scandal seem to be taking up a sizeable portion of talk about politics in the media nowadays. Sometimes, also, there are "real" political consequences – people lose their seats (like Neil Hamilton in Tatton), they have to resign from office, they get thrown out of their parties in order to avoid further damage, and so on.

Structurally, these four reports occur in a cluster of identical genres which are loosely held together by being human interest items with a touch of the scandalous. Their sequential order might just as well be otherwise. This is a **paradigmatic genre chain**. Matters are more complicated with the two setting-the-scene reports. While they also form a chain of identical genres with identical topics, the sequence is still ordered, though in an unexpected way. It is striking that the constituency of John Major, who is after all the Prime Minister, is not placed in first position. The fact that the first report of the night comes not from the incumbent's seat but from that of his challenger Tony Blair reverses the expected order based on status and replaces it by one of expected winner over expected loser. The communicative benefit of this is that, by violating conversational expectations, the BBC can give a hint as to the winner (via Gricean inference). For of course they know which way the exit polls are going, but they are not allowed to say before the polls close. Structurally, the fact that there is hierarchy in play here makes this a **syntagmatic chain**.

4.2   Reporting the exit poll result: Hard news

The first real news report of the night comes from the presenter himself when at exactly 10 pm, after the polls have closed, he announces the exit poll results. His field are the results of the exit polls, tenor is presenter to audience, mode is audiovisual, presenter speaking to camera. His announcement is extremely important, the results of the exit polls are the first indication of the way the election is going, and they are sensational. Great care is called for in their presentation. The announcement is virtually packed with source references, both in the verbal and in the visual channel. There are many voices in play here: that of the presenter, who gives the results, that of the National Opinion Polling organization providing them, that of the BBC's institutional voice as well as that of its political, technical and graphics staff responsible for the way the information is presented visually. One of the interesting questions of this genre is the relation between the verbal and the visual channel and the footings adopted in each (Goffman 1981).

Excerpt 2. Reporting the exit poll result

00:04:50	David Dimbleby in front of video wall with LS of Big Ben taking up 2/3 of video wall, two smaller images to the (r), one on top of the other; zoom-in on Big Ben's clock, reading 10 o'clock	DD: Thanks, Kate. And as Big Ben strikes ten, the polls close, we can give you the results of our exit poll, we've spoken to (.) fourteen thousand people in two hundred constituencies tonight, and er we hope they've been telling us the truth.(2.0) [*a loud strike of Big Ben*] There it is,
shot 1	picture of Big Ben changes to a graphic, set in red: a photo of Tony Blair (CU); a red rose (turning); URC election '97 logo; video wall heading: "BBC/NOP Exit Poll – Forecast"; text at bottom: "BLAIR TO BE PRIME MINISTER"; "LANDSLIDE LIKELY"	(*to camera* (ten o'clock and we say (.)) Tony Blair is to be Prime Minister
00:05:07 shot 2	red graphic takes up entire TV screen	and a **landslide** [*two more strikes*]) (.5) is likely.) And reactions
00:05:11	David Dimbleby in front of video wall as before; small image LRC bears video wall heading: "*B B C* Sedgefield" and shows people applauding; image on TOS (r) shows large room titled "BBC Conservatives"; Dimbleby looking at video wall	from Sedgefield already, down there on the right in the Labour club, (.5) (all applauding there, Conservative Party headquarters,
shot 3		
00:05:18 shot 4	back to full view of red graphic Tony Blair	rather more sombre scenes [*applause audible in the BG*]). (.5) So, here are the details,

| 00:05:22 | graphic against red BG; video wall heading: "BBC/NOP Exit Poll" *"Share of the Vote"*; graphic reads: Lab 47% <red bar>, Con 29% <blue bar>, LibDem 18% <yellow bar>, Others 6% <grey bar>; bars vertical; at BOS: "Margin of Error +/−2%" | Tony Blair will be Prime Minister and this (.) is (.) why. Labour, forty-seven percent. The Conservatives, twenty-nine percent, according to our exit poll. That would be the worst result not just this century but if you care to go back that far (.) to the Tory vote after the Great Reform Act in nineteen thirty-two where they were led by the Duke of Wellington. The Liberal Democrats on eighteen percent, pretty much what they did at the last election, |
| shot 5 | | others, on six. (2.5) |

As the presenter begins to speak, we see him, in shot 1, sitting at his desk in left foreground of the large video wall, with an image of Big Ben taking up most of its space. He opens with remarks on the reliability of the BBC's exit poll. While the camera zooms to the clock reading 10 and we can hear Big Ben striking ten o'clock, the presenter looks into the camera and says: "And as Big Ben strikes ten, the polls close, we can give you the results of our exit poll". This sounds as if the BBC had their own polling organization or as if BBC staff had done the polling. The data come however from GfK NOP, who describe themselves on their website as "a leading market research and consumer insight agency" (www.gfk.com). No doubt the BBC commissioned the poll and paid a substantial sum for it. This may account for the presenter's proprietory mode.[7] Then comes his announcement to camera in an almost perfect explicit performative formulation: "Ten o'clock and we say (.) Tony Blair is to be Prime Minister and a landslide is likely". The visuals behind him, meanwhile, are changing to a large head-and-shoulders image of Blair, with the heading "BBC/NOP Exit Poll – Forecast", and at the bottom of the screen two captions say: "BLAIR TO BE PRIME MINISTER" and "LANDSLIDE LIKELY". The relation between the information given in the visual and the auditory channel is one of correspondence.

It is clear that Dimbleby is the animator of this announcement in shot 1, but who is the author, and who is the principal of it? The question is easier to answer if we first look at the visual text, that is, the verbal text visually presented in the shot that accompanies the presenter's statement. In the heading of the visuals, the BBC and NOP are cited as joint source, i.e. as principals of the results of exit poll. This clarifies visually the presenter's auditory reference to "our exit poll" at the beginning of the shot. However, it is the BBC alone, as the media company which has control over what is broadcast and how things go on air, which animates and has, as author, formulated the visual text. A similar mix of principal, author and animator holds for the verbal text: BBC/NOP as principals are responsible for the facts of the poll, the BBC's political editor for the authorship of the formulation and the presenter for animating the words. So the institutional "we" of the presenter's announcement ("we say …") is heard as the voice of the BBC (and not of the NOP as well), especially as the presenter speaks directly to camera. The relations are shown in (1).

(1)   Production format: Reporting the exit poll results

Visual discourse		Verbal discourse	
principal	NOP/BBC	principal	NOP/BBC
author	BBC	author	BBC
animator	BBC	animator	presenter

What is the relation between the BBC's two institutional voices, the verbal and the visual? Is the one quoting the other, as if the presenter were reading off the screen? No, he is speaking to camera, and the visual text is shown behind him. What the audience is presented with is the two voices of the BBC in parallel – the audio-visual one of the presenter speaking to camera and the visual one on the screen behind him. In fact, where there are two voices in play, new meanings can arise inferentially from the type of relation between them (cf. Meinhof 1984; Holly 2006; Lauerbach 2010). Here, the two voices are not just in parallel, they are also in almost exact informational overlap. This is not the rule in news genres, where the gap between the verbal information transmitted on the auditory channel and the images provided by the visual one have often been criticized as producing a "scissor effect" which can impair comprehension and recall (Wember 1976). The surplus meaning which should arise from the two channels working in overlap is one of mutual reinforcement – an effect aimed for in all kinds of verbal/visual didactic and presentational discourse.

In shot 3, the presenter then turns to the video wall and briefly comments on reactions to the exit poll news in two locations visible there: applause in the Sedgefield Labour Club, which everywhere by now knows is in Tony Blair's constituency, more somber scenes in the headquarters of the Conservative Party. This piece of talk is a typical presenter's sub-genre in which presenters not only "anchor" (Barthes 1977) what is shown in the images in its context, naming persons, place and/or time in the first part. As we can see in shots 3 and 4, the presenter also goes on to provide descriptions of what the people shown are doing or what they look like. After establishing reference through the verbal channel, something can then be said about them. This information may be self-evident, because everyone can see what is going on, or it may be necessary for audience comprehension. In our case, the verbal information is helpful as the images on the video wall are very small. It is important to realize that this kind of interaction between visual and verbal channel in television news is no different from deictic communication in the real world. Presenter and audience share a visual context just as communicators do in a face-to-face situation. There as well, if you want to talk about something visible in the context, you have to identify it before you can talk about it: "See this dog there? Well, it's mine." The difference is that it is one-way communication, so the audience cannot ask questions ("Which dog? There are two."). It follows that the presenter has to take special care in establishing reference. How he does this is up to him. He does not merely animate someone else's words, he is also the author who has decided what to say and how to say it, as well as principal in the sense of the one whose position is expressed.

In the second part of the report, the presenter delivers the details of the poll, which are shown full screen as "share of the vote" in a bar graph in shot 5. What is different here from the first part of the report is that he now goes beyond what is shown on the screen. Onscreen, we see the figures per party, above them the reference to the BBC/NOP exit poll as source and below them the margin of error of this poll as +/–2%. The presenter not only gives each party's share of the vote as it is presented visually, he also provides brief comments: Blair will be Prime Minister due to Labour's percentage. The Conservative's is the worst result since 1932 (there is a slip of the tongue here, it should be 1832), and the Liberals have stayed more or less the same. The presenter's voice thus supplements the information given by the authorial voice of the BBC in the visuals by providing further details regarding consequences, historical context, evaluation of what is shown visually. What we have here is a change in the presenter's footing: in reading the figures, he is mere animator, the BBC is author and BBC/NOP are principals. In commenting on the figures, the presenter becomes also author. And with his footing change from mere reporter to one who assesses what has been reported, the genre changes from report to comment. Thus it is only in his first dramatic announcement that he is unambiguously mere animator. This is probably due to the fact that his opening statement was obviously scripted, or at least well prepared and rehearsed. As the broadcast goes on, the presenter becomes more and more the author of his words.

The structural analysis of the discourse in excerpt (2) yields a complex chain of syntagmatic and paradigmatic genre relations, as shown in (2):

(2)   Generic chain structure of excerpt 2: report of the exit polls results
1.   opening
2.   report (claim)
     a.   announcement: Blair to be the winner, landslide likely (claim)
     b.   comment: reactions Labour, Conservatives
3.   report (evidence)
     3.1. number of votes for Labour

3.2. a. number of votes for the Conservatives
      b. comment (evaluation)
3.3. a. number of votes for the Liberal Democrats
      b. comment (comparison)
3.4. number of votes for other parties

The sequential order of the genres in (2) is tightly bound to the events happening outside the studio, which are transformed into a live audiovisual broadcast text. The sequence mirrors the order in which those events have happened. That people have been voting all day, have been interviewed as to how they had voted as they came out of the voting booths – all this is not news, and it serves as a preamble in the presenter's opening. The news is what the exit poll says, so the report starts with the end of a long chain of events, the results of the exit poll. It consists of two major parts, the first announcing that Tony Blair will be Prime Minister, the second supplying the details.

The relation between parts (2) and (3) follows from Grice's (1975) maxim of quality, part two: "Do not say that for which you lack adequate evidence" (Grice 1975; for a brief survey, cf. Yule 1996, 36ff.). In everyday talk, we assume that people generally adhere to this norm and could produce the evidence for their claims **if challenged**. In other genres, this has to be modified, so that it is obligatory to exhibit the evidence for the truth-claims made right away and without challenge. They range from general discourse genres such as argument to institutional genres like hard news reports. The relation between reports (2) and (3) is like the structure of argumentation – a claim is made in the first part, and the evidence for it supplied in the second. It is the requirement of producing the evidence for the claim made in part (2) that produces a syntagmatic relation between (2) and (3).

The internal order of the sub-genres (a, b) in part (2), is likewise syntagmatic. Their order follows a natural order of things – you cannot react to something before it has happened, and you cannot comment on reactions before they occur. And even the two comments on the reactions of Labour and Conservative supporters in (2) are ordered – as to status: winners before losers. Likewise in the structure within which the evidence is supplied in part (3), reports 1 to 4 are ordered according to status and size of parties, their internal structure (a, b) is hierarchically ordered according to something like "you can't comment on something before you know what it is".

What is not shown in Fig. (2) are the presenter's discourse organizers "so here are the details" and "this is why". If presenting is also a genre (and why should it not be?), then such organizers would be one of its central discourse practices, together with reading news items, talking over and about images, introducing participants in and outside of the studio, organizing turn-taking in studio talk, and so on.

4.3   Interpreting the exit poll results: Interacting with computer animated graphics

After the presenter's announcement of the exit poll results, there is another report on the poll by the BBC's statistics analyst, Peter Snow. It was preceded by an interview between David Dimbleby and John Prescott, the Labour Deputy Leader. This interview was interrupted after two brief exchanges by Dimbleby for "the full details of our exit poll from Peter". In his report, the analyst repeats and comments on the results and then embarks on a series of "what would happen if" – projections to illustrate – on his legendary "swingometer" – the effect of various swings in the vote on the number of seats for Labour.[8]

Following again Hasan's (1985a–c) model for analyzing genre, the field of the analyst's text is provided by the results of the 1997 parliamentary elections in the UK, as broadcast in BBC's election night special. The analyst's topics are the results of the exit poll, the changes on the last election, the swing in the vote to Labour and what that means for the constitution of the new parliament. His goal is to present these topics clearly and in a way comprehensible to his audience. Part of this is to clarify the source of the poll results. What is also important for this genre is that exit polls are not real results. They just show how people responded when asked how they had voted as they were leaving the polling station. Exit polls can be wrong and they have been wrong in the past. So a further goal of the analyst must be to leave the audience in no doubt about this. His report is not the first one of the night on the exit poll results as the presenter has announced these already, but it is the first one on converting the results into wins and losses and into possible Labour majorities.

In terms of tenor, the analyst is neither the "principal" of the poll results – the person or institution who takes responsibility for them in Goffman's (1981) sense – nor is he the "author" of how they are formulated. In fact, he is mere "animator" of the figures provided by the polling agency. Also, the analyst is embedded into a configuration of role-specific interaction obligations. He has to take over the floor from the presenter, and return it to him when he has finished. He has to interact with the audience, who is his primary addressee. These are constraints that his genre shares with many other television genres. The third requirement, which is genre-specific and makes his genre an essentially audio-visual one, over and above being on television, is that he also has to interact with the animated visuals of the swingometer shown on the video wall in order to explain their contents to the audience. Each time he changes his addressee or target of his gaze between visuals and camera, he changes his footing in Goffman's sense.

In terms of mode, the analyst has various semiotic systems at his disposal for fulfilling these genre-specific constraints: language, para-verbal means like e.g.

chuckling, and non-verbal means like gaze, facial expression, gesture, and kine-sics. How does the analyst realize these resources? How can this be shown in an integrated transcript?

Excerpt 3. Interpreting the exit poll results

6:24	LS of Peter Snow in front of framed section of video wall. Wall shows BBC election logo, which dissolves into map of the UK with bar graph across bottom, heading TOS: :BBC/NOP EXIT POLL – SHARE: Lab 47% \<red bar> Con 29% \<blue bar> LibDem 18% \<yellow bar> Others 6% \<grey bar> BOS: BBC/NOP Sample Size 10,400 Margin of Error: +/–2%	Peter Snow. PS: (*keeps looking back and forth between cam. and video wall throughout unless indicated otherwise*) ((*arms folded*)) Well, I mean David, John Prescott is of course **absolutely** right, this is just an exit poll, but **my goodness!** It has to be terribly wrong for the Tories to win this election. **Forty** (.)-**seven** (.) percent (.) the Labour share of the vote if our exit poll is anywhere near right. The best since nineteen sixty-six. **Twenty**(.)-**nine** percent for the Conservatives, as **you** said,
shot 1		
6:44 shot 2	zoom to close-up of bar graph	we've never had anything like that since **eigh**teen thirty-two when the Duke of Wellington led his party to defeat then. In/ eighteen percent for the Liberal Democrats and six percent for the others). **Also** incidentally, the (eighteen percent **lead** by Labour over the Conservatives ((*r*) *arm points from the Labour block in the diagram to the Conservative block*)), bigger **even** than the record (.) lead that (Clement Attlee ((*r*) *hand briefly points in direction of Labour block*)) had over Winston Churchill in nineteen forty-five.
shot 3	bar graph changes to Lab +12% \<red bar> Con –14% \<blue bar> LibDem +0% \<yellow bar> Others +1 \<grey bar> BOS: BBC/NOP Sample Size 10,400 Margin of Error: +/–2%	Now the changes that would represent on the last general election, here they go! (Labour up twelve percent on last time ((*r*) *arm points at Labour bar and moves upwards*)), (the Tories down fourteen percent ((*r*) *arm points at Cons. bar, moving down*)), (no change for the Liberal Democrats ((*r*) *hand points at the LibDem percentage points*)), (and one percent up for the others. = You expect that, lots of other people contesting

7:16 shot 4	map of the UK and bar graph disappear, swingometer moves into view (= section of large, scales-like disk, outer edge bears numbers: 10 to 0 from left to centre against red background, 0 to 10 from centre to right against blue background; blue and red lines going from outer edge to centre represent Tory (left) and Labour seats (right). Needle points to zero) - - - - - - - - - - - - - - - -	this time ((r) hand points at the others' percentage points)) like the Referendum Party. Now let's bring down our swingometer and see what all that (.) means. (1.0) Here it comes, **now**, (these are all the vulnerable **red** Labour MPs, vulnerable to a Tory swing, needn't worry about them (dismissive gesture with (r) arm)) I don't think, (these are the **blue** Conservative MPs (walks over to blue section of swingometer, (r) hand moves across it)) (vulnerable to each point of swing to Labour ((r) hand quickly points at the numbers 1-2-3. What (.)
shot 5	zoom to section of disk , disk tilts back, rim moves into view, showing below 0: Con Maj 27 below 2: Hung Parl below 3: Con Maj 100	would happen if there were no swing at all? (There'd be a Conservative majority we estimate on the new boundaries
7:38 shot 6	needle moves to (l), pointing to: 4: Lab Maj 1 and 6: Lab Maj 50 - - - - - - - - - - - - - -	of something like twenty-seven ((r) hand points at centre of rim labelled "Con Maj 27," underneath 0)). (Now, these are the **blue** Conservative Mps who turn to **red** seats for Labour ((r) hand points at the disk, then to the (l), as needle starts moving to the (l)) (for a swing of four and a half percent ((r) hand indicates the 4.5% section of the swingometer)), something like fifty-five of them would go red (and that would be Mister Blair [back] ((r) hand points at label "Lab Maj 1")) with a bare majority. But the swing our (**exit poll** (adds emphasis with (r) arm)) is suggesting, just watch this:
shot 7	Needle moves further to the (l): 10 Lab Maj 100 13 14 Lab Maj 200 come into view	((l) shoulder towards cam, he is looking at the (l) side of the swingometer, faces cam. only briefly)) on it goes, **look** at those blue seats turning red, they go **on** and **on** and **on**, more than a hundred of them, until you get to **thirteen** percent. (Now that

8:04 shot 8	zoom on 10–14 section of swing-ometer	swing, if it was precisely accurate (*(r) hand points at "13"*), *(to camera till end of shot)* (**uniform** all over the country (*large, sweeping gesture with (r) arm*)), would see (Labour [win with] a majority of very nearly two hundred (*(r) hand moves down from "13" to "Lab Maj 200"*). *(to camera)* But just take the bound of error, don't forget these exit polls can be (two percent out in either direction (*quickly moves (r) arm back and forth*)), they can be even more than that when they're (very wrong (*chuckles*)), but if they're two percent out of the marginal error,
shot 9	needle moves from 13 back to 11, the area between 13 and 11 is shaded white	(then at the **bottom** end of our swing, (.) it's **eleven** percent to Labour (*(r) arm moves from "13" to "11"*). (But look, (.) Labour with a
8:23 shot 10	zoom on section 13–11	majority of **more** than a hundred with an eleven percent swing (*(r) arm points down at "Lab Maj 100"*).
shot 11	needle moves past 12, 13, 14, to 15, area it passes is shaded white	(**If** the swing was at the **top end** of our bound of error (*(r) arm points to the (l) section of the swingometer, following the needle*)), (at **fifteen** percent, then Labour would be in with a majority of over two hundred (*walks over to the (l), (r) arm points at "Lab Maj 200"*). It'd be something (.) quite **unique** for the Labour Party and a **record** (.) certainly since nineteen forty-five. (.5) (*takes a few steps back, so that the centre of the swingometer is fully visible*)
shot 12	needle moves back to 13	*(to camera till end of shot)* There we are then, (a **thirteen** percent swing, and it's even **worse** than that for the Tories if our exit poll is anywhere near (*(r) arm points in direction of "13"*)) right because we are getting messages from the (.) **detail** of the poll, that there was a lot of (**tactical** voting going on, that the **Liberal** Democrats may do **better** (*adds emphasis to stressed words with clenched fist*)) than the national swing in the seats **they're** chasing, (and also the **Tories** are doing **badly** in their own seats (*quickly moves (r) arm, fist clenched, up and down*)). David

The analyst interacts with the written information and the images shown on the video wall. These visuals are described in the middle column of the transcript. His interaction with the visuals is expressed verbally and non-verbally. His verbal text is shown in the right column of the transcript, with emphatic word stress printed in bold. His non-verbal interaction with the visuals is expressed through a series of extra-linguistic means like gestures of pointing, of explanation and of emphasis, and by kinesics when he moves about in front of the swingometer. He also keeps looking back and forth between camera and video wall, that is, he also interacts by gaze with the visuals, with the (for the audience) invisible presenter in the opening and closing phases, and with the visuals and the audience in the middle part. Some longer passages however are delivered straight to camera throughout. All of the non-verbal expressions go hand in hand with the expert's verbal text. In the transcript, they are integrated into the verbal text, marked off by brackets where they begin and end relative to the words, and by descriptions printed in italics. Visually, there are twelve shots in all. Not all of the shots are separated by cuts, sometimes the previous image dissolves into the next. This is indicated by half a line in the visual column and by a dotted line in the verbal one. The number of shot is shown in the left column, which also notes the time.

Let us take shots 1 and 2 first. In accepting the floor by saying "David" the expert opens his report and then establishes continuity by indirectly quoting John Prescott with something he said in his interview immediately before ("it's just an exit poll"). In doing this, he has changed footing from being principal, author and animator in "David" to being mere animator of John Prescott's words, Prescott being principal and author. By continuing with, "but, my goodness, it has to be terribly wrong for the Tories to win this election", he swiftly returns to the principal/author/animator footing. What he has also done is acknowledge the element of uncertainty and conditionality adhering to exit poll results in general and at the same time establishing that this exit poll is somehow special in being more certain than others.

This enables him to do two contradictory things. He announces the share of the vote for the parties with a note of caution – "if our exit poll is anywhere near right" – and then goes on to comment on the Labour and Tory figures with very emphatic and highly up-graded remarks just how exceptional the Labour results are. Some of these are phrased in moodless clauses, which may suggest factuality. These statements engage dramatic historical comparisons to put into perspective not only Labour's win and their lead over the Tories, but also the Conservatives' loss: "47% the Labour share of the vote – the best since nineteen sixty-six" (shot 1); "29% for the Conservatives ... – we've never had anything like it since eighteen thirty-two when the Duke of Wellington led his party to defeat then"; "the 18% lead by Labour over the Conservatives – bigger even than the record lead Clement Atlee had over Winston Churchill in nineteen forty-five". As in the presenter's report before in Section 4.1, this series of figures-plus-comment statements entails constant changes of footing between animator of the figures which Snow reads after a quick glance at the video frame, and author and animator of the comments. It is even more complicated, since for the Duke of Wellington comment he briefly addresses David Dimbleby and quotes him from his previous announcement, slipping in a repair of the latter's slip of the tongue (from "1932" to "1832").

What seems strange at first glance is that in shots 1 and 2 the analyst does not refer to the source of the figures and the poll's credentials like sample size and the margin of error. But this has been done already by Dimbleby before, and it seems that Snow treats this as **old** information, not worthy of repeating. He also saves himself any pointing at the figures on the video, standing in front of the frame with folded arms. The result is that the series of up-graded evaluation statements receives full attention. Here we have an effect of information management on the form of the report, which in this instance is a contextual effect of its place in the chain of genres. When it comes to the lead of Labour over the Tories however, this is **new** information and receives a lengthy pointing gesture. The same goes for the changes on the last election in shot 3. They are again **new** information and as such accompanied by pointing gestures as each figure is read. These cases warrant a hypothesis that in reading out loud written visual information which is visible to the audience, old information does not require reinforcement by pointing gestures and other non-verbal signals, but new information does. This cannot be pursued here, however. The production format shows again, as in (1), two voices in play, the relation between the two channels is in parallel, and the additional inferential meaning is that they mutually reinforce each other.

(3)   Production format for shots 1 to 3: Interacting with visual text

Visual discourse		Verbal and non-verbal discourse	
principal	NOP/BBC	principal	NOP/BBC
author	BBC	author	BBC/analyst
animator	BBC	animator	analyst

In shots 4 to 11, the analyst interacts with the swingometer, the field is the swings in the vote and the Labour majority, the tenor is the expert's interaction with the visuals and the audience, with constant footing change between the visuals and the camera, i.e. audience address, the mode is audiovisual. The visuals show the swingometer, which is computer animated, with the expert in front of the video wall. The verbal discourse follows the computer animation. The production format is as shown in (4). The relation between the two channels is in parallel, complemented by comments from the expert, the inferential surplus meaning may be reinforcement, but could also be confusion for some recipients, due to the fast delivery.

(4)   Production format for shots 4 to 11: Interacting with computer animation

Visual discourse		Verbal and non-verbal discourse	
principal	NOP/BBC	principal	NOP/BBC and expert
author	BBC	author	analyst
animator	BBC	animator	analyst

This format allows the expert much more freedom in authoring and being responsible for his text than the previous one. The relation between the verbal/non-verbal channel and the visual one is again in parallel and the inferential surplus meaning is again mutual reinforcement.

The report ends with shot 12. The shot starts with a clear discourse marker ("there we are then"), which is followed by a clear summary ("a thirteen percent swing"). And it ends with a parting comment, again accompanied by emphasis expressed both verbally and gesturally, which introduces more complexity. This last comment is announced in the same sensationalist tone the audience knows already from the up-graded statements of the first part of the report: "But it's even worse than that for the Tories, if our exit poll is anywhere near right".

The field of shot 12 is the summary of the swing-topic, plus a qualification that things may be even more complex. The tenor is expert speaking to audience; there are no footing changes regarding the addressee. The mode is audiovisual, the visuals show the analyst standing to the side of a still of the swingometer with the needle at 13. The verbal discourse is delivered to camera in direct audience address. The production format is as in (4), the channels are partially in parallel, the surplus meaning is mutual reinforcement for the first clause in the shot. For the rest of the complicated comment on tactical voting going on, etc., there is no visual support, apart from the analyst's gestures providing emphasis at certain points.

The analysis of mode as regards how the language is used with respect to topic and the visuals throughout the text yields interesting insights. The expert's delivery is fast and lively and his style approaches the familiar variety assumed to be spoken by his audience. His text however is very professionally organized in terms of structure and comprehension signals and of deictic expressions referring to what is shown or happening on the video wall, as shown in (5).

(5)   Discourse organizers

shot 2	also
shot 3	now the changes that would represent on the last general election
shot 4	now let's bring down our swingometer
	here it comes now

these are …

needn't worry about them, I don't think

these are …

shot 5   what would happen if …

shot 6   now these are …

but the swing our exit poll is suggesting …

shot 7/8   now that swing …

shot 9   then at the bottom end of our swing

shot 11   if the swing was at the top end of our bound of error …

shot 12   there we are then

In shots 6–9, when working with the swingometer, the expert also uses a number of urgent-sounding imperatives addressed directly to the audience to direct their attention, as shown in (6).

(6)   Audience imperatives
    shot 6   just watch this!
    shot 7   look at these blue seats turning red
    shot 8   but just take the bound of error
    don't forget these exit polls can be out two percent in either direction
    shot 9   but look at Labour …

Most of these verbal discourse markers are accompanied by gestural ones: expressive gestures of pointing, of emphasis or illustration, and these in turn correspond with emphatic word stress in the verbal text. Sometimes the analyst also moves about in front of the video wall to be better able to point at something.

Also, the up-graded comments at the beginning and later in the text may address an audience need to be witness to an event of historical dimensions. They are repeated in (7).

(7)   Upgraders
    shot 1   47% the Labour share of the vote – the best since nineteen sixty-six
    shot 1+2   29% for the Conservatives … we've never had anything like it since eighteen thirty-two when the Duke of Wellington led his party to defeat then
    shot 2   the 18% lead by Labour over the Conservatives – bigger even than the record lead Clement Atlee had over Winston Churchill in nineteen forty-five
    shot 11   it'd be something quite unique for the Labour party and a record certainly since nineteen forty-five

And there is yet another element of mode that is relevant for the genre of this text, apart from verbal emphasis and gestural reinforcement, namely the grammatical one of mood and conditionality. The exit poll is mentioned frequently in the text, and mainly in conditional mode. By the formulation "if our exit poll is anywhere near right" in the first shot, which is mirrored word by word in the last, the whole text is framed as conditional on the exit poll. The conditional mode is also particularly noticeable where the swingometer comes into play. In fact, its very design is to allow conclusions of the sort shown in (8).

> (8)   The swingometer: Designed to illustrate conditionality
>   If there is an x percent swing to Labour, then Labour will gain y Tory seats.
>   If Labour gains y Tory seats, then Labour will have a majority of z seats.

Overall, in terms of mode, this text is nicely balanced between emphasis and conditionality. And if we look at tenor also in terms of what kinds of interpersonal identities and relations are constructed by these elements of mode, then what comes across in Peter Snow's performance is not just a desire to be clear and didactic for the sake of the audience, but also a strong interpersonal motivation to entertain and keep his viewers riveted (as well as the fun he himself seems to be having with his newly computer-animated toy). For to keep the audience at their screens is a problem for television this particular night: from 10 o'clock on, viewers know who has won the election – why should they keep watching?

Yet there is also something more general going on: the familiar register, the superlative historical comments, the audience imperatives, the frequent stress in language and gesture, the expansive gestures and quick movements – all this points to a strong current of dramatization, conversationalization and personalization flowing through this text. In other words, the analyst is putting on a pretty good show. This may not however have helped achieve the goal of making the audience understand, especially if one takes the night's context of reception into account.[9]

Turning to global structure, the middle section of the expert's contribution is a composite, tri-partite report, framed by opening and closing sections, as shown in (9).

> (9)   Generic chain structure of excerpt 3: interpreting the exit polls results
>   opening
>   a.   report and comment: exit poll results
>   b.   report and comment: changes on the last election
>   c.   report and comment: swings in the vote and Labour majorities
>   closing

The chain of genres a-c within the report is syntagmatic – their sequence could not be otherwise. The underlying logic is again not merely a Gricean "be orderly" one (report events in the order they happened), but also a logic of action and cognition: you cannot do (b) until you know (a), and you cannot do (c) if you do not know (b). This nicely illustrates that while genres are the points of articulation between society and discourse, chains of genres engage with orders inherent to various logics of (inter)action and of cognition.

In the macro-structure of the election night, the analyst's report comes after the presenter's announcement of the winner of the election, after his report on the share of the vote at 10 o'clock and after his brief interview with John Prescott, the Labour Deputy Leader. Again the order is syntagmatic and not paradigmatic, as shown in (10).

(10) Syntagmatic genre chain of reporting exit polls results
        presenter   a. announcement: the winner
                        b. report and comment: share of the vote
                        c. interview: John Prescott, first reaction from Labour
        stats. analyst d. report and comment: share of the vote
                        e. report: changes on the last election
                        f. report and comment: swing in the vote and Labour
                            majority

However, the argument of a strict "syntactic" constraint does not hold for the relation between b-c-d: the interview with Prescott could just as well have been done after the analyst's report. Indeed the interview was interrupted by the presenter to delegate the floor to the analyst – a hint that this was indeed the planned sequential order and that some hitch might have intervened in this live broadcast. A further indication for this is that after the analyst's report, there followed an interview of the presenter with the Conservative campaign manager Brian Mawhinney for a first reaction from the Tories. So the planned order could well have been a-b-d-e-f, followed by the Prescott and the Mawhinney interviews as reactions from the two major parties. And the order of the latter two would not have been due to some (inter)actional logic but to social matters of protocol: winner before loser.

4.4   Production formats in television genres (audiovisual reports)

On the basis of the analysis of the genres in Section 4, production formats for audiovisual reports in general can be formulated as shown in (11).

(11)   Production formats in audiovisual reports

1a. The television company is the principal of the visual image and text, unless indicated otherwise (as in "BBC/NOP exit poll").

1b. The television company is the author of the visual image and text, unless indicated otherwise (as by quotation marks, attribution to source).

1c. The television company is the animator of the visual images and text, unless indicated otherwise (as in caption "footage from Al Djazeera" or "live from CNN International").

2a. The television company and/or the journalist is the principal of the verbal text, unless indicated otherwise (as by quoting, source attribution; texts by other participants as in political speeches, interviews, talk shows, etc.).

2b. Television journalists are the authors of the verbal text, unless indicated otherwise (as in 2a or in scripted text like the news).

2c. Television journalists are the animators of the verbal text, unless indicated otherwise.

With regard to 2a, one could assume that the television organization is in any case the institution responsible in the "legalistic sense" (Goffman 1981) for any text that is broadcast under its name. However, as experience shows, whenever things become difficult TV-companies tend to hold their journalists responsible to avoid damage to their image or litigation costs. In the next section, some genres will be dealt with which may make it necessary to rethink this paradigm further.

5.   Declaration sequences

Declaration sequences consist, in the normal case, of two parts – a sequence of talk, usually from the studio, while waiting for the Declaration to begin, and the Declaration itself, in which the results of all candidates in a particular constituency are announced and the winner is declared the elected Member of Parliament for the constituency.

5.1   "Waiting for …" – the running-up sequence

There is a tension between live broadcasting and events which take a long time to prepare and whose exact starting time cannot be precisely predicted. It takes ages before the athletes are properly lined up at the starting line, and when they're finally off, the 100 meters are over in no time at all. It is a bit like that with Declarations. Declarations are an ancient ritual which has its roots in an age long before the ascendancy of the electronic media. The precise point at which the counting process is finished and all the candidates and the Returning Officer are assembled on the stage of a constituency's count cannot be predicted. Yet the *raison d'etre* of live broadcasting is to be there at the very moment when things are starting to happen. Therefore on occasion live television has to wait around a little.

What does live television do while it waits? It produces waiting talk. The status of the genres that make up waiting talk is unclear. They inherit the property of waiting talk from their place in a generic sequence leading up to an event which is about to happen. Could they nevertheless appear in a different context as genuine expert interviews in their own right, as proper reports on historical or political background or as comments on what is happening elsewhere? Or do these genres exhibit properties which reveal that they are in some manner made to serve as fillers in a running-up sequence leading up to the "real thing"? Running-up sequences are not like pre-sequences, which have been defined in conversation analysis as the strategic and tentative preparation of certain speech actions such as requests. Running-up sequences lead up to a generic event without preparing it as such. Also, the event is one which is performed by participants other than the ones in charge of the running-up sequence and it begins at a time which is not under the control of these participants.

My data in excerpt 4 are from the run-up to the declaration of the third result of the night. The constituency is Wrexham, the time is about twenty minutes to eleven.

Excerpt 4. Running-up sequence

1.37:19 shot 1	MS of DD	DD: (We're about to get a **third** result of the night declared by the returning officer (*to camera and repeatedly looking down on monitor in table*))
shot 2	MLS of studio, DD front left at desk from side; on video wall behind, LS of candidates on podium, banner above "Wrexham/Wrecsam", BBC-logo and "Wrexham" top of video wall	in Wrexham, only **two** results have so far been declared in this general election (.)
shot 3	MLS of Wrexham candidates on podium	at the: (.) eh at the counts and Wrexham is coming up, and this is **North** East Wales, and it's a **safe** Labour seat, mining area, and it's held by Dr. John Marrick who's actually a mathematician, rather a quiet presence in the House of Commons, for seventeen years

shot 4	MS of Dr. John Marrick talking to candidate on his left	or so he taught mathematics down at the University in Aberystwyth,
shot 5	MLS of candidates as before	and (.) what'll be interesting **here**/again it's **Labour** in first place, fifty per cent of the vote they got last time round, (.) the Conservatives got thirty two per cent, the Liberal Democrats **fifteen** per cent. So (.) it'll be an indication for us whether that exit poll is still standing up **as it has so far**, Tony King, hasn't it? ANTHONY KING <AK>: It stood up **very** well so far,
1.38:10 shot 6	MLS of studio, DD front left from side, looking at table monitor; then at AK and into camera behind him; AK at desk front right, LS of Wrexham podium on video wall, between AK and DD	it'll be interesting to see whether John Marrick gets, depending on the turnout, about twenty-three or twenty-four thousand votes (.)
shot 7	MS of AK, video wall displaying AK	if turnout **has** stayed at its previous level, then that's what he should do. (.) That did **not** happen in Sunderland South which is why (.)
shot 8	MLS of studio as before but DD turning away to look at table monitor	Chris Mullin didn't get quite as many votes as we were supposing- DD: But the swing we'll be looking for would be sort of eleven (.) eleven per cent //<u>roughly, something like</u> that. AK: //<u>Will be (.) will be</u> between (.) ten and twelve per cent, //<u>absolutely</u>. DD: //<u>Ye:s</u>. They all seem to be standing there without much going on. = I don't know what's happening because (.) all the candidates are there and the returning officer in the center (1.0) it's like a sort of
	MLS of Wrexham podium as before, Returning Officer <RE> RE: I just mention as they finish the uh the bits and pieces that the/the turnout has been seventy-one per cent	(2.0) it's like a sort of uhm rather embarrassed school prize-giving. (2.0) They are early declarers by **design**, that's to say (.) they're one of those places, Torbay used to be one but isn't this year because of the local elections, which makes a point of getting its **face** on the television screen by being an early declarer.

shot 9		DD: Turnout of seventy-one per cent (.) he says. Well (2.0) Robin, what do you make of this eh (1.0) the reports we've been having from our own correspondents
1:39:21 shot 10	MLS of studio as before, includ-ing now Robin Oakley <RO> , expert in studio on the left of AK	out in the field (.) that the (0.5) landslide doesn't **feel** to them (.) in line with our exit poll. Do you think that's just
	MS of RO, BG video wall with election logo	RO: (2.0) ((*waiting for DD to finish sentence*)) I think that's what they're being told by Tory Party workers and Tory agents. **All** through this campaign we've had Tories saying they're absolutely baffled by the opinion poll figures, they can't understand why there isn't more **feel**good factor coming through, and I think we ['re] probably not getting as good a quality of canvasser as we used to in the old days, particularly if too many people are doing telephone canvass-ing and not seeing the whites of their eyes. Because if you go around as a **jour**nalist on a by-election you follow the canvassers to the doorstep, people on the doorstep are **very** polite, the British are a po**lite** nation, they don't like to say they're not gonna vote for something- DD: I mean the first- RO: (.) and when you speak to them afterwards they say I wouldn't vote for that [...] if they came down the driveway with a barrow //<u>full of</u> fivers DD: //<u>Ye:s</u>. RO: [...]
shot 11		DD: And the first reports
shot 12	MS of DD, looking at table RO, table monitor	from Conservative Central Office where they were (**shattered**) by (.) (*nodding*)) the exit poll and they were **shattered** by what/ what they were hearing from their own (.) constituencies.
shot 13	MS of RO	RO: I think they are quite **genuinely** surprised DD: Ye:s RO: because (that's not the message (*underlining each word with a sweep of right hand*)) they got on the //<u>doorsteps</u>. DD: //<u>Yeah</u>.

1:40:16 shot 14	MS Robin Oakley remains	DD: Tony Blair, first glimpse of
1:40:18 shot 15	MS David Dimbleby, looking at table monitor	him (.) at his
1:40:19 shot 16	heading ULC: "*B B C* Tony Blair's House" outside shot through window, flowers on window sill, within Alistair Campbell visible from behind	house, Myrobella in Trimdon. He's going (.) **from** there to: the count.=There he is. (The man who will be Prime Minister (1.0) tomorrow (.) [*camera zooms to PA Alistair Campbell*]) when he goes (.) to Buckingham Palace ([*Tony Blair joins Alistair Camp- bell*]), probably late tomorrow morning, (2.0) and that's Alistair Campbell, his First Secretary, **there** is Mister Blair, **behind,** (1.0) where we/ (.) there we are.
1:40:41 shot 17	MS David Dimbleby bent over table monitor	(Just a **brief** (*straightening up*)) (.) glimpse (.) of Tony Blair. A:nd he'll be going down to his count, he's then going to go to the: Trimdon: Labour Club and we'll hear from him there and then [he] planned to go down (.) **South** later on today.

Immediately adjoining shot 17 the presenter goes on to interview George Brown, Labour Shadow Chancellor of the Exchequer via a live two-way to his constituency in Dunfermline, Scotland. This interview will not be dealt with in detail here since it does not seem to be different from other political interviews of the night, except for the fact that it is almost one minute shorter than the usual duration of such exchanges (which is about three minutes, and thirty seconds). There are 17 shots in excerpt (4), taking up 3 minutes and 41 seconds of time. The interview, on the other hand, has 16 shots in only 2 minutes and 30 seconds. The high frequency of shots is due to the short turns in political interviews and the cuts from one speaker to the other in two-ways. The entire running up sequence thus takes up 6 minutes and 11 seconds of live broadcasting time on election night. How does the BBC fill this time? In terms of field, tenor and mode, what is being talked about by whom and how? What kinds of genres are constructed and what sorts of generic chains?

The sequence is opened by presenter David Dimbleby who in shot 1 announces to camera the declaration of the third result of the night coming up. In shot 2, he frequently changes his footing between speaking to camera and looking down at his table monitor, while on the video wall behind him we see the candidates and the Returning Officer lined up on the stage of Wrexham count. In shots 3 to 5 he is speaking from the off over images of the candidates lined up on the stage of the Wrexham count shown full screen. He does not at first describe what is to be seen on the screen but provides information of a geographical (North Wales), political (safe Labour seat) and socio-economic kind (mining area), plus personal information on the Labour candidate John Marrick. This information is presumably supplied by his monitor. When he mentions the name of the sitting member, the camera picks out John Marrick from the candidates standing in line on the stage of Wrexham count. The footing of presenter talk over images of Wrexham count is maintained to the end of shot 5. The presenter here establishes the relevance of focusing on this particular constituency at this particular point of time in the night, and at the same time prepares the ground for a question to his expert Anthony King: the constituency is comparable to the others declared so far and "what'll be interesting **here**" is if the Wrexham result will support the prediction of the exit poll regarding the swing to Labour. This opens the first expert interview of the sequence. Visually, there follows with some delay in shot 6, what usually serves as an establishing or framing shot for speaker change, namely a shot that shows both co-present speakers together. After that comes, in shot 7, the visual focus on the second speaker Anthony King, shown in middle shot while all units of the video wall behind him combine to display his image. This brief expert "interview" of two question-answer exchanges ends visually with a framing shot showing both speakers, and verbally by the expert – not confirming, as the presenter insists, that the swing will be around 11 percent – but insisting on "between ten and twelve percent". During the expert's answers, the presenter can be seen checking his monitor (shots 6 and 8).

Before the expert has finished speaking, the presenter turns away in shot 8 to the video wall where Wrexham count is still displayed and wonders aloud what is going on. These remarks, framed by two pauses of two seconds each, are delivered at a slow rate and are interspersed with more filled and unfilled pauses. The last remark overlaps into shot 9: "it's like a sort of uhm embarrassed school prize giving". However, as soon as the Wrexham count is again shown full screen, the presenter delivers more information from the off on the images in a manner which is prosodically and stylistically in marked contrast to this previous stretch of speech – his talk is faster and the register more formal. We cannot see the presenter of course, but it sounds very much as if the information on Wrexham being "early declarers by design" for example (which definitely sounds like written mode) is supplied in print by the monitor. At this point, and still in shot 9, the Returning Officer, who is standing in the middle of the candidates on stage, can be heard saying, in low volume: "I just mention as they finish the uh the bits and pieces that the/the turnout has been seventy-one percent". The presenter repeats this statement for the benefit of the audience and, still from the off over the image of Wrexham count, begins his second interview of this running-up sequence by asking political expert Robin Oakley his opinion on reports from correspondents about how "they" feel about the landslide and the exit poll. The second part of his question overlaps into shot 10 which shows presenter and the two experts in front of the video wall still displaying Wrexham count. The expert seems to know that "they" refers to the Tories and delivers discourse on how what canvassers hear at the doorstep and the way people actually vote can diverge. But this is not what the presenter meant: "I mean the first …", he tries to interrupt, and responds to the end of the expert's answer with a "ye:s" that signals "go on", like a teacher who has not yet heard the desired answer. This not being successful, he finally comes out with what he wants in a follow-up question – he wants to hear about the first reports of the night about the Tories being **shattered**. But the expert's response "I think they are quite **genuinely** surprised", which tones down the language considerably – is still not completely satisfactory. He is once more egged on by a "ye:s" and delivers the reason. "Yeah", says the presenter and lets the matter rest.

In shot 14, there comes an abrupt transition to quite a different topic, although the previous speaker Robert Oakley remains in full view: The first glimpse of the night of Tony Blair at his home in Trimdon. Framed by two shots which show the presenter looking at the table monitor, the visuals in shot 16 display a sneak view through a groundfloor window. The presenter describes what can be seen in this short sequence of film. First one man is visible from behind, then another joins him. The presenter's job is to "anchor" the images (Barthes 1977), that is, establish reference, tell the audience the identity of the people they are seeing, i.e. establish reference for talk to follow. But it is dark outside, and the light inside is dim. Dimbleby takes Alastair Campbell, one of Blair's campaign managers, for Blair and Blair for Alastair Campbell. As he realizes his mistake and repairs it ("**there** is Mister Blair, **behind**") he straightens up from his monitor and delivers the rest of his text in shot 17 about Blair's plans that night straight to camera/audience – for the first time since opening the sequence.

To sum up, in terms of field, the initial topic of this running-up sequence is the third result of the night, to be declared at Wrexham. The relevance of Wrexham for the BBC's election night broadcast is that the results at this safe Labour seat may confirm or disconfirm the 11% swing to Labour forecast by the exit poll. This topic is announced in the presenter's opening and dealt with in the two reports on the constituency which frame the expert interview with Anthony King, as well as in the interview itself. The second expert interview however addresses the Tories' reactions to the forecast of the poll, and the report which follows this presents a sneak-view into Tony Blair's house, the home of "the man who will be Prime Minister tomorrow" (shot 16), and a report on his plans for the night. In the political interview with George Brown, which concludes the sequence, the fact that Labour has won the election in a landslide victory is taken for granted. There is then a cline of topical relevance, from the focus on the results of

Wrexham and the forecast of the exit poll, to topics that take the result of the election as a foregone conclusion. This topical progression shows that the longer the wait for the up-coming event, the more irrelevant to the event itself the contributions become. By the time the Wrexham results are at last declared, the question of just how many percent swing to Labour they document is not really of much interest anymore.[10]

As regards the participants and their interaction (tenor), there is the presenter in the studio, who addresses the audience, who talks on the visuals shown and who enters into dialogue with his two co-present experts, as well as with an absent politician in a live two-way interview. He also repeats what the Returning Office of Wrexham says about the figures of the turn-out. The presenter, however, is not only a speaker, he is also a recipient of the verbal and visual information supplied by participants who do not perceivably enter the discourse. In this genre of live "waiting talk" of uncertain duration, he receives background information and directions from the monitor built into his table, i.e. from the BBC journalists in charge of it behind the scene. The monitor seems to be in use more extensively in this relatively unpredictable sequence than in the other genres studied. But even in the political interview with Gordon Brown, which follows the sequence shown in excerpt 4 and which the presenter does from his desk in front of the video wall, we cannot decide if the monitor is used or not. The presenter looks at his interviewee as he addresses him. He may well be consulting his monitor while his interviewee is shown full-screen answering, as some quotes inserted in one of the presenter's questions which go back into the history of Labour suggest. Such things are relevant for determining authorship. In the running-up sequence at any rate, some considerable portion of the presenter talk seems to come from the monitor, making other, uncredited BBC journalists the authors of much of what he says. Especially in talk from the off over visuals, we can in general assume that the monitor is in play. Presenter authorship in this running-up sequence prevails in passages addressed to the audience, in the questions he asks from his expert interviewees, and in spontaneous remarks he makes while waiting and watching people waiting in Wrexham.

Regarding mode or the way in which the communicative means are used, written language is employed, as in BBC captions in the visuals, and presumably via the monitor to the presenter. This latter communication is however not accessible to the audience, nor to the author of this study. However, since these resources influence what the presenter says and how he may put it, it has to count as a feature of the genre. Spoken language is used either dialogically or in monologue, either in the studio or via two-way interview to outside locations. There may also be an acoustic one-way communication from journalists in charge of the monitor via earpiece to the presenter. This cannot be determined, no earpiece being visible, but we only see the presenter from the right throughout. The images are mostly static, showing talking heads and people standing about waiting. The relations between the verbal and the visual channel are presenter close-up for audience address; for dialogue, framing shots show both speakers for openings and closings and current speaker middle shots or close-ups tracking speaker change. This means that during interviewee responses the presenter is free to consult his monitor. Monologue is the exclusive domain of the presenter (this changes much later in the night when occasionally political victory or concession speeches are shown). It is used in this sequence in three modes: the presenter addresses the audience to camera, he can be seen while talking about images shown on the studio video wall, or he speaks from the off over images that take up the screen. In shot 1 he introduces the imminent Declaration at Wrexham. In 2 to 5, he identifies from the off the place shown on the screen as Wrexham count and provides further information to identify and characterize the place and its incumbent Member of Parliament. He then goes on to provide the reason for choosing to focus on just this place at this point in the broadcast. These are the features of the classical news report: who, where, what, why (plus, later, how). In providing the answers to the who and where, the presenter furnishes the persons shown with identities and a place in the world. In dealing with the what and why of it he supplies from the off information which goes beyond what is to be seen on-screen. In this manner, the images and the presenter's discourse together tell a story. The end of the story will be revealed in the Declaration.

Dialogue is used in the two expert interviews and in the political interview at the end. As for the expert interviews, the analysis has shown they hardly warrant the term. The experts in this sequence do try to give their reflected opinions on the basis of specialist knowledge, but the presenter nudges them into the direction of the answers he wants to hear. With Anthony King this is to confirm the predicted swing of 11 percent, with Robin Oakley to confirm that the Tories are "shattered". But both experts insist on their own, more cautious and reflected formulations. The result is a sort of "light" (and short) version of the expert interview. This may be due to the BBC's particularly "light" entertaining audience design on election night. Also, these "interviews" have an air of being pre-arranged. What sort of genre are they then, if they are not real expert interviews? Are they like talk show interviews? No, they are too narrowly controlled for that, they are far too short and they are topically tied into a live news program. They seem to be indeed "filler interviews", designed to provide supplementary information and to fill the time until the event finally happens.

The generic sequence or chain is shown in (12). The political interview with Gordon Brown in (2g) is kept short to switch to Wrexham for the Declaration.

(12)   Generic chain structure of excerpt 4: running-up sequence
  1.   opening
  2.   waiting
    a.   report on Wrexham count
    b.   filler interview with expert 1
    c.   report on Wrexham count
    e.   filler interview with expert 2
    f.   report on Blair in Trimdon
    g.   political interview with Gordon Brown

A few remarks on (12) are in order: Firstly, there is no closing to the sequence, since the event it is leading up to has not yet happened – the sequence is open-ended. Secondly, sequence (2) is called "waiting" and not "preparation" because only (2a), (2b) and (2c) actually prepare the audience with information relevant to the up-coming Declaration (cf. the cline of topical relevance described above). Thirdly, only the relations between (1) and (2) and between (2a), (2b) and (2c) are syntagmatic ones and thereby construct topical coherence. (2e) to (2g) are paradigmatic to one another and as a block to the rest of the sequence. The cline of topical relevance leads to increasing topical incoherence. And last but not least, there is a clear sequential pattern in a chain of report and interview pairs. This established format of television news provides scaffolding in an unpredictable situation.

5.2   The Declaration

Political science makes a difference between symbolic politics and real politics, that is, between the presentation of politics and its production (Sarcinelli 1987). The greatest part of the political discourse disseminated by the mass media is the presentation of political decisions made in backrooms and behind closed doors. Even parliamentary debates are prepared by deliberations of the political parties beforehand to which the media have no access. Great political speeches are the work of a team of gifted writers. Political interviews, even if broadcast live, may be prearranged. The one genre where we can witness politics in the making on election night is that of the Declaration of the winner by the election official at the level of the local constituency. It is there that the figures on the ballots are converted into political facts: a new member of parliament is created, or a sitting member confirmed. This does not mean that Declarations are held in high esteem by the media, as we have seen in excerpt 4. They are just not – to use a term of the Blair era – sexy enough, and since they are an old prescribed ritual, there is no way to "sex them up a bit". The Wrexham Declaration is shown in excerpt 5.

Excerpt 5. Declaration

1:43:25	Wrexham returning officer on stage at mike, reading out results; to his left and right election candidates; in BG large banner reading "WREXHAM / WREC-SAM"; in front of stage people; screen heading in ULC: *B B C Wrexham* ° screen heading disappears	DD: (//<u>Wrexham about to declare</u>. RETURNING OFFICER <RE>: (//<u>[…], Con- servative Party</u> candidate, eight thousand (.) six hundred an ei/ and ° eighty eight.
1:43:29	MS smiling man (John Cronk?)	Cronk, John
1:43:30	Wrexham returning officer and others on stage	Edwards/ Edward, the Referendum Party candidate, one
1:43:35	MS man (Nicholas Low?)	thousand one hundred and ninety five.
1:43:37	Wrexham returning officer and others on stage	Low, Nicholas John, Natural Labour Party, eighty six.
1:43:42	MS three men on stage	
1:43:44	Wrexham returning officer and others on stage	Marek, John, the Labour Party candidate, twenty thousand (.)
1:43:48	MS John Marek	four hundred (.) and fifty.
1:43:50	Wrexham returning officer and others on stage ° flashing Labour rose appears in LLC	° Plant, James Kevin, Plaid Cymru, one
1:43:54	MS smiling James Plaid	thousand one hundred and seventy.
1:43:57	Wrexham returning officer and others on stage	Thomas, Andrew Martin, Liberal Democrat, four thousand (.)
1:44:00	MS Andrew Thomas	eight hundred and (.) thirty three.
1:44:03	Wrexham returning officer and others on stage	And that John Marek (.) has been duly elected (.) to serve as Member (.) for the Wrexham constituency. The
1:44:09	screen displaying Wrexham returning officer and others on stage gets reduced to insert headed "Wrexham". To the right of the live picture five lines, read-ing top to bottom: "Lab" in red bar "20450", "Con" in blue bar "8688", "LibDem" in yellow bar "4833", "Ref" in light blue bar "1195" and "Others" in grey bar "1256".	number of ballot papers rejected ([…] (*voice fades out*)) DD: So John Marek holds his seat, his majority eleven thousand (.) seven hundred. Con-servatives in second place **but but but**, and a big **but**, this is the swing (.) (in this **third** result [*"LibDem"*, *"Ref"* and *"Others"* get re-placed by three-dimensional semicircle that is black on top, the outside is coloured red from left to middle and blue from middle to right. A needle points to 7% in red half. "SWING" written above semicircle*].). **Seven percent**

	Then some free space, followed by "HOLD" in red bar "Maj 11762". In BG a detail of the UK-map in black, with Wrexham highlighted in red	(.) from Conservative to Labour. So a lower swing, well above the amount that's needed (.) for a substantial (.) Labour victory, but below the kind of eleven percent swing that we got from the first two seats. Tony, what d'you make of that? ANTHONY KING <AK>: That's absolutely
1:44:37	MS David Dimbleby, sitting at desk in LLC of screen in FG, in LRC MS Tony King; to DD's left large video screen split in 1 big screen displaying MS John Marek; to the right nine small screens displaying people at different locations; underneath table: "Con" in blue bar "0", "0"; "Lab" in red bar "3", "0"; "Lib Dem" in yellow bar "0", "0"	right. Er it does look as though there's going to be a considerable
1:44:39	MS Tony King	drop in the turnout in these **very** safe Labour seats. And it's **very** hard to say what the **effect** of/ er on the swing of that is going to be. Er but **notice**, as you said a moment ago, a swing of seventy percent would ((//have Mister Blair- DD: (//Of seven percent! AK: Seven percent, [what did I say, yes, yes]. DD: Seventy percent would have/ yes.
1:44:55	MS David Dimbleby, as before, video screen displays Falmouth count; screen heading in ULC: B B C Falmouth & Camb., rest as before	AK: ((laughs)) It's the kind of language we've been talking till now.
1:44:58	MS Tony King	Wou/ would have Mister Blair **very** comfortably in Downing Street indeed. DD: Tony uhm Peter ([laughter Tony King]).

The last genre in the running-up sequence, the filler interview with Gordon Brown, although kept shorter than usual, proved to be too long after all to catch the beginning of the Declaration. When the BBC gets there, the Returning Officer is already in the middle of reading the result of the first of Wrexham's six candidates, the one for the Conservative party. So the presenter's "Wrexham about to declare" does not quite fit the facts. The visuals show the Wrexham stage, the Returning Officer standing in the middle of the row of candidates. The relations between the visual and the verbal channel are different from those in the running-up sequence. The object of the news everyone has been waiting for is given voice and face through the Returning Officer and the candidates shown on the Wrexham stage. In this short sequence of film, it is the camera that performs Barthes' anchoring function. We see and hear the Returning Officer speak and as he mentions each candidate's name, party and result, the camera picks out the corresponding face and visually establishes for the audience the referents of his assertions. The Returning Officer himself is never identified beyond his function and authority in this phase of the democratic process. Nor is he the author or principal of his text. The words to be uttered are wholly prescribed with empty slots for the candidates' names, party and the number of votes. The full Declaration formula is as quoted in (13).

(13)   Declaration formula
I hereby give notice the total number of votes given for each candidate at the election was as follows: name 1, party 1, number of votes 1; name 2, party 2, number of votes 2; etc., and that (name, party) has been duly elected to serve as the Member for the (name) constituency.

With this explicit performative speech act by a person with the authority to utter it, a number of ballots as expression of the will of the people are converted into a social fact. It takes all of forty-four seconds.

What happens at a count after the Declaration is that the winner and the runner-up deliver a speech thanking their supporters and so on. The BBC however decides not to stay for this, nor does the presenter read aloud the results shown on the video wall, he just briefly summarizes the result of the winning Labour candidate. Given the landslide victory for Labour forecast by the exit poll, the percentage of the swing to Labour at Wrexham remains the only topic of interest. The Wrexham swing of seven percent is below the eleven expected. So the expert Tony King is asked for his opinion on that. We do not learn whether this might have developed into a full-blown expert interview beyond the connection between a safe Labour seat, low turnout and low swing, because Tony King produces a whopping slip of the tongue and speaks of "a swing of seventy percent". When this has been repaired, he laughs and says revealingly "it's the kind of language we've been talking till now".

The "superlative" talk of the BBC which we already noted in the reports and interpretations of the exit poll in Section 4 seems to be contagious, and it is one of the studio experts who falls victim to this exaggeritis. He has, however, the presence of mind to name and explicitly criticize what he believes to be the cause. We may also remember how Robin Oakley, the second studio expert, insisted on his sober formulation of "genuinely surprised" against the presenter's "shattered" when referring to the Tories in the running-up sequence. So it seems that both experts show signs of linguistic resistance. But slips of the tongue can be catching as well and in the end it is the presenter himself who produces the last one in this text by calling on "Tony" as he delegates the floor to Peter Snow for another round on the swingometer. By way of a comment on the news just received, the expert "interview" rounds the Declaration sequence off. The presenter's transition to the statistics analyst Peter Snow closes it and at the same time opens a new one. The relations in the Declaration core are all syntagmatic and the generic chain of the entire Declaration sequence looks like this:

(14)   Generic chain structure of excerpts 4 and 5: running-up sequence and Declaration
   1.   opening
   2.   waiting
       a.   report on Wrexham count
       b.   filler interview with expert 1
       c.   report on Wrexham count
       e.   filler interview with expert 2
       f.   report on Blair in Trimdon
       g.   political interview with Gordon Brown
   3.   Declaration (core)
       a.   opening
       b.   Declaration
       c.   summary
       d.   "interview" with expert 2
   4.   closing

6.   Summary and conclusion

Election night broadcasts as a macro-genre exhibit the articulation between social practices and discourse practices (Fairclough 1995), contextual configuration and genre (Hasan 1985a–c), external and internal structure of a genre (Luckmann 1986) in an exemplary manner. The election system in use, the organization of the election and of the counting of the votes, the number of political candidates and correspondingly the number of results to be presented, the journalistic personnel and technical wherewithal on the media side – all these strongly influence, almost determine the generic characteristics of this television genre. As to the theoretical model of genre on which the analyses in Sections 4 and 5 are based, this was first of all the systemic tri-partite model of Hasan (1985a–c), according to which genre can be identified and analyzed through the meaning potentials provided in the semantic, interpersonal and textural domains by a typical contextual figuration of field, tenor and mode. This was supplemented by Goffman's (1967, 1981) concept of footing and footing change and his deconstruction of the speaker role into animator, author and principal. The latter was particularly valuable in audiovisual analysis, and led to an unexpected outcome. What also proved necessary were general pragmatic principles like those of Grice's conversational logic, as well as general practices of conversational organization as described in conversation analysis (such as global and local practices). The audio-visual analysis profited from concepts and methods developed in semiotics (Barthes 1977), media studies (Graber 1990; Graddol 1994; van Leeuwen and Jewitt 2001), discourse analysis (Meinhoff 1994; Holly 2005), from work done in our television discourse project (cf. Note * and Schieß 2007) and from the author's own work (cf. Note 5).

The genres analyzed in Sections 4 and 5 of this chapter do not of course exhaust the full catalogue of genres of election nights. The selection criteria were heterogeneous, as described in Section 3. The genres selected deal explicitly with the processes after an election: waiting for the ballot boxes to arrive in the constituencies of the two party leaders John Major and Tony Blair (4.1); reporting the exit poll results and evaluating them (4.2). In the UK parliamentary election of 1997, the exit poll left no possible doubt that Labour had won the election. The only questions left open were how big the Labour majority and the swing from the Conservatives to Labour would be. One of the reports analyzed deals explicitly with this, in a manner rich in audio-visual interaction (4.3). Another genre selected as typical for the UK election television nights was the live official Declaration of the winner at constituency level (5.2). The Declaration not only constitutes an old political and ritualized genre of the democratic process, the instance analyzed was also typical for the liveness of election night broadcasts in that it was situated towards the end of a chain of genres in a protracted running-up sequence rich in "waiting talk" (5.1). Another feature that the genres analyzed have in common is that they do not predominantly deal with the discourse of politicians but with that of journalists talking about politicians or about the democratic process of elections and parliamentary representation.

The results of the analyses in Section 4 yielded three different sub-genres of audiovisual news reports: first the "soft" report which seems to be exempt from the generic requirement of news reports to attribute statements to their sources, both in the visual and the verbal domain (4.1). Secondly, the report of "real" or hard news, i.e. the exit poll results, in which great care was taken to source the figures to both the National Polling Organization and the BBC, both verbally and visually (4.2). In this sub-genre, the visual and the verbal voice of the BBC spoke in parallel, so that they mutually reinforced each other. This also holds for the third sub-genre, the interpretation of the exit poll results (4.3). The difference between the second and the third type was that in the second, the presenter interacted with a still of the numerical results shown on the screen, while in the third, a statistics expert interacted with the computer animated "swingometer", explaining the correlations between the percentage of the swing from Conservatives to Labour, the number of seats gained by Labour and the majority for Labour to be expected.

In terms of the speaker roles of Goffman's production format, the statistics expert, in his more dynamic verbal-visual interaction, could be shown to be more in authorial control of his own discourse than the presenter in his. What was also interesting in this section was the increasing amount of knowledge which the journalists could take as shared between themselves and the audience as the sequence of reports unfolded. This was documented in the reduction of verbal references to the sources of the exit poll results as well as of pointing gestures to their display on the screen. Different footings and footing changes between modes of relating image and talk were also noted. As regards the sequential order of genre chains, differences were found between paradigmatic and syntagmatic ones. The genres in the latter are constrained in their sequential occurrence by Gricean maxims (be orderly), based on what I have termed a "natural logic", and semantic coherence. The genres in paradigmatic chains could also potentially occur in a different sequence.

The micro-analysis of audio-visual reports in Section 4 of this chapter, while answering some questions, has also raised a few new ones. One concerns the status of the genres in the chains shown in examples (2), (9) and (10). Can they be analyzed as genres in their own right or should they rather be categorized as subgenres that realize particular stages, phases, discourse paragraphs etc. of the report in question? What are the criteria for doing the one and the other? Another question is: what exactly is it that defines a genre? Just what is the difference for example between report and comment? When does a genre change into a different one, not over time, but in the course of talk – does a footing change suffice? A change in field, tenor, or mode? Or do all three have to change? Or two? And how? Or is this irrelevant? After extensive micro analysis one might well wish to look elsewhere, high up on the scale of abstraction, for generic prototypes, pre-genres (cf. Swales 1990; Fairclough 2003), formulate felicity conditions, find where the differences lie for example between report and comment, apart from the fact that the one has to come before the other.

In Section 5 we looked at a sequence which regarding mode is very typical for the liveness of election night broadcasts and regarding field touches on their innermost purpose: waiting for the live Declaration of the winner of a constituency. This involves a "running-up" sequence while the television audience, the studio journalists, the Returning Officer and the candidates lined up on the stage of their count wait for the Declaration. More than in the genres studied in Section 4, the running-up sequence involved the presenter's use of a monitor. Sometimes he could be seen consulting the monitor in the visuals, and in one very significant instance, where the presenter changed from speaking on camera to speaking from the off, the change between spontaneous presenter talk and monitor talk was noticeable by changes in tempo, pausing and register. As for the expert interviews in this sequence, they could be shown to be a reduced variant of such interviews, both in seriousness, purpose and length, as well as by their quality of being overly controlled by the presenter. Their reduced status arises from their positioning in the running-up sequence whose dominant goal is to fill the time while waiting for the Declaration to get under way – they are "filler" interviews.

The analysis of waiting talk in 5.1 was a first exploration of what such talk comprises and of how it could be done. Waiting talk is complex in its tenor and mode constellations while its field is the up-coming event. What had not turned up in our previous work as a major factor was the noticeable influence of the presenter's monitor and audio feed on his speech. Whether this is a particular property of waiting talk or a property much more widespread in news and news magazine genres needs to be explored. The outcome will certainly have consequences on how the participant roles of the production format of audiovisual reporting and other genres are to be assessed (cf. Section 4.4). The analysis of waiting talk is not easy – in fact one wonders how it could be done without having, in addition to the audio-visual product that goes on air, parallel recordings of the visuals on the presenter's monitor and of the verbal text on his audio feed.

Waiting talk is obviously also not easy to do. It requires a good deal of uncertainty tolerance from the participants on top of flexibility and fast reactions. No wonder our data exhibited quite a few hitches and glitches. As a result, the analysis sometimes turned into a kind of deviant case study – that is, an analysis that draws attention to an underlying order on the basis of the things that go wrong (cf. Garfinkel's [1967] crisis experiments). Another surprise was the presenter's lack of respect for the old ritual of the Declaration – even if it does appear like something dropped into the text from another time.

The Declaration with its ritual character and narrowly prescribed procedure is in fact a genre that might well be a generic prototype. It crucially involves the basic speech act type of declarative. Interestingly, the Declaration also raises questions regarding Goffman's production format: the returning officer who speaks the declarative formula that creates a new social fact on the basis of the ballots cast is mere animator of the words, albeit with great effect. But who is the author? Who the principal? Presumably one would have to go far back in British parliamentary history to look for the author and most likely one would find a committee, a commission, a collective. And for the principal one is bound to find a development from privileged groups with a vested interest in sending their man to Westminster to political institutions with their collection of political and discourse practices. Monitor talk, as described in this chapter, poses similar questions: Who is the author? A team, a collective. And principal? An institution, a collection of media and discourse practices. Roland Barthes not only gave us the distinction between anchoring and relay for the difference between two image-text relations, he also deconstructed the concept of author in his essay "The Death of the Author" (Barthes 1977). Is it time to deconstruct Goffman's production format for certain discourse domains and their genres? Who is the author of a political speech? Or of a press statement? A policy statement? Or of what a politician says in an interview? Or how a presenter opens a political magazine on television?

Notes

* The research reported on in this chapter arises from the project "Television Discourse: Election Nights", funded by the German Research Council (DFG) in the years 2003 to 2005 and directed by the author. The goal of the project was the cross- and trans-cultural analysis of discourse practices used during election night broadcasts in the UK (1997), Germany (1998) and the US (2000) on national and international channels, as well as the genres and generic configurations which were constructed by the participants through these practices. For further information, see http://web.uni-frankfurt.de/zenaf/projekte/TVdiscourses/ lauerbach.htm.

1. See Schieß (2007) for the electronic studio of election nights, Malkmus (2010) for gesture and gaze in political speeches, Lauerbach (2010) for audio-visual rhythm in a political talk show interview.

2. Many thanks go to Gunter Kress for kindly providing the eight hour-long video-recording.

3. The first 15 minutes of the middle section have been analyzed with respect to metaphor (Scheithauer 2007), interviews (Becker 2007), the visual component (Schieß 2007) and presenting practices (Lauerbach 2007).

4. Annette Becker, Eleonore Emsbach, Martin Hampel, Raimund Schieß, Vanessa Tomalla and others.

5. Extensive analytical and comparative work has been done on the audio-visual discourse of political interviews, political speeches and of argument, and of presenting. See Becker (2005, 2007), Fetzer (2007), Hampel (2003), Lauerbach (2000a, 2000b, 2001, 2003a, 2003b, 2004, 2006, 2007a, 2007b, 2010), Malkmus (2010), Scheithauer (2007), Schieß (2003, 2007).

6. For transcription conventions please refer to the Appendix.

7. BBC's commercial rival ITV, presented by David Dimbleby's brother Jonathan, opens as follows: "Good evening. The votes are cast, the polling stations are closed. Our prediction based on the Mori Poll for ITV is that Labour have clearly won this election with what appears to be a massive majority". ITV thus makes a clear distinction between their company and the polling agency they are using.

8. The swingometer is a device for illustrating swings in the vote from one party to another and for interpreting what this means in terms of seats won or lost and for the resulting constitution of parliament. In a rudimentary version it was first used by the BBC in the general election of 1955, which was the first to be televised. After various modifications, it was changed from an actual swingometer, which had to be worked by several men, to a virtual reality one for the election night broadcast of 1997. In 2001, it was changed to a laser-beam projection (cf. Wikipedia 2010).

9. Here is a quote from Helen Fielding's novel *Bridget Jones: The Edge of Reason,* referring to sometime later in the night:

> "When we went to bed Peter Snow was striding marvellously but incomprehensibly about and it seemed pretty clear the swingometer was to Labour but … Oh-oh. Maybe we misunderstood. We were a bit squiffy and nothing made any particular sense other than all the blue Tory buildings on the map of Britain being blown up".

(Fielding 1999, 206)

10. This points to a general problem of the night's broadcast: with a landslide election victory, the pressure on television to keep the audience in front of the screen is immense. To watch the election night coverage of an election whose results are known early on is a little like reading a detective novel and knowing who did it, or watching the recording of a soccer match and knowing who won, and by a large margin. You do it out of genuine interest for the thing, for the love of its narrative, of its aesthetics and entertainment, of its idiosyncrasies of style, and of the personal traits and fates of its protagonists – and the BBC tries its best to cater to these needs.

References

Barthes, Roland. 1977. *Image, Music, Text.* London: Fontana.

Barthes, Roland. 1994. "The Death of the Author." In *Media Texts: Authors and Readers*, ed. by David Graddol, and Oliver Boyd-Barrett, 166–170. Clevedon: The Open University.

BBC. 2005. "Peter Snow's Swingometer." Retrieved June 12, 2011 from http://news.bbc. co.uk/2/ shared/vote2005/swingometer/html/labcon.stm

Bell, Allan. 1991. *The Language of News Media.* Oxford: Blackwell.

Bakhtin, Michail M. 1986. "The Problem of Speech Genres." In *Speech and Other Late Essays*, ed. by Michail Holquist, and Caryl Emerson, 60–102. Austin, TX: University of Texas Press.

Becker, Annette. 2005. "Interviews in TV Election Night Broadcasts: A Framework for Cross-Cultural Analysis." In *Dialogue Analysis IX: Dialogue in Literature and the Media*, ed. by Anne Betten, and Monika Dannerer, 65–75. Tübingen: Niemeyer.

Becker, Annette. 2007a. "'Are You Saying…?'. A Cross-Cultural Analysis of Interviewing Practices in TV Election Night Broadcasts." In *Political Discourse in the Media*, ed. by Anita Fetzer, and Gerda Lauerbach, 109–137. Amsterdam: Benjamins.

Becker, Annette. 2007b. "The Appropriateness of Questions." In *Context and Appropriateness*, ed. by Anita Fetzer, 147–166. Amsterdam: Benjamins.

Crystal, David and Derek Davy. 1969. *Investigating English Style.* London: Longman.

Fairclough, Norman. 1988. "Discourse Representation in Media Discourse." *Sociolinguistics* 17: 125–139.

Fairclough, Norman. 1995. *Media Discourse.* London: Arnold.

Fairclough, Norman. 2003. *Analysing Discourse. Textual Analysis for Social Research*. London: Routledge.

Fetzer, Anita. 2007. "Challenges in Political Interviews: An Intercultural Aanalysis." In *Political Discourse in the Media*, ed. by Anita Fetzer, and Gerda Lauerbach, 163–195. Amsterdam: Benjamins.

Fielding, Helen. 1999. *Bridget Jones: The Edge of Reason*. London: Picador.

GfK NOP. 2011. www.gfk.com. Retrieved June 12, 2011.

Garfinkel, Harold. 1967. *Studies in Ethnomethodology*. Englewood Cliffs, NJ: Prentice Hall.

Goffman, Erving. 1981. "Footing." In *Forms of Talk*, ed. by Erving Goffman, 124–157. Oxford: Blackwell.

Graber, Doris A. 1990. "Seeing is Remembering: How Visuals Contribute to Learning from Television News." *Journal of Communication* 40: 134–155.

Graddol, David. 1994. "The Visual Accomplishment of Factuality." In *Media Texts: Authors and Readers*, ed. by David Graddol, and Oliver Boyd-Barrett, 136–160. Clevedon: The Open University.

Günthner, Susanne, and Thomas Luckmann. 2001. "Asymmetries of Knowledge in Intercultural Communication." In *Culture in Communication. Analyses of Intercultural Situations*, ed. by Aldo di Luzio, Susanne Günthner, and Franca Orletti, 55–85. Amsterdam: Benjamins.

Habermas, Jürgen. 1984. *Theory of Communicative Action, vol. 1*. London: Heinemann.

Hasan, Ruqaiya. 1985a. "The Structure of a Text." In *Language, Context and Text: Aspects of Language in a Social-Semiotic Perspective*, ed. by M. A. K. Halliday, and Ruqaiya Hasan, 52–69. Victoria: Deakin University Press.

Hasan, Ruqaiya. 1985b. "The Texture of a Text." In *Language, Context and Text: Aspects of Language in a Social-Semiotic Perspective*, ed. by M. A. K. Halliday, and Ruqaiya Hasan, 70–96. Victoria: Deakin University Press.

Hasan, Ruqaiya. 1985c. "The Identity of a Text." In *Language, Context and Text: Aspects of Language in a Social-Semiotic Perspective*, ed. by M. A. K. Halliday, and Ruqaiya Hasan, 97–116. Victoria: Deakin University Press.

Heritage, John, and David Greatbatch. 1991. "On the Institutional Character of Institutional Talk: The Case of News Interviews." In *Talk and Social Structure*, ed. by Deirdre Boden, and Don H. Zimmerman, 93–137. Cambridge: Polity Press.

Holly, Werner. 2006. "Mit Worten sehen. Audiovisuelle Bedeutungskonstitution und Muster transkriptiver Logik in der Fernsehberichterstattung." *Deutsche Sprache* 34: 135–150.

Kress, Gunther. 1993. "Genre as Social Process." In *The Powers of Literacy – A Genre Approach to Teaching Writing*, ed. by Bill Cope, and Mary Kalantzis, 22–37. London: Falmer.

Lauerbach, Gerda. 2004. "Political Interviews as a Hybrid Genre." *Text* 3: 353–397.

Lauerbach, Gerda. 1993. "Qu'est-ce qui permet de comprendre le discours de la classe en langue étrangère? Quelques types de connaissances sur lesquels s'appuient les élèves." *AILE* 2: 61–83.

Lauerbach, Gerda. 2006. "Discourse Representation in Political Interviews. The Construction of Identities and Relations through Voicing and Ventriloquizing." *Journal of Pragmatics* 38: 196–215.

Lauerbach, Gerda. 2007. "Presenting Television Election Nights in Britain, the United States and Germany: Cross-Cultural Analyses." In *Political Discourse in the Media*, ed. by Anita Fetzer, and Gerda Lauerbach, 315–375. Amsterdam: Benjamins.

Lauerbach, Gerda. 2010. "Manoeuvring between the Political, the Personal and the Private: Talk, Image and Rhythm in TV Dialogue." *Discourse and Communication* 4: 124–159.

Levinson, Stephen C. 1979. "Activity Types and Language." *Linguistics* 17: 365–399.

Levinson, Stephen C. 1983. *Pragmatics*. Cambridge: Cambridge University Press.

Luckmann, Thomas. 1986. "Grundformen der gesellschaftlichen Vermittlung des Wissens: Kommunikative Gattungen." *Kölner Zeitschrift für Soziologie und Sozialpsychologie Sonderheft 27 (Kultur und Gesellschaft)*: 191–211.

Malkmus, Thorsten. 2010. *Der Wahlkampf ist vorbei – ist der Wahlkampf vorbei? – Diskursanalytische Untersuchung und interkultureller Vergleich britischer und deutscher Wahlnachtreden*. Unpublished dissertation, University of Frankfurt.

Marriott, Stephanie. 1997. "The Emergence of Live Television Talk." *Text* 17: 181–198.

Marriott, Stephanie. 2000. "Election Night." *Media, Culture & Society* 22: 131–150.

Meinhof, Ulrike H. 1994. "Double Talk in News Broadcasts: A Cross-Cultural Comparison of Pictures and Texts in Television News." In *Media Texts: Authors and Readers*, ed. by David Graddol, and Oliver Boyd-Barrett, 212–223. Clevedon: The Open University Press.

Montgomery, Martin. 2007. *The Discourse of Broadcast News. A Linguistic Approach*. London: Routledge.

Sacks, Harvey, Emanuel A. Schegloff, and Gail Jefferson. 1974. "A Simplest Systematics for the Organization of Turn-Taking for Conversation." *Language* 50: 696–735.

Sarcinelli, Ulrich. 1987. *Symbolische Politik*. Opladen: Westdeutscher Verlag.

Schegloff, Emanuel A. 1972. "Sequencing in Conversational Openings." In *Directions in Sociolinguistics*, ed. by John Gumperz, and Dell Hymes, 45–77. New York, NY: Holt, Rinehart and Winston.

Schegloff, Emanuel A., and Harvey Sacks. 1973. "Opening up Closings." *Semiotica* 7: 289–327.

Scheithauer, Rut. 2007. "Metaphors in Election Night Television Coverage in Britain, the United States and Germany." In *Political Discourse in the Media*, ed. by Anita Fetzer, and Gerda Lauerbach, 75–106. Amsterdam: Benjamins.

Schieß, Raimund. 2007. "Information Meets Entertainment: A Visual Analysis of Election Night TV Programs across Cultures." In *Political Discourse in the Media*, ed. by Anita Fetzer, and Gerda Lauerbach, 275–313. Amsterdam: Benjamins.

Stiehler, Hans-Jörg. 2000. " 'Nach der Wahl ist vor der Wahl': Interpretationen als Gegenstand der Medienforschung." In *Wahlen und Politikvermittlung durch Massenmedien*, ed. by Hans Bohrmann, Otfried Jarren, Gabriele Melischek, and Josef Seethaler, 105–120. Frankfurt: Westdeutscher Verlag.

Swales, John. 1990. *Genre Analysis. English in Academic and Research Settings*. Cambridge: Cambridge University Press.

van Leeuwen, Theo, and Carey Jewitt. (eds). 2001. *Handbook of Visual Analysis*. London: Sage.

Wember, Bernward. 1976. *Wie informiert das Fernsehen? – Ein Indizienbeweis*. München: List.

Wikipedia. 2010. Retrieved June 12, 2011 from http://en.wikipedia.org/wiki/Swingometer.

Appendix

Transcription conventions

column 1	time-line, number of shot
	cuts between shots: horizontal line; dissolve: no line
column 2	visual/screen content:
	headings, images (stills or moving), print or graphics, captions
	cuts: horizontal line; dissolve: half a broken line

types of shots:

CU	close-up
MCU	medium close-up
MS	medium shot
MLS	medium long shot
LS	long shot

column 3	verbal text, including filled (erm) and unfilled ((.) or (number of secs.)) pauses	
	boldface	marked stress
	. ? ,	punctuation signs: intonation contours (falling, rising, level)
	/	cut-off
	=	latching
	-	interruption
	//	start of overlapping talk
	underline	stretch of overlapping talk
	[…]	unintelligible text
	[text]	uncertain transcription
	°	heading/caption in visual text disappears
	paraverbals	(e.g. laughter), and nonverbals (e.g. gestures/postures: "points at", "to camera", and kinesics) – these are integrated into the text, marked with brackets where they begin and end relative to the words; descriptions are supplied where they end and printed in italics; (r) stands for "right", (l) for "left", (c) for "corner", (u) for "upper", (TOS) for "top of screen", (BOS) for "bottom of screen"
	cuts in the visual text: horizontal line; dissolves: broken line	

CHAPTER 5

Analyzing meetings in political and business contexts

Different genres – similar strategies?

Ruth Wodak

Lancaster University, UK & University of Vienna, Austria

This chapter compares various instances of everyday routine meetings in political institutions (such as the European Parliament and the European Commission) with meetings in business organizations, with the aim of, first describing
similarities and differences in the genre (and subgenres) of meetings across
organizations and social fields; and of secondly investigating the impact of organizational knowledge of the genre on presuppositions and context models of the
participants related to the interaction and intended outcome of the meetings.

I argue that the concept of a "prototype genre of meeting" is adequate for
an integrated, interdisciplinary discourse-analytical and sociolinguistic theoretical framework which allows understanding and explaining the intricate dynamic of meetings in a systematic, in-depth, and context-dependent way. Moreover,
I claim that organizational knowledge of the genre is part and parcel of successful interaction strategies; and that much miscommunication and problems
could be avoided if manifest and latent genre conventions were sufficiently
acknowledged.

Drawing on transcribed data of 36 meetings in the European Parliament
and European Commission, on the one hand, and of 6 meetings (2 away days, 4
regular) in one large business organization, on the other hand, I illustrate the salience of the genre characteristics in the interaction and its intended, expected,
and actual outcome.

1. Introduction: Strategic discussion and decision-making, power and knowledge in meetings[1]

As Boden (1994, 82) observed, meetings are "the very stuff of management and, as
such, play an oddly central role in the accomplishment of the organization". However, while meetings occupy a significant proportion of any organizational praxis –

around 70 per cent according to one study (McCall et al. 1978) – as Schwartzman (1986, 249) has stressed, there is a "... need to produce field studies that examine what naturally occurring meetings do for individuals in specific organizations (...) how meetings affect individuals in specific settings (...) and to compare the structure and use of meetings across organizations and cross-culturally".

The sociologist Niklas Luhmann characterizes organizations primarily in terms of their decisions and the processes of decision making. He claims that these decision processes determine the everyday life in organizations. Organizations, he says, are constantly reproduced through decisions: "Organizations produce decision options which otherwise would not exist. Decisions serve as contexts for decisions" (Luhmann 1997, 830). Thus, for example, the European Union is a much differentiated system with an extremely complex structure. "With increasing complexity of decision-making on decisions on decisions", Luhmann says about such organizations, "the *autopoesis* creates conforming structures and develops a growing tendency towards a decision not to decide" (1997, 839). This may sound confusing at first, but what it means is that decisions are postponed, delegated, or shifted to other bodies by an organization. Organizations may even choose not to take any decision at all, and this also is a decision. Such processes happen at numerous meetings; the feeling that yet again "nothing has been achieved" simply means that there has been a decision not to decide anything definite and to postpone the decision.

Decisions are taken at many points in an organization, at meetings, in the corridors, during telephone conversations or on social and informal occasions, thus on frontstage or on backstage, or in transition from frontstage to backstage (or vice versa) (Goffman 1959). Hence, it is difficult to reconstruct individual incidents. Organizations also frequently tend to stage their decision processes, much like a drama, orally at meetings as well as through their protocols, directives and other written bureaucratic genres (Wodak 2000a, 2000b; Wodak 2011, 7f.). At least for an insider these scenes are comprehensible; they are hierarchically structured as not everyone has unlimited access to everything, accordingly status and power are produced and reproduced. Meetings are thus usually the sites where decisions are taken and where conflicts evolve and are resolved through decisions in more or less democratic ways (through debates, through voting procedures, through majorities or through the decisions of the powerful).

Individual managers and politicians pick up and read environmental signals differently (Hodgkinson and Sparrow 2002; Wodak 2011), potentially generating ambiguity (Weick 2001) as they expose their cognitive "schemas" in the process of decision-making, brainstorming or strategic change.[2] *Strategic discussion* – variously characterized as a strategic "choice process" (March and Olsen 1976), "challenging debate" (Bowman 1995), "self-organizing discussion" (Hendry and Seidl 2003), an "animated process" (Maitlis 2005), and as "free discussion" (Jarzabkowski and Seidl 2008) – is challenging because it generates discomfort when agents' perceptions are at odds with those of others. Without it, however, important organizational processes such as *sense-making* (Maitlis and Lawrence 2007) and *decision-making* (Pettigrew 1973; Eisenhardt and Bourgeois 1988) would be stymied. Thus, strategic discussion is a necessary precursor to strategic change and decision-making.[3] Of course, much organizational discussion is simply about keeping the "machine" running. Or, as Wodak et al. (2011) illustrate, much discussion also serves the construction of a corporate identity and specific bonding processes which function as pre-condition to more complex activities (see also Wodak 2000a, 2000b).[4]

An important dimension underpinning the enactment of strategic discussion is the continued negotiation of power in organizations through meetings. According to Mumby (1988, 68), meetings "function as one of the most important and visible sites of organisational power, and of the reification of organisational hierarchy". Power cannot be defined as a discrete entity but a relational process (Faubion 2000) that is inherently tied to communicative practices. Following Holzscheiter (2005), I view *power in discourse* as "actors' struggles with different interpretations of meaning" (2005, 69). This struggle for *semiotic hegemony* relates to the selection of "specific linguistic codes, rules for interaction, rules for access to the meaning-making forum, rules for decision-making, turn-taking, opening of sessions, making contributions and interventions" (2005, 69). *Power over discourse* is defined as the general "access to the stage" in macro- and micro contexts (Holzscheiter 2005, 57), i.e. processes of inclusion and exclusion. Finally, *power of discourse* relates to "the influence of historically grown macro-structures of meaning, of the conventions of the language game in which actors find themselves" (2005, 57). The individual influence of actors might contribute to changing these macro-structures (cf. also Wodak 2011, 34–36). Power struggles are obviously not always related to observable behavior.

Power is linked to *knowledge*. "Knowledge", in the view of Jäger and Maier (2009, 37), refers to "all kinds of contents that make up a human consciousness, or in other words, all kinds of meanings that people use to interpret and shape their environment". People derive this knowledge from the discursive surroundings into which they are born and in which they are enmeshed throughout their life. A consistent theme throughout Foucault's work is the idea that belief systems gain momentum and therefore power through their normalization such that they become "common knowledge" and that certain contradictory thoughts or acts can become "abnormal" or "impossible". Because this form of power covertly works through individuals and has no particular locus, resistance to this power actually serves to define it and in itself is only possible through knowledge (Foucault 1995;

Foucault and Rabinow 1984). "Knowledge management", then, involves several different dimensions of knowledge of groups or individual social actors which are informed by acquired and internalized event models, context models, and experience models, thus part of the socialization into a professional habitus and the many communities of practice to which people belong (see Wodak 2011, 45–49). Firstly, we can distinguish shared knowledge about preceding events and debates, rules and routines, and about the positions and opinions of specific managers or politicians, political parties or businesses. Moreover, experience and socialization into the profession are indicated through quick references to time and space (where events take place or have taken place, and in which documents with important topics are elaborated). It is possible to characterize this form of knowledge as *organizational knowledge* which can be either manifest or tacit (Polanyi and Grene 1969). Secondly, knowledge of specific agenda is necessary in order to participate actively in current debates and push ideological agenda, in specific meetings. Here the knowledge of expectations (i.e. *context models*; van Dijk 2008) as well as specific expertise in various domains becomes salient. Many utterances, insinuations and inferences cannot be understood without shared presuppositions and substantial knowledge in these areas. This dimension, therefore, could be defined as *expert knowledge*.

Finally, intensive organizational-political work on backstage is necessary and occurs continuously, and more or less explicitly: convincing and persuading others of one's opinion, lobbying, debating, arguing, struggling to win in motions, forming alliances, advising (and persuading) outsiders of one's ideas, and preparing and influencing decision making. This knowledge could be labeled *political knowledge* (or "know-how") and presupposes the knowledge of tactics and strategies, of ideologies and positions, of the strengths and weaknesses of colleagues; in sum, one has to know the "rules of the game". As will be illustrated below (Sections 4 and 5), politicians and managers perform several roles at once, and simultaneously draw on knowledge from all three dimensions. Hence, following Jäger and Maier's (2009) summary of the interdependent processes and relationships between discourse, knowledge, and power, I assume that

> [d]iscourses exert power because they transport knowledge on which collective and individual consciousness feeds. This knowledge is the basis for individual and collective, discursive and non-discursive action, which in turn shapes reality.
>
> (Jäger and Maier 2009, 39)

So how can we define strategic discussion in meetings and which factors contribute to it? To be able to investigate these issues, I propose a *prototype genre – meeting* – which is defined in abstract and general, schematic terms, thus elaborating on Bax's (2011) assumptions. In specific organizational contexts and social fields, organizational and expert knowledges as well as context models contribute to the actual interaction in a specified meeting. I claim that *organizational, expert and political knowledges* of the prototype genre meeting and related meeting types are part and parcel of successful interaction strategies; and that much miscommunication and problems could be avoided if manifest and latent *prototype genre conventions* and detailed *context models* were sufficiently acknowledged.

This chapter is set out in three parts. First, I review important theoretical and empirical work on interaction in meetings. In particular, I focus on: (i) the organizational discourse literature on the strategic dimension of meetings; and (ii) the linguistic literature on language in the workplace, in order to identify the main factors that appear to affect the emergence and development of, and the micro-level linguistic features that characterize strategic discussion. This provides two main conclusions for the definition of the *prototype genre of meeting*: (a) the *physical and social context* of the meeting and the *nature of the strategic issue* (i.e. the topic) being discussed matters; and (b) how these influences get manifested in the following constitutive characteristics: (i) the *behavior of the chair*; (ii) the level and form of *participation*; and (iii) the way in which different participants attempt to *argue and legitimate their respective viewpoints*.

In the second part of the chapter, I first present my model for analyzing text and talk in meetings combining the *Discourse-Historical Approach* (DHA) in Critical Discourse Studies (CDS) with *socio-cognitive approaches to genre* (see Bax 2011; van Dijk 2008; Wodak 2008, for extensive summaries). Having compared extant research on political and business meetings,[5] I then proceed – thirdly – to illustrating some key discursive strategies which are highly influential in strategic discussion and decision-making and thus also form an integral, stable part of the genre prototype meeting and related meeting types: *Bonding to create co-operate identities; establishing Salience via Urgency;* and *Mobilizing via threat and scenarios of danger.* I provide examples for these strategies while drawing on the range of meeting data from EU organizations and business companies from our fieldwork.

2.   Strategic discussion in meetings

In this chapter it is important to review the literatures from the domains of organization studies and linguistics (primarily, discourse studies and sociolinguistics). Within the former, we can distinguish theoretical and empirical work that touches upon the role of meetings in facilitating strategic change[6] and discourse analyses of strategy and strategic change. Within the latter, I focus primarily on linguistic studies of the use of language in the workplace, particularly large-scale empirical studies focused on linguistic-pragmatic, sociolinguistic, and argumentative behaviors within meetings.[7] It is possible to identify several categories which bridge factors known to influence strategic discourse within the Management Studies literature, and micro-level characteristics of naturally occurring talk in meetings within organization from the linguistics literature.[8]

2.1   Contextual factors: Participation

Recently, researchers have begun to focus on the role of the discussion context in influencing the conduct of strategic discussion within meetings. For example, Hendry and Seidl (2003) theorized that episodes of strategic discussion were more likely to emerge in *away-day meetings* – which are typically held in off-site locations – because these occasions created a sense of separation through different norms of dress and interpersonal interaction, which allowed individuals the time and space to escape from the constraints of organizational routines and structures in order to engage in critical reflection on strategic issues. Conversely, bracketing participants in a centralized organizational location served to reinforce the *authority of top managers* (Jarzabkowski and Seidl 2008). More recently, Bourque and Johnson (2008) argued that away-day workshops could be conceptualized as *ritualistic structures*, which create a sense of separation so as to allow participants to enter a state of *liminality*[9] unconstrained by regular routines and structures. This in turn establishes the conditions for: a relaxation of hierarchical norms; a sense of collegiality; and thus a greater willingness to engage in strategic discussion, also of novel and unexpected issues.[10] Bourque and Johnson (2008) also observed that the sense of de-coupling created by workshops combined with a high degree of ritualization encourage discussions with high levels of questioning and challenging of issues, but are less likely to lead to grounded decisions. Conversely events less decoupled from the workplace that are more concerned with practical implications are more likely to lead to decisions that allow change.

What is not addressed within the management literature on meetings however is how the *nature of the issue* (the *topic*) itself can influence strategic discussion. While not addressing how an issue is discussed *per se*, insight on this matter might be found within previous research on *strategic decision-making as a political process*. For a strategic discussion to be considered "strategic", it must involve discussion of an issue that is perceived by at least some participants as being *strategically salient* (and thus also *urgent*) to the future direction of the organization. Of course, the relative strategic importance of issues is socially constructed (Daft and Weick 1984; Feldman 1989). It begins with the diagnosis of perceived problems by individuals (Dutton 1993) who recruit support by selling the issue to others

(Dutton, Ashford, O'Neill, and Lawrence 2001; Rouleau 2005), and if successful, bring it to the attention of organizational decision-makers. These processes combined with *bounded rationality* (March and Simon 1958; Cyert and March 1963) serve to shape an organization's investment in time and attention towards a given issue and thus the subsequent ensuing actions (Ocasio 1997). Thus, issues that are allocated significant organizational attention, and invested with the self-interests of discussion participants, are more likely to lead to the emergence of episodes of strategic discussion and to successful decision-making. But does the *nature of the topic* itself influence the development of strategic discussion, and is this affected by the context in which it occurs?

2.2   Contextual factors: Topic, salience, urgency and threat

Organizational cognition researchers suggest that when faced with *salient threats,* participants will attempt to regain control by rigidly pursuing organizational routines, thus implying that the form of issues has some impact on strategic discussion. This hypothesis of "threat-rigidity" (Staw et al. 1981) suggests that *issues that are interpreted as urgent and immediate, and thus potentially threatening to the organization, are likely to be met with reflex responses,* while issues perceived as more "blue skies" in nature are seen as less dangerous and may lead to more open debate and discussion. Further, because particular organizational discourses enable some individuals more than others to establish their subject positions (van Leeuwen and Wodak 1999), such issues are likely to lead to these participants having a "louder voice" within a given interaction, with the effect that they may exclude or silence others (Hardy and Philips 1999) and make certain actions possible while delimiting others (Hardy and Philips 2004). Hence, it is probable that discourses around certain strategic issues (topics) – those defined as salient to a group of actors – are more likely to have individuals involved where their positions are socially tied to the issue (Knights and Morgan 1995). In other words, certain participants may be "automatically" tied into some discourses, because of their organizational or professional roles (Laine and Vaara 2007), with each person's talk reflecting their personality and interest (Taylor and Robichaud 2007).

This brief review suggests that the *context in which the meeting occurs* is likely to have a bearing on how strategic discussion and decision-making develop, in three ways. First, issues tend to be discussed if they have previously been subjected to *organizational attention* (i.e. *salience* is constructed). Second, those involved in discussion are more likely to be involved if the issue links closely to their *role and identity* in the organization (*urgency* and *imminent threat* are created). Third, patterns of interaction and decision-making will tend to align with the *structural type of meeting* in which they occur; with, for example, away-days leading to less constrained discussion than regular meetings inside the organization.

2.3   Level and means of involvement of participants

As Boden (1994) notes, while organizational meetings are characteristically associated with decision-making, observing them is difficult because of their diffuse and incremental nature within and across meetings. Consequently, it is important to unpack how strategic thinking and decision-making develop through linguistic interaction. Unfortunately, few studies have focused on how strategizing and decision-making are facilitated through talk. Notable exceptions are, for example, the "Language in the Workplace" project in New Zealand (e.g. Holmes 2000; Stubbe et al. 2003; Vine 2004), Bargiela-Chiappini and Harris's (1997) study of Italian and English corporate discourse; investigation of meetings in a big Australian company (Kwon, Clarke, and Wodak 2009, 2013) and various studies on meetings in national and transnational political organizations (e.g. Krzyżanowski and Oberhuber 2007; Menz 1999; Muntigl, Weiss, and Wodak 2000; Wodak 2011; Wodak, Krzyżanowski, and Forchtner 2012).

Drawing on these projects, three linguistic strategies can be seen to underpin participants' level of involvement in strategic discussion: (a) their *mode of participation*; (b) the degree to which they have *access to the floor*; and (c) their mode of *self-presentation*. The single most basic factor affecting individual involvement is the mode of participation in a meeting. Boden (1994), for example, commented that meetings are necessary to get key personnel all looking at the same problem at the same time (see Section 2.1).

A second aspect of *involvement* is the degree to which individuals have *access to the floor* to speak. Studies of gendered workplace participation have found, for example, that the distribution of talk and negotiation of access to the "floor" helps construct professional identities and power relations (Holmes 1992; Woods 1989). So-called negotiation of the floor is well documented, as is the role of *interruptions* (West and Zimmerman 1975, 1983) as a linguistic strategy for "doing power" (e.g. Bargiela-Chiappini and Harris 1997; Edelsky 1981; Schnurr et al. 2006). But while the literature in this field has grown, there is no clear picture that emerges, probably because of the absence of a widely accepted definition of what counts as an interruption as distinct from other types of overlapping speech (Talbot 1992; Beattie 1983). In order to identify interruptions, researchers typically focus on the Conversation Analysis notion of a *transition relevance place* (TRP) – the point where the speaker (turn-holder) may change. As Bargiela-Chiappini and Harris (1997) have shown, this can be particularly problematic when observing corporate meetings where several participants typically compete to gain access to the floor. Such *competitive bidding* for the floor has been held to be a critical means of accomplishing power (Hopper 1992), typified by interruptive speech overlap, which occurs when TRPs are not respected. In empirical terms, this type of competitive bidding – when participants offer "supportive feedback" that "does not constitute an attempted speaker-switch" (Talbot 1992, 459) – needs to be distinguished from overlapping talk which is purely facilitative.[11]

Finally, a third dimension of involvement in strategic discourse is the *mode of self-presentation*. The mode or manner by which individuals present themselves in meetings is important, since utterances not only convey information but also help negotiate social relations and construct identities, allowing speakers to perform several different social functions at once (Halliday 1978). Among the most salient linguistic resources for self-representation is the choice of the first person that helps construct the way the speaker represents themselves in relation to one or more others (Goffman 1959; Triandafyllidou and Wodak 2003) as well as to perform bonding processes.

2.4   Means of control over interactions: The influence of meeting chairs

A final crucial dimension of strategic discussion is the extent to which it is constrained or enabled by techniques of control over the interaction. This can operate through two main linguistic means: (a) *management of the meeting* by the chair by composing the agenda and controlling interactions by participants; and (b) by the innate *discursive structure* that might characterize different types of meetings.

As Holmes and Stubbe (2003) have amply demonstrated, management of meetings by the *chair* or a senior participant tends to be characterized by four discursive mechanisms: (a) setting the agenda, (b) summarizing progress, (c) keeping the discussion on track, and (d) reaching decisions (see also Angouri and Marra 2010). In terms of the agenda, it is well known to practitioners that the management of the meeting through presence or absence of an agenda and the role of the chair is important in exercising control over strategic discussion and decision-making processes. Senior managers have considerable discretion in determining what issues are "strategic" and therefore worthy of organizational attention, and the setting of the meeting agenda in advance allows them to exert control over what will be discussed (Kieffer 1988). Insights from practitioners suggest that a narrow agenda with a selection of issues increases the probability of substantial engagement with strategic issues (Mezias et al. 2001; Frisch and Chandler 2006). Related to the agenda, the behavior of the meeting chair can govern discussion of topics and the turn-taking pattern of speakers. The chair's ability to regulate turn-taking can therefore serve to reinforce hierarchical control, enabling organizational decision-makers to impose strategic agendas (Samra-Fredericks 2005) by reducing the scope of strategic discussion. These conclusions were reinforced by Jarzabkowski and Seidl (2008), who found that when the chair refrained from intervention, strategic discussion was more likely to occur.

Wodak, Clarke, and Kwon (2011) identified five salient *discursive strategies* which meeting chairs employ in driving decision-making: (1) Encouraging; (2) Directing; (3) Modulating; (4) Re/committing; and (5) Bonding. They found that the chair of the meetings (and leading manager) influences the outcome of the meetings in both negative and positive ways, through the choice of specific *discursive strategies*. It also became apparent that the specific context and related meeting type mediate participation and the ability of the chair to control interactions within the team. Moreover, the authors argue, a more hierarchical authoritarian or a more interpersonal egalitarian leadership style can be identified via specific combinations of these five discursive strategies. Wodak et al. (2011) conclude that the *egalitarian leadership style* increases the likelihood of achieving a durable consensus. I will come back to these five strategies below, when attempting to arrive at a decision in the meeting dynamics.

Another means of controlling interactions in meetings is by *orchestration of the overall structure of the discussion*. For instance, Holmes and Stubbe (2003) identified two broad types of topical structural patterns in meetings: *linear and cyclical*, in which linear discussion patterns tend to follow an agenda quite closely, whereas cyclical discussion deviates from it in a more exploratory fashion. They argue that *linear patterns* typically occur in meetings when information giving or reporting occurs. It tends to be associated with "rubber stamping" exercises and discussion in which the chair takes a prominent role. Significantly, this yields a correlation between decision-making and interactional patterns. Importantly, however, linear discussion also tends to occur in the final stages of decision-making during which topic-management and turn-management by the chair is important for decision-making.

Cyclical patterns of discussion tend to be more associated with planning meetings involving "brainstorming" and creative problem solving, in which the same point may recur several times, tackled from different perspectives as elaboration occurs through competing arguments being marshaled. Given the prominent focus on "free thinking" associated with away day meetings, this suggests that strategic discussion in such contexts is likely to represent a "spiral" pattern of topic-management, and that the chair's control over the interaction will be less prominent than in regular meetings (see Kwon et al. 2009). It is probable, therefore, that the chair can exert high-level control on the overall nature of strategic discussion simply by choosing a different format or type of meeting.

Kwon, Clarke, and Wodak (2013) investigate how conflict over ideas within the team is stimulated by actors' deploying discursive strategies that shape consensus. They illustrate that the overall management of meetings is indeed salient. Furthermore, they argue that four discursive strategies used by actors are instrumental in shaping consensus formation around strategic issues. *Re/Defining* provides a new proposition/perspective; *Justifying/Legitimizing* gives support to a proposition; *Challenging* confronts the propositions of other actors; and *Mobilizing* is used to identify practical actions to address the issue. Using detailed illustrations, the authors show how repetition of these strategies leads to clear outcomes from strategic discussion in terms of the *salience* and *urgency* of the issue being identified, and the *feasibility* of plans to address the issue being assessed (see also Section 2.1).

I will come back to these four discursive strategies (as well as the five strategies of getting people on board) and the dimensions of salience, urgency, and threat related to the topic discussed in a meeting (either political or business or both) below when illustrating them with text extracts (Section 4). These examples serve to illustrate, on the one hand, the vast range of context-dependent meeting types as realizations of the *prototype genre "meeting"*; on the other hand, these examples also allow detecting differences and similarities between the fields of business and politics in respect to these three dimensions. It is, of course, not possible to conduct any representative or standardized modes of comparison here. This is also not the aim of this chapter. Rather, these examples serve to point to – as I argue – *constitutive factors of the prototype genre of meeting and the specificities of the meeting type.* As the fields of business and politics interact and overlap more and more (e.g. Mautner 2010),[12] it would also be of interest for future research to investigate interdiscursive and intertextual relationships in-depth (Fairclough and Wodak 2008; Wodak and Fairclough 2010) and establish *empirically* if and how interaction in meetings and other discursive practices from the fields of business and politics are converging.

3. The Discourse-Historical Approach (DHA) – Defining discourse, genre, context, and text

> The 'doing' of discourse analysis requires us to attend to aspects of bounded space and multiple locales – the landscapes within which discourse is conducted (…) this process involves a robust delineation of text and context where the focal discourse is uncoupled and investigated independently of the physical surroundings and the wider social context in which it occurs (…) these contexts (that is, other

spaces) are not simply a backdrop to text, they are actually embedded within it: the text actually forms part of the context and vice versa.

(Keenoy and Oswick 2003, 139–140)

In this section, I briefly outline the Discourse Historical Approach (DHA) because it provides a robust set of discourse constructs and a heuristic framework for analyzing the important issue of contextual influences on talk in empirically systematic ways. The DHA is different from other forms of CDA in that it enables analysis of the historical (i.e. intertextual) dimension of discursive actions by exploring the *ways in which particular genres of discourse are subject to change through time, and also by integrating social theories to explain context.* Following Foucault (1972), "historical context" includes the history and subsystem of meetings and narratives in the organization as well as wider forces. Consequently, "history" can involve studying how language use changes over shorter timescales, for example, during one meeting (over a certain amount of time) or over several meetings, as part of latent and manifest rules and norms that serve to rationalize, explain, and make sense of organizational events (e.g. Lalouschek et al. 1990; Linde 2008; Mumby and Clair 1997). Thus, the contextual knowledge about the individual team members, the organization, and its industry that is gained through ethnographic field research is a necessary prerequisite for gaining substantive insight into the dynamics of a strategy meeting.

Figure 1 illustrates the relation between the conceptual scaffolding of DHA and its practical application as a methodology. Thus, I view the empirical event under investigation (decision-making in a meeting in an organization as part of the prototype genre meeting) as a phenomenon that has discursive manifestations across four heuristic "levels of context" (Wodak 2011):

i. the *immediate, co-text of the communicative event* in question (e.g. the transcript of a business or political meeting);
ii. the *intertextual and interdiscursive relationship* between utterances, texts, genres and discourses (e.g. transcripts of individual interviews with members of the respective organization, other meetings, meeting minutes and agendas of meetings, powerpoint presentations);
iii. the *extralinguistic social* (e.g. physical gestures, facial expressions, posture) and *environmental* (e.g. location, room size and layout) *variables and institutional frames* (e.g. formal hierarchical structure, informal power relations, institutional imperatives) of a specific *context of situation* (derived from observer notes and reflections on direct observations of the communicative event);

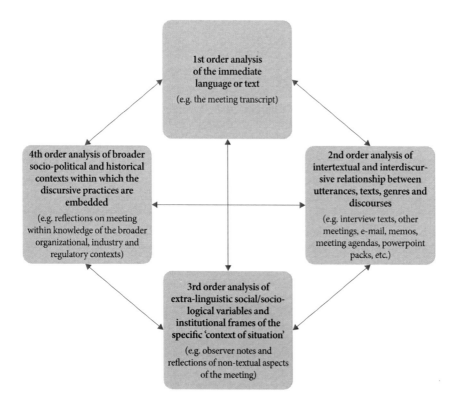

Figure 1. Recursive analysis between four context levels (adapted from Clarke, Kwon, and Wodak 2011)

iv. the broader *sociopolitical and historical context* which discursive practices are embedded in and related to (e.g. knowledge derived from ethnographic study of the organization and aspects of the broader social and cultural macro-environment that influence the direction and sustainability of the respective business or political, national or transnational organization).

Understanding the empirical phenomenon as having hierarchical levels of context allows unpacking the relationship between the motivations/ideologies (e.g. underlying agendas, ingrained attitudes and practices) of organizational actors and their actions (i.e. what they say and do). This relationship between intent and action can be understood through the linguistic concepts of discursive strategies and linguistic devices. By use of the term "strategy" the DHA implies a more or less intentional plan of practices (including discursive practices) adopted to achieve a particular goal, a definition which draws on Bourdieu's (1972) conception of the strategies of individuals as a dynamic interaction between habitus, internalized disposition, social structures and a historically determined set of potential actions (see Reisigl and Wodak 2009). This distinction between *discursive strategies* and *linguistic devices* is key to making sense of episodes of social interaction in that (planned or subconscious) intentions of actors are translated into action through discursive strategies, which are operationalized through linguistic devices. This distinction overcomes the tendency to conflate devices and strategies, which can result in an overly mechanical and deterministic view of the dynamics of discursive interaction (see Samra-Fredericks 2003; Wodak et al. 2009, for differentiated critique; Section 1).

In the DHA, "discourse" is not viewed as simply determining social action but also as integrating a voluntaristic element. These two aspects are intertwined or, as Fairclough and Wodak (1997) put it, discourse (and *semiosis* in general) is

> a form of 'social practice'. Describing discourse as a social practice implies a dialectical relationship between a particular discursive event and the situation(s), institution(s) and social structure(s), which frame it. (…) To put the same point in a different way, discourse is socially *constitutive* as well as socially shaped.
>
> (Fairclough and Wodak 1997, 258)

Moreover, Reisigl and Wodak (2009, 89) define *discourse* as being

- related to a macro-topic (and to the argumentation about validity claims such as truth and normative validity which involves social actors who have different points of view);
- a cluster of context-dependent semiotic practices that are situated within specific fields of social action;
- socially constituted as well as socially constitutive;
- integrating various differing positions and voices.

Furthermore, I distinguish between *discourse* and *text*. *Discourse* implies patterns and commonalities of knowledge and structures, whereas a *text* is a specific and unique realization of a *discourse*. Texts relate to *genres* (or *prototype genres* – such as the prototype genre of meeting postulated in this chapter). The full sense of a text only becomes accessible when its manifest and latent meanings (inter alia implicature, presupposition, allusion) are made sense of in relation to one's wider knowledge(s) of the world and specific organizational contexts (see also Section 1).[13]

Bakhtin's early work (1986, 60) defined genre as, initially, *each separate* utterance, but emphasized that each sphere in which language is used tends to develop its own relatively *stable types* of these utterances – which he defined as "speech genres". Systemic Functional Linguistics, sociolinguistic studies on language in the professions, Discourse Studies, and Applied Linguistics have also extensively discussed the concept of genre.[14] For example, Martin (1996) states that

> topological description [of genres …] is organised around prototypes; it associates phenomena with cores, with phenomena treated as more or less closely associated with each other.   (Martin 1996, 364)

Such a concept of cognitive schemata available as *proto-types of genres* lends itself well to be related both to van Dijk's concept of *context models* (2008) as well as to the DHA's assumptions of discursive strategies and context-dependent realization of strategies via linguistic devices.[15] I thus agree with Bax's definition (which draws on Artificial Intelligence categories) that

> [g]enres are *ideals*, texts are real (…), share *mental constructs*, and are characterised first and foremost by the *functions* which they perform; the function of a genre then guides the *features* of the genre (…); genres have structure, as one of their main features (…); genres are identified not only by formal criteria, but also by *social* and *contextual* factors (…); genres are highly *flexible,* and they can change, blend, evolve and die out.   (Bax 2011, 60–61; italics original)

Moreover, Bax (2011, 61f.) makes clear distinctions between *genres* and *discourse modes* such as narrative, reporting, interacting or argumentative modes. Modes are inherent in genres, but they do not have a specific social function. If we relate this discussion to the prototype genre of meeting, we are able to distinguish distinct structures, modes, and functions which are realized in specific texts, i.e. a unique meeting. Thus meetings have clear, manifest and latent, social functions (such as decision-making), clear structures (set by the agenda, the rules of procedure, hierarchy of participants, knowledges of participants, location, space and time), various modes (interacting, interspersed with narrative and argumentative modes), shared expectations and context models of the participants, and are flexible in that structures may also change (e.g. due to new meeting chairs, new locations, and new functions). As I argue below, meetings with the function of decision-making also require nine discursive strategies as constitutive factors, to be judged as successful; i.e. of achieving a consensual decision.

4.   "Meeting" and meeting types: Salient discursive strategies

In Wodak, Clarke, and Kwon (2011) and in Kwon, Clarke, and Wodak (2013), we were able to abductively identify a range of (five) discursive strategies which characterize styles of leadership (when attempting to "get people on board", thus creating a cooperate identity) and, in the latter paper, (four) strategies to arrive at consensually taken decisions on the background of such a cooperate identity (which serves as precondition for arriving at a consensus). For this research, meeting and interview data were collected in a large Australian aerospace company by ethnography, tape-recordings, and interviews. In re-analyzing political meetings in EU organizations, it became obvious that similar discursive strategies were salient when supporting bonding processes and attempting to "get people on board" (Wodak 2000a, 2000b, 2011; Wodak, Krzyżanowski, and Forchtner 2012) even though these meetings were conducted in totally different settings (in the European Parliament (plenary discussion and committee meetings) and in the European Commission). Thus, in the following, I will first shortly present the nine discursive strategies mentioned above (see Section 2.4) and then proceed to illustrating the three dimensions of *salience, urgency and threat* in relationship to the discursive strategies of negotiating consensus in more detail as they contribute to the specific meeting type (related to the prototype genre of meeting) (Figure 2 summarizes all nine discursive strategies).

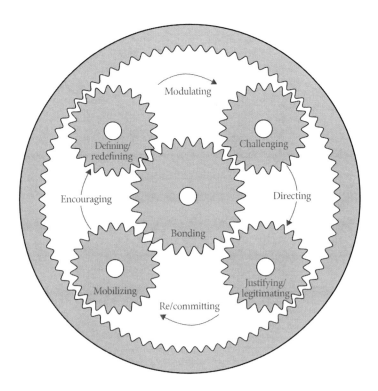

Figure 2. Interplay of discursive strategies in driving decision-making and forming consensus (see also Section 2.4)

Strategies to arrive at consensus:
Re/Defining – Formulating a perspective or changing it to make it align with own interests;
Justifying/Legitimating – Expressing a logic or rationale using arguments or supporting validity of others' ideas;
Challenging – Negating a view of Others to provoke explanation or modifying of ideas;
Mobilizing – Moving from general understanding towards specific action, operationalizing a decision.

Strategies to "get people on board":
Encouraging – Stimulating participation of other speakers to explore new ideas/ synthesize with others;
Directing – Bringing discussion toward closure and resolution by reducing equivocality of ideas;
Modulating – Regulating the perception of external environmental threats or institutional imperatives to act;
Re/Committing – Moving from consensual understanding of issue towards commitment to action to address it;
Bonding – Support to promote (or undermine) cohesive group identity around the issue.

As shown in Text 1 below, *Bonding* serves the discursive construction of group identity that supports motivation to reach consensus and a decision. Bonding is thus constitutive of the specific meeting type where decisions are supposed to be taken via reaching a consensus. The distribution of use of personal pronouns among the different participants in each meeting is of importance, as well as the transitivity of their respective collocates. For example, the selection of the singular "I" versus the plural "we" in discussion has considerable sociological and rhetorical implications (Mulderrig 2011; Petersoo 2007; Wodak 2011; Wodak et al. 2009): while the singular form claims personal responsibility for the remainder of the sentence, the plural form collectivizes it, so it could be used to emphasize authority, avoid or accept responsibility, and minimize or expand claims made by the speaker. In respect to the bonding strategy, the so-called "theory of group-think" argues that too much accommodation and internalization of group norms prevents successful decision-making because no arguments or deliberations take place. In this way, quasi-decisions that are reached fast rarely tend to hold over time (Janis 1972). People who tend to disagree are usually marginalized in group-think and cohesive bonding processes.

Establishing *Bonding* through self/other-presentation, *legitimation* and *justification* strategies: Text 1 – Competitiveness Advisory Group Meeting (European Commission) (see Wodak and Weiss 2002)

[....]

M9   I think, another strong point ehm, which we're just beginning to see, is, in the context of a global market place. Ehm, Europe's historical positioning around the world. And the fact that uniquely in terms of the main blocks of economic activity, the United States, Europe and Japan, ehm, we in Europe are best positioned to cover the world with cultural and commercial links. And if I can turn to my left, you take Spain, I mean, Spain has rediscovered an Hispanic market which extends not just throughout most of Latin America but also of course in the United States. Ehm, and we're beginning to find in other parts of the world that we have links, which are old links, which have been dormant and which can come forth, and in terms of, you know Europe in a global market place, that inheritance is very very strong. But we got to capitalize it, and use it.

Paye Just, a, a sentence adding to that point. European is more international than, than other ones, and ….

M9   Exact, and it's very much easier as a European to develop commercial partnerships outside your domestic country than it is for Americans, or Japanese. And that's partly because of our inheritance and history.

M4   … maybe, our diversity …

M9   … that too …

M3   Diversity is a richness, not a weakness, to a large extent.

M9   There are two layers to it: I mean, the, the, there is the diversity and that in one sense or another we cover the globe, eh, but there is also the, the history and the way in which we have operated, we, we do have a more global view of the world than the Americans, far more so.

M3   Exact, it is the long-term favour of fall-out of our colonial past. Yeah, after 30 years of independence of all our former colonies we can say that now, today. Without being accused of neo-, neo-colonialism. Yeah.

F1   In a more friendly way, in our entrepreneurship. Our ancestors went out, sailing, to do business.

M6   Well, American multinationals have done well but, I mean you, I mean the, the, the, many sectors, I'm not saying your sector, but I mean, one cannot forget that … …

M9   I, I, I'm not xxx the Americans, in that sense, and eh, all I'm saying is that ehm, they do have a blind spot. And their blind spot is often their ability to make partnerships outside their domestic base. Ehm, and they have significant blind spots within Europe, in, Europe is Europe is Europe, except there is an English speaking bit in the UK, and the, they ha, they have difficulty in sensing the differences between countries, and it, it's much tougher for them. Where as we have something which we haven't used for a long time, but is, is, is coming forward here, and, I, I, I do take the Hispanic point is very strong as you know and me too well, in eh, in all sorts of businesses, telecommunications, financial services, you name it, it's eh, they've found a new market.

Paye   Alright, that, you, do, do you see any other eh, strong eh, points, or should we move to the next session?

This sequence is one of the few in a EU meeting where spontaneous discussion occurs although the Competitiveness Advisory Group is obviously meeting backstage (it is a closed meeting, nobody – apart from the selected members of the committee – has access). Nevertheless, clear rules of conduct and procedure govern such meetings – the meeting chair Paye calls on the speakers, and speakers' turns are returned to the chair again. This extract illustrates a brainstorming session where everybody contributes to the characteristics of a new European identity, one which stands in contrast to the USA and Japan. The rules of procedure are suddenly obsolete as a huge *Bonding* starts: the members of the committee try to convince each other that specific European aspects are actually to be viewed as positive and not negative. This sequence thus functions to emphasize group solidarity and establish a constructive working atmosphere between agonistic players, the employers' side and delegates from trade-unions (see Muntigl et al. 2000; Wodak 2000a, 2000b for detailed analysis). Here, I would like to point out two salient linguistic strategies employed to establish Bonding and subsequently a positive corporate identity: constructing positive self-presentation and negative other-presentation, primarily via the use of "I, we", and "they", and legitimation and justification strategies. All the characteristics mentioned in this short dialogue point to Europe's traditions in justice and welfare, education and professional expertise, thus to traditional values. Specifically, Europe's internationalism is mentioned, its tradition in contacting other parts of the world, in contrast to the USA which does not have this history.

Some other characteristics are added on during this brainstorming session: diversity and knowledge. Moreover, the debate about "diversity" is of interest here. Diversity is defined in a positive way, as richness of cultures and traditions and languages, not as something negative – which frequently confronts all European citizens in rightwing populist rhetoric (Wodak and Köhler 2010). All the positive characteristics reassure the members of the committee that Europe has a chance in the world market even though taxes are higher and labor laws stricter. In the entire sequence, we also encounter a clear argumentative schema: If Europe has all these positive values and if "they" (i.e. the US and Japan) do not have these values and traditions, then Europe ("we") will be stronger and win (in the economic competition). The evidence (*datum*) is spelt out in detail (the range of positive values), and even an *argumentum ad exemplum* is presented to substantiate the conclusion (the Hispanic case).

The specific Europeanness is co-constructed interactively. The second strategy of identity construction consists in distinguishing oneself from others, the USA and Japan, thus in creating uniqueness, which is quite typical of discourses on identity (see Wodak et al. 2009). The above passage is salient for the positive outcome of the meeting which has to arrive at a consensual decision on a policy paper combating unemployment. It has the function of creating optimism and showing solutions to the European economic problems. The positive self-assessment, realized in the frequent use of the plural pronoun "we" makes everybody "stronger". Thus, the passage vastly contributes to constructing positive identities and self-presentations of the committee members. Towards the end of it, the chair moves to the next topic and Re/defines the agenda.

It is apparent that meeting participants tend to respond to issues that represent either opportunities or threats by developing an initial formulation of a proposition to introduce a new perspective, or by the reformulation of an existing proposition (*Re/Defining*; see analysis of Text 2 below). Speakers tend to do this to shape the issue under discussion to make it congruent with their own interests (i.e. knowledge, practices, vested material interests, etc.), to make it more acceptable to the other participants, either by simply stating their view as a definition, or by emphasizing it to make it *salient*. Moreover, Kwon, Clarke, and Wodak (2013) found that members of a meeting tended to express a rationale or logic for a proposition through justifying, giving reasons, and/or supporting the validity of an existing proposition, by signaling the legitimacy of the speaker to talk about the issue at hand (*Justifying/Legitimating*). Frequently, this is backed up by the *topos of threat* (defined as a warrant of the form "If X, then Y"; i.e. *If we don't do that, we will fail*).[16] That implies that the other meeting participants then are forced to state goals, give reasons and explain the causality of a situation in response to the "threats", which produces "positive energy" and momentum (Pettigrew et al. 1992). Such strategies can be used to legitimate/delegitimate/re-legitimate actions within the context of a specific setting (van Leeuwen and Wodak 1999).

Redefining/Justifying by creating *Urgency*: Text 2 – Lines 185–192,
Business Meeting
185 Mike: Yeah, we do it (*redistributing agenda around the company; RW*) all the time
and – with David, for example, we have one
186   lawyer, and a fine lawyer he is, and it's held at the centre, and his expertise – such as
187   it is [laughter] – is shared across the business. But we've never done it with engineers

188	Really, with output producers. So we'll find that much more difficult. And we did with
189	FSG, and maybe it's a lot better now, but we certainly did it at the start. And what's
190	more here is we've got a very finite – we've got a burning platform, if you like –
191	which we need to put out, maybe before we can reach a level of maturity that – is that
192	going to work? What do you think, Will and Charlie?

In this brief turn, the Australian CEO Mike employs several strategies at once: he has to get the other team members on board, thus he has to provide evidence for the decision to tackle the potential job. Mike does this in several steps; first, by praising the lawyer of the firm who has all the necessary expertise and experience (*predicational strategy, topos of authority*). Simultaneously, he provides evidence for the *feasibility* of taking a new project on board, as legal expertise would be available. Secondly, he concedes that it might be more difficult to work with engineers (lines 187–189), but recurs to some other positive shared experience (*topos of history*). Moreover, he unifies the team via witty remarks (lines 186–187). Thirdly, he redefines the decision which has to be taken now and quickly by defining it as "finite", thus concise, and urgent. *Urgency* is created by employing a metaphor: "burning platform which has to be put out". Thus, he indirectly implies: if this decision is not reached now, then they will remain immature (line 191) and be potentially destroyed (set on fire) (*topos of threat*).

In this way, Mike's turn can be conceived as indirect latent argument, in the form of "if we do not take this job on, we will be destroyed". This argument (if p then q) is realized in three steps as outlined above. At the end, Mike attempts to mitigate the directive force of his turn by allowing Will and Charlie to voice their opinions (lines 191–192). He addresses them directly, with open questions. On the other hand, the emphasis and force of the argument would probably defy resistance by other team members as is illustrated immediately by the further dynamics of this meeting, in Text 5 below (lines 265–279).

Text 3 (and Text 4) also demonstrate that sometimes participants identify actions to address their understanding of issues, a strategy Kwon, Clarke, and Wodak (2013) label *Mobilization*. The intent of this strategy is to provoke further discussion related to the commitment of organizational resources required, specific people, or the responsibilities and timescales associated with each action by attributing responsibility to individuals (Sillince and Mueller 2007), thus providing the initial impetus to act upon the issue.

Mobilizing by creating *Salience* and *Danger*: Text 3 – Committee Meeting
in the European Parliament (see Wodak 2011)

MEP 1 (Hans):   uhm I am very thankful for this working paper of the (xxx) science
directorate we probably could have used that much earlier,
for example when we began the Eastern enlargement discussions
on a parliamentary level … in reality we would have had better
management at the European level then we could have like at the
time of the single market when we began with the single market
concept (   )[and] thoroughly discussed what the possibilities
[and] chances are then we could have (   ) very very differently
in terms of Eastern enlargement

At the beginning of this short statement in the Committee of Social Affairs (a
standing committee in the European Parliament), Hans *Re/defines* the topic: he
wants to talk about the costs of Enlargement. He presupposes that everybody
knows and has read the document he is referring to; he also presupposes that
every committee member is well informed about the problems related to Eastern
Enlargement and about the many debates and decisions which have already taken
place. He employs the discursive strategies of *Challenging* and *Justifying* by painting an "unreal scenario" – "what would have happened if" – in order to highlight
how much better it would have been had the debate on the enlargement issue begun much earlier, thus creating *danger* and *urgency*. He also refers intertextually
to past debates on the Single Market, where he claims better procedures had been
used. By drawing on this as a *shared* past experience ("when *we* began with (…)
and thoroughly discussed") as a model of how things should have been done in
relation to enlargement, he is assuming not only that this event is shared knowledge but also that everybody agrees with his evaluation of it (*topos of history*).
His brief account also serves as *Justification* for the *feasibility* of the agenda. The
macro argumentative strategy consists in a justification for missed opportunities
and obviously wrong decisions and policies, in Hans' view. He shifts the blame to
the Commission (a well-known and frequently occurring fallacy in politicians'
persuasive rhetoric), which serves to unite the committee members and also re-
lieves them of responsibility (*Bonding*). In this way, his brief introduction sets the
ground for more detailed criticism and some constructive proposals.

Mobilizing by creating *Salience*: Text 4 – Lines 1–15, Business Meeting

1   Mike: Alright then. Can we have a – can we just – Avionics. Can we talk about
Avionics?

2   Will: Yep.

3   Larry: OK. Do you want me to …

4   Mike: Yeah [talking together, laughter].

5   Larry: Um – well – perhaps, my comments will be around resources / Mike: Resourcing? /

6   Rather than the technical issues, which is a separate but related issue?

7   So I'll address the resource issue –

8   Charlie: Are you going to have a meeting with us and then a meeting with Gerald?

9   Larry: OK, that might be the better way to do it. Get the big picture first and

10   then drill down into it.

11   [talking together, laughter, joking]

12   Mike: Alright, knock yourself out there.

13   Adam: We got the process right.

14   Charlie: [indistinct]

15   Mike: Go ahead.

In this extract, it becomes apparent that Mike wants everybody to focus on just one topic – the new project, and that secondly this topic is of huge importance for the team and company. In using his leadership role and by acting as chair (a role which he delegates later on; see Wodak et al. 2011), he takes the floor and introduces the topic by repeating a rhetorical question which – as a speech act of request – also has a slightly less directive meaning in this context than a direct command would have had: "Can we have a – can we just – Avionics? Can we talk about Avionics?" (line 1). In this way, he precludes resistance to the topic; Larry feels addressed by Mike and starts introducing one aspect of the topic, namely resources. Mike, who would like to talk about the more urgent overall picture, *challenges* Larry's choice by interrupting Larry and asking "resourcing?" (line 5). Charlie intervenes, intending to co-construct the specific topical dimension by proposing an alternative route; in this way, Charlie indirectly rejects Mike's attempt at discussing the new project and suggests having meetings with other people first (line 8). Larry seems to agree with Charlie's proposal and *re/defines* it as if it would allow getting the big picture (lines 9–10). This brief negotiation leads to casual joking which implies that Mike has not succeeded as yet in establishing the *salience* and *urgency* of the agenda. Thus, in line 12, Mike reframes his turn and agenda, this time with a direct command by using a quite casual idiom: "knock yourself out there" (line 12). Adam immediately supports this second attempt, and Mike reinforces his agenda in line 15 by requesting Larry to speak.

This brief interaction illustrates that it took Mike two attempts to establish the *salience* of the agenda; and that he had to overcome resistance by shifting from a more indirect mode to a very direct mode of command. The interaction also points to the team member who will probably cause most resistance in the course of this meeting, namely Charlie – out of various motives which only become clearer when more context information is available.

Moreover, Kwon et al. (2013) found that although salience and feasibility of the issue were also established in a regular meeting which had to decide on two alternatives, the creation of a *strong sense of urgency* to address the issue became relevant. As Text 5 shows, only *after* a sense of urgency was created and the salience of the issue was established, was the team able to move on to consider the *feasibility* of its plan of action to address it.

Justifying feasibility: Text 5 – Lines 265–279, Business Meeting

265 Mike: Well, on the other hand … / Adam: Well my / – there's nothing like a
266   burning platform to get people to …
267 Adam: My variation on Larry's thing would be to incentivize people on
268   resources, to share resources with the enterprise, not just on projects, to
269   make them more responsible.
270 Larry: Oh, oh, OK, you mean incentivize managers. I thought you were
271   talking about incentivizing these individuals / Adam: no /, OK.
272 Mike: So are we talking about Hobson's choice here, really? Do we have any
273   other option what to do, this way, other than saying we're not going to
274   take the PEREGRINE contract? That's the two options.
275 Will: I believe what Larry's saying about sharing the resources across the
276   projects is fundamental. If we don't do that, we will fail.
277 Mike: Right, and then at some level of abstraction I agree with that, and
278   absolutely. But now we've got this [bangs table for emphasis] cast-iron,
279   concrete case that we have to do something about.

In this brief extract, the CEO and chair of the meeting Mike first intertextually refers to his use of the "burning platform" metaphor in line 190 (see Text 2); explaining why he had thought that it would be an effective device to stress *urgency*. This utterance serves as a meta- comment on his previous turn (see Text 2) and thus validates our analysis and interpretation. Adam agrees with Mike and provides another justification for using such powerful language: such metaphors, etc., would be able to *Mobilize* the team to share responsibility (lines 267–269).

In this way, lines 265–269 reinforce the previous arguments. Then Mike shifts the frame of discussion and returns to *Mobilizing* the team. He creates a clear choice by reducing complexity: two options to choose from! Will agrees this time by repeating Larry's argument about sharing responsibility (and resources). Only if that works, the new contract would be feasible. *He creates even more salience by providing a topos of threat*: "If we don't do that, we will fail". Mike agrees partially, but then *Re/defines* the decision by reiterating the *urgency* and *feasibility*. This time he employs another metaphor, "cast-iron concrete case", which emphasizes the materiality of the decision as well as the concreteness (in contrast to Will's abstractness).

5. Discussion and conclusion

As illustrated above, the specific *type of meeting* (derived from the *prototype genre of meeting*), with the social function of consensual decision-making, is dependent on the ability of participants to establish *not only* the *salience* of the issue and the *feasibility* of their plan to address it, *but also* a strong sense of *urgency* to move people and resources to actually mobilize that plan. *Urgency* thus appears an essential outcome in the co-construction of actionable consensus in both social fields, in business and in politics, in particular settings and with chairs who have succeeded in creating a corporate identity of the participants. Therefore, multilateral negotiation between team members as opposed to the domination by powerful actor(s) is a necessary and crucial aspect of the process through which urgency is created. Figure 3 summarizes the process of co-construction of consensus, applicable across social fields.

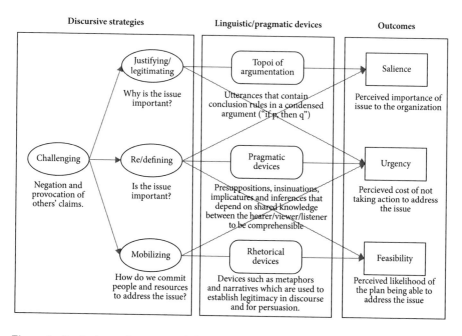

Figure 3. Strategies and outcomes (adapted from Kwon, Clarke, and Wodak 2013)

Figure 3 illustrates the conceptual framework of the co-construction of consensus (Kwon et al. 2013).[17] The authors argue that "[S]*alience* of an issue is defined as its perceived relative importance to the ongoing survival and future prospects of an organization" (Kwon et al. 2013). It is a discursively constructed reason or purpose through the interaction of two strategies. Moreover, Kwon et al. (2013) state that "*[R]e/defining* simultaneously serves as a sensegiving and a sensehiding mechanism that privileges some agenda and related discourses or actors while simultaneously marginalizing others (Gioia and Chittipeddi 1991)". Accordingly, more powerful actors have more space for *Justifying/Legitimating* their proposed actions through the accumulation of logical arguments and appeals to emotion (Weick 1995) in order to enhance commitment to change and increase motivation to act (Sillince 2005). Finally, the authors emphasize that

> *[F]easibility* is the assessment of the likelihood that a proposed plan of action to address an issue will succeed. Assessments of *feasibility* are made in conjunction with the definition and interpretation (*Re/Defining*) of an issue – feasible and urgent issues are more likely to lead to the *Mobilization* of people and resources for a plan of action, more likely to result in significant organizational change.
>
> (Kwon et al. 2013)

Most importantly, the *Urgency* of a strategic issue is the perceived cost of not taking action to resolve or mitigate its negative consequences (Miller 1982). In sum, the authors conclude that more urgent issues receive greater organizational attention and resources, while those issues that are not urgent may become inactive for lack of attention (Ocasio 1997).

Importantly for defining the specific meeting type, I argue that when establishing the entire procedure of arriving at a consensual decision, *Bonding* is first used by the meeting chair (leader) to create a constructive and cooperative atmosphere. *Re/Defining* is then secondly employed to create an *urgent* issue. *Justifying/Legitimating* is thirdly used to establish *why* and *when* something must be done. *Mobilizing* is simultaneously employed to explain *how* and *when* something must be done. Thus, the *discursive construction of time pressure* (see also Lalouschek et al. 1990; Wodak 1996) is integral to this meeting-type with the social *function of achieving a consensual decision* as the issue is *Re/Defined* in terms of deadlines or *threats* of impending danger in order to *Justify/Legitimate* the reason *why* something must be done, and to *Mobilize* the commitment of people and resources to a given plan of action.

If we now return to Bax's criteria for defining the prototype genre (see Section 3), then the specific meeting type which has the social function of achieving a consensual decision possesses a clear structure, displays shared collective experience and expectations, has characteristic features (such as the interacting and argumentative modes as well as typical discursive strategies), and these meetings – both "political" and "business" ones – are also defined contextually and socially in their respective fields and organizations. The social fields and organizations influence the choice of conversational styles, the choice of language, the specific professional and technical language, and the specific shared knowledges which are presupposed and necessary for efficient decision-making. Moreover, bonding occurs in all such meetings, as do the construction of salience of topic, urgency for arriving at the decision, and predictable threat if no decision is achieved. Of course, the topics and agenda differ in different social fields and organizations (in business and politics) as do the specific realizations of the texts.

Notes

1. This chapter draws on research on meetings in a large business company, conducted by the author at Lancaster University primarily with Ian Clarke (now Management School, Edinburgh University) and Winston Kwon (Management School, Lancaster University); and – for a brief period of several months in 2009 – also with Jane Mulderrig (now Sheffield University) in the years 2008–2011 (see Clarke et al. 2011; Kwon et al. 2009, forthcoming; and Wodak et al. 2011, for detailed presentations of the results). Moreover, the chapter also draws on research conducted during the DYLAN project 2006–2011 (see http://www.dylan-project.org/Dylan_en/home/home.php for more details). The author was the PI of the Lancaster team (consisting of Michał Krzyżanowski and Bernhard Forchtner) and also Manager of Workpackage 2 which investigated the organizations of the European Union (see Wodak et al. 2012, for an extensive analysis of various meetings in the European Parliament and the European Commission). At this point, I would like to express my gratitude to all project partners, both in the DYLAN project and at Lancaster University. Indeed, the specific research for this chapter would not have been possible without them. Of course, the entire responsibility for the final version remains solely with the author. The chapter also draws on previous research on political meetings conducted by the author in the European Commission (see Wodak 2000a, 2000b, 2011; Muntigl et al. 2000) and on meetings in various other organizations (in Austria) (hospitals, schools, crisis intervention centers, and so forth; see Lalouschek et al. 1990; Wodak 1986, 1996).

2. See, for example, Balogun and Johnson (2004), Vacek (2008), Mautner (2010), Menz (1999), Bargiela-Chiappini and Harris (1997), Bargiela-Chiappini et al. (2007), Holmes and Stubbe (2003), Stubbe et al. (2003), Iedema et al. (2003), Iedema and Wodak (1999), Wodak (1996, 2011), Kwon, Clarke, and Wodak (2009, 2013), Sarangi and Roberts (1999), Firth (1995).

3. It is important to note that the terms "strategic" and "strategy" are used differently in the fields of linguistics (pragmatics, sociolinguistics, discourse studies, cognitive linguistics) and sociology than in organization studies. In the case of linguistics, it refers epistemologically to agents' purposive and calculated plans of goal-oriented action (see Habermas 1984, 85, 87f., for further explanation), while in the latter it refers to theories of intelligence (Schank and Abelson 1977), elaborated, for example, by van Dijk and Kintsch (1983) in their socio-cognitive approach to discourse analysis (see also Wodak 1986, 1996, for extensive discussion). In organization studies, by comparison, it refers to the internal plans and activities as well as external trends and events that have the potential to affect organizational performance (Ansoff 1968; Dutton 1993; Johnson, Langley, Melin, and Whittington 2007), and is concerned with the long-term direction of the organization. Hence, for the purposes of this chapter, I use the notion of "strategic discussion", within which organizational strategy is constantly *re-contextualized* through micro-discursive interaction (see Wodak and Fairclough 2010; Wodak 2011).

4. As this chapter focuses on the proto-genre and sub-genres of *meetings* and their more general and more specific characteristics, I will illustrate some features with examples from the above mentioned previous studies without being able to elaborate on the entire fieldwork, ethnography and context of the respective organization or on the various implicit and explicit "rules of the game". I have to refer readers to our publications mentioned above which summarize the empirical studies, methodologies, and detailed results on which I draw in this chapter.

5. See Wodak (2000a, 2000b, 2011), Wodak et al. (2011, 2012), Clarke et al. (2011), Kwon et al. (2009).

6. See Hendry and Seidl (2003), Jarzabkowski and Seidl (2008), Bourque and Johnson (2008), Hodgkinson, Whittington, Johnson, and Schwartz (2006), Maitlis (2005), Maitlis and Lawrence (2007).

7. See Bargiela-Chiappini and Harris (1997), Bargiela-Chiappini, Nickerson, and Planken (2007), Holmes and Stubbe (2003), Stubbe, Lane, Hilder, Vine, Marra, Holmes, and Weatherall (2003).

8. See Clarke et al. (2011), Kwon et al. (2009, 2013), Wodak et al. (2011, 2012), for more details and extensive discussion of specific phenomena and episodes in meetings, such as negotiation of consensus, chairing and styles of leadership, power negotiations and manifestations of power in language choice, and the "un/making" of a decision. Moreover, the precise stages of our abductive methodology (ethnography, DHA, and the integration of corpus linguistic methods with qualitative analysis) are also spelt out in these publications in much detail (see also Reisigl and Wodak 2009). Again, I have to refer readers to these publications for more details on the triangulation of methodologies and data sets.

9. Turner (1977) defined *liminality* as a social space that is, "betwixt and between the original positions arrayed by law, custom, convention and ceremony" (1977, 95). Adapting this to organizational contexts, Sturdy, Schwartz, and Spicer (2006) re-defined liminality as a space where the regular routines of the organization are suspended.

10. This research is supported by practitioner oriented literatures which identify other characteristics such as: (a) the adequacy of time and organizational resources given over to planning and preparation; (b) a limited scope of strategically salient issues on the meeting agenda; and (c) a downplaying of political agendas and hierarchical authority (e.g. Mezias, Grinyer, and Guth 2001; Frisch and Chandler 2006), as further factors which influence the staging of successful away-days.

11. Bargiela-Chiappini and Harris (1997) modified the model used by West and Zimmerman (1975, 1983), to arrive at a number of basic types of overlapped speech, based on their function (to support the existing turn or to take over the turn) and their position (at/near or not near a TRP).

12. See also discussions of "political" communication in Okulska and Cap (2010, Ch. 1), and in Section 3 of this volume's Introduction.

13. In the concrete discourse analysis, the DHA also considers *intertextual* and *interdiscursive relationships* between utterances, texts, genres and discourses, as well as extra-linguistic social/sociological variables, the history of an organization or institution, and situational frames. Intertextuality refers to the fact that all texts are linked to other texts, both in the past and in the present. Such links can be established in different ways: through continued reference to a topic or main actors; through reference to the same events; or by the transfer of main arguments from one text into the next. This process is also labeled *recontextualization* (see Bernstein 1990). By taking an argument and restating it in a new context, we first observe the process of *decontextualization*, and then, when the respective element is implemented in a new context, of recontextualization. *Interdiscursivity* indicates that discourses are linked to each other in various ways. Consequently, the DHA emphasizes why discourses are open and hybrid, with new sub-topics frequently being created at many points (see Reisigl and Wodak 2001, 2009; Wodak 2011; for details).

14. See, for example, Gruber et al. (2006, 86f.), Gruber in this volume (Section 2), Cap and Okulska's Introduction to this volume (Section 2), Martin (1996), Bax (2011, 47–57).

15. See also the *Socio-Psychological Theory of Text-Planning and Text Production* put forward in Wodak (1980, 1986) and in Wodak and Schulz (1986), as a socio-cognitive model combining concepts from Artificial Intelligence with text-linguistics and sociolinguistics. In this theory, cognitive frames were related to prototypical genres, schemas to specific types of genres, and scripts to realized unique texts. Of course, much research since the 1980s has vastly elaborated these concepts (see Note 10).

16. There exist many different theoretical approaches in argumentation theory to the use and definition of *topos* (see, for example, van Eemeren 2010, 101–108). I use the concept of *topos* following Kienpointner's (1996) proposal (see also Reisigl and Wodak 2009, 101–110). In Kienpointner's approach, *topoi* are defined as field-specific and content-related warrants, with an underlying structure "If X, then Y". They usually refer to shared knowledge (and commonsense) warrants in arguments where the evidence (*datum*) is not spelt out explicitly but presupposed (see also Wodak 2011, 44).

17. This framework distinguishes between: outcomes (i.e. Salience, Feasibility and Urgency), which are the constituent "building blocks" of consensus; discursive strategies (i.e. Re/Defining, Justifying/Legitimating, Challenging and Mobilizing), which are the "processes" through which these outcomes are developed; and the linguistic/pragmatic devices (e.g. *topoi* of argumentation, metaphors, narratives, etc.), which are discursive resources that actors draw upon to affect their individual discursive strategies (see Kwon et al. 2013 for more details of theory, methodology, and the specific case study). I have to neglect elaborating this framework here as this is not the focus of the chapter. Rather, I restrict myself to the presentation of relevant characteristics of the prototype genre of meeting, in the social fields of business and politics, with the function of achieving consensual decisions.

References

Angouri, Jo, and Meredith Marra. 2010. "Corporate Meetings as Genre, and the Role of the Chair in Corporate Meeting Talk." *Text & Talk* 30: 615–636.

Ansoff, Igor. 1968. *Corporate Strategy: An Analytic Approach to Business Policy for Growth and Expansion.* New York, NY: McGraw-Hill.

Bakhtin, Michail. 1986. "The Problem of Speech Genres." In *Speech Genres and Other Late Essays*, 60–102. Austin, TX: University of Texas Press.

Balogun, Julia, and Gerry Johnson. 2004. "Organizational Restructuring and Middle Manager Sensemaking." *Academy of Management Journal* 47: 523–549.

Bargiela-Chiappini, Francesca, and Sandra Harris. 1997. *Managing Language: The Discourse of Corporate Meetings.* Amsterdam: Benjamins.

Bargiela-Chiappini, Francesca, Catherine Nickerson, and Brigitte Planken. 2007. *Business Discourse.* Basingstoke: Palgrave.

Bax, Stephen. 2011. *Discourse and Genre. Analysing Language in Context.* Basingstoke: Palgrave.

Beattie, Geoffrey. 1983. *Talk.* Milton Keynes: Open University Press.

Bernstein, Basil. 1990. *The Structuring of Pedagogic Discourse.* London: Routledge.

Boden, Deirdre. 1994. *The Business of Talk: Organizations in Action.* Cambridge: Polity Press.

Bourdieu, Pierre. 1972. *Outline of a Theory of Practice.* Cambridge: Cambridge University Press.

Bourque, Nicole, and Gerry Johnson. 2008. "Workshops and 'Away-Days' as Ritual." In *The Oxford Handbook of Organizational Decision*, ed. by Gerard Hodgkinson, and William Starbuck, 552–564. Oxford: Oxford University Press.

Bowman, Cliff. 1995. "Strategy Workshops and Top-Team Commitment to Strategic Change." *Journal of Managerial Psychology* 10: 4–13.

Clarke, Ian, Winston Kwon, and Ruth Wodak. 2011. "A Context-Sensitive Approach to Analysing Talk in Strategy Meetings." *British Journal of Management* 23(4): 455–473.

Cyert, Richard, and James March. 1963. *Behavioral Theory of the Firm.* Englewood Cliffs, NJ: Prentice Hall.

Daft, Richard, and Karl Weick. 1984. "Toward a Model of Organizations as Interpretation Systems." *Academy of Management Review* 9: 284–296.

Dreyfus, Hubert, and Paul Rabinow. 1982. *Michel Foucault: Beyond Structuralism and Hermeneutics.* Sussex: The Harvester Press.

Dutton, Jane. 1993. "Interpretations on Automatic: A Different View of Strategic Issue Diagnosis." *Journal of Management Studies* 30: 339–357.

Dutton, Jane, Susan Ashford, Regina O'Neill, and Katherine Lawrence. 2001. "Moves that Matter: Issue Selling and Organizational Change." *Academy of Management Journal* 44: 716–736.

Edelsky, Carole. 1981. "Who's Got the Floor." *Language in Society* 10: 383–421.

Eisenhardt, Kathleen, and Jay Bourgeois. 1988. "Politics of Strategic Decision Making in High-Velocity Environments." *Academy of Management Journal* 31: 737–770.

Fairclough, Norman, and Ruth Wodak. 1997. "Critical Discourse Analysis." In *Discourse Studies: A Multidisciplinary Introduction, Volume 2*, ed. by Teun van Dijk, 258–284. London: Sage.

—. 2008. "The Bologna Process and the Knowledge-Based Economy." In *Education and the Knowledge-Based Economy in Europe*, ed. by Bob Jessop, Norman Fairclough, and Ruth Wodak, 109–126. Amsterdam: Sense Publishers.

Faubion, James (ed.). 2000. *Michel Foucault – Power: Essential Works of Foucault.* New York, NY: The New Press.

Feldman, Martha. 1989. *Order without Design.* Stanford, CA: Stanford University Press.

Firth, Alan (ed.). 1995. *The Discourse of Negotiation: Studies of Language in the Workplace.* Oxford: Elsevier.

Foucault, Michel. 1972. *The Archeology of Knowledge.* London: Routledge.

—. 1981. *The History of Sexuality.* Harmondsworth: Penguin.

—. 1995 [1974]. *Discipline and Punish.* New York, NY: Random House.

Foucault, Michel, and Paul Rabinow. 1984. *The Foucault Reader.* New York, NY: Pantheon Books.

Frisch, Bob, and Logan Chandler. 2006. "Off-Sites that Work." *Harvard Business Review* 84: 117–126.

Gioia, Dennis, and Kumar Chittipeddi. 1991. "Sensemaking and Sensegiving in Strategic Change Initiation." *Strategic Management Journal* 12: 433–448.

Goffman, Erving. 1959. *The Presentation of Self in Everyday Life.* London: Penguin.

Gruber, Helmut, Peter Muntigl, Martin Reisigl, Markus Rheindorf, Karin Wetschanow, and Christine Czinglar. 2006. *Genre, Habitus und wissenschaftliches Schreiben.* Münster: LIT Verlag.

Habermas, Jürgen. 1984. *The Theory of Communicative Action.* Cambridge: Polity Press.

Halliday, Michael A. K. 1978. *Language as Social Semiotic: The Social Interpretation of Language and Meaning.* London: Edward Arnold.

Hardy, Cynthia, and Nelson Philips. 1999. "No Joking Matter: Discursive Struggle in the Canadian Refugee System." *Organization Studies* 20: 1–24.

—. 2004. "Discourse and Power." In *The Sage Handbook of Organizational Discourse,* ed. by David Grant, Cynthia Hardy, Clifford Oswick, and Linda Putnam, 299–316. London: Sage.

Hendry, John, and David Seidl. 2003. "The Structure and Significance of Strategic Episodes: Social Systems Theory and the Routine Practices of Strategic Change." *Journal of Management Studies* 40: 175–196.

Hodgkinson, Gerard, and Paul Sparrow. 2002. *The Competent Organization.* The Open University Press.

Hodgkinson, Gerard, Richard Whittington, Gerry Johnson, and Mirela Schwarz. 2006. "The Role of Strategy Workshops in Strategy Development Processes: Formality, Communication, Co-ordination and Inclusion." *Long Range Planning* 39: 479–496.

Holmes, Janet. 1992. "Women's Talk in Public Contexts." *Discourse & Society* 3: 131–150.

—. 2000. "Women at Work: Analysing Women's Talk in New Zealand Workplaces." *Australian Association of Applied Linguistics* 22: 1–17.

Holmes, Janet, and Maria Stubbe. 2003. *Power and Politeness in the Workplace. A Sociolinguistic Analysis of Talk at Work.* London: Longman.

Holzscheiter, Anna. 2005. *Power of Discourse and Power in Discourse. An Investigation of Transformation and Exclusion in the Global Discourse of Childhood.* Unpublished PhD dissertation, FU Berlin.

Hopper, Robert. 1992. *Telephone Conversation.* Bloomington, IN: Indiana University Press.

Iedema, Rick, Pieter Degeling, Jeffrey Braithwaite, and Les White. 2003. "'It's an Interesting Conversation I'm Hearing': The Doctor as Manager." *Organization Studies* 25: 15–33.

Iedema, Rick, and Ruth Wodak. 1999. "Introduction: Organizational Discourses and Practices." *Discourse & Society* 10: 5–19.

Jäger, Siegfried, and Florentine Maier. 2009. "Theoretical and Methodological Aspects of Foucauldian Critical Discourse Analysis and Dispositive Analysis." In *Methods of CDA, 2nd revised edition,* ed. by Ruth Wodak, and Michael Meyer, 34–60. London: Sage.

Janis, Irving. 1972. *Victims of Groupthink*. New York, NY: Houghton Mifflin.

Jarzabkowski, Paula, and David Seidl. 2008. "The Role of Meetings in the Social Practice of Strategy." *Organization Studies* 29: 1391–1426.

Johnson, Gerry, Ann Langley, Leif Melin, and Richard Whittington. 2007. *Strategy as Practice: Research Directions and Resources*. Cambridge: Cambridge University Press.

Keenoy, Tom, and Cliff Oswick. 2003. "Organizing Textscapes." *Organization Studies* 25: 135–142.

Kieffer, George D. 1988. *The Strategy of Meetings*. New York, NY: Warner.

Kienpointner, R. 1992. *Alltagslogik. Struktur und Funktion von Argumentationsmustern*. Stuttgart-Bad Cannstatt: Frommann-Holzboog.

Knights, David, and Glenn Morgan. 1995. "Strategy under the Microscope: Strategic Management and IT in Financial Services." *Journal of Management Studies* 32: 191–214.

Krzyżanowski, Michał, and Florian Oberhuber. 2007. *(Un)Doing Europe. Discourses and Practices of Negotiating the EU Constitution*. Brussels: Peter Lang.

Kwon, Winston, Ian Clarke, and Ruth Wodak. 2009. "Organizational Decision-Making, Discourse, and Power: Integrating across Contexts and Scales." *Discourse & Communication* 3: 273–302.

—. 2013. "Micro-level Strategies for Constructing Shared Views around Strategic Issues in Team Meetings." *Journal of Management Studies* (in press).

Lalouschek, Johanna, Florian Menz, and Ruth Wodak. 1990. *Alltag in der Ambulanz*. Tübingen: Niemeyer.

Laine, Pikka-Maaria, and Eero Vaara. 2007. "Struggling over Subjectivity: A Discursive Analysis of Strategic Development in an Engineering Group." *Human Relations* 60: 29–58.

Linde, Charlotte. 2008. *Working the Past: Narrative and Institutional Memory*. Oxford: Oxford University Press.

Luhmann, Niklas. 1997. *Soziale Systeme*. Frankfurt: Suhrkamp.

Maitlis, Sally. 2005. "The Social Processes of Organizational Sensemaking." *Academy of Management Journal* 48: 21–49.

Maitlis, Sally, and Thomas Lawrence. 2007. "Triggers and Enablers of Sensegiving in Organizations." *Academy of Management Journal* 50: 57–84.

March, James, and Johan Olsen. 1976. *Ambiguity and Choice in Organizations*. Oslo: Universitetsforlaget.

March, James, and Herbert Simon. 1958. *Organizations*. New York, NY: Wiley.

Mautner, Gerlinde. 2010. *Language and the Market Society*. London, Routledge.

McCall, Morgan, Ann Morrison, and Robert Hannan. 1978. *Studies of Managerial Work: Results and Methods, Technical Report No. 9*. Greensboro, NC: Centre for Creative Leadership.

Menz, Florian. 1999. "'Who Am I Gonna Do This With?': Self-Organization, Ambiguity and Decision-Making in a Business Enterprise." *Discourse & Society* 10: 101–128.

Mezias, John, Peter Grinyer, and William Guth. 2001. "Changing Collective Cognition: A Process Model for Strategic Change." *Long Range Planning* 34: 71–95.

Miller, Danny. 1982. "Evolution and Revolution: A Quantum View of Structural Change in Organizations." *Journal of Management Studies* 19: 131–151.

Mulderrig, Jane. 2011. "The Grammar of Governance." *Critical Discourse Studies* 8(1): 45–68.

Mumby, Dennis. 1988. *Communication and Power in Organizations: Discourse, Ideology and Domination*. Norwood, NJ: Ablex.

Mumby, Dennis, and Robin Clair. 1997. "Organizational Discourse." In *Discourse Studies, Volume 2: Discourse as Social Interaction*, ed. by Teun van Dijk, 181–196. London: Sage.

Muntigl, Peter, Gilbert Weiss, and Ruth Wodak. 2000. *European Union Discourses on Un/employment: An Interdisciplinary Approach to Employment Policy-making and Organizational Change*. Amsterdam: Benjamins.

Ocasio, William. 1997. "Towards an Attention-Based View of the Firm." *Strategic Management Journal* 18: 187–206.

Okulska, Urszula, and Piotr Cap. (eds). 2010. *Perspectives in Politics and Discourse*. Amsterdam: Benjamins.

Petersoo, Pille. 2007. "National Deixis in the Media." *Journal of Language and Politics* 6: 419–436.

Pettigrew, Andrew. 1973. *The Politics of Organizational Decision-Making*. London: Tavistock.

Pettigrew, Andrew, Ewan Ferlie, and Lorna McKee. 1992. *Shaping Strategic Change. Making Change in Large Organizations*. London: Sage.

Polanyi, Michael, and Marjorie Grene. (eds). 1969. *Knowing and Being: Essays by Michael Polanyi*. Chicago: University of Chicago Press.

Reisigl, Martin, and Ruth Wodak. 2001. *Discourse and Discrimination: Rhetorics of Racism and Antisemitism*. London: Routledge.

—. 2009. "The Discourse-Historical Approach." In *Methods of CDA, 2nd revised edition*, ed. by Ruth Wodak, and Michael Meyer, 87–121. London: Sage.

Rouleau, Linda. 2005. "Micro-Practices of Strategic Sensemaking and Sensegiving: How Middle Managers Interpret and Sell Change Every Day." *Journal of Management Studies* 42: 1413–1443.

Samra-Fredericks, Dalvir. 2003. "Strategizing as Lived Experience and Strategists' Everyday Efforts to Shape Strategic Direction." *Journal of Management Studies* 40: 141–174.

Samra-Fredericks, Dalvir. 2005. "Strategic Practice, 'Discourse' and the Everyday Interactional Constitution of 'Power Effects'." *Organization* 12: 803–841.

Sarangi, Srikant, and Celia Roberts. (eds). 1999. *Talk, Work and Institutional Order: Discourse in Medical, Meditation and Management Settings*. Berlin: de Gruyter.

Schank, Roger, and Robert Abelson. 1977. *Scripts, Plans, Goals and Understanding*. Hillsdale, NY: Erlbaum.

Schnurr, Stephanie, Meredith Marra, and Janet Holmes. 2006. "Being (Im)polite in New Zealand Workplaces: Maori and Pakeha Leaders." *Journal of Pragmatics* 39: 712–729.

Schwartzman, Helen. 1986. "The Meeting as a Neglected Social Form in Organizational Studies." In *Research in Organizational Behavior*, ed. by Larry Cummings, and Peter Frost, 233–258. Greenwich, CT: JAI Press.

Schwartzman, Helen. 1989. *The Meeting: Gatherings in Organizations and Communities*. New York, NY: Plenum Press.

Scollon, Ron. 2008. *Analysing Public Discourse*. London: Routledge.

Sillence, J. A. A. 2005. "A Contingency Theory of Rhetorical Congruence." *Academy of Management Review* 30: 608–621.

Staw, Barry, Lance Standelands, and Jane Dutton. 1981. "Threat-Rigidity Cycles in Organizational Behavior: A Multi-Level Analysis." *Administrative Science Quarterly* 26: 501–524.

Stubbe, Maria, Chris Lane, Jo Hilder, Bernadette Vine, Meredith Marra, Janet Holmes, and Ann Weatherall. 2003. "Multiple Discourse Analyses of a Workplace Interaction." *Discourse Studies* 5: 351–388.

Sturdy, Andrew, Mirela Schwarz, and Andre Spicer. 2006. "Guess Who's Coming to Dinner? Structures and the Uses of Liminality in Strategic Management Consultancy." *Human Relations* 59: 929–960.

Talbot, Mary. 1992. "'I Wish You'd Stop Interrupting Me!': Interruptions and Asymmetries in Speaker-Rights in Equal Encounters." *Journal of Pragmatics* 18: 451–466.

Taylor, James, and Daniel Robichaud. 2007. "Management as Metaconversation: The Search for Closure." In *Interacting and Organizing: Analyses of a Management Meeting*, ed. by Francois Cooren, 5–30. Mahwah, NJ: Lawrence Erlbaum.

Triandafyllidou, Anna, and Ruth Wodak. 2003. "Conceptual and Methodological Questions in the Study of Collective Identities." *Journal of Language and Politics* 2: 205–223.

Turner, Victor. 1977. *The Ritual Process*. Ithaca, NY: Cornell University Press.

Vacek, Edelgard. 2008. *Wie man über Wandel spricht*. Wiesbaden: VS Research.

van Dijk, Teun. 2008. *Discourse and Context: A Sociocognitive Approach*. Cambridge: Cambridge University Press.

van Dijk, Teun, and Walter Kintsch. 1983. *Strategies of Discourse Comprehension*. New York, NY: Academic Press.

van Eemeren, Frans. 2010. *Strategic Maneuvering*. Amsterdam: Benjamins.

van Leeuwen, Theo, and Ruth Wodak. 1999. "Legitimating Immigration Control: A Discourse-Historical Analysis." *Discourse Studies* 1: 83–118.

Vine, Bernadette. 2004. *Getting Things Done at Work: The Discourse of Power in Workplace Interaction*. Amsterdam: Benjamins.

Weick, Karl. 1979. *The Social Psychology of Organizing*. London: Addison-Wesley.

—. 1995. *Sensemaking in Organizations*. Thousand Oaks, CA: Sage.

—. 2001. *Making Sense of the Organization*. Oxford: Blackwell.

West, Candace, and Don Zimmerman. 1975. "Sex Roles, Interruptions and Silences in Conversations." In *Language and Sex: Differences and Dominance*, ed. by Barrie Thorne, and Nancy Henley. Rowley, MA: Newbury House.

—. 1983. "Small Insults: A Study of Interruptions in Cross-Sex Conversations between Unacquinted Persons." In *Language, Gender and Society*, ed. by Barrie Thorne, Cheris Kramarae, and Nancy Henley, 102–117. Rowley, MA: Newbury House.

Wodak, Ruth. 1980. *Das Wort in der Gruppe*. Vienna: Austrian Academy of Sciences.

—. 1986. *Language Behavior in Therapy Groups*. Los Angeles, CA: University of California Press.

—. 1996. *Disorders of Discourse*. London: Longman.

—. 2000a. "From Conflict to Consensus? The Co-Construction of a Policy Paper." In *European Union Discourses on Unemployment. An Interdisciplinary Approach to Employment Policy-Making and Organisational Change*, ed. by Peter Muntigl, Gilbert Weiss, and Ruth Wodak, 73–114. Amsterdam: Benjamins.

—. 2000b. "Recontextualization and the Transformation of Meanings: A Critical Discourse Analysis of Decision Making in EU-Meetings about Employment Policies." In *Discourse and Social Life*, ed. by Srikant Sarangi, and Malcolm Coulthard, 185–206. Harlow: Pearson Education.

—. 2008. "Introduction". In *Qualitative Discourse Analysis in the Social Sciences*, ed. by Ruth Wodak, and Michał Krzyżanowski, 1–29. Basingstoke: Palgrave.

—. 2011 [2009]. *The Discourse of Politics in Action: 'Politics as Usual'*. Basingstoke: Palgrave.

Wodak, Ruth, Ian Clarke, and Winston Kwon. 2011. "'Getting People on Board': Discursive Leadership for Consensus Building in Team Meetings." *Discourse & Society* 22: 592–644.

Wodak, Ruth, Michał Krzyżanowski, and Bernhard Forchtner. 2012. "The Interplay of Language Ideologies and Contextual Cues in Multilingual Interactions: Language Choice and Code-Switching in European Union Institutions." *Language in Society* 41: 157–186.

Wodak, Ruth, Rudolf de Cillia, Martin Reisigl, and Karin Liebhart. 2009 [1999]. *The Discursive Construction of National Identity.* Edinburgh: Edinburgh University Press.

Wodak, Ruth, and Norman Fairclough. 2010. "Recontextualising the Bologna Declaration: The Austrian and Romanian Case." *Critical Discourse Studies* 7: 19–40.

Wodak, Ruth, and Katharina Köhler. 2010. "Wer oder Was ist »Fremd«? Diskurshistorische Analyse Fremdenfeindlicher Rhetorik in Österreich." *Sozialwissenschaftliche Studien* 1: 33–55.

Wodak, Ruth, and Muriel Schulz. 1986. *The Language of Love and Guilt.* Amsterdam: Benjamins.

Wodak, Ruth, and Gilbert Weiss. 2003. ""We Are Different than the Americans and the Japanese!" Critical Discourse Analysis of Decision-Making in European Union Meetings about Employment Policies." In *Negotiation and Power in Dialogic Interaction*, ed. by Edda Weigand, and Marcelo Dascal, 39–63. Amsterdam: Benjamins.

Woods, Nicola. 1989. "Talking Shop: Sex and Status as Determinants of Floor Appportionment in Work Setting." In *Women in their Speech Communities: New Perspectives on Language and Sex*, ed. by Jennifer Coates, and Deborah Cameron, 141–157. London: Longman.

CHAPTER 6

Presenting politics

Persuasion and performance across genres of political communication

James Moir
University of Abertay Dundee, UK

The study of political persuasion has traditionally examined the components of communication in terms of the source, nature and recipients of messages. This approach is based on the assumption of communication as a psychological process involving a mental system that operates upon different political messages. However, another research tradition has examined performative aspects such as the use of metaphors, three-part lists, intonation of voice and so on. Bull (2007) argues that these two different approaches need not be incompatible and that they could be brought together to strengthen research across different genres of political communication. Whilst this would be a laudable attempt to build bridges between these two different approaches, it is argued that their underlying philosophical commitments cannot be glossed. These tensions are explored in terms of focusing on whether political communication should be considered as a matter of persuasion or as a matter of performance.

1. Introduction

This chapter considers the philosophical commitments that underlie two main approaches to the analysis of political communication as a form of persuasion. One approach focuses upon political communication as what might be colloquially referred to as "winning hearts and minds". In other words, its concern is with the *process* of persuasion as it affects individual recipients and how they *think*. However, a quite different approach examines political communication as performative in relation to cultural practices and in the way that these are traded upon. This approach eschews any commitment to the notion of political communication as influencing minds and instead supplants this with a focus on the actions and practices involved in such discourse. These two approaches therefore offer different modes of analytical engagement with the various genres of political communication although there has been an attempt to bring the two together, if only to consider what each has to offer and if their findings can be combined in some way. The chapter considers, and ultimately rejects, this aim given the fundamental divergence between the two on the acceptance or rejection of a Cartesian position on the notion of discourse and mind.

In the conclusion to his review of key aspects of the study of political language use and its rhetorical effects, Bull (2007) invites a rapprochement between this research tradition and that of social psychological research on persuasion. As he puts it:

> Currently these two research traditions exist as if in a parallel universe, there has been no interplay between them. [...] Analysis of the major dimensions of traditional persuasive communication research – message source, message characteristics, message, receivers, and cognitive models of persuasion – would benefit greatly from the application of techniques used in the study of political language.
>
> (Bull 2007, 273)

This is indeed a laudable aim and there is much to be learned from the mutual interaction of research traditions between different disciplines, particularly where there is a common focus on language. However, whilst this may be desirable in terms of attempting to strengthen the explanatory power of findings, and perhaps in gaining new insights into how such communication "works", there are nevertheless long-established theoretical and methodological preferences that could prove a stumbling block. It is therefore clear that in order to overcome these we need to get "down" to the various mediated levels where political communication takes place. This is all the more pressing when we consider the explosion in internet-based and social networking media as a relatively new and expanding genre for political communication. Consider for example, how President Obama made extensive use of blogs and Twitter in his first and second presidential campaigns in order to reach a variety of audiences, and which included posts and tweets that were tailored to those audiences. His blend of controlled and candid videos (e.g., YouTube), provided a means of political communication that worked on several levels but with a net effect of "humanizing" him for various audiences. Indeed it is apparent that he had a high degree of trust in internet-based political communication (Obama 2008, 41; Castells 2009, 389). In Obama's case, his use of new media was in itself a rhetorical act and a persuasive one given that he attracted a significant majority of the youth vote (Castells 2009, 368-369) in his first campaign. In his second campaign, the weak health of the U.S. economy and higher unemployment, made his task of gathering support and mobilizing the electorate through such communication much more difficult, although he has been highly effective in agenda setting around issues of inequality (Bennett 2012). Indeed the use of such communication and its familiarity with younger voters has been found to create engagement with political communicative practices (Rice, Moffet, and Madupalli 2012). The expansion of social networking communication as a distinct genre or style of political communication begs the question about its analysis as a social practice or as a means of mindful persuasion. It is perhaps telling that as of November 1 2012 Obama's Twitter account (BarackObama) reports over 21.5 million followers whilst Mitt Romney's account (MittRomney) reports over 1.6 million followers. Based on these figures there is little doubt that Obama has managed to tap into a source of political communication that his presidential opponent cannot match. The key issue is the assumptions that lie behind the approaches to analyzing this type of communication: as a social practice or as a means of persuasion.

This chapter does not address the use made of different sources of media in acts of political communication, but the Obama example above drives home the point that it is important to examine these genres of communication as sites for different forms of performance and persuasion. With this caveat in mind, and in returning to Bull's argument, the aim of this chapter is to map out some of the theoretical and associated empirical terrain that has to be covered in considering the possibility of this integration. The key issues under consideration are (i) the assumption of a communication model in which messages are packaged, transmitted and received between politicians and their audiences, and (ii) a performative model based on a view of researching language at the "surface" level without, or explicitly against, any notion of a telementational model of mind.

2.   The microanalysis of political language

To begin with, it is worth offering a brief summation of the research tradition of what Bull refers to as the *microanalysis* (2007, 272) of political communication. In his overview of this he charts three key aspects of the study of the ways in which politicians speak when talking politics in different settings such as television interviews, political party conferences, and during times of election speeches. The first of these is the study of equivocation, which, according to Bavelas et al. (1990), is the communication that is ambiguous, contradictory, tangential or evasive. Bull (1994) found in a study of four British party leaders that the reply rate (the proportion of questions receiving direct answers) was on average 46% (or slightly more than two out of five questions). In a further study, Bull and Fetzer (2006) examined 21 political interviews from British general elections 1997–2001 and found 17 examples where politicians avoided replying to questions where they were invited to respond in personal terms but avoided this by responding in terms of the collective "we".

These examples of the study of equivocation highlight a mix of approaches based on frequency counts and an examination of pronoun use. However, the message for Bull is clear: politicians appear to equivocate much more than non-politicians. In order to explain this higher incidence of equivocation Bull suggests that politicians run the risk of making face-damaging responses during televised interviews and therefore equivocation can be seen as being the least face-threatening option. A further study by Bull (2003) found that politicians are far more likely to respond to audience questions directly (73% reply rate) than to those of political interviewers (47% reply rate). Bull interprets this in terms of questioning styles, with political interviewers' questions being more aimed at exposing inconsistencies in policy on the one hand, and "ordinary" voters' questions attempting to establish party political positions on the other. Finally, Bull (2008) suggests that equivocation is problematic for politicians in terms of the potential for being viewed as lacking commitment. He suggests that they must therefore engage in face management in order to negotiate this issue.

Bull then turns to the conversation analytic tradition of research on political language use in terms of Atkinson's (1984) studies of how politicians invite applause (or "claptrap"). Atkinson's work identified particular rhetorical devices employed to elicit such applause, including, for example the use of three-part lists or contrast structures. Bull goes on to argue that Atkinson's work only partly accounts for the elicitation of applause and that speech content, delivery and spontaneous applause are also crucially important.

Finally, the role of metaphors on political communication is considered. Bull draws upon Lakoff and Johnson's (1980) argument that human thought processes are to some extent intrinsically metaphorical. However, in the context of political communication he notes that metaphors can obscure as much as they reveal about an issue and that we may be talked into focusing on one aspect of a concept or issue whilst overlooking other aspects that are inconsistent with the metaphor used. This is a common theme in much cognitive social psychology: the danger of cognitive processes that attempt to simplify the world and in so doing lead us astray. It is an argument that clearly trades upon the idea that political communication taps into a top-down processing system in some way or other in that information provided is then used to complete the picture.

3. Political communication as persuasion

The above foray into cognitive social psychology leads to a consideration of how political communication "works" as persuasion. However, this approach is based on an assumption about political communication in terms of what Edwards (1997) refers to as something akin to sending letters through the post, where there is a sender who has a message packaged as a letter, which is then sent through the post, and finally safely received by the recipient, who then reads the contents and "understands" the message. It is what Harris (1981) refers to as "telementational-ism", i.e., a system for conveying "thoughts". This is a key assumption in treating political discourse in terms of persuasion.

Given the above view, the logical outcome of such an approach is to con-sider aspects of the components of persuasive messages (Hovland, Janis, and Kelly 1953; Stiff and Mongeau 2003). Typically, this is configured in terms of a mes-sage source (e.g., credibility); message characteristics (e.g., one-sided versus two-sided messages); and message receivers (e.g., involvement). Much of the focus of this area has been concerned with the routes to persuasion in terms of careful scrutiny of message content (central route) versus aspects such emotional appeals (peripheral route) (Petty and Cacioppo 1986). In a similar vein, Chaiken (1987) suggests a distinction between systematic processing and heuristic processing. In considering Bull's argument about the integration of approaches to political communication that approach the study of genres in diverging ways, a combina-tion of the microanalysis of political language alongside these kinds of models is seen as a way of providing an over-arching structure to understanding political persuasion.

However, there is another research tradition in which persuasion is treated more in terms of its ideological effect, namely critical discourse analysis. For those who take this approach, persuasion is part-and-parcel of an examination of the discursive construction of attitudes. Here then, cognition is linked to ideology in terms of the exercise of manipulative power and control (van Dijk 2006). More-over, the focus of analysis in such work often involves exposing the operation of such attempts at persuasion as founded upon ideological commitments that the analyst considers in some way or other as unjust or oppressive.

This ideological examination of political communication can involve an ex-amination of how attempts are made to forge connections between message source and recipients in terms of identities, and in particular national identities. In her study of how politicians characterize the European Union, Wodak (2007) notes how attempts to construct a single historical narrative revolve around the vague notion of "culture" or "tradition". This was particularly evident in the case of the entry of Turkey into the Union and in the opinion that such widening should be curtailed as it does not sit within the predominately Christian European "culture". Turkey is a predominately Muslim country and therefore was characterized as an out-group. Similarly, Capdevila and Callaghan (2008) studied how a speech made by the then Conservative party leader in the United Kingdom, Michael Howard, during the 2005 election addressed his party's plans to curb immigration. This was, and still is, a sensitive issue and Howard drew upon notions of "Britishness" in terms of fair play, tolerance, generosity and compassion as the cultural basis for accepting immigrants. However, his speech also suggested that immigrants should also strive to live up to these values and they must *want* to work hard to make a positive contribution to Britain. He also pointed out in the same speech that his parents were immigrants thereby aligning himself both with "Britishness" and with immigrants. These kinds of identity construction can therefore be considered as persuasive in terms of the creation of identifications and alignments between political sources and their audiences.

Another example of a study of political communication that is concerned with ideological import is the analysis of speeches and texts produced by what can be considered far right-wing politicians in the U.K. and their pronouncements about immigration (Charteris-Black 2006). This work focused on the use of metaphors commonly used by these politicians and, in particular, those that characterize immigration in terms of the excessive or damaging flow of water ("limitless flow of immigration", "flood of asylum seekers", "tide of immigration"; Charteris-Black 2006, 570–571). It is suggested that these metaphors are powerful in the service of ideology in that they draw upon an understanding of nature and water and its sometimes necessary control in order to prevent damage. In the context of the U.K. there is a further layer of meaning in terms of its island status and the notion of immigrants having to come ashore.

The interesting point here is that this kind of work could potentially be considered as shedding light on key aspects of "message characteristics" within the communication model of persuasion preferred by Bull. Perhaps of interest here is the role that such metaphors play through their rhetorical power. As McKinlay and McVittie (2008, 124–125) point out, this neither depends on any kind of logical argument, nor on the presentation of supporting evidence. The key point about the use of metaphors in such contexts is that they are rhetorically self-sufficient (Wetherell and Potter 1992) and can be regarded as operating in much the same way as proverbs (Gandara 2004) in terms of their unchallenged status as distillations of wisdom.

Work in this vein was also conducted by Augoustinos, Le Couteur, and Soyland (2002) in their examination of the then Australian Prime Mimister's, John Howard's use of self-sufficient discourse to defend his government's position on not considering issuing a national apology to the indigenous Aboriginal people for their subjection to human rights abuses by previous settler generations. In the course of his speech on this issue, Howard drew a distinction between symbolic gestures and practical needs. He argued that it was the latter that mattered most in terms of access to housing, education, health and employment. This he suggested was being "realistic", whereas a national apology was in effect characterized as being merely symbolic and was in danger of being accompanied by unrealistic expectations. Thus he was able to characterize the case for a national apology as a form of rhetoric offering little value in itself. The persuasiveness of this argument is based on the rhetoric of being realistic and coming down on the side of material needs rather than fine words. The authors of the study suggest that the creation of this division, between the symbolic and the material, offers a means of being against a national apology on the grounds of focusing instead on the contrasting issue of practical needs.

This kind of discursive focus can therefore fit neatly into a cognitive model in which persuasion is viewed as operating on mental objects such as attitudes. In taking up this perspective, van Dijk (2006) suggests that dominant groups or those who hold political power seek to control the attitudes of people in such a way as to manipulate how issues are to be framed and perceived. For example, in his analysis of a speech by the then British Prime Minister, Tony Blair, justifying his government's involvement in the Iraq war, van Dijk (2006) notes that Blair frames the issue in terms of contrast between those who support the British and the upholding of democracy in terms of the necessity of troops in Iraq, and the unstated but nonetheless implicit counter-position of failing to do so. This message characteristic is further bolstered by Blair's positioning of himself as a credible message source in terms of being someone who stands firm in making difficult decisions on the basis of his own commitment.

4. Political communication as performance

There is little doubt that Bull's suggested alignment with cognitive models of persuasion has an affinity with the critical discourse analytic position outlined above. This provides structure to what can seem an area that abounds with an apparently piecemeal approach to studying political language. However, the microanalysis that Bull refers to covers a variety of approaches with differing theoretical and methodological allegiances. These range from Bull's own eclectic approach involving a mix of frequency counts and lexical analysis to studies that connect the study of persuasion to ideological concerns. Other non-cognitive approaches vary in terms of the extent to which they leave theoretical space for the potential integration with cognitivist approaches, and much of owing to the extent to which they align themselves with linguistic philosophy of Ryle (1963) and Wittgenstein (1953).

As previously noted, Bull evaluates Atkinson's work on political claptrap. This research stems from the conversation analytic approach in terms of turn-taking (Sacks 1992). The idea here is that although political speeches may seem as if they are unidirectional based on a speaker delivering a political message to an audience, that audience is nevertheless part of an interactive turn-taking process. Such speeches allow for cues for the audience to let them know that the orator's performance constitutes their turn, so to speak. In this case the turn is not necessarily a signal to respond verbally, but may be an invitation to show approval by clapping. Bull notes that Atkinson's work does not account for such instances of synchronous "elicited" applause or for instances of asynchronous applause, including spontaneous and unexpected responses to content. Bull therefore distinguishes between invited and uninvited applause. This is an important distinction, for it allows him to argue that although the format of political speeches admits the possibility to punctuate them with cues for the audience to respond, their nature is not entirely based on the interactional architecture of turn-taking.

Whilst political speeches offer less of an interactive dimension, political interviews can be considered as more akin to what would be expected in conversational turn-taking. In such settings it is usually the interviewer who is in control of the question agenda and question framing. However, it is not uncommon for participants to skillfully challenge or deflect the interviewer's questions and prior turns through various means such as not being the legitimate person to ask a question (Dickerson 2001), or subverting the question frame by transforming it into an answer (Leon 2004; see also Okulska 2004). The latter would overlap with the problem of equivocation as studied by Bull, who pays special attention to its nuances in the turn-by-turn sequencing of the question-and-answer format of the interview. The point here is that political communication is viewed as operating within the ongoing performance of such interviews. This focus on performance does not tend to adopt an agnostic stance on the status of cognition, particularly where there is an interest in the strategic deployment of political language (Hopper 2005). Others who utilize the conversational analysis methodology at the same time maintaining a focus on discursive psychology (e.g., Edwards and Potter 2005) likewise adopt an agnostic stance on the status of an underlying cognitive machinery of mind, but prefer to examine how people orientate to each other in terms of both explicit and implicit reference to cognition. Here the focus is on language as performance rather than a window to communication between minds.

This leads on to the final position of anti-cognitivism. Clearly, Bull's affinity for a source-message-receiver model stems from his own disciplinary background in psychology. This treats people as engaged in cognitive operations such as formulating what to say or interpreting what has been said. However, those who take an ethnomethodological stance combined with the linguistic philosophy of Ryle and Wittgenstein, reject outright a set of cognitive operations being performed on talk (Coulter 1979, 1990, 2005). Thus, Coulter (2005) argues that although it is possible to slide into analyzing hearers as "analysts" and speakers as "designers" of what they say, "mind" is commonly used in vernacular expression or is treated as a philosophical reification. At the same time, Coulter asserts that it is people who do things as "agents" rather than as "minds". This position poses serious questions for an approach to the study of political communication as involving "concepts" or "ideas". Following this line, it can be argued that such a focus on mental architecture arguably deflects attention away from political language as something that "works" as part of a series of practices, and instead tries to postulate what is "behind" speaking and hearing. To accept this view then would be to reject any linkage of political communication as being bound up with persuasion as a cognitive process.

Instead, analysis is concerned with ways of communicating that relate to cultural practices. These "performances" are what is taken to count as persuasion in that they offer audiences a means of taking part in various practices through a variety of linguistically and visually constructed scenes and frames (Goffman 1974). It is this inclusion in these various modalities of practice where political communication takes place that is the focus of study in terms of a grammar of engagement. This is considered as a cultural capacity to engage in various language games (Wittgenstein 1953) rather than the interior processing of information.

5. Conclusion

McKinlay and McVittie (2008, 254–273) lay out in turn the arguments in favor of what they refer to as "research independence" or "research integration" in the study of the social psychology of language. They note that as social psychology has emphasized, in common with much of psychology, the role of cognition, there has been a resulting atomization of the study of people's conduct in terms of "stereotyping", "categorization", "attribution", etc. This view of people as "information processors" pervades much of social psychology and of course can be found in models of persuasion. The danger of such an approach is that persuasion may become decoupled from the world of practice, from where it is happening. On the other hand, they note that there has been some attempt by critical discourse analysts, such as Wodak (2006), to recast this cognitive perspective by, for example, considering stereotyping and prejudice as cultural "frames". Meanwhile, those working within the research traditions of discourse and conversational analysis have conducted their work on the basis of an agnostic or explicit anti-cognitivist stance.

Bull's suggestion for an over-arching framework for the microanalysis study of political communication glosses over these important philosophical commitments and distinctions. Whilst he is to be commended for setting out a research integration position, it is still the case that he suggests that the study of political language and communication can be accommodated *within* an over-arching cognitivist framework. For some this may be a desirable viewpoint, but others will adhere to the research independence position based upon a commitment to a non- or anti-cognitivst approach to the study of discourse.

Of course in putting across these matters through the rhetoric of a contrast structure, this chapter can be seen as being engaged in a typical persuasive maneuver. The discerning reader will no doubt be aware that drawing attention to one's own rhetorical construction is in itself a (not so) deft attempt at persuasion. Rather than becoming ensnared in this pointless exercise, there is another analytic position worth pursing in the analysis of genres in political communication, and that is to ensure that analysts appreciate the range and variety of political communication.

As noted in the early part of the chapter it is evident that social media and internet-based communication is transforming the political communication landscape. Political communication is now freed from that of a one-way channel from the politician or party to the citizen or potential voter. It can now be almost instantaneous, with feedback and response in a dialogic manner (see, e.g., Janoschka 2010; Kopytowska, this volume). Indeed, political communication has moved beyond the realm of party politics to include social movements that involve direct action. This kind of seismic shift has forced politicians to rethink their communication strategies. Just as radio and television forced politicians into dealing with these media in various ways, then so is it the case that they are now confronted by new media. The "old ways" of dealing with the media are being disturbed just as politicians have become familiar with, or perhaps even complacent in their techniques of performance and persuasion.

Of course, like a city and its transport network, both old and new methods of movement take place all at once as each technology comes along and is added to others. Trams, buses, cars, metro trains and so on are all running at one and the same time. Likewise, political communication also takes place through both "old" and "new" modalities at one and the same time: constituency meetings, hustings, televised speeches, radio broadcasts, televised debates, journalist interviews for newspapers, blogs, tweets and YouTube videos. These different forms of media elicit different political communication techniques and strategies. The manner in which politics is conducted across these different modalities is of course what forms the basis of analytic work within the study of presenting politics. However, the extent to which performance and persuasion manifest themselves within these different mediated formats and how this connects with the notion of genres is a complex matter. For example, in what forms of media and in what contexts does political communication involve the use of metaphors? It is for this reason that we require a "bottom-up" approach that keeps our analytic feet on the ground (to use a familiar metaphor). The extent to which we focus on performance or persuasion is a theoretical commitment but nonetheless we should be clear about grounding our work *in situ* rather than seeking regularities and patterns on the basis of imposing pre-formed analytic conceptions that may apply in one political communication context and genre but not another.

References

Atkinson, Max. 1984. *Our Masters' Voices*. London & New York: Methuen.

Augoustinos, Martha, Amanda LeCouteur, and John A. Soyland. 2002. "Self-Sufficient Arguments in Political Rhetoric: Constructing Reconciliation and Apologizing to the Stolen Generations." *Discourse & Society* 13: 105–142.

Bavelas, Janet B., Alex Black, Nicole Chovil, and Jennifer Mullett. 1990. *Equivocal Communication*. Newbury Park: Sage.

Bennett, W. Lance. 2012. "The Personalization of Politics: Political Identity, Social Media, and Changing Patterns of Participation." *The ANNALS of the American Academy of Political and Social Science* 644: 20–39.

Bull, Peter E. 1994. "On Identifying Questions, Replies, and Non-Replies in Political Interviews." *Journal of Language and Social Psychology* 13: 115–131.

—. 2003. *The Microanalysis of Political Communication: Claptrap and Ambiguity*. London: Routledge.

—. 2007. "Political Language and Persuasive Communication." In *Language, Discourse and Social Psychology*, ed. by Ann Weatherall, Bernadette M. Watson, and Cindy Gallois, 255–275. Basingstoke, Hampshire, U.K. & New York, U.S.A.: Palgrave.

—. 2008. "Slipperiness, Evasion and Ambiguity: Equivocation and Facework in Noncommittal Political Discourse." *Journal of Language and Social Psychology* 27: 333–244.

Bull, Peter E., and Anita Fetzer. 2006. "Who are *We* and Who are *You*? The Strategic Use of Forms of Address in Political Interviews." *Text and Talk* 26: 1–35.

Capdevila, Rose, and Jane E. M. Callaghan. 2008. "'It's not Racist. It's Common Sense': Critical Analysis of Political Discourse Around Asylum and Immigration in the UK." *Journal of Community and Applied Social Psychology* 18: 1–16.

Castells, Manuel. 2009. *Communication Power*. Oxford: Oxford University Press.

Chaiken, Shelly. 1987. "The Heuristic Model of Persuasion." In *Social Influence: The Ontario Symposium. Vol. 5*, ed. by Mark P. Zanna, James M. Olson, and C. Peter Herman, 3–39. Hillsdale, NJ: Erlbuam.

Charteris-Black, Jonathan. 2006. "Britain as a Container: Immigration Metaphors in the 2005 Election Campaign." *Discourse & Society* 17: 563–581.

Coulter, Jeff. 1979. *The Social Construction of Mind: Studies in Ethnomethodology and Linguistic Philosophy.* London: Macmillan.

—. 1990. *Mind in Action.* Oxford: Polity.

—. 2005. "Language without Mind." In *Conversation and Cognition*, ed. by Hedwig te Molder and Jonathan Potter, 79–92. Cambridge: Cambridge University Press.

Dickerson, Paul. 2001. "Disputing with Care: Analysing Interviewees' Treatment of Prior Turns in Televised Political Interviews." *Discourse & Society*, 3: 203–222.

Edwards, Derek. 1997. *Discourse and Cognition.* London and Beverly Hills: Sage.

Edwards, Derek, and Jonathan Potter. 2005. "Discursive Psychology, Mental States and Descriptions." In *Conversation and Cognition*, ed. by Hedwig te Molder, and Jontahn Potter, 241–259. Cambridge: Cambridge University Press.

Gandara, Lelia. 2004. "'They that Sow the Wind…': Proverbs and Sayings in Argumentation." *Discourse & Society*, 15: 345–359.

Goffman, Erving. 1974. *Frame Analysis: An Essay on the Organization of Experience.* Boston: Northeastern University Press.

Harris, Roy. 1981. *The Language Myth.* London: Duckworth.

Hopper, Robert. 2005. "A Cognitive Agnostic in Conversation Analysis: When Do Strategies Affect Spoken Interaction." In *Conversation and Cognition*, ed. by Hedwig te Molder, and Jonathan Potter, 134–158. Cambridge: Cambridge University Press.

Hovland, Carl I., Irving L. Janis, and Harold H. Kelly. 1953. *Communication and Persuasion.* New Haven, CT: Yale University Press.

Janoschka, Anja. 2010. "Direct E-Communication: Linguistic Weapons in a Political Weblog." In *Perspectives in Politics and Discourse*, ed. by Urszula Okulska, and Piotr Cap, 215–236. Amsterdam/Philadelphia: John Benjamins.

Lakoff, George, and Mark Johnson. 1980. *Metaphors We Live By.* Chicago: Chicago University Press.

Leon, Jacqueline. 2004. "Preference and "Bias" in the Format of French News Interviews: The Semantic Analysis of Question-Answer Pairs in Conversation." *Journal of Pragmatics* 36: 1885–1920.

McKinlay, Andrew, and Christopher McVittie. 2008. *Social Psychology and Discourse.* Chichester, West Sussex, UK: Wiley-Blackwell.

Obama, Barack. 2008. *The Audacity of Hope: Thoughts on Reclaiming the American Dream.* Edinburgh: Cannongate Books.

Okulska, Urszula. 2004. "Globalisation on the Polish Radio. The Case of Political Interviews." In *Speaking from the Margin. Global English from a European Perspective*, ed. by Anna Duszak, and Urszula Okulska, 239–259. Frankfurt am Main: Peter Lang.

Petty, Richard E., and John T. Cacioppo. 1986. *Communication and Persuasion: Central and Peripheral Routes to Attitude Change.* New York: Springer-Verlag.

Rice, Laurie, Kenneth W. Moffett, and Ramana Madupalli. 2012. "Campaign-Related Social Networking and the Political Participation of College Students." *Social Science Computer Review* DOI: 10.1177/0894439312455474

Ryle, Gilbert. 1963. *The Concept of Mind.* Harmondsworth: Penguin.

Sacks, Harvey. 1992. *Lectures on Conversation*. Oxford: Blackwell.

Stiff, James B., and Paul A. Mongeau. 2003. *Persuasive Communication* (2nd edition). New York: The Guilford Press.

Van Dijk, Teun A. 2006. "Discourse and Manipulation." *Discourse & Society* 17: 359–383.

Wetherell, Margaret, and Jonathan. Potter. 1992. *Mapping the Language of Racism: Discourse and the Legitimation of Exploitation*. London & New York: Harvester Wheatsheaf.

Wittgenstein, Ludwig. 1953. *Philosophical Investigations*. Oxford: Blackwell.

Wodak, Ruth. 2006. "Mediation between Discourse and Society: Assessing Cognitive Approaches in CDA." *Discourse Studies* 8: 179–190.

—. 2007. "Discourses in European Union Organizations: Aspects of Access, Participation and Exclusion." *Text and Talk* 27: 707–726.

PART II

Data-driven approaches

CHAPTER 7

Legitimizing the Iraq War through the genre of political speeches

Rhetorics of judge-penitence in the narrative reconstruction of Denmark's cooperation with Nazism*

Bernhard Forchtner
Humboldt University, Berlin, Germany

> 'I have done that,' says my memory.
> 'I cannot have done that' –
> says my pride, and remains adamant.
> At last – memory yields.
>
> (Friedrich Nietzsche 1973, §68)

In Albert Camus' novel *The Fall*, the main character Jean-Baptiste Clamance introduces himself as a *judge-penitent*, following the motto "[t]he more I accuse myself, the more I have a right to judge you". In this chapter, I operationalize such behavior in order to understand the strategy of persuasion used by Denmark's then Prime-Minister Anders Fogh Rasmussen when he legitimized the Iraq-invasion in 2003. In contrast to self-righteous myths, Rasmussen did so by self-critically addressing the policy of Danish collaboration with Nazi-Germany during World War Two. He thereby became able to claim, like Clamance, to have learnt the lessons from history, thus occupying the moral high ground from which he discursively constructed the opponents of the invasion as being morally inferior.

1. Introduction

In a commemorative speech in August 2003, the then Danish Prime Minister, Anders Fogh Rasmussen, criticized the Danish policy of cooperation during the country's occupation in World War II. His speech contradicted decades of official silence over the role Denmark played in (indirectly) supporting German war efforts (cf. Judt 2006 on the silence concerning collaboration and cooperation in most occupied European countries after 1945). Indeed, the consensus of having been a small but resisting nation was crucial for a positive Danish post-war self-image and had only very rarely been challenged within the political mainstream. In fact, Denmark, for most parts of the second half of the 20th century, confirmed Nietzsche's above-quoted aphorism, as selectively constructed memories of the past supported a positive self-representation and a negative representation of an external "other".

However, in particular since the fall of the Berlin Wall, it has become clear – not only in Denmark – that Nietzsche does not have the final word when it comes to the narrative construction of memory and identity (cf. Eder 2009 for a recent discussion of the narrative construction of collective identities). Since communism as the token of evil has vanished, a new discursive space has opened up, enabling the admission of human rights and their violations. In consequence, a post-heroic "politics of apology" (Brooks 1999; Barkan 2001; Olick 2007; Gibney et al. 2008) has become increasingly significant as in-groups construct their collective identities more than ever through admissions of past wrongdoing, instead of through positive self-representations and negative representations of an external "other". Can Rasmussen's speech thus best be understood when placed within this wider trend of *post-heroic identity* construction? Here, one's own history is no longer solely positively and uncritically imagined, e.g. in terms of heroic resistance, innocence, etc., whilst representing the out-group as guilty, barbaric, etc. Instead, the in-group recognizes its mistakes and the harm done to others which enables a more inclusive *we*. In other words: whilst collective identity has previously been narrated through the demarcation of a negative, *external* "other", the contemporary in-group now demarcates itself from its *own* evil past.

Bernhard Giesen further develops such notions of public apologies in his concept of *perpetrator trauma*: the latter are founded in "public rituals of confession of guilt" (2004, 130) which are successfully narrated and thereby become a significant part of the official and public self-understanding of the in-group. It is the "symbolic surplus value" of such performances – which are not necessarily only part of highly visible political apologies but also of more mundane self-critical reflections in, e.g., newspapers – which appeals to the victims as their suffering is (partly) recognized. In contrast to rituals and performances which uncritically frame national identities as success stories, such attempts to reframe the nation redraw the moral boundaries in a more universal and egalitarian way by performing an "exorcism", often via commemoration ceremonies of past wrongdoing. Such a self-representation, in turn, enables the recognition of one's own identity through others as the previously excluded "other" is now recognized instead of offended.

Some scholars have, however, criticized the increasing significance of this way of relating to one's past as, e.g., reproducing structural inequalities and racism (e.g. Trouillot 2000; LeCouteur 2001). This article is an attempt to elaborate further on potential misuses of admissions of wrongdoing by outlining *rhetorics of judge-penitence*. I elaborate on such a development by following Jean-Baptiste Clamance, the main character in Albert Camus' novel *The Fall*, who lives by the motto "[t]he more I accuse myself, the more I have a right to judge you" (Camus 2006, 88). By confessing wrongdoing, this rhetorical strategy enables Clamance *self-righteously* to claim the moral high ground from which he is able to legitimize his own position and judge others through constructing them as morally inferior.

In sum, this case study, a data-driven contribution to the study of the genre of political speeches (cf. Gruber [this volume], for a more theoretical account), aims to inform the theory of the genre by a thematic finding: in political speeches, in particular in symbolically highly significant ones such as a commemorative speech, "politics of apology" or "saying sorry", can be counter-intuitively used as a means of legitimizing the alleged moral inferiority of "others". I start by conceptualizing rhetorics of judge-penitence and operationalize this phenomenon through Toulmin's scheme. In Section 2, I outline the methodological framework I rely on, i.e. Ruth Wodak's discourse-historical approach (DHA), in order to understand its linguistic realization. Section 3 extensively introduces the Danish historical context, showing how Danish debates over the policy of cooperation with Nazi-Germany have developed. This enables me, in Section 4, to analyze Rasmussen's speech mentioned above, which triggered one of the major debates over the nation's past, asking if the concept of judge-penitence helps to understand the force of the Prime Minister's argument. It is here that I also elaborate on the genre of political speeches, in particular the sub-genre of commemorative speeches. Finally, I summarize my findings.

2. Rhetorics of judge-penitence

2.1 Conceptualizing judge-penitence

My conceptualization of rhetorics of judge-penitence is oriented towards Jean-Baptiste Clamance, a figure from Camus' novel *The Fall*. Camus presents Clamance's thesis through a staged dialogue between Clamance who narrates and a silent listener. The former is a previously successful and altruistic Parisian lawyer. But, through a series of incidents, most importantly his reluctance to help a probable suicide victim, Clamance recognizes the pure vanity behind a facade of altruism and becomes haunted by memories of his own failure and self-pity. Suddenly, his pride in being an altruistic lawyer strikes him as being purely selfish in order to feel good. He takes the outbreak of World War II as an opportunity to cross over to Africa, where he is soon interned by German forces. In front of comrades, he publicly confesses his weaknesses and thereby becomes their leader. Within their community, he is now responsible for the distribution of water. When on one occasion he is drinking the water of a dying comrade, he recognizes that nobody, not even Christ, can stay innocent in this world and that justice has become necessarily disconnected from innocence. He therefore concludes that since

> one could not condemn others without at the same time judging oneself, one should heap accusations on one's own head, in order to have the right to judge others. Since every judge eventually becomes a penitent, one had to take the opposite route and be a professional penitent in order to become a judge.
>
> (Camus 2006, 86)

Thus, judge-penitents admit a painful and problematic historical past and thereby construct the in-group as morally superior: while *we* learnt the painful lessons from the past, *they* stubbornly refuse to accept these lessons and are therefore uncivilized. Thus, self-reflection is regressively instrumentalized and replaced by an instrumental self-righteousness which blocks the tendencies inherent in admissions of wrongdoing towards a more inclusive identity. This subtle shift represents an instrumentalization based on a "pride in atonement", a "pathology of pride" as Robert Solomon puts it. He (Solomon 2004, 48) characterizes *The Fall* as a "condemnation of resentful pride and superiority, pride that refuses to recognize itself as such and superiority that proves itself only by stealth and subversion". Admissions of past wrongdoing become problematic as soon as they serve as a means to construct others as morally inferior.

Instead of widening the circle of the *we* by admitting the harm *we* have caused to others, and thereby transforming the moral boundaries of the community in an egalitarian and universal direction, this closes the process of communicating *with* the "other". It becomes an argument *about* or even *against* the "other". *Our* wrongdoings are no longer the primary focus. Rather, the claim that we have successfully dealt with our painful past enables the positive self-representation as a penitent sinner. At the same time, it is only through contextualizing oneself within a burdened past that rhetorics of judge-penitence can be adopted. This represents a gradual but substantial shift. Whilst "public rituals of confession of guilt" construct the in-group's own past as the evil "other", from which it has to demarcate itself, rhetorics of judge-penitence construct the in-group via the exclusion of an external, now morally inferior, "other".

Consequently, rhetorics of judge-penitence cannot be understood in terms of traditional strategies of shifting blame as it crucially depends on admitting guilt – or at least the acceptance of wrong elements within the in-group's own tradition. Rhetorics of judge-penitence do not construct one's own past in a traditional, i.e. uncritical, way. At the same time, it is precisely the admission which serves as a premise in order to create the illocutionary force characterizing judge-penitence: by humbling oneself, the agent is ultimately exalted and thus enables to construct the other as morally inferior. It is therefore a subtle strategy of justification and self-legitimation which probably only appeals to a limited audience but might, nevertheless, become a significant element in an increasingly fragmented public sphere. Without doubt, collective and individual narratives of innocence, heroic sacrifice and bravery often remain at the core of a community's self-understanding. However, I claim that even welcome admissions of failure might ultimately block more inclusive and egalitarian moral boundaries, as in the case of judge-penitence in which new exclusionary symbolic boundaries are drawn.

This does certainly not imply that admissions of wrongdoing are problematic per se – quite the contrary: they are normatively welcome as they mark the inclusion of those previously excluded and enable recognition between former enemies. As Habermas (1994, 13) put it: only if we admit to ourselves that we have failed are communities able to progress morally, which requires rather open and egalitarian modes of communication. Arguably, it could well be that the confessor rightly claims the moral high ground. That is to say, a negative evaluation of the "other" due to one's own historical experience is not necessarily a regressive instrumentalization. Instead, it might be justifiable and principled. But even if this is the case, the discursive realization could still aim for a regressive positive self- and negative "other" construction.

2.2   Operationalizing judge-penitence

The above ideal-typical conceptualization of rhetorics of judge-penitence consists of three separate elements: firstly, there has to be an implicit or explicit admission of guilt or at least an intertextual reference to a self-critical acknowledgment of one's own wrong past. Secondly, there has to be an implicit or explicit claim that "We learnt the lessons from the past". Thirdly, another party has to be nominated or brought into the picture who has, allegedly, not (yet) learnt these lessons. In order to clarify this subtle argument, let me operationalize judge-penitence via Stephen E. Toulmin's (2003) argumentation scheme (Figure 1).

Given the purely heuristic function of his scheme here, I avoid a full discussion of Toulmin's extended model but restrict myself to the most important

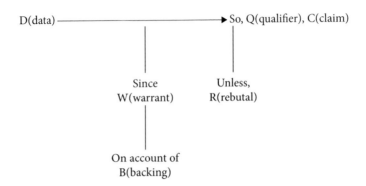

Figure 1. Toulmin's (2003, 97) extended scheme

aspects, i.e. his so-called simple model, which consists of *data, warrant* and *claim*. However, even such a heuristic use of Toulmin's simple scheme is illuminating as it makes transparent the crucial elements of the argumentative form of judge-penitence by illustrating its structural composition. The *claim* describes the point of arrival, i.e. what is at stake. It can be identified by asking, e.g., "What exactly are you claiming?". In the case of judge-penitence, this concerns self-legitimation through a claim for moral superiority. The data on which this claim is based can be identified by asking: "On what grounds is your conclusion based?". In the case of judge-penitence, this might include more or less explicit references to historical crimes committed by the in-group, which have become increasingly common in the recent rise of the "politics of apology". Finally, *warrants* are those kinds of "statements indicating the *general ways of arguing* being applied in each particular case and *implicitly relied on* as ones whose *trustworthiness* is well established" (Toulmin et al. 1979, 43). They can be identified by asking "How is this claim justifying the conclusion?" and are, thus, those elements which determine the acceptance of an argument. To that extent, warrants enable inference from an argument by every audience which holds the relevant background knowledge. In other words: as soon as the audience lives by such a warrant – and different audiences have different warrants although some might be more general than others and be even universally shared – the conclusion appears almost natural. Although "warrants are not self-validating" (Toulmin et al. 1979, 58), there is generally little backing needed as they form common background knowledge. In the case of rhetorics of judge-penitence, the widely shared warrant is that those who humble themselves by admitting wrongdoing get credit for doing so (for the relevance of the Christian doctrine on this issue, cf. Forchtner 2011b).

Although everyday arguments are hardly spelt out in such an abstract manner but are mostly conducted on the basis of incomplete syllogisms, what Aristotle

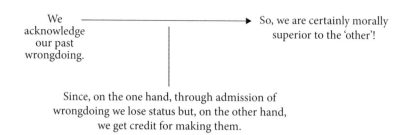

Figure 2. Reconstruction of rhetorics of judge-penitence via Toulmin's simple model

(1982, I, 2, 8) called a "rhetorical syllogism" or an enthymeme, rhetorics of judge-penitence, can be helpfully illustrated via this scheme (Figure 2).

3. Methodology

Critical Discourse Analysis (CDA) provides a general framework to *problem-oriented social research* (for a history of the field and the particular approach adopted in this chapter, the DHA, cf. Reisigl and Wodak 2001, 2009; Wodak and Meyer 2009). The DHA offers a broad understanding of *texts* as semiotic entities – i.e. not only written texts – which influence and are influenced by *discourses*, embedded in a *text-internal co-text* as well as a *socio-political* context. Further salient concepts outlined in the following are: *intertextuality, interdiscursivity, re-contextualization, genre, critique* and *power*.

The concept of *text* is not restricted to written materials alone but entails spoken and visual materials as well. Texts are basic units of discourse and discourses materialize and reproduce themselves in texts. They are therefore sites of power struggles (Reisigl and Wodak 2009, 89). Texts belong to *genres*, the choice of the latter is also related to power as not everybody has access to influential means of symbol production. Different genres are defined by different rules which are socially (re)produced. Participants can expect regularities when approaching a particular genre and can observe differences between, e.g., a newspaper in contrast to an action movie. As Mikhail M. Bakhtin (1986, 60) famously put it: "[e]each separate utterance is individual of course, but each sphere in which language is used develops its own *relatively stable types* of these utterances. These we may call speech genres". In the case of this data-driven study the genre in question is that of commemorative speeches, a sub-genre of political speeches in general. Texts and genres are elements of discourse (Figure 3), and thus the former are specific events via which the flow of *discourses* is (re)produced or challenged. The DHA considers "discourses" to be (a) macro-topic-related, (b) socially constituted and

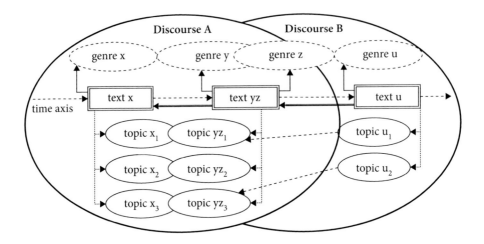

Figure 3. Interdiscursive and intertextual relationships between discourses, discourse topics, genres and texts (taken from Reisigl and Wodak 2009, 92)

socially constitutive, as well as (c) argumentative (Reisigl and Wodak 2009, 89). As such, discourses are identifiable by the analyst as analytical concepts which empirically overlap and are interwoven with other discourses.

The concept of *interdiscursivity* indicates that discourses are linked to each other in various ways. As discourses, following the DHA, are topic-related, e.g. a discourse on (un)employment, discourses often refer to topics or subtopics of other discourses, such as gender or racism: arguments on systematically lower salaries for women or migrants might be included in discourses on (un)employment. *Intertextuality*, on the other hand, refers to the fact that all texts are linked to other texts. Julia Kristeva (1986, 37), who coined the concept views texts as "constructed as a mosaic of quotations; any text is the absorption and transformation of another". Hence, no text is seen as a monological self-sufficient unit, which follows Bakhtin (1986, 91), who states that any concrete utterance "is filled with echoes and reverberations of other utterances (…). Every utterance must be regarded primarily as a *response* to preceding utterances". Thus, "[a]ny concrete utterance is a link in the chain of speech communication" (Bakhtin 1986, 91). Such links can be established in different ways: through reference to a topic or actors; through reference to the same event; or by transferring arguments from one text to another. The latter process is also labelled *recontextualization*. By taking an argument and restating it in a new context, an element of a text is de-contextualised and then, when implemented in a new context, re-contextualised (Reisigl and Wodak 2009, 90). The element then partly acquires a new meaning as meaning is formed in use (e.g. Wittgenstein 1968, §432). Therefore, analysis has to take into account the *intertextual and interdiscursive relationships* between utterances, texts, genres and discourses, as well as the extra-linguistic social variables and specific contexts of situation, e.g. the history of an institution. The DHA is therefore a holistic approach which is interested in contextualized data, and the relation between text and the wider socio-political context, in order to analyze dominance, discrimination and power as they are manifested in language.

Its *critique* is thus directed "*for* emancipation, self-determination and social recognition" (Reisigl and Wodak 2001, 34). This notion of critique goes beyond self-reflexivity and making its political stance explicit. By itself, such an *intellectually honest* attitude when engaging with data alone would not justify the DHA's aims. Rather, its notion of critique is predominantly rooted in Jürgen Habermas' language philosophy (cf. Forchtner 2011), providing a grounding of the norms and principles of the DHA. Against such a background, the DHA is able to identify manipulative practices, *überreden*, aiming to legitimize one's own position, and demarcate them from *überzeugen*, i.e. rational acts of deliberation (Reisigl and Wodak 2001, 70).[1] Here, the DHA connects with van Eemeren and Grootendorst's (2003, 158–186) pragma-dialectical approach in order to provide a toolkit for how arguments become fallacious (for a critical discussion of this connection and the underlying theoretical traditions – Critical Rationalism and Critical Theory – cf. Forchtner and Tominc 2012).

It is the discursively exercised use of *power* seeking to demarcate *us* from *them* via strategies of nomination, predication, argumentation, perspecitivization and mitigation/intensification (Reisigl and Wodak 2001, 45ff.) – strategies we will also find in the example below – which is the focus of the DHA. Power is signaled not only by grammatical forms within a text but also by a person's control of a social occasion by means of the genre, or by access to certain arenas in the public sphere and the position the speaker takes. It is often exactly within the genres associated with given social occasions, e.g. the possibility to speak at a commemorative event as in the analysis below, that power is exercised or challenged. Those groups who are in control of the most influential public discourses, i.e. *symbolic elites*, such as politicians, journalists, scholars, teachers and writers, play a special role in the reproduction of dominant knowledge (van Dijk 2001, 17). A critical attitude towards elites is indeed necessary but this should not overlook the often symbiotic mutual relationship between discourses from above and below (Reisigl and Wodak 2001, 24). In any case, it is important to emphasize that the DHA does not necessarily perceive power as a bad thing as power and its use might be adequately legitimized, e.g. through deliberation. However, the DHA is primarily interested in the ways in which power "comes to life" in various linguistic forms in order to manipulate the audience.

4. Denmark – the historical context

4.1 1523–1864

Danish history is a history of imperial decline. For most of the second millennium, Denmark was one of the major players in the European North. The Danish king ruled an empire which, over the years, spanned from Greenland, Iceland, the Faroe Islands, Norway, (large parts of) Sweden and North Germany (the Duchies of Slesvig, Holstein and Lauenburg) to some Caribbean and Indian territories. Particularly notable in Denmark's steady imperial decline was, firstly, the British bombardment of Copenhagen in course of the Napoleonic wars (1807), which also resulted in the loss of the Danish fleet and the subsequent loss of Norway to Sweden in 1814/1815. Secondly, and more important for contemporary Denmark, the Kingdom of Prussia and the Austrian Empire defeated the Danish army in a war over the rights of Denmark's German duchies in 1864, whereby Denmark had to sign away the three aforementioned duchies. Denmark was now reduced to a much smaller area (although it got back Northern Slesvig after a plebiscite in 1918).

4.2 1864–1989

The defeat of 1864 made the Danish establishment aware that the

> next conflict in which Denmark will be involved (with allies or alone) against Germany in all probability will be Denmark's *last* conflict. I am therefore of the conviction that *in due time* we will approach Germany to a degree that Germany will have no doubt whatsoever that Denmark will be on her side – under *no circumstances* against her.
> (conservative Prime Minister J. B. S. Estrup in 1878, quoted in Bjørn 2000, 121)

Whilst Denmark had managed to stay neutral during World War I, the country became a protectorate when German forces occupied Denmark on 9 April 1940. A policy of cooperation – *samarbejdspolitikken* – was negotiated by which the country's internal affairs remained largely under the control of a national unity government formed by the four major parties: *Det Konservative Folkeparti* (Conservatives), *Venstre* (Liberals), *Det Radikale Venstre* (Social Liberals) and *Socialdemokraterne* (Social Democrats). Whilst all four parties opposed German occupation, the unity government nevertheless encompassed a broad range of positions concerning policies and militant resistance (Lund 2003). For example, both the Social Liberals and Social Democrats supported *samarbejdspolitikken,* exploited in particular by *Venstre*, which insisted on farmer-friendly policies, thereby securing vast profits by selling agricultural products to Germany. This went largely at the expense of the Social Democrats (their clientele) which backed down repeatedly in order to hold the government together. At the same time, *Venstre* was least involved of all major parties in the resistance movement.

By and large, the fact that the unity government kept working from 1940 to 1943 was due to its public acceptance. This is illustrated by the outcome of the national elections in 1943 which, given the context, were surprisingly free and fair and resulted in approximately 90% of the electorate voting for parties in the unity government. The reasons for this satisfaction on the part of the wider population are manifold, including there being no nazification attempt in Denmark. Copenhagen and other Danish cities were not destroyed, there was no collective punishment such as mass executions, no general conscription and the population remained relatively well supplied. The country's institutions survived as did a democratic ethos that was visible in, e.g., public demonstrations against Nazi policies in 1941 and 1942 as well as serious uprisings in 1943 and 1944. Finally, it was also due to this policy that the rescue of Jews in Denmark was possible in 1943 and, furthermore, the crucial support for those deported to the concentration camp at Theresienstadt. Nevertheless, cooperating with Nazi-Germany did also involve political and morale failure such as the banning of the Communist Party and the detention of many of their members (more than the Germans had asked for) by the Danish police in June 1941, in violation of the Danish constitution, and the subsequent signing of the *Anti-Comintern Pact* in November 1941. Furthermore, there was expulsion and rejection of refugees (see below) and condemnation of anti-German sabotage by leading politicians in September 1942 in order to accommodate Germany.

Due to popular unease with the occupation, the changing fortunes of war and increasing economic hardship for ordinary employees, *samarbejdspolitikken* came under increasing pressure, ultimately resulting in an uprising during the summer of 1943 (Kirchhoff 2004, 194–206), which led to the collapse of the policy of cooperation. Although Nazi-Germany now administered directly, its measures remained modest and the administration was mostly carried out by Danish civil servants in accordance with the political parties. The historian Henning Poulsen (1995, 17, my translation) has thus described Denmark's occupation as follows: "we collaborated with the occupying power, obtained first of all the best and uncontrolled conditions of life in occupied Europe, further a resistance movement for half the price, and finally became part of the Allies without experiencing warfare".

Another consequence of the collapse of *samarbejdspolitikken* in 1943 was the attempted deportation of the Jews in Denmark (Danish citizens as well as some of other nationalities) who had, so far, lived under Danish law und were not subject to Nazi policies. Given that the German representative Werner Best wanted to avoid public unrest, he probably prompted the German official Georg Ferdinand Duckwitz to inform Danish Social Democrats to warn the Jewish community (Mogensen 2003). In consequence, when German forces attempted to capture the entire Jewish population on the night of 1–2 October, "only" 284 Jews of about 7,000 were captured. Supported by decentralized resistance groups, most non-captured Jews were shipped to Sweden by 14 October, whereby 246 more Jews were captured in the course of these rescue-efforts (cf. Mogensen et al. 2003 for an overview of the events). Of the 7,000 potentially imprisoned, fewer than 500, of which ca. 300 were Danish citizens, were deported to Theresienstadt. Due to support by the Danish government and the wider public, most of the captured survived the war.[2] Those who "returned home to Denmark in the summer of 1945 found that not that much was missing and that they were very well received by the neighbors" (Vilhjálmsson 2005, 318, my translation).

Thus, after Denmark was liberated on 5 May 1945 by the British, there were legitimate reasons for a positive Danish self-representation. Not only had Denmark succeeded in rescuing its Jewish population but an active resistance movement had also existed. However, the subsequently constructed self-image depicted the rescue as an act of moral heroism without recognizing its more ambiguous aspects, and it overestimated the actual relevance of the resistance as well as its popular support. Instead of facts, the post-war compromise between the resistance movement, on the one hand, and the political elites on the other facilitated unifying the nation around a consensual narrative of "heroically resisting Danes".

Although there were conflicts between these two poles immediately after 1945, they remained within the consensual frame of this basic narrative. Even historical research, arguing in favor of either the resistance movement or political parties, stayed within these confines (Bryld and Warring 1996, 60). Only in the 1970s did this hegemonic narrative start to fragment. Scientists such as Aage Trommer and Hans Kirchhoff questioned the importance of the resistance and prompted (academic) debates. However, since 1945, the main narrative – small Denmark ambushed by Germany but staying true to its values and fighting heroically – was not successfully challenged and "with some minor rhetorical changes, the story was the same 50 years later. Most Danes gathered around this narrative and did not raise many questions, at least not in public" (Bryld 2001, 40, my translation). This narrative of the period of occupation had been central and it is "presumably [still] the period in Denmark's history which is most widely propagated" (Bryld and Warring 1996, 55, my translation). Claus Bryld and Anette Warring (1966, 478) consequently point to the fact that Danes did not critically engage with the policy of cooperation itself but were still caught up within a narrative of resistance until the end of the last millennium.

4.3   1989–present

After 1945, *Aldrig mere en 9. april!* ("Never again a 9th April!") became the guid-
ing political motto and central point of reference for the nation. It was the fall of
the Berlin Wall which changed the scene as it helped bring about the end of one of
the central distortions of the Western European public sphere: anti-communism.
Now, values and narratives were no longer justified by the existence of the communist other but had to be legitimized through other means. Thus, Denmark has
experienced

> since the end of the 1990s the onset of a self-critical and self-reflective process
> which in two to three years has radically transformed the public understanding
> of the period of occupation and thereby contributed to changing the Danish self-
> image.   (Bryld 2001, 41f., my translation)

This rather self-critical process is illustrated in the following via reference to major debates:

1. A state-funded research project looked into the expulsion of about 130 state-
    less persons of which about 21 of them, Jews, died as a result in German
    concentration camps. This issue was first raised in 1998 by Vilhjálmur Örn
    Vilhjálmsson (2005, 8–13) and the project ultimately led to an official public
    apology by Prime Minister Rasmussen on 4 May 2005 (Rasmussen 2005).
2. In 1999, a series of articles was published in the newspaper *Berlingske Tidende*
    on the issue of Danish business enterprises and their trade with Nazi-Ger-
    many (summarized in a subsequently published book by Jensen et al. 2000;
    cf. Andersen 2005 for a more general assessment of Danish industrial co-
    operation). Collaboration was even more significant in the area of agricul-
    ture which helped to stabilize the German war effort (cf. Giltner 2001; Lund
    2005).
3. Although the significance of the resistance movement had already been ques-
    tioned in the 1970s, Peter Øvig Knudsen (2001) showed that the glorified
    resistance had even killed innocent people (although it remains unclear to
    what extent the resistance movement was officially involved in signing off
    the killing of alleged informers). These killings have not been investigated
    by the courts. Knudsen also pointed to the involvement of resistance groups
    in more profane criminal activities, in particular, after the disbanding of the
    Danish police in September 1944. Research has also dealt with the immedi-
    ate aftermath of the war. Already in 1985, Ditlev Tamm published a study on
    the so-called *retsopgør*, i.e. the juridical treatment of alleged collaborators.
    Most of the ca. 13,500 sentenced – including 78 death penalties of which 46

were executed – were responsible for minor offences, those who collaborated on a large scale were often able to avoid conviction. Warring (1994) showed how Danish women who had relationships with Germans during the occupation were badly treated after the war. Helge Hagemann (1998) investigated how some 500 German soldiers died while clearing the Danish West coast of mines shortly after 1945 – under extremely dangerous conditions. Kirsten Lylloff (1999) showed that Danish doctors actively and passively avoided treating German refugees. As a consequence, 13,741 people, of whom 7,859 children, died of minor illnesses such as diarrhea (58–61).

4. Research has also self-critically addressed the rescue of the Danish Jews. It has been shown that it was not so much the Danish resistance but rather Best's act of deception – in order to maintain public peace and keep the Wehrmacht out – that enabled the rescue in the first place. The fact that boat skippers did not act out of collective altruism but out of a desire for profit when helping Jews escape to Sweden contrasted with the traditional image of the rescue and provoked public debate (Mogensen 2003, 47–50). Furthermore, researchers have shown that, although of minor influence, anti-Semitism also occurred in Denmark (Mogensen 2001).

5. Cecilie Stockholm Banke (2005) linked the emergence of the Danish welfare state to exclusionary policies towards (Jewish) refugees in the 1930s. Capping the number of refugees – about 2,000 were allowed to enter the country between 1933 and 1940 – aimed not only to appease Germany and prevent the emergence of a Danish "Jewish question" but sought to secure social planning and the creation of a national labor market by the then Social-Liberal government. Banke's criticism of this particular rationale behind the implementation of the welfare state led her to conclude that not just governments but the very idea of liberal democracy failed.

These examples illustrate that there has been an increasingly lively and self-critical debate amongst the Danish public over the nation's role under occupation since around the 1990s. However, as I show in the analysis below, a self-critical debate of the in-group's national past *can*, counter-intuitively, provide a background for instrumentalizing such references of wrongdoing by claiming the moral high ground and constructing the "other" as "having not learnt the lessons from the past".

5. Denmark and the Iraq crisis

5.1 The context of the debate

Like many other (non-)European countries, the war against Iraq was heatedly debated in Denmark at the beginning of 2003, whereby its centre-right-wing government, headed by Prime Minister Anders Fogh Rasmussen, decided to join the *Coalition of the Willing*. This was initially justified via the apparent danger from Iraqi weapons of mass destruction (WMD). In September 2002, Rasmussen had even warned of deadly gas attacks on Danish cities by Saddam Hussein (Kaae and Nissen 2008, 25f.) and, in a newspaper article in March 2003, Rasmussen (2003a) still referred to issues of security and WMD (cf. Farbol 2011 for an overview). Given the collapse of this argument in mid-2003 and the emergence of new problems (the insurgency in Iraq and rising unemployment in Denmark), the government increasingly needed new arguments in order to legitimize its position.

Although Rasmussen (2003a) tried to link his foreign policy to Denmark's resistance against German occupation and Danish cooperation in March 2003, and had already even indicated such in November 2002 (Rasmussen 2002), this was first and foremost achieved through a speech at the navy's Officers Candidate School. The speech was given on the 60th anniversary of the end of the policy of cooperation, i.e. when the unity government was dissolved on 29 August 1943, and in honor of the navy which sank its fleet so that German forces could not take control of it. His argument was widely perceived as an attempt to legitimize Danish participation in the Iraq War. This became even more obvious in two flanking articles published in the same month. In a foreword to the veterans anniversary paper, Rasmussen (2003c, my translation) claimed that "the lesson of 29 August 1943 is still pertinent [also] in connection with the war that has just ended against Saddam Hussein's tyrannical regime in Iraq". This claim was repeated in the same words in an educational paper distributed to all Danish pupils in the 9th and 10th grades which included an article by Rasmussen (2003d).

By constructing the policy of cooperation as wrong and, subsequently, equating resistance to it with the war against Iraq, Rasmussen aimed to legitimize the latter. On the one hand, the speech was controversial as Rasmussen was the first prime minister openly to question the historical consensus that cooperation was necessary (Stockholm-Banke 2009, 274). His remarks were directly relevant to the discourse on Danish behavior during World War II. On the other hand, the text was also an intervention in the discourse on Denmark's role in the attack on Iraq, explicitly linking both discourses.

5.2   The genre of Rasmussen's intervention: A political speech

It is in this context that Rasmussen gave a speech at Søværnets Officerskole in order to honor the navy which sank its fleet so that German forces could not take control of it after the unity government stepped down on 29 August 1943. The major liberal broadsheet *Politiken* brought the speech to the public's attention by printing it, thereby triggering one of the major debates over Denmark's behavior during the Second World War.

The function of political speeches in general – as well as this one in particular – is not simply to inform (or entertain) but to pursue, change attitudes, strenghen convictions, create identities, etc. A political speech "creates community in all its complexity, of discourse that creates identity, and of discourse that creates shared definitions of reality" (Brummett 2004, quoted in Dedaić 2006, 701). They aim to represent the world in a particular way is often driven by particularly strong perlocutionary aims, such as the creation of in-group solidarity and/or the construction of exclusionary (symbolic) boundaries. As the orator attempts to be seen as the voice of a group and to project his particular message as the group message, so political speeches are indeed exemplary political interventions through language use. This is particularly clear in what Graham et al. (2004) identify as one sub-genre of political speeches: *call to arms speeches*. Here, the appeal to an external authority, such as God, "race" or national honour, paradigmatically supports the construction and exclusion of an external "other" against the background of the unity of the in-group.

Drawing on the three forms of oratory in classical rhetoric, political speeches can be primarily situated at the crossroads of the deliberative and the epideictic genres (Aristotle 1982, I, 3; for a more detailed discussion, cf. Reisigl 2008, 245). The three classical genres are the:

-   *forensic* genre, being concerned with the past, focusing on (in)justice and subsequent accusation or defense;
-   *epideictic* genre, being concerning with the present, focusing on honor and disgrace and subsequent praise or blame; and
-   *deliberative* genre, being concerned with the future, focusing on expediency and harmfulness and subsequent exhortation or dissuasion.

As Reisigl (2008, 244) notes, classical genre theory should be understood as ideal-typical, i.e. as providing, first and foremost, heuristic guidance. Empirical examples, however, will always consist of more or less overlapping genres. For example, Rasmussen's speech below has strong commemorative aspects and thus inclines towards the epideictic genre with its strong educational undertones. Indeed, it can be claimed that the latter is the main function of such speeches, given to redrawing the moral boundaries of the community. In that sense, rhetorics of judge-penitence with their highly non-profane, non-everyday elements is obviously related to the epideictic genre. Simultaneously, educational undertones also concern the future (deliberative genre) and even include reassessments of the past (forensic genre). Accordingly, the speech below, at least in its entirety, includes recalling, thanking, congratulatory, promising and teaching elements (epideictic functions of commemorative speeches whereby the latter two – congratulation and promising – overlap with the deliberative genre), but also accusing elements, a forensic purpose in commemorative speeches (Reisigl 2008, 254f.). Another difference to classical explorations, which will also be noted in the example discussed below, is that modern political communication, including commemorative speeches, is much more complex than its classical predecessor (257f.). Most relevant here is that references to past, present and future are mixed and that multiple intertextual and interdiscursive references can be found which account for the plurality of audiences in modern societies.

Against the background outlined above, it is understandable that rhetorics of judge-penitence will be found first and foremost in highly symbolic texts such as a commemorative speech or an editorial instead of, e.g., a profane parliamentary announcement or a simple newspaper article. In other words: rhetorics of judge-penitence, representing the world in a particular way in order to articulate a particular identity, require a particular scene in which *symbolic speculation* about the community in question can occur.

5.3   Analysis

The following focuses only on the final two paragraphs of Rasmussen's speech. In the preceding part of his speech, Rasmussen presented his interpretation of historical events, i.e. the policy of cooperation and its ultimate collapse. He criticized the then Danish policy of political, economic and agricultural cooperation, painting the ruling elite as irresponsible. This description could be contested on a factual basis. However, an analysis which focuses on this would lead in a different direction, away from the very particular argumentative pattern of judge-penitence whose existence and linguistic realization I am interested in. I therefore restrict the analysis to the two final paragraphs in which rhetorics of judge-penitence become apparent.

[1] Even judged against the assumptions of the time, the Danish policy appears
[2] naive and it is totally unacceptable that the political elite in Denmark pursued

[3]   not only a neutral but an active policy of adjustment to that extent. In the fight
[4]   between democracy and dictatorship, one cannot stay neutral. One has to support
[5]   democracy and oppose dictatorship. This is why the policy of active
[6]   alignment of the time represented political and moral betrayal.

In the first sentence of the second last paragraph, Rasmussen summarizes his previous interpretation of events (lines 1–3). The first part of the sentence serves to
fend off accusations of applying contemporary standards to past events that he
did not experience personally. The use of "even" strengthens this further. To that
extent, Rasmussen is able to take the wind out of potential critics' sails. This is all
done to make his interpretation seem balanced so that, in the second half of the
sentence, he can predicate the "elite" as "naive". Firstly, singling out the "political
elite" overlooks that they had, most of the time, massive public support. Ignoring
this aspect distorts the argument as it suggests that not only can blame be easily
shifted to a small clearly demarcated group, but also that everything would have
been different if only this group had decided to make it so. Furthermore, Rasmussen states that its policy was not only "unacceptable" but "totally" unacceptable
(strategy of intensification, also via "to that extent" in line 3). Secondly, "naive"
is not used for the first time in this paragraph. Rather, the term has already been
used three times in the previous paragraph when characterizing the actions of
the "political elite", making it the second most frequent adjective after "active"
(five times). Having described the allegedly neutral stance as "naive", Rasmussen
is now able to proceed and claim that "one cannot stay neutral" and "one has to
support democracy". Based on Rasmussen's interpretation of the past, this condemnation of Danish cooperation appears logical or, in other words, formally
deducible from what had previously been presented.

   However, it seems as if it is following this sentence that the whole focus of the
speech starts to shift. While the subject of the debate so far was a particular historical event, the Danish cooperation with Nazism, the claim raised in lines 3–5 is
rather generalized: "one has to support" democracy and oppose dictatorship. The
deontic dimension of such a remark transcends the boundaries of the past but
claims universal importance. Similarly, sentence three (lines 4–5) speaks of "[o]ne
has to". It is only after Rasmussen introduced this generalization that he moves
back to his particular theme, a move which enables him to predicate the policy of
cooperation as "moral betrayal". Additionally, using "That is why" (explicit causality) makes the argument appear even more coherent. Again, it is important to
note that he refers to the "active" alignment. Critics are thus not able to accuse
him of putting forward an unrealistic position as he is seemingly not condemning
alignment in general but only "active alignment". Furthermore, stressing "active"
carries a crucial presupposition, namely, that neutral alignment was possible in

the first place. However, Rasmussen never discusses to what extent a different policy might have served, or might serve, the democratic cause better.

[7]   All too often over the course of history, we Danes simply sailed under a flag of
[8]   ease and convenience and let others fight [*ladet andre slås*] for our freedom and
[9]   peace. The lesson to be drawn from 29 August 1943 is that, if we set store by
[10] our values, by our freedom, democracy and human rights, then we too should
[11] contribute actively in the effort to defend them. Even when the odds are
[12] difficult. Even when unpopular and dangerous decisions have to be made. Let us
[13] honor our countrymen's involvement in the resistance movement and the
[14] armed forces for freedom and democracy.

What has already been indicated in the second half of the previous paragraph now becomes even more explicit: that not only are issues of the past addressed but that generalized claims are made which affect the present. In other words: Rasmussen is no longer concerned simply with the 1940s. This is not only in-dicated by the fact that "over the course of history" (line 7) is not restricted to the short period of occupation but also by the inclusive use of "we Danes". This addresses the contemporary community directly and overcomes the previously stressed internal diversion between a naive elite and the people. Whilst it could be argued that, previously, Rasmussen did not acknowledge wrongdoing but rather shifted the blame to the elite, this inclusiveness ("we") marks a shift in his argu-ment. Whilst the predication of an elite as irresponsible might well serve as an externalization of one's own wrongdoing, this new argument rather self-critically assesses the nation's past.[3] The use of "too often" further intensifies his judgment.

Whilst the previous sentence self-critically refers to the in-group's own past, lines 9–11 activate the topos *History is life's teacher (Historia Magistra Vitae)*. Rasmussen appeals to experiences of the early 1940s (line 9) and, enabled by his role as a speaker and unchallenged due to the particularities of the genre, offers the lesson to be drawn. Three details are of particular interest in this sentence. Firstly, he talks in terms of causality ("if", "then"). This conditional clause leaves the reader little space to draw alternative meaning from the utterance. Addition-ally, who would reject values such as "freedom, democracy and human rights"? Thus, an affirmation of these values in combination with the sentence's structure leads to and legitimizes an active contribution to the US war efforts (see below). Secondly, the use of the personal pronoun "we" includes the audience – and sub-sequently makes it difficult to position oneself in opposition to this conclusion. Thirdly, the use of "actively" links with what Rasmussen said previously: one has to fight (lines 3–5). As indicated above, this metaphor carries a surplus value: after all, it does not bring to mind concepts such as discussion or negotiation. In lines

11–12, Rasmussen frames the path he proposes, i.e. the active fight to defend our values, in terms of a "difficult" "unpopular and dangerous discussion". To draw lessons is always hard and Rasmussen here presents himself as a true leader who is able to teach the nation the lessons from the past whilst, subsequently, taking tough decisions.

The final sentence might seem the least controversial but, in the context of the Danish post-Iraq War debate, ultimately caused the whole controversy. Honoring the resistance was not problematic though the unspecified predication of the army as fighting for "freedom and democracy" was (line 14). All participants in the subsequent debate, critics as well as supporters of Rasmussen, understood this passage, i.e. his recontextualization of the 1940s, in terms of a retroactive legitimation of the Danish participation in the war against Iraq. It could be argued that Rasmussen referred to the armed forces' fight for "freedom and democracy" solely because the navy sank its fleet in 1943 so that the German Wehrmacht could not commandeer those vessels. However, this would not only run contrary to the main line of his speech, i.e. that not enough was done. It would furthermore represent an implausible retreat into the particular case of Denmark in the 1940s – though Rasmussen has made efforts to generalize his interpretation of these events. If the context of this speech, i.e. heated discussions over the war against Iraq, are further taken into consideration, it is plausible to assume that most of the audience understood line 14 as indeed referring to the current fighting in Iraq. In any case, Rasmussen has made this link explicit in a simultaneously published booklet dedicated to former resistance fighters (2003c) and educational material which promoted his policy to schoolchildren (2003d).

Still, although the speech entails a general acknowledgement of wrongdoing and a claim of having learnt the lessons, it apparently lacks the third aforementioned argumentative element of judge-penitence, i.e. an "other". This is striking, since it is no longer a past elite which can be identified and excluded from today's in-group. Instead, Rasmussen explicitly uses inclusive "we" as having made mistakes. In this way, he establishes a continuity between the past and the present, thereby committing the current population to learn from "its" past wrongdoings. However, taking the context of the speech into account, the attack on the policy of cooperation was directed against the centre-left opposition to the war. Rasmussen's predecessor, the Social-Democrat Poul Nyrup Rasmussen, thus even felt obliged to defend the policy of collaboration, in an interview, by saying that he also would have negotiated with Hitler (Rehling 2003). Whilst Anders Fogh Rasmussen played on the field of history in order to justify an active policy for freedom, democracy and human rights, including the use of force, the left also pointed to history and outlined that it was only through continuous engagement with the Germans that Denmark survived as a nation. Thus their lesson from

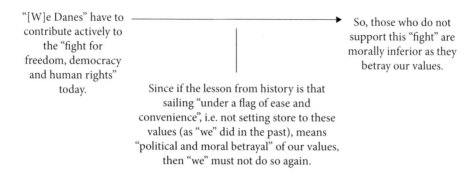

Figure 4. Rasmussen's argument following Toulmin's simple model

history was that dialogue should also be at the centre of conflict resolution in 2003, e.g. through the United Nations. To that extent, the reference by Nyrup Rasmusen to cooperation with Hitler was consistent. However, such a move seems doomed to fail given the fact that Hitler is predominantly perceived as a token of evil nowadays. To align oneself with him means to pollute one's own message, i.e. make it less attractive to the audience. Consequently, the social-democratic argument was never able to set the agenda – although it probably had a lot of public support. Thus, Anders Fogh Rasmussen, adopting rhetorics of judge-penitence, was able to drive his opponents into a corner from which they had little chance to define the political agenda (Figure 4). Although it is impossible to specify the significance of this rhetoric for Rasmussen's political survival, it is crucial to recognize that he was the only European head of government who survived the public debates over the war in Iraq relatively unharmed and was reelected twice.

6. Conclusion

Denmark has adhered to a narrative of externalization, i.e. silencing in-group wrongdoing and shifting blame to the outside, for many years since 1945 – with some legitimate reasons as Danes, in a widely supported effort, rescued its Jewish population. However, public debates show – not only in Denmark – that national narratives now, more and more, include the in-group's wrongdoing as well. In this chapter I have analyzed how the prime minister (mis)used acknowledgments of past wrongdoing in order to justify the war against Iraq. It is thus a centre-right voice which applies rhetorics of judge-penitence in order to construct the "other", the centre-left opposition, as morally inferior. Of course, discourse analysis provides no access to the intentions of Rasmussen and the truthfulness of these acknowledgments. Nevertheless, it is important to recognize that a tendency to view the in-group's past self-critically has also affected the Danish national audience in such a way that arguments to exclude others on the grounds of acknowledging the in-group's own mistakes, such as rhetorics of judge-penitence, have become possible. Again, the fact that admissions of wrongdoing are able to legitimize one's claims is by no means generally recognized. The sheer possibility that a politician can make an argument based on self-criticism suggests that Nietzsche's aphorism is not the last word.

The rhetorical force of the speech as well as his particular argument seems to have benefitted from Rasmussen's (ambivalent) acknowledgements of past wrong-doing. A more traditional reference to a solely heroic past – as was possible un-til the 1990s – would have made it much easier for critics to attack Rasmussen. However, by choosing a different path, Rasmussen could dismiss his critics as doing "old politics" whilst he was appealing to a broader, rather liberal Danish public which accepts self-criticism and is open to human rights, pro-democracy and freedom arguments. By becoming a judge-penitent, Rasmussen also avoided legitimizing the Iraq War through references to the policy of appeasement in the 1930s. After all, judge-penitence depends on an acknowledgement of one's own wrongdoing and is thus less vulnerable to criticism than much more blatant uses of historical analogies.

The fact that he was able to perform this in a political speech is not surpris-ing. The function of recalling is of utmost importance, given the emphasis on past failure (as well as thanking and congratulating the resistance and the military). The function of accusing is equally central and visible in his attempts to single out an elite and the opposition by leftist parties against the war as well as against rightist policies in the 1980s (Note 3). This last note also illustrates the fact that modern political speeches are supposed to address and satisfy multiple audiences at once. Finally, the function of teaching (and to a degree even promising) can be found in Rasmussen's speech in which he represents himself as a leader who, even in difficult circumstances, claims to act in accordance with the lessons he has identified.

Although other authors have looked at Rasmussen's speech (cf. Bryld 2007, 100f.; Kaae and Nissen 2008, 214–235), my conceptualization provides a frame-work which helps to classify such argumentative patterns when comparing dif-ferent contexts. Beyond the use of the model of judge-penitence in this paper, the scheme can easily be adapted to other contexts. Rhetorics of judge-penitence are not even bound to issues of national identity or the past. In other words: both what was wrong in the past (which is now confessed) as well as who is (allegedly) wrong now are flexible (cf. Forchtner and Kølvraa 2012 for European examples, and Forchtner 2014 for a general account). The conceptualization and operation-alization of rhetorics of judge-penitence I have presented in this chapter should thus help to understand new attempts at self-legitimation in ever more post-heroic societies.

Notes

*   I am thankful to Ruth Wodak and Michał Krzyżanowski for their comments on an earlier version of this chapter. All mistakes remain of course my own. The author was the recipient of a DOC fellowship from the Austrian Academy of Sciences and an ESRC studentship at the Department of Linguistics and English Language at Lancaster University.

1.   Legitimizing is understood as a process of putting forward reasons to justify one's claim. In contrast, legitimacy, e.g. of a social order, refers to the internalization of reasons given in such a process. The listener has therefore accepted these arguments, values, etc. and made them his own (cf. Chilton 2004 for a general discussion of legitimation and/through language use).

2.   About 50 of those imprisoned did not survive; whereby exact numbers are still disputed. For slightly diverging accounts, cf. Sode-Madsen (2003) and Goldbaum Tarabini Fracapane (2008).

3.   There might be a second rationale behind this acknowledgement of the nation's failing. For parts of the audience, lines 7–9 call to mind the footnote policy (*fodnotepolitikken)*, a still virulent highly-contested political issue of the 1980s, when the Danish centre-left opted for nuclear disarmament and against the deployment of further US rockets (DIIS 2005, 74ff.). Ever since then, the centre-right parties have denounced the other side for appeasing the Soviet Union and, thereby, repeating the mistakes of the period of occupation. However, by not making the point explicit, Rasmussen might please certain segments of his electorate, whilst the implicit character of this interdiscursive reference does not damage the construction of his image as non-partisan.

References

Alexander, Jeffrey C. 2002. "On the Social Construction of Moral Universals. The Holocaust from War Crime Trauma to Drama." *European Journal of Social Theory* 5 (1): 5–85.

Andersen, Steen. 2005. *De gjorde Danmark større… De multinationale Danske entreprenørfirmaer i krise og krig 1919–1947* [They made Denmark bigger… Multinational Danish Companies during Crisis and War 1919–1947]. Copenhagen: Gyldendale.

Aristotle. 1982. *The 'Art' of Rhetoric*. London: Heinemann.

Barkan, Elazar. 2001. *The Guilt of Nations: Restitution and Negotiating Historical Injustices.* Baltimore: The John Hopkins University Press.

Blüdnikow, Bent, and Vilhjálmur Örn Vilhjálmsson. 2006. "Rescue, Expulsion, and Collaboration: Denmark's Difficulties with Its World War II past." *Jewish Political Studies Review* 18 (3&4): http://www.jcpa.org/phas/phas-vilhjalmsson-f06.htm [24.08.2008].

Bjørn, Claus. 2000. "Modern Denmark: A Synthesis of Converging Developments." *Scandinavian Journal of History* 25 (1&2): 119–130.

Bryld, Claus. 2001. "Med besættelsen som spejl [Occupation as a mirror]." In *Kampen om historien. Brug og misbrug af historien siden Murens Fals* [The struggle over history. Use and misuse of history since the Fall of the Wall], ed. by Claus Bryld, 39–56. Frederiksberg: Roskilde Universitetsforlag.

—. 2007. "'The Five Accursed Years'. Danish Perception and Usage of the Period of the German Occupation, with a Wider View to Norway and Sweden." *Scandinavian Journal of History* 32 (1): 86–115.

Bryld, Claus, and Annette Warring. 1998. *Besættelsestiden som kollektiv erindring* [The occupation as collective memory]. Frederiksberg: Roskilde Universitetsforlag.

Camus, Albert. 2000. *The Fall.* London: Penguin Books.

Chilton, Paul. 2004. *Analysing Political Discourse. Theory and Practice.* London. Routledge.

Dedaić, Mirjana. N. 2006. "Political Speeches and Persuasive Argumentation." In *Encyclopedia of Language and Linguistics. Vol. 9*, ed. by Keith Brown, 700–707. Amsterdam: Elsevier.

DIIS. 2005. *Danmark under den Kolde Krig. Den sikkerhedspolitiske situation 1945–1991* [Denmark during the Cold War. Security Policy 1945–1991]. *Bind 3: 1979–1991.* Copenhagen: DIIS.

Eder, Klaus. 2009. "A Theory of Collective Identity. Making Sense of the Debate on a 'European Identity'." *European Journal of Social Theory* 12 (4): 427–447.

Farbol, Rosanna. 2011. "Irakkrigen og den historiske legitimering [The Iraq war and its legitimation through history]". *Slagmark* 60: 73–85.

Forchtner, Bernhard. 2011. "Critique, the Discourse-Historical Approach and the Frankfurt School." *Critical Discourse Studies* 8 (1): 1–14.

—. 2014. "Rhetorics of Judge-Penitence: Claiming Moral Superiority through Admissions of Past Wrongdoing." To appear in *Memory Studies* 7 (4).

Forchtner, Bernhard, and Christoffer Kølvraa. 2012. "Narrating a 'New Europe': From 'Bitter Past' to Self-Righteousness". *Discourse & Society* 23 (4): 1–24.

Forchtner, Bernhard, and Ana Tominc. 2012. "Critique and Argumentation: On the Relation between the Discourse-Historical Approach and Pragma-Dialectics". *Journal for Language and Politics* 11 (1): 31–50.

Giesen, Bernhard. 2004. "The Trauma of Perpetrators. The Holocaust as the Traumatic Reference of German National Identity." In *Cultural Trauma and Collective Identity*, ed. by Jeffrey C. Alexander, 112–154. Berkeley: University of California Press.

Giltner, Phil. 2001. "The Success of Collaboration: Denmark's Self-Assessment of Its Economic Position after Five Years of Nazi Occupation." *Journal of Contemporary History* 36 (3): 485–506.

Graham, Phil, Thomas Keenan, and Anne-Maree Dowd. 2004. "A Call to Arms at the End of History: A Discourse-Historical Analysis of George W. Bush's Declaration of War on Terror." *Discourse and Society* 15 (2–3): 199–222.

Habermas, Jürgen. 1998. "Can We Learn from History?" In *A Berlin Republic: Writings on Germany*, ed. by Jürgen Habermas, 3–13. Cambridge: Polity Press.

Hagemann, Helge. 1998. *Under tvang. Minerydningen ved den Jyske Vestkyst 1945* [Under coercion. The demining of Jutland's West Coast 1945]. Copenhagen: Akademisk Forlag.

Jensen, Christian, Tomas Kristiansen, and Karl Erik Nielsen. 2000. "Krigens købmænd [The war's merchants]." *Berlingske Tidende* 2.12.2000: 1.

Judt, Tony. 2006. *Postwar: A History of Europe since 1945.* London: Penguin.

Kaae, Martin, and Jesper Nissen. 2008. *Vejen til Iraq – Hvorfor gik Danmark i krig* [The road to Iraq – Why did Denmark go to war]? Copenhagen: Gads Forlag.

Kirchhoff, Hans. 2004. *Samarbejde og modstand under besættelsen – En politisk historie* [Co-operation and resistance during the occupation – A political history]. Odense. Syddansk Universitetsforlag.

LeCouteur, Amanda. 2001. "On Saying 'Sorry': Repertoires of Apology to Australia's Stolen Generations." In *How to Analyse Talk in Institutional Settings. A Casebook of Methods*, ed. by Alec McHoul, and Mark Rapley, 146–158. London: Continuum.

Lund, Joachim. 2003. "Mellem fædreland og flæskepriser. Partiet Venstre under besættelsen [Between fatherland and pork prices]." In *Partier under pres – Demokratiet under besættelsen* [Political parties under pressure – Democracy during the occupation], ed. by Joachim Lund, 130–166. Copenhagen: Gyldendal.

—. 2005. *Hitlers spisekammer. Danmark og den Europaeiske nyordning 1940–43* [Hitler's Pantry. Denmark and the European Reallignment 1940–1943]. Copenhagen: Gyldendale.

Lundtofte, Henrik. 2003. "Den store undtagelse – Gestapo og jødeaktionen [The big exception – Gestapo and the Jewish campaign]." In *I Hitler-Tysklands skygge. Dramaet om de Danske Jøder 1933–1945* [In the shadow of Hitler-Germany. The Drama of the Danish Jews], ed. by Hans Sode-Madsen, 182–201. Oslo: Aschehoug.

Lylloff, Kirsten. 1999. "Kan lægeløftet gradbøjes? Dødsfald blandt og lægehjælp til de tyske flygtninge i Danmark 1945 [Is there any limit to the Hippocratic Oath? Deathrates and medical care of the German refugees in Denmark 1945]." *Historisk Tidsskrift* 99 (1): 33–67.

Mogensen, Michael. (ed.). 2001. *Antisemitisme i Danmark* [Anti-semitism in Denmark]. Copenhagen: Dansk Center for Holocaust- og Folkedrabsstudier.

Mogensen, Michael, Otto Rühl, and Peder Wiben. 2003. *Aktion mod de Danske Jøder, Oktober 1943. Flugten til Sverige* [Campaign against the Danish Jews, October 1943. The escape to Sweden]. Århus: Systimer.

Nielsen, Jakob. 2003. "Danskerne har accepteret krigen [The Danes have accepted the war]." *Politiken* 19.07.2003: 6.

Nietzsche, Friedrich. 1973. *Beyond Good and Evil. Prelude to a Philosophy of the Future.* London: Penguin.

Olick, Jeffrey. 2007. "The Politics of Regret: Analytical Frames." In *The Politics of Regret: On Collective Memory and Historical Responsibility*, ed. by Jeffrey Olick, 121–138. London: Routledge.

Poulsen, Henning. 1995. "Dansk modstand og tysk politik [Danish resistance and German policy]." *Den Jyske Historiker* 71: 7–18.

Rasmussen, Anders Fogh. 2002. "Fogh: Opgør med tilpasningspolitik [Fogh: Confronting the policy of adjustment]." *Politiken* 08.11.2002: 4.

—. 2003a. "Hvad kan det nytte [What good would it do]?" *Berlingske Tidende* 26.03.2003: 4.

—. 2003b. "60 år efter: Samarbejdspolitikken var et moralsk svigt [60 years after: The policy of cooperation was a moral failure]." *Politiken* 29.08.2003: 6.

—. 2003c. "Forord [Foreword]." *Frihedskampens Venner* 29.08.2003: 2–3.

—. 2003d. "Det drejer sig om at turde handle [It is about daring to act]." In *Fred i frihed. Skoleavis til 9. og 10. klasserne i folke- og efterskolerne i anledning af 60 året for den 29. August 1943* [Peace and freedom. School-newspaper for school classes 9 and 10 at the instance of 60 years 29. August 1943], 2.

—. 2005. "Dokumentation: Statsminister Anders Fogh Rasmussens tale i mindelunden 4. maj 2005 [Documentation: Prime minister's Anders Fogh Rasmussen's speech at the memorial grove 4. May 2005]." Online: http://www.berlingske.dk/ apps/pbcs.dll/article?aid=/ 20050505/abmdanmark/105050041/ [25/04/2009].

—. 2009. ""Når vi danskere ønsker frihed og fred, så skal vi også selv yde en indsats. Det kan vi ikke bare overlade til andre at slås for" [When we Danes desire freedom and peace, we must also ourselves make an effort. We can't just let others fight for this]." *Politken Weekly* 20.05.2009: 4.

Rehling, David. 2003. "Nyrup: Jeg ville føre forhandlingspolitik over for Hitler [Nyrup: I would have negotiated with Hitler]." *Information.* 14.11.2003, http://www.information.dk/87672 [29.04.2009].

Reisigl, Martin. 2008. "Rhetoric of Political Speeches." In *Handbook of Communication in the Public Sphere*, ed. by Ruth Wodak, and Veronika Koller, 243–270. Berlin: Mouton de Gruyter.

Reisigl, Martin, and Ruth Wodak. 2001. *Discourse and Discrimination. Rhetorics of Racism and Antisemitism.* London: Routledge.

—. 2009. "The Discourse-Historical Approach." In *Methods of Critical Discourse Analysis* (2nd edition), ed. by Ruth Wodak, and Michael Meyer, 87–121. London: Sage.

Stockholm-Banke, Cecilie Felicia. 2005. *Demokratiets skyggeside. Flygtinge og menneskerettigheder i Danmark før holocaust* [Democracy's dark side: Refugees and human rights in Denmark before the holocaust]. Odense: Syddansk Universitetsforlag.

Sode-Madsen, Hans. 2003. "Theresienstadt og de danske jøder [Theresienstadt and the Danish Jews]." In *I Hitler-Tysklands skygge. Dramaet om de Danske Jøder 1933–1945* [In the shadow of Hitler-Germany. The drama over the Danish Jews], ed. by Hans Sode-Madsen, 226–268. Oslo: Aschehoug.

Solomon, Robert C. 2004. "Pathologies of Pride in Camus's *The Fall.*" *Philosophy and Literature* 28 (1): 41–59.

Sørensen, Nils Arne. 1995. "En traditions etablering og forfald. Befrielsen fejret 1946–1985 [The rise and decline of a tradition. Celebrating the liberation 1946–1985]." *Den Jyske Historiker* 71: 113–124.

Tamm, Dieter. 1985. *Retsopgøret efter besættelsen* [*The purge after the occupation*]. Copenhagen: Jurist- og Økonomforbundets Forlag.

The New American Bible. Oxford: Oxford University Press.

Toulmin, Stephen E. 2003. *The Uses of Argument.* Cambridge: Cambridge University Press.

Toulmin, Stephen, Richard Rieke, and Allan Janik. 1979. *An Introduction to Reasoning.* New York: MacMillan.

Trouillot, Michel-Rolph. 2000. "Abortive Rituals: Historical Apologies in the Global Era." *Interventions: International Journal of Postcolonial Studies* 2 (2): 171–186.

van Dijk, Teun. 2001. "Theoretical Background." In *Racism at the Top. Parliamentary Discourses on Ethnic Issues in Six European States*, ed. by Ruth Wodak, and Teun A. van Dijk, 13–30. Klagenfurt: Drave.

van Eemeren, Frans H., and Rob Grootendorst. 2003. *A Systematic Theory of Argumentation: The Pragma-Dialectical Approach.* Cambridge University Press.

Vilhjálmsson, Vilhjálmur Örn. 2005. *Medaljens bagside. Jødiske flygtningeskæber i Danmark 1933–1945* [The Reverse of the Medal. The Fate of Jewish Refugees in Denmark 1933–1945]. Copenhagen: Forlaget Vandkunsten.

Warring, Anette. 1994. *Tyskerpiger – Under besættelse og retsopgør* [*German Girls – During occupation and the purge*]. Copenhagen: Gyldendal.

Wittgenstein, Ludwig. 1968. *Philosophical Investigations*. Oxford: Basil Blackwell.

Wodak, Ruth and Michael Meyer. 2009. "Critical Discourse Analysis: History, Agenda, Theory and Methodology." In *Methods of Critical Discourse Analysis. Second Edition*, ed. by Ruth Wodak, and Michael Meyer, 1–33. London: Sage.

Wodak, Ruth, Rudolf de Cillia, Martin Reisigl, and Karin Liehart. 1999. *The Discursive Construction of National Identity*. Edinburgh University Press.

CHAPTER 8

Macro and micro, quantitative and qualitative

An integrative approach for analyzing (election night) speeches

Thorsten Malkmus

University of Frankfurt am Main, Germany

The aim of this work is to present an integrative approach for analyzing discursive strategies in political speeches and for characterizing British and German election night speeches as a subgenre of political speech on the generic, discursive and cross-cultural level. The study deals with Blair's speech after winning the British General Election of 1997 and Schröder's speech after the German *Bundestagswahlen* in 1998. The quantitative and qualitative analyses focus on the interplay of the following linguistic macro- and micro-phenomena with regard to van Dijk's "ideological square": speech acts, pronouns, metaphors, evaluative expressions, rhetorical formats/applause. The analysis demonstrates that cross-cultural similarities on the micro level do not have to correspond to similarities on the macro level. The numerous implicit messages identified illustrate the hybrid character of the genre of election night speeches.

1. Introduction

"Der Wahlkampf ist vorbei" – "*The election campaign is over*"; this is the German Conservative Chancellor candidate Angela Merkel's response to a very polarizing 2005 election night speech given some minutes before by one of her opponents, Social Democrat Party leader Franz Müntefering. Although all projections saw the hitherto Chancellor Gerhard Schröder and his Social Democrats (SPD) behind Merkel and the Christian Democrats (CDU), Schröder and Müntefering presented a highly polarizing discourse in the election night speeches. According to Schröder, German Chancellor during the years 1998–2005, the CDU had a disastrous result, the SPD were the winners of the elections, and Merkel would therefore not become Chancellor. Thus he followed the discourse strategies of positive self-presentation and negative other-presentation that are so typical of election campaigns (Arduç 2002; Stiehler 2000; Hetterich 2000; Hategan 2005; Althaus 2001).

This chapter deals specifically with British and German election night speeches (cf. Lauerbach, this volume, for a macro account of election night genres). There are typical differences between British and German election night speeches such as length, degree of institutionalization, tradition, structure, time and place of delivery, rhetorical construction and staging by the respective television stations (Schieß 2007, 276). Many studies have already dealt with cross-cultural comparisons of British and German discursive strategies in various contexts (for example House 1996). Yet, no investigations of election night speeches can be found (except for Malkmus to appear) and it is interesting to see how comparative analyses of other genres relate to the findings of this study. This chapter will discuss some significant questions concerning the rhetoric of election night speeches,

a. particularly on the generic level:
    – Are election night speeches a special subgenre of political speech with particular rules for self-presentation and the presentation of other individuals and groups?
b. on the discursive level:
    – What is the speech act design of winner speeches on election nights?
    – How are the identities of the individual and collective participants construed? What is the nature of their relationship with one another?
    – Which linguistic formulas (evaluations, metaphors, etc.) are used, and how often?
    – Do politicians tend to employ polarizing discursive strategies immediately after the election results are announced, as opposed to employing such strategies in election campaigns?
c. on the cross-cultural level:
    – What similarities and differences can be found between British and German winner speeches?
    – Are German politicians less inclined to polarize than British ones, as has been postulated so often in comparable studies (Ueding 2000; House 1996)?
    – Are the British speeches more ritualized (for example with respect to speech act sequences) than the German ones?
    – What role does (political) culture play in this context?

In order to answer these questions, this chapter will center on quantitative and qualitative analyses and comparisons on the macro level (of speech acts) and micro level (of pronouns, metaphors, evaluations and rhetorical formats).[1]

2. Theory and methodological approach

Critical Discourse Analysis (CDA) is the approach used to examine the speeches. Teun van Dijk's socio-cognitive version of CDA, with the analytical tool of the ideological square, provides a workable model, as the four corners WE, THEY, GOOD and BAD serve best to identify (non-)polarizing discursive strategies (van Dijk 1995, 1998). Wodak (2008) illustrates the discursive construction of US and THEM when analyzing discriminatory prejudices and stereotypes in the language of politics. She claims people can be racialized by the way they are named and categorized by "others" (Wodak 2008, 294). The field of action (e.g. political advertising, as in election campaign speeches, or forming of public opinion and self-presentation, as in inaugural speeches) decisively contributes to the choice of discourse topics and their linguistic construction (Wodak 2008, 297). This analysis of election night speeches is centered around strategies to establish the respective identities and relationships between speaker and addressees as well as strategies to create an appropriate recipient design.

The examination of form and function of speech acts, speech act sequences, presuppositions and conversational implicatures describes the pragmalinguistic macro structure of the speeches (Austin 1962; Searle 1969/1975; Grice 1975). On this basis, the respective micro structures can be presented in their pragmatic dimensions. These microstructures are pronouns and referential strategies (Wilson 1990; Yule 1996), metaphors and metonymies (Lakoff and Johnson 1980), and evaluative expressions (White 1999, 2001a, 2001b). With these linguistic means, speakers can evaluate individuals and groups either positively or negatively. White's Appraisal Theory is a particularly suitable tool for this analysis, since it distinguishes between various kinds of evaluations that can be located at each of the four corners of the ideological square. Rhetorical formats like three-part-lists, contrasts and their combinations and techniques to create fluent transitions between talk and applause can have evaluative functions as well. Through the evocation of applause rhetorical formats may underline the communicative success of the respective utterances (Atkinson 1984).

In combination with speech acts, all these micro-parameters contribute to the identification of discursive strategies of election night speeches (Figure 1).

The "new" aspect of this integrative approach lies in the principled consideration of the interaction between speech acts and the various micro parameters. Also, in my method, rhetorical formats play an important role, since they contribute most to the interactional character of the speeches (for example by the elicitation of applause and its management). The most important micro analytical tool is Appraisal Theory which focuses on various types of evaluations. Fløttum and

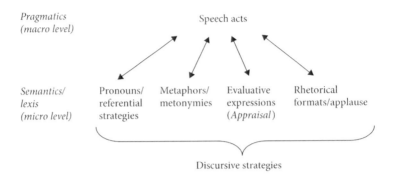

Figure 1. Relationship of the criteria applied in the analysis of election night speeches

Stenvoll (2009) illustrate the importance of the analysis of evaluations. They show in their analysis of two speeches given by PM Blair in the British (2004) and the European Parliament (2005) how important the interplay between pronouns and evaluative terms is (i.e. in particular the integration of internal and external voices in discourse). In their polyphonic perspective (comparable to the categories of intra-vocalization and extra-vocalization of White's Appraisal Theory) they show very clearly how Blair integrates implicitly the voices of others with the help of the contrastive connective "but" (in its concessive use) and the negation "not" (in its polemical use) to present his visions. Cap (2010) also concentrates on speech acts and evaluative terms and shows that they represent crucial features in the legitimization of policies, especially in the construction of individual and collectives identities as in the poignant US vs. THEM dichotomy (Cap 2002; Cap 2010, 119–142).

In this analysis, not only speech act types like Representatives or Expressives, but also illocutionary acts like thanking or promising are identified (Levinson 1983, 240; Yule 1996, 55). In general, it is quite difficult to identify and analyze speech acts in election night discourse because their identification highly depends on the context. Since election night speakers often mean more than they say and thus perform indirect speech acts, the context of the election nights is taken into consideration to identify speech acts and illocutionary points (Searle 1975, 59). Grice's (1975) theory of conversational implicature is another feasible approach to understand how hearers activate relevant background knowledge in a particular context (Fetzer 2002, 179) to understand the communicative intention of indirect speech acts on the basis of pragmatic inferences (Sbisà 1995, 497).

Election nights constitute very peculiar contexts in which election night speeches are performed. An election night speech consists of several speech acts, but its entire discourse is much more than the sum of these speech acts. Accordingly, speech acts are not analyzed as isolated phenomena, but it is necessary to focus on speech act sequences (as shown in the transcripts in the Appendix). This is due to the fact that speakers often prepare the ground for a speech act with the utterances preceding it and sometimes react to a speech act with the utterances following it (Yule 1996, 57). In their election night speeches, Blair and Schröder often perform several similar speech acts consecutively. Thus these speech acts can be considered as a speech act sequence. For example Schröder interprets the election result in detail at the beginning of his speech and praises Helmut Kohl as a tough political opponent only briefly. This sequence can be characterized as a sequence concentrating on the interpretation of the election result that stands in stark contrast to the following sequence in which he presents the aims of the Social Democrat Party as part of the new government. This exemplary distribution of speech acts within a sequence shows that in many cases one speech act sequence can be discerned clearly from another one. Hence an overarching function of the respective sequence (for example interpreting, presenting or thanking) or even of an entire speech can be identified (van Dijk 1997, 14).

Yet, speech act sequences are not to be mixed up with speech events (Hymes 1974, 24f.). Speech events comprise speech acts and speech act sequences, but also further social and contextual elements. These elements are for example the speech situation (a classroom, a party), the aim (a diagnosis, a verdict), the means (spoken or written language, variety of speech) or the tone (serious, ironic). Therefore a speech act is only one part of a speech event (Yule 1996, 47). In general, speech events are sociolinguistically oriented (Hymes 1974, 24f.) and describe speech communities on their terms instead of looking only for the universal in language as pragmatics does (Johnstone and Marcellino 2011, 65). So pragmatics is far more philosophically oriented, concentrates on language use per se, is less empirically oriented than sociolinguistics (van Dijk 2009, 13ff.) and is more delimited from grammar than from sociolinguistics (Ariel 2010, 97).

Consequently speech events cannot explain why people (for instance politicians in election night speeches) behave differently in similar situations (like in election nights). Instead of trying to explain individual ways of talking, they focus, like activity types (Levinson 1979, 368), on how the contextual factors restrict the range of potential utterances of an individual in a particular context. But in order to understand implicit meanings like presuppositions and inferences, a pragmatic approach is necessary to identify genre-specific realizations of universal models like speech acts and to show how genre-specific coherence is established. Thus on the generic level this discourse analytical work can only be a first attempt to establish particular rules for self-presentation and the presentation of other individuals and groups in election night speeches.

3. Election night speeches as one part in a chain of events

Election nights are part of a chain of events. They are preceded by election campaigns of various parties competing for power (Reisigl 2008a, 260). For the
audience, election night speeches are only a part of a chain of numerous other
speeches that were already held during the election campaign and that are seen
in the context of other genres, such as interviews, statements to the press, etc.
(generic chains, see Fairclough 2000, 174). The orators and their styles are already
known by the audience, whose knowledge of the genre is largely based on their
experience of other texts (Bax 2011, 45).

The election night begins after the closing of the polling stations and with the
announcement of the first predictions and projections. In Great Britain the polling stations close at 10 pm, in Germany at 6 pm. Throughout the night, more and
more results come in. It may take the whole night until it becomes clear which
party won the elections and is able to form a new government. In the course of
this time, top-rank politicians give several speeches on different forums. Genres
like speeches, interviews, news stories, commentaries and waiting discourse
(among others) constitute *the macro genre of the election night* (cf. Lauerbach, this
volume). Their paradigmatic or syntagmatic relations to each other are construed
by the media coverage of the various broadcast channels (Martin and Rose 2008).
Like in election campaigns in which the macro-goal of winning an election race
may be realized, the macro genre of election night speeches may serve to solicit
legitimization of policies. In this chapter, only the contextual constraints of one
particular genre (i.e. the election night speech) can be taken into consideration.
Lauerbach (this volume) concentrates on the description of various election night
(sub-)genres, their relations to each other and the constraints on their order of
sequential chaining. Particularly in Anglo-American cultures, election night
speeches are a well-established ritual, and in Germany as well this genre has attracted much more attention in recent years.

4. Election night speeches as a subgenre of political speech

4.1   Definition

This chapter follows a data-driven approach to analyzing the political genre of
election night speeches. Levinson (1979, 1992) defines genre as

> a fuzzy category whose focal members are goal-defined, socially constituted,
> bounded events with *constraints* on participants, setting, and so on, but above all
> on the kinds of allowable contributions.   (Levinson 1979, 368; 1992, 69)

Genres are socio-culturally conventionalized and represent in parts ritualized schemata enabling people to deal with social problems. They deliver standardized frames of interpretation and genre-specific inference potentials in order to understand implicit meanings (Lauerbach and Fetzer 2007, 11). Genres are akin to concepts and ideals and display the following features (Bax 2011, 60–61): they may be linguistic or not; they are shared as mental constructs; they are often referred to by particular names; they are characterized by their functions; their function guides their features; they are structured; they include not only formal, but also social and contextual factors; they are highly flexible.

Election night speeches are a particular subgenre of political speech. They are part of a media discourse that is not only directed at those present, but also (and maybe predominantly) to an absent mass media audience (ratified overhearer, Goffman 1981, 132). Thus they have a specific recipient design whose form and function is oriented to both audiences. On the one hand, applause and cheering show the immediate effects of the speech on the people physically present. On the other hand, no reactions of the mass audience in front of their television screens can be directly observed. Thus it is only the potentially intended effects on the minds of the television viewers and not the immediate effects themselves that form the basis for the analysis of election night speeches as mediatized events (see Lauerbach and Fetzer 2007, 21). It is vital to stress this difference between observable and intended effects since it is one of the most important characteristics of election night speeches that, for the vast majority of the TV audience, they take place only on the record (Scannell 1998, 260).

Election night speeches are particularly suited for a cross-cultural comparison of discursive practices, partly because of their genre-specific characteristics. First of all, they represent a form of traditional political speech taking place on the level of national politics (for further analyses see also Cap 2002, 2010; Schäffner 1997; Sauer 2002; Fairclough 2000; Charteris-Black 2005; Dedaić 2006; Reisigl 2008b; Bastow 2010; El-Hussari 2010). They are limited in time, and are imbued with (implicit or explicit) interpretations of the election results and of the policies of the rival parties. In addition, election night speeches are ideologically-loaded and comprise typical discursive patterns that are representative of the discourse of a political group or party. Politicians concentrate on similar topics, pursue the same aims and use similar discursive strategies to a certain extent (Lauerbach 2007, 315). The dispute over the social and political consequences of the election result begins in these speeches (Lauerbach 2007, 316). The winners and the losers are named as well as the expected political actions and their consequences for the nation. Strengths and weaknesses of the election campaign are analyzed and individuals and/or groups are blamed or praised. In many cases, election night speeches already show characteristics of subsequent genres like news interviews

(Lauerbach 2007, 318). Extracts of the speeches (so-called soundbites) often appear in the news and are printed by the newspapers.

All these observations hold particularly true for the British and the German election night speeches analyzed in this chapter. Both in Great Britain and in Germany, these speeches represent a highly ritualized genre that constitutes a very important part of the media coverage of election nights (Schieß 2007, 276) which in turn have the potential of generating a unified mass audience (Gurevitch and Kavoori 1992, 415). The similar political circumstances in the 1997 Great Britain and the 1998 Germany (see Sections 6 and 8) enhance their comparability even more (Fetzer and Bull 2006, 17). The political conditions were very similar (Strohmeier 2002, 215ff, 259ff.): in both countries, Conservative governments had been in office for almost two decades and the leading politicians faced many difficulties (Kohl for example because of his old-fashioned (political) style, Major because of his dwindling authority). In the 1990s, the Labour Party and the German SPD led successful election campaigns, and a change of government did not seem to be a high risk. Major and Kohl distanced themselves from modern ways of campaigning (cf. Strohmeier 2002, 159ff.) and were no longer supported by the conservative media, whereas Blair and Schröder and their respective spin doctors Mandelson and Hombach/Machnig led very innovative campaigns.

4.2   Genre expectations

There are certain general expectations of the genre of a political speech. In general, people accept that only the politician (and not the audience) speaks (see Reisigl 2008a, 257 for a comparison of classical and modern political rhetoric). It is also a convention that orators do not state solely objective facts and the audience expects a subjective message. The particular expectations depend on the context of the speech. The context is made up of a number of components, described by Levinson (1983, 49ff.) as follows: temporal, spatial and social relations between the participants and their assumptions, knowledge and intentions, the media used and the cultural context. The relationship of these components to each other varies at each stage of the election night. For example in the speech in his constituency in Sedgefield early in the election night, Blair is expected to predominantly thank his (local) supporters. Yet, in his speech in front of the Royal Festival Hall at the end of the election night, the (television) audience expects him to present his policies and prospects for the future. This shows that there are certain expectations of the genre of the election night speech that are activated through relatively predictable language forms and speech act sequences (segments of the speech like thanking) which then materialize in conventionalized forms. However, there may also be individual realizations of the typical features of the genre (for example Blair's conviction rhetoric, see Section 6.2). An educated audience with a knowledge of a particular genre can anticipate the nature of the planned interaction (see also Luckmann 1995, 185) taking both conventional and individual features into consideration. It is quite obvious that election night speeches are different to election campaign speeches because the contexts, the roles of the participants and the communicative goals are different. The interesting question to be analyzed in this work is which similarities and differences in the self- and other-presentation of the respective participants can be identified in the cross-cultural comparison of election night speeches and how they can contribute to a definition of the genre of the election night speech.

Context is a decisive concept to approach this question and different approaches to context have been established by discourse analysts. In general, approaches to media texts have become more "decentralized", i.e. in recent approaches contexts play a preponderant role to understand the meaning of media texts (Wodak and Busch 2004, 106). Chilton (2004, 154) follows a cognitive and recipient-oriented approach to context. According to him, context is no objective social situation. He defines context as "representations of the world stored in the mind and accessed when presumed relevant" (Chilton 2004, 155). Recipients choose cognitively which contextual dimensions they consider relevant. This choice is influenced by their background knowledge, interests and presumptions that interact constantly between texts and themselves (Chilton 2004, 154). Van Dijk (2008, 218) has refined this approach to context by a general theory of context. Van Dijk adds the mental properties of contexts to the notions of Field, Tenor and Mode used by Halliday and Hasan (1985) in their Systemic Functional Grammar to define context. Van Dijk sees contexts as recipients' mental representation of the communicative situations in which they participate (van Dijk 2008, 218). This pragmatic model is sensitive to social influences, particularly to daily experiences. It is these pragmatic context models that control the production and reception of language and its contextual appropriateness and they constitute the decisive link between language and society (van Dijk 2008, 221). In other words, context models are mental constructs "of the relevant aspects of the communicative situation by the participants themselves" (van Dijk 2009, 239). So participants themselves define what they consider relevant to construct their own mental representation of a context. As a consequence, contexts are subjective, evaluative, dynamically construed (and updated) during interaction. As a result, they may also be incomplete, biased or prejudiced (van Dijk 2009, 241). Fairclough and Fairclough (2012, 17) show that the notion of context is essential to understanding political discourse. This is because political contexts are institutional contexts in which political agents can use their power to exert an influence on a variety of matters, including mental matters. The context of election night speeches is an institutional one in which the speakers use their power to influence matters like the political agenda, the discourse of winning and losing and the way the political opponents are delineated and (mentally) represented.

The data to be analyzed in this work are the winner speeches held by Tony Blair on the occasion of the British General Elections 1997 and by Gerhard Schröder at the German Bundestagswahlen (General Elections) 1998 (see transcripts in Appendix). Blair performs his speech in front of the Royal Festival Hall in London and Schröder talks in front of the Party headquarters of the SPD in Bonn.

5. Political background of the British General Election in 1997

At the British General Elections in 1997, New Labour ended 18 years of Conservative government under Margaret Thatcher and John Major with a landslide victory, giving them an unprecedented majority of 179 seats (Hames 2001, 45). The following analysis is based on the transcript of Tony Blair's speech included in the Appendix.

6. Tony Blair's winner speech in front of the Royal Festival Hall in London

6.1   Quantitative analysis

(Political) promises, though in most cases indirect ones, make up about 50% of all speech acts in Tony Blair's address. Thus Blair's speech focuses on the future rather than on an interpretation of the election results and on thanking various people (as he does in his winner speech in his constituency of Sedgefield). "We" is the pronoun that is most often used (almost 60%) and almost four out of five of them refer to the Labour Party. More than 60% of the metaphors used display WE-explicit-GOOD-references, only less than 10% refer (implicitly) to BAD aspects of THEM (i.e. the Conservatives). Appraisal-expressions are used with very similar references to the four corners of the ideological square, with highly-graded and moral evaluations forming the majority. Blair often integrates (with or without making them explicit) internal and external voices in his speech, thus his speech takes on a very conversational tone. More than 90% of the rhetorical formats used (in particular three-part lists with abundant WE-GOOD-references) elicit applause. In general one can say that short, simple and general WE-GOOD-promises tend to be applauded enthusiastically by the audience, thus showing the communicative success of the construction and delivery of Blair's speech.

6.2   Qualitative analysis

The following excerpts from Blair's election night speech illustrate the most important findings according to the analytical criteria applied. The analysis focuses first on the form and functions at the macro level of speech acts and then proceeds to the micro level of evaluating linguistic means.

At the beginning of his very lively and enthusiastic winner speech in front of the Royal Festival Hall in London at about 5 am, Blair makes indirect promises in the name of the future New Labour government. While doing this, he implies a critical position towards the policies of the former Conservative government. For this purpose, he uses metaphors of UNITY that represent US, New Labour, explicitly GOOD, and metaphors of SEPARATION that represent THEM, the Conservatives, implicitly as the BAD ones.

(1)   And where we build a nation with <u>common</u> purpose, <u>shared</u> values, with <u>no</u> <u>one shut out, no one excluded</u>, no one told that they do not matter. [14 sec. applause][2]

Blair often makes promises with antithetical metaphorical concepts ("shared" vs. "shut out") in order to create a coherent impression in his audience's minds and thus delineates the WE- and THEY-groups (i.e. New Labour and the Conservatives) with their respective evaluations. The "conviction rhetoric" of the "preacher-politician Blair" (Charteris-Black 2005, 143), moralizing politics through values that are characterized by the moral contrast of good vs. evil and through the conceptual metaphor MORALITY IS CONFLICT (Charteris-Black 2005, 148), can be observed in (1) as well. Charteris-Black's (2004) corpus analysis of speeches given by Labour politicians such as Blair and Brown corroborates these findings: POLITICS is metaphorically conceived from RELIGION and constitutes the lexical field for morality and ethics, comprising ideas such as commitment, mission, faith, doctrine and dogma (Charteris-Black 2004, 64). One reason for this may lie in Labour's attempt to distinguish its political behavior from the sleaze of the previous Conservative government.

Most political promises follow the pattern "we will (work)…" or patterns that are similar to the one just mentioned. In general, these promises themselves are not highly-graded:

(2)   We will govern for the whole of this nation, every single part of it.

Yet, Blair grades the political aims of his and his party's efforts a lot, for instance through the use of adjectives and/or superlatives:

(3)   dynamic and enterprising economy

(4)   the good practical things

(5)   just and decent society

(6)   a nation united with common purpose

(7)   the finest ideals of public service

These examples illustrate the pragmatic output-orientation of Blair's political visions. He does not only distinguish the Labour Party from the Conservative Party on the basis of the way political actions are pursued, but also on the basis of political results.

Nevertheless, the WE-GOOD-aspect of the landslide victory of New Labour in general is given little attention and is hardly graded (for example, Blair renounces superlatives or intensifying adverbs):

(8)   We always said that if we have the courage to change then we could do it and we did it. And let me say this to you. The British people have put their trust in us. It is a moving and it is a humbling experience and the size of our likely majority now poses a special sort of responsibility upon us. We have been elected as New Labour and we will govern as New Labour.

Through the use of this strategy, Blair is able to avoid any impression of complacency that the past Conservative government was so often accused of.

The lack of emphasis on the election result (evaluations there are little graded), coupled with his focus on the political achievements of the new Labour government (evaluations there are highly graded) shows that the time dimension decisively influences the WE-GOOD-aspects. This evaluative scheme becomes also salient when examining the rhetorical formats and the applause that is elicited by them. Blair's speech is, in that respect, a rhetorical masterpiece: the audience applauds 19 times whilst Blair repeatedly interrupts the end of the applause to continue talking. The WE-GOOD-aspects, but also some of the THEY-implicit-BAD-aspects, are reinforced by the applause of the audience. Interestingly enough, applause is not only elicited by rhetorical formats (claptraps, cf. Atkinson 1984) such as the three-part list in (1), but also by contrasts between the WE-GOOD- and THEY-BAD-aspects as the following example shows:

(9)   Extending educational opportunity not to an elite but to all our children.

Through the use of intonation, increased speed and accentuated mimics and gestures Blair manages to establish a very intense interaction on the I-YOU level.
Since the direct audience mainly consists of supporters of New Labour, journalists as well as the audience in front of their television screens are invited to perceive New Labour (personified by Tony Blair and its direct audience) as a GOOD
UNITY (compare the metaphorical analysis above).

Towards the end of his speech, Blair's promises become more and more direct
and are also addressed to the British nation as a whole. Blair constructs the voice
of the direct audience with the help of the pronoun "we" and addresses the British
people with the pronoun "you". While doing this, shifting references of the pronoun "we" can be observed (for instance, "we" first denotes the present audience
and later on the new Labour government):

> (10)   And it is with real pride that <u>we, all the people here</u>, young and old from every
>   part of the country, from every background, <u>we</u> say tonight: "<u>You</u> the British
>   people have given <u>us</u> the chance to serve <u>you</u>, <u>you</u> have put your trust in <u>us</u>",
>   and <u>we</u> say to <u>you</u>, "<u>We</u> shall repay that trust for <u>you</u>, <u>we</u> govern for <u>you</u>". [13
>   sec. applause]

Through these vague and shifting references of the pronoun "we", a feeling of being
in power and of governing the country is suggested to the direct audience. It is no
longer an unaddressed recipient of speech whom the viewers see in front of their
television screens (compare the participation framework, Goffman 1981, 137).
The people in front of The Royal Festival Hall become addressed recipients and
even indirect animators, because Tony Blair constructs and animates their voice
in a way that suits his needs. Hence Blair invokes the will of the entire British
nation (rather than only the will of those who voted for the Labour Party) and
invites his audience to share the impression that New Labour represents Great
Britain as a whole.

All in all, the following general tendency can be observed: utterances containing explicit WE-GOOD-messages and implicit-THEY-BAD-messages are
increasingly utilized and graded in the course of Blair's speech. This holds true
for the quantitative as well as for the qualitative level of his address. Yet, the time
dimension of the WE-GOOD-utterances plays a decisive role: on the one hand,
utterances underlining the present good situation of the Labour Party, like the
election result, are hardly mentioned and graded. On the other hand, aspects
displaying the promised results of the future achievements of the New Labour
government are highly emphasized and graded. Thus an impression of complacency about the landslide victory can be avoided and the projected policies of
the Labour government serve to strengthen the pragmatic force of the implicit

criticisms of the past Conservative government. Hence the intensity of the explicit and/or implicit polarizations in Blair's discourse is amplified.

As illustrated in the example above (taken from the end of the speech), this tendency (increasing enthusiasm and gradation of evaluations) is also reflected by the enhanced dialogical orientation of Blair's speech; the longer his speech goes on, the more applause breaks can be observed and the more intense gets the clapping. This may be partly caused by the fact that Blair interrupts more and more the beginning and/or end of the applause and that he relies more and more on rhetorical formats like three-part lists, contrasts and the combination of the two. These claptraps are delivered with amplified stress and increased speed and are accompanied by resolute mimics and gesticulation. As a consequence, the interpersonal function of communication gets a preponderant role. This tendency intensifies the WE-explicit-GOOD- and THEY-implicit-BAD-messages.

7.   Background to the German Bundestagswahlen 1998

Before elaborating comparatively on certain discourse strategies typical of the British and the German political culture, Schröder's winner speech at the 1998 German Bundestagswahlen will be analyzed. After 16 years of a Conservative-Liberal coalition under Chancellor Kohl, the Social Democrats together with the Green Party won the elections and Schröder became the new Chancellor. These elections are historically significant, in the sense that they were the only German elections in which all governing parties were voted out of office and had to form the new opposition.

8.   Gerhard Schröder's winner speech in front of the Parteizentrale of the SPD in Bonn

Almost one hour and a half after the closing of the polling stations, the new Chancellor Schröder held his victory speech in front of the headquarters of the SPD, the German Social Democrat Party (see transcript in Appendix).

8.1   Quantitative analysis

Only a quarter of Schröder's speech acts are promises, whereas the remaining speech acts (thanking, interpreting the result, representing himself and his political aims) constitute 20–25% each. Schröder focuses on traditional Conservative topics and interprets the election result with regard to Kohl's term of office.

Still, no ritualized speech act schemata are evident. There are three times more first person singular pronouns in the speech than first person plural pronouns (60%–20% respectively). Schröder never uses "we", only changing references of the pronoun *our* can be observed. Almost two-thirds of the metaphors, evaluations and rhetorical formats used can be identified with the WE-GOOD-field of the ideological square. Highly conventionalized and inactive WAR-metaphors and non-confrontational source domains like STABILITY, SPACE and TRAFFIC are the most frequently used. Moral and emotional evaluations occur less often than aesthetical appraisal-formulations (61%) and only moderate gradations can be observed. Schröder never uses isolated contrasts and prefers three-part lists. Only half of the rhetorical formats employed elicit applause.

8.2 Qualitative analysis

The qualitative analysis of his speech shows that he presents himself as the new "firm and stable" Chancellor, through pronouns of the first person singular in combination with STABILITY- and STANDING-metaphors:

(11) Ich <u>stehe</u> für ökonomische <u>Stabilität</u> und Entwicklung, für innere Sicherheit, aber vor allem auch für außenpolitische Kontinuität.
I <u>stand</u> for economic <u>stability</u> and development, for internal security, but particularly for continuity with regard to external affairs as well.

In addition, he expresses his gratefulness to his own party through expressive speech acts in the first person singular:

(12) <u>Ich bin froh und dankbar</u> für all die Unterstützung, ja Zuwendung, die ich erfahren habe, vor allem aus meiner Partei, der SPD.
<u>I am glad and thankful</u> for all the support, even affection, that I have experienced, particularly from my party, the Social Democrats.

The positive presentation of his party stands in the foreground. For this purpose, Schröder uses evaluations with reference to the election results:

(13) Die Neue Mitte hat sich entschieden, <u>sie ist von der SPD zurück gewonnen worden</u>.
The "New Center" is decided, <u>it has been won back by the Social Democrats.</u>

These evaluations are used more often than WE-GOOD-evaluations with regard to political aims of the new government led by the Social Democrats. Through shifting references of the pronoun "our", Schröder creates a common knowledge basis as well as distance to his own party:

(14)   <u>Unsere</u> Aufgabe wird sein, <u>unser</u> Land durchgreifend zu modernisieren. [10
Sek. Applaus]
It will be <u>our</u> task to modernize <u>our</u> country radically. [10 sec. applause]

When presenting his election victory and his political aims, Schröder always creates links, through shifting references of the pronoun "our", to the electorate and
to the German nation. Thereby Schröder avoids any presentations of his own
party as an autonomously acting political force.

There are very few THEY-BAD-implicatures in Schröder's speech. They only
serve as background in order to underline the dominant WE-GOOD-presenta-
tion (for instance through metaphors):

(15)   Ich hatte schon im Wahlkampf gesagt, dass es Aufgabe einer neuen Regierung
unter einem sozialdemokratischen Bundeskanzler sein wird, <u>das Volk zusam-
menzuführen</u> und <u>die innere Spaltung zu überwinden.</u>
*I had already said during the election campaign that it will be the task of a
government under a social democrat Chancellor <u>to unite the people</u> and to
<u>overcome the internal division.</u>*

Schröder's speech is thus a true "Chancellor speech", since it is quite personalized on the quantitative and the qualitative level (for example when he utters his
thanks or states his political aims), though collective identity constructions and
evaluations still form the majority of his utterances. Many inner links to the electorate are formed, be it on the individual or the collective level. Yet, the electorate,
the direct audience, or the viewers in front of their television sets, are never addressed directly, for instance through pronouns. All in all, only a very low degree
of explicit or implicit collective polarization can be observed in Schröder's speech.
It is only occasionally and implicitly that Schröder dissociates himself from his
political opponent, Chancellor Helmut Kohl.

9.   Comparison of Blair's and Schröder's speeches

The two speeches yield both similarities and differences, on the quantitative and
the qualitative levels.

9.1   Quantitative comparison

In *quantitative* terms, speech act types (i.e. Representatives, Expressives, Com-
missives, etc.) and illocutionary acts (i.e. thanking, promising, etc.) are quite
similar in both speeches. It is also obvious that both speakers concentrate on the

positive representation of their own party, hardly mention the political opponent(s) and avoid an explicit confrontation with them. In general, winners avoid talking about their victory. That means that there are relevant similarities on the level of discursive strategies of their speeches. Thus winner speeches seem to fulfill an integrative rather than an informative-persuasive function (Girnth 2002, 40), i.e. they are a modern means by which political leaders define and communicate the ethos of their party and suggest an efficient formula of public relations (Ensink 1999, 98; Kopperschmidt 1999, 16f.). The THEY-BAD-messages are communicated only implicitly, through presuppositions and particularized conversational implicatures (in Blair's speech more frequently and more intensely than in Schröder's). However, there are also important quantitative *differences* that can be observed. The WE-GOOD- and THEY-BAD-aspects can be found much more often in Blair's than in Schröder's speech, whereas Schröder uses more often WE-BAD- or THEY-GOOD-phrases.

9.2   Qualitative comparison

There are numerous and important *qualitative* differences between the two speeches. First, Blair delivers many direct, emphatic and highly-graded promises, whereas Schröder presents himself as the new Chancellor through plain and non-graded statements and claims. Secondly, Blair gives the positive self-presentations and the negative other-presentations a more intense pragmatic force than Schröder does. Correspondingly, Blair does *not* formulate any negative evaluations of his own party and positive evaluations of the opposing party policies as directly as the German Chancellor does. Furthermore, Schröder orients his thanks to himself, whereas Blair's expressives are oriented more to others. It becomes obvious that in this context Blair addresses the recipients of his speech (be it the direct audience or the viewers in front of their television screens) more often, more informally and in a more personal way. Thus in Blair's speech, a more intense interaction between speaker and addressees occurs than in Schröder's speech. Finally, Schröder's winner speech is much more personalized, and fewer examples and fewer gradations of the WE-GOOD-phrases can be observed than in Blair's winner speech. Accordingly, Blair also uses more THEY-BAD-implicatures, whose pragmatic force is much greater than Schröder's.

Overall, it becomes obvious that Blair dissociates his own party more often and more obviously from the political opponent, whom he implicitly presents as BAD, than Schröder does. The latter presents himself as part of a chain of Social Democratic Chancellors, and assures his audience that Conservative political ideas will be put into practice without combining them with classical social-democratic topics. Compared to Blair, Schröder tends to present himself, his party and his opponents in a more balanced and self-critical way. So in contrast to Schröder's rhetorical reservation, there are linguistic routines in Blair's speech which imply a confrontation with the collective political opponent, the Conservatives.

In general then, there are *quantitative similarities and qualitative differences between the two speeches*. These results demonstrate that the combination of quantitative and qualitative analytical tools seems to be fertile enough, not only for this case study but for further pragmatic studies focusing on the analysis of (non-)polarizing discursive strategies in other genres as well. It can also be said that similar results on the micro level do not have to correspond to similarities on the macro level. In conclusion, polarizing discursive strategies that are so typical of election *campaign* speeches are continued to a greater extent in Blair's than in Schröder's election *night* speech. The question to be asked now is: why is that so?

10. Conclusion

In this case study, (political) culture cannot serve as a universal explanation of the discursive strategies employed. The social and political context (for example the voting system), genre-specific constraints, socially shared background knowledge (for instance about the latest voting results) and possible individual dispositions may have a certain influence. Also the fact that political parties compete permanently with their respective political opponents may contribute to the fact that the two winner speeches are different in many ways. Thus Tony Blair defines the Labour Party in relation to the Conservative Party in a different way from how Gerhard Schröder presents the SPD with regard to the German Conservative Party, the CDU/CSU. This importance of the self- and other-representation of political individuals and groups couples with the fact that the voting behavior in recent elections in the United Kingdom is influenced by opinions (on politicians and policies), rather than by sociological factors (Moir 2010, 253).

However, there are also numerous indications that (political) culture *does* play an important role regarding the discursive construction of the two winner speeches. Particularly the observations concerning the cultural differences (recipient design, self- vs. other-orientation, implicit self- and other-presentation) correspond to the results of studies about discursive strategies in both cultures in everyday situations (House 1996) and to results of studies of other election night genres undertaken – for instance – in the Election Night Project led by Professor Gerda Lauerbach at the Goethe-University in Frankfurt (Lauerbach 2007; see also Fetzer 2007; Becker 2007; Scheithauer 2007; Schieß 2007). Finally, the similarities between Blair's and Schröder's winner speeches and the respective loser speeches given by John Major and Helmut Kohl indicate that certain discursive patterns (for example self-orientation vs. other-orientation of expressive speech acts) are typical of the respective (political) culture.

This comparison of British and German election night speeches has shown that election night speeches represent a subgenre of political speech that is neither the climax of the preceding nor the start of the next election campaign. In particular the numerous implicit messages with reference to one's own or to the opponent's party illustrate the autonomous character of the genre of election night speeches. As a consequence, they can be defined as a repose between the preceding and the following election campaign.

The analysis of the two winner speeches marks some preliminary characteristics that typify election night speeches. It has already become clear that there are monologic as well as dialogic patterns (for example rhetorical formats and claptraps) and it can be assumed that their interplay involves both obligatory and optional elements (regarding for example speech act sequences).

In order to characterize the genre of election night speeches more specifically and to delineate them from other subgenres of political speech, it is helpful to take a look at different categorizations of political speeches and not to stick exclusively to the analytical tool of the ideological square. Reisigl (2008a, 249f.) for example characterizes political speeches according to ten criteria comparing modern political communication to classical rhetorical type with the help of the following questions: Who? On what occasion? Where? When? To whom? Via what media? For what purpose? In what form? About what? Belonging to which rhetorical genre? It has already been shown that there are various subgenres of political speeches that are culturally-specific or even culturally-unique depending on which answers are given to Reisigl's analytical questions. Labor Day or State of the Union addresses given by American Presidents (Goetsch and Hurm 1994, 28) or inaugural speeches (Regierungserklärungen) held by German Chancellors (Stüwe 2005) or British Prime Ministers (Grond 1994) are well-known examples of culturally-specific or culturally-unique speeches. In these analyses it has been shown that there is a mixture of conventional genre-specific constraints and contextual factors influencing the definition of these speeches. The same holds true for the subgenre of election night speeches.

Schröter's classification (2006, 52f.) seems to be very fruitful for taking these conventional and contextual factors into account. She distinguishes between various types of speeches on domestic affairs by taking into consideration different degrees of addressee orientation. Considering her criteria, it becomes clear that election night speeches are a hybrid genre of political speech: on the one hand, they can be characterized as speeches expressing a huge degree of political advertising directed to a mass audience since they are broadcast live by the mass media. They address, among others, the viewers in front of the TV screens and many sequences are not specific to the winning or losing of an election but aim at eliciting agreement. On the other hand, election night speeches also show features of speeches that are aimed at a medium-size public: the addressees are in many cases political actors (for instance political campaigners) themselves spreading political messages. The hybrid character of election night speeches can thus be explained – at least partly – in terms of the presence of multiple addressees (those actually present vs. the TV audience). Finally, the sequences referring to victory or defeat of an election show characteristics of integrative speeches (almost like epideictic speeches) identifying addressees as part of a (winning vs. losing) community. It is not their aim to realize political advertising through a (non-)polarizing discourse, but to create a communal spirit within a particular political group. This does not mean that election night speeches do not have any clear or direct aims. They rather combine (like epideictic speeches) the aims of persuading a particular audience by reference to the election result and by trying to create "consensus regarding norms and values" (Sauer 1997, 48).

The hybrid character of the genre of election night speeches can also be illustrated with van Dijk's (2009, 149) distinction between context genres (that are defined especially in terms of their contextual features like setting, participants, kind of political activity, etc.) and discursive genres (defined in terms of the structures of text and talk like schematic structures, speech acts, etc.). These two genres combine in election night speeches. The winning and losing sequences are context-specific and the sequences related to party politics show properties that are also partly shared with other genres (WE-GOOD). Yet, it should be noted that the latter sequences are not just taken over from other speeches, but they are also modified for the respective context in order to be considered appropriate. This phenomenon is not that surprising because politicians' habitus as campaigning and governing changes and because the hybridity of the election night speech as a genre "arises from its positioning in generic chains" (Fairclough 2000, 175). Although the positioning of the British and German election night speeches is quite similar, the generic chains with the respective implicit and explicit self- and other-presentations are very culture- and context-specific. Thus it is too general to say that there is always an election campaign going on (Merkel 2000, 663), even in election night speeches. The various phases of election campaigns and the respective positioning of speakers and addressees should be taken into account (see von Alemann's (2003, 48) and Arduç's (2002, 181–182) characterizations of the various phases of election campaigns).

Yet, this analysis has shown that the habitus of politicians during election night speeches cannot only be explained by the positioning of election night speeches in a generic chain or by a politician's individual character, but also by cultural aspects. In order to describe and analyze the genre of election night speeches more comprehensively, the concept of (cross-cultural) interdiscursivity in the development of genre theory (Bhatia 2008) should be taken into consideration. Since election night speeches (at least the winner speeches) seem to be positioned somewhere between election campaign speeches and inaugural speeches, more research is necessary to account for the interdiscursive processes and for the (cross-cultural) mixing, embedding and bending of generic norms (Bhatia 2008) in election night speeches.

Also, a larger database is necessary to define individual preferences in the employment of specific discursive strategies (Bhatia 1993). A corpus methodology like the one applied by Bastow (2010), who focuses on binomials in the U.S. defense speeches, might be a suitable tool for such an analytical approach. The results of this case study of two election night speeches can only provide preliminary and tentative hypotheses on culturally specific or individual language use. On the basis of these hypotheses statistically significant results from a larger corpus could be expected. In addition, the results of the analysis of election *night* speeches could also be compared to the findings on other subgenres of political speech, for instance election *campaign* speeches. Thus, generic chains, consisting of election *campaign* speeches and election *night* speeches, would be the next natural focus of interest. Finally, a comparison of election night speeches with other genres of an election night (e.g. interviews) could reveal to what extent election *campaigns* conclude during election *nights* (i.e. to what extent polarizing discursive strategies are abandoned) and how far established conventions or resources of other genres are utilized or exploited in this particular genre. A larger database is also needed to find out how far cultural factors can be held responsible for the hybridization and change of the genre of the election night speech. But what has already become obvious in this preliminary analysis is that the definition of this genre will vary relative to culture. A cross-cultural comparison of British and/or German election night speeches with election night speeches from completely different cultures may contribute even more to the way this genre can be defined without running the risk of a Western bias.

Notes

1.   This work is part of the research project "Television Discourse" financed by the Deutsche Forschungsgemeinschaft (DFG) and directed by Prof. Dr. Gerda Lauerbach (University of Frankfurt/Main). The aim of this project is a comparative analysis of American, British and German election nights and their coverage on television. For further information see http://web.uni-frankfurt.de/zenaf/projekte/TVdiscourses/lauerbach.htm (Lauerbach 2001). In this

chapter, only the British and German election night speeches will be taken into consideration, since the political context of the American elections in 1996 was completely different and during the elections of 2000 no speeches were made.

2.   Underlined words serve to highlight the linguistic criterion applied.

References

Althaus, Marco. 2001. "Strategien für Kampagnen – Klassische Lektionen und modernes Targeting." In *Kampagne! Neue Strategien für Wahlkampf, PR und Lobbying*, ed. by Marco Althaus, 11–44. Münster: LIT Verlag.

Arduç, Maria. 2002. "Linguistische Strategien in österreichischen Wahlkämpfen am Beispiel des Nationalratswahlkampfes." In *Wahlkämpfe – Sprache und Politik*, ed. by Robert Kriechbaumer, and Oswald Panagl, 181–214. Wien: Böhlau.

Ariel, Mira. 2010. *Defining Pragmatics*. Cambridge: Cambridge University Press.

Atkinson, Max. 1984. *Our Masters' Voices. The Language and Body Language of Politics*. London: Methuen.

Austin, John. 1962. *How to Do Things with Words*. Oxford: Clarendon Press.

Bastow, Tony. 2010. "*Friends and Allies*: The Rhetoric of Binominal Phrases in a Corpus of U.S. Defense Speeches." In *Perspectives in Politics and Discourse*, ed. by Urszula Okulska, and Piotr Cap, 143–154. Amsterdam: Benjamins.

Bax, Stephen. 2011. *Discourse and Genre: Using Language in Context*. Basingstoke: Palgrave.

Becker, Annette. 2007. "'Are You Saying …?' A Cross-Cultural Analysis of Interviewing Practices in TV Election Night Coverages." In *Political Discourse in the Media*, ed. by Anita Fetzer, and Gerda Lauerbach, 109–137. Amsterdam: Benjamins.

Bhatia, Vijay. 1993. *Analysing Genre: Language Use in Professional Settings*. London: Longman.

—. 2008. *Advances in Discourse Studies*. London: Routledge.

Cap, Piotr. 2002. *Explorations in Political Discourse. Methodological and Critical Perspectives*. Frankfurt am Main: Peter Lang.

—. 2010. "Axiological Aspects of Proximization." *Journal of Pragmatics* 42: 392–407.

Charteris-Black, Jonathan. 2004. *Corpus Approaches to Critical Metaphor Analysis*. Basingstoke: Palgrave.

—. 2005. *Politicians and Rhetoric: The Persuasive Power of Metaphor*. Basingstoke: Palgrave.

Chilton, Paul. 2004. *Analyzing Political Discourse: Theory and Practice*. London: Routledge.

Dedaić, Mirjana. 2006. "Political Speeches and Persuasive Argumentation." In *Encyclopedia of Language & Linguistics 2nd Edition, vol. 5*, ed. by Keith Brown, 700–707. Oxford: Elsevier.

El-Hussari, Ibrahim. 2010. "President Bush's Address to the Nation on U.S. Policy in Iraq: A Critical Discourse Analysis Approach." In *Perspectives in Politics and Discourse*, ed. by Urszula Okulska, and Piotr Cap, 99–117. Amsterdam: Benjamins.

Ensink, Titus. 1999. "Epideiktik mit fehlendem Konsens. Die Tischrede der niederländischen Königin Beatrix beim Staatsbesuch in Indonesien im August 1995." In *Fest und Festrhetorik. Zu Theorie, Geschichte und Praxis der Epideiktik*, ed. by Josef Kopperschmidt, and Helmut Schanze, 75–102. München: Fink.

Fairclough, Norman. 2000. *Analysing Discourse: Textual Analysis for Social Research*. London: Routledge.

Fairclough, Isabela, and Norman Fairclough. 2012. *Political Discourse Analysis. A Method for Advanced Students*. London: Routledge.

Fetzer, Anita. 2002. "'Put Bluntly, You Have Something of a Credibility Problem.' Sincerity and Credibility in Political Interviews." In *Politics as Text and Talk: Analytic Approaches to Political Discourse*, ed. by Paul Chilton, and Christina Schäffner, 173–201. Amsterdam: Benjamins.

—. 2007. "Challenges in Political Interviews. An Intercultural Analysis." In *Political Discourse in the Media*, ed. by Anita Fetzer, and Gerda Lauerbach, 161–194. Amsterdam: Benjamins.

Fetzer, Anita, and Peter Bull. 2006. "Who Are We and Who Are You? The Strategic Use of Forms of Address in Political Interviews." *Text & Talk* 26: 1–36.

Fløttum, Kjersti, and Dag Stenvoll. 2009. "Blair Speeches in a Polyphonic Perspective: NOTs and BUTs in Visions on Europe." *Journal of Language and Politics* 8: 269–286.

Girnth, Heiko. 2002. *Sprache und Sprachverwendung in der Politik. Eine Einführung in die linguistische Analyse öffentlich-politischer Kommunikation*. Tübingen: Niemeyer.

Goetsch, Paul, and Gerd Hurm. 1994. *Important Speeches by American Presidents after 1945*. Heidelberg: Universitätsverlag C. Winter.

Goffman, Erving. 1981. "Footing." In *Forms of Talk*, ed. by Erving Goffman, 124–159. Oxford: Blackwell.

Grice, Paul. 1975. "Logic and Conversation." *Syntax and Semantics 3: Speech Acts*: 41–58.

Grond, Petra. 2004. *When Maggie speaks. Die Reden der britischen Premierministerin Margaret Thatcher – eine Studie in politischer Rhetorik*. Passau: Verlag Karl Stutz.

Gurevitch, Michael, and Anandam Kavoori. 1992. "Television Spectacles as Politics." *Communication Monographs* 59: 415–420.

Halliday, M. A. K., and Ruqaiya Hasan. 1985. *Language, Context and Text: Aspects of Language in a Social-semiotic Perspective*. Victoria: Deakin University Press.

Hames, Tim. 2001. "Election Round-up." *The Times*. 9th June: 42–54.

Hategan, Christa. 2005. "Auf den Mundfunk kommt es an. Wahlkampflegenden über Umfragen, Berichterstattung und Entscheidung." *Die Neue Gesellschaft/Frankfurter Hefte* 12: 33–35.

Hetterich, Volker. 2000. *Von Adenauer zu Schröder – der Kampf um Stimmen: Eine Längsschnittanalyse der Wahlkampagnen von CDU und SPD bei den Bundestagswahlen 1949 bis 1998*. Opladen: Leske + Budrich.

House, Juliane. 1996. "Contrastive Discourse Analysis and Misunderstanding: The Case of German and English." In *Contrastive Sociolinguistics*, ed. by Marlis Hellinger, and Ulrich Ammon, 345–361. Berlin: de Gruyter.

Hymes, Dell. 1974. *Foundations in Sociolinguistics – An Ethnographic Approach*. Philadelphia, PA: University of Philadelphia Press.

Johnstone, Barbara, and William Marcellino. 2011. "Dell Hymes and the Ethnography of Communication." In *The Sage Handbook of Sociolinguistics*, ed. by Ruth Wodak, Barbara Johnstone, and Paul Kerswill, 57–66. London: Sage.

Kopperschmidt, Josef. 1999. "Zwischen Affirmation und Subversion. Einleitende Bemerkungen zur Theorie und Rhetorik des Festes." In *Fest und Festrhetorik. Zu Theorie, Geschichte und Praxis der Epideiktik*, ed. by Josef Kopperschmidt, and Helmut Schanze, 9–22. München: Fink.

Lakoff, George, and Mark Johnson. 1980. *Metaphors We Live by*. Chicago, IL: University of Chicago Press.

Lauerbach, Gerda. 2001. "Fernsehdiskurse. Nationale Wahlnachtsendungen im interkulturellen Vergleich und die US Post Election 2000 als globales Medienereignis." http://web. uni-frankfurt.de/zenaf/projekte/TVdiscourses/antrag.pdf [retrieved on August 31, 2012].

—. 2007. "Presenting Television Election Nights in Britain, the United States and Germany. Cross-Cultural Analyses." In *Political Discourse in the Media*, ed. by Anita Fetzer, and Gerda Lauerbach, 315–375. Amsterdam: Benjamins.

Lauerbach, Gerda and Anita Fetzer. 2007. "Political Discourse in the Media. Cross-Cultural Perspectives." In *Political Discourse in the Media*, ed. by Anita Fetzer, and Gerda Lauerbach, 3–28. Amsterdam: Benjamins.

Levinson, Stephen. 1979. "Activity Types and Language." *Linguistics* 17: 364–399.

—. 1983. *Pragmatics*. Cambridge: Cambridge University Press.

—. 1992. "Activity Types and Language." In *Talk at Work*, ed. by Paul Drew, and John Heritage, 66–100. Cambridge: Cambridge University Press.

Luckmann, Thomas. 1995. "Interaction Planning and Intersubjective Adjustment of Perspectives by Communicative Genres." In *Social Intelligence and Interaction: Expressions and Implications of the Social Bias in Human Intelligence*, ed. by Esther Goody, 175–188. Cambridge: Cambridge University Press.

Malkmus, Thorsten. to appear. *"Der Wahlkampf ist vorbei" – Ist der Wahlkampf vorbei?: Diskursanalytische Untersuchung und interkultureller Vergleich britischer und deutscher Wahlnachtreden*. Frankfurt: Lang.

Martin, James, and David Rose. 2008. *Genre Relations: Mapping Culture*. London: Equinox.

Merkel, Angela. 2000. "Strategische Wahlkampf-Planung." In *Der moderne Medienwahlkampf – Professionelles Wahlmanagement unter Einsatz neuer Medien, Strategien und Psychologien*, ed. by Otto Altendorfer, Heinrich Wiedemann, and Hermann Mayer, 663–670. Eichstätt: Media Plus Verlag.

Moir, James. 2010. "The Language of Political Opinion: Discourse, Rhetoric and Voting Behaviour." In *Perspectives in Politics and Discourse*, ed. by Urszula Okulska, and Piotr Cap, 237–254. Amsterdam: Benjamins.

Reisigl, Martin. 2008a. "Rhetoric of Political Speeches." In *Handbook of Communication in the Public Sphere*, ed. by Ruth Wodak, and Veronika Koller, 243–270. Berlin: Mouton de Gruyter.

—. 2008b. "Analysing Political Rhetoric." In *Qualitative Discourse Analysis in the Social Sciences*, ed. by Ruth Wodak, and Michał Krzyżanowski, 96–120. Basingstoke: Palgrave.

Sauer, Christoph. 2002. "Ceremonial Text and Talk. A Functional-Pragmatic Approach." In *Politics as Text and Talk: Analytic Approaches to Political Discourse*, ed. by Paul Chilton, and Christina Schäffner, 111–142. Amsterdam: Benjamins.

Sbisà, Marina. 1995. "Speech Act Theory." In *Handbook of Pragmatics*, ed. by Jef Verschueren, Jan-Ola Östman, and Jan Blommaert, 495–506. Amsterdam: Benjamins.

Scannell, Paddy. 1998. "Media – Language – World." In *Approaches to Media Discourse*, ed. by Allan Bell, and Peter Garrett, 142–162. Oxford: Blackwell.

Schäffner, Christina. 1997. *Analysis of Political Speeches*. Clevedon: Multilingual Matters.

Scheithauer, Rut. 2007. "Metaphors in Election Night Television Coverage in Britain, the United States and Germany." In *Political Discourse in the Media*, ed. by Anita Fetzer, and Gerda Lauerbach, 75–106. Amsterdam: Benjamins.

Schieß, Raimund. 2007. "Information Meets Entertainment. A Visual Analysis of Election Night TV Programs Across Cultures." In *Political Discourse in the Media*, ed. by Anita Fetzer, and Gerda Lauerbach, 275–313. Amsterdam: Benjamins.

Schröter, Melani. 2006. *Adressatenorientierung in der öffentlichen politischen Rede von Bundes-kanzlern. 1951–2001.* Frankfurt: Lang.

Searle, John. 1969. *Speech Acts. An Essay in the Philosophy of Language.* Cambridge: Cambridge University Press.

—. 1975. "Indirect Speech Acts." In *Syntax and Semantics 3: Speech Acts*, ed. by Peter Cole, and Jerry Morgan, 59–82. New York, NY: Academic Press.

Stiehler, Hans-Jörg. 2000. "'Nach der Wahl ist vor der Wahl': Interpretationen als Gegenstand der Medienforschung." In *Wahlen und Politikvermittlung durch Massenmedien*, ed. by Hans Bohrmann, 105–120. Wiesbaden: Westdeutscher Verlag.

Strohmeier, Gerd. 2002. *Moderne Wahlkämpfe – Wie sie geplant, geführt und gewonnen werden.* Baden-Baden: Nomos.

Stüwe, Klaus. 2005. *Die Rede des Bundeskanzlers. Regierungserklärungen von Adenauer bis Schröder.* Wiesbaden: Verlag für Sozialwissenschaften.

Ueding, Gert. 2000. *Moderne Rhetorik – Von der Aufklärung bis zur Gegenwart.* München: Beck.

van Dijk, Teun. 1995. "Discourse Semantics and Ideology." *Discourse and Society* 6: 243–289.

—. 1997. "The Study of Discourse." In *Discourse as Structure and Process*, ed. by Teun van Dijk, 1–34. London: Sage.

—. 1998. "Opinions and Ideologies in the Press." In *Approaches to Media Discourse*, ed. by Allan Bell, and Peter Garrett, 21–63. Oxford: Blackwell.

—. 2008. *Discourse and Context. A Sociocognitive Approach.* Cambridge: Cambridge University Press.

—. 2009. *Society and Discourse. How Social Contexts Influence Text and Talk.* Cambridge: CUP.

von Alemann, Ulrich. 2003. "Der Zittersieg der SPD: Mit einem blauen und einem grünen Auge davon gekommen." In *Die Parteien nach der Bundestagswahl 2002*, ed. by Oskar Niedermayer, 43–70. Opladen: Leske + Budrich.

White, Peter. 1999. *Appraisal and a Grammar of Solidarity: New Developments in the Theory of Modality, Evidentiality, Hedging and Attitude.* Unpublished manuscript.

—. 2001a. "An Introductory Tour Through Appraisal Theory." http://www.grammatics.com/appraisal/AppraisalGuide/Framed/Frame.htm_[retrieved on December 7, 2001].

—. 2001b. "Appraisal: An Overview." Available at: http://www.grammatics.com/appraisal/AppraisalGuide/Framed/Frame.htm [retrieved on December 7, 2001].

Wilson, John. 1990. *Politically Speaking. The Pragmatic Analysis of Political Language.* Oxford: Blackwell.

Wodak, Ruth. 2008. "The Contribution of Critical Linguistics to the Analysis of Discriminatory Prejudices and Stereotypes in the Language of Politics." In *Handbook of Communication in the Public Sphere*, ed. by Ruth Wodak, and Veronika Koller, 291–316. Berlin: Mouton de Gruyter.

Wodak, Ruth, and Brigitta Busch. 2004. "Approaches to Media Texts." *In The SAGE Handbook of Media Studies*, ed. by John Downing, 105–122. London: Sage.

Yule, George. 1996. *Pragmatics.* Oxford: Oxford University Press.

Appendix

Transcript of Tony Blair's speech in front of Royal Festival Hall in London on May 2, 1997 at 05:09 am

Speech act sequence	Blair's speech
(1) short thanks; interpretation of the election result; Blair's emotional reactions to New Labour's victory; promise that the Labour Party will govern as New Labour	Thank you, thank you very much indeed. Well, thank you very much. Thank you. Well, a new dawn has broken, has it not and it is wonderful. We always said that if we have the courage to change then we could do it and we did it. And let me say this to you. The British people have put their trust in us. It is a moving and it is a humbling experience and the size of our likely majority now poses a special sort of responsibility upon us. We have been elected as New Labour and we will govern as New Labour.
(2) Political promises of the future New Labour government (education, welfare state, National Health System, economy, united society, powerful Great Britain)	We were elected because as a party today we represent the whole of this nation and we will govern for the whole of this nation, every single part of it. We will speak up for that decent, hard-working majority of the British people whose voices been silent for all too long in our political life. And we'll set about doing the good practical things that need to be done in this country, extending educational opportunity, not to an elite, but to all our children, modernizing our welfare state, rebuilding our National Health Service as a proper National Health Service to serve the needs of Britain. We will work with business to create that dynamic and enterprizing economy we need, and we will work with all our people for that just and decent society that the British people have wanted for so long. This vote tonight has been a vote for the future, for a new era of politics in Britain, so that we can put behind us the battles of this past century, and address the challenges of the new century. It will be a Britain renewed where through education and technology and enterprise, we equip our country for the future in a different and new economic world, and where we build a nation united with common purpose, shared values, with no one shut out, no one excluded, no one told that they do not matter. In that society, tolerance and respect will be the order of the day, as we watch our children growing strength, and our elderly rest easy and secure in old age. That is the country we have wanted for so long, a Britain whose politics starts once again to live up to the finest ideals of public service. And a Britain that stands tall in the world whose sense of its future is as certain and confident as its sense of its own history.

(3) Presentation of New Labour as a party comprising the entire British nation	Today on the eve of this new millenium, the British people have ushered in this new era of politics. And a great thing about it is that we have won support in this election from all walks of life, from all classes of people, from every single corner of our country. We are now today the people's party, the party of all the people, the many not the few, the party that belongs to every part of Britain, no matter what people's background or their creed or their colour, the party that can stand up for what is a great country. And I want everyone to feel proud in their country tonight, because they all have a stake in its success. I believed in Britain, and tonight, the people of Britain are united behind New Labour. They are united around basic British values, uniting to put the divisions of the past behind us, uniting to face the challenges of the future, uniting at long last as one nation. Three days ago, I quoted one of my predecessors John Smith. He said "all we ask is the chance to serve". Tonight, the British people have given us the chance to serve, and serve we will, with all our heart and all our mind.
(4) Thanks to the direct audience and to Neil Kinnock	And to you, all of you that have come here this evening I say thank you for all your work and for all your help. It's been a long journey for this party, has it not. It's been a long journey. I'm delighted that Neil Kinnock is here tonight as well with us.
(5) Promise to serve the British nation	Neil took us back, Neil took us back from the brink of extinction and helped make this party what it is today, and it is with real pride that we, all the people here, young and old from every part of the country, from every background we say tonight: "You the British people have given us the chance to serve you, you have put your trust in us", and we say to you, "We shall repay that trust for you, we govern for you". Finally, all these years, we have been people saying but never given the chance to do. And yet, the only purpose of being in politics is to do, to get things done, to make things happen. Now we have the chance to make things happen, and we take that responsibility upon us, and we say we shall discharge it and we shall make this country as proud of us as tonight we are proud of them. Thank you very much indeed.

Transcript of Gerhard Schröders's speech in front of the headquarters of the Social Democratic Party in Bonn on September 27, 1998, at 07:23 pm

Speech act sequence	Schröder's speech
(1) Interpretation of the election result	Meine Damen und Herren, liebe Freundinnen und Freunde, nach 16 Jahren ist heute die Ära Helmut Kohl zu Ende gegangen. Die Neue Mitte hat sich entschieden, sie ist von der SPD zurückgewonnen worden. Das ist Verpflichtung für unsere Politik in den nächsten vier Jahren. Ich möchte, meine Damen und Herren, liebe Freundinnen und Freunde, an dieser Stelle Helmut Kohl Respekt bezeugen. Er war der erwartet harte Gegner, aber die Wählerinnen und Wähler haben geklärt, wer unser Land in Zukunft führen soll.
(2) Presentation of the aims of the Social Democrat Party as part of the new government	Unsere Aufgabe wird es sein, unser Land durchgreifend zu modernisieren und den Reformstau im Land zu überwinden. Die Wählerinnen und Wähler in Deutschland haben mit dieser Wahl einen Generationswechsel vollzogen. Der Wahlkampf, liebe Freundinnen und Freunde, meine Damen und Herren, war auch ein Wahlkampf der Polarisierung und der Versuch, unser Land in zwei Lager zu spalten. Ich hatte schon im Wahlkampf gesagt, dass es Aufgabe einer neuen Regierung unter einem sozialdemokratischen Bundeskanzler sein wird, das Volk zusammenzuführen und die innere Spaltung zu überwinden. Das gilt vor allem, und das sage ich besonders den Menschen im Osten unseres Landes, das gilt vor allem für die Notwendigkeit, der staatlichen Einheit Deutschlands die innere Einheit hinzuzufügen.
(3) Schröder's thanks to his own party	Ich bin froh und dankbar für all die Unterstützung, ja Zuwendung, die ich erfahren habe, vor allem aus meiner Partei, der SPD. Auf diese Partei bin ich stolz und ich bin glücklich darüber, wie ich unterstützt worden bin.
(4) Schröder's self-presentation as part of a chain of Social Democrat chancellors	Die deutschen Sozialdemokraten mit Willy Brandt und Helmut Schmidt haben zweimal den Kanzler gestellt. Beide standen in ihrer Zeit für Erneuerung und für Aufbruch. Ich stehe in dieser Kontinuität. Helmut Schmidt bin ich besonders dankbar für Rat und Unterstützung, die er mir in den letzten Monaten hat zuteil werden lassen.

(5) Political promises for his term of office	Unser Konzept hieß, auf die Neue Mitte zu setzen. Ganz offenkundig ist geworden, dass dieses Konzept richtig war. Das bedeutet, ich wiederhole es, für unsere Regierungsarbeit eine unabdingbare Verpflichtung. Für mich heißt das vor allem: Ich stehe für ökonomische Stabilität und Entwicklung, für innere Sicherheit, aber vor allem auch für außenpolitische Kontinuität. Mein wichtigstes Ziel, liebe Freundinnen und Freunde, ist der Kampf gegen die Geißel der Massenarbeitslosigkeit. Dafür werde ich zu einem Bündnis für Arbeit und Ausbildung nach Bonn einladen. Ich bin überzeugt davon, dass alle großen Akteure in der Volkswirtschaft, und das sind neben der neuen Bundesregierung vor allem die Gewerkschaften und die Arbeitgeber, sich der gemeinsamen Verantwortung für Deutschland und für Recht und Ordnung, vor allem auf dem Arbeitsmarkt, nicht entziehen werden. Den Menschen in den neuen Bundesländern verspreche ich, alles, aber auch wirklich alles zu tun, um ihre Lebensbedingungen zu verbessern und die innere Einheit Schritt für Schritt zu vollenden.
(6) Thanks to all supporters, thanks to Lafontaine	Noch einmal an alle meinen herzlich empfundenen Dank. Ich bin, das wird jeder verstehen, froh und glücklich über die Unterstützung, die ich erfahren habe, froh und glücklich auch über die, die hierher gekommen sind. Herzlichen Dank, und ich will, und ich will, liebe Freundinnen und Freunde, mit einem Wort abschließen. Unser gemeinsamer Erfolg, mein eigener, wäre ohne die Arbeit meines Freundes Oskar Lafontaine, dem Parteivorsitzenden, nicht denkbar gewesen.

CHAPTER 9

Reframing the American Dream

Conceptual metaphor and personal pronouns
in the 2008 US presidential debates

Michael S. Boyd
University of Roma Tre, Italy

Lakoff (2002) maintains that US political divisions are shaped by competing
interpretations of the NATION AS FAMILY conceptual metaphor, which create
fundamentally different moral models for conservative and liberal politicians
to articulate their values and worldviews. Such differences are realized through
various underlying and surface linguistic means. Based on the 2008 presidential
election debates between Barack Obama and John McCain, the work provides
empirical evidence for the existence of two different morality models. From a
theoretical perspective, the work argues that the family-based models are further consolidated through the strategic use of personal reference and pronouns.
Moreover, it considers the importance of various recontextualization strategies
used to frame the competing worldviews. Finally, the work posits that it is precisely the hybrid nature of the genre of the debate that favors the emergence of
the two models, offering an innovative approach not only to conceptual metaphor theory but also to the study of the genre of political debates.

1. Introduction

The final televised debate between the 2008 presidential candidates, Barack Obama
and John McCain, broadcast on 15 October 2008, focused primarily on domestic policy and the economy. During the debate, both candidates made reference
to "Joe the Plumber" (JTP), a figure thrust into the spotlight in ensuing media
descriptions (Rohter 2008). Although based on a real person, Joe Wurzelbacher,
with whom Barack Obama had briefly spoken while campaigning in Ohio, JTP
was invoked in the debate by McCain and subsequently recast as an embodiment
"working-class white everyman" both in the debate and in the ensuing mass media descriptions (Crowley 2009).

In the meeting between Obama and Wurzelbacher, the latter had voiced concern about Obama's tax plan which would have apparently affected incomes of over $250,000/year, allegedly complaining that such a plan was un-American. In the debate, McCain strategically recast this exchange as a means of delegitimizing Obama's tax and health care plans, while legitimizing his own policies and worldview. In the subsequent turns in the debate, McCain continued to demonize Obama's proposed policies, depicting them as fundamentally immoral and un-American, while addressing – both directly and indirectly – JTP. In this way, JTP was recontextualized as the quintessential working-class American who was only trying to realize the American Dream. While Obama also made reference to JTP in the debate, he did so less often and, for the most part, as a direct response to McCain's constant invocations. Nevertheless, two clearly distinct JTPs emerge from the debates shaped by the candidates' political ideals, personal message and worldviews.

2.   Aims and scope

This chapter is interested in comparing the two competing notions of JTP that emerged in the debate, arguing that the differences were the result of two opposing worldviews expressed in the candidates' discourse practices. More specifically, in line with Lakoff (2002), it is maintained that the different representations (and recontextualizations) of JTP stem from distinct family-based moral systems. Thus, while McCain's conservative (Republican) worldview is shaped by Lakoff's Strict Father (SF) model, Obama's progressive (Democrat) one is shaped by the Nurturant Parent (NP) model. These models frame the various discourses and "force a certain logic" (Lakoff 2004, 17) or ways of thinking, which are clearly evident in the differing ways the two candidates recontextualize JTP. Furthermore, differences in framing are realized not only through conceptual metaphor, but also by the lexical, syntactic and pragmatic means afforded by the genre of political debate.

The main research question addressed in the work is to what extent the recontextualizations of JTP draw upon and adapt the conceptual SF and NP models and their underlying conceptual metaphors. The discourses regarding JTP, it is argued, are based on opposing understandings of "moral action as fair distribution" vs. "immoral action as unfair distribution", which are influenced, specifically, by different conceptualizations of the MORALITY AS FAIR DISTRIBUTION metaphor (Lakoff 2002, 66) and the diametrically opposed moral notions of fairness that this metaphor entails. To support this claim, the work also attempts to provide empirical evidence for the existence of certain underlying conceptual metaphors.

These differences, it is further argued, are realized through various (surface) linguistic means. In a departure from most conceptual metaphor analyses, the chapter posits that the family-based models are further consolidated and propagated through strategic use of personal reference and pronouns determined by the two candidates' family-based worldviews. While the metaphoric nature of pronouns has been widely noted in the literature (see, for example, Malone 1997; Wales 1996; Wodak, De Cillia, Reisigl, and Liebhart 2009), their (strategic) use in relation to Lakoff's proposed family-based models appears not to have been fully explored. The work also highlights the importance of recontextualization as an important (re-)framing strategy. In fact, it is the combination of conceptual metaphors, linguistic features and recontextualization that frames the candidates' discourse and, ultimately, legitimizes the candidates' personal view of working-class Americans and the American Dream. Furthermore, it is precisely the hybrid nature of the genre of political debate that favors such recontextualization practices. In the debate, JTP comes to represent, both metaphorically and metonymically, all working class Americans according to the individual family-based frames adopted. In the next section the most salient theoretical claims are discussed.

3.   Theoretical background

3.1   The genre of presidential debates

US presidential election debates have been studied from a number of different perspectives in the literature (see, e.g., Airne and Benoit 2005 for an overview of the literature; Cienki 2005a, 2005b; Halmari 2008; Myers 2008; Wilson 1990). However, while these debates are closely followed by discourse analysts, political observers and the mass media, their significance in the overall campaign remains, to a certain extent, uncertain (Myers 2008, 121). Most likely, interest in debates is inspired by the fact that they "seem to promise insight into what the candidates are like and how they think on their feet" (Myers 2008, 121), which can be used at times by (undecided) voters to evaluate candidates (Adams 2009, 184).

Debates can be seen as a hybrid genre which mixes aspects of both political interviews and speeches (Halmari 2008, 258; see also Gruber [this volume] and Fetzer and Bull [this volume]). Similarly, Myers (2008, 140) situates debates on a continuum between speeches, which are more oratorical and rhetorical, and interviews, which are more conversational and spontaneous. Such hybridity arises from the fact that presidential debates are not really debates, i.e. there is very little direct interaction between the two candidates and between the candidates, and the audience. The format, content and questions are pre-determined and regulated by the two candidates and the Committee for Presidential Debates (Myers 2008, 124–125).

As in other forms of political (electoral) discourse, the candidates draw on rhetorical "appeals" for positive self-presentation and negative other-presentation, which may include metaphor and metonymy as determined by various ideological considerations (Myers 2008; see also Reisigl 2006 and Van Dijk 2001). In addition, the registers adopted by the candidates also shift greatly, ranging "from the more formal and serious to the occasional joking, and from statements which [are] more prepared and often reused to responses which were more spontaneous" (Cienki 2005a, 284). Such variation is due to the candidates' conflicting desire to demonstrate their knowledge about the issues on the one hand, and to prove that they can talk "one-to-one to ordinary folk" and treat them with due respect on the other (Myers 2008, 130). Furthermore, for Cienki (2005a, 244) debates represent "the supra-individual level" because many of the issues under discussion have already been framed strategically by the campaign team.

An important factor in debates is the way participants address each other and the audience. Ostensibly, the two debating parties form a relationship of speaker/addressee, which varies according to who is speaking and who is being addressed. Other participants in this relationship are the moderator, as well as various audiences – the co-present, primary audience, a secondary audience that is watching or listening to the speech via the mass media, and a tertiary audience that watches the debates in a later transmission, on the Internet or mediated text (Reisigl 2008, 256; Boyd, 2011; for more about participant roles see Goffman 1967; Goffman and Best 2005; Levin 1985). However, since the speakers in the debate are more concerned with making appeals to their voting public and winning over undecided voters, the audience is more often the main addressee, while the opposing candidate can be either the addressee or the referent in a candidate's projected dialogue with the audience. Such behavior is determined by a number of different factors. First, the candidates' communication with the audience is usually one-way, since co-present audience members are rarely allowed to ask questions, and when they are, the questions have been previously scripted and approved by the campaign teams. Thus, the presidential debate can be seen as an example of what Goffman calls "platform format", i.e. an activity enacted before an audience "whose job is it to observe, not to interact" (in Malone 1997, 9). Second, the role of the co-present primary audience is generally less unimportant than that of the much larger secondary and tertiary audiences. Third, even when the opposing candidate becomes a referent, he/she theoretically can still respond directly to the speaker.

There are two other features in the genre of (presidential) debates that need to be considered. First, the choice of reference terms plays an important role in signaling participant relationships. Since reference terms are determined by the speaker's attitude towards the referent and the audience (Murphy 1988, 343), they may also be used strategically to legitimize or delegitimize an adversary. Second, all participants in public discourse must maintain their "public self-image" or face (Brown and Levinson 1987, 61; see also Chilton 2004, 40–41; Goffman 1967; Goffman and Best 2005). In public encounters in general there is a tendency for a speaker to conduct himself/herself in such a way as to maintain his/her face as well as that of the other participants, which, according to Goffman, is due to the "combined effect" of the rules of self-respect and considerateness (Goffman and Best 2005, 11). In political contexts such as debates, participants are constantly trying to maintain a balance between positive-face and negative-face strategies (Chilton 2004, 40) as part of what Chilton and Schäffner (2002, 13) call a "balancing act". Such strategies imply certain linguistic choices, such as, e.g., using the first person plural pronoun over the singular or simply avoiding reference to certain face-threatening elements or referring to them indirectly.

3.2   Metaphor in political discourse

In cognitive approaches, metaphor is treated as a basic mechanism of the mind rather than purely linguistic or literary phenomenon (Chilton 2006, 63; Chilton 2008). In such a view, first illustrated by Lakoff and Johnson in their seminal *Metaphors We Live By* (2003 [1980]), metaphor is seen as the result of cognitive processes through which a known source domain is mapped onto another conceptual domain (Chilton 2008, 236; Lakoff and Johnson 2003 [1980]). A conceptual metaphor creates a correspondence between different conceptual domains, so that forms of reasoning from a source domain can be used in another one (Lakoff 2002, 63). Similarly, Chilton and Schäffner (2002, 29) view metaphor in political discourse as the conceptual structure for "a systematized ideology" that can be used to create inter- and intra-textual coherence. Such coherence can arise both through the use of metaphor and certain lexical items, that, when taken together, create "a conceptual coherence through a common underlying metaphorical schema" (Chilton and Schäffner 2002, 29).

Although similar to metaphor, metonymy represents a fundamentally different process. While metaphor is primarily a way of imagining one thing in terms of another, its most important function is understanding (Lakoff and Johnson 2003 [1980], 36). In the case of metonymy the primary function is referential, i.e. "it allows us to use one entity to *stand for* another" (Lakoff and Johnson 2003 [1980], 36). Metonymy also provides an understanding function, as, e.g., in the metonymy THE PART FOR THE WHOLE, the one part that is chosen out of the many possibilities determines the focus (Lakoff and Johnson 2003 [1980]). Like metaphor, metonymic concepts also shape not just language but also "thoughts, attitudes, and actions" (Lakoff and Johnson 2003 [1980], 39). In other words, metonymy creates a material, causal or cognitive shift between "adjacent fields of reference" (Reisigl 2006, 601).[1]

Not surprisingly, the importance of metaphor and metonymy in political rhetoric has long been recognized (Chilton 2004), and politicians are often perceived as more persuasive when they use metaphors in combination with other linguistic means to legitimize their own policies (Charteris-Black 2005, 17) or to delegitimize those of their adversaries. Furthermore, metaphors represent ways of thinking and speaking about the world that reveal "a shared system of belief as to what the world is, and culture-specific beliefs about mankind's place in it" (Charteris-Black 2007, 43). In politics, these beliefs are disclosed in the way that candidates frame their political message and how such models or frames "organize political thought, politics, and discourse" (Van Dijk 2001, 360). Political (and personal) values and attitudes are then transferred metaphorically to ideologies and policies (Chilton 2008, 233).

Thus, on the one hand, politicians employ traditional figures of speech as "effective rhetorical means of constructing, representing, and transforming political 'reality', as well as a means of political persuasion" or for positive self-presentation and negative other-presentation (Reisigl 2006, 598–599). On the other hand, deeper lexical "metaphorical mappings" can be used in quite complex ways to frame "stores of structured cultural knowledge" (Chilton 2004, 52).

A particularly insightful discussion of political discourse from a cognitive perspective can be found in Chilton (2004), who sees political texts as the "intersecting" of various cognitive, deictic dimensions exploited through language use (Chilton 2004, 204). He proposes the three axes of space, time and modality that combine to form spatial metaphors "conceptualising the speaker's and/or hearer's relationship to the interlocutor(s), to their physical location, to the point of time of the ongoing utterance, and to where they are in the ongoing discourse" (Chilton 2004, 56). Particularly relevant for the present discussion is how these coordinates are accessed by speakers and/or hearers, which, in fact, occurs through the (strategic) use of linguistic expressions, such as prepositions, pronouns and modals in combination with "frame-based knowledge" (Chilton 2004, 61).

In *Moral Politics*, Lakoff (2002) applies conceptual metaphor theory to politics. He uses cognitive models of morality based on two competing "idealized" (Cienki 2005a, 280) interpretations of the NATION AS FAMILY metaphor, which, he claims, is predominantly exploited in the conservative and liberal political worldviews in the US political system. Lakoff argues that unconscious cognitive models are fundamental to understanding (and reproducing) politics, exactly as in other areas in our lives (Lakoff 2002, 159). Furthermore, these cognitive models help us to 'fill in' what is not explicitly said in political discourse. More-over, conservative and, to a much lesser degree, liberal political actors *consciously* draw upon the models linguistically to articulate a unifying system of moral and family values in their political rhetoric (Lakoff 2004).

The two versions of family underlying the model determine "which meta-phorical ways of thinking and morality have priority" (Cienki 2005a, 280) and, consequently, how the public discourse of the Democrats and Republicans is framed (Chilton 2008, 233). The NATION AS FAMILY is a natural metaphor: large social groups such as nations are conceptualized in terms of smaller ones like families or communities (Lakoff 2004, 5). Thus, on the one hand, the conservative or Republican worldview and discourse are shaped by the Strict Father [SF] mod-el. This model is grounded in the notion that the world is a difficult and dangerous place and, therefore, a child should be raised in a traditional nuclear family by a father who has "primary responsibility for supporting and protecting the family as well as the authority to set overall family policy" (Lakoff 2002, 65–66). A child raised in such an environment, however, should never be coddled lest he/she not learn the proper morals of self-discipline, self-reliance and respect for legitimate authority (Lakoff 2002, 65–71). One of the entailments of this model is a natu-ral disdain for "meddling" parents who assert their authority when they have no business doing so (Lakoff 2002, 79). Furthermore, according to SF morality, the rich should have moral authority over the poor, which nourishes the myth of the American Dream, according to which "America is truly a land of opportunity where anyone with self-discipline can, through hard work, climb the ladder of success" (Lakoff 2002, 83).

The Nurturant Parent [NP] model, which Lakoff associates with the liberal worldview, is based on a very different notion of parenthood (and childhood), producing different moral values. Underlying this model are the basic childhood experiences of being cared for and cared about by a caring and nurturant parent or parents. In such a view, a child grows up (and is nurtured) through interaction and care, which instills a strong sense of empathy for others and potential for achievement and enjoyment. Empathy, in turn, is viewed metaphorically as "the capacity to project [...] consciousness into other people so that you can feel what they feel" (Lakoff 2002, 114). Children raised in such a model develop a strong sense of community and, consequently, feel responsibility for those members of the community who need help (Lakoff 2002, 118).

One of the central metaphors underlying these models, based on the competing notions of what constitutes fair distribution, is MORALITY AS FAIR DISTRIBUTION. From this metaphor, it follows that liberals should see the federal government as a strong, nurturant parent that provides basic needs for all of its citizens. Govern-ment-supported social programs, in turn, both help and strengthen people, and such programs are seen as a form of civic duty and conceptualized metaphorically as investments (Lakoff 2002, 179). For conservatives, however, the very same programs are seen as unnatural and immoral because they "coddle" people who should be learning to fend for themselves, which is a natural consequence of the "myth of America as a Land of Opportunity", or the American Dream (Lakoff 2002, 181, 180). In the conservative worldview taxes are seen as a form of punishment rather than investments, and when people are taxed more for making more money they "are [...] being punished for being model citizens, for doing what, according to the American Dream, they are supposed to do" (Lakoff 2002, 181, 180).

Lakoff's family-based models have been applied to the analysis of election debates (Adams 2009; Cienki 2005a; Cienki 2005b), presidential speeches (Ahrens 2011) and Senate debates (Ahrens and Lee 2009). In two complementary studies about the 2000 presidential debates between Bush and Gore, Cienki (2005a, 2005b) found that the actual incidence of conceptual metaphors was quite low, concluding that "the genre of the political debate is not one which lends itself to the characterization of political issues, via the nation as a family metaphor, in terms of SF and NP family metaphors" (Cienki 2005a, 288). In response to this apparent lack of conceptual metaphors, Ahrens (2011) proposes a corpus-based approach aimed at uncovering patterns of lexical usage that may reflect the underlying cognitive models of the speaker.

Bar-Lev (2007, 462, 464) offers several criticisms of Lakoff's models, noting the simplicity of the NP model compared to the SF one: "[the NP model] seems to be missing local elements ('frames') that are clearly necessary to explain the linguistic and cognitive behavior of liberals". Moreover, he complains about the general lack of discourse data in Lakoff's analysis, suggesting the need for more empirical data to support the two models (Bar-Lev 2007, 463). One of the goals of this work is to provide more empirical data to demonstrate the existence of these models.

3.3   Personal reference and pronouns

The use and meaning of pronouns in political discourse is highly influenced by the social and political "spaces" within which people and groups are positioned or position themselves (Chilton and Schäffner 1997, 216), closely tied to the notions of identity and ideology. Indeed, pronouns can be used to indicate or obscure collectivity and individuality (Fairclough 2003, 162), for referencing "self" or "others", or as a means of polarizing representations of ingroups and outgroups (Suleiman and O'Connell 2008; Van Dijk 2001, 103). The choice and interpretation of the pronominal form is mediated by a number of different social and personal factors including (in)formality, status, solidarity, power, class, sex and race (Wilson 1990, 45–46). To return to Goffman (1967), pronouns change according to "how people build particular types of footings or alignments not only between speakers and hearers, but also between a speaker and his or her own utterance" (Malone 1997, 44).

While the most salient pronominal distinctions in political discourse include "I" vs. "we", inclusive vs. exclusive "we", and "us" vs. "them", third person pronouns can also be used in a variety of ways to create or obfuscate agency. Chilton's approach (2004, 57–59) sheds some light on pronoun analysis. In his three-dimensional approach, pronouns are employed deictically to represent people's position in the world on the space axis, in a process that is often called "pronominal scaling":

> The speaker (Self, which may be *I* or a *we*-group) is at *here*. The entities indexed by second-person and third-person pronouns are 'situated' along *s*, some nearer to, some more remote from *self*. It is not that we can actually measure the 'distances' from Self; rather, the idea is that people tend to place people and things along a scale of remoteness from the self, using background assumptions and indexical cues.   (Chilton 2004, 58)

In Wales's (1996, 26) equally insightful approach, pronouns are interpreted according to pragmatic and cognitive factors which are part of "ongoing discourse-world creation". The speaker and the addressee are involved cooperatively in the creation of a discourse universe "based on the assumption of a body of knowledge, held in common to a greater or lesser degree and bearing some relationship to a 'real' world, 'out there'" (Wales 1996, 26). This definition highlights the indexical function as well as the pragmatic power of pronoun distinctions: "*We* and *they* may well reflect a social and cultural climate, but as deictic elements they have the pragmatic power to delimit and oppose groups for political expediency" (Wales 1996, 61). Furthermore, the indexicality of discourse, as also noted by Malone (1997, 58), is reinforced by the pronominal choices that speakers make to "create alignments between talkers and their topics and their hearers that must be attended to in order that conversation continue".

As far as the first person pronouns are concerned, the decision to use "I" or "we" is determined by the degree of responsibility the speaker wants to claim: "I" is used "to gain the people's allegiance", while "we" is often used to evade complete responsibility (Wilson 1990, 45). Thus, in her analysis of the 1996 presidential debates between Clinton and Dole, Halamari (2008, 260) notes that, "*I* is more transparently audience-exclusive than *we*, even though *we* is sometimes used without including the audience as in reference to 'I and some others'". The first person plural pronoun "we" can also convey different meanings depending on the inclusion or exclusion of the addressee(s) and whether inclusion is partial or total (Wilson 1990, Chapter 3; Wodak et al. 2009, 45–47), creating a sort of ambivalence that can be useful for political ends (Wales 1996, 58). Furthermore, "we" can be used for cohesive purposes, providing a sense of unity not only at the purely textual level but also pragmatically (cf. Wales 1996, 62 and Boyd 2009a, 2009b for a discussion of Obama's use of "we"). In debates, as noted by Wilson (1990, 52), "we" can be used to "spread the load of responsibility", a strategy he considers as "a useful ploy" since the opponent will almost certainly question any positive claims that are made.

Finally, we need to consider the fundamental differences between the first and second person pronouns as against the third person ones. While the first and second person pronouns are generally used "in the situational context, and refer normally to human beings in the 'dialogue'" (Wales 1996, 3), third person pronouns are typically used anaphorically (or "prototypically" as Wales observes). The variable nature of the first and second person pronouns is well captured by Jakobson's (1990) term "shifters",[2] since they cannot be defined without reference to the message. The third person pronoun, on the other hand, as noted by Malone (1997, 71, citing Lyons [1977, 638]), does not correspond to "any positive participant role". Moreover, since the meaning of third person pronouns is established by exclusion from direct address, they can naturally be used metaphorically to represent others: "Their use means that 'I', 'we', and 'you' are defined not simply as people who are present and engaged in this interaction, but, more significantly, as people who are connected to those 'others' in particular ways" (Malone 1997, 73).

As already mentioned, pronouns can be used strategically in political debates in various ways. For example, an opponent can be referred to by using the third person pronoun instead of direct naming (Wilson 1990, 61), while the use of vocative forms (with the corresponding second person pronoun) is often employed to engage the audience (Halmari 2008, 263). We should recall, however, that the meaning of the second person pronoun may vary according to its location on Chilton's distancing scale.

Pronouns can also be used strategically to create metaphor and metonymy. Chilton (2004, 56) remarks on the use of the third person plural pronoun to encourage "interpreters to conceptualise group identity, coalitions, parties and the like, either as insiders or outsiders". Similarly, Wodak et al. (2009, 45–46) refer to the "synecdochal realizations" of "we" with a generalizing meaning: "all seem to include a second person into the 'we' group; that is they seem to be cases of addressee-inclusive 'we', whereas in fact they are addressee-exclusive". In addition, there are "metonymic realizations" of "we" when "*we* pretends to include the speaker and perhaps also the addressee as well as the third persons who are not present" (Wodak et al. 2009, 46).

3.4   Recontextualization

Speakers use intertextuality to bring other voices into a discourse (Myers 2008, 134), most often through a process of recontextualization (Wodak and De Cillia 2007, 323). In the latter, elements of one social practice are appropriated within another (Fairclough 2003, 32) for some strategic or ideological purpose (Chilton and Schäffner 2002, 17).[3] Fairclough (2010, 79) hints at the metaphorical nature of recontextualization: "A discourse decontextualised from its dialectical relationship with other elements of a field or network of social practices becomes an imaginary, very often working in a metaphorical way in the re-imagining of aspects of the field or practices it is recontextualised within [...]". Furthermore, recontextualization implies a twofold process of "suppression" and "filtering" of meanings (Chouliaraki and Fairclough 1999), making recontextualization a powerful tool in transforming discourses and creating new ones (Busch 2006, 613). This, in turn, may lead to struggles between social actors who pursue "different strategies within the recontextualized context" (Fairclough 2010, 77).

Recontextualization often occurs through the use of lexical substitution, re-semanticization and rhetorical figures such as metaphor and metonymy (Boyd 2009a; Van Dijk 1993, 261; Wodak and De Cillia 2007). Discourses can also be recontextualized in represented discourse, when speakers make reference to other speakers and contexts: "In the co-construction of meaning, the speakers recontextualize material from other contexts, usually the other speaker's utterances, in some manner in the on-going interaction" (Johansson 2006, 217; see also Myers 2008). Important to this notion is how social actors are represented and, consequently, how "anthropomorphized social actors" are constructed (Wodak et al. 2009, 35). Finally, recontextualization is also an important part of discourse-world creation through pronominal use as we shall see in the discussion that follows.

4.   Analysis

4.1   Data and methodology

The corpus data in the analysis are based on the transcript downloaded from the Commission for Presidential Debates website.[4] Separate files containing the turns by Obama and McCain were created and a word count was performed using Wordsmith Tools 4 (Scott 2004). In addition, the video podcast version of the debate was downloaded from CBS[5] news to determine appropriate times. The final presidential debate lasted 1:29:45, with individual speaker times almost equally

Table 1. Word distribution in the final 2008 presidential debate

Value	Total	McCain	Obama
Tokens	15,419	6682	7292
Types	2,122	1311	1382
Token/Type ratio	14	20	19

Table 2. References to Joe the Plumber

	McCain	Obama
Joe Wurzelbacher	1	–
Joe	12	3
Joe the Plumber	5	2
Other	3	–
Personal noun	21	5
he	7	2
him	6	1
his	3	–
Third person sg.	16	3
you subj.	16	8
you obj.	6	3
your	8	4
Second person	30	15
they	–	–
them	–	1
their	3	–
Other pl. nouns	6	1
Third person pl.	9	1
First person pl.	3	1
Total	79	26

distributed between the two candidates. Table 1 shows the individual number of tokens and types used, which are quite similar.

The transcripts were subsequently searched for all turns in which JTP was mentioned (and addressed) both by name and indirectly. In fact, while the political and media analyses following the debates were focused on the number of times Joe the Plumber was mentioned directly, actual pronominal reference to JTP was much greater. Finally, the transcripts of the turns were matched with the video version to determine the total time devoted to JTP, which amounted to 7:48, or 6.8% of the total debate time. Interestingly, McCain spent three times as much time as Obama on the topic (approximately 6:03 vs. 1:45), as illustrated by the word counts in Table 2.

4.2   Data analysis

We will now look at some of the relevant turns chronologically. In (1) below, the first mention of JTP, McCain recontextualizes Joe Wurzelbacher as a sort of *argumentum ad exemplum*.[6] This turn takes place almost at the beginning of the debate (6:07), when McCain was answering a question about his economic plans:

> (1)   [McCain] I would like to mention that a couple of days ago Senator Obama was out in Ohio and he had an encounter with a guy who's a plumber, his name is Joe Wurzelbacher.

In this example, the full name, *Joe Wurzelbacher* is used only at the end, presumably to lend legitimacy to his words. More importantly, it is preceded by a familiar, cataphoric noun phrase *a guy who's a plumber*, which lends a more familiar tone to the entire turn. We should also note McCain's strategic use of the personal noun *Senator Obama* coupled with the third person pronoun *he*, transforming Obama into a referent in the debate and creating more distance.

In what follows, in (2) below, McCain reverts to the more familiar first name, *Joe*, as a referent, in addition to the more formal, and distance-creating, title form, *Senator Obama* we saw in (1). In the second sentence *he* now refers to *Joe* in contrast to the *he* used to refer to Obama. To create more distance, however, the deictic second person possessive *your* and subject *you* are used, transforming Obama into the addressee:

> (2)   [McCain] Joe wants to buy the business that he has been in for all of these years, worked 10, 12 hours a day. And he wanted to buy the business but he looked at your tax plan and he saw that he was going to pay much higher taxes. You were going to put him in a higher tax bracket which was going to increase his taxes, which was going to cause him not to be able to employ people, which Joe was trying to realize [*sic*] the American dream.

The use of second person pronoun with no address term allows McCain to put Obama in the role of the accused and to delegitimize him further (Murphy 1988, 318). In fact, McCain's accusatory, "finger-pointing" other-depiction is reinforced through the repeated use of the second person pronoun with no vocative appellative. Interestingly, (2) ends with a rather transparent metaphorical reference to the SF morality model, *the American Dream*, through which McCain implies that Obama's tax plan would make it impossible for JTP to employ people and, consequently, to realize such a dream. It should be recalled that the SF model places great importance in the virtues of self-discipline and hard work as the basis of this myth.

In the same turn, as illustrated in (3) below, McCain later switches back to the more distancing third person proper noun *Senator Obama*, making his opponent the referent once again, thus allowing him to directly address *Joe* with the "audience-engaging", familiar vocative form:

(3)   [McCain] Now Senator Obama talks about the very, very rich. Joe, I want to tell you, I'll not only help you buy that business that you worked your whole life for and be able – and I'll keep your taxes low and I'll provide available and affordable health care for you and your employees. And I will not have – I will not stand for a tax increase on small business income. That's 16 million jobs in America. And what you want to do to Joe the plumber and millions more like him is have their taxes increased and not be able to realize the American dream of owning their own business.

This switch also allows McCain to create an extended imaginary dialogue with Joe; in fact, McCain uses the first person singular *I* so that he can directly address the second person *you*. Although ostensibly speaking to *Joe*, the meaning can clearly be extended to include the wider audience(s), as we can see at the end of the turn, when *Joe the Plumber* is coupled *with millions more like him*. Here, once again the accusatory, deictic *you* is used with prominent stress and with no vocative form to create a negative contrast between Obama and the expanded Joe addressee group. It is at this point in the debate that JTP comes to represent all working-class Americans. The repetition of the third person plural possessive demonstrative *their* further strengthens the extended Joe group as representing all Americans. Moreover, *the American Dream* is repeated with a negative verb to stress the immorality of Obama's tax plan (and, consequently, the superiority and morality of his own). This, in turn, reinforces the American Dream Myth and the importance that it gives to the virtue of self-discipline, as well as that of industry and perseverance (Lakoff 2002).

At this point in the debate, Obama has no choice but to respond to McCain's criticisms, which we can find in (4). Although his turns about JTP are much shorter, a number of elements of the NP morality still emerge. Firstly, even though he was the one to meet the real Joe Wurzelbacher, Obama also makes use of an extended *Joe the Plumber* epithet. Moreover, he recontextualizes his original conversation to provide a sense of both familiarity and legitimacy:

(4)   [Obama] Now, the conversation I had with Joe the plumber, what I essentially said to him was, "Five years ago, when you were in a position to buy your business, you needed a tax cut then." And what I want to do is to make sure that the plumber, the nurse, the fire-fighter, the teacher, the young entrepreneur who doesn't yet have money, I want to give them a tax break now. And that requires us to make some important choices.

By reproducing his conversation he can directly address Joe with the less distancing second person *you*. In the following sentence, he extends the metonymy "Joe
the Plumber" to include other professions, opening his message to workers and
young professionals alike. The repetition of the particularizing synecdoches such
as *the plumber* and *the nurse* with the definite article and singular noun form serve
a "leveling" function (Reisigl 2006, 603). This particular use can also be analyzed
as an example of what Fairclough calls "synthetic personalization" (2001, 52) because it gives people the impression that they are being treated as individuals,
and, at the same time, it helps Obama to extend his message of unity to everyone
(Boyd 2009a; Suleiman and O'Connell 2008). By focusing on diverse yet equally
important members of the American public, JTP becomes a template for all working Americans. This message is further reinforced through the use of the third
person plural object pronoun *them*, which, however, is immediately contrasted
with an inclusive "we" form (*us*). It is also interesting to note the repeated use
of the first person singular pronoun *I*, rather than Obama's preferred *we*. In fact,
in a corpus-based study about Obama's 2008 campaign discourse, Boyd (2009b)
notes the high incidence of "we" in both the presidential debates and election
speeches.[7] Such usage of "I" instead, I would argue, can be attributed to the simulated dialogue and face-saving strategy. By the end of (4) Obama has returned
to the plural pronoun: *that requires **us** to make some important choices*. It should
also be noted that when referring to JTP, Obama rarely includes McCain in the
conversation for delegitimization purposes. I would argue that the absence of another referee in his personal pronominal paradigm allows him to focus more on
his underlying message.

The strategic use of the inclusive "we" continues in what follows, as in (5):

(5)   [Obama] So here's what we do. We exempt small businesses. In fact, what,
      Joe, if you want to do the right thing with your employees and you want to
      provide them health insurance, we'll give you a 50 per cent credit so that you
      will actually be able to afford it.

In the following, however, there is a slight hesitation between an object and vocative *Joe* due to the fact that Obama evidently wants to make a direct appeal to JTP
and the various audiences. Nevertheless, Obama continues with the repetition of
the second person pronoun *you*, so that he can directly address the extended Joe
group and, therefore, metonymically all Americans.

This strategy is exemplified in (6), in which Obama also addresses McCain
using the rather neutral first name *John*. This example also illustrates oscillation
between the first person singular and plural pronouns. In this example Obama
switches to *I* so that he can engage in a rare direct exchange with McCain. As we
can see, however, he soon switches back to the safer inclusive "we", which, once

again, is paired with the vocative + second person pronoun to address directly the expanded Joe group:[8]

(6) [Obama] And I'm happy to talk to you, Joe, too, if you're out there. Here's your fine – zero. You won't pay a fine, because… // Zero, because as I said in our last debate and I'll repeat, John, I exempt small businesses from the requirement for large businesses that can afford to provide health care to their employees, but are not doing it. // So here's what we do. We exempt small businesses. In fact, what, Joe, if you want to do the right thing with your employees and you want to provide them health insurance, we'll give you a 50 per cent credit so that you will actually be able to afford it.

As mentioned above, the conceptualization of MORAL ACTION AS FAIR DISTRIBUTION and IMMORAL ACTION AS UNFAIR DISTRIBUTION is influenced by different versions of what constitutes fairness in the SF and NP models. Example (7) strikingly represents the differences in the two models:

(7) [McCain] You know, when Senator Obama ended up his conversation with Joe the plumber – we need to spread the wealth around. In other words, we're going to take Joe's money, give it to Senator Obama, and let him spread the wealth around. I want Joe the plumber to spread that wealth around. You told him you wanted to spread the wealth around. // The whole premise behind Senator Obama's plans are class warfare, let's spread the wealth around. […]

Here, Obama is portrayed by McCain as an immoral actor or "meddling parent" who, unfairly and immorally, wants "to spread the wealth around" thereby "restricting freedom and posing a threat to the moral order" (Lakoff 2002, 95). Such a notion fits in perfectly with the SF model of morality that sees socialism, communism or anything that smacks of a controlled market economy as immoral. The moral division is further highlighted through pronominal use: the exclusive *we* in *we need to spread the wealth around* and *we're going to take Joe's money* creates a mocking tone, most likely to mimic Obama's prevalent use of *we* as an inclusive strategy. The mocking tone is further reinforced by the continued use of the third person proper noun *Senator Obama* and the distancing *him*, which are eventually abandoned in favor of the more direct second person pronoun, which allows McCain, once again, to attack Obama directly. The turn ends with further moral criticism of Obama's tax plan by comparing it to "class warfare", another important metaphor.

The final example, provided in (8), further demonstrates McCain's recontexualization of JTP:

(8) [McCain] Who – why would you want to increase anybody's taxes right now? Why would you want to do that, anyone, anyone in America, when we have such a tough time, when these small business people, like Joe the plumber, are going to create jobs, unless you take that money from him and spread the wealth around.

In this example McCain continues to adopt an accusatory tone against Obama through the repeated use of the second person *you* without a vocative. This use also underlines Obama's agency while extending it to others who are against SF morality with the indefinite pronoun *anyone*. Thus, Obama metonymically comes to represent a demon for SF morality, as he, and everyone like him, are the ones who want to *take the money away from* JTP and *spread the wealth around*. On the other hand, JTP is grouped with *these small business people* who *are going to create jobs*, thereby propagating the SF model bases on prosperity, hardworking self-discipline and self-reliance. The metaphorical use of pronouns, in fact, reinforces these underlying moral systems.

5. Discussion and conclusion

As we have seen in the discussion of the examples in the previous section, through various recontextualization strategies employed by both candidates, JTP comes to represent – both metaphorically and metonymically – working Americans. Both candidates use various means to appropriate JTP into their own moral world-views, which are clearly moulded by the SF and NP models, as proposed by Lakoff (2002). The analysis has provided further empirical data to support the existence of these two models and, more importantly, in the context of presidential debates, where both points of view clearly emerge. It has also demonstrated that the hybrid nature of the genre of debates, which allows the candidates to express themselves on many different levels both spontaneously and not, tends to favor the emergence of different worldviews. From a theoretical perspective, then, the work provides insight into both Conceptual Metaphor Theory and the genre of political debate.

The most salient metaphor in the discussions about JTP appears to be MORALITY AS FAIR DISTRIBUTION, and, consequently, this metaphor determines the conservative and progressive metaphorical ways of thinking and morality in regard to fair distribution. The analysis demonstrates that McCain exploited the SF model more extensively, which can be explained due to a number of reasons. First of all, it was McCain who first recontextualized JTP in the debate and continued to refer to him, which points to a pre-determined plan that was most likely well studied and prepared by his campaign team. Secondly, as noted by Lakoff (2002; 2004), conservatives are more aware of their underlying family model and, therefore, consciously exploit it to frame the important issues, such as taxes and health care. It can be assumed, then, that the choice of Joe Wurzelbacher to become JTP and, consequently, a representative of working class Americans, was also strategic. We can further postulate that his home state (Ohio), his race and his profession also influenced this choice: Ohio has recently become an important swing state in presidential elections, the issue of Obama's race was considered to be an important factor in the elections, although often overlooked by the two candidates in the 2008 elections (see, for example, Boyd 2009a, 77, 80), and Joe was a self-employed citizen trying to realize the American Dream. Thus, Joe Wurzelbacher could more easily become a representative of the Americans most likely to support the SF model and hence vote for McCain. This was achieved, in part, by the use of the Morality As Fair Distribution metaphor. On the one hand, taxation is depicted by McCain and his supporters as an unfair form of punishment for hard-working Americans like JTP and a way for a meddling NP-model supporter like Obama to assert his moral authority by unfairly redistributing hard-earned wealth and prosperity. On the other hand, through this metaphor Obama portrays taxation as an investment for the future and for all hard-working, responsible and caring Americans like JTP. Obama, however, does not use JTP strategically to demonize the SF model, while McCain's disparaging use of such phrases as *we're going to spread the wealth around* serve not only to condemn the NP principles of fair distribution but also to mimic Obama's frequent use of inclusive-"we" as part of his message of unity. This last example also demonstrates further use of recontextualization to enhance the values underlying the SF model. Nevertheless, both of the candidates use metonymy The Part For The Whole to create a cognitive shift so that one person (Joe Wurzelbacher) comes to represent two distinct extended JTP groups, which embody the relevant model-based qualities.

The analysis also calls attention to the strategic use of pronouns, which are often employed metaphorically and metonymically to reinforce the underlying moral models. The examples presented in the previous section reveal certain alignments that are maintained or avoided by the use of specific pronominal strategies. As far as the first person pronouns are concerned, although "we" is used by both speakers, Obama tends to prefer "we" over "I" for cohesive purposes thereby reinforcing the notions of group identity and unity. As noted in example (7), this use is mimicked by McCain as a way to demonize NP morality, also providing an insightful example of the truly shifting nature of the first person plural pronoun. At the same time, however, McCain uses inclusive "we" to frame JTP and others like him within the SF worldview. Thus, Obama appears to use "we" more with a positive function, while McCain uses it for both positive self- and negative other-referencing. Furthermore, both speakers oscillate between the third and second persons when addressing JTP stressing both the importance of pronouns in the construction of the ongoing discourse world (Wales 1996), and the instability of third person pronouns as a marker of deixis. Moreover, the examples provided appear to contradict Malone's (1997, 73) claim that the meaning of third person pronouns is established by exclusion from direct address. In this case, in fact, the third person singular pronoun is mostly used metonymically to appeal to the various audiences, and it is also for this reason that JTP is an addressee rather than a referent. Due to both grammatical and pragmatic pressures he is often transformed into *Joe* with a second person pronoun. However, the third person pronoun is still used quite often with a second person pragmatic meaning, which appears to provide evidence for a deictic rather than purely anaphoric third person singular pronoun. At the same time, McCain generally uses the third person pronoun for exclusionary purposes in referring to Obama and he often uses the formal term of address, *Senator Obama*. By transforming Obama into the referent, he places him further away from himself (the speaker) and from JTP (the addressee) on the distancing scale. If we analyze this in terms of Chilton's space axes, then *I* is at the center of the *s* axis, at *self*, while *he* and *you* are indexed closer or further to the *self* depending on who the addressee is and who the referent is. All of these distinctions, it is argued, come to the fore in the genre of the political debate.

To conclude, the various discourses dealing with JTP in the final 2008 presidential debate, and, more generally, in the genre of presidential debates, represent a useful test case for the existence of Lakoff's family-based models in the US political system. By concentrating on a limited set of data with a common theme afforded, crucially, by the genre of political debate, evidence of underlying metaphors and moral priorities can be better ascertained and tested. The data presented in this work appear to provide further empirical evidence for the existence of two different models of morality. The analysis was particularly concerned with the different conceptualizations of MORAL ACTION AS FAIR DISTRIBUTION and IMMORAL ACTION AS UNFAIR DISTRIBUTION enacted by the two models, and the data appear to provide evidence demonstrating two fundamentally different ways of thinking metaphorically about taxes and taxation. However, the paper is focused on how certain linguistic realizations are used in relation to the underlying family-based moral models. Specifically, pronominal choice and use are seen as being closely tied to the moral values inherent in the models. Finally, the paper demonstrates the various ways that recontextualization is used to frame discourses about JTP, thereby offering further evidence for a wider understanding of recontextualization.

In hindsight, it is probably safe to assume that McCain's many references to JTP in the debate, although closely tied to the values embodied by SF morality, did not make him the stronger, or more persuasive candidate. Thus, while McCain may have been more successful in applying SF morals to his recontextualization of JTP, this did not ultimately lead to his victory. The real winners of the debate were, of course, Barack Obama, who less than three weeks later became the 44th President of the United States, and, to a lesser extent, Joe Wurzelbacher. In fact, after the debate, Joe Wurzelbacher was transformed into a media and political personality. Interestingly, however, he recently claimed that McCain had ruined his life by using him for political gains, while Obama was "un-American, but [...] one of the more honest politicians. At least he told us what he wanted to do" (Zimmerman 2010).

Notes

1. Another important distinction, but beyond the scope of this work, is that between metonymy and synecdoche, which Wodak et al. (2009, 43) see as having more to do with semantic "widening or narrowing" (or generalizing vs. particularizing), such as when the name of the referent is replaced by "the name of an entity which is closely associated with it in either concrete or abstract terms" (see also Reisigl 2006; Wodak et al. 2009, 43).

2. The term originally comes from Jespersen (1922).

3. The term originally comes from Bernstein (1981, 1986), who applied the notion of recontextualization to educational practices (Van Leeuwen 2008).

4. www.debates.org/index.php?page=october-15-2008-debate-transcript

5. The podcast was downloaded using iTunes, but was also available at the time of writing (January 2010) in streaming at www.cbsnews.com and on YouTube.

6. I wish to thank an anonymous reviewer for pointing this out.

7. In all three debates Obama's total "we" frequency was 4.4% vs. McCain's 3.0% (Boyd 2009b).

8. Obama's preference of *we* over *I* has been noted in the literature. See Boyd (2009a, b) and Suleiman and O'Connell (2008).

References

Adams, Karen L. 2009. "Conceptual Metaphors of Family in Political Debates in the USA." In *Politics, Gender and Conceptual Metaphor*, ed. by Kathleen Ahrens, 184–206. Basingstoke: Palgrave Macmillan.

—. 2011. "Examining Conceptual Worldviews through Lexical Frequency Patterns: A Case Study of U.S. Presidential Speeches." In *Windows to the Mind*, ed. by Hans-Joerg Schmid, 167–184. Berlin: Mouton De Gruyter.

Ahrens, Kathleen, and Sophia Yat Mei Lee. 2009. "Gender versus Politics: When Conceptual Models Collide in the US Senate." In *Politics, Gender and Metaphor*, ed. by Kathleen Ahrens, 62–82. Basingstoke: Palgrave Macmillan.

Airne, David, and William L. Benoit. 2005. "2004 Illinois U.S. Senate Debates: Keyes versus Obama." *American Behavioral Scientist* 49: 343–353.

Bar-Lev, Zev. 2007. "Reframing Moral Politics." *Journal of Language and Politics* 6 (3): 459–474.

Boyd, Michael S. 2009a. "De-constructing Race and Identity in US Presidential Discourse: Barack Obama's Speech on Race." *Atlantis. Journal of the Spanish Association of Anglo-American Studies* 31 (2): 75–94.

—. 2009b. "Regrammaticalization as a Restrategization Device in Political Discourse." Paper presented at Corpus Linguistics Conference CL2009, Liverpool, July 21–23.

—. 2011. "(New) Political Genres for the Masses? YouTube in the 2008 US Presidential Elections". In *Genres on the Move: Hybridization and Discourse Change in Specialized Communication*, ed. by Srikant Sarangi, Vanda Polese, and Giuditta Caliendo, 27–44. Naples: Edizioni Scientifiche Italiane.

Brown, Penelope, and Stephen C. Levinson. 1987. *Politeness: Some Universals in Language Usage.* Cambridge/New York: Cambridge University Press.

Busch, Birgitta. 2006. "Media, Politics, and Discourse: Interactions." In *Encyclopedia of Language and Linguistics. Vol. 7*, ed. by Keith Brown, 609–616. Oxford: Elsevier.

Charteris-Black, Jonathan. 2005. *Politicians and Rhetoric: The Persuasive Power of Metaphor.* Basingstoke: Palgrave Macmillan.

—. 2007. *The Communication of Leadership: The Design of Leadership Style.* London/New York: Routledge.

Chilton, Paul. 2004. *Analysing Political Discourse: Theory and Practice.* London/New York: Routledge.

—. 2006. "Metaphors in Political Discourse." In *Encyclopedia of Language and Linguistics*, ed. by Keith Brown, 63–65. Oxford: Elsevier.

—. 2008. "Political Terminology." In *Handbook of Communication in the Public Sphere*, ed. by Ruth Wodak, and Veronika Koller, 225–242. New York/Berlin: Mouton de Gruyter.

Chilton, Paul, and Christina Schäffner. 1997. "Discourse and Politics." In *Discourse as Social Interaction*, ed. by Teun A. Van Dijk, 206–230. London: Sage.

—. 2002. "Introduction: Themes and Principles in the Analysis of Political Discourse." In *Politics as Text and Talk. Analytic Approaches to Political Discourse*, ed. by Paul Chilton, and Christina Schäffner, 1–41. Amsterdam: John Benjamins.

Chouliaraki, Lilie and Norman Fairclough. 1999. *Discourse in Late Moderinity. Rethinking Critical Discourse Analysis.* Edinburgh: Edinburgh Univeristy Press.

Cienki, Alan. 2005a. "Metaphor in the 'Strict Father' and 'Nurturant Parent' Cognitive Models: Theoretical Issues Raised in an Empirical Study." *Cognitive Linguistics* 16 (2): 279–312.

—. 2005b. "The Metaphorical Use of Family Terms versus Other Nouns in Political Debates." *Identifying Information and Tenor in Texts: Special Issue of Information Design Journal + Document Design* 13 (1): 27–39.

Crowley, Michael. 2009. "Obama, Crowley, and White Guy Politics." *The New Republic*, August 8. http://blogs.tnr.com/tnr/blogs/the_plank/archive/2009/07/26/men-in-uniform.aspx

Fairclough, Norman. 2003. *Analysing Discourse: Textual Analysis for Social Research*. London/New York: Routledge.

—. 2010. *Critical Discourse Analysis. The Critical Study of Language*, 2nd ed. Harlow: Pearson Education Limited.

Goffman, Erving. 1967. *Interaction Ritual*. New York: Doubleday.

Goffman, Erving, and Joel Best. 2005. *Interaction Ritual: Essays in Face-to-Face Behavior*. New Brunswick, NJ: Transaction Publishers.

Halmari, Helena. 2008. "On the Language of the Clinton-Dole Presidential Campaign Debates: General Tendencies and Successful Strategies." *Journal of Language and Politics* 7 (2): 247–270.

Jakobson, Roman. 1990. "Shifters and Verbal Categories." In *On Language*, ed. by Linda R. Waugh, and Monique Monville-Burston, 386–392. Cambridge, MA/London: Harvard University Press.

Jespersen, Otto. 1922. *Language: Its Nature, Development and Origin*. London: Allen and Unwin.

Johansson, Marjut. 2006. "Constructing Objects of Discourse in the Broadcast Political Interview." *Journal of Pragmatics* 38: 216–229.

Lakoff, George. 2002. *Moral Politics: How Liberals and Conservatives Think*. Chicago: University of Chicago Press.

—. 2004. *Don't Think of an Elephant: Know your Values and Frame the Debate*. White River Junction, VT: Chelsea Green Publishing.

Lakoff, George, and Mark Johnson. 2003. *Metaphors we Live by*, 2nd Ed. Chicago: University of Chicago Press.

Lyons, John. 1977. *Semantics*. New York: Cambridge University Press.

Malone, Martin J. 1997. *Worlds of Talk: The Presentation of Self in Everyday Conversation*. Malden, MA/Cambridge: Polity Press.

Murphy, Gregory L. 1988. "Personal Reference in English." *Language and Society* 17: 317–349.

Myers, Greg. 2008. "Analyzing Interaction in Broadcast Debates." In *Qualitative Discourse Analysis in the Social Sciences*, ed. by Ruth Wodak, and Michał Krzyżanowski, 121–144. Houndmills, Basingstoke; New York: Palgrave Macmillan.

Reisigl, Martin. 2006. "Rhetorical Tropes in Political Discourse." In *Encyclopedia of Language and Linguistics*, Vol. 10, ed. by Keith Brown, 597–604. Oxford: Elsevier.

—. 2008. "Rhetoric of Political Speeches." In *Handbook of Communication in the Public Sphere*, ed. by Ruth Wodak, and Veronika Koller, 243–269. Berlin/New York: Mouton de Gruyter.

Rohter, Larry. 2008. "Plumber from Ohio is Thrust into Spotlight." *The New York Times*, October 15. http://www.nytimes.com/2008/10/16/us/politics/16plumber.html

Scott, Mike. 2004. *WordSmith Tools version 4*. Oxford: Oxford University Press.

Suleiman, Camelia, and Daniel C. O'Connell. 2008. "Race and Gender in Current American Politics." *Journal of Psycholinguistic Research* 37: 373–389.

Van Dijk, Teun A. 2001. "Multidisciplinary CDA: A Plea for Diversity." In *Methods of Critical Discourse Analysis*, ed. by Ruth Wodak, and Michael Meyer, 95–120. London: Sage.

Van Leeuwen, Theo. 2008. *Discourse and Practice. New Tools for Critical Discourse Analysis*. Oxford: Oxford University Press.

Wales, Katie. 1996. *Personal Pronouns in Present-Day English*. Cambridge: Cambridge University Press.

Wilson, John. 1990. *Politically Speaking. The Pragmatic Analysis of Political Language*. Oxford: Blackwell.

Wodak, Ruth, and Rudolf De Cillia. 2007. "Commemorating the Past: The Discursive Construction of Official narratives about the 'rebirth of the Second Austrian Republic.'" *Discourse & Communication* 1 (3): 315–341.

Wodak, Ruth, Rudolf De Cillia, Martin Reisigl, and Karin Liebhart. 2009. *The Discursive Construction of National Identity*. Edinburgh: Edinburgh University Press.

Zimmerman, Eric. 2010. "Joe the Plumber Goes off on McCain, Says He 'Screwed up my Life.'" *The Hill's Blog Briefing Room*, February 15. http://thehill.com/blogs/blog-briefing-room/news/81035-joe-the-plumber-tears-into-john-mccain

The late-night TV talk show as a strategic genre in American political campaigning

Katarzyna Molek-Kozakowska
University of Opole, Poland

This chapter focuses on the functions and properties of the American late-night TV talk show as used during the 2008 presidential campaign. It analyses some interviews with presidential candidates (Barack Obama, Hillary Clinton and John McCain) broadcast on CBS's *Late Show with David Letterman*, CNN's *Larry King Live* and NBC's *Tonight Show with Jay Leno* in order to demonstrate the ways the talk show's generic conventions tend to be recruited to suit politicians' aims. This case study illustrates how the semi-institutional nature of the talk show allows candidates to implement such campaigning strategies as the performance of sociability, the management of impressions, the manufacture of authenticity, and the tactical maneuvering between institutional and personal discourse. The study identifies and critiques some discursive practices enabled by the talk show's generic formula which can be used manipulatively by campaigners.

1. Introduction

American media outlets are known for prioritizing the entertainment value of broadcast messages, even if such messages are related to the country's most significant political issues. For example, media researchers concerned with the quality of American mass-mediated political discourse have criticized the "shrinking" of the political soundbite, the prevalence of "soft" news over "hard" facts, and the increase in the volume of political advertising, especially during presidential campaigns (cf. Capella and Jamieson 1997; Płudowski 2008). At the same time, data show that a substantial part (21–22%) of the younger section (18–29-year-olds) of the voting public in the US tended to rely mainly on late night talk show and entertainment programming to get information about 2004 and 2008 presidential candidates (Pew Research Center 2004, 2008). As a result, the question that arises is no longer "if", but "how" the popularity of televised talk shows has influenced American political discourse.

This chapter focuses on the functions and properties of the American late-night TV talk show as used during the 2008 presidential campaign. It ought to be reminded that satirical late-night talk shows are much different from current affairs programs, and they only occasionally host political figures, usually in relation to widely-publicized political events. This case study demonstrates in what ways the talk show's generic conventions tend to be recruited to suit politicians' campaigning efforts. It analyses a collection of interviews with 2008 presidential candidates (Barack Obama, Hillary Clinton and John McCain) broadcast on CBS's *Late Show with David Letterman*, CNN's *Larry King Live* and NBC's *Tonight Show with Jay Leno*, and subsequently made available on the Internet. It will be demonstrated that appearing on popular talk shows allows candidates to implement such campaigning strategies as the performance of sociability, the management of impressions, the manufacture of authenticity, and the tactical maneuvering between the institutional and the personal. To identify the properties that make the talk show useful for strategic purposes, attention is paid, for example, to characteristic patterns of interaction, thematic and stylistic choices, narrative and argumentative moves, small talk and verbal humor and speech contours that make the interview appear as if it were unscripted and thus revealing the candidate's "true" self.

On this basis, it is argued that, with the increasing demand – particularly in the US – for political discourse that values presidential candidates' authentic emotional expressiveness rooted in personal integrity and credibility, the strategic potential of satirical televised talk shows for political campaigning should not be underestimated. In fact, the critical interrogation of emergent, hybrid, semi-institutional and mediated genres that tend to take over public communication is needed (cf. Gruber and Muntigl 2005; Wodak 2009; Myers 2010). At this point it must also be stressed that the chapter does not aim to characterize the talk show genre in its abstract, idealized entirety, or to suggest that it has a fixed or stabilized generic structure, or to exhaustively list the semiotic resources that can be put to politically motivated aims in this genre. This case study has been designed as a data-driven illustration (rather than a full taxonomy) of the key strategic functionalities of the late-night TV talk show genre in the context of American political campaigning (cf. Boyd [this volume]). It aims at capturing the current state of the evolution of the genre, but focuses on its social relevance rather than formal properties. In particular, it critically spotlights those generic conventions of the late-night talk show that have the capacity to be used manipulatively by campaigners.

2.   Delimiting and approaching genres

Public discourse is often investigated according to its genre. For instance, many research projects dealing with political discourse explore collected samples of texts/talk, be they manifestoes and documents, reports and editorials, talk radio and televised broadcasts, mass-mediated speeches and debates, multimodal advertisements, or blogs and websites. Such samples are then examined quantitatively or qualitatively with respect to the application of specific semiotic resources, rhetorical devices or discursive strategies (and their likely persuasive and/or ideological effects). In many such analyses the notion of genre is taken for granted as an unvarying, "controlled" variable. Frequently, *genre* is simply defined as a text type, or as a class of communicative events sharing the same communicative purpose, a property that "shapes the schematic structure of the discourse and influences and constrains choice of content and style", to use a classic definition (Swales 1990, 58).

If we assume, following a broad functional perspective,[1] that genres are recurrent configurations of meanings (content) and forms (style) used to enact social practices, then genre as an analytic category is placed at a relatively high level of abstraction. It is an intertextual and socio-pragmatic conceptual category that cannot be non-reductively operationalized in formal linguistic terms. In Systemic-Functional Linguistics, for example, genre is an overarching category of the "cultural context", even beyond register (i.e. field+tenor+mode) of the "situational context" (Martin and Rose 2008). In the socio-cognitive model of discourse, genre is theorized as a complex category conjoining "textual and contextual aspects of discursive practice" (van Dijk 2008, 149–151). The notion of genre also inheres a historically developed, conscious and situationally appropriate choice of semiotic resources, which is key to the enactment of social relations (Scollon 1998) and the exercise of power (Chilton and Schaeffner 2002, 19–21).

Current approaches in genology vary from the classification of extant genres, to the chronicling of genre evolution; from the description of culturally prominent genres, to the tracing of emergent hybrid genres. However, until fairly recently genre studies were mostly descriptively or pedagogically oriented (cf. Bakhtin 1986; Bernstein 1990; Swales 1990; Bhatia 1993; Grzmil-Tylutki 2007). Many focused on abstracting generic types from textual tokens derived from ever larger collections of linguistic data (Mauranen 1998) and systematically "compartmentalizing" them (Martin and Rose 2008). On this basis, prospective students could be introduced to genre "prototypes" in an effort to broaden their competence of some of the culturally dominant and prestigious genres. Naturally, a well-developed generic competence facilitates construing the meanings of particular texts, since having a "mental model" of a given genre functions as an interpretative heuristic in the processing of incoming information (van Dijk 2008). However, introducing a critical component to such competence also seems crucial. For example, critical generic awareness helps one to "see through" attempts at manipulating generic conventions, as is the case with "promotorials" in which political advocacy is disguised as editorial evaluation, "open letters" that are in fact advertisements, or sponsored "academic reports" that favor particular company's technological solutions over the competition's.

That is why the notion of genre is of significance to CDA/CDS,[2] since genres are responsible for configuring (and regulating) meaning and power relations in a culture (Martin and Rose 2008). At the same time, genres constitute a resource for negotiation and change, and any attempt at tracing genre evolution, for example in mass-mediated discourse, reveals how creative rather than reproductive genre applications can now be (cf. docudrama, dramedy or confrontainment). Apart from identifying and analyzing various kinds of extant, emergent or hybrid genres in public discourses (cf. Gruber and Muntigl 2005), CDA/CDS practitioners may look at their interrelations and constellations to see if they are likely to either reinforce or change a society's power relations. For example, the rise of *macrogenres,* to borrow Martin and Rose's (2008) term, is characteristic of contemporary mass-mediated political communication. From this perspective, a political campaign may be regarded as a macrogenre which draws on generic conventions and semiotic resources typical of political discourse on the one hand and popular culture on the other, to realize its aims.

Since this chapter undertakes a critical genre analysis, which is a type of meta-analysis, it aims at interrogating the generic conventions of the late-night satirical TV talk show – an increasingly significant exemplar of American mass-mediated political discourse. This case study is not likely to capture all aspects of the talk show genre in all its present instantiations (though some descriptive and historical background will be offered). But, as generic conventions are potentially power-invested, it is crucial to move beyond genre description and interpretation (as in typological or diachronic genological studies) to the stage of explanation (cf. Fairclough 1989, 1995) of social consequences of the rise, popularity, proliferation, or cross-fertilization of certain genres. In accordance with the overall philosophy of CDA/CDS (van Dijk 1993, 2011), the strategic potential of discourses should be demystified and not just documented or expounded.

3.   The history and properties of the talk show in the American context

Originally, the talk show genre was designed as a relatively casual, personality-oriented conversation between a host and a public figure. It emerged in the 1950s in the US radio and television broadcasting as an alterative to newscasting and current affairs. In due course, talk show producers started employing new media technologies to increase the genre's popularity through both the access to celebrities (teleconferencing) and wider audience participation (call-in, instant polling). Today, according to Hume (2000), the political environment in the United States has been largely pervaded by "the talk show culture", with mixed results for the society. On the one hand, talk show programs, inexpensive to produce and choreographed by charismatic hosts, expand the political agenda beyond elite voices and offer a close-up view of public figures, but on the other hand, they degrade American public discourse with a focus on the personal and the trivial.

Media scholarship demonstrates that, since the advent of electronic media, infotainment genres, including TV talk shows or political advertisements, have gradually become a primary venue for mass-mediated political discourse, replacing televised evening news and debates as sources of citizens' knowledge of campaign issues (Płudowski 2008). Critics of this trend (e.g. Postman 1986; Cappella and Jamieson 1997) claim that the subsequent trivialization of political coverage prevents audiences from developing a rational and critical competence needed for a democratic public sphere (cf. Habermas 1989; Bourdieu 1998). However, other studies indicate that framing politics as entertainment can also have a democratizing effect, as it allows people not accustomed to deliberative discourse to access political information through lighter and more enjoyable genres (Lee 2002). Perhaps an alternative conception of the public sphere – replacing the bourgeois culture of deliberation and consensus-seeking with a mass-mediated arena of expression and compromise – will envision a more positive role for such genres as TV or radio talk shows (Livingstone and Lunt 1994).

Historically, the launching moment for the rise in importance of *political* celebrity talk show in the US campaign context was Ross Perot's announcement on CNN's *Larry King Live* show on November 20, 1992 that he would be willing to run for president. At that time Larry King hosted one of the most popular talk shows of the 1990s, despite his failure to challenge his guests with difficult questions of policy and program. It was also one of the few programs with friendly atmosphere, in contrast to Jerry Springer's shock-and-ambush shows popular at that time. At the same time King's ingratiating style and flattery often disarmed his guests and made them say more than they intended (Hume 2000). Soon after,

Bill Clinton responded in bringing some of his presidential campaigning to the late-night comedy and talk shows, playing his saxophone on *Arsenio Hall* and showing his informal, "human" side on *Larry King Live* (Chafe 1999). Nowadays any campaign to sway public opinion, promote ideas, or run for public office in the US requires appearances on radio and television talk shows and sometimes involves entertainment-driven "staging" of politics.

The current format of a typical talk show on American television involves merging deliberate socializing with elements of revelation, satire and promotion.[3] That is why the talk show as a genre is said to exemplify "semi-institutional" discourse: a hybrid type of mediated discourse in which some established conventions of public broadcasting are flaunted to allow for "spontaneous intervention and unpredictable outcomes" (Ilie 2001, 218). The generic hybridity of the televised talk show is informed by its indeterminate status both as an infotainment media product and as a public/private conversation encounter.[4] The CDA/CDS literature on the talk show has so far been rather sketchy but it problematizes some key discursive aspects of the genre, for example self-identity and face management techniques (Thornborrow 2001; O'Sullivan 2005); dominant patterns of interaction (Tolson 2001); audience participation mechanisms (Lee 2002); the projection of broadcaster-audience relation and the construction of the norm (Hutchby 2006), the genre's potential for therapeutic self-expression (Yan 2008); and the linguistic devices of TV broadcasting instrumental in the production of seemingly authentic, unscripted, "fresh" talk to use Goffman's (1981) term (Montgomery 2001; Lorenzo-Dus 2009). With special relevance for the present study, Ilie (2001) identifies the main pragma-linguistic features that frame the talk show conversationally and institutionally, notably the tensions between spontaneous and purposeful talk, the choices between negotiated and monitored topic selection and turn-taking, or the shifts between real-life or institutional roles assumed by participants.

In this context, the aim of the following section of this chapter is to map out the late-night talk show's strategic potential for political campaigning activated through its generic formula. To do this, salient discursive practices reflecting the talk show's strategic capacity are identified, discussed and illustrated with excerpts from late-night TV talk show interviews with 2008 presidential candidates broadcast on CBS's *Late Show with David Letterman*, CNN's *Larry King Live*, or NBC's *Tonight Show with Jay Leno*. Extracts that exemplify strategic uses of certain generic conventions of the talk show are used to discuss critical points about presidential campaigning, rather than to provide a formal delineation of the talk show genre. The extracts have been transcribed "parsimoniously," that is without attempting to faithfully reproduce all aspects of multi-modal discourse in televised talk shows, but with a focus on intelligibility and interpretative accessibility (cf. Lorenzo-Dus 2009).

4. The strategic potential of the late-night TV talk show: A case study of 2008 campaign

According to Fairclough, *strategic* discourse, unlike communicative or deliberative discourse in Habermasian sense, "is oriented towards achieving specific ideological purposes" (1989, 164), such as persuasion or positive self-presentation, which lie at the core of political campaigning. In the talk show interview, the message is "designed to reach, appeal to, impress, or activate" the viewers (Hillier 2004, 189), even though the audience is hardly ever explicitly addressed. This enables the viewing audience to experience a sort of "voyeuristic" pleasure, supposedly derived from "overhearing" the interviewees' self-disclosures (cf. Goffman 1981).

The overall strategic potential of the late-night TV talk show lies in its entertaining function obscuring the ideological investments always inherent in political discourse. In addition, the satirical frame of the talk show genre tends to put audiences in the state of uncritical disposition, arguably making them more susceptible to persuasion. Its double purpose – infotainment – is realized mainly through the type of host–guest interaction that resembles informal, humorous or ironic conversation in which the celebrity politicians' personal matters are expected to be taken up, while their public role is never invalidated. Incidentally, the talk show's verbal exchanges are interpreted as entertaining performances because they largely rely on the transgression of the principles of "serious" news interview. As mentioned above, the late-night talk show is predicated on gross deviations from institutionalized conventions of public discourse in terms of, for example, topic selection, projection of participant roles, staging of conversational routines, as well as register- and style-cueing (cf. Ilie 2001; Tolson 2001; Rama Martinez 2003).

In this case study, four generic conventions of the late-night TV talk show that testify to its strategic potential for political campaigning have been identified: (1) the performance of sociability, (2) the personalization of politics, (3) the manufacture of authenticity and (4) the management of impressions, mainly through verbal humor. These discursive strategies can be said to have pervaded the collected sample of talk show episodes. In addition, they seem to be closely linked to the generic conventions of the talk-show. Since they are not claimed to be typical of one program/episode or another, nor to work in isolation, the following sections mark them as separate only for the sake of analytic clarity.

4.1   The performance of sociability in talk shows

According to Scannell (1996), the communicative ethos of non-fictional programming on TV is the "performance of sociability", i.e. creating the impression
of social closeness and "togetherness" for the audience. Hence, unlike "serious"
political newscasting and interviewing, late-night talk show programs with political celebrities tend to be driven by "the interpersonal" rather than "the ideational"
(what is talked about), or "the textual" (how well managed is the talk) (Lorenzo-
Dus 2009, 63). Thus, the staging of a friendly and non-confrontational rapport
between the host and the interviewee is of central importance to this genre. It is
often pre-constructed with the aid of specific generic structures and interaction
patterns, and then performed on air more or less successfully.[5]

Unlike political interviews, whose value is derived from the performance of
adversarial stances through staged conflict talk (face-threatening acts, uncooper-
ativeness, evasiveness, impoliteness, and provocation), satirical TV talk shows are
predicated on host–guest affiliation, which facilitates emotional disclosure. The
genre is mainly realized in the form of a "simulated conversation" with an abun-
dance of small talk (i.e. various realizations of phatic communion) (cf. Coupland
2000). For example, the conjunction of small talk and self-expression is evident in
the following short exchange on the *Late Show with David Letterman*:

(1)   David Letterman: How do you like being a Senator?
      Barack Obama: Being a Senator has been terrific. We now are a majority, so
      at least we can stop some bad things from happening.
      Audience: *clapping and cheers.* (1)[6]

In small talk, both the private ("How do you like...") and public ("...being a
Senator?") persona of the interviewee can be "interpellated" at the same time.
The performance of small talk is also indispensible for the building of sociability and rapport with the overhearing audience. The characteristic signals of the
talk show's fostering such social bonding come in the form of reactions, even if
directed, from the in-studio audience, such as clapping or cheers.

Besides emotional disclosure ("mood reporting"), expressed in (1) with the
colloquial adjective "terrific", or the evaluative expression "bad things", politicians
can project the sense of commonality of purpose. Such a maneuver is evident in
all accounts where they position themselves as agents of positive change (heroes),
acting on behalf of the community. Here, the sense of sociability is enhanced by
the strategic use of the inclusive pronoun "we", which tends to conflate the interests of the political elites with those of the society at large, as demonstrated below
(emphasis added):

(2) DL: Other than wanting to lead your country and make things better. Is this a good time now to be wanting this office?

BO: *Laughter*

DL: Look what you, or anybody for that matter, what you have ahead of you!

BO: Yes, I suspect Iraq is still on the table when the next president is sworn in. I think *we* have major budget problems. *We* have a healthcare system that is broken. But I also think there are enormous opportunities right now. The American people are paying attention (…). They really understand that *we* have a series of choices to make in terms of fixing *our* education system, *our* healthcare system. And when you mobilize millions of Americans and say: let's think about solving *our* problems in practical commonsense ways, let's get beyond the partisanship, the bickering, the slash-and-burn politics, people are really responding. And that's why *we* are doing pretty well in this campaign.

DL: Yes (1)

Except for the last sentence, in which "we" refers to Barack Obama's 2008 campaign management or, more generally, the Democratic Party, the use of "we", "our" and "us" is inclusive of all Americans. In addition, the sequence of assertions ("people are paying attention", "they really understand", "people are really responding") and the repetitive use of imperatives ("let's…"), implies that there is an overwhelming agreement with the candidate's political platform and that divisive "partisanship" is an expression of ill-will rather than ideological differences. The audience is also likely to be caught in the idealistic enthusiasm generated by the list of things that could be "fixed" by the new administration that promises to work together with various interest groups on healthcare, education, budget, or Iraq.

The performance of sociability is also enabled by conversational story-telling, which is one of the basic structures of the talk show genre. The cultural prominence of stories has long been shown as instrumental for the reproduction of ideologies. The narratives told by the interviewees can be dramatized or co-constructed by the hosts, who are usually acquainted with them before the program. This routine practice helps to present the story as less monologic. These properties of the talk show genre also confirm the tendency towards "conversationalization" of public discourse, as envisioned by Fairclough (1989, 1995). However, the host's interjections are far from hostile takeovers of the floor; in fact, in (3) they tend to include references to common experience (e.g. Iraq), articulations of widely shared feelings (e.g. anxiety), manifestations of agreement with the speaker's arguments (e.g. repetitions, reformulations), or supportive paralinguistic signals (e.g. nodding, hand gestures), as illustrated below:

(3) DL: [Iraq] is a horrible mess. But what happens once we leave? (...)

BO: I don't think we can be as careless getting out as we were careless getting in (...). We've got to do it in a phased fashion; we've got to add
some flexibility, make sure our commanders are on the ground and our
troops are actually protected (...). We've got to train up the Iraqi forces
effectively. But what we CAN'T do is simply stay the course that we've
been on over the last several years. It's not working.

DL: *nodding*: It's a horrible, horrible mess.

BO: There are no good options in Iraq. At this point there are bad options
and worse options.

DL: (...) whether you believe we should've gone there or not, still it's our
mess, it's our war, and we have to do something. And, I think, self-pres-
ervation, as you pointed out, is first... *extends an arm in BO's direction*

BO: ...we have a strategic interest there. We have a humanitarian interest
there in making sure it's not a complete bloodbath, but if we continue
on this course, we could be there for the next ten years (1)

As can be noticed here, the talk show genre does not allow for an extensive elaboration of specific aspects of policy (e.g. Barack Obama's specific plans as to the
timetable and logistics of the US withdrawal from Iraq). Instead, the conventions
of the genre favor using memorable labels ("a mess"), catchy phrases ("there are
bad options and worse options"), and syntactic parallelisms ("we can [not] be as
careless getting out as we were careless getting in"). The level of generalization
about policy ("it's not working", "we have to do something") adopted in the talk
show makes it difficult for the viewers to question it.

Notably, the satirical talk show genre does not admit of significant challenges
to the statements or actions of the guest. Conventionally, it is not designed to impose on the interviewee's "face":

(4) BO: (...) I think Americans are ready for a change. We have had enough over
the last eight years. We need something fundamentally new. Whoever
makes that case to the American people will be the next president.

DL: You are campaigning now, aren't you?

BO: *Laughter, inaudible concession.*

Audience: *Laughter, clapping* (4)

Here, the guest's quick-paced, "fresh" (in Goffman's [1981] sense) speaking turn,
finished with a falling intonation that makes it sound more authoritative, is not
interrupted or questioned by the host. On the contrary, the host acknowledges
Obama's need to seize every opportunity to promote himself.

To summarize, it can be noticed that the talk show's interactional patterning
(both at the level of host/guest and at the level of performers/audience) facilitates

co-operation in the maintaining of face and communion, and, hence, in the performance of sociability. During the show, narratives are co-constructed, friendly rapports are nurtured through small talk, and common identities and purposes are implied and accepted through clusivity. As a result, persuasive messages can be inserted smoothly and political candidates can easily project positive self-images of sociable individuals and community leaders in order to self-advertise more effectively.

4.2   Replacing the issues of public concern with personal information

It is almost a truism to say that political talk shows tend to combine conventional themes of public discourse (e.g. political platform or election process) with topics that are typical of private conversation (e.g. personal experiences, feelings or intentions). Personalization of politics has long been observed as one of the main features of mediatization of the public sphere (cf. McAllister 2007). The choice of personal themes (semantic macrostructures) is but one way in which the conflation of information-seeking and entertainment is instantiated. For example, political talk show interviews can seamlessly merge campaign themes with those regarding family relationships or even clothing preferences, as the following extract demonstrates:

(5) DL: This is a tremendous suit that you have.
     BO: You like this one?
     DL: It's beautiful…
     BO: It's a presidential suit.
     DL: That is an electable suit. I would vote for that suit.
     Audience: *Laughter*
     DL: I'll be right back. *Music* (1)

Extract (5) illustrates how a personal compliment can easily transfigure into a political endorsement. Arguably, the wit and absurdity ("I would vote for that suit") involved in the exchange distract audiences from noticing the strategic potential of such maneuvers for campaigning.

Apart from the strictly thematic choices (of which more below), there is a generic convention and a general expectation that "serious" content is to be limited. The point seems to be to cover a range of politics-related subjects in a rather cursory and general way, so that awkward repetitions can be avoided and the audience's attention is not tested with details of policy. Unlike current affairs interviews, which are designed to provide the audience with a deeper understanding of a selected issue of public concern, an important convention of the talk show is to keep swift pacing and to change topics of conversation frequently. Such style is claimed to be a general characteristic of television discourse, which offers instantaneous and superficial coverage (determined by the visual mode), as opposed to more abstract and in-depth coverage of print discourse (Postman 1986). For example, to keep audiences engaged in a talk show, speculation and drama are favored over verified information:

(6) DL: What would you have done then [after 9/11 attacks]? What kind of a situation would we be now if you had been president? (…)

BO: (…) the big difference between myself and George Bush would've been to stay focused on Afghanistan. Not get distracted by Iraq. We could've tracked down Al-Qaeda (…), captured, if not killed, Bin Laden (…)

BO: [After 9/11] Here in the US people wanted to do something…

DL: Sure.

BO: … and George Bush asked them to shop. And if I'd stood there I would've told them: we are going to reduce our dependence on Middle Eastern oil, or we are going to build an energy-efficient economy (…) to weaken the forces of terror. That would have made an enormous difference. (5)

In this example, a personalized vision of "what might be" is offered by Obama. The heavy use of counterfactuals and contrastive structures helps him project an alternative political reality that is much more attractive than the current situation. Thus, besides the preoccupation with speculation rather than fact, the talk show genre offers opportunities for ideological work, particularly for positive self-presentation and negative other-presentation, to use van Dijk's terminology (1998). As shown above, the host's question is designed to facilitate the candidate's self-appraisal of his (hypothetical) political decisions and the denigration of the political opponent's. Again, unlike in political interviews, there is no trace of generically constructed adversarial relation between the host and the interviewee, which is often instantiated by political journalists' offering competing "versions of events" in response to politicians' talking points.[7]

The infotaining frame of the talk show genre is ideally suited for a selective choice of personal details to be revealed in order to show "the essence of the candidate's self". During a talk show episode, a candidate is likely to share information about personal habits, daily routines, family relationships or likes and dislikes. In the same vein, talk show hosts' questions are conventionally designed to provoke self-disclosure and facilitate sharing feelings, expectations and intentions rather than to communicate positions on public issues. This is evident in the following exchange on *Larry King Live*, in which the host is insistent on extracting as much personal information as possible:

(7)   Larry King: Are you ready to become the first black First Lady?
      Michelle Obama:[8] Yes, I am ready.
      LK: Do you feel the pressure?
      MO: Of course, I do. (…) But I try to be positive, not to think what might go wrong. (…) I thought through everything and kind of prepared myself for anything that might go wrong.
      LK: You have not been surprised?
      MO: I have not been surprised by anything; by the good and the bad. (…) You know, we are not new to politics. (…) You are not surprised if you are secure in yourself, and you know who you are. We know what we stand for. (…) We are in our forties, we are pretty grounded and this helps us through all the ups and downs. (…)
      LK: Did you, as many wives do, try to put a damper on it?
      MO: Of course, that's my job. We have often talked about the practical aspects of the race: how it would affect the kids (…) How we would manage our lives to make sure their lives stay on track (9).

This question-fuelled interaction between Larry King and Michelle Obama is confessional and confidential in both topic and tone, which makes it different from an institutionally framed news interview with a prospective First Lady. The host's questions are casual ("Do you feel the pressure?"), if not colloquial ("Did you […] try to put a damper on it?"), which also helps to diminish the distance between the audience and the interviewee. She is allowed to share as much information about her family, her marriage and her own feelings as she pleases.

It should be noted that by carefully foregrounded personal information shared in a rather relaxed situation, candidates have even more opportunities to persuade a prospective voter to accept their constructed "personas". This is especially striking in the contemporary US political culture, where what is increasingly appreciated by audiences of mediated political discourse is the candidate's emotional expressiveness, personal integrity and clearly articulated ethos (cf. spontaneous, unequivocal and apparently "more sincere" George W. Bush beating emotionally "colder" and ideologically more complex Al Gore in 2000, and John Kerry in 2004 presidential debates). It can be concluded that the talk show as a genre allows the participants to strategically perform their institutional roles (a presidential candidate) when it suits them, activating their non-institutional identities (a parent, a spouse, a neighbor, a sibling, a smoker) alongside.

4.3   Manufacturing authenticity

The talk show genre allows politicians to appear as more spontaneous and au-thentic than they would be able to present themselves via traditional genres of mass-mediated political discourse, e.g., addresses, statements, speeches, and even replies at press conferences. However, media scholars note the potential for generically "manufactured authenticity" and carefully managed appearance of sincerity, as was the case with Bill and Hillary Clinton's famous appearance on CBS's *60 Minutes* to "talk away" their marital problems and to reverse the failing prospects of the 1992 presidential campaign (Chafe 1999, 506–507; Płudowski 2008). CDA/CDS analysts, including Fairclough (1995) and Thornborrow (2001) for example, notice the growth of informal, conversational patterns of interaction in mass-mediated public discourse, which they see as an artful "performance" of interpersonal intimacy rather than its authentic expression. The notion of the very definition of authenticity in broadcast discourse is a topical issue as well (cf. Montgomery 2001).

Naturally, production teams of the most popular televised talk shows ensure that the conversation is going well and that it sounds as if it were largely un-scripted (often through particular camera angles and editing), despite the fact that in most cases the hosts are fed with the issues the politicians are willing to discuss before the program (cf. O'Sullivan 2005; Lorenzo-Dus 2009). The follow-ing exchange resembles a casual, authentic conversation; yet it is highly unlikely for David Letterman not to have consulted the topic and not to have prepared his comic routine in advance:

(8)   DL: Are you still smoking cigarettes? Because…
       BO: Nicorette.
       DL: Is it the gum?
       BO: It's my wife actually. She gave out my secret to the world and told America: if you see him, turn him in to me. And I'm terrified of her.
       DL: How long have you been smoking cigarettes?
       BO: Oh, you know, on and off. You pick it up when you are writing a book, or campaigning, or… (…)
       Audience+DL+BO: *Laughter*
       DL: It's certainly not a good thing to be smoking…
       BO: No, no.
       DL: It's a nasty habit. But it might be fun if we had a president who smoked (mimes a smoker for a few seconds).
       Audience: *Laughter*
       BO: *smiling*: Blowing smoke in the face of the Iranian president (…)
       DL: You are using the gum. So, are you still smoking?

> BO: No, the gum's working good.
> DL: Working good. Oh, boy!
> BO: I could use one now.
> Audience+DL+BO: *Laughter*. (1)

Apart from being highly personal in topic, the exchange above is also marked by hedges and hesitations ("you know"), interruptions (DL: Are you still smoking cigarettes? Because… BO: Nicorette"), unfinished clauses ("you pick it up when you are writing a book, or campaigning, or…"), exclamations ("Oh, boy!"), which characterize naturally occurring conversations rather than mediated interviews. Needless to say, in political talk shows both the guest and the host are professional communicators who have been trained how to speak and act naturally on air (controlling the tempo, loudness and length of their utterances, as well as their body language). What the talk show audiences enjoy is witnessing a casual conversation that is non-argumentative and emotionally involving, rather than purely "purposeful talk" that is characteristic of institutional discourse (Ilie 2001, 220).

Authenticity is also manufactured through leaving space for unexpected queries and allowing witty, self-effacing replies, usually at the beginning and the end of the interview:

> (9)   DL: Hallo John. Can you stay? (alluding to McCain's cancellation of the previously scheduled appearance on the show)
>   John McCain: Depends how bad it gets (…). It's been some time since my last interrogation (McCain was PoW in Vietnam). (6)

The embedded allusion (instantly recognized by *Letterman*'s fans) and the reciprocal ironic banter reveal a different side of McCain's, who can be appreciated as someone willing to joke about his dramatic war experiences. This is a type of self-effacing humor that Americans tend to value most (Płudowski, 2008). Authenticity is also at stake in the following exchange between Hillary Clinton and Jay Leno on *The Tonight Show*, in which the presidential candidate shows modesty and warmth that is largely contradictory to the popular perception of her public persona.[9]

> (10)   JL: [Chelsea Clinton] said that YOU would be a better president than her DAD!
>   Audience+HC: *Laughter*
>   HC: *smiling*: Oh, she's such a smart young woman. (8)

In this exchange, Chelsea's remark is recontextualized as both a compliment and a relatively face-threatening comment to respond to by Hillary. The threat is successfully mitigated by laughter and a returned compliment, allowable in a genre that meshes the personal perspective and the public issue. Indeed, the flaunting of the maxim of relation in Hillary's response produces a conversational implicature that amounts to a concession to Chelsea's view.[10]

In the talk show genre, it is precisely these apparently unscripted humorous situations that draw audiences and that have replaced staged conflict situations typical of many shock-and-ambush talk shows and political interviews specializing in confrontainment. Additionally, through the generic conventions that help to manufacture authenticity, politicians are able to project the impression of credibility and integrity as speakers. These properties are central to all types of persuasive communication that requires not only an effective argumentation (logos), but also a socially and morally acceptable source (ethos).

4.4   Impression management and image building

The talk show genre is notable for offering the opportunity for "the entrepreneurship of the self" for the participants, be they public figures, celebrities or members of the audience (O'Sullivan 2005). For example, in order to enhance their personal image, politicians are likely to recount personal stories or entertaining anecdotes (or make them up for the show) to make a specific point. Such stories sometimes include explicit evaluations of the experiences recounted, or leave clues for the audience to evaluate them in an intended manner. (11) is a nostalgic recount of Barack Obama's childhood vacation, complete with an expression of amazement for America's "treasures":

(11)   BO: When I was eleven years old we went to the mainland for the first time. We went to Seattle (…) to the Disneyland (…). The Grand Canyon was great. Also on that trip I first went to Chicago. I still remember in the field museum in Chicago, they had, mind you, ten-year-old boys are pretty strange, they had those shrunken heads (…). These were cool. They were almost as cool as the Disneyland. (…) What many people don't realize is how spectacular this country is. (5)

Following a personal story such as this one, with its spatial details, emphatic evaluations ("cool"), even inconsistencies ("eleven" or "ten-year-old") and sideline comments ("mind you"), may well foster solidarity, sympathy and appreciation.

The same image-enhancing sense of affiliation is achieved by means of jokes,[11] as in:

(12)   BO: When I tell my kids to clean their room, I end up by saying I'm Barack Obama and I endorse this message. (3)

This succinct, witty, personal joke is designed to provoke a sense of affiliation with audience members who can discern a parallel between the routines of parenting and endless campaigning.

The talk show genre also offers a strategic opportunity for candidates to explain away misstatements or blunders and clarify issues behind current media scandals. This helps them to maintain a positive image in the face of campaign attacks and even to ridicule the opponents' tactics. For example, on *Letterman* Obama is enabled to clarify what he meant when he used the expression "put lipstick on a pig" a few days before:

(13)   DL: Let me ask you a question now. Have you ever actually put lipstick on a pig?
　　　Audience: *Laughter*
　　　BO: The answer would be no. But it might be fun to try. (…) Yeah, it's a common expression, at least in Illinois. I don't know about NYC. I don't know where you put lipstick on here.
　　　Audience+DL: *Laughter*
　　　BO: In Illinois the expression connotes the idea that if you have a bad idea, in that case I was talking about John McCain's economic plans, that just calling them change, calling them something different, wouldn't make them better. Hence, lipstick on a pig. It's still a pig.
　　　DL: What I like about this scenario is, because Republicans demanded an apology…
　　　BO: Yes, they did.
　　　DL: So it means there's been a meeting at some point (…) and they said, you know, he called our vice-presidential candidate [Sarah Palin] a pig. (…)
　　　BO: Had I meant it this way, she would've been the lipstick.
　　　Audience: *Laughter*
　　　BO: The failed policies of John McCain would be the pig. (4)

Here, Obama "comes clean" from a media-generated outrage over the meaning of his idiomatic comment in a witty and polite manner, criticizing McCain in an non-offensive way and even managing to imply a compliment about Palin.

Typically, in order to boost their image, politicians will also try to orient themselves to the conventions of the genre and project friendly relations with the host, for example by calling him by his first name, responding to compliments, engaging in banter, etc.:

(14)   Jay Leno: Are you getting much sleep?
　　　Hillary Clinton: Not enough.

> JL: (alluding to a recent campaign ad that features HC answering a phone call at 3 a.m. in the White House) Answering a phone at 3 a.m. That's got to be tough.
>
> HC: And it happens every SINGLE night! Somebody calls up and they have something to say. Like, YOU got to stop calling me. (8)

(15) David Letterman: Top ten reasons why Hillary Clinton loves America

> HC: (…) Thanks to the Internet I can order new pantsuits 24/7. *Laughter.* Here is your pantsuit joke, David. Are you happy now? (7)

These exchanges allow Hillary Clinton to take up and defuse some of the criticisms from pundits obsessing about her looks, her mannerisms and her campaign management's publicity strategy. Her joking participation in this kind of "political discourse" proves two things: for one, she is not too aloof to respond to such gross criticisms; for another, the criticisms are demonstrated to be absurd and have little to do with what she stands for politically.

At the same time, it is to be noted that on a talk show candidates tend to use more casual speech registers, more varied intonation contours and more expressive body language than in most other televised contexts (e.g. rallies, interviews, panel discussions, press conferences). Naturally, the talk show's relatively informal and humorous exchanges do not eliminate the deference and politeness required in a mass-mediated encounter between a host and a high-profile politician. As shown above, the generic conventions of the late-night talk show allow for, even demand, displays of humor, irony and sarcasm, provided these are within the boundaries of good taste and tact. Politicians are generally willing to play by those rules in an attempt to improve their image, which tends to be constantly undermined by more hostile and critical media coverage during campaigns.

This is why some talk shows have specific generic structures that allow self-advertising through displays of wit and humor, as is the case with the popular "Top Ten List" on the *Late Show with David Letterman*, here selected to demonstrate examples of ironic banter with the host:

(16) DL: Top ten reasons why Hillary Clinton loves America
      HC: (…) Apparently, anyone can get a talk show. (7)

(17) DL: Barack Obama's top ten campaign promises.
      BO: (…) I'll find money in the budget to buy Letterman a decent hairpiece. (2)

It can be noted that collaboration in "doing humor" on air is another generic convention of the late-night TV talk show. It requires the tacit understanding of the primarily jocular nature of the interaction between the host and the participant and the acceptance of entertainment as the genre's communicative priority. The strategic potential of the talk show genre lies in the unobstructed opportunity to disseminate specifically contrived positive images of the candidates, which is, after all, a key purpose of any campaign.

5.   Conclusion

It can be noted that the genre of late-night televised talk show is of specific cultural importance in the US (Hume 2000; Płudowski 2008). The genre's steady rise in popularity and significance is reflected not only by its viewing figures, but also by the growing academic research devoted to its multiple aspects (review, e.g., in Tolson 2001; Ilie 2001). However, the constant diversification of realizations of the talk show genre precludes all-encompassing generalizations about its structure as a text-type. That is why this paper adopts a functional perspective to demonstrate in what ways the talk show's politically oriented variant has become a strategic genre in the US presidential campaigning. In the course of the above analysis of widely circulated records of popular TV talk shows from 2008 presidential race, it has been shown how the genre's conventions provide new opportunities for the candidates to sway public opinion and win voters through such discursive strategies as the performance of sociability, the personalization of politics, the manufacture of authenticity, and impression management (image building).

This case study has taken a functional, rather than formal, perspective to the genre of the talk show: it looks at what it is capable of doing for the political actors and audiences, rather than what it looks like. In fact, despite their relatively stabilized status as a televised genre, late-night satirical talk shows, as any entertainment programs, tend to have a very flexible structure and must strive to answer to various contextual, institutional and cultural constraints. The study both identifies and critically evaluates the discursive practices enabled by the talk show's generic formula, as they can be used manipulatively by campaigners. For example, since the entertaining conventions of the talk show are likely to obscure the ideological investments of campaigners, attention needs to be drawn to structures that purport to inform while they misinform (speculation, revelation, personal opinion). Moreover, the infotaining frame of the talk show had been designed to impede critical reflection, which is evident in the premium put on sociability, informality and humor (non-confrontational interactive patterns, small talk, self-effacing wit and ironic banter). The thematic preferences of the genre displace serious deliberation and political argumentation for the sake of anecdotal narration, personalization, and positive self-presentation. Presumably, the image-boosting potential of the genre, particularly its capacity for the manufacture of authenticity, is the main reason why politicians entangled in media-generated scandals and worried about the way they are perceived by voters flock to late-night TV talk shows.

It would be wrong to assume that there is not much to gain politically in a talk show because there is no argument to win against an opponent (as in a debate), no attack to repel from an adversarial reporter (as in a political interview), no strategic talking points to publicize (as in a press conference, press release or news broadcast). Indeed, it has been shown that the talk show genre can become an effective resource for the politically relevant purposes of persuasion, comparable to eloquently delivered speeches or impeccably designed advertisements. With the current demand, at least in the US, for political rhetoric that values authentic emotional expressiveness rooted in clearly articulated personal ethos, the potential of televised entertainment talk shows in political campaigning cannot be underestimated. Apparently, the synergetic relationship between the media and the political elites (cf. Fairclough 1995) has been strengthened – through yet another genre. In a wider perspective, the hybridized nature of the talk show genre – where political campaigning is meshed with satirical entertainment – is emblematic of media-saturated postmodern societies, where pop-cultural forms have been increasingly colonizing the public sphere (Postman 1986; Livingstone and Lunt 1994; Fairclough 1995; Płudowski 2008). This trend deserves to be not only thoroughly documented but also critically interrogated.

Notes

1.   A concise, yet comprehensive, comparison of various functionally oriented approaches to the notion of genre can be found in Duszak (1998, 213–219).

2.   Critical Discourse Analysis/Critical Discourse Studies – an interdisciplinary field of language-oriented research focusing on the relations between communicative practices, their epistemic bases and socially/institutionally delimited contexts. It aims at exposing ideological investments in naturalized and conventionalized language uses. Its main principles were laid out by Fairclough (1989) and van Dijk (1993) among others, and its methodologies are being constantly diversified and enriched. For recent comprehensive overviews see for example Schiffrin, Tannen and Hamilton (2001), Wodak and Meyer (2009), van Dijk (2011).

3.   A similar conjunction is evident in the recently popular type of parody news bulletin exemplified by Jon Stewart's *The Daily Show*.

4.   Specifically, Ilie (2001, 209–212) notes that, as a semi-institutional genre, the TV talk show tends to be institution-defined (e.g. by broadcasting conventions and corporate strategies), host-controlled (e.g. as to the monitoring of interaction patterns and roles), participant-shaped (e.g. with respect to subtopic selection) and audience-evaluated (e.g. in terms of achieved goals).

5.   E.g. Hillary Clinton's 2008 appearances on popular late-night talk shows were criticized as staged, stilted and insincere by her opponents (Molek-Kozakowska 2010).

6. The numbers refer to the list of primary sources in the Appendix.

7. Admittedly, in the recorded episodes under analysis in this study, one can see that David Letterman is being slightly more prickly towards John McCain than towards Barack Obama, but this can be attributed to their personal animosity rather than to the generically prescribed conflict staging (on 24 Sept. 2008 McCain cancelled his appearance on *Letterman* claiming he was going to Washington, yet appeared on that night's *CBS Evening News with Katie Couric*).

8. Obviously, Michelle Obama herself was not a presidential candidate; however, she was a First Lady candidate, which is the focus of this interview, and in general she was heavily involved in Barack Obama's campaign by attending media events and talk shows.

9. The imagery and techniques used by Hillary Clinton's media strategists in the 2008 campaign are explored in Molek-Kozakowska (2010).

10. More on verbal humor from a pragmatic perspective can be found in Dynel (2009).

11. This effect has been documented by Ekstrom (2009).

References

Bakhtin, Mikhail M. 1986. *Speech Genres and Other Late Essays.* Trans. by Vern W. McGee. Austin, TX: University of Texas Press.

Bernstein, Basil. 1990. *The Structuring of Pedagogic Discourse.* London: Routledge.

Bhatia, Vijay. 1993. *Analyzing Genre: Language Use in Professional Settings.* London: Longman.

Bourdieu, Pierre. 1998. *On Television and Journalism.* London: Pluto.

Cappella, Joseph, and Kathleen H. Jamieson. 1997. *Spiral of Cynicism. The Press and the Public Good.* New York/Oxford: Oxford University Press.

Chafe, William H. 1999. *The Unfinished Journey: America since Word War II.* New York/Oxford: Oxford University Press.

Chilton, Paul, and Christina Schaeffner. (eds). 2002. *Politics as Text and Talk: Analytic Approaches to Political Discourse.* Amsterdam/Philadelphia: John Benjamins.

Coupland, Justine. (ed.). 2000. *Small Talk.* London: Pearson Education.

Duszak, Anna. 1998. *Tekst, dyskurs, komunikacja międzykulturowa* [Text, discourse, intercultural communication]. Warszawa: Wydawnictwo Naukowe PWN.

Dynel, Marta. 2009. *Humorous Garden-Paths: A Pragmatic-Cognitive Study.* Newcastle: Cambridge Scholars Publishing.

Ekstrom, Mats. 2009. "Power and Affiliation in Presidential Press Conferences: A Study of Interruptions, Jokes and Laughter." *Journal of Language and Politics* 8 (3): 386–414.

Fairclough, Norman. 1989. *Language and Power.* Harlow: Longman.

—. 1995. *Media Discourse.* London: Arnold.

Goffman, Erving. 1981. *Forms of Talk.* Oxford: Blackwell.

Gruber, Helmut, and Peter Muntigl. (eds). 2005. *Approaches to Genre.* Berlin/New York: Mouton de Gruyter.

Grzmil-Tylutki, Halina. 2007. *Gatunek w świetle francuskiej teorii dyskursu* [Genre in the context of French discourse theory]. Kraków: Universitas.

Habermas, Jurgen. 1989. *The Structural Transformation of the Public Sphere.* Cambridge MA: MIT Press.

Hillier, Hilary. 2004. *Analyzing Real Texts. Research Studies in Modern English Language.* Basingstoke: Palgrave Macmillan.

Hume, Ellen. 2000. "Talk Show Culture." Retrieved on 10 June 2009 from http://www.ellen-hume.com/articles/talkshow1.htm

Hutchby, Ian. 2006. *Media Talk: Conversation Analysis and the Study of Broadcasting.* Maidenhead: Open University Press.

Ilie, Cornelia. 2001. "Semi-Institutional Discourse: The Case of Talk Shows." *Journal of Pragmatics* 33: 209–254.

Livingstone, Sonia, and Peter Lunt. 1994. *Talk on Television: Audience Participation and Public Debate.* London: Routledge.

Lee, Francis. 2002. "Radio Phone-in Talk Shows as Politically Significant Infotainment in Hong Kong." *The Harvard International Journal of Press/Politics* 7 (4): 57–79.

Lorenzo-Dus, Nuria. 2009. *Television Discourse: Analyzing Language in the Media.* Basingstoke: Palgrave Macmillan.

Martin, J. R., and David Rose. 2008. *Genre Relations. Mapping Culture.* London/Oakville: Equinox Publishing.

Mauranen, Anna. 1998. "Another Look at Genre: Corpus Linguistics vs. Genre Analysis." *Studia Anglica Posnaniensia* 33: 303–315.

McAllister, Ian. 2007. "The Personalization of Politics." In *The Oxford Handbook of Political Behaviour,* ed. by Russell Dalton and Hans-Dietrich Klingemann, 571–587. Oxford: Oxford University Press.

Montgomery, Martin. 2001. "Defining Authentic Talk." *Discourse Studies* 3 (4): 397–405.

Molek-Kozakowska, Katarzyna. 2010. "Personalization in Political Discourse: Its Pragma-linguistic Realizations and Potential Persuasive Effects." In *Pragmatic Perspectives on Language and Linguistics,* ed. by Iwona Witczak-Plisiecka, 51–64. Newcastle: Cambridge Scholars Publishing.

Myers, Greg. 2010. *The Discourse of Blogs and Wikis.* London: Continuum.

O'Sullivan, Sara. 2005. "'The Whole Nation is Listening to You': The Presentation of the Self on a Tabloid Talk Radio Show." *Media, Culture, Society* 27 (5): 719–738.

Pew Research Center for the People and the Press. 2004. *The State of the News Media 2004.* Washington, D.C.

—. 2008. *Internet's Broader Role in Campaign 2008.* Washington, D.C.

Płudowski, Tomasz. 2008. *Komunikacja polityczna w amerykańskich kampaniach wyborczych* [Political communication in American election campaigns]. Warszawa: Wydawnictwo Naukowe PWN.

Postman, Neil. 1986. *Amusing Ourselves to Death: Public Discourse in the Age of Show Business.* London: Methuen.

Rama Martinez, Esperanza. 2003. "Accomplishing Closings in Talk Show Interviews: A Comparison with News Interviews." *Discourse Studies* 5 (3): 283–302.

Scannell, Paddy. 1996. *Radio, Television and Modern Life.* Oxford: Blackwell.

Schiffrin Deborah, Deborah Tannen, and Heidi Hamilton. (eds). 2001. *The Handbook of Discourse Analysis.* Oxford: Blackwell.

Scollon, Ron. 1998. *Mediated Discourse as Social Interaction: A Study of News Discourse.* New York: Longman.

Swales, John. 1990. *Genre Analysis: English in Academic and Research Settings.* Cambridge: Cambridge University Press.

Tolson, Andrew. (ed). 2001. *Television Talk Shows. Discourse, Performance, Spectacle.* London/ Mahwah NJ: Laurence Earlbaum.

Thornborrow, Joanna. 2001. "Authenticating Talk: Building Public Identity in Audience Participation Broadcasting." *Discourse Studies* 3 (4): 459–479.

Van Dijk, Teun A. 1993. "Principles of Critical Discourse Analysis." *Discourse and Society* 4: 247–283.

—. 1998. *Ideology: A Multidisciplinary Approach.* London/Thousand Oaks: Sage.

—. 2008. *Discourse and Context.* Cambridge: Cambridge University Press.

Van Dijk, Teun A. (ed). 2011. *Discourse Studies: A Multidisciplinary Introduction.* London/ Thousand Oaks: Sage

Wodak, Ruth. 2009. *The Discourse of Politics in Action. Politics as Usual.* Basingstoke: Palgrave Macmillan.

Wodak, Ruth, and Michael Meyer. (eds). 2009. *Methods of Critical Discourse Analysis.* 2nd Revised Edition. London: Sage.

Yan, Xiaoping. 2008. "TV Talk Show Therapy as a Distinct Genre of Discourse." *Discourse Studies* 10 (4): 469–491.

Appendix: List of primary sources

1. Barack Obama on the *Late Show with David Letterman* (11 April 2007)
   www.youtube.com/watch?v=MAVauLsJ56Q
2. Barack Obama's Top Ten campaign promises on the *Late Show with David Letterman* (24 January 2008)
   www.youtube.com/watch?v=rOWlpvOPKXc
3. Top Ten surprising facts about Barack Obama on the *Late Show with David Letterman* (1 May 2008)
   www.youtube.com/watch?v=dVy6z7gwydU
4. Barack Obama on the *Late Show with David Letterman*, part 1 (10 September 2008)
   www.youtube.com/watch?v=QkM66VEfJYk
5. Barack Obama on the *Late Show with David Letterman*, part 3 (10 September 2008)
   www.youtube.com/watch?v=MOLRrdnBZ0Y
6. John McCain on the *Late Show with David Letterman* (16 October 2008)
   www.youtube.com/watch?v=jiBqHczYJYo
7. Top Ten reasons Hillary Clinton loves America on the *Late Show with David Letterman* (6 May 2008)
   www.youtube.com/watch?v=sdsaiTkJx1g
8. Hillary Clinton on *Tonight Show with Jay Leno* (3 April 2008)
   www.youtube.com/watch?v=_0RnRHLL76g
9. Michelle Obama on *Larry King Live* (11 February 2008)
   www.youtube.com/watch?v=pyBc33UjvDU

CHAPTER 11

Multimodal legitimation

Looking at and listening to Obama's ads

Rowan R. Mackay
University of Edinburgh, UK

In this paper I look at legitimation in multimodal texts. By focusing first upon genre analysis from a social semiotic perspective, and highlighting the complications it presents for genre identification, I lay a conceptual framework for looking at the specific genre of political spot ads. Analyzing a small selection of such ads used in the 2008 American presidential campaign, I show how the legitimating features they contain, although recognizable from more traditional studies, have been strikingly and successfully adapted to a new context. Furthermore, I suggest that this reworking marks a shift in the hierarchy of legitimating tools: a shift away from the unquestioned primacy of text and talk.

1. Introduction

In this paper I look at legitimation in multimodal texts. By focusing upon the genre of political spot ads, and analyzing a small selection of these used in the 2008 campaign, I show how the legitimating features they contain, although recognizable from more traditional studies, have been strikingly and successfully adapted to a new context. Furthermore, I suggest that this reworking marks a shift in the hierarchy of legitimating tools: a shift away from the unquestioned primacy of text and talk. Obama's campaign and subsequent election have led to a renewed interest in oratory and rhetoric, classical tools which are concerned with legitimation. The election of a President compared to Cicero (Higgins 2008), a "man of ideas", a lawyer, an "intellectual heavyweight", shows that oratorical and rhetorical qualities are still highly valued for someone holding the office of President – but have tended to overshadow other notable features of the Obama campaign.

The campaign was revolutionary in the way it used the internet: not only to raise money, but also by exploiting its viral quality. Social networking and video-sharing sites were utilized, multimodal messages were freed into cyberspace and left to do their work, and other multimodal texts were picked up from cyberspace and redeployed in more formal settings. The official advertisements aired on television were only one part of the advertising offensive: other ads were released as "web-only", and of course there was the utilization of other advertising genres: the more traditional billboards, bumper stickers, T-shirts etc. It is worth remembering that multimodality itself is not new, but the ways of realizing multimodality are changing in line with the affordances of the new technology (cf. Kopytowska's discussion of political blogs [this volume]). It is in this socio-political-technological context that my study is situated.

Legitimation is a broad concept which has been heavily theorized, but not deeply analyzed in terms of its workings, structure or makeup. Teun van Dijk, while concentrating on ideology, has attempted to answer the question: "if ideologies are being developed to 'legitimate' power or social inequality, what is the precise nature of these legitimation processes and practices?" (van Dijk 1998, 8). Theo van Leeuwen has similarly worked upon this gap in understanding by "set[ting] out a framework for analyzing the language of legitimation" (van Leeuwen 2007, 91–92) in which he identifies four categories of legitimation: authorization, moral evaluation, rationalization, and mythopoesis. Despite these inroads, there is still work to be done on understanding how legitimation functions. The work that has been done in discourse analysis on legitimation has tended to be on institutional texts, which are usually formal, written documents. Thus, the language of multimodality has not been focused on as much as the pervasiveness of multimodal texts would seem to justify. Van Leeuwen has led a growing interest in this area through his work on social semiotics (van Leeuwen 2005) but, as yet, there have been few focused studies on legitimation in multimodal texts. In this chapter, through analyzing a small number of ads, I shall try to lay the ground for such a project.

2. Conceptual framework

2.1 Genre

Before discussing the genre of political ads, the very concept of genre needs to be touched upon. As discussed in the Introduction to this collection, genre is a highly theorized and complex area of study, and "political genre" no less so. Poon (2010), in surveying the use of the term "genre" (and several associated terms including "style", "register", "dialect", "sociolect", and "language" itself) uncovers a tremendous lack of agreement in the definition and domain of the term. This concords with Lemke who, in writing specifically about the place of genre, writes:

> Constructs like community, dialect and sociolect, semiotic cultural formation and genre, all of which describe systems of practices/processes that directly participate in both semiotic and material types of relations/couplings, must be conceptualized as trajectory entities, i.e. as being defined in terms of meta-stable, dynamic open systems that are continually in the process of developing themselves, creating conditions that require them to change and reorganize themselves in interaction with their environments.   (Lemke 1999, 14)

In acknowledgment of the breadth of the topic, and what Santini has termed the "still unsolved genre riddle" (Santini 2010), what I attempt here is to briefly situate my own position for the purposes of later discussion.

Lemke's paper "Typology, Topology, Topography: Genre Semantics" (1999) locates genre within social semiotics, in fact he states that genres are "social semiotic formations, that is, they are social constructions, the products of conventional social meaning-making practices that belong to a community's system of intertextuality" (Lemke 1999, 1). For anyone acquainted with the scholarship of Social Semiotics, Lemke's statement will flag-up a triad of concerns: first, the tension between the system within which genre is an identifiable part, and the indeterminable range of its use by creative users; second, its social constructedness; and third, its role in intertextuality and "dialectic", culturally specific, meaning-making.

The title of Lemke's paper prefigures his concentration upon the conceptual "places" genre inhabits – and the distinction between the identification and definition of that (topological) space, and the topography of (any specific) genre as it is realized through actual use. The importance of this distinction shall be seen in the analysis as texts are reclassified, being transposed (at least temporarily) from one genre to another (e.g. pop song to political ad). I focus upon Lemke's work, but several of Lemke's points have been reiterated, with distinctive slants, by Bateman (2008) who focuses particularly on multimodality and genre, and van Dijk (2008) who makes a distinction between "context genres" (characterized by the context in which they exist) and "discursive genres" (characterized by the internal structures they exhibit), which, although they "usually combine" (van Dijk 2008, 149), goes some way to explaining the two ends of the genre spectrum. Lemke's own formulation takes inspiration from Threadgold and Kress's (1988, 1989) discussion of genre as an "intertextual resource".

Lemke's first point is an important one: he is using, he writes, "the term topography here to remind us that texts and text formation patterns like genres unfold in a space of many semantic dimensions" (Lemke 1999, 2). "Prior deployments" of both the system of genre, and specific "textual semiotic formations" inform each newly realized instance. In an ambitious "ecosocial" framework, Lemke employs an evolutionary metaphor with genre evolution being dependent upon the requirements, demands and environmental features of each cultural ecosystem, with the attendant notions of "agnation", "specialization", and "redundancy". This way of analyzing genre easily admits the further recognition of "hybrids" and "sub-genres". Lemke states that "[g]enres change over historical time. Like species, some may persist over long periods in relatively stable forms and come to co-exist with their own 'descendants'" (Lemke 1999, 10). We shall see that this is indeed the situation in the case of spot ads, where more traditional forms of the spot ad co-exists with newly realized manifestations of the shifting genre (or are we experiencing/ can we now identify a new (sub)genre?)

The way in which genre is conceived of by Lemke allows for the flexibility necessary to accommodate the fluidly changing realizations of genre, while maintaining it as a useful concept. He writes:

> An 'ideal genre' can be represented by definite points in such a topological space, marking the centers of clusters of other points representing actual texts. Those clusters ('fuzzy sets' or distributions) may overlap, representing ambiguity (or 'multiple inheretance' cf. Stillar 1992) in the genre classification of texts.
>
> (Lemke 1999, 4)

He further highlights that in the evolution of a genre – or adjacent genres – the centre of a cluster (the prevalent defining features) may shift due to "polarizing social pressures" (Lemke 1999, 11), and thus create a (refreshed) genre with a different topographical contour. This leads to the re-alignment of texts with genres: on occasion producing a gap, or a split into which a new genre, or a sub-genre comes to be seen as such. Lemke explains:

> new genres arise from old ones by processes of differentiation and specialization, and their reverses (coalescence, neutralization of semantic distinctions). Any particular feature we use to trace the history of a genre will be subject to change.
>
> (Lemke 1999, 13)

What is not explained here – and I do not offer an answer – is what forms the catalyst for actual change. Does a new (sub)genre (of, say, political advertisement) come into being when a scholar such as Lemke, or Iyengar, suggests the change? Even then, how many subsequent acknowledgements, uses, refutals, mentions of the new (sub)genre are necessary for it to *be* one? Or is this the wrong way of looking at it? Ought we instead attempt to track – necessarily retrospectively – the moment of creative innovation, which marked the first instance of the new (sub)genre? If the latter is the case, the (possible) precedents of new (sub)genre spot ads analyzed in this chapter will be of relevance not only to political genre analysis, but to the theoretical study of genres.

2.2   Genre of political ads

The genre of the political spot ad is – or at least until very recently has been – close to an "ideal" genre under Lemke's definition, the texts so classified possessing relatively stable shared features. Van Dijk notes that the "point of the discourse-structural manifestations of genres […] is that these structures appear in specific combinations, collocations, frequencies and distributions" (Van Dijk 2008, 150). Van Dijk lists some of the contextual and discursive features of parliamentary debates, noting that there is not one specific characteristic, but a combination of features which is unique – and thus genre specific.

Spot ads share a temporal context in relation to the election, the campaign of which such ads form a part. From this we can see that in the traditional formulation, such ads are created in response to a demand *for* a spot ad. However, as we shall see below, Obama's campaign requisitioned (and in the process "re-genred") pre-existing texts. Other features are expected length (generally between 30 secs and 2 mins although with increased financial wherewithal, Obama was able to run on seven networks with his 30 min, $4 million "special", "American Stories, American Solutions"), ideological import (Self-legitimation, Other de-legitimation), contextual limitations (can only present what is – or can be presented as – politically relevant), and the institutionalized "Stand By Your Ad" 2002 provision of the Bipartisan Campaign Reform Act which requires candidates and special interest groups to include, as part of their television or radio ads, a statement that gives their identity and declares that the message has been approved by them. This institutional requirement can, in some way, ground the genre in the sense that, being enshrined in law, this feature, unrequired (and prohibited by being potentially libelous) by and in other genres, can stand as the defining centre of the cluster. If this is the case, the genre of the political spot will take a more static identity, more commonly accorded to message "type", yet will manifest characteristics of other genres (e.g. comedy sketch, movie trailer etc.).

The history of the spot ad, from the first movie-theatre airing of a prototype in 1934,[1] through the first proper TV-spot ad during the 1952 presidential campaign, to the Bush vs. Clinton 1992 campaign is documented by Diamond and Bates in their book *The Spot* (1993). The subject of the political spot (from a U.S. perspective) has had a great deal of expert and scholarly time spent on it, from an academic, a journalistic, an advertising-science, a political, and a lobbying perspective. For the purposes of this paper, I shall assume a reasonable knowledge of the basic (political advertising) concept, and discuss in more detail the impact of the internet upon the spot (already mentioned above) which is where Diamond and Bates left off. Shanto Iyengar has written and spoken a great deal about political ads and, in particular (with Ansolabehere 1997), the ramifications of negative advertising. Together with Kathleen Hall Jamieson (Jamieson 1984; Jamieson and Campbell 2008; Jamieson, Kenski, and Hardy 2010), Iyengar is probably the most public, prolific, and respected scholar in the area. His opinion of the "advent of online media" (Iyengar 2011), therefore, is of particular interest here.

Whereas many of us may view campaigns through a spectator's lens of watching a contest between two (or more) contestants, Iyengar uses a different frame. His abstract for the paper reads as follows:

> Campaigns are strategic contests between candidates and reporters. While candidates have proven to be adept at gaining news coverage of their campaign advertisements, journalists have maintained their autonomy by curtailing coverage of the candidates' stump speeches.   (Iyengar 2011, online)

This introduces to the already complicated notion of genre, questions of the manipulation of genre through technology or/and through a mediatization (necessarily ideologically driven, but often explicitly so). One could certainly say that a political speech was a genre, but to what extent is a news clip showing 30 seconds of that speech a neutral genre (the news – *supposedly* neutral) with another "unviolated" genre (the political speech) embedded within it? Such interdiscursivity has been discussed by Fairclough (1992, 1995) and van Leeuwen (1987). A connected query asks to what extent the genre of the political speech maintains its genre integrity if its dissemination comes not through direct experience (not many people actually attend such speeches) but via technological channels (TV, radio, newsprint, internet) with such different affordances? In a recent article Lazar (2010) has discussed some of these issues with reference to public education campaigns in Singapore. Her article "examines how in two fairly recent campaigns, a new approach to campaign communication is used that involves media interdiscursivity, viz., the mixing of discourses and genres in which the media constitute a significant element" (Lazar 2010, 285).

The role of the media in relation to political ads is traced by Iyengar. He describes the field of battle:

> Each side has clearly defined and conflicting objectives. Candidates covet the free and "objective" publicity provided by news reports. Reporters, for their part, are motivated to maintain their autonomy by debunking campaign rhetoric and "spin". In the ensuing tussle over whose voice is to be heard, which side comes out ahead?   (Iyengar 2011, online)

He then goes on to "update the strategic dance" (Iyengar 2011, online) which he has followed, analyzed, and, indeed, been part of. He talks of the see-saw of the media willingness to "give voice to" the politicians. Feeling initially duped into presenting "advertising as news" (Iyengar 2011, online) broadcasters and journalists came back with "a new genre of campaign reporting known as the adwatch" (Iyengar 2011, online). However, the balance these items were supposed to provide was somewhat – and on occasion greatly – undermined by the maxim "all advertising is good advertising". Exposure, even if it came at the cost of some criticism, was often worth it: "candidates responded to adwatches by developing ads that would deliberately elicit adwatch coverage" (Iyengar 2011, online). This media manipulation has, however, been matched by the press "successfully stifl[ing] candidate voices" in "more extensive forms of campaign communication".

The internet changes the game – and the game-plan – for all contestants. "Unmediated" (Iyengar 2011, online) coverage is, again, (illusively?) attainable. A candidate can now have their own "channel" onto which hours and hours of material may be placed, framed, (internally) commented upon and analyzed (the channel itself becoming one big political ad). And for a miniscule fraction of the price! Ads can be – and are – now constructed for web-only viewing. Journalists may prefer "to rely on the voices of the analysts rather than the candidates, since the latter are seen as self-serving", but it became clear in the 2004 presidential election that there was a demand from the public to "hear it straight from the horse's mouth". The ad-watching did not stop, but became far more democratic, as viewers could use the "comment" function, either directly (if comments were enabled), or through the multiple re-postings of the ads on YouTube and similar platforms. Iyengar views this new development, not with the kneejerk response often elicited when the public are to be left "unguided" to traverse political rhetoric, but rather with a degree of optimism:

> Against this backdrop, technology at least makes it possible for voters to bypass or supplement media treatment of the campaign and access information about the issues that affect them [...] Thus, there is some reason to hope that the spread of new forms of unmediated communication will eventually provide a better way to inform and engage voters.   (Iyengar 2011, online)

2.3   Legitimation

The O.E.D. definition of "legitimation" has five strands:

1. The action or process of rendering or authoritatively declaring (a person) legitimate.
2. The condition of being legitimate; legitimacy. Obs.
   (...)

b. transf. Of a literary work: The fact that it is the work of its reputed author; authenticity, genuineness. Now rare.

3. The action of naturalizing (an alien). Obs.

4. The action of giving a lawful character to something forbidden by law; a dispensation. Obs.

5. gen. The action of making lawful; authorization; rarely concr. a document of authorization.

From this we can see that legitimation can be an action or a condition. Furthermore, legitimation can be rendered and declared. It can even be performative in nature – the stating of it being so makes it so. Although the vagaries of these definitions are beyond the scope of this paper, the fact that legitimacy is wrapped up with legal declarations, yet is also a disputed and debatable quality, informs all but its very narrowest conceptions. In discourse analysis, legitimation is largely redefined with each new study undertaken. Van Leeuwen states that "[l]egitimation is always the legitimation of the practices of specific institutional orders" (van Leeuwen 2007, 92) and seems to accept Berger and Luckmann's view that "a decontextualised study of legitimation is not possible" (1966, 111). However, the title for van Leeuwen's paper is "Legitimation in discourse and communication" – not "Legitimation in discourse and communication concerning compulsory education" or some other specific institutional order. Indeed, van Leeuwen's paper ends with a generalized discussion of legitimation and context. In this he looks at an analysis of Kress's (1985) which, he says, shows that "a single text can invoke many different, sometimes even contradictory, discourses" (van Leeuwen 2007, 108). He goes on to say that "[v]iewing these discourses as legitimation discourses can add a further dimension, as the concept of legitimation can link, on the one hand, social practices, and on the other hand, discourses of value" (van Leeuwen 2007, 109). That is, legitimation as a process is all-encompassing: a category which applies to all discourses. This sweeping inclusivity differs from van Dijk's position that everyday language does not "legitimate", but institutional language does. However, on further inspection, the two positions are not that different. Van Dijk states that

> Legitimating discourse is usually accomplished in institutional contexts. Although people may perhaps be said to 'legitimate' their everyday actions in informal conversations, such usage would probably count as being derived from a more formal lexical register. In everyday informal talk, we would rather speak of justifications, explanations or accounts. In all these cases, the crucial point is that speakers explain why they did or do something and why such an action is reasonable or, in general, socially acceptable... People justify or account for their actions mostly if they know or expect that others might be puzzled or, more

strongly, if others disagree, condemn, challenge or attack them because of these actions.

Legitimation, then, is the institutional counterpart of such justifications.

(van Dijk 1998, 256)

In this chapter I shall be looking at institutional texts for the most part, but I think it is important to remember that texts which could hardly be called institutional (such as Obama Girl's music video) can, in any case, legitimate an institution. Moreover, the institutional nature of the ads is downplayed where the intended message would seem dissonant with the formality that comes with institutional settings and registers. Consequently, the institutionality of a text is not as black and white as may first be thought.

2.4   Legitimation in CDA

Legitimation as a practice is fundamental to Critical Discourse Analysis (CDA), yet, generally, it informs the context, rather than being itself the subject. Here is Chilton setting the ground for his book, *Analysing Political Discourse*:

> We shall see throughout this book that political discourse involves, among other things, the promotion of representations, and a pervasive feature of representation is the evident need for political speakers to imbue their utterances with evidence, authority and truth, a process that we shall refer to in broad terms, in the context of political discourse, as 'legitimisation'.   (Chilton 2004, 23)

The need for a meta-level analysis of what legitimation is and how it works has been less pressing, perhaps, than the actual analysis of political discourse itself. As Joseph points out,

> CDA marries critical linguistics with the perspectives of Foucault and Bourdieu, and sees itself as capturing the 'dynamic' nature of both power relations and text production by uncovering the hegemonic structures within texts. This is in contrast with earlier analyses, including those of critical linguistics, which concerned themselves with static relations and how they are encoded.   (Joseph 2006, 127)

In CDA, legitimation garners attention through the analyses of political discourses. With an understanding of legitimation in some sense carried forward from Bourdieu and Habermas, it is through textual analysis itself that any discussion of legitimation comes up: the political urgency and commitment to effect change – the applied nature of CDA – has steered it away from drier theorizing. Chilton's focus on "foreigners" and Van Dijk's focus on racism have provided the most detailed discussions of legitimation in political texts.

3.   Method

For the analyses a number of spot ads have been chosen which illustrate the multimodal features that will be discussed. The selection process is driven by what can be illustrated; therefore only a handful of ads have been taken into account, each of which allows the highlighting of certain features interesting for a discussion of multimodal legitimation. The ads are freely available on the web and, being part of the most recent election campaign, are relatively safe in terms of continued accessibility for the foreseeable future.

The formula of an academic text like the present one necessitates tackling the ads through written descriptions, but part of the point I make here is that the other modes are not dispensable or replaceable with words on paper. Therefore, the reader of this chapter is encouraged to view each of the ads under discussion:

1.   "Yes We Can": <www.livingroomcandidate.org/commercials/2008/yes-we-can-web> (Will.i.am and Dylan 2008)
2.   "Don't Vote Alone": <www.livingroomcandidate.org/news/perma/obama-web-video-recommends-voting-as-a-social-activity> (VoteForChange.com 2008)
3.   "Don't Know Much": <www.livingroomcandidate.org/commercials/2008/dont-know-much> (Team 2008)

The Living Room Candidate, as part of the Museum of the Moving Image, has a wonderful archive of presidential campaign commercials from 1952–2008. The Political Communication Lab at Stanford University, too, has a well-maintained and thorough online ad archive (http://pcl.stanford.edu/).

4.   Analyses

4.1   Multimodal legitimation of a speech

4.1.1   *Background*
Legitimacy draws on contextual knowledge, as well as being achievable in the moment. Barack Obama's concession speech in New Hampshire was made during the primaries, while he was competing with Hilary Clinton, John Edwards and Bill Richardson for the Democratic nomination. This formal position – as a contender in a formal and heavily institutionalized competition – is already a legitimating one. It is understood that Obama is there after going through due process and succeeding where others have failed. It is also contextually understood that he has respectable financial backing, both in terms of amounts and in terms of sources.

A plethora of other background details are almost certainly known and add to the consideration of legitimacy before the New Hampshire speech is even begun. These legitimating features are absolutely crucial, yet are so taken as a given that it is easy to dismiss them. Legitimacy is accrued by Obama being:

- A U.S. citizen
- College-educated
- A man
- Able-bodied
- A lawyer
- Married with kids
- Straight
- Healthy
- Clever

Hopefully this is not a non-controversial list. Yes, of course some people would attach more legitimacy to Obama if he was gay, or female, or anything but a lawyer. But the fact remains that Obama does not appear on that stage as an unknown quantity, and the context we perceive him in is highly relevant to our consideration of his legitimacy.

Van Dijk has recently proposed a detailed "framework for a theoretical *concept* of 'context' that can be used in theories of language, discourse, cognition, interaction, society, politics and culture" (van Dijk 2008, 15). The theory espoused in this two-book monograph

> emphasizes that the relation between society and discourse is indirect, and mediated by the *socially based but subjective definitions of the communicative situation as they are construed and dynamically updated by the participants*.
>
> (van Dijk 2009, vii)

Contextual knowledge relevant to Obama's speech will vary from person to person, and the evaluation of such knowledge will inform each individual's judgment as to the legitimacy of Obama's position. Normative pressures created and applied socially lead to a consensus in many areas. It is a truth almost universally acknowledged that elected leaders ought to be adults (*pace* generations of teenagers). This is at the uncontroversial end of a huge spectrum. There is no comparable consensus that the leader of a multiracial nation ought to belong to a particular race, but the fact that Obama is black certainly lends him a degree of legitimacy with some – and none with others (Sinclair-Chapman and Price 2008). And it is this play upon the elements which differentiate him from his competitors, and sell him to (enough of) the American public that matters most here.

It is important to note that the dialectical nature of context not only means that we shape our contexts and that they shape us, but that we can project contradictory notions. Thus, I may believe that class ought not to signify legitimacy, since I believe in meritocracy rather than aristocracy. This would imply that class indicators were of no interest to me when judging the legitimacy of someone's position. However, if I were to judge two candidates, one of whom spoke RP and one who spoke Manc (an English regional dialect), I may decide that the RP candidate sounded more politically experienced and accord them more legitimacy, but this may simply be because I am used to the politically experienced having an RP accent. Clearly this is an area with inexhaustible permutations: the point is that, as individuals, we do not make simple binary judgments.

Working out what is relevant, what is concerned with legitimation, in the context of Obama's speech is incredibly difficult. The fact that he is from Chicago legitimates him in the eyes of those who feel that belonging to a certain place *means* something: unique features of that city giving him by environmental osmosis certain qualities of the city which they hold dear. Van Dijk wryly notes the need to "define (delimit) the notion of 'context', lest the theory becomes a Theory of Everything" (van Dijk 2009, 3). That being said, as analysts we have to be aware that the dog Obama chooses (Maltzmana et al. 2012), the look in his eye, or even something so undefined as the "I just really [don't] like him" gut response, remain factors at which we can only guess – together with Obama's image consultants and advertising teams paid to pick up on such elusive appeal. Van Dijk moves away from this conundrum by saying that in his understanding of context, it is the discursively relevant – as opposed to simply the socially relevant – which is important.[2] I shall take van Dijk's definition as my own working definition: "a context is what is defined to be relevant to the social situation by the participants themselves" (2009, 5).

4.1.2   *Ad 1*

This ad was originally a viral music video, released on February 2, 2008 by musician will.i.am, member of a popular and influential hip-hop band. The lyrics are almost entirely taken from Obama's New Hampshire Concession speech, apart from the Hebrew, Spanish and Sign Language translations of the slogan "Yes We Can", and the addition of "I want change". The order of the text is slightly different, and some repetitions not in the original speech have been added. These very minor changes mean that throughout the ad we hear and see Obama's speech as it was given and broadcast on the U.S. national and international news. The video is in stark black and white, the frame division varies from none to a triptych, with the placement of Obama giving his speech varying within that. The guest appearances are all young American celebrities of varied race, cultural heritage, and gender, ranging from musicians to actresses; basketball players to models, singing the words of the speech, chanting "Yes We Can", or playing instruments. The use of text in the video is limited: four phrases appear in different parts of the frame in temporal keeping with the call-and-response style of the song. These phrases are: "YES WE CAN", "CHANGE", "HOPE", and "VOTE". The last of these is the only use of color in the video and ends the video – "HOPE" in black changes letter by letter to "VOTE" in red.

4.1.3   *Multimodal re-contextualization in a supporting role*

The cornerstone of this ad is Obama's speech, as it is seen and heard, not as it is written. Oratory, in this televisual age, is clearly multimodal: we listen and watch. Obama's speeches have been analyzed a great deal in terms of their rhetorical power, and his skill as an orator is much discussed. I must limit my discussion of these two subjects in order to give myself space to discuss the multimodality of the ad. It is important, however, to summarize where the power lies in the speech given and I do that below. However, this ad is not simultaneous with the speech. The speech's context has changed in a retrospective fashion. What is important about this speech has altered, and keeps altering depending on when it is viewed. One of the qualities of the viral video is that re-interpretation, re-contextualization continues upon viewing which is unprogramed but openly available. This video was released just before super Tuesday, a day when many primaries occur and therefore, crucial to the nomination. Fast forward to Obama's nomination though and the video becomes an ad for the presidency, rather than for the primary. Fast forward to today and the video, again, is thrown into a different light.

Keeping in mind that such re-contextualizing occurs, for an ad to be both viral and effective over time (at least until the election is over) the legitimating features need to withstand the changes that will occur in the remaining timescale. For example, if the ad had mentioned the need to vote in the primaries, its use in the subsequent presidential election would be limited. Similarly, Obama's speech, looked at retrospectively, stands as a powerful speech advocating voting for Obama, rather than a poignant concessionary speech, linked solely to a defeat in the primaries. In the speech, and ad, we get the following uses of tense:

(1)   We know the battle ahead *will be* long. But always *remember that*, no matter what obstacles stand in our way, *nothing can stand* in the way of the power of millions of voices calling for change.
We *have been told we cannot do thi*s by a chorus of cynics. And *they will* only grow louder and more dissonant…
there is something happening in America…
Yes, *we can*…

And, together, *we will begin* the next great chapter in the American story, with three words *that will* ring from coast to coast, from sea to shining sea: Yes, we can.

This unspecific futurity is linked with a very conscious reflection on the history of America leading up to this point. The notion of history in the making, with the momentum and forward-looking impression that this calls up, is a significant theme of the speech. Obama placed himself very consciously within the narrative of the Civil Rights Movement – and also painted himself as the result of the patchwork history, and unfettered potential (to be realized once again through him) of the United States. The legitimation which comes from tradition, and from the "rightness" of conforming to that tradition (thus also showing a high regard for it) is two-fold. First, it is a powerful source of ideological legitimation, and social legitimacy (society in general being receptive to the more conservative following of past tradition). Secondly, as noted at the beginning, legitimacy can be performative, and in following tradition and the rules set down, legitimation is bestowed upon Obama.

It is worth looking at this in more detail as regards the multimodality of the ad. Obama gains legitimacy through placing himself not only within the tradition of America politically, but also more personally. Politically he aligns himself with Martin Luther King, who, although not named, is heavily alluded to: "a king who took us to the mountaintop and pointed the way to the Promised Land". This is a clear signal to the civil rights movement, and although at no time in the speech does he discuss his own race, the fact that he is the first African American to run for president makes his place as heir to King's "kingdom" visually more legitimate than that of any of the other presidential hopefuls.[3] The soundtrack here is one mixing hip hop and black gospel call-and-response: this is not a *white* soundtrack. Of course, one could argue that there is no such thing as a black or white soundtrack, but I think this would be missing the point. This music situates and legitimates Obama as King's heir apparent and also as something new in politics: a *change*! For when have we seen a presidential candidate congruent with black youth culture? We will see later on in this paper how Obama uses the age of a genre of music to his advantage – and to McCain's disadvantage.

Any analysis of the meaning of music faces the challenge of grounding opinion. Unlike with spoken and written language, which has recourse (or rather, *more* recourse) to authoritative texts defining (and delimiting) meaning, music – although it does have dictionaries – has no such notion of one-to-one relation. Musical analysis in social semiotics, therefore, has been a little tentative. Following on from van Leeuwen (1999), Machin and Richardson (2012) have been less apologetic in their social semiotic analysis of two fascist songs set to the same melody.

The position they take is an associative one: music gains meaning through our experience of it, not through its inherent quality. This being the case, music also functions to "implicitly index" a plethora of further associations (the cognition involved in these mental linkages has been a focus of much work by van Dijk).

The video emphasizes several of the themes within his speech which are themselves legitimating. Obama's rhetoric and oratory have been much discussed and this speech is a good example of why. The formal rhetorical devices used are multiple (and these are just a few):

- Molossus (three stressed syllables: "Yes we can")
- Triad (threesomes: repetition of "we are")
- Syntheton (balanced doubles: "the hopes of the little girl who goes to the crumbling school in Dillon are the same as the dreams of the boy who learns on the streets of L.A.")
- Anaphora (repetition of words at the beginning: "We")
- Epistrophe (repetition of words at the end: "Yes we can. Yes we can. Yes we can.")
- Alliteration (words starting with similar sounds: "documents that declared the destiny")
- Assonance (words with similar consonantal sounds: "whispered by slaves and abolitionists as they blazed a trail towards freedom (through the darkest of nights'))
- Imagery (emotive images for the audience: "sung by immigrants as they struck out from distant shores and pioneers who pushed westward against an unforgiving wilderness")

These are often emphasized by Obama's delivery, reminiscent of gospel sermons. As Graham says, "[t]o hear Obama speak is to be vividly reminded of the language and cadences of the African-American pulpit, transposed into public oratory" (Graham 2009, 157).

The cadences are highlighted and emboldened by the singing of the soundtrack. The sung harmony brings out the musicality of the Obama speech. These are stylistic points but also become part of the legitimation strategy. On several levels, Obama needs us to read between the lines, or rather "do the math": he talks about civil rights and Martin Luther King and we are expected to put him into that narrative (Frank 2009). To some extent, the success of such legitimation comes from it not being explicit but from our putting him in the frame. Similarly, Obama does not discuss his own religious beliefs, but in his speech he becomes the implied (yet not ambiguous) vehicle of deliverance. The ad highlights the religious style of his speech and places him as the pastor – his "we", therefore, becomes one of a religious and visionary leader and his congregation. Of course, if this was made explicit, Obama would be attacked for arrogance (even more than he already was being). This religious tone legitimates his position not only with the black Christian community, but also, in the U.S., with the Christian community at large.

The catchphrase "Yes we can", driven home *repeatedly* has a history itself. It is a slogan of the organized labor movement in the United States stemming from *Sí, se puede* (Spanish for "yes, it can be done"), the motto of the United Farm Workers who, in 1972, brought it to widespread attention by the fasting of César Estrada Chávez. For the large Latino minority in the States, Obama's use of this national hero's catchphrase will legitimate his position, associating Obama to the values of change by peaceful means (which Chávez and King both espoused). Appealing to the racial minorities in the States is extremely important for any Presidential campaign, and in this ad, the multiracial presence of young and attractive people, singing Obama's words and chanting "we want change", is an appeal to the masses.

Framing is also very important in this ad: not only do we have rapidly shifting frames, but we have a constant play upon the triptych structure. The stylistic features of the speech which have to do with timing are highlighted once again, not this time by the harmony of the singers, but by the rhythm of the changing frames. Kress and van Leeuwen (1996) say this about framing and its role in composition:

> In temporally integrated texts framing is, again, affected by rhythm. From time to time the ongoing equal-timed cycles of rhythm are momentarily interrupted by a pause, a *rallentando*, a change of gait, and these junctures mark off distinct units, disconnect stretches of speech or music or movement from each other to a greater or lesser degree.   (Kress and van Leeuwen 1996, 214)

The frames themselves are variations upon the triptych. This compositional tool is not only aesthetic – it also contains information which we need in order to decode the message, that is, it deals in social semiotics. The triptych is a frame divided into three (normally equal) parts, either vertically or horizontally. Thus, in this ad it is so:

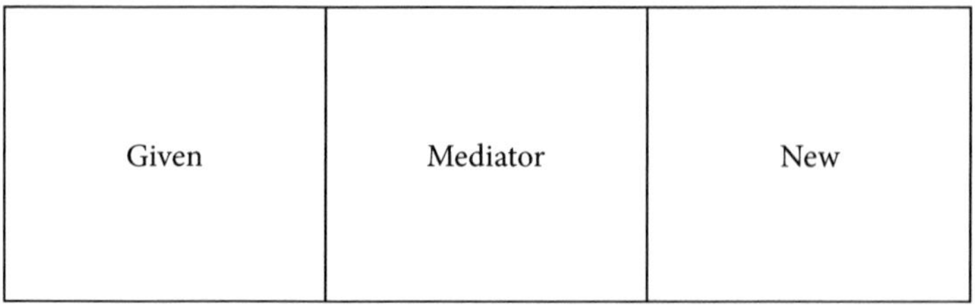

Given	Mediator	New

Figure 1. Horizontal triptych (Kress and van Leeuwen 1996, 211)

That is, the left hand side of the frame tells us what is already known, the right hand side of the frame is the new information, and the middle frame is the method by which we get from the given to the new. There is also the vertical triptych structure of Ideal at the top, Mediated in the middle, and Real at the bottom. In terms of political advertising, clearly, there are two projected scenarios: one, the advertised wins and the ideal becomes the new; two, the advertised opponent does not win and the new dystopia begins. This also explains, visually, why an incumbent has to struggle to break away from the present "real", to promise a new, enhanced, ideal. A concrete example of this is the way in which the Obama campaign "threatened" that a vote for McCain was "more of the same".

As applied to this ad, the message seems to be less clear-cut. The frames play with thirds, sometimes being divided with two-thirds on the left and a third on the right, sometimes being in even thirds, sometimes being one-third on the left and two-thirds on the right, and sometimes being a full frame.

Figure 2. Obama in all three triptych positions

Obama is pictured in all these positions, as are the others in the ad. This signals equality and continuation: that everyone is in all these positions and Obama, particularly, fills all three. How should we interpret this? I think this is a reinforcement of Obama as preacher and the responders as his congregation: going together as equals, yet led by Obama. There are some crucial instances in which the traditional formulation applies – and that is with the reference to Martin Luther King in which the screen is, for the first time, made whole.

Figure 3. Traditional full screen formulation

With the text, "YES WE CAN" varies its position, "CHANGE" is on the right and "HOPE" is in the center, until the last frame in which the letters "O" and "E" from "HOPE" are carried through to become "VOTE" in red (which is the only use of color in the video). I would suggest this interpretation: ability (existing now as real and given – thus empowering) symbolized by "Yes we can", mediated by hope, will lead to the new and ideal of "Change", if hope can extend into the action of voting. Interestingly, it is also in this very last frame that the borders between the middle and the right become crossable, which again reinforces the possibility that with hope as mediator, the ideal can be realized.

4.2 Legitimation through genres

4.2.1 Background

The existence of the red and the blue states in the U.S., the fact that certain demographics indicate a certain voting behavior means that Presidential campaigns work within their budget to convert those swing voters, or lightly allied voters, and also work to "bring out the vote". It is the expressed aim of most politicians that they would like to see more voting turnout, regardless of whether that favors them. However, a Democratic campaign will not spend money in bringing out Republican voters, and vice versa. Indeed, there is fear of lethargy among the converted, and the likelihood that a candidate is getting through to the more politically inactive influences the pollsters. There are also demographic tendencies

Figure 4. Positioning text within the triptych and in relation to borders

influencing who is likely to care enough about any election to actually get to a ballot box and vote. Furthermore, in the States, every state except North Dakota requires that citizens who wish to vote be registered.[4] Some states allow citizens to register to vote on the same day of the election, but others do not.

Political commentary leading up to an election habitually uses these generalized (but nonetheless useful) demographic tendencies, together with the notion of generational cohorts. For example, Jon Bruner wrote in a *Forbes* blog called "Trailwatch" (Bruner 2008) as follows:

> Successive generations are more liberal in their views toward minorities, Hansen said, and baby boomers, who are substantially more liberal on race than their parents, have reached the age bracket of maximum voter participation, making their attitudes particularly influential at the polls… The generational effects continue into the cohort that has just reached voting age. Obama is particularly popular with college students, whose support may obviate one of the Clinton

> campaign's biggest knocks against him: that Obama can't connect with white, blue-collar voters.   (Brunner 2008)

He goes on to say that if we pair these relevant demographics with the idea that "Americans have generally become more liberal on race regardless of generation" (because of increased exposure to African-Americans in prestigious positions), we get the following result:

> Americans are more willing than ever to vote for a black presidential candidate. A 1958 Gallup poll found that just over 40% of Americans would be willing to vote for a qualified black presidential candidate. That percentage broke the 70% mark in the late 1960s; today, about 95% of Americans tell pollsters that they would vote for a qualified black presidential candidate.   (Brunner 2008)

What is interesting here is the matrix of group belonging it concocts. In the "Comments" section of the blog, there is this comment:

> And there is another demographic – it comprises all those 'immigrants' (oh yes, legal, of course) who came here over the last 20–40 years. Many of us are baby boomers, doubling the effect described above. We are definitely considering someone with more diversity, and if Obama doesn't embody diversity of almost all kinds, I don't know who does.   (Brunner 2008)

The analysis of demographic tendencies is important to this study in that the same demographics influencing voting behavior of a particular group often overlaps with the preferred musical and visual genres of that group. Matching demographic makeup with the genre chosen to communicate is extremely important.

4.2.2   *Ad 2*

This ad, "Don't Vote Alone" was released as a web video on the 30th October, 2008 – that is, five days before election day, and was the second last ad released by the Obama team. It contains a small amount of text, is 40 seconds long, has no narrator, and is an animation with a soundtrack. The same soundtrack was used in another web-only ad released five days earlier and is similar enough in style to be seen as a follow-up, although both ads can stand alone. A simplified, description of the ad would be the following:

1. Text: TENNIS ANYONE? – appearing character by character onscreen as in instant messaging.
    Simultaneously, the music starts – it is heavy on bass, electronic/house music with a simple electronic melody.
2. The frame now overlaps and then fades into another frame with a tennis net and some ground drawn as if by hand. A racket hits the ball from our (near)

side of the court to the other side. The camera pans around to the head of a female, again drawn sketchily, mouth downturned unhappily.

3. The frame changes again and we see the same girl sitting on a seesaw by herself looking dejected.

    The picture pans out to her in the play park.

    Text: HOW ABOUT SEESAW? – appears similarly.

4. The one cloud in the sky moves above the girl and she is seen shaking her hand with nobody.

    Text: NICE TO MEET YOU – the text is not typed out this time.

    The music here gains another strain in a higher register, accompanying the melody.

5. Then she is pictured holding an end of a tin-can phone to her ear.

    Text: HELLO?

    The picture pans out to show the other end of the "phone" hanging down over a branch.

    Text: SOME THINGS ARE FUNNER WITH SOMEONE ELSE

6. The cloud which has been moving through the sky (viewer left to right) morphs in the next frame into a box labeled: VOTE HERE on one face of the cube, and POLLING LOCATION on another (under which is a drawn in door). To the right of this box is the text BRING.

7. The box then starts to fade out, lines turning from black to red, and faint red and yellow beams emanating from the box (in a way viewers will associate with the iconic "Hope" image of the Obama campaign) rotate clockwise. At the same time, the text is increased word by word in time with the rhythm to: BRING A FRIEND TO VOTE.

8. As soon as this text is completed, it moves closer into the foreground, increases in size, and below this message is the text: TUESDAY, NOVEMBER 4th, 2008, and then immediately after that in red the words VOTE FOR "written" along the bottom of the date, and the word CHANGE appears, also in red. When these text features have arrived, the rest of a web address appears making the red text read: www.VOTEFORCHANGE.COM. The faint rotating beams continue and the words VOTE FOR are underlined, as if by hand, in red.

9. Centralized at the bottom the "Hope" image (or logo)[5] appears and the music simplifies.

4.2.3   *Legitimation through multimodally realized genre and register*

This ad uses animation, music and language simultaneously, to identify with, and persuade, its target audience. The brevity of the ad – the complete text which follows – contrasts starkly with the previous one:

(2) TENNIS ANYONE?
    HOW ABOUT SEESAW?
    NICE TO MEET YOU
    HELLO?
    SOME THINGS ARE FUNNER WITH SOMEONE ELSE
    VOTE HERE / POLLING LOCATION
    BRING A FRIEND TO VOTE
    TUESDAY, NOVEMBER 4TH, 2008
    www.VOTEFORCHANGE.COM

The power of the ad does not lie in any rhetorical flourish, indeed its apparent simplicity in terms of typeface, uppercase lettering and vocabulary is clear.

Figure 5. "Simple" genre and register

But something more complex is going on: informal and youth-orientated slang phrasing "SOME THINGS ARE FUNNER", changes the register in which the ad is placed from simple to more self-consciously casual. The relationship between the portrayed character and the intended audience is interesting. To vote in the U.S. you need to be eighteen or above. In the ad, the figure looks very much like a young girl: she is in the play park, trying to play two-person games on her own.

The gender seems clear and with the ponytail attached to a stick figure betraying no curves, the figure does not seem to be nearing voting age. Why this discrepancy? If we follow through the logic of the ad, the character would go with a friend from tennis, to the play park, to the poling station, her day just getting funner and funner. Yet not many kids would actually find voting fun and they are not permitted to vote anyway. Why is the youth *so* youthful? The style of the drawing and writing is also childish: does this signal naivety, simple hope? And what is the relationship of young voters, eligible to vote for the first time perhaps, to this stick girl? Do they relate to her youth? Perhaps, the stereotypical teenager would

Figure 6. "Some things are funner"

not have the right semiotic associations. The child must have afforded something which another figure could not. Furthermore, the discrepancy between the age of the character and any intended audience (of voting age) allows for the phrase, "some things are funner with someone else" to be recontextualized into an older, yet still youthful space. The fun of the play park could easily be replaced by the fun of sex.

This ad does not come with an "intended audience certificate" so its identification is debatable. Moreover, a viral ad may have several different demographic groups making up a more complicated intended audience which we have to differentiate among. Audience design, as Lazar (2010) points out, takes the "layers of interaction", "involved beyond the immediate interactional setting", into account when choreographing the use of genre. This was a web-only ad, which already delimits its primary viewers. Only those who watch videos on the web will be exposed to this ad initially. I would suggest that this is the part of the intended audience to which the ad appeals. The genre of music, graphic design and animation should, therefore, also appeal to these people, as should the message, put succinctly on The Living Room Candidate website:

(3)   This Web video/animation urges supporters to turn voting into a social activity and bring friends along.   (VoteForChange.com 2008)

Note that even though the text of the ad does not specify until the end who it would like to follow this advice (the web address specified at the end, <www.voteforchange.com>, is identified with the Obama team enough to make it tantamount to an endorsement), it does not come across as a cross-party call to the ballot box.

Figure 7. Voting as a social activity

The political identification is realized multimodally. We can see the demographic reflected through some of the comments made by viewers on YouTube about the video:

(4)   Already voted – alone – absentee. It was fun. But it could've been funner.

(5)   already voted with my 5 friends it was fun, obama 08!

(6)   this video is really good its not just telling u to vote its telling u to vote with a friend and for obama! GO OBAMA!!!!!!!

(7)   I brought a friend. And yes, it was more fun.

(8)   it was funner for me lol

(9)   Like this ad, it is positive, short, sweet and simple. I refuse to live in fear

(10)   Thank you so much for all this fun, positive, creative work.

(11)   my mom is 50 and has NEVER voted. ever. i printed out a slip had her sign it she mailed it and she received her first voter card last weekend. she was so proud. i then sat and watched these videos with her and then she was excited. then i took her to vote. the first time in many elections that she is able to say she felt motivated enough to go vote. im so proud of her.

(12)   Funner is a word. It's just not often used. Cute ad, vote Obama!

(13)   Some things are "funner"?? And these are the people who want to run our educational system??

(14)   which if obama is elected, he will bring an extreme leftist view, such as making funner, aint and tubular a word, where as mccain will keep english the way way it was when he was a kid, like thee and ye

(15)   ¨¤ø„, ¨°°¤ø„, , „ø¤°°¨ „ø¤°°¨
         ¨°°¤ø„ Obama & Biden „ø¤°°¨ (this was clearly a banner made of text)
              , „ø¤°°¨ ` `°°¤ø„,
         ø¤°°¨ , „ø¤°°¨¨°°¤ø„, ¨°°¤ø

This is clearly a multimodally realized demographic, successfully attracted by and responding to the ad.

This brings us onto a counterpart of intended audience – namely, that part of the audience which is likely to feel isolated in some way by the message being put across. Web-based ads released virally quickly make it onto the television news, newspaper websites and further afield through news agencies. This second round of viewers is also part of the intended audience. If the language in this ad jars for a certain demographic, or the playfully sexual overtones are disapproved of, it is possible that the ad succeeds on two fronts: the core intended audience feels like the "in" group, cutting-edge, liberal and enthused; while those actively put off by the ad may be demotivated, their apathy increasing as they feel "out of touch" with the world the ad represents. The former group are those likely to vote Democrat, and the latter group are those likely to vote Republican. Obviously this could be a dangerous game since the right type of negative feeling needs to be created. A stirring of righteous anger may motivate voters to actively go out and vote against the values represented in the ad. This tendency to vote as much against something as for something was evident in this election. McCain was tarred by the similarities between himself and Bush. A vote against McCain was seen by many as a vote away from what Bush represented. Even McCain presented himself as a "maverick", not a natural heir to Bush. But the positivity of this ad, and its apparent lack of political allegiance are both factors which have been acknowledged as less likely to galvanize voters to vote against it (although the effect of negative and positive advertising is not agreed upon – see Heldman 2009; Iyengar and McGrady 2006; McClurg 2009; Wattenberg and Brians 1999).

4.3   Legitimation and semiotic simultaneity

4.3.1   *Background*
Much of the post-ad analysis and dissection aired on television and radio and published on websites and in newspapers concerns the question of negativity. There is much academic discussion (on the whole stemming from Ansolabehere and Iyengar 1997) about whether negative advertising works, but it is certainly the case that media accusations of negative campaigning are frequent, and campaign teams seem to feel obliged to defend themselves against such a judgment. The multimodal components of an ad can be used to carefully balance the negative and positive impressions and messages it gives viewers. Both humor and music can counteract an ad with a predominantly negative message (see Bush's 2004 "Windsurfing" ad criticizing Kerry). Similarly, a visually positive ad can be accompanied by harsh commentary (see Johnson's 1964 "Ice Cream" ad attacking

Goldwater's nuclear policy). The juxtaposition between the different modes and tones are used for legitimation and delegitimation, attack and self-defense. Many stock clichés can be employed regardless of the subtlety of production. Children, happy music, the U.S. flag, bright, saturated color, and beautiful scenery are all rough and ready positivity signs. Ominous music, black and white color, stormy skies, and war are all negativity signs.

The background to the following ad is clearly the financial crash, but it also requires the cultural knowledge of a specific song, "Wonderful World" by Sam Cooke. The referencing of popular culture has to be carefully done: judgments of taste, inaccurate assumptions of knowledge, or any sense of cultural inappropriacy is a minefield of (sometimes) slightly trivial, but nonetheless, politically lethal gaffes (recall Howard Dean's "Yee Haw!" exclamation in the 2004 primaries).

4.3.2   Ad 3

Instead of taking a paragraph to describe this ad, labeled "Don't know much", it is easier to present its multilayering in the form of a three-column figure (see Figure 8 below). Although it still conflates and reduces the many tiers which are interrelated and inter-signifying (for example the spoken endorsement is put in the same column as the sung lyrics and the music), it goes some way to illustrating the simultaneity of the modes used.

Spot ad: 'Don't know much'

VOICE	TEXT	IMAGE WITH TEXT
I'm Barack Obama and I approve this message.	BarackObama.com	
I'm not up on the economy,	"Economics is not something	
Don't know much about industry,	I've understood as well as I should" –John McCain	
Really can't explain the price of gas,	December 2007	(On signs) ADVANCE REALTY
Or what has happened to the middle class,		598-212 FORECLOSURE
But I know that one and one is two,	Voted with Bush 90% of the time.	
And if I could be just like you,		
What a wonderful world this would be.	APPROVED BY BARACK OBAMA. PAID FOR BY	
"Do we really want four more years of the same old tune?"	OBAMA FOR AMERICA We can't afford more of the same.	

Figure 8. "Don't know much": multilayering and simultaneity of modes

4.3.3   *Legitimation through semiotic simultaneity*

The ad "Don't know much" emphasizes the importance of semiotic simultaneity – by which I mean that the practice of legitimation is realized in different modes of expression simultaneously. A stylistic analysis of the words – written, spoken, and sung – would need to be brought together with a visual and musical analysis. Again, it is useful to look at this ad in the light of the grid adapted from Kress and van Leeuwen (1996):

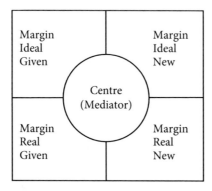

Figure 9. The dimensions of visual space (Kress and van Leeuwen 1996, 208)

To reiterate, very simply, on the left hand side of the screen is what is given – what we already know. On the right is what is new. This ad uses this semiotic language in complex ways. More specifically, the ad starts with Obama on the right and when it changes, McCain is situated on the left – this is basic projection: Obama as future, McCain as past. Moreover, note the color and saturation choices of the two different faces: Obama is in the sunlight (outdoors, with the red, white, and blue of the flag blurred in the background?) which, although strong, shows Obama to his advantage, with his facial definition highlighted, and his color healthy. Contrasting with this is McCain, pictured with darkness around him, his thinning white hair reflecting bright artificial light. A light which also manages, literally, to highlight the folds of skin around his neck. Although not a bad picture of McCain (that would be an overly heavy-handed comparison) it does rather emphasize the age (and implied health) difference between the two.

It is clear that Bush and McCain are interchangeable in terms of position – and the dividing line (present–given/future–new) is compromised by their bodily contact. This is exactly the message the Obama team tried repeatedly, throughout the campaign, to get across. Furthermore, when pictured together, Bush appears dominant physically – taller, bigger, younger. This physical representation easily slips into a wider, metaphorical comparison, of say policy and influence, not to mention that the reiterated "chumminess" of McCain towards Bush, out of context as it is here, seems obsequious. The importance of presenting physical stature in political advertising is great, although remains implicit. Camera angle, lighting, posture and relative height are all employed to manipulate our impression of a candidate's stature. The importance of stature, I suggest, comes from this metaphorical importance attached to it. The age-old belief that there is a connection between the body, mind and morals of individuals has gone through many stages but has never quite disappeared.[6] The fact that stature is sometimes taken as analogous to moral state, social status, physical virility and mental agility is used by advertisers – including political ones.

Figure 10. Presenting McCain and Bush physically and metaphorically

A part of negative campaigning is concerned with scaremongering – or warning, the authoring camp may say. In this ad we see the McCain quote about economics ("Economics is not something I've understood as well as I should") in the "new", right hand side position, and the Foreclosure sign in the "given", left hand side position. By this simple placement McCain's claim to be economically competent is de-legitimated and, simultaneously, placed into the projected future. Furthermore, by initially inserting a dividing white line between right and left in these first frames concerning McCain, there is a sense of duality: an old McCain/ Bush's present escalating fuel costs/ middle-class foreclosures in the present, and McCain's implied economic incompetence in the future. This strong linear divide is broken by the close physical proximity and body contact between Bush and McCain (interchangeably placed) in the next three frames, hammering home the "more of the same" message.

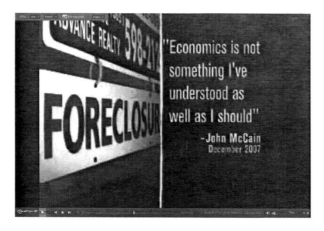

Figure 11. De-legitimating McCain's economic competence

The defining feature of this ad – that which makes it work – is the use of the old (1960) song "Wonderful World". This cultural appropriation of a "golden oldie" allows for the allusions made about McCain's age and his similarity and closeness to Bush to be made explicit through the use of irony and humor.

In the ad, the lyrics of this song have been changed, but it is highly unlikely that the original lyrics are not known, thus making the change itself foregrounded. The original lyrics are placed beside those of the ad:

Don't know much about geography	I'm not up on the economy,
Don't know much trigonometry	Don't know much about industry,
Don't know much about algebra	Really can't explain the price of gas,
Don't know what a slide rule is for	Or what has happened to the middle class,
But I do know that one and one is two	But I know that one and one is two,
And if this one could be with you	And if I could be just like you,
What a wonderful world this would be	What a wonderful world this would be.

Figure 12. "Wonderful World" satire

This satirizing is only effective because of the assumed knowledge of the original. Insofar as it assumes some knowledge and rewards comparison, it legitimates the Obama camp for cleverness, and also flatters the viewer for recognizing the satire. Clearly, the song's narrator's intellectual weakness is directed at McCain – with the quote about economics emphasizing this (viewers will probably also know and anticipate the next line of the song "now I don't claim to be an 'A' student"), but the values attached to the song more generally are ambiguously attached to both camps. It is a much loved song; the Obama team is using it. But also, it is old – just like McCain. This attempt to split the legitimating function indicates the richness of this as semiotic currency.

5. Conclusion

I have attempted to illustrate the importance of multimodality to legitimation within the complex genre environment of political advertising. By trying to show various ways in which legitimation is achieved in these multimodal texts, I hope to highlight the depth and dimension which such a full study would take. The three sections in this paper focus on the unique characteristics of the multimodal text and how these can be used to legitimate. The ability to re-contextualize a speech is the first example, and I point out how the visual and auditory elements foreground certain features (of an already strong and symbolically rich text) to legitimate Obama. I then use a very different ad to show that the written – or spoken – text is not a necessary base to which multimodal adornment is added. Furthermore, I point out that the careful selection and use of genres can single out demographic groups which can then be appealed to or otherwise. The ad I analyze aims to appeal to one group while, at the same time, demotivate a politically opposed demographic. This ability to do several different things simultaneously is the focus of the last section. In this I emphasize the importance and efficiency of semiotic simultaneity – that is the inextricably entwined semiotic layers which work together, and at the same time, to achieve different things. I think it is important to note that the sum of the parts does not equal the whole here: the interaction between the different modes affords more than the different modes could have taken separately. The present investigation also raises another question: Can music and image themselves legitimate, or are they necessarily held to supporting roles? In an open-ended enquiry such as this one I can only answer that it seems, from this small study, that the modes are not in any necessary hierarchy – and that multimodality allows for a certain semiotic richness to be exploited for legitimation – and de-legitimation.

Notes

1.   The description given of this ad demonstrates, paradoxically, how little has changed, and yet how far the genre has come (this now reading as a self-conscious "spoof" ad, using humour

and genre choice to mask the negative message being promoted, yet it still sounds very plausible). Diamond and Bates write: "In 1934 the muckraker and Nativist Radical Upton Sinclair became the Democratic candidate for governor of California. Businessmen and conservatives, who regarded Sinclair's program to end poverty as a Bolshevik plan to redistribute the wealth were horrified [...] Whitaker & Baxter [the ad agency commissioned] produced phony newsreels of staged events. In one, dozens of bedraggled hoboes leap off a freight train, presumably having arrived in the Promised Land of California. Explains one bum: 'Sinclair says he'll take the property of the working people and give it to us.' In another, a bearded man with a Hollywood-Russian accent explains why he will vote for Sinclair: 'His System vorked vell in Russia, so vy can't it vork here?'" (Diamond and Bates 1993, 37).

2.   Interestingly, it is here, at this early point in his Introduction, that van Dijk indicates that semiotic studies may have a different take on what is relevant: "That is, usually our clothes are seldom *discursively* relevant, although they may often be *socially* relevant, for instance in order to 'flag' aspects of our current social identity ('doing feminine'), or to adapt (as does our discourse) to formal vs. informal social events. Politicians are very conscious about their 'image' and no doubt their clothes (ties etc.) are consciously selected and adapted to the occasion in which the politicians are going to speak. This also suggests that besides discourse there are other (semiotic) aspects of interaction and communication that may have their own contextual constraints. These, however, shall not be the main focus in this book" (2009b, 4).

3.   Is it echoes of anti-miscegenation sentiment which leads Obama to be called – and call himself – black, or is it a consequence of the not-so-distant "blood fraction statutes" or the "one drop rule"?

4.   It seems that "an unregistered voter could still appear at the polls and vote by filing an affidavit supported by the oath of a householder or registered voter attesting that the prospective voter was in fact a resident entitled to vote". See http://www.nd.gov/ sos/electvote/voting/vote-history.html.

5.   A full analysis of the logos used by the Obama campaign is beyond the scope of this study. There is however much discussion about their importance, significance, success, and rapid proliferation (see, for example, Smith 2009).

6.   Plutarch, in his essays, has a familiar illustration, which he borrows from some philosopher more ancient than himself: "Should the Body sue the Mind before a court of judicature for damages, it would be found that the Mind would prove to have been a ruinous tenant to its landlord" (D'Israeli 1791–1823).

References

Ansolabehere, Stephen and Shanto Iyengar. 1997. *Going Negative: How Political Advertisements Shrink and Polarize the Electorate.* New York: Simon & Schuster Free Press.

Bateman, John. 2008. *Multimodality and Genre.* London: Palgrave Macmillan.

Berger, Peter, and Thomas Luckmann. 1966. *The Social Construction of Reality.* Harmondsworth: Penguin.

Bruner, Jon. 2008. For Obama, Demographics May be Key to the White House [electronic version]. *Forbes Online.* Retrieved 2009 from http://blogs.forbes.com/trailwatch/2008/ 05/for-obama-demographics-may-be-key-to-the-white-house/.

Campbell, Karlyn, and Kathleen Jamieson (eds). 2008. *Presidents Creating the Presidency: Deeds Done in Words*. Chicago: University of Chicago Press.

Chilton, Paul. 2004. *Analysing Political Discourse: Theory and Practice*. London: Routledge.

Diamond, Edwin, and Stephen Bates. 1993. *The Spot: The Rise of Political Advertising on Television*. Cambridge, MA; London: MIT Press.

D'Israeli, Isaac. 1791–1823. *Medicine and Morals*. From http://www.spamula.net/col/ archives/2006/01/medicine_and_mo.html.

Fairclough, Norman. 1992. *Discourse and Social Change*. London: Polity.

—. 1995. *Critical Discourse Analysis: The Critical Study of Language*. London: Longman.

Frank, David A. 2009. "The Prophetic Voice and the Face of the Other in Barack Obama's 'A More Perfect Union' Address, March 18, 2008." *Rhetoric & Public Affairs* 12(2): 167–194.

Graham, Elaine. 2009. "A Window on the Soul: Four Politicians on Religion and Public Life." *International Journal of Public Theology* 3(2): 145–164.

Heldman, Caroline. 2009. "Campaign Advertising and American Democracy. By Michael M. Franz, Paul B. Freedman, Kenneth M. Goldstein, and Travis N. Ridout. (Temple University Press, 2007)." *The Journal of Politics* 71(2): 760–761.

Higgins, Charlotte. 2008. "The New Cicero." *The Guardian* 26/11/08: 10.

Iyengar, Shanto. 2011. "The Media Game: New Moves, Old Strategies". *The Forum* 9(1). Retrieved 2011 from http://pcl.stanford.edu/research/2011/iyengar-mediagame.pdf

Iyengar, Shanto, and Jennifer McGrady. 2006. *Media Politics: A Citizen's Guide*. Stanford: W.W. Norton & Co.

Jamieson, Kathleen. 1984. *Packaging the Presidency* Oxford: Oxford University Press.

Joseph, John E. 2006. *Language and Politics*. Edinburgh: Edinburgh University Press.

Kenski, Kate, Bruce Hardy, and Kathleen Jamieson. 2010. *The Obama Victory: How Media, Money, and Message Shaped the 2008 Election*. Oxford: Oxford University Press.

Kress, Gunther. 1985. *Linguistic Processes in Sociocultural Practice*. Geelong: Deakin University Press.

Kress, Gunther, and Theo van Leeuwen. 1996. *Reading Images: The Grammar of Visual Design*. London: Routledge.

Lazar, Michelle. 2010. "Performing the 'Lifeworld' in Public Education Campaigns: Media Interdiscursivity and Social Governance." *Pragmatics and Society* 1(2), 284–310.

Lemke, Jey L. 1999. Typology, Topology, Topography: Genre Semantics [Electronic Version]. *Author's Homepage*. Retrieved 25/09/12 from http://academic.brooklyn. cuny.edu/education/jlemke/papers/Genre-topology-revised.htm.

Machin, David, and John Richardson. 2012. "Discourses of Unity and Purpose in the Sounds of Fascist Music: A Multimodal Approach." *Critical Discourse Studies* 9(4): 329–345.

Maltzmana, Forrest, James Lebovica, Elizabeth Saundersa, and Emma Furth. 2012. "Unleashing Presidential Power: The Politics of Pets in the White House." *Political Science & Politics* 45(3): 395–400.

McClurg, Scott D. 2009. "In Defense of Negativity: Attack Ads in Presidential Campaigns. By John G. Geer. (University of Chicago Press, 2006.)." *The Journal of Politics* 71(2): 758–760.

Poon, Wing. 2010. The Linguistic Norms of Hong Kong English in Computer-mediated Communication. Unpublished PhD Thesis. University of Edinburgh.

Santini, Marina. 2010. "Review: Pragmatics; Text/Corpus Linguistics: Bateman (2008) [Electronic Version]." *Linguist List, 21:1606*. Retrieved 26/09/12 from http://linguistlist.org/issues/21/21-1606.html.

Sinclair-Chapman, Valeria, and Melanye Price. 2008. "Black Politics, the 2008 Election, and the (Im)possibility of Race Transcendence." *Political Science & Politics* 41(4): 739–745.

Smith, Marquard. (ed.). 2009. *The Journal of Visual Culture: The Obama Issue* 8(2): 123–233.

Stillar, Glenn. 1992. Phasal Analysis and Multiple Inheritance. (Manuscript).

Threadgold, Terry. 1989. "Talk about Genre: Ideologies and Incompatible Discourses." *Cultural Studies* 3(1): 101–127.

Threadgold, Terry, and Gunther Kress. 1988. "Towards a Social Theory of Genre". *Southern Review* 21(3), 215–243.

Van Dijk, Teun A. 1998. *Ideology: A Multidisciplinary Approach*. London: Sage.

—. 2008. *Discourse and Context: A Socio-Cognitive Approach*. Cambridge: Cambridge University Press.

—. 2009. *Society and Discourse: How Context Controls Text and Talk*. Cambridge: Cambridge University Press.

Van Leeuwen, Theo. 1987. "Generic Strategies in Press Journalism". *Australian Review of Applied Linguistics* 10(2): 199–220.

—. 1999. *Speech, Music, Sound*. London: Macmillan.

—. 2005. *Introducing Social Semiotics*. Oxford: Routledge.

—. 2007. "Legitimation in Discourse and Communication." *Discourse & Communication* 1(1): 91–112.

Wattenberg, Martin P., and Craig L. Brians. 1999. "Negative Campaign Advertising: Demobilizer or Mobilizer?" *The American Political Science Review* 93(4): 891–899.

CHAPTER 12

Blogging as the mediatization of politics and a new form of social interaction

A case study of 'proximization dynamics' in Polish and British political blogs

Monika Kopytowska
University of Łódź, Poland

The present chapter takes under scrutiny political blogs with a view to establishing their generic profile, both in terms of structure and functions. This relatively new genre in political communication is discussed in the context of "mediatization", a meta-process transforming the relationship between media, society and politics through creating a common spatiotemporal, cognitive and axiological sphere of shared experience, and supplementing the social activities which previously took place only face-to-face with virtual interaction. The study demonstrates that what makes this process possible is the mechanism of "proximization", allowing for the reduction of the temporal, spatial, axiological, cognitive and emotional distance between the blogger and his or her audience, and thus for the mediation of experience and the creation of a virtual community around the "networked public sphere." On the theoretical level, the chapter offers a new integrated approach towards the discourse of the political blogosphere, combining pragmatic and cognitive linguistic perspectives with insights from social semiotics and media studies. Quantitative (e.g. keyword analysis, concordance analysis, semantic vectors) and qualitative methods are used to explore "proximization dynamics" in political blogs written by active party politicians: the corpus of Polish- and English-language data comprises the two most prominent political blogs in each country along with their readers' comments from the left and right ends of the political spectrum.

1. Introduction[1]

The emergence and rapid development of new media and the growth of political blogosphere has over the last decades become a key concern of theorists, journalists and policy makers, stimulating research in the socio-political potential and communicative nature of cyberspace. The near-instantaneous, dialogic, and decentralized nature and interactivity make this part of MediaSpace[2] an ultra-attractive site for extended political debate, citizen participation, and a more direct and effective communication between political elites and the rest of the society (McKenna and Pole 2004, cit. in McKenna and Pole 2008; Keren 2010; Coleman and Wright 2008; Street 2011). At the same time, hybridization of (on-line) genres, non-linearity of textual forms, and a new dimension of interactivity and intertextuality, have brought about, to use Kress's (2005) words, the "crisis" of the traditional *status quo* within the domain of representation and communication, creating the need for redefining traditional forms and for generating new methods of critical study to be applied to texts structurally and functionally different from the (political) genres traditionally studied in the past:

> In the domain of representation and communication, the crisis manifests itself at every point: genres are insecure; canonical forms of representation have come into question.   (Kress 2005, 17, cit. in Warnick 2007, 13)

Hence, attempts have been made to investigate and assess the persuasive potential of online political communication (Louw 2005; Chadwick 2006; Warnick 2007; see also Mackay [this volume]), and, at a more general level, to classify and delimit genre boundaries in cyberspace (Herring et al. 2004; Kress 2005; Giltrow and Stein 2009; Dean 2010; Myers 2010; Lehti 2011; Yus 2011). The concepts of "mediated society", or even "mediatized society" have been frequently used to account for "the ways in which the media have infiltrated into the rhythms and practices of everyday life" (Cottle 2006, 9), transforming, in consequence, not only the media-politics-society interface, but also the prototypical roles of sender/receiver, author/audience, along with the nature of authorship, feedback, and even text itself.[3] These changes, in turn, have had a considerable bearing on the form and function of political communication and, what follows, on the three dimensions of "political reality", namely (a) an *objective* political reality, comprising political events as they actually occur, (b) a *subjective* reality – the "reality" of political events as they are perceived by actors and citizens, and (c) a *constructed* reality – images of events as they are covered by the media (Kaid et al. 1991, cit. in McNair 2003, 12).[4]

One of the new media genres that has gained prominence within the domain of political communication and received positive attention from an increasing number of Western scholars is the "political blog".[5] The term has been used to refer to blogs "about politics", written by both active party politicians and individuals from outside the formal political establishment. Although the present study focuses only on the former type, both types have been discussed in the literature in the context of a "limitless public sphere" in the Habermasian sense (1989, 2006) and the "network society", as defined by Castells (1997, 2007), and analyzed in terms of their communicative and transformative power in the process of democratization and the "reframing" of political interaction. While blogs written by active politicians have become a new way of communicating with voters and appealing to mass audiences, blogs "about politics" by non-politicians have allowed citizens "to create their own coverage [of politics] and to use new media to enact forms of political activism and leadership" (Street 2011, 261).[6]

Castells (2007) refers to political blogs as a form of "mass self communication" and another weapon in "informational politics struggle", where access to and skillful use of information technologies translate into political power, while Coleman (2005, 274) sees them as "sophisticated listening posts of modern democracy" and a manifestation of the changing nature of political communication:

> A relentless desire to reconnect with the public – or even connect for the very first time – has become a contemporary preoccupation of the political elite. Everywhere technologies, techniques, and styles [...] are being employed to generate circuits of connectivity, porousness, recognition, and sympathy between rulers and ruled, representatives and represented, the remote Them and the disenchanted Us.
> (Coleman 2005, 273)

The rapidly increasing number of blogs has been accompanied by a surge in the amount of research in the phenomenon of political blogging. Much of what has been written, however, comes from the area of journalism and mass communication studies, as well as political science. Political blogs have been analyzed, both quantitatively and qualitatively, in terms of their impact on mainstream media coverage (Hennessy and Martin 2006; Hewitt 2005; Schiffer 2005; Smolkin 2004; Wallsten 2005, 2008), election campaigns and domestic politics (Hopkins and Matheson 2005; Kerbel and Bloom 2007; Downey and Davidson 2007; Janack 2006; Campbell 2009), and international affairs (MacKinnon 2007; Zuckerman 2007). More recently, studies in the political blogosphere have reached beyond the Anglo-American context to include blogging practices and their implications in Egypt (El-Nawawy and Khamis 2011), China (Zhou 2009), Arab countries (Etling et al. 2010), and East Asia (Sullivan and Cheon 2011). The analyses of the linguistic dimension of blogs, in particular political blogs, have been relatively scarce, and so has been the research in blogging discourse and the media-society interface (Lehti 2001; Suomela Salmi 2009; Vesnic-Alujevic 2011).

The aim of the present chapter, situated within the area of critical discourse studies, is to identify and discuss the key characteristics of the political blog as a new emerging genre in the ever-changing new media environment. With the blogosphere conceptualized as a vast virtual agora enabling interaction between political elites and ordinary citizens, and thus extending the scope of political deliberation (Bruns 2008; Coleman and Blumler 2009),[7] the blog is seen as a new way of relating to the networked public sphere, through undermining the onto-logical divisions between the public and the private, the official and the informal, the mediated and unmediated experience. Adopting a new integrated approach towards the discourse of political blogosphere, combining pragmatic and cog-nitive linguistic perspectives with the insights from social semiotics and media studies, I examine the communicative and representative profile of blogs in terms of its structural and functional features. Importantly, blogging discourse is un-derstood here as both "product" and "process", which entails analyzing the mo-tivations behind producing a blog, blogging practices, and the blogger-audience interaction.

The potential of political blogs to negotiate specific meanings and references and to exercise control over audience's involvement will be approached within the context of "mediatization" and accounted for by the concept of "proximization". Mediatization is understood as a meta-process transforming the relationship be-tween media, society and politics through creating a common spatiotemporal, cognitive and axiological sphere of shared experience, and supplementing the so-cial activities which previously took place only face-to-face with virtual interac-tion. Proximization is defined as a discursive tool allowing for the reduction of the temporal, spatial, axiological, cognitive and emotional distance between the blogger and his or her audience, and thus for the mediation of experience and creation of virtual community. "Proximization dynamics" as a genre delimiting factor will be explored here from both qualitative and quantitative perspectives.

In its pragma-cognitive approach, relying on the insights from mass commu-nication and political communication research, the study combines quantitative (e.g. keyword analysis, concordance analysis, etc.) and qualitative methods in its analysis of the Polish and British political blogs. The analysis of bloggers' posts and readers' comments has two, interrelated methodological objectives: firstly, to identify and describe proximization mechanisms in political blogosphere, and, secondly, to establish the generic profile (both structural and functional) of political blogs. The basis of the analysis is the corpus of Polish and English-language data, which comprises the two most prominent political blogs in each country along with readers' comments from the left and right ends of the political spectrum.

2. Defining the genre

Although blogs take numerous forms, and there is an ongoing debate about their generic features (cf. e.g. Herring et al. 2005; Boyd 2006), blogs (shortened from

Weblogs), which came into existence in the mid-1990s when programmers posted journals online and linked to one another (Keren 2004), may be defined as an online diary, or more specifically, "frequently updated websites where content (text, pictures, sound files, etc.) is posted on a regular basis and displayed in a reverse chronological order" (Schmidt 2007 – see also Blood 2002; Herring et al. 2004; Lomborg 2009; Myers 2010).[8] Thus, their main characteristics include: (i) the blogger's posts and general ownership and administration of the blog, hence its author-driven character; (ii) regular posts in (typically) a reverse chronological order; (iii) posts/comments from readers following the blogger's posts and the resulting asynchronicity of communication; (iv) hyperlinks either to internal pages within the blog, or (v) to external blogs, sites, pages, posts as a form of intertextuality. As stated by Francoli and Ward (2008), these characteristics, on the one hand, mark a certain continuity between the blog and other new media forms (through the hyperlink architecture, interactive features, and user-generated content), and on the other, make the blog distinct from other online genres (its temporality, a specific combination of blogger and guest-generated content resulting from blogger-guest and guest-guest interaction).[9] As regards the first point, in the words of Wallsten (2008, 22), a defining feature of blogs – and something that increases their attractiveness as a political communication tool – is that "they are subject to almost no external editing and, therefore, provide the blogger with complete control over when and what to post". This is in contrast with political discourse production and presentation in its traditional form, entailing pre-scheduling in terms of time and space, and various forms of editorial supervision. With respect to blog's (dis)similarity to traditional news, it has to be emphasized that most political bloggers do not subscribe to journalistic norms of objectivity, making their writings imbued with strong ideological bias (Hennessy and Martin 2006). Secondly, although the style of blog communication has its roots in the journalistic tradition, the significant difference in the style of journalists and the blogger lies in the latter's emotive quality. Hence, in the words of Stoller (2004):

> Big Media does "human interest" stories – but this is mere sensationalism. There remains the essential failure to connect politics to the human, to us; a failure to tell us why and in what ways any of it matters to us. Blogs take up this important slack.
>
> (Stoller 2004, 12)

It has been frequently pointed out that political blogging has blurred the lines between public and private spheres, or, as Gunter (2009, 120) puts it, has become the space where "private becomes public and public becomes personalized". According to Cohen (2006, 164–165), it results from the fact that "blogs sit irregularly between familiar modes of address, never quite addressing a person (dialogue), never quite addressing a crowd (speech, public address), never quite speaking to oneself (diary, monologue, soliloquy)."[10] Consequently to this bridge between the private subjective form of self expression and the civic sphere, as pointed out by Coleman (2005, 277), blogs allow people to express incomplete thoughts in contrast to certainties that dominate political discourse. There is also a certain continuity and overlap between blog posts and audience's comments. The latter, despite expressing different positions in different ways, often involve a return to some of the issues raised by the original post. In this sense, the blogger becomes engaged in a dialogue with the audience mostly on themes he or she has raised. Hence, blogging emerges as a social activity (Nardi et al. 2004) and "collaborative co-creation" (Baumer et al. 2011). Additionally, blogs potentially open the debate for a wide range of participants, and, in contrast to traditional media offer space for greater interactive communication. Accordingly, it may be concluded that while being thematically situated in the official or public domain, blogs weave into political discourse the informal and the personal.[11] In reference to the above features, Lomborg (2009, 6) puts forward a template for blog classification acknowledging three structural-functional dimensions, namely: (i) a content axis: internal-topical (Does the blog deal with personal themes, experiences, and emotions, or with topics of general interest?); (ii) a directional axis: monological-dialogical (Is it primarily used for dissemination of ideas to an audience, or highly conversational and densely networked?); (iii) a style axis: intimate-objective (Is it confessional and personal, or rather objective in tone?). Irrespective of the blog's position on the three axes, it may be stated that functionally, a blogger performs three discursive roles, those of "author-critic-diarist" (Lawson-Borders and Kirk 2005). This observation has been confirmed by Lehti's (2011) study of French politicians' blogs, where several function and form related sub-genres are distinguished, namely: diary, scrapbook, notice-board, essay and polemic.

While Coleman (2005, 276) sees blogs as "vehicles for self-presentation" and "a channel for authentic expression that is free from repressive controls of traditional media", Francoli and Ward (2008) point out that blogs written by politicians serve five different functions: "solving", which consists in introducing substantive problems with the explicit intention of raising and discussing potential solutions; "explaining" policy positions or the actions of the individual or her party; "promoting" points of view, activities, and achievements; "criticizing" an opponent or the opposing party, and, finally, "informing", where the purpose is simply to provide information about an issue or event. Likewise, in his function oriented classification, Wallsten (2008) categorizes blogs as: "soapboxes", "transmission belts", "mobilizers", or "conversation starters". The first type is meant to provide the audience with a record of thoughts, observations, experiences, and opinions of the blogger; in this sense it resembles a political diary or a political confessional. The second group provides links to Web sites or quotes sources with no commentary from the blogger, thereby providing the reader with an efficient way to separate out the interesting political stories and links from the vast number of uninteresting stories. The third group, "mobilizers", is aimed at encouraging readers to take political action, for example voting for a particular candidate or supporting a certain political party. Finally, political blogs can be used as "conversation starters" that try to elicit feedback from readers. In order to encourage such a feedback, bloggers may provide an e-mail address and a comments section, and ask direct questions to their readers in the body of their posts. Importantly, it should be noted that the functions are not mutually exclusive, and political blogs may simultaneously act as soapboxes, mobilizers, and conversation starters (Wallsten 2008).

One possible conclusion that might be drawn from the above overview of political blog classifications is that it is a hybrid and dynamic genre. Whichever of the two subsets we consider – blogs written by active politicians or blogs written by non-politicians – most functional characteristics of the genre can be linked to the process of reducing the "distance", in its various dimensions, between the public and the private, the individual and the mass, the formal and the informal, the layman and the expert. This is both manifested in and enabled by the political blog's structural features, which facilitate interactivity and, as a consequence, contribute to creating cognitive and emotional proximity.

3. The networked public sphere, the mediatization of politics, and proximization

The discussion of the blogosphere as a forum for public discourse or a virtual agora has often been linked to Habermas's notion of the public sphere. As defined by Habermas (1989, xi), the "public sphere" denotes the space "between civil society and the state, in which critical public discussion of matters of general interest was institutionally guaranteed". Originally, it manifested itself in the intellectual discussions and deliberations among members of the aristocracy or the "bourgeois" at the salons and coffee houses in the 17th and 18th century, when it was a "sphere of private people [coming together] as a public" to discuss matters of shared interest and to engage in stimulating debates" (Habermas 1989, 27). Even more importantly, Habermas distinguished between two kinds of actions accompanying the debate in the public sphere, namely strategic action and communicative action. While the former is meant to influence the behavior of the audience by means of the "threat of sanctions or the prospect of gratification in order to cause the interaction to continue as the first actor desires", the latter, perceived by Habermas as "ideal speech situation", is intended to "motivate [rationally] another by relying on the illusionary binding/bonding effect of the offer contained in his speech act" (Habermas 1989, 58). In this context, Dahlgren (2001, 40) argued that "strategic action is goal-oriented and manipulative; communicative action aims for mutual understanding, trust, and shared knowledge".

Bourdieu (1993, 2005), though he does not often name the public sphere as such, relates "social space" and interactions within this space to various "fields", including the political field and the journalistic field. Fields are arenas of struggle for symbolic power in which individuals and organizations compete, unconsciously and consciously, to valorize the forms of capital, both material and symbolic, which they possess. Struggles are enacted in the course of communicative interaction and such interaction is socially constitutive, including positions within and relations between social fields. For politicians it means attempts to establish and preserve coherent discourse, determined both internally, by the position in the field of politics, and externally, by relations with the outside world: citizens, voters, journalists, etc. Blogging provides users – both politicians and journalists – with various forms of cultural capital, enabling them to participate more effectively in the process of public deliberation, which Bourdieu considers crucial for contemporary societies:

> The question is to make the rigorous use of reason, and thus of language, a political virtue, indeed the first of all political virtues, and thus to give intellectuals the sole power that they have a right and a duty to claim, that of exercising a ceaseless and effective vigilance against the abusive words – and grand words most of all.
> (Bourdieu 2008, 219)

Discourse of political blogs can be regarded as both a manifestation and consequence of two processes: constant evolution of fields as dynamic terrains of struggle and change, and their growing interdependence.[12] The "networked public sphere" (Benkler 1998; Friedland, Hove, and Rojas 2006; Pfitser 2011) constitutes an online space where members of society can exchange political opinions and observations, and collaborate as watchdogs over powerful social institutions, all via peer production. It is here that the field of politics interacts and overlaps with other fields, including the field of media and the field of citizens' private lives. Hence, it may be said that it stretches the "public sphere" in its traditional sense, beyond the "geospatial" (territorially bounded) configuration via the "sociospatial" (virtual space online) one (Youngs 2009). The phenomenon responsible for that virtual stretch is that of "mediatization", understood both as the meta process of creating a common spatiotemporal, cognitive and axiological sphere of shared experience in the cyberspace (Krotz 2007, 2009), and as a substitution of the social activities which previously took place face-to-face (Schulz 2004). According to Thompson

(1995), "mediated quasi-interaction", where the co-involvement of large numbers of spatially and temporally dispersed people is coupled with the time-space distantiation of mediated interaction, is a salient feature of modernity.

Both traditional and new media have often been linked to the concept of "mediatizing politics", or, to use Ekström's words (2001, 564), "[politics] mediating between the politicians and the public". Mediated or mediatized politics has "lost its autonomy, has become dependent in its central functions on mass media, and is continuously shaped by interactions with mass media" (Mazzoleni and Schulz 1999, 250; see also Livingstone 2009; Hjarvard 2008; Mazzoleni 2008a, 2008b; Strömback 2008, 2010, 2011). The scale of this process has resulted in numerous discussions concerning the process of mediatization, from both linguistic (cf. Borchers 2005; Chouliaraki and Fairclough 1999; Fairclough 2000) and political/mass communication studies perspectives (Asp 1990; Bennet and Entman 2001; Ekström 2001; Hjarvard 2008; Lilleker 2006; Schulz 2004), as well as a whole body of research in the media-politics interface (cf. Bazzi 2009; Fetzer and Lauerbach 2007; Hodges and Nilep 2007; Okulska and Cap 2010; Triandafyllidou et al. 2009).

Although theorists agree that mediatization is a dynamic process through which media transform society, some relate it to changes associated with the development of communication media, entailing the new demands and expectations politicians as individuals and political institutions have to face (Hajer 2009), while others see it as a process "through which core elements of a social or cultural activity [...] assume media form" (Hjarvard 2004, 48). Trying to systematize different approaches to this meta-process, Strömback (2008, 2010, 2011) and Strömback and Esser (2009) propose a four-dimensional conceptualization of the mediatization of politics, in which the first dimension is related to the increasing importance of the media as a source of information and a channel of communication, the second to the media independence from other social and political institutions, the third is concerned with the degree to which media content is governed by media logic and political logic, and the fourth one, in which political actors are governed by media logic and political logic. Together, these four dimensions form, according to the authors, "a spiral of mediatization" (Asp 1986, 361, cit. in Strömback 2011, 423).

It is also important to acknowledge that mediatization is a special case of mediation. In the words of Agha (2011, 163), "to speak of communicative mediation is to observe that communicative signs formulate a bridge or connection among those they link, mediating social relations through activities of uptake and response at different scales of social history," while "to speak of mediatization is to speak of institutional practices that reflexively link processes of communication to processes of commoditization."

One of the underlying assumptions of this chapter is that mediatization of politics, in either of its two dimensions, would not be possible without the mechanism of "proximization" allowing for the symbolic construal of relations between entities within the Discourse Space (DS) (Chilton 2005) and convergence of the "deictic centers" of the speaker/author and the audience through the process of symbolic discursive shifts (Chilton 2004, 2005, 2010; Cap 2006, 2008, 2010). This methodological construct, regarded by its original proponent as the main tool of legitimization (Cap 2006, 2008), has been so far applied, within a number of different theoretical frameworks, to account for the persuasive potential of both mediated and unmediated political discourse (Hart 2010; Filardo Llamas 2010; Cienki, Kaal, and Maks 2010; Kopytowska 2010).

Both the structural and functional properties of blogs, conditioned by the semiotic environment in which they are produced and read, as well as the power of this genre in negotiating political meanings can be accounted for by the proximization mechanism, understood as reducing spatial, temporal, axiological, cognitive, and emotional distance between the blog writer and the audience. Blogs transcend geographical (spatial) barriers, and their reverse presentation, and fluid and ever-changing content may be seen as one of the manifestations of temporal proximization. The following analysis is meant to demonstrate that both the semiotic profile of the blogosphere, and the conscious discursive strategies of bloggers are manifestations of the proximizing mechanism inherent in the blog genre.

4. Data and methodology

The material analyzed in the study comprises 4 blogs maintained by 2 Polish and 2 British politicians, along with comments following the posts. As already mentioned, this is only a subset of political blogs, including blogs written by the representatives of political establishment. While it is acknowledged here that political blogging in general both reflects and enables the mediatization of politics and employs proximization strategies, this study is primarily interested in how politicians bring their views and party ideology "closer" to their audiences. The blogs in question have been selected for two reasons; firstly, their authors – active politicians and political commentators – represent the opposing poles of the political spectrum, right and left-wing parties; secondly, their blogs rank among top most visited political blogging sites in the two countries. Janusz Korwin-Mikke (www.korwin-mikke.blog.onet.pl) is a Polish conservative politician and the leader of the Congress of the New Right (*Kongres Nowej Prawicy*), formed in 2011 from Freedom and Lawfulness (*Wolność i Praworządność*) and the Real Politics Union (*Unia Polityki Realnej*). He was a Member of Parliament during the first term of the Sejm of the Third Republic of Poland, and ran for president several times. Being known for his sharp tongue and an eccentric way of voicing his political views, he receives a lot of media publicity, and his blog (maintained since 2006) was in 2007 voted the best political blog of the year,[13] and in 2008 chosen as the most popular political blog in Poland (Rogowicz 2008).[14] In addition to his blog, Korwin-Mikke maintains his personal website (www.korwin-mikke.pl). Joanna Senyszyn (www.senyszyn.blog.onet.pl) is a Polish left-wing politician, vice-president of the Democratic Left Alliance (SLD), the former member of the Sejm and the current member of the European Parliament. Her public appearances, due to her biting, provocative, and satirical style, often attract considerable media attention. Her political blog was granted the title of the Blog of the Year 2008 in the Onet.pl contest.[15] Tim Montgomerie (www.conservativehome.blogs.com), the founder and editor of the ConservativeHome website (established in 2005 before the general election campaign), has been described as "one of the most important Conservative activists of the past 20 years" (Finkelstein 2009) and "emerging as a major player in Tory politics" (*Independent* 2006). In the present study his blogs were selected from among other blogs on the ConservativeHome website.[16] Kerry Gillian McCarthy (www.kerrymccarthy.wordpress.com) is a British Labour Party politician who has been the Member of Parliament for Bristol East since 2005. She got into the center of media attention in 2010, when, after revealing election results on Twitter, she was cautioned for electoral fraud (*BBC* 2010). In addition to her blog, she maintains her personal website (www.kerrymccarthymp.org).

The data that was chosen met the following criteria: (a) it has been written by the politician who is active on the Polish or British political scene, preferably a former or current MP, (b) it has been regularly updated, (c) it possesses a commentary section and an archive, and (d) it ranks among top most political blogs in the two countries. Since the four blogs were established at different times, to normalize the data from 8 corpora (with separate corpora created for each blogger's posts and subsequent comments), the material analyzed was limited to blogs posted between 1st January 2010 and 31st July 2011. The statistical data concerning the blogs is presented in Table 1.

The objective of the study was to establish the structural-functional genre profile of political blog. To achieve that, several sub-goals were set, viz. (a) identifying new media "input" vs. traditional communication modes (e.g. in terms of interactivity and non-linearity); (b) identifying "proximization dynamics" at the level of the semiotic characteristics of the medium/channel and the blog discourse itself; (c) describing the transformative potential of the media to blur or reconfigure hitherto fundamental distinctions: public/private, self/other and local/global; (d) identifying the manifestations of mediated society/public sphere.

Table 1. Blogs analyzed: statistical data

Blog	conservativehome. blogs.com	kerrymccarthy. wordpress.com	korwin-mikke. blog.onet.pl	senyszyn.blog. onet.pl
Period (from)	2010-01-02 22:36	2010-01-01 01:18	2010-01-01 14:14	2010-05-11 11:57
Period (to)	2011-07-31 00:00	2011-06-19 14:49	2011-07-31 23:47	2011-07-19 11:52
Posts per day	1.22	0.64	2.57	0.31
Posts (total)	735	397	1554	147
Comments (total)	46644	685	81182	22093
Comments per post	63.46	1.73	52.24	150.29
Standard deviation (comments)	33.62	4.91	65.10	94.20
Coefficient of variation (comments)	52.98%	284.70%	124.61%	62.67%
Commenters	22995	276	20324	6489
Commenters per post	31.29	0.70	13.08	44.14
Standard deviation (commenters)	29.61	2.60	32.63	47.36
Coefficient of variation (commenters)	94.64%	373.90%	249.50%	107.29%
Replies	28347	117	39229	13455
Replies per comment	0.61	0.17	0.48	0.61
Comments per author	2.03	2.48	3.99	3.40
Words (posts)	258087	119474	208177	39028
Words per post	351.14	300.94	133.96	265.50
Words (comments)	217.82	232.27	234.79	214.60
Words per comment	62.03	77.18	175.27	80.83
Standard deviation (posts)	3036984	47682	3070842	944566
Coefficient of variation (posts)	65.11%	69.61%	37.83%	42.75%
Standard deviation (comments)	71.80	85.85	147.02	127.64
Coefficient of variation (comments)	110.28%	123.32%	388.67%	298.54%

The analysis, conducted from a pragma-cognitive perspective, and relying on the insights from semiotics, mass communication studies and political science, combined quantitative and qualitative methods. The underlying methodological assumption here was that corpus linguistics tools along with other statistical data exploration methods, when used in combination with qualitative approaches, can become a valuable tool for blog discourse analysis, as they allow for the quantification of recurring linguistic features necessary to substantiate qualitative insights and for reliable generalizations concerning the effects of various linguistic choices (Stubbs 1997, 107, 111; O'Keeffe 2006, 51; see also Kopytowska 2009).

Custom web crawlers were developed to parse the respective websites and extract the text of posts and comments along with meta-data. Subsequently, the data were uploaded to a relational database, which allowed for the representation of the nested structure of the comments and for quantitative analyses. Additional software was developed to export the data for further processing, including three procedures: (1) concordance and keyword analysis with WordSmith tools; (2) latent semantic analysis and cluster analysis with the software Semantic Vectors (Widdows and Ferraro 2008); and (3) the analysis of the interconnectedness and interactivity patterns among the blog author and users with the open source Gephi package. The Yifan Hu layout algorithm (Hu 2005; Bastian et al. 2009) was employed to create the visualizations of the large networks of interrelated comments.

Given that political texts render a particular meaning system through the key words they employ, one of the steps in the process of identifying and describing proximization techniques was to examine such words and their semantic import. Keyword analysis served as a starting point for the discussion of the motivation behind and the possible implications of using various lexical items as proximization triggers. WordSmith Tools 5.00 was used to generate wordlists on the basis of the text files in all corpora. The lists were then used as an input to the KeyWord program, which compares frequencies with a reference corpus (British National Corpus/National Corpus of Polish) to produce lists of keywords manifesting a measure of saliency, i.e. the importance of the word in the corpus.

The analysis of "proximization dynamics" included both the semiotic properties of the medium/channel and the discursive patterns within text itself. Drawing on the insights from Chilton's (2004, 2005) and Cap's (2006, 2008, 2010, 2013) theoretical models, a new analytical framework was developed specifically for the new media discourse (see also Kopytowska 2009, 2010). Proximization dynamics for blogs are presented in Figure 1. For the analysis of semiotic and discursive variables in the proximization process, Ungerer's (1997) model of emotional inferencing was also adapted. The model, originally designed for news discourse, includes the following principles of proximization: (a) principle of proximity/us vs. them principle relying on deictic terms, kinship terms, direct speech, rhetorical questions; (b) homocentric principle, relying on personalization, personification, reference to the negative frames; (c) principle of emotional evaluation,

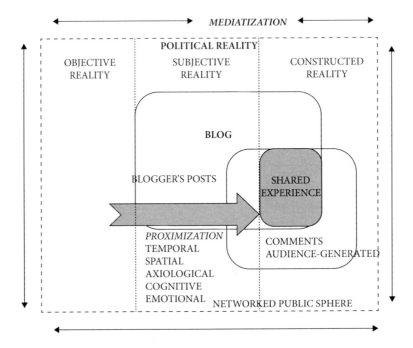

Figure 1. Proximization dynamics for blog discourse

relying on evaluative adjectives, loaded lexical items, comparison and contrast; (d) principle of intensity of presentation employing vivid details and intensifying metaphors, metonymy, contrast. In the analysis it is used simultaneously with Lomborg's (2009) template for blog classification (see Section 2 above).

5. Analysis

The semiotic properties of the Internet medium, within which the blogosphere is situated, make it an ideal proximizing environment, both from the perspective of the blogger and the readers of his/her texts. Hypertextuality, manifested mostly in interactivity and non-linearity, plays a key role as regards spatial and temporal proximization. All the blog sites analyzed present the user-reader with an opportunity to (a) select from among the links offered (for example from the blogroll, a list of other blogs the authors recommend or follow themselves), and (b) produce content in the form of comments. In the former case, they can be, at any time, shifted automatically to another discourse space, while in the latter they can incorporate their discourse spaces into the text of the blog. This spatial and temporal proximization is correlated with the axiological one, as the hyperlinks "transport" the reader to other discourse spaces within the blogosphere, which are related in terms of values, opinions and beliefs. Senyszyn's blog is a good example here. The author is known for her anti-religious atheistic stance, and her openly demonstrated prejudice against Church representatives is reflected in such post titles as: "Przepraszam za Kościół" ["I apologize for the Church"], or "Zakon ojców pedofilów" ["The order of pedophile friars"]. On the blog site we will find hyperlinks to *Fakty i Mity*, a Polish anticlerical daily, and to www.boskiateista.pl, which is a blog written from an atheistic perspective. Likewise, Korwin-Mikke's website abounds in hyperlinks to websites with conservative and monarchist ideology, including those maintained by political parties and other organizations, and individuals' blogs. McCarthy's blogroll includes only her own personal website, in contrast to Montgomerie's blog site, and the blog itself which is highly hyperlinked within the author's posts.

The strongest manifestation of interactivity, and thus spatial, temporal, and axiological proximization, lies in the possibility offered to the reader to add comments after each post. The statistical data breakdown (Table 1) shows high interactivity for three of the blogs analyzed, manifested in the number of comments. The interactivity patterns for all blogs, both in the case of individual posts and the whole corpus, are visualized in the following graphs (Figures 2–9). The higher the density of interconnections, the more interactive a particular blog (for analysis of interactivity in Polish political blogs see Lewandowska-Tomaszczyk 2011; Lewandowska-Tomaszczyk and Zeller 2012). Some structures (in this study Senyszyn's and Korwin Mikke's) are characterized by significant concentration in foci other than the center (author), which signifies the existence of influential commenters whose (often provocative) remarks serve as stimuli for further discussion. This can be seen more clearly in the graphs representing an individual post with the structures branching out and generating connections other than those stemming directly from the blog author (e.g. Figure 3, where we can see an influential commenter of Korwin-Mikke, generating a network of connections). The highest degree of interactivity can be observed in Senyszyn's blog, both in terms of the number of comments and the number of replies (defined as comments on comments). The latter is correlated with another semiotic property of blogs, namely non-linearity; the blog posts and the associated comments at a given point of time do not form a chronological narration, but rather a branching structure of comments and replies.

Interestingly, the number of comments and replies seems to be more dependent on the style of the blogger than on the number of posts (Montgomerie with 735 comments vs. Senyszyn with 147), which highlights the potential of axiological, cognitive, and emotional proximization techniques applied by bloggers. The visualization of McCarthy's blog interactivity (Figure 8 and Figure 9) shows the dialogic blogger-commenter nature of interaction in contrast to Senyszyn's blog

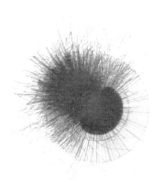

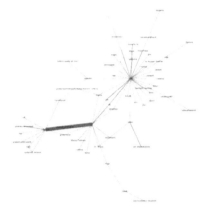

Figure 2. Korwin-Mikke's blog-interactivity pattern

Figure 3. Korwin-Mikke's post-interactivity pattern

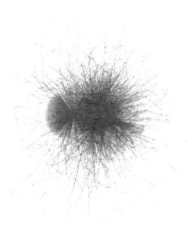

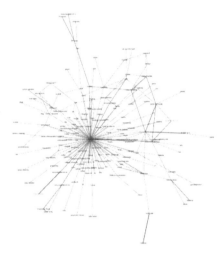

Figure 4. Senyszyn's blog-interactivity pattern

Figure 5. Senyszyn's post-interactivity pattern

where commenters are involved in discussion with one another. It is worth noticing that McCarthy replies to the comments (out of 117 replies to comments, 59 are McCarthy's), while Senyszyn does not get engaged in the dialogic interaction with her commenters.

Another interesting statistical observation is that the number of words per post and per comment is higher in the British blogs than in the Polish ones, and that greater differences in length can be observed in the Polish comments. As demonstrated by further qualitative analysis, this, at least in the case of

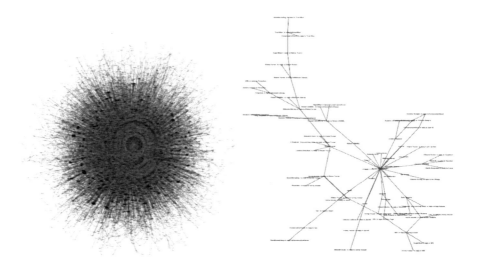

Figure 6. Montgomerie's blog-interactivity pattern

Figure 7. Montgomerie's post-interactivity pattern

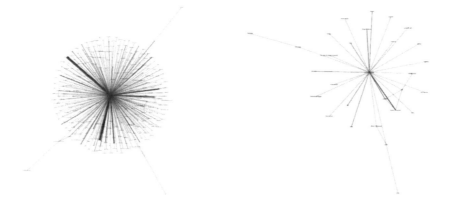

Figure 8. McCarthy's blog-interactivity pattern

Figure 9. McCarthy's post-interactivity pattern

comments, translates into greater facticity and topic- rather than author-orientation of the British commenters' posts.

Several interesting regularities can be observed as regards other semiotic characteristics of the blog sites. In terms of colors used they conform to the traditionally established color preferences in politics, with blue being associated with Conservative parties and red with Social Democrats and Labour. Hence, the colors act as cognitive proximization trigger, evoking the familiar frames of representation. Polish politicians' blogs demonstrate greater degree of personalization

Figure 10. Korwin-Mikke's blog site

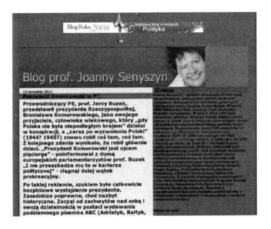

Figure 11. Senyszyn's blog site

and informality, which gives them a less professional and official character. They feature authors' photographs and bios, and, in the case of Korwin-Mikke's posts, a special color notation system, e.g. different colors for parties' names. The photo of Senyszyn, which is a facial close-up with a direct gaze performs the emotionally proximizing function. There is something more to the red color predominant on her site than just political party associations. It attracts attention as the most salient color for human beings (Miller 1997) whose connotations include: aggression, intensity, and power, and correspond perfectly with the author's aggressive style.

As regards discursive similarities of proximization in the four blogs, several regularities can be observed on the basis of keyness values and concordance patterns. Firstly, among 500 keywords identified for each corpus, a considerable

Figure 12. Montgomerie's blog site

Figure 13. McCarthy's blog site

number of lexical items (or at least concepts) was shared by a given blog corpus and the accompanying comments corpus, which might be an indication of the fact that the blogger successfully proximizes selective aspects of subjective political reality, to the extent that they are shared in constructed political reality within common discourse space. The us vs. them principle of proximity can be noticed in all the corpora analyzed, with the world divided along the conservative/liberal, right/left wing ideologies. An interesting difference between Polish and British politicians, however, is that while the former tend to create positive self-images and a group-shared system of values through vilifying and denigrating political opponents, the latter proximize *generally* shared values and objectives without necessarily resorting to mudslinging and personal attacks.

Both Korwin-Mikke and Senyszyn tend to use emotionally loaded words (principle of emotional evaluation and intensity of presentation) while referring to individuals or parties from the opposing side of the political spectrum. Among Korwin-Mikke's keywords we will find "**kracja" standing for "dupokracja" ["democr-ass-y"], "zwyrodnialcy" ["degenerates"], "bandy" ["gangs"], "lewacy" ["lefties"], as well as dehumanizing metaphors like "bydlaki" ["swine"], and "chwasty" ["weeds"]. Some of these reappear in the comments corpus, though the commenters seem to be even more hostile in their comments, using such terms as "ubecy" [a pejorative term for a secret police agent], "przychlasty" ["half-wits"], "idioci" ["idiots"], and such metaphor-evoking expressions as "plankton" ["plankton"], "kanalie" ["scoundrels"], etc. In a similar way, Senyszyn uses derogatory terms to refer to Church representatives: "klechy" ["Holy Joes"], "pedofile" ["pedophiles"], or otherwise neutral terms with contextually determined negative slant, e.g. "kler" ["clergy"]. And so do her blog commenters: "pedały"/ "pedalstwo" ["fags"], "dupcyngier" ["shag around"], "debil" ["moron"], "kaczy-chuj" ["duckprick"], "katomatoł" ["catho-moron"]. If we look at concordances with "kler" ["clergy"] in Senyszyn's posts, the following examples can be found: "przemoc stosowana przez kler" ["violence exercised by the clergy"], "na polski kler nie ma mocnych" ["nothing can be done about Polish clergy"], "utwierdza kler w bezkarności" ["consolidates the impunity of the clergy"], "pazerność kleru" ["greed of the clergy"], "stopnia klerykalizacji" ["the degree of clerical influence"], "pazernego, spasionego kleru" ["greedy, obese clergy"]. It is then not only through forms of reference, but also through pre/post-modification and semantic roles/ transitivity patterns that the clergy is presented as a threat to Polish society. This axiological and emotional proximization apparently has its effect on the commenters' discourse and its construction of the image of the clergy. Concordances from the comments include: "po co klerowi dobra ziemskie?" [why would the clergy need earthly goods?"], "przestępstw seksualnych kleru" ["sexual offences of the clergy"], "klerykalna Polska" ["clerical Poland"], "masowa pedofilia kleru katolickiego w Polsce" ["mass pedophilia of the Catholic clergy in Poland"], "kler ujarzmił rząd" ["the clergy have enslaved the government"], etc. Likewise, when we look at the results of Latent Semantic Analysis, which shows terms appearing in similar contexts as the query word, in the posts we will find such terms as: "wyrok" ["verdict"], "odrzucenie" ["rejection"], "państwo" ["state"], "obłudnie" ["hypocritically"], "seksualnie" ["sexually"], "problem" ["problem"], "klerykalny" ["clerical"], and "Kościół" ["Church"], while in the comments these will be: "demoralizuje" ["demoralizes"], "gadatliwe" ["talkative"], "kombinuje" ["is up to"], "szkodą" ["harm"], and "księdzu" ["priest"]. It can thus be observed that the "clergy" is often semantically linked with concepts like sex, money, law and the state. Similar observations can be made for the word "klecha" in both corpora.

Although both politicians discuss topics of general interest, political and so-cial actors and events, their perspective is highly biased and subjective, which is manifested primarily in the lexical dimension of the text (patterns of reference and predication), and which is, for the most part, echoed in the comments follow-ing the posts. Axiological and emotional proximization, responsible for creating the discursive space of shared experience is thus predominantly achieved through the reference to the negative, and an evil-Other image construction. This very distinctive and aggressive style of both politicians might lead us to the conclu-sion that the main objectives behind, and thus functions of their blog discourse are self-presentation and political polemics. Korwin-Mikke frequently makes his presence in the discursive space visible by the use of first person pronouns and verb forms, e.g. "przypominam" ["(I) remind"], "proszę" ["(I) demand"]. He also uses first person plural imperative forms, e.g. "pokażmy" ["let's show"], "zrób-my" ["let's do"], "przemyślmy" ["let's reflect on"], thereby creating the sense of unity with his audience and merging his deictic center with that of his readers. He frequently uses the word "uwaga" ["attention"], when he wants to make an an-nouncement and motivate his audience to act.

In contrast to the Polish blogs, the British ones create a space of shared expe-rience through axiological and cognitive proximization of *generally* shared val-ues and viewpoints, which emerges from the keywords, concordances, and their resulting frames. Keywords (see Appendix) in the four corpora manifest greater salience (as compared to the Polish texts) of concepts related to the democratic processes (e.g. "election", "campaign", "polls", "voters", "debate", "referendum"), in-ternational and national policy (e.g. "coalition", "tax", "budget", "reform", "deficit", "Obama", "Afghanistan"), and social issues (e.g. "immigration", "NHS"). Interest-ingly, the posts and the accompanying comments share almost all the keywords, which might be an indication of the fact that political, economic, and social issues are framed in a similar way, or, which is even more probable, that politicians' frames shift from their subjective political reality to the constructed reality, and then perhaps to the subjective reality of the audience. What can be stated with a high degree of certainty is that the elements prominent in politicians' picture (to use Lippmann's [1922, 29] claim about creating "pictures" in people's minds) become prominent in the audience's picture. Given that readers not only acquire factual information about public affairs, but also learn how much importance to attach to a topic on the basis of the emphasis placed on it in the blogs, the blog discourse (as is the case with other new media-dependent political genres) can influence what issues people pay attention to, and determine the audience's judgments about political and social problems and their remedies. In the words of Berelson (1949, 117), "some kinds of issues, brought to the attention of some kinds of people, under some kinds of conditions, have some kinds of effects."[17] As pointed out by Lakoff (2004), negating the frame still evokes the frame, bringing up (in audience's minds) certain images and feelings. The concept of immigration may be a good example here. In the Conservative blog discourse it is framed mostly as a threat, which is manifested in concordances both in the posts and comments, e.g.: "tough immigration policy", "immigration cut", "avoid immigration", "controlled immigration". In contrast to this, in McCarthy's blog posts and comments, immigration is framed more as a problem that needs to be solved, e.g.: "funding for immigration", "immigration cases", "areas of high immigration", "immigration is something that crops up", "immigration issue". Interestingly, if we look at semantic vectors, demonstrating the issues discussed in the same context as "immigration", for Conservatives we will find "nightmare", "gangleaders", "minuses", "antidotes", "apocalyptic", while for Labour "free", "European", "pollution", "power", and "conflict", which might be yet another indication that in the former case immigration is cognitively and axiologically proximized as a threat, and in the latter as a problem to be confronted like other salient problems, for example pollution.

Looking up concordances with "Labour" in the Conservative blog, we will find that the most critical comments directed at Labour are: "Labour 'hypocrisy'", "Labour is actually the nasty party",[18] and few derogatory forms are used. This applies also to the corpus with comments. Conversely, the most critical statements about the Conservatives in McCarthy's blog will be: "So why are the Conservatives so obsessed with structures rather than outcomes?", and, in the corpus with comments: "The support for the Conservatives doesn't seem to be as strong as was suggested." No instances of mudslinging can be found as regards political opponents. A conclusion may be drawn here, that the axiological proximization within British political blogs is correlated more with cognitive proximization, consisting in operating within the same frame schemata (which is manifested by keywords), than with the emotional one (which is the case with Polish blogs).

A higher degree of homogeneity observed in the British blog discourse, both in terms of topics covered and posts-comments interface might be an interesting indication as to their functional profile and its discursive manifestation. Referring back to Lomborg's (2009) classification we might thus say that they are more topical and more objective. What also deserves attention is their dialogical character, whose forms are, however, different for the two blog corpora. Both Montgomerie and McCarthy (in contrast to Polish politicians) reply to their commenters' remarks, engaging at times in longer exchanges of opinions. Yet, the former's posts and comments generate more user – user interactions, manifested in a more complex network of interconnections (Figures 6, 7), while in the case of the latter communication is, for the most part, bi-directional (Figures 8, 9).

6. Conclusion

The blog, as a new emerging genre in political communication, seems to be an answer to, on the one hand, demands of a new networked public sphere, and, on the other, the potential offered by the new media environment. Its success, and at the same time, generic profile, as the analysis has shown, consists firstly, in the blogger's ability to remove traditional boundaries between the public and the private, the official and the informal, the mediated and the unmediated, and secondly, in proximizing (and thus shifting) various elements from the subjective political reality to the discursive space of shared experience (constructed political reality), where the blogger makes the audience involved in political deliberation. Various dimensions of proximization may be at work here. Spatial and temporal proximization are to a large extent conditioned on the semiotic properties of the Internet medium, and linked to both non-linearity and hypertextuality of the blog text. Axiological proximization, entailing bringing into common discursive space shared values, viewpoints and worldviews, can be correlated with the emotional one, as strong feelings of identification are often evoked by means of a provocative and aggressive style, vilifying and denigrating political opponents. It can also be linked to cognitive proximization, which is operating within the same conceptual frames.

The border between blogs serving as a tool for self-presentation and a vehicle for polemics appears to be fluid, with the result that blogs often serve the two functions. Self-presentation frequently entails a more distinctive and provocative style, and results in greater diversification of the audience's interactivity and more user – user replies. It is this interactivity that makes blogs distinct from the so-called traditional political genres, allowing both the author and the audience to fully exploit the "proximization dynamics".

Blogs as a genre tell us a lot about the nature of public deliberation, and thus about the mediated public sphere and mediatized society. Differences between Polish and British blogs demonstrate that such deliberation may vary along Lomborg's (2009) variables, with various degrees of personalization and bias. Blogging practices may thus range from simple denigration of political opponents or opposing world views (Polish blogs) to a highly structured dialogic interaction. This is probably the reason why political blogs, along with other new media genres have both their advocates and critics in the debate over "the promise of e-democracy" (Street 2011, 268). In the view of the former, new media facilitate political participation and popular deliberation. For the latter, the kind of democracy they offer is "a debased, impoverished version" (Street 2011, 272). Whichever of the two opinions one embraces, one has to acknowledge the fact that "[p]olitical ideas cannot be separated from the medium in which they are thought" as "[t]echnical change brings with it new ideas and possibilities, and new notions of democracy" (Street 2011, 282).

Notes

1. I would like to thank Ruth Wodak, Greg Myers and John Heywood for their comments on earlier versions of this chapter. Special thanks to Łukasz Dróżdż for assistance with statistical analyses.

2. The term "MediaSpace" is "a dialectical concept, encompassing both the kinds of spaces created by media, and the effects that existing spatial arrangements have on media forms as they materialize in everyday life" (Couldry and McCarthy 2004, 2).

3. The phenomenon of blurring the boundaries between producers and consumers of texts has been referred to as "prosumption", which Ritzer and Jurgenson (2010) consider a salient characteristic of Web 2.0. with its user generated context.

4. Street (2011, 262–265) discusses five ways in which new media transform the political landscape; firstly, they influence the operation of the government, in particular the way in which it circulates information, delivers services and implements policy; secondly, they impact on campaigning and the conduct of elections; thirdly, they change the dynamics of political and social movements, enabling new forms of political activism; fourthly, they transform the interface of politics and journalism, through blogosphere and user-generated content; finally, they enable the state to exercise greater control over citizens in an Orwellian "Big Brother"-like manner;

5. As a political communication tool, blogging considerably grew in prominence with Howard Dean's campaign for the Democratic presidential nomination in 2004 (Meraz 2007, cit. in Sullivan and Cheon 2011, 10–20).

6. In the United States blogging has been regarded as a form of "citizen journalism" (Wright 2009). As pointed out by Carlson (2007, 275, cit. in Street 2011, 208) it has exerted an impact on both the understanding and practice of traditional journalism: "Journalists are now faced with a competing form of political discourse, but one that challenges journalism's formative foundations. It is more than a competition for eyeballs; it is a different way of producing and consuming political communication."

7. For a discussion on the role of blogging in e-democracy see Street (2011, 261–282).

8. Due to structural and functional differences various typologies of blogs have been suggested; for example Herring et al. (2004) list "filter blogs", "diary blogs", "k-logs" (highly specialized knowledge logs), "mixed purpose blogs" and others. For detailed typologies see Miller and Shepherd (2004) and Lomborg (2009).

9. Herring et al. (2005) locate blogs in the middle of a continuum between HTML documents (with highly asymmetrical reader/writer relations) and asynchronous CMC (with symmetric relations). See also Karlsson (2006) who points to greater immediacy and interactivity of blogs when compared to web pages.

10. According to Dean (2010, 46) a blog, which differs from both mass communication and one-to-one or one-to-list communication, "enables the production of content potentially accessible to anyone who happens to find it".

11. The UK Tory leader David Cameron's domestic scenes in his video blog can be given as an example here (Youngs 2009).

12. Bourdieu (1998a, 76) points to this interdependence when he says that "in a certain way, the journalistic field is part of the political field on which it has such a powerful impact."

13. The "Blog of the Year" contest has been organized by Onet.pl, Poland's no.1 web portal, since 2005. Voting is done by both the Internet users and members of a committee elected each year, consisting of representatives of media and cultural institutions. As demonstrated by the study conducted by Webb et al. (2012), what influences users' choices and thus blog popularity is not only political ideology, but also blog complexity, interactivity, user-friendliness, and navigability.

14. The blog's popularity was measured by the number of visitors: 20 million hits during the period of two years.

15. See Note 13.

16. For an overview of the British political blogging scene see Dale (2009).

17. While some researchers believe that frames are to be found in media coverage/public discourse (Entman 1991, 2003, 2004; Pan and Kosicki 1993; Schaefer 2003), others claim they are in the recipient's mind (Scheufele 2004), or both in the sender and recipient (Scheufele 1999). Entman (1993, 52) argues that "frames have at least four locations in the communication process: the communicator, the text, the receiver and the culture."

18. The term "nasty party" was first used by the Tory chairwoman, Theresa May in October 2002, when she commented on the Conservative Party of the United Kingdom in the following way: "There's a lot we need to do in this party of ours. Our base is too narrow and so, occasionally, are our sympathies. You know what some people call us – the Nasty Party" (Hasan 2010).

References

Agha, Asif. 2011. "Meet Mediatization." *Language & Communication* 31: 163–170.

Asp, Kent. 1990. "Medialization, Media Logic and Mediarchy." *The Nordicom Review of Mass Communication Research* 2: 47–50.

Bastian, Mathieu, Sebastien Heymann, and Mathieu Jacomy. 2009. "Gephi: An Open Source Software for Exploring and Manipulating Networks." In *Proceedings of International AAAI Conference on Weblogs and Social Media*, ed. by Eytan Adar et al., 12–23. San Jose: AAAI Press.

Baumer, Eric, Mark Sueyoshi, and Bill Tomlinson. 2011. "Bloggers and Readers Blogging Together: Collaborative Co-Creation of Political Blogs." *Computer Supported Cooperative Work* 20: 1–36.

Bazzi, Samia. 2009. *Arab News and Conflict*. Amsterdam: Benjamins.

Benkler, Yochai. 1998. "Over-Coming Agoraphobia: Building the Commons of the Digitally Networked Environment". *Harvard Journal of Law and Technology* 11: 287.

Bennett, Lance, and Robert Entman. 2001. *Mediated Politics: Communication in the Future of Democracy*. Cambridge: Cambridge University Press.

Berelson, Bernard. 1949. "What 'Missing the Newspaper' Means." In *Communications Research 1948-1949*, ed. by Paul F. Lazarsfeld and Frank N. Stanton, 111–128. New York: Harper & Brothers.

Blood, Rebecca. 2002. "Weblogs: A History and Perspective." In *We've Got Blog: How Weblogs Are Changing Our Culture*, ed. by John Rodzvilla, 33–50. Cambridge, MA: Perseus.

Borchers, Timothy A. 2005. *Persuasion in the Media Age*. Boston: McGraw-Hill.

Bourdieu, Pierre. 1993. *The Field of Cultural Production*. Cambridge: Polity.

—. 1998. *On Television*. New York: New Press.

—. 2005. "The Political Field, the Social Science Field, and the Journalistic Field." In *Bourdieu and the Journalistic Field*, ed. by Rodney Benson, and Erik Neveu, 29–47. Cambridge, England: Polity.

—. 2008. *Political Interventions: Social Science and Political Action*. London: Verso.

Boyd, Danah. 2006. "A Blogger's Blog: Exploring the Definition of a Medium." Retrieved May 21, 2011 from http://www.danah.org/papers/ABloggersBlog.pdf

Bruns, Axel. 2008. "Life Beyond the Public Sphere: Towards the Networked Model for Political Deliberation." *Information Polity* 13.1–2: 71–85.

Campbell, Vincent. 2009. "Blogs in American Politics: From Lott to Lieberman." *Aslib Proceedings: New Information Perspectives* 61: 139–154.

Cap, Piotr. 2006. *Legitimisation in Political Discourse: A Cross-Disciplinary Perspective on the Modern US War Rhetoric*. Newcastle: Cambridge Scholars Press.

—. 2008. "Towards the Proximization Model of the Analysis of Legitimization in Political Discourse." *Journal of Pragmatics* 40: 17–41.

—. 2010. "Axiological Aspects of Proximization." *Journal of Pragmatics* 42: 392–407.

—. 2013. *Proximization: The Pragmatics of Symbolic Distance Crossing*. Amsterdam: Benjamins.

Cappella, Joseph B., and Kathleen Hall Jamieson. 1997. *Spiral of Cynicism: The Press and the Public Good*. New York: Oxford University Press.

Carlson, Matt. 2007. "Blogs and Journalistic Authority: The Role of Blogs in US Election Day 2004 Coverage." *Journalism Studies* 8.2: 264–279.

Castells, Manuel. 1997. *The Power of Identity*. Oxford: Blackwell.

—. 2007. "Communication, Power and Counter-Power in the Network Society." *International Journal of Communication* 1: 238–266.

Chadwick, Andrew. 2006. *Internet Politics: States, Citizens and New Communication Technologies*. Oxford: Oxford University Press.

Chilton, Paul. 2004. *Analysing Political Discourse: Theory and Practice*. London: Routledge.

—. 2005. "Discourse Space Theory: Geometry, Brain and Shifting Viewpoints." *Annual Review of Cognitive Linguistics* 3: 78–116.

—. 2010. "From Mind to Grammar: Coordinate Systems, Prepositions, Constructions." In *Language, Cognition and Space: The State of the Art and New Directions*, ed. by Vyvyan Evans, and Paul Chilton, 499–514. London: Equinox.

Chouliaraki, Lilie, and Norman Fairclough. 1999. *Discourse in Late Modernity: Rethinking Critical Discourse Analysis*. Edinburgh: Edinburgh University Press.

Chovanec, Jan. 2010. "Legitimation through Differentiation: Discursive Construction of Jacques *Le Worm* Chirac as an Opponent to Military Action." In *Perspectives in Politics and Discourse*, ed. by Urszula Okulska, and Piotr Cap, 61–82. Amsterdam: Benjamins.

Cienki, Alan et al. 2010. Mapping World View in Political Texts Using Discourse Space Theory: Metaphor as an Analytical Tool. Paper presented at RaAM 8 conference, Vrije Universiteit Amsterdam.

Cohen, Kris. 2006. "A Welcome for Blogs." *Continuum* 20: 161–173.

Coleman, Stephen. 2005. "Blogs and the New Politics of Listening." *The Political Quarterly* 76: 272–280.

Coleman, Stephen, and Jay Blumler. 2009. *The Internet and Democratic Citizenship: Theory, Practice and Policy*. Cambridge: Cambridge University Press.

Coleman, Stephen, and Scott Wright. 2008. "Political Blogs and Representative Democracy." *Information Polity* 13: 1–5.

Cottle, Simon. 2006. *Mediatized Conflict*. Berkshire: Open University Press.

Couldry, Nick, and Anna McCarthy. (eds). 2004. *MediaSpace: Place, Scale and Culture in a Media Age*. London: Routledge.

Dahlgren, Peter. 2001. "The Transformation of Democracy?" In *New Media and Politics*, ed. by Barrie Axford, and Richard Huggins, 64–89. London: Sage.

Dale, Iain. (ed.). 2010. *Guide to Political Blogging in the UK 2009/2010*. London: Biteback Publishing.

Davies, Richard. 1999. *The Web of Politics: The Internet's Impact on the American Political System*. New York, NY: Oxford University Press.

Dean, Jodi. 2010. *Blog Theory: Feedback and Capture in the Circuits of Drive*. Cambridge: Polity Press.

Downey, John, and Scott Davidson. 2007. "The Internet and the UK General Election." In *Political Communications: The General Election Campaign of 2005*, ed. by Dominic Wring, Jane Green, Roger Mortimore, and Simon Atkinson, 93–107. Basingstoke: Palgrave.

Ekström, Mats. 2001. "Politicians Interviewed on Television News." *Discourse and Society* 12: 563–584.

El-Nawawy, Mohammed, and Sahar Khamis. 2011. "Political Blogging and (Re)envisioning the Virtual Public Sphere: Muslim-Christian Discourses in two Egyptian Blogs." *International Journal of Press/Politics* 16: 234–253.

Entman, Robert. 1991. "Framing U.S. Coverage of International News: Contrasts in Narratives of KAL and Iran Air Incidents." *Journal of Communication* 41: 6–27.

—. 1993. "Framing: Toward Clarification of a Fractured Paradigm." *Journal of Communication* 43: 51–58.

—. 2003. "Cascading Activation: Contesting the White House's Frame after 9/11." *Political Communication* 20: 415–432.

—. 2004. *Projections of Power: Framing News, Public Opinion, and U.S. Foreign Policy*. Chicago, IL: University of Chicago Press.

Etling, Bruce, John Kelly, Robert Faris, and John Palfrey. 2010. "Mapping the Arabic Blogosphere: Politics and Dissent Online." *New Media & Society* 12: 1225–1243.

Fairclough, Norman. 2000. *New Labour, New Language?* London: Routledge.

Fetzer, Anita, and Gerda Lauerbach. (eds). 2007. *Political Discourse in the Media*. Amsterdam: Benjamins.

Filardo Llamas, Laura. 2010. "Discourse Worlds in Northern Ireland: The Legitimisation of the 1998 Agreement". In *Political Discourse and Conflict Resolution. Debating Peace in Northern Ireland*, ed. by Katy Hayward, and Catherine O'Donnell, 62–76. London: Routledge.

Finkelstein, Daniel. 2009. "The Coup behind the Tories' Clap for Poverty." Retrieved May 15, 2001 from http://www.timesonline.co.uk/tol/comment/columnists/daniel_finkelstein/article6873422.ece

Francoli, Mary, and Stephen Ward. 2008. "21st Century Soapboxes? MPs and Their Blogs." *Information Polity* 13: 21–39.

Friedland, Lewis A., Thomas Hove, and Hernando Rojas. 2006. "The Networked Public Sphere." *Javnost – The Public* 13. 4: 5–26.

Giltrow, Janet, and Dieter Stein. (eds). 2009. *Genres in the Internet: Issues in the Theory of Genre*. Amsterdam: Benjamins.

Gunter, Barrie. 2009. "Blogging – Private Becomes Public and Public Becomes Personalized." *Aslib Proceedings: New Information Perspectives* 61: 120–126.

Habermas, Jürgen. 1989. *The Structural Transformation of the Public Sphere: An Inquiry into a Category of Bourgeois Society*. Cambridge: MIT Press.

—. 2006. "Political Communication in Media Society: Does Democracy Still Enjoy an Epistemic Dimension? The Impact of Normative Theory on Empirical Research." *Communication Theory* 16: 411–420.

Hajer, Maarten. 2009. *Authoritative Governance. Policy-Making in the Age of Mediatization*. New York, NY: Oxford University Press.

Hart, Christopher. 2010. *Critical Discourse Analysis and Cognitive Science: New Perspectives on Immigration Discourse*. Basingstoke: Palgrave.

Hasan, Mehdi. 2010. "The Tories Are Still the Nasty Party." Retrieved December 15, 2012 from http://www.newstatesman.com/uk-politics/2010/06/david-cameron-party-budget

Hennessy, Cari Lynn, and Paul S. Martin. 2006. "Blogs, the Mainstream Media, and the War in Iraq." Retrieved June 30, 2011 from http://www.journalism.wisc.edu/~dshah/blog-club/Site/Hennessy.pdf

Herring, Susan, Lois Scheidt, Sabrina Bonus, and Elijah Wright. 2004. "Bridging the Gap: A Genre Analysis of Weblogs." Retrieved July 31, 2011 from http://csdl.computer.org/comp/proceedings/hicss/2004/2056/04/205640101b.pdf

Herring, Susan, Lois Scheidt, Elijah Wright, and Sabrina Bonus. 2005. "Weblogs as a Bridging Genre." *Information Technology & People* 18.2: 142–171.

Hewitt, Hugh. 2005. *Blog: Understanding the Information Reformation That's Changing Our World*. Nashville: Nelson.

Hjarvard, Stig. 2008. "The Mediatization of Society. A Theory of the Media as Agents of Social and Cultural Change." *Nordicom Review* 29: 105–134.

Hodges, Adam, and Chad Nilep. (eds). 2007. *Discourse, War and Terrorism*. Amsterdam: Benjamins.

Hopkins, Kane, and Donald Matheson. 2005. "Blogging the New Zealand Election: The Impact of New Media Practices on the Old Game." *Political Science* 57: 93–105.

Hu, Yifan. 2005. "Efficient and High Quality Force-Directed Graph Drawing." *The Mathematica Journal* 10: 37–71.

Janack, James A. 2006. "Mediated Citizenship and Digital Discipline: A Rhetoric of Control in a Campaign Blog." *Social Semiotics* 16: 283–301.

Kaid, Lynda Lee, Jacques Gerstlé, and Keith R. Sanders. (eds). 1991. *Mediated Politics in Two Cultures: Presidential Campaigning in the United States and France*. New York: Praeger.

Karlsson, Lena. 2006. "Acts of Reading Diary Weblogs." *Human IT* 8.2: 1–59.

Kerbel, Matthew R., and Bloom, Joel. 2005. "Blog for America and Civic Involvement." *International Journal of Press/Politics* 10: 3–27.

Keren, Michael. 2004. "Blogging and the Politics of Melancholy." *Canadian Journal of Communication* 29: 5–23.

—. 2006. *Blogosphere: The New Political Arena*. Toronto: Lexington Books.

—. 2010. "Blogging and Mass Politics." *Biography* 33: 110–126.

Koop, Royce, and Harold J. Jansen. 2009. "Political Blogs and Blogrolls in Canada Forums for Democratic Deliberation." *Social Science Computer Review* 27: 155–173.

Kopytowska, Monika. 2009. "Corpus Linguistics and an Eclectic Approach to the Study of News – The Mechanism of Framing." In *Studies in Cognitive Corpus Linguistics,* ed. by Barbara Lewandowska-Tomaszczyk, and Katarzyna Dziwirek, 83–109. Frankfurt am Main: Peter Lang.

—. 2010. "Kognitywno-afektywne aspekty komunikacji masowej – Proksymizacja w dyskursie wiadomości telewizyjnych [Cognitive-affective aspects of mass communication – Proximization in television news discourse]." In *Prace Komisji Nauk Filologicznych Oddziału Polskiej Akademii Nauk we Wrocławiu. II* [Proceedings of the Philological Committee of the Polish Academy of Sciences, Wrocław Branch. Vol. II], ed. by Piotr Chruszczewski, and Stanisław Prędota, 191–193. Wrocław: PAN.

Kress, Gunter. 2005. "Gains and Losses: New Forms of Texts, Knowledge and Learning." *Computers and Composition* 22: 5–22.

Krotz, Friedrich. 2007. "The Meta-Process of Mediatization as a Conceptual Frame." *Global Media and Communication* 3: 256–260.

—. 2009. "Mediatization: A Concept with Which to Grasp Media and Societal Change." In *Mediatization: Concept, Changes, Consequences,* ed. by Knut Lundby, 21–40. New York: Peter Lang.

Lakoff, George. 1996. *Moral Politics: What the Conservatives Know that Liberals Don't.* Chicago, IL: University of Chicago Press.

—. 2004. *Don't Think of an Elephant! Know Your Values and Frame the Debate.* White River Junction, VT: Chelsea Green Publishing.

Lawson-Borders, Gracie, and Rita Kirk. 2005. "Blogs in Campaign Communication." *American Behavioral Scientist* 49: 548–559.

Lehti, Lotta. 2011. "Blogging Politics in Various Ways: A Typology of French Politicians' Blogs." *Journal of Pragmatics* 43: 1610–1627.

Lewandowska-Tomaszczyk, Barbara. 2011. "Blurring the Boundaries: A Model of Online Computer-Mediated Communication Activities (OCA)." In *Interdisciplinary Perspectives in Cross-Cultural Communication,* ed. by Adam Bednarek, 8–37. Muenchen: Lincom.

Lewandowska-Tomaszczyk, Barbara and Frauke Zeller. 2012. "The Media in Transforming Audiences and Societies." In *Corpus Data Across Languages and Disciplines,* ed. by Piotr Pęzik, 127–148. Frankfurt am Main: Peter Lang.

Lilleker, Darren G. 2006. *Key Concepts in Political Communication.* London: Sage.

Lippmann, Walter. 1922. *Public Opinion.* New York, NY: Harcourt, Brace and Co.

Livingstone, Sonia. 2009. "On the Mediation of Everything." *Journal of Communication* 59: 1–18.

Lomborg, Stine. 2009. "Navigating the Blogosphere: Towards a Genre-Based Typology of Weblogs." *First Monday* 14. Retrieved June 30, 2011 from http://firstmonday.org/htbin/cgiwrap/bin/ojs/index.php/fm/article/view/2329/2178

Louw, Eric. 2005. *The Media and Political Process.* London: Sage.

MacKinnon, Rebecca. 2007. "Flatter World and Thicker Walls? Blogs, Censorship and Civic Discourse in China." *Public Choice* 134: 31–46.

Mazzoleni, Gianpietro. 2008a. "Mediatization of Politics." In *The International Encyclopedia of Communication,* ed. by Wolfgang Donsbach, 3047–3051. Malden, MA: Blackwell.

—. 2008b. "Mediatization of Society." In *The International Encyclopedia of Communication,* ed. by Wolfgang Donsbach, 3052–3055. Malden, MA: Blackwell.

Mazzoleni, Gianpietro, and Winfried Schulz. 1999. "Mediatization of Politics: A Challenge for Democracy?" *Political Communication* 16: 247–261.

McKenna, Laura, and Antoinette Pole. 2004. Do Blogs Matter? Weblogs in American Politics. Paper presented at the American Political Science Association's annual meeting, Chicago, IL.

—. 2008. "What Do Bloggers Do: An Average Day on an Average Political Blog." *Public Choice* 134: 97–108.

McNair, Brian. 2003. *An Introduction to Political* Communication. London: Routledge.

Miller, Mary C. 1997. *Color for Interior Architecture*. New York: John Wiley & Sons, Inc.

Miller, Carolyn R., and Dawn Shepherd. 2004. "Blogging as Social Action: A Genre Analysis of the Weblog." In *Into the Blogosphere: Rhetoric, Community and Culture of Weblogs*, ed. by Laura J. Gurak, Smiljana Antonijevic, Laurie Johnson, Clancy Ratliff, and Jessica Reyman. Retrieved November 30, 2012 from http://www.firstmonday.org/htbin/cgiwrap/bin/ojs/index.php/fm/article/view/2329/2178

Myers, Greg. 2010. *Discourse of Blogs and Wikis*. London: Continuum.

Nardi, Bonnie, Diane Schiano, Michelle Gumbrecht, and Luke Swartz. 2004. "Why We Blog." Communications of the ACM 47: 41–46.

O'Keeffe, Anne. 2006. *Investigating Media Discourse*. New York, NY: Routledge.

Okulska, Urszula, and Piotr Cap. (eds). 2010. *Perspectives in Politics and Discourse*. Amsterdam: Benjamins.

Pan, Zhongdang, and Gerald Kosicki. 1993. "Framing Analysis: An Approach to News Discourse." *Political Communication* 10: 55–75.

Pfitser, Damien S. 2011. "The Logos of the Blogosphere: Flooding the Zone, Invention, and the Attention in the Lott Ombroglio." *Argumentation and Advocacy* 47: 141–162.

Ritzer, George, and Nathan Jurgenson. 2010. "Production, Consumption, Prosumption: The Nature of Capitalism in the Age of the Digital 'Prosumer'." *Journal of Consumer Culture* 10.1: 13–36.

Rogowicz, Michał. 2008. "Blog Janusza Korwina Mikke najpopularniejszy w Internecie [Janusz Korwin Mikke's blog the most popular in the Internet]." Retrieved May 15, 2011 from http://media2.pl/badania/44293-Blog-Janusza-Korwin-Mikke-najpopularniejszy-w-Internecie.html

Scheufele, Dietram. 1999. "Framing as a Theory of Media Effects". *Journal of Communication* 49: 103–122.

—. 2004. "Framing-Effects Approach: A Theoretical and Methodological Critique." *Communications* 29: 401–428.

Schiffer, Adam. 2005. Blogswarms and Press Norms: News Coverage of the Downing Street Controversy. Paper presented at the Annual Meeting of the American Political Science Association, Washington, DC.

Schmidt, Jan. 2007. "Blogging Practices: An Analytical Framework." *Journal of Computer-Mediated Communication* 12: 1409–1427.

Schulz, Winfried. 2004. "Reconstructing Mediatization as an Analytical Concept." *European Journal of Communication* 19: 87–101.

Smolkin, Rachel. 2004. "The Expanding Blogosphere." *American Journalism Review* 26: 38–44.

Stanyer, James. 2005. "Online Campaign Communication and the Phenomenon of Blogging: An Analysis of Weblogs during the 2005 British General Election Campaign." *Aslib Proceedings: New Information Perspectives* 58: 404–415.

Stoller, Matt. 2004. "Presidential Session at Bloggercon." Retrieved June 16, 2010 from http://www.bopnews.com/archives/000581.html

Street, John. 2011. *Mass Media, Politics & Democracy* (2nd edition). Basingstoke: Pallgrave Macmillan.

Strömbäck, Jesper. 2008. "Four Phases of Mediatization: An Analysis of the Mediatization of Politics." *International Journal of Press/Politics* 13: 228–246.

—. 2010. "Mediatization of Politics: Towards a Conceptual Framework for Comparative Research." In *Sourcebook for Political Communication Research: Methods, Measures, and Analytical Techniques*, ed. by Erik P. Bucy, and R. Lance Holbert, 34–55. New York, NY: Routledge.

—. 2011. "Mediatization and Perceptions of the Media's Political Influence." *Journalism Studies* 12: 423–439.

Strömbäck, Jesper, and Frank Esser. 2009. "Shaping Politics: Mediatization and Media Interventionism." In *Mediatization: Concepts, Changes, Consequences*, ed. by Knut Lundby, 205–233. New York, NY: Peter Lang.

Stubbs, Michael. 1997. "Whorf's Children: Critical Comments on Critical Discourse Analysis (CDA)." In *Evolving Models of Language*, ed. by Ann Ryan, and Alison Wray, 110–116. Clevedon: Multilingual Matters.

Sullivan, Jonathan, and Sehun Cheon. 2011. "Reconnecting Representatives in two East Asian Democracies." *East Asia* 28: 21–36.

Suomela-Salmi, Eija. 2009. "La construction de soi dans les blogs des politiciens francais." In *Du côté des langues romanes: Mélanges en l'honneur de Juhani Härmä*, ed. by Eva Havu, Mervi Helkkula, and Ulla Tuomarla, 265–281. Cambridge: Cambridge University Press.

Thompson, John. 1995. *The Media and Modernity*. Cambridge: Polity Press.

Triandafyllidou, Anna, Ruth Wodak, and Michał Krzyżanowski. (eds). 2009. *The European Public Sphere and the Media: Europe in Crisis*. Basingstoke: Palgrave.

Ungerer, Friedrich. 1997. "Emotions and Emotional Language in English and German News Stories." In *The Language of Emotions*, ed. by Susanne Niemeier, and Rene Dirven, 397–328. Amsterdam: Benjamins.

Vesnic-Alujevic, Lucia. 2011. "Communicating with Voters by Blogs? Campaigning for the 2009 European Parliament Elections." *Discourse & Communication* 5.4: 413–428.

Wallsten, Kevin. 2005. Political Blogs: Is the Political Blogosphere an Echo Chamber? Paper presented at the American Political Science Association's Annual Meeting, Washington, D.C.

Wallsten, Kevin. 2008. "Political Blogs: Transmission Belts, Soapboxes, Mobilizers, or Conversation Starters?" *Journal of Information Technology & Politics* 4 (3): 19–40.

Warnick, Barbara. 2007. *Rhetoric Online: Persuasion and Politics on the World Wide Web*. New York, NY: Peter Lang.

Webb, Lynne M., Tiffany E. Fields, Sitthivorada Boupha, and Matthew N. Stell. 2012. "U.S. Political Blogs: What Aspects of Blog Design Correlate with Popularity?" In *Blogging in the Global Society: Cultural, Political and Geographical Aspects*, ed. by Tatyana Dumova, and Richard Fiordo, 179–199. IGI Global.

Widdows, Dominic, and Kathleen Ferraro. 2008. "Semantic Vectors: A Scalable Open Source Package and Online Technology Management Application." *Proceedings of Language Resources and Evaluation (LREC'08)*, 17–42.

Wright, Scott. 2009. "Political Blogs, Representation and the Public Sphere." *Aslib Proceedings: New Information Perspectives* 61: 155–169.

Youngs, Gillian. 2009. "Blogging and Globalization: The Blurring of the Public/Private Spheres." *Aslib Proceedings: New Information Perspectives* 61: 127–138.

Yus, Francisco. 2011. *Cyberpragmatics. Internet-Mediated Communication in Context.* Amsterdam: Benjamins.

Zhou, Xiang. 2009. "The Political Blogosphere in China: A Content Analysis of the Blogs Regarding the Dismissal of Shanghai Leader Chen Liangyu." *New Media & Society* 11: 1003–1022.

Zuckerman, Ethan. 2007. "Meet the Bridgebloggers." *Public Choice* 134: 47–65.

Appendix

Korwin-Mikke's blog – keywords

Key word	Freq.	%	RC. Freq.	RC. %	Keyness
PRAWICY	104	0.134952769	3737		488.4801331
NOWAPRAWICA	29	0.037631061	0		400.6345215
PAŃSTWO	101	0.1310599	18851	045	174.2619934
PRZYPOMINAM	42	0.054500155	3337		134.8735657
LEWACY	16	0.020761965	107		126.1620483
KRACJA	9	0.011678604	0		124.3325119
UWAGA	33	0.042821553	2435		110.4447327
BANDA	17	0.022059588	254		108.3070984
RP	39	0.050607286	4040		106.5437469
PRZYPOMINAMY	17	0.022059588	343		98.55600739
BANDY	17	0.022059588	361		96.89372253
PALIKOTA	6		0		82.8881073
TUSK	27	0.035035815	2324		82.76099396
POKAŻMY	9	0.011678604	31		81.74146271
PALIKOTEM	5		0		69.07335663
KACZYŃSKI	23	0.029845323	2082		68.39930725
BYDLAKÓW	6		6		66.2645874
SOCJALIZMU	21	0.027250078	1810		64.3167572
TU	136	0.176476702	63418	265	62.12145996
CHWASTY	9	0.011678604	105		61.57115936
GEJÓW	10	0.012976227	175		60.6927948
ZBIERAMY-PODPISY	4		0		55.25863647
PROŚBA	13	0.016869096	621		54.03887558
ZWYRODNIALCÓW	5		6		53.92716599
PROSZĘ	91	0.118083671	38073	21	52.54171371

Korwin-Mikke's comments – keywords

Key word	Freq.	%	RC. Freq.	RC. %	Keyness
JANUSZU	2409	0.188015699	50		19328.42773
PIS	713	0.055647653	276		4701.865234
PRAWICY	892	0.069618098	3737		2922.016357
PRAWICA	751	0.058613446	2332		2830.106689
UBECKIE	349	0.027238471	32		2651.44873
TUSKA	286	0.022321498	99		1916.368042
POLSKE	237	0.018497186	4		1908.466309
MISTRZU	260	0.020292271	175		1557.665894
BANDA	256	0.019980082	254		1406.697388
GŁUPI	348	0.027160425	1054		1325.463623
POPIERAM	264	0.02060446	379		1312.911133
WOLNOŚĆ	582	0.045423467	5495		1130.948975
PALIKOT	141	0.011004655	6		1109.616577
ZGADZAM	383	0.029892076	2346		1013.539734
LIBERAŁ	180	0.014048495	230		925.614502
PRZYCHLASTY	106		0		871.71875
LICHWIARZY	131	0.010224183	48		870.7533569
BANDĘ	145	0.011316843	122		828.3217773
BANDY	183	0.014282637	361		822.0651855
LIBERALIZM	193	0.015063109	443		821.1162109
PEDOFILII	111		35		753.1707764
PLANKTON	106		35		714.8477783
DEMOKRACJA	329	0.025677528	2787		696.37854
MONARCHIA	127		173		641.3257446
PRAWICĘ	169	0.013189976	602		598.7835693
POLAKOW	84		18		596.3251953
PEDOFILIA	74		12		539.444519
SOCJALISTÓW	186	0.014516778	982		537.913208
SOCJALISTYCZNA	135	0.010536372	399		519.5397339
PRAWICOWIEC	74		23		503.0565796
PRZYCHLASTÓW	61		0		501.6473694
SOCJALISTO	61		0		501.6473694
JANUSZKU	65		10		475.9715576
LEWAK	58		18		394.3638306
LEWACTWO	53		8		388.7168274
IDIOTÓW	75		102		378.9095459

Senyszyn's blog – keywords

Key word	Freq.	%	RC. Freq.	RC. %	Keyness
PIS	51	0.291411906	276		572.8161011
TUSKA	31	0.177132741	99		377.394165
KACZYŃSKIEGO	36	0.205702528	870		301.6826782
RP	38	0.217130452	4040		208.4692841
KOBIET	42	0.239986286	8806	0.011443477	175.5411682
KACZYŃSKI	27	0.154276893	2082		164.99617
RYDZYKA	9	0.051425632	282		70.84465027
HOMOSEKSUALIZMU	6	0.034283753	122		52.28692627
KARŁY	5	0.028569795	56		49.32313156
JAROSŁAW	13	0.074281469	3387		48.97923279
BEATYFIKACJĘ	4	0.022855837	13		48.56787491
KACZYŃSKIM	6	0.034283753	168		48.54710388
SMOLEŃSKIEM	4	0.022855837	16		47.10335922
DUCHOWNYCH	8	0.045711674	714		46.59840393
KLERU	6	0.034283753	242		44.26529694
KULTU	8	0.045711674	833		44.19880676
JAROSŁAWA	8	0.045711674	902		42.96272278
HOMOSEKSUALNEJ	4	0.022855837	34		41.55396271
WATYKANU	6	0.034283753	384		38.84367752
ZEMSTA	6	0.034283753	414		37.96136093
REPRODUKCYJNEJ	3	0.017141877	8		37.44664383
SEKSUALNEJ	6	0.034283753	506		35.61081696
PEDOFILIA	3	0.017141877	12		35.3273468
EPISKOPAT	6	0.034283753	581		33.99546051
PEDOFILII	3	0.017141877	35		29.35936928
BEATYFIKACJI	3	0.017141877	44		28.04045868
KLECHY	3	0.017141877	46		27.78317261
ORGAZMU	3	0.017141877	47		27.65858269
POLACY	13	0.074281469	8610	0.011188773	27.12582588
RYDZYK	4	0.022855837	231		26.69935989
KOŚCIOŁA	15	0.085709386	11941	0.015517438	26.69734573
PAZERNOŚĆ	3	0.017141877	76		24.85890198

Senyszyn's comments – keywords

Key word	Freq.	%	RC. Freq.	RC. %	Keyness
PANI	2980	0.631075144	58624	0.076182425	7260.450195
TOWARZYSZKO	518	0.109696954	4		5236.893066
PIS	507	0.107367486	276		4158.647949

SLD	1230	0.260477334	17885	0.023241721	3638.561523
JOANNO	198	0.041930497	6		1965.472412
TOWARZYSZKA	220	0.046589442	66		1935.750732
RYDZYKA	243	0.051460154	282		1757.089722
RYDZYK	192	0.040659875	231		1378.360107
MATOLE	124	0.026259502	3		1236.375977
PEDALY	105	0.02223587	0		1070.946045
TOWARZYSZU	141	0.029859597	173		1008.224731
PRZYGŁUPIE	97	0.020541709	2		969.8057861
TOWARZYSZE	177	0.037483323	659		950.2596436
PZPR	330	0.069884159	5098		940.6491699
MATOŁ	82	0.017365156	9		777.739563
DUPCYNGIER	66	0.013976832	0		673.1607056
PEDALOW	66	0.013976832	0		673.1607056
WATYKANU	110	0.023294721	384		602.7360229
KACZYCHUJU	59	0.012494441	0		601.7639771
GIERKA	117	0.024777113	606		560.6331787
DEBIL	63	0.013341522	21		548.3466797
KACZEŚCIERWO	48	0.010164969	0		489.5695801
PEDOFILÓW	58	0.01228267	27		485.6306458
KOŚCIÓŁ	288	0.060989812	9157	0.011899604	472.0114136
PEDAŁY	62	0.013129751	69		451.9763489
POPIERAM	88	0.018635776	379		450.1802063
KSIĘŻY	123	0.026047733	1389		418.605957
KLER	64	0.013553292	159		387.35672
KATOSKURWYSYNIE	37		0		377.3757019
TOWARZYSZ	84	0.017788695	539		370.5924988
KATOCHUJU	36		0		367.1763
CZARNYCHUJU	31		0		316.1792603
PIEPRZYSZ	33		8		296.2035828
UBECKIE	37		32		282.4755249
MATKOJEBCU	26		0		265.182312
KLECHA	29		8		257.2446289
KOMUCHY	37		54		255.0781403
KOSCIOLA	25		0		254.9829559
LEWAK	31		18		251.9616699
JOASIU	26		7		231.1622314
LEWACTWO	26		8		228.1797791
WATYKAŃCZYKÓW	20		0		203.986145
GÓWNIATYKLECHA	20		0		203.986145

Montgomerie's blog – keywords

Key word	Freq.	%	RC. Freq.	RC. %	Keyness
CAMERON	4585	0.382458776	868		35885.14063
TORY	2543	0.212124899	3579		14313.45117
CONSERVATIVE	2808	0.234229937	7099		13245.125
CONSERVATIVES	1588	0.132463366	2328		8840.849609
COALITION	1588	0.132463366	2379		8789.47168
ELECTION	2161	0.180260286	9684		8129.411621
LABOUR	2917	0.243322194	25263	0.025398808	7705.306641
PARTY	3427	0.285863966	37720	0.037922774	7681.725098
MPS	1333	0.111192487	2548		6880.665527
GOVERNMENT	3610	0.301128954	56343	0.056645889	6059.717773
VOTERS	1131	0.094342612	1956		6013.25
TORIES	1086	0.090588927	1987		5679.489258
LIBERAL	1353	0.112860791	5566		5285.218262
EU	619	0.051634021	44		5162.545898
TAX	1865	0.155569389	16339	0.016426835	4888.967773
BROWN	1310	0.10927394	8206		4179.526855
NHS	883	0.073655635	2448		4030.735596
POLL	882	0.073572226	2834		3811.014404
DEMOCRATS	795	0.0663151	1979		3768.685303
SPENDING	1117	0.0931748	6593		3676.950928
CUTS	953	0.079494707	4074		3660.426514
DEMS	449	0.037453432	87		3505.376953
IMMIGRATION	629	0.052468173	1081		3350.06543
MP	811	0.067649744	3456		3119.278076
VOTE	1001	0.083498634	7052		2993.094482
POLICY	1631	0.136050224	25803	0.025941711	2701.495117
MINISTER	1527	0.127375036	23008	0.023131685	2645.92041
CAMPAIGN	1009	0.084165953	9381		2543.670166
REFERENDUM	538	0.044877388	1429		2493.465332
LEADER	952	0.079411291	9003		2372.782715
REFORM	796	0.066398516	5848		2323.239258
DEFICIT	570	0.047546674	2348		2224.9729
PARLIAMENT	897	0.074823454	9441		2075.656006
COALITION'S	244	0.020353314	19		2026.117554
ANTI	339	0.028277759	378		2021.143921
COMMONS	616	0.051383775	3664		2019.440186
PUBLIC	1739	0.145059064	38393	0.038599394	2011.890625
DEMOCRAT	406	0.033866581	982		1943.420776
BLOG	216	0.018017687	0		1913.992798
CABINET	724	0.060392618	6360		1894.080688

BRITAIN	1198	0.099931434	19935	0.020042166	1890.058594
MANIFESTO	371	0.030947046	754		1879.020996
POLLS	401	0.033449505	1063		1859.768555
MINISTERS	723	0.060309205	6754		1816.771973
BUDGET	776	0.064730212	8283		1777.537598
POLITICS	738	0.061560433	7387		1769.287598
DEM	286	0.023856753	321		1702.513184
AFGHANISTAN	320	0.026692871	613		1650.433472
POLLING	291	0.02427383	514		1537.528442
LEADERSHIP	564	0.047046185	4688		1528.031616
OBAMA	155	0.012929359	1		1361.390015
BLAIR	240	0.020019652	416		1275.023193
SEATS	497	0.041457362	4612		1254.345703
TAXES	403	0.033616334	2814		1210.939453
DEBATES	291	0.02427383	1186		1141.095825
TAXPAYERS	247	0.02060356	676		1132.61438
WELFARE	468	0.039038323	4804		1102.273071
ECONOMY	653	0.054470137	10365	0.01042072	1077.869629
BACKBENCHERS	176	0.014681078	198		1047.108398
VOTING	330	0.027527023	2201		1017.337463
DEBATE	535	0.044627141	7285		1012.844788
CONSERVATISM	205	0.01710012	476		994.7427979
MEDIA	548	0.04571154	7862		991.7675171
POLITICAL	1113	0.092841141	30168	0.030330177	973.7577515
ELECTORAL	317	0.026442625	2147		968.9682617
REFORMS	347	0.028945081	2800		957.468689
PLEDGE	212	0.017684026	658		928.1196899
BRITAINS	117		19		927.1870728

Montgomerie's comments – keywords

Key word	Freq.	%	RC. Freq.	RC. %	Keyness
CAMERON	27955	0.221026987	868		114468.9844
LABOUR	36271	0.286777675	25263	0.025398808	81088.89844
EU	15788	0.124828257	44		68321.875
CONSERVATIVE	20441	0.161617339	7099		59497.07422
PARTY	31079	0.245726973	37720	0.037922774	49975.39063
TORY	14186	0.112162001	3579		44927.34375
VOTE	15144	0.119736455	7052		40040.70703
LIB	8675	0.068589129	439		34448.92969
CONSERVATIVES	9637	0.07619521	2328		30827.63086
TORIES	9353	0.073949754	1987		30773.41797

ELECTION	13201	0.104374073	9684		28755.54883
BROWN	12206	0.09650708	8206		27732.78516
COALITION	7667	0.060619347	2379		23034.65625
DEMS	5082	0.040180974	87		21317.51367
CLEGG	4919	0.03889221	126		20319.95313
TAX	12861	0.101685852	16339	0.016426835	19981.22656
PEOPLE	36182	0.286073983	116196	0.116820648	18706.16406
VOTERS	6069	0.047984716	1956		18042.69531
GOVERNMENT	22763	0.179976285	56343	0.056645889	17897.05078
REFERENDUM	5545	0.043841697	1429		17469.39844
AGREE	8874	0.070162527	8060		17224.11328
TIGER	4895	0.038702454	842		16779.88281
LEFTIE	3861	0.030527104	5		16775.35156
IMMIGRATION	4876	0.038552228	1081		15896.88574
MPS	5825	0.046055526	2548		15742.74902
UK	10633	0.084070109	16534	0.016622882	13996.87695
NHS	5237	0.041406486	2448		13824.27051
BLAIR	3585	0.028344901	416		13075.10254
CUTS	5829	0.04608715	4074		12999.54688
COUNTRY	13190	0.104287103	27959	0.028109301	12638.01465
VOTING	4187	0.033104632	2201		10572.41895
THINK	24970	0.197425991	88700	0.089176834	10525.68359
ANTI	2917	0.023063341	378		10473.19434
POLLS	3458	0.027340773	1063		10414.6875
DEM	2748	0.021727139	321		10013.16797
LIBDEMS	2297	0.018161295	8		9919.927734
BNP	2475	0.019568656	117		9875.893555
MP	4521	0.035745412	3456		9642.554688
ELECTORATE	3113	0.024613021	1052		9130.041992
PUBLIC	13718	0.108461745	38393	0.038599394	8986.654297
PARLIAMENT	6305	0.049850658	9441		8577.517578
VOTES	4023	0.031807963	3119		8518.007813
CONSERVATIVEHOME	1921	0.01518844	0		8383.604492
LIBERAL	4828	0.038172714	5566		8046.629883
LISBON	2273	0.017971538	328		8027.246094
EURO	2464	0.019481685	617		7815.437988
PM	2855	0.022573138	1355		7494.327148
RESIDENT	3185	0.02518229	2070		7349.072266
POLICIES	5571	0.044047266	8778		7245.885742
SPENDING	4808	0.038014587	6593		7037.305176
POLITICIANS	3611	0.028550472	3264		7027.455566
TAXES	3407	0.026937541	2814		6975.12207
WING	3343	0.026431521	2869		6701.027832
POLL	3311	0.026178513	2834		6646.72998

POLITICS	4836	0.03823597	7387		6465.724609
SEATS	3813	0.03014759	4612		6141.327637
ECONOMY	5443	0.043035232	10365	0.01042072	5879.851563
SECTOR	4940	0.039058246	8623		5834.257324
DEFICIT	2750	0.021742951	2348		5528.078125
POLICY	8859	0.070043929	25803	0.025941711	5437.770996
LIBDEM	1248		12		5313.739258
WIN	5215	0.041232541	10485	0.010541365	5308.651367
VICTOR	2043	0.016153036	1013		5276.056152
VOTER	1466	0.01159097	282		4920.598145
GOVT	1188		31		4903.158203
LEADER	4634	0.036638848	9003		4899.001465
VOTED	2519	0.019916544	2283		4894.561523
NATION	2902	0.022944743	3567		4619.379395
PAY	7459	0.058974791	21712	0.021828718	4582.817871
PARTIES	5384	0.042568747	12581	0.012648633	4569.909668
MANIFESTO	1680	0.013282967	754		4499.374023
MONEY	10219	0.080796808	36425	0.036620814	4272.605957
ELECTED	3329	0.026320832	5335		4263.456543
OBAMA	943		1		4099.904297
CORPOREAL	1019		44		4091.172363
LEADERSHIP	2996	0.023687957	4688		3920.765381
LIBERTARIAN	1100		152		3911.158447

McCarthy's blog – keywords

Key word	Freq.	%	RC. Freq.	RC. %	Keyness
BRISTOL	485	0.279262066	2799		3422.819336
BLOG	127	0.073126353	0		1613.536377
LIB	146	0.084066518	439		1199.095703
THEME	232	0.133585155	3826		1182.725464
TORY	208	0.119765997	3579		1043.705933
POST	276	0.158920258	9426		1030.636963
MPS	184	0.105946839	2548		998.5333862
CAMERON	132	0.076005347	868		899.7493896
LABOUR	362	0.208438903	25263	0.025398808	884.8053589
DEMS	85	0.048942834	87		841.7893677
TORIES	148	0.085218109	1987		811.7646484
DEBATE	207	0.119190201	7285		761.4005127
BILL	255	0.146828502	13297	0.013368482	754.8799438
MP	155	0.089248702	3456		702.1221924
BACKBENCHER	61	0.03512368	70		594.2409058

VEGAN	57	0.032820489	45		584.3326416
DEM	72	0.041457459	321		541.5482788
VOTE	152	0.087521307	7052		482.0101929
CAMPAIGN	158	0.090976089	9381		430.9807129
PARLIAMENT	151	0.086945504	9441		398.0560303
TWEET	36	0.02072873	20		384.4345703
SHARE	170	0.097885668	13362	0.013433831	380.4321594
PEOPLE	528	0.304021388	116196	0.116820648	359.4907532
ELECTION	137	0.078884333	9684		331.6680603
CONSTITUENCY	72	0.041457459	1862		306.088501
PARLIAMENTARY	92	0.052973419	4238		292.90802
EU	31	0.01784974	44		292.2843933
WHIP	53	0.030517297	824		276.027832
WEB	48	0.027638307	570		274.3279419
TWEETS	22	0.012667557	1		271.2735596
BACKBENCHERS	36	0.02072873	198		257.1290588
PARTY	228	0.131281957	37720	0.037922774	241.4376984
RIOTS	43	0.024759317	888		200.9544678
LETS	43	0.024759317	909		199.0642395
QUESTIONS	123	0.070823163	14067	0.014142621	198.7975006
LAB	40	0.023031922	708		198.5464478
DAVID	125	0.071974754	14556	0.01463425	198.4473419
UK	132	0.076005347	16534	0.016622882	194.4450989
CONSTITUENTS	41	0.02360772	830		193.1436615
BLOGGER	15		0		190.5654907
CAMPAIGNING	40	0.023031922	840		185.6735382
KIDS	69	0.039730065	4198		185.1968994
WEST	144	0.082914919	20977	0.021089768	179.0524139
VEGGIE	17		12		176.6801453
SOMEONE	127	0.073126353	16947	0.017038103	174.6886292
COMMITTEE	132	0.076005347	18268	0.018366205	174.2618713
THINK	346	0.199226126	88700	0.089176834	173.7926941
GOVERNMENT	252	0.145101115	56343	0.056645889	166.5422668
BALLOT	37	0.021304527	987		155.1415558
BACKBENCH	22	0.012667557	128		154.8785248
UPDATE	40	0.023031922	1286		153.8018799
VEGFEST	12		0		152.4521942
YOUTUBE	12		0		152.4521942
ACTUALLY	149	0.085793912	25455	0.025591841	151.0094604
EAST	120	0.069095768	17313	0.017406071	150.9232788
ONLINE	31	0.01784974	597		148.9466095
ISSUES	99	0.057004008	12188	0.01225352	148.4899597
COMMONS	57	0.032820489	3664		147.4488831
VOTES	53	0.030517297	3119		145.3792725

VOTING	45	0.025910912	2201		138.3675385
PIECE	81	0.046639644	9039		134.0786896
ASHCROFT	18	0.010364365	86		133.1467438
WESTMINSTER	42	0.024183519	2106		127.254509
CONSERVATIVE	68	0.039154269	7099		119.8730316
MEDIA	69	0.039730065	7862		111.9149475
CANDIDATES	49	0.028214104	3983		106.8154068
BILLS	41	0.02360772	3015		96.42912292
VOTERS	34	0.019577134	1956		94.63176727
MINISTER	116	0.066792578	23008	0.023131685	94.14053345
SOMALILAND	11		30		92.16506958

McCarthy's comments – keywords

Key word	Freq.	%	RC. Freq.	RC. %	Keyness
BRISTOL	66	0.134933457	2799		380.2191467
BLOG	23	0.047022264	0		350.4393921
RAPE	51	0.104266763	2051		299.0330505
ANONYMITY	27	0.055200048	267		231.2710419
LABOUR	97	0.198311284	25263	0.025398808	229.4065552
LIB	28	0.057244495	439		215.1785431
RAPISTS	20	0.040888924	83		203.4129181
DEMS	18	0.036800034	87		178.1303101
PEOPLE	178	0.36391142	116196	0.116820648	162.9668121
TWITTER	12	0.024533356	11		151.004776
VEGAN	14	0.028622247	45		148.6963959
CAMERON	24	0.049066711	868		145.6412659
FATHERLESSNESS	9	0.018400017	0		137.125885
OUTSIDERNESS	8	0.01635557	0		121.8895111
ANTI	17	0.034755588	378		119.17939
UK	54	0.110400096	16534	0.016622882	112.6571655
EU	11	0.022488909	44		112.5977325
CLEGG	13	0.026577801	126		111.843605
INNOCENT	26	0.053155601	2394		111.0453873
VOTE	36	0.073600069	7052		103.2857132
MPS	25	0.051111158	2548		101.9636383
ACCUSED	30	0.061333388	4783		97.31406403
JUSTICE	34	0.069511175	7321		91.77902222
CRIME	33	0.067466728	6929		90.56336212
SOMALI	12	0.024533356	292		82.03142548
THINK	115	0.235111326	88700	0.089176834	80.25569153
RAPIST	11	0.022488909	233		78.14732361

MP	23	0.047022264	3456		77.11417389
FATHERS	16	0.032711141	1192		74.79393768
RAPED	13	0.026577801	590		73.17289734
FRECKLES	9	0.018400017	115		72.69354248
DEM	11	0.022488909	321		71.32358551
AGREE	30	0.061333388	8060		69.30001068
MILIBAND	7	0.014311124	46		65.32521057
TORY	20	0.040888924	3579		60.65063477
TORIES	16	0.032711141	1987		59.30892944
CONVICTION	16	0.032711141	2008		58.99448776
WELFARE	22	0.044977818	4804		58.8323822
VICTIMS	18	0.036800034	2837		58.76497269
PARLIAMENT	29	0.059288941	9441		57.49074554
RIDICULOUS	15	0.030666694	1779		56.89488602
FALSELY	8	0.01635557	228		52.23771667
ACCUSATION	9	0.018400017	430		49.76345062
MOTHERS	17	0.034755588	3225		49.75274658
GOVT	5	0.010222231	31		47.19933701
IDEA	39	0.079733402	21067	0.021180252	46.09597397
KIDS	18	0.036800034	4198		46.03266525
LIBDEMS	4		8		45.67595291
RIOTS	10	0.020444462	888		43.39534378
WRONG	32	0.065422282	15513	0.015596394	42.9958992
VEGGIE	4		12		42.96149826
BLAIR	8	0.01635557	416		42.9257164
IDS	4		13		42.40699005
ELECTION	25	0.051111158	9684		42.39884186
RIOTERS	6	0.012266678	137		41.75389862
ACCUSATIONS	9	0.018400017	695		41.45271683
VOTES	15	0.030666694	3119		41.42237091
VOTING	13	0.026577801	2201		40.73412704
BRITAINS	4		19		39.70940781
SURE	39	0.079733402	23750	0.023877675	39.39051819
MILKED	5	0.010222231	78		38.47073746
PROVEN	9	0.018400017	845		38.10306168
ACTUALLY	40	0.081777848	25455	0.025591841	37.95989609
PARENT	15	0.030666694	3579		37.75667191
CANDIDATE	15	0.030666694	3772		36.37394333
INTERNET	5	0.010222231	97		36.36985779
CYCLIST	6	0.012266678	229		35.78262711
JERK	6	0.012266678	234		35.53165817
CRITICISE	7	0.014311124	445		34.85083389
ETHNICITY	6	0.012266678	250		34.76339722
CONSTITUENCY	11	0.022488909	1862		34.4711113

GUILTY	15	0.030666694	4109	34.14286804
RESTORATIVE	5	0.010222231	123	34.07354736
BENEFITS	20	0.040888924	7711	34.06925583
GANG	10	0.020444462	1483	33.76818085
VOTERS	11	0.022488909	1956	33.48312378
CONSTITUENCIES	8	0.01635557	796	32.98941422
MILLIONAIRES	5	0.010222231	142	32.68232727
PROTECT	16	0.032711141	5047	32.56532669
CUTS	14	0.028622247	4074	30.41205597
FEMINISM	7	0.014311124	665	29.47925949

Index